1000
Portrait
Illustrations

1000 **Portrait** Illustrations

Contemporary Illustration from Pencil to Digital

Julia Schonlau

Quarry Books
100 Cummings Center, Suite 406L
Beverly, MA 01915

quarrybooks.com • craftside.typepad.com

ISBN: 978-1-59253-809-6

Digital edition published in 2012

eISBN: 978-1-61058-609-2

Publisher: Paco Asensio

Editorial coordination: Cristian Campos

Editor and texts: Julia Schonlau

Art director: Emma Termes Parera

Layout: Maira Purman

English translation: Cillero & de Motta

Editorial Project:

maomao publications

Via Laietana, 32 4th fl. of. 104

08003 Barcelona, España

Tel. : +34 93 268 80 88

Fax : +34 93 317 42 08

www.maomaopublications.com

10 9 8 7 6 5 4 3 2 1

Printed in China

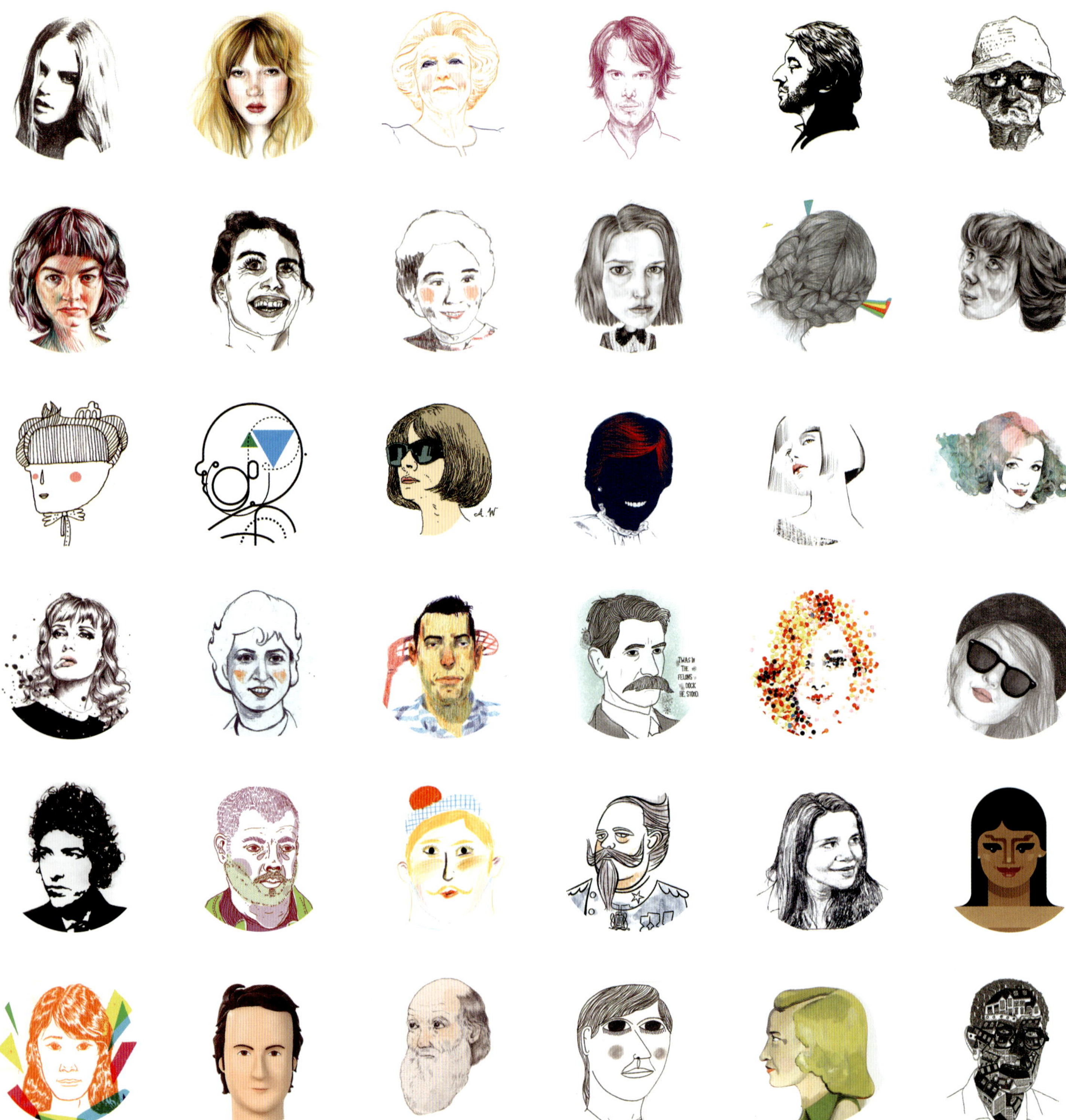

Should portrait illustration not be obsolete in this day and age, when even the most basic mobile phone has a built-in camera? Surely a photographic image is the most accurate representation of a human being. Yet it seems as though more illustrators than ever are specializing in portraiture. And maybe the importance lies not in depicting what is on the surface but what is hidden within the person— or the artist's imagination. In the long history of portraiture there are only brief moments when verisimilitude was of chief importance.

Portraiture always had one primary function – to keep us present among the living, even after we have perished. Some of the earliest examples of standardized but impressively realistic portraits have been found in Egypt. Painted on wood, these images covered the face of the mummified body.

Medieval art only allowed the depiction of saints and biblical scenes. But the wealthy merchants who commissioned these paintings asked to be included in the work—at first only as silent worshippers, and later as participants within the scenes. During the Renaissance, portraiture was reaching a peak. The wealthy bourgeoisie had the means and confidence to commission their own portraits. New techniques such as oil painting allowed for a greater realism and detail. A growing number of increasingly skilled artists were eager not only to produce a lifelike representation, but also to infuse the painting with their artistic intention.

Self-portraits have only been around since the late 15th century when glass mirrors became more widely available. But they also attest to a newfound confidence within the artists. Their status in society had been elevated from simple craftsmen to artistic geniuses.

In the late 19th century, portrait painting was challenged by the invention of photography. Art was freed from literal representation and, consequently, the artist's perspective turned inwards. Portraiture became a reflection of the innermost thoughts of the artists and a mirror held up to society.

If we look at today's portrait illustration we see a fragmented society, which is highly individualized. There is a stark contrast between the outside and the inside world. It is a constant striving for authenticity and self-reflection. But most of all, it is a battle against our ephemerality, and the ultimate reaffirmation of our existence.

Realistic

It seems straightforward and rather simple to produce a portrait,
which should predominantly be a recognisable person. But as this
chapter shows, even within these narrow boundaries there are
endless possibilities. Most realistic portraits these days are based on
photographs, but they create an altogether different effect. Just take,
for example, the way in which celebrities are depicted over and over
again, with a different twist depending on the individual artist.

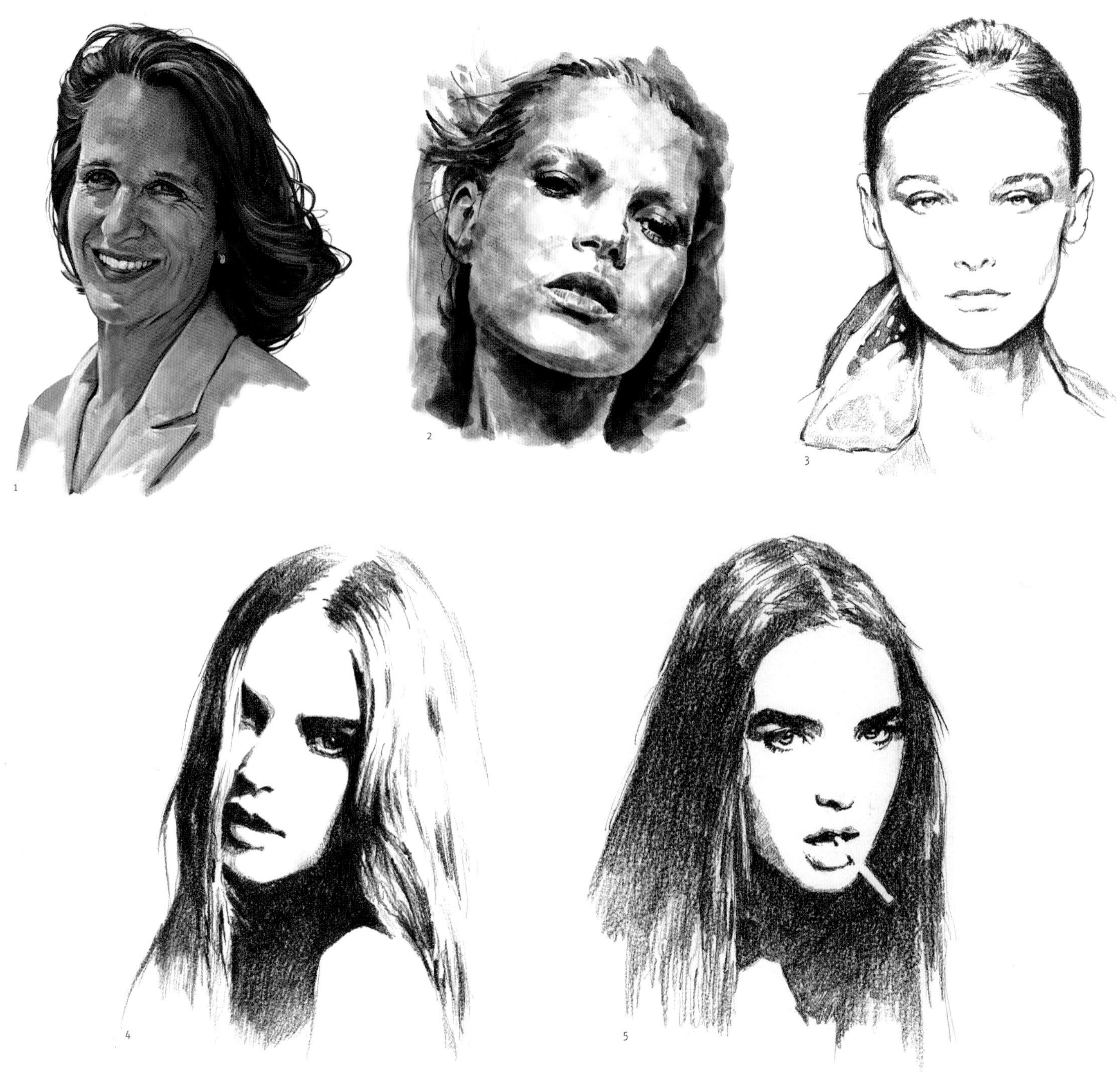

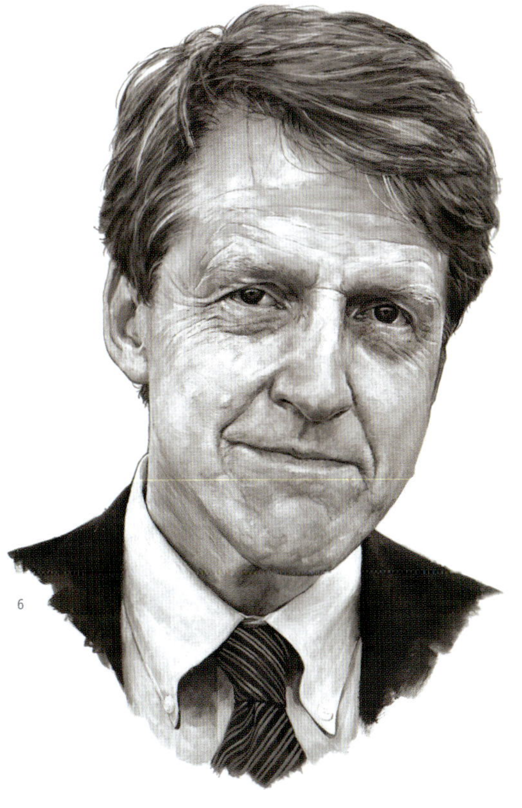

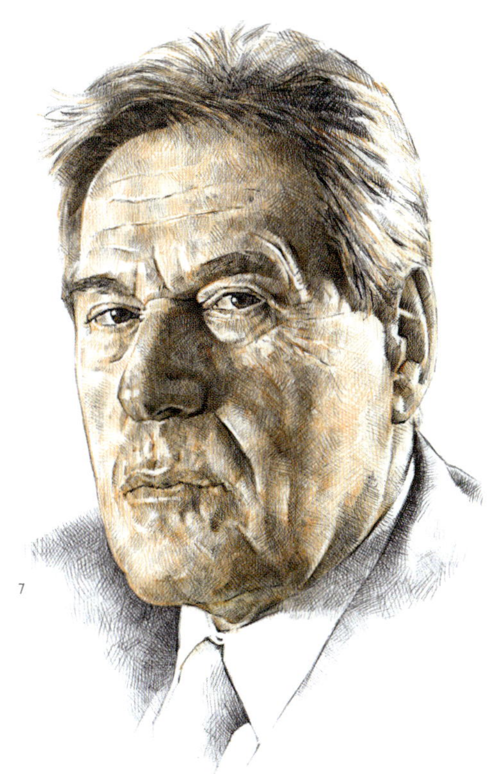

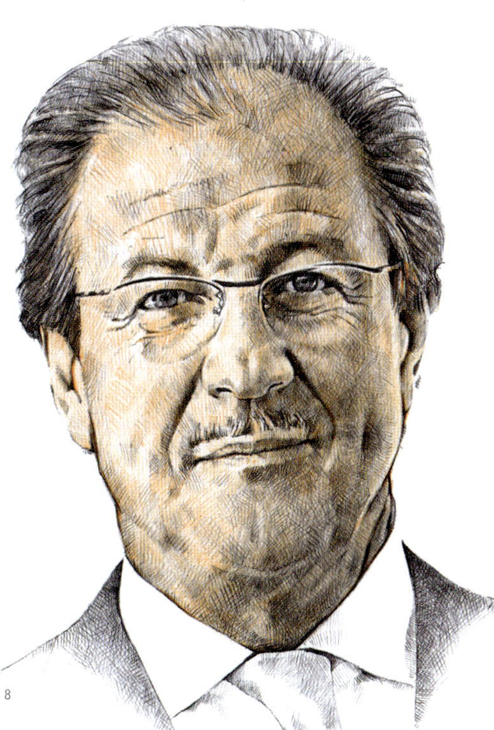

Bernd Schifferdecker

Germany

www.berndschifferdecker.com

1. **Mitarbeiter** (2006). Columbus Bank And Trust Company. Acrylic

2. **Kate Moss** (2007). *E&A The Glossy Zine.* Watercolor

3. **Models** (2009). *E&A The Glossy Zine.* Pencil

4. **Models** (2009). *E&A The Glossy Zine.* Pencil

5. **Models** (2009). *E&A The Glossy Zine.* Pencil

6. **Robert Shiller, Interview** (2009). *SAP FIVE.* Acrylic

7. **Michael Glos** (2006). *WirtschaftsWoche.* Ball pen, pencil

8. **Manager des Jahres, Wolfgang Reitzle** (2006). *WirtschaftsWoche.* Ball pen, pencil

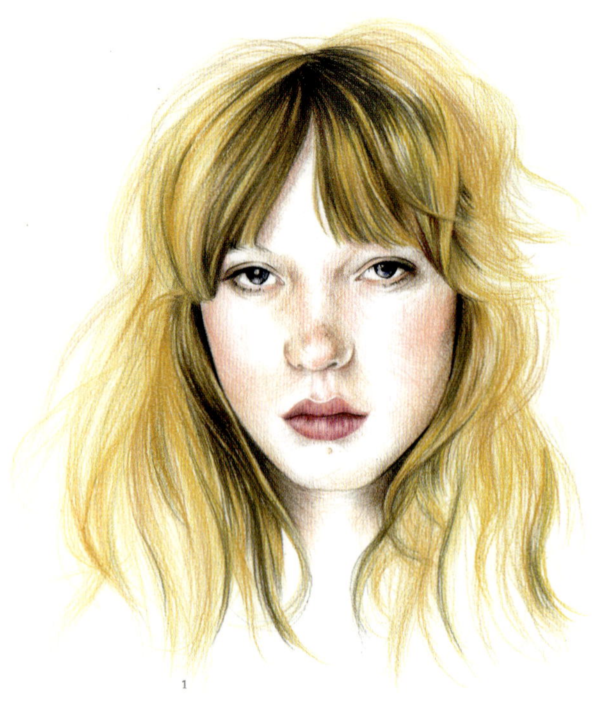

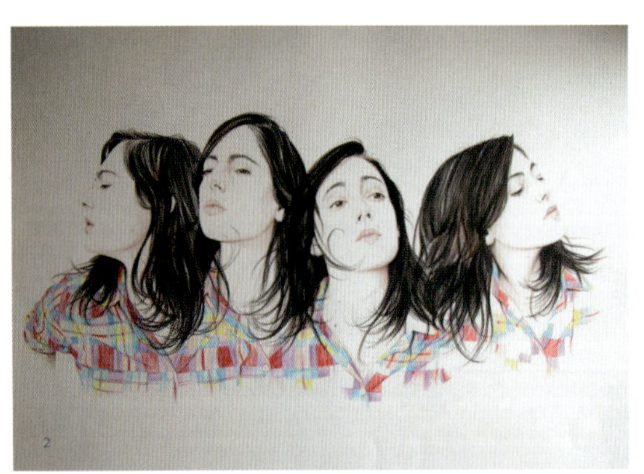

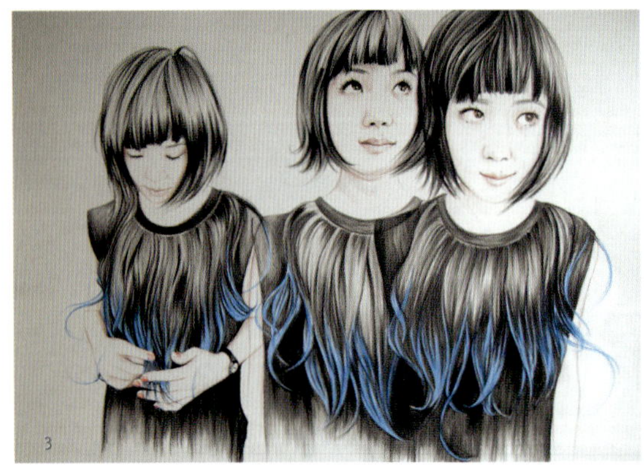

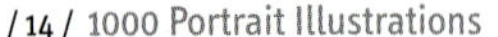

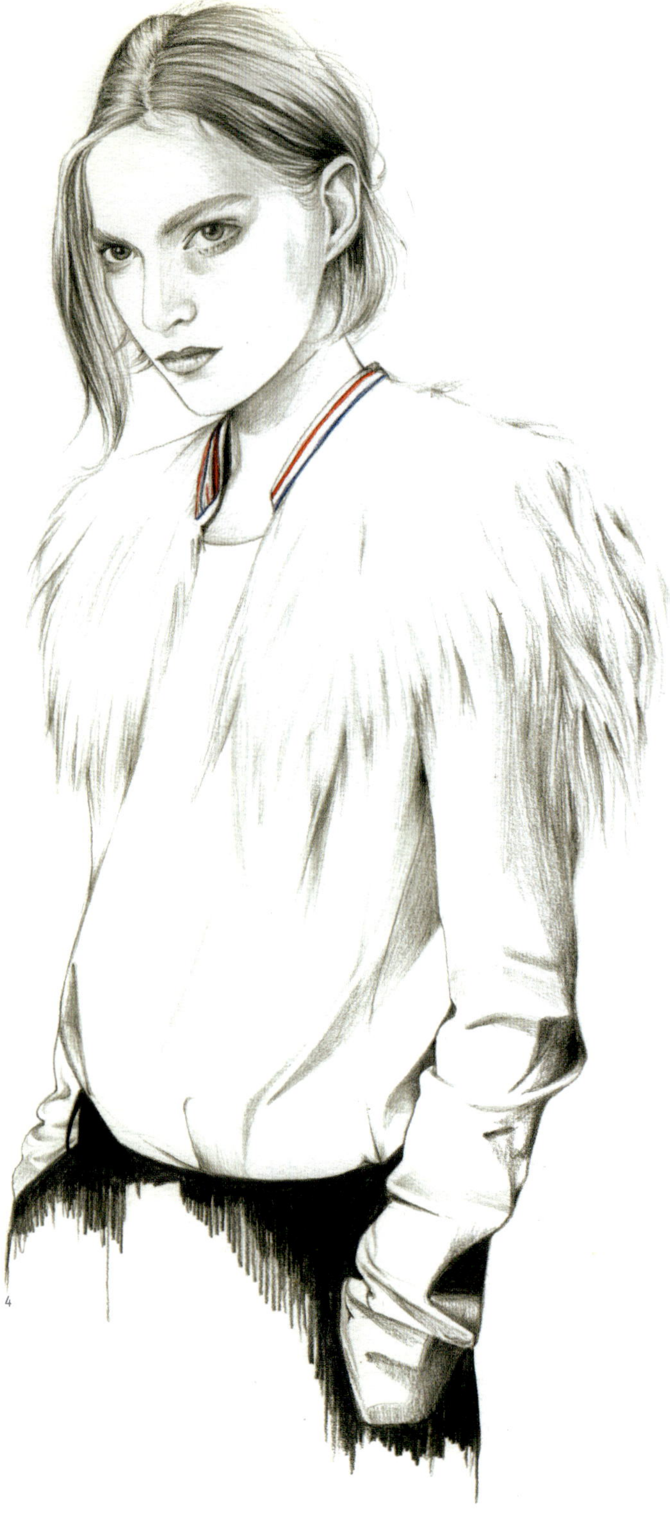

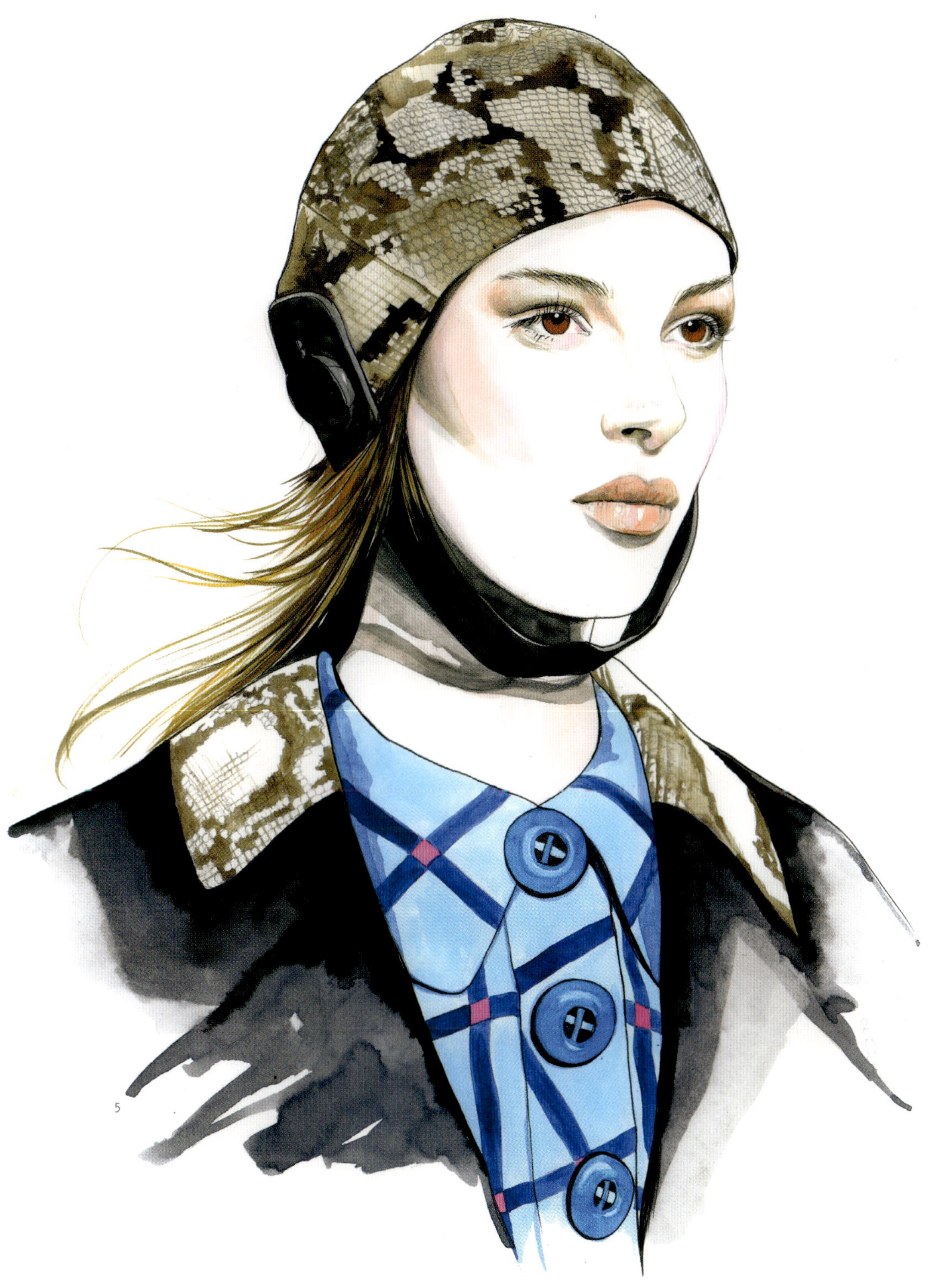

Caroline Andrieu

France

www.untitled-07.com

1. **Lea** (2011). Personal work. Colored pencil

2. **3 Kumis** (2010). Personal work. Colored pencil

3. **Arizona for Balmain** (2011). Personal work. Pencil, ink

4. **Mariacarla & Maryna for Louis Vuitton** (2011). Personal work. Pencil

5. **Tati for Marni** (2011). *Vogue* France. Ink

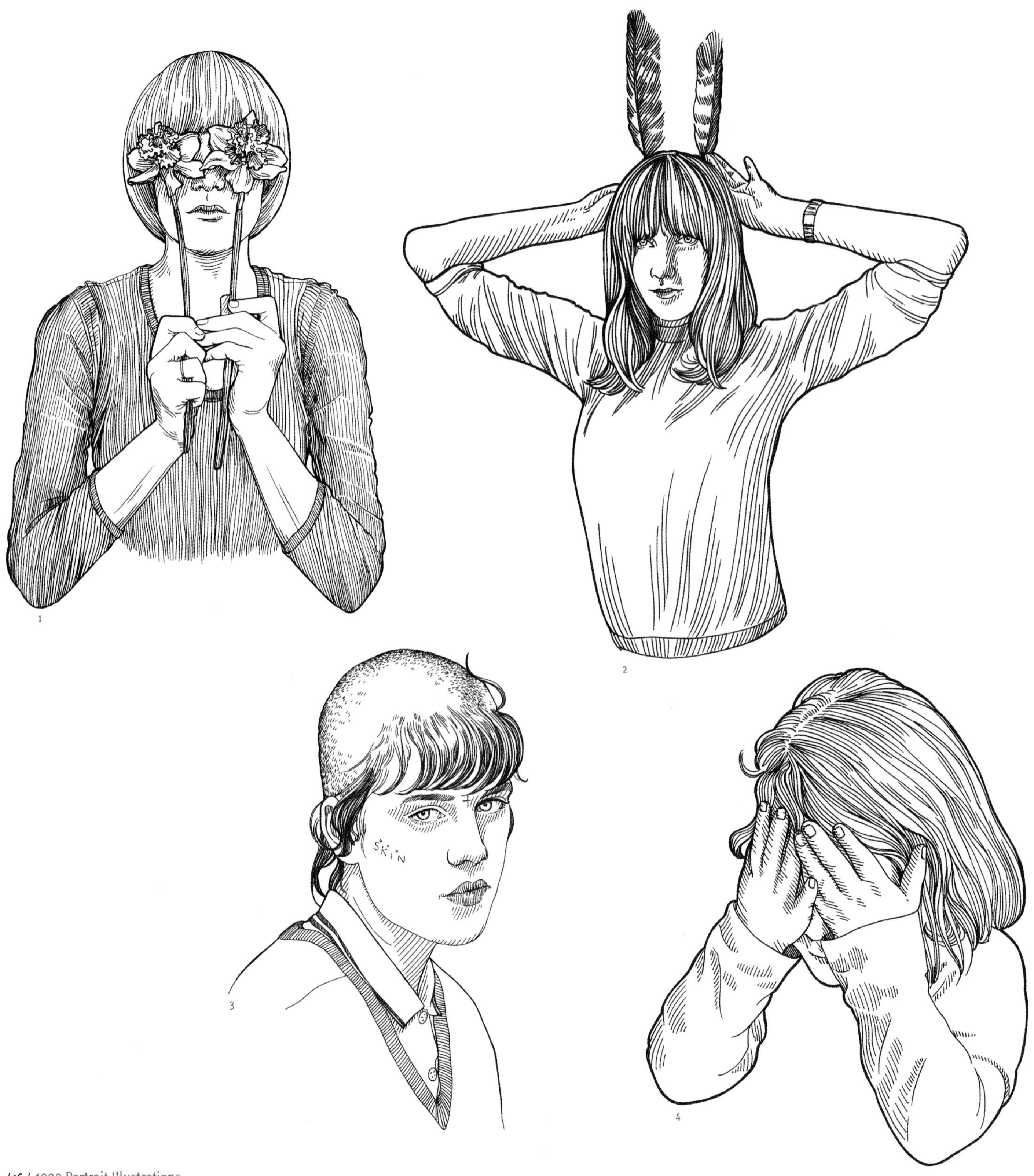

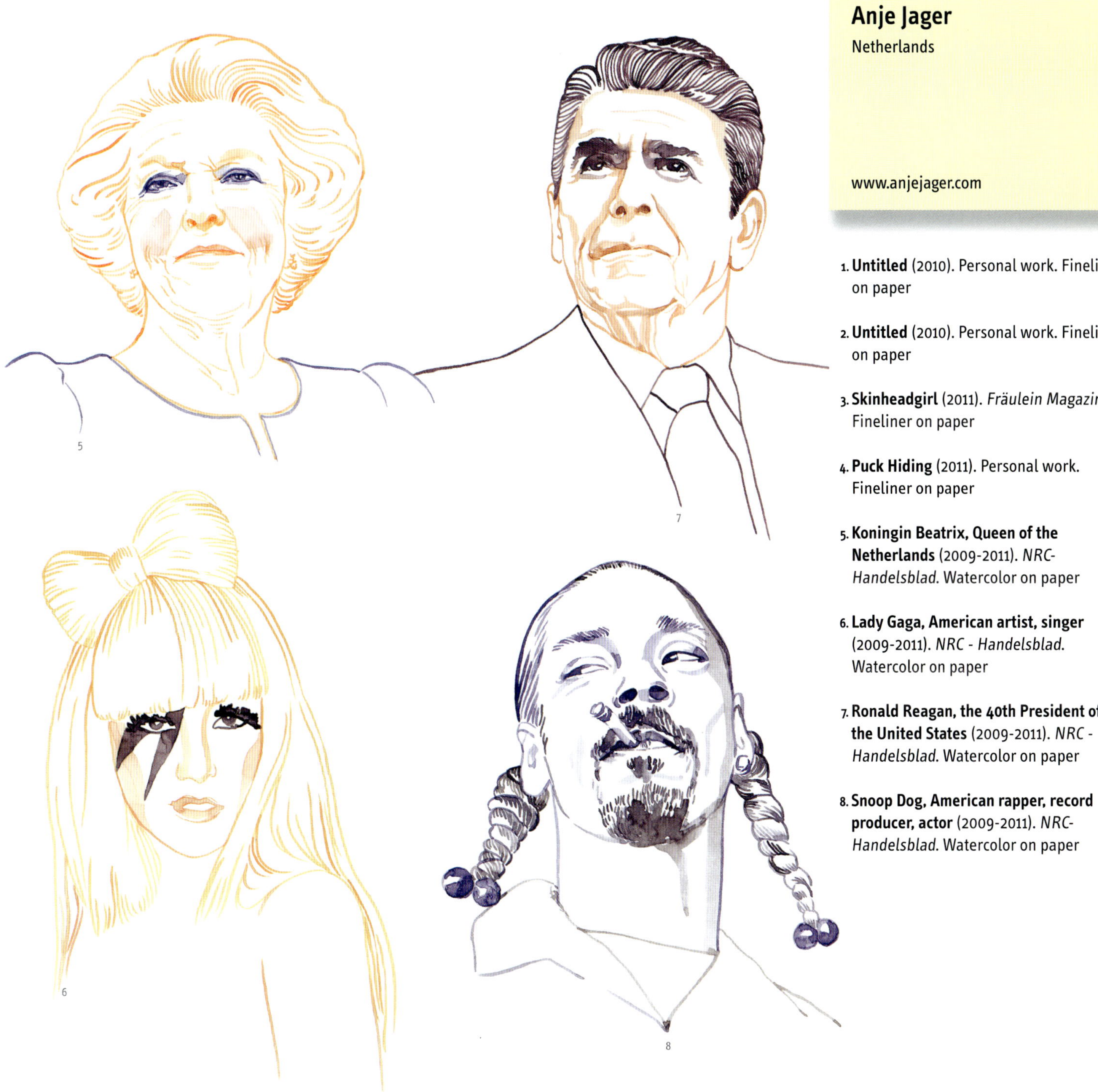

Anje Jager
Netherlands

www.anjejager.com

1. **Untitled** (2010). Personal work. Fineliner on paper

2. **Untitled** (2010). Personal work. Fineliner on paper

3. **Skinheadgirl** (2011). *Fräulein Magazin.* Fineliner on paper

4. **Puck Hiding** (2011). Personal work. Fineliner on paper

5. **Koningin Beatrix, Queen of the Netherlands** (2009-2011). *NRC-Handelsblad.* Watercolor on paper

6. **Lady Gaga, American artist, singer** (2009-2011). *NRC - Handelsblad.* Watercolor on paper

7. **Ronald Reagan, the 40th President of the United States** (2009-2011). *NRC - Handelsblad.* Watercolor on paper

8. **Snoop Dog, American rapper, record producer, actor** (2009-2011). *NRC-Handelsblad.* Watercolor on paper

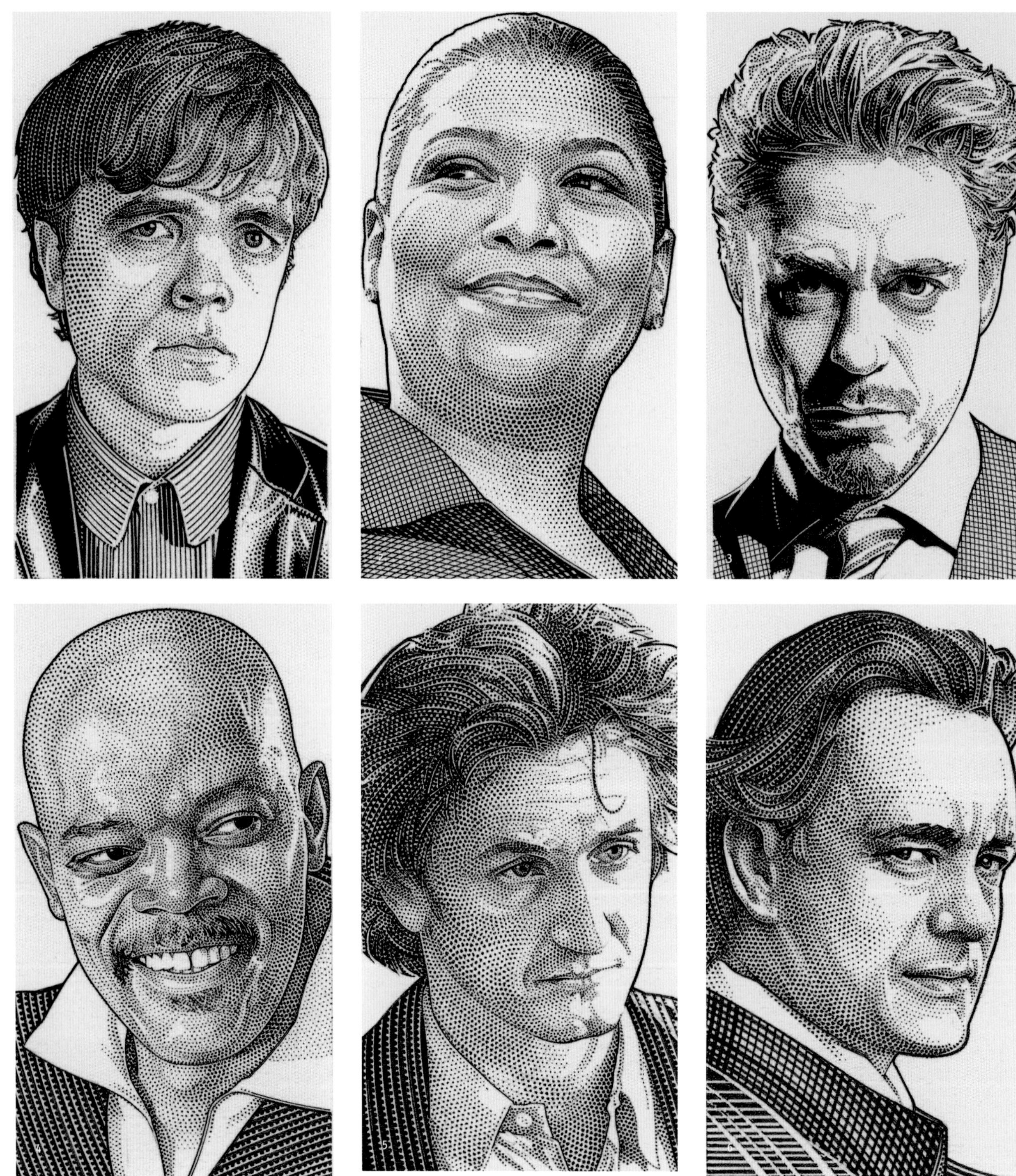

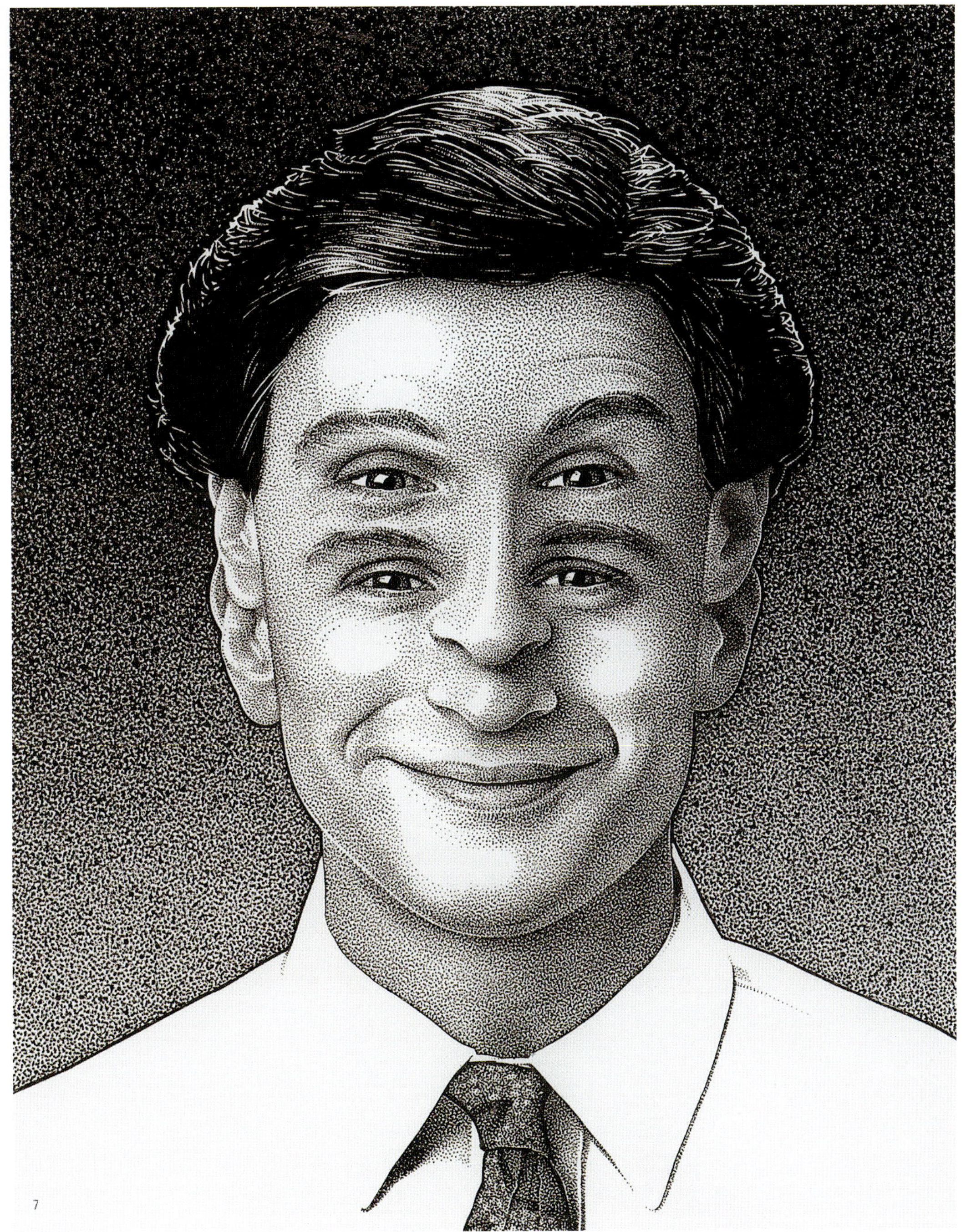

Randy Glass
USA

www.randyglassstudio.com

1. **Peter Dinklage** (2007). *Wall Street Journal*. Pen, ink

2. **Queen Latifah** (2008). *Wall Street Journal*. Pen, ink

3. **Robert Downey Jr.** (2008). *Wall Street Journal*. Pen, ink

4. **Samuel L. Jackson** (2006). *Wall Street Journal*. Pen, ink

5. **Sean Penn** (2004). *Wall Street Journal*. Pen, ink

6. **Tom Hanks** (2006). *Wall Street Journal*. Pen, ink

7. **2-Faced** (2008). Kinko's. Pen, ink

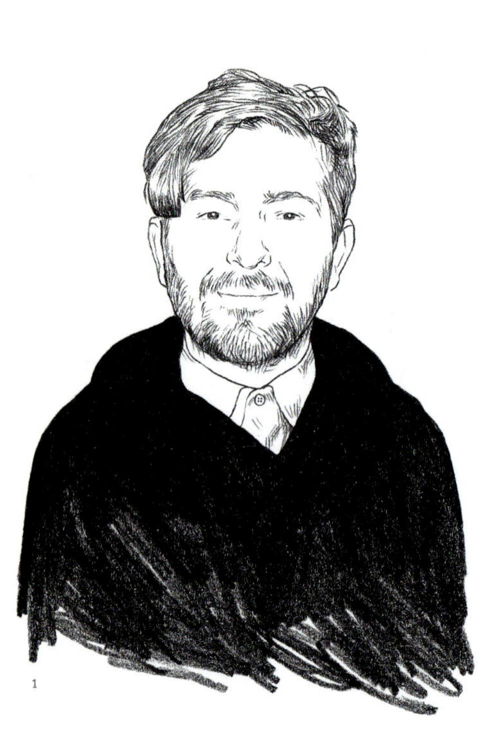

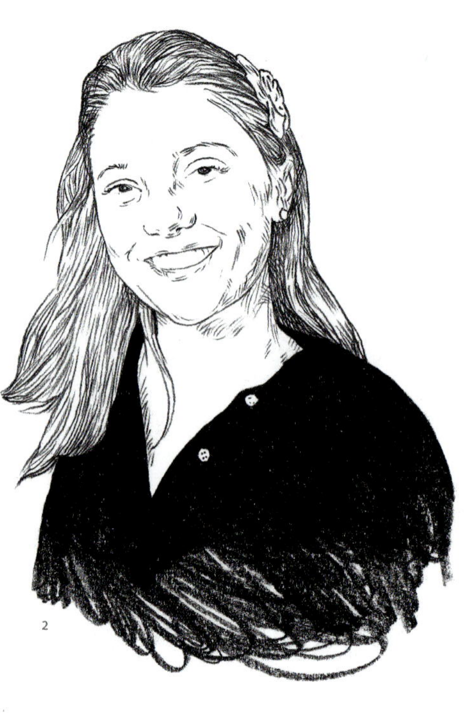

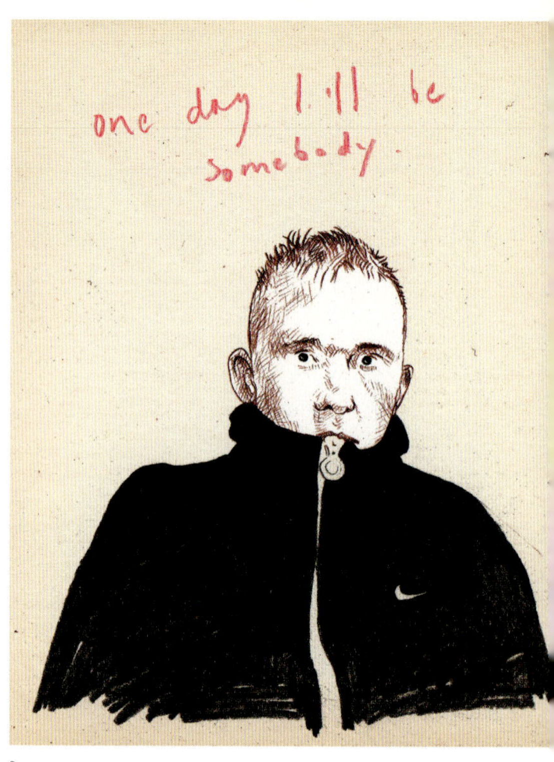

one day I will be
somebody.

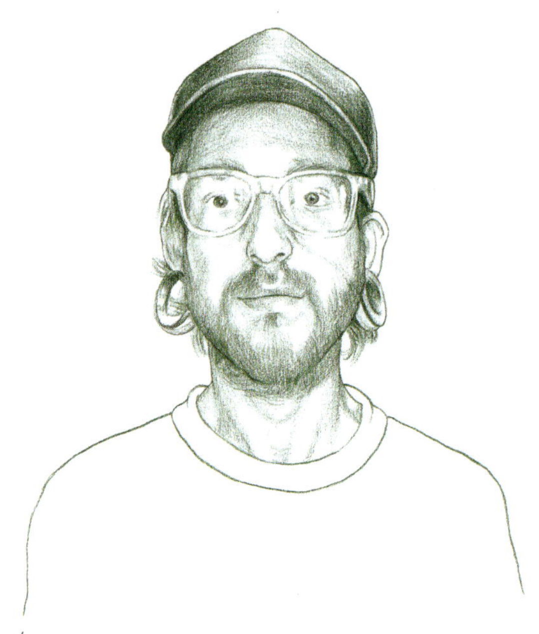

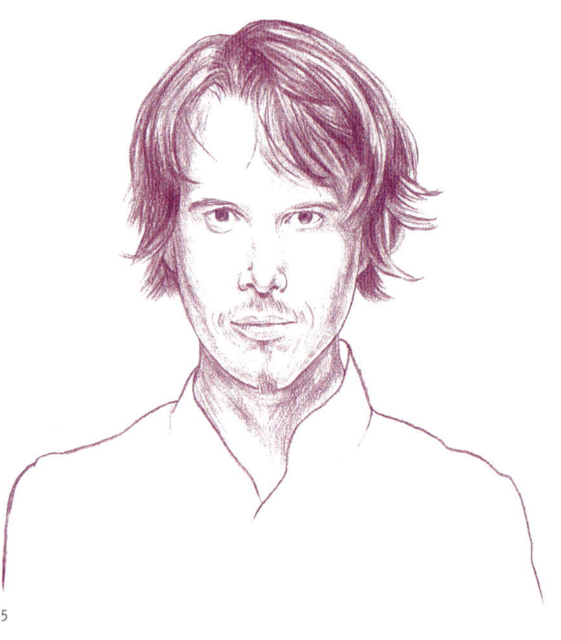

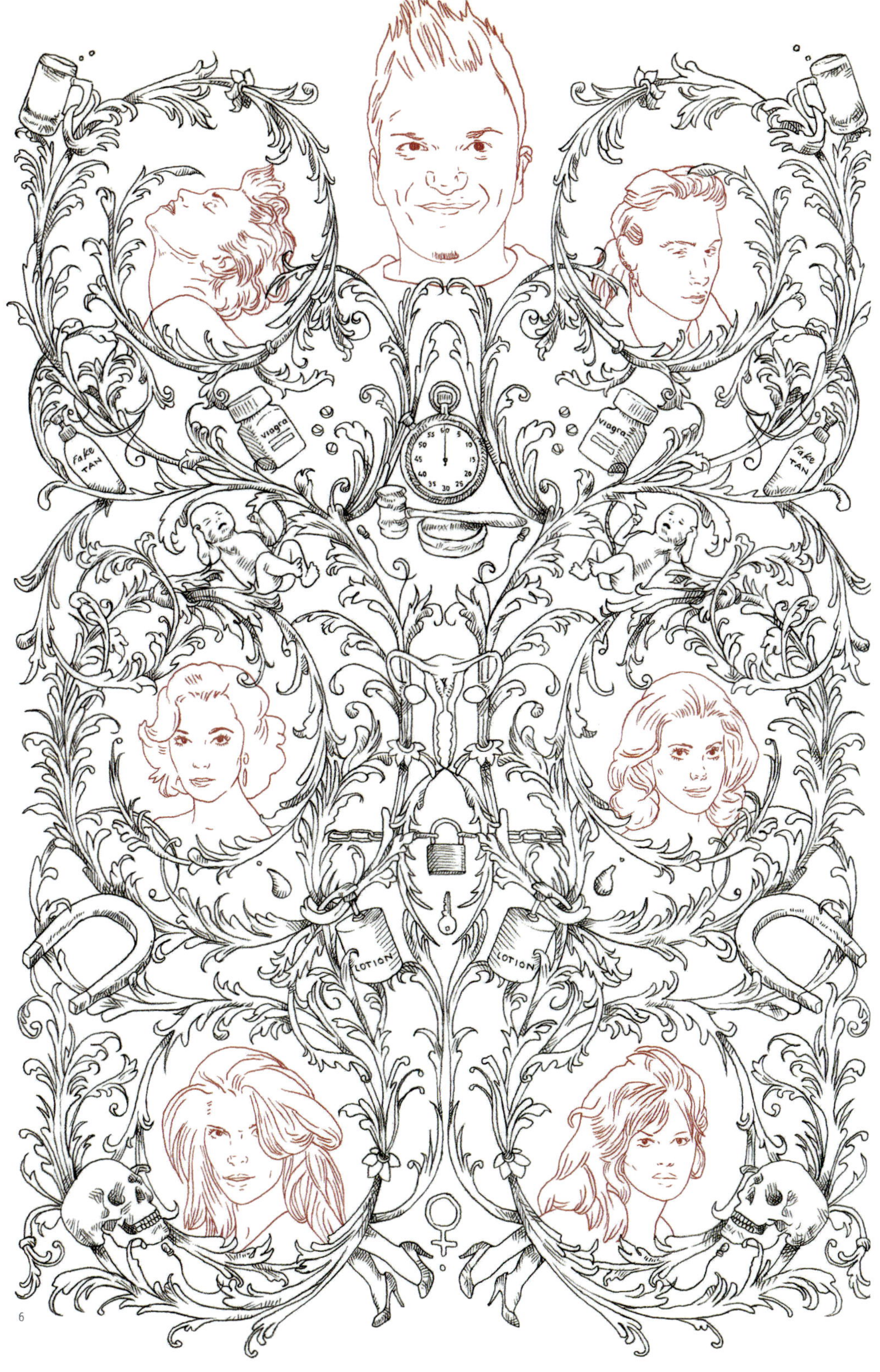

Peter James Field

UK

www.peterjamesfield.co.uk

1. **Contributors to *3 Perfect Days* column** (2010-11). *United Airlines Hemispheres* magazine. Pencil

2. **Contributors to *3 Perfect Days* column** (2010-11). *United Airlines Hemispheres* magazine. Pencil

3. **Somebody** (2009). Personal work. Pencil and digital

4. **Contributors to *3 Perfect Days* column** (2011). *United Airlines Hemispheres* magazine. Colored pencil

5. **Contributors to *3 Perfect Days* column** (2011). *United Airlines Hemispheres* magazine. Colored pencil

6. ***Saliva Tree*** Book Cover (2011). Personal work. Pencil

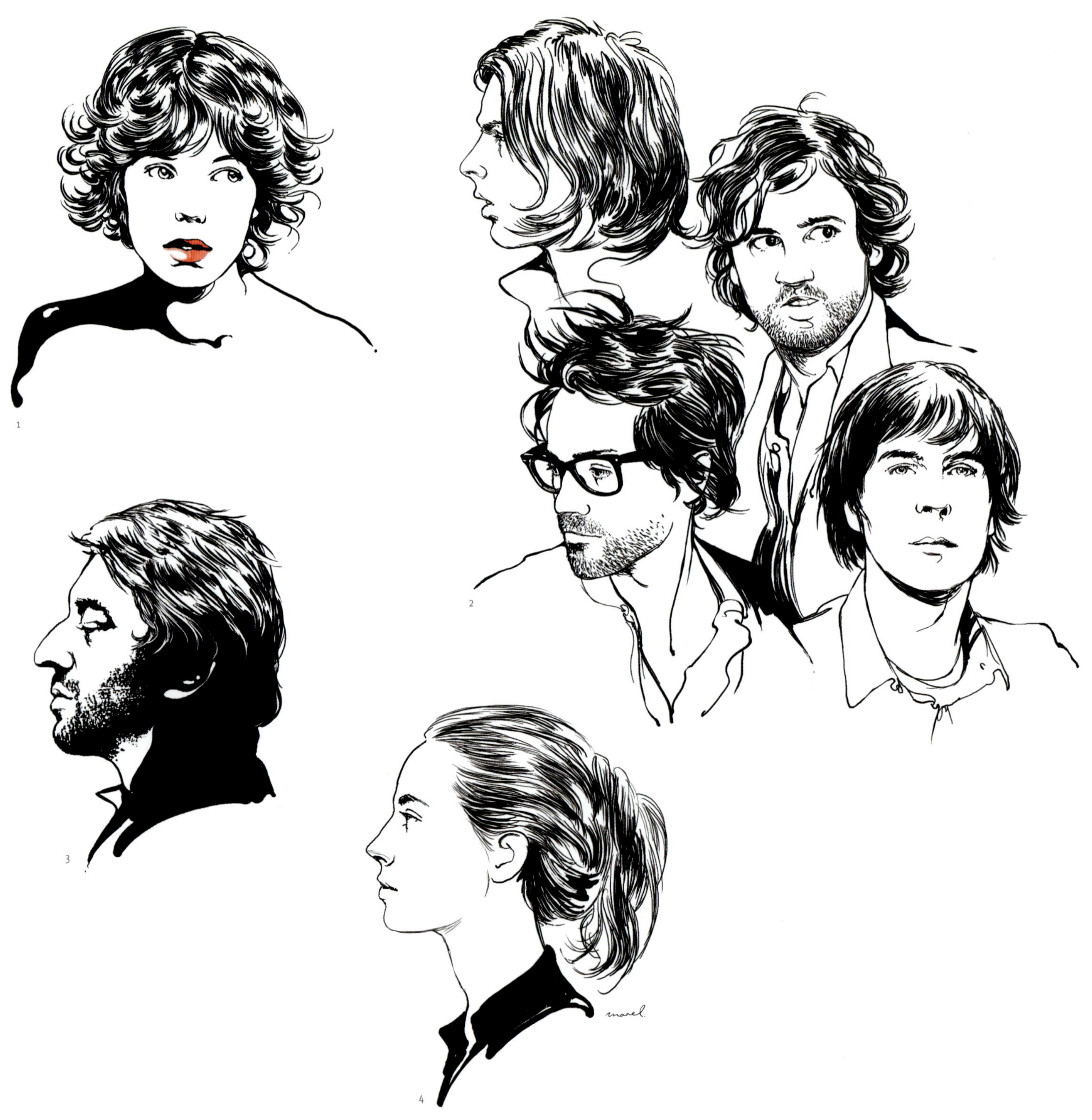

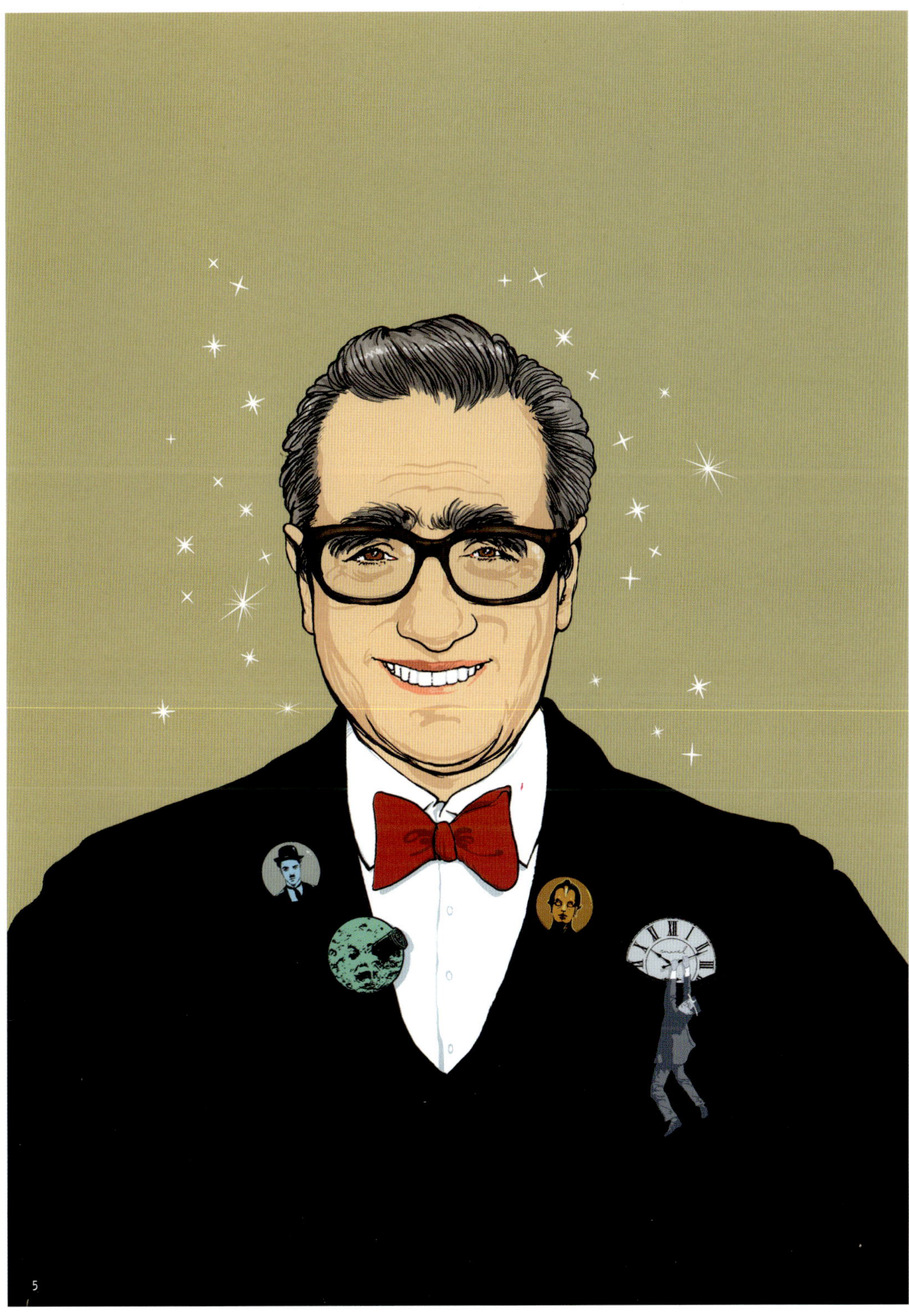

Stéphane Manel

France

www.stephanemanel.com

1. **Amiral Nelson** (2010). *Social Club Magazine*. Ink on paper

2. **Phoenix** (2009). *Magic Magazine* Hors Série. Digital

3. **Serge Gainsbourg** (2011) *L'integrale Gainsbourg* by Gilles Verlant & Loic Picaud, Fetjaine Editions. Ink on paper

4. **Anne** (2009). Personal work. Ink on paper

5. **Martin Scorsese** (2011). *3 Couleurs*. Digital

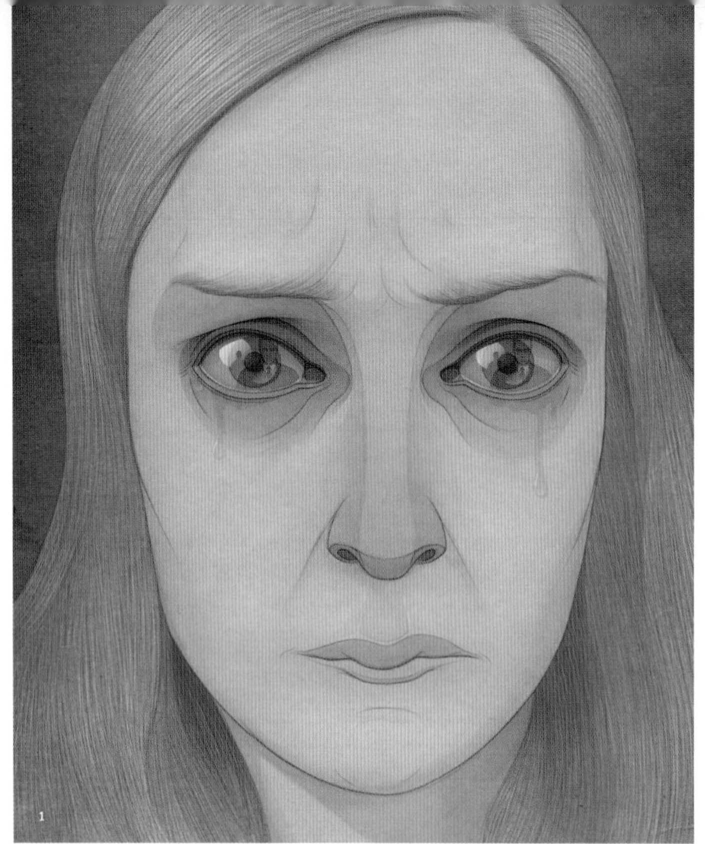

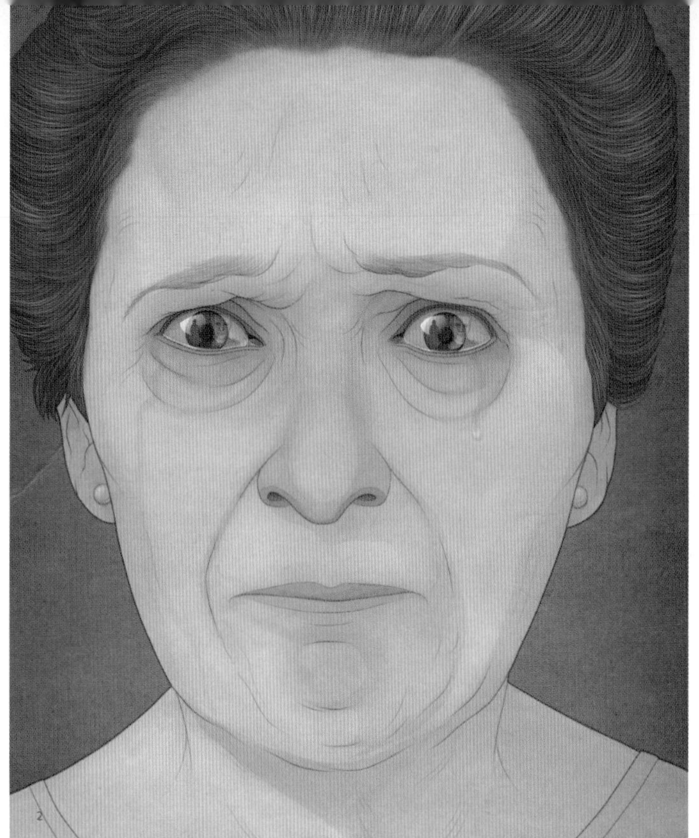

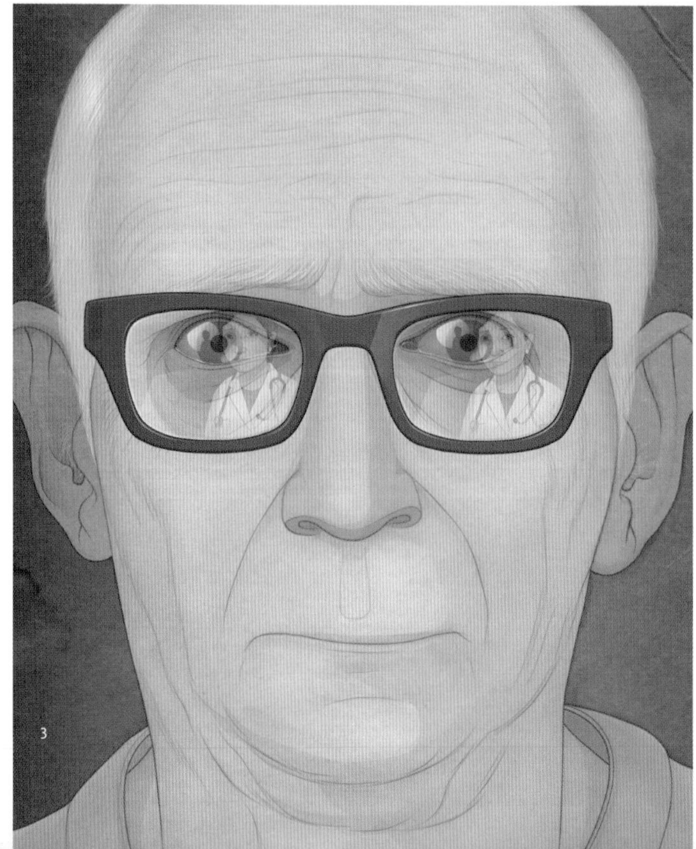

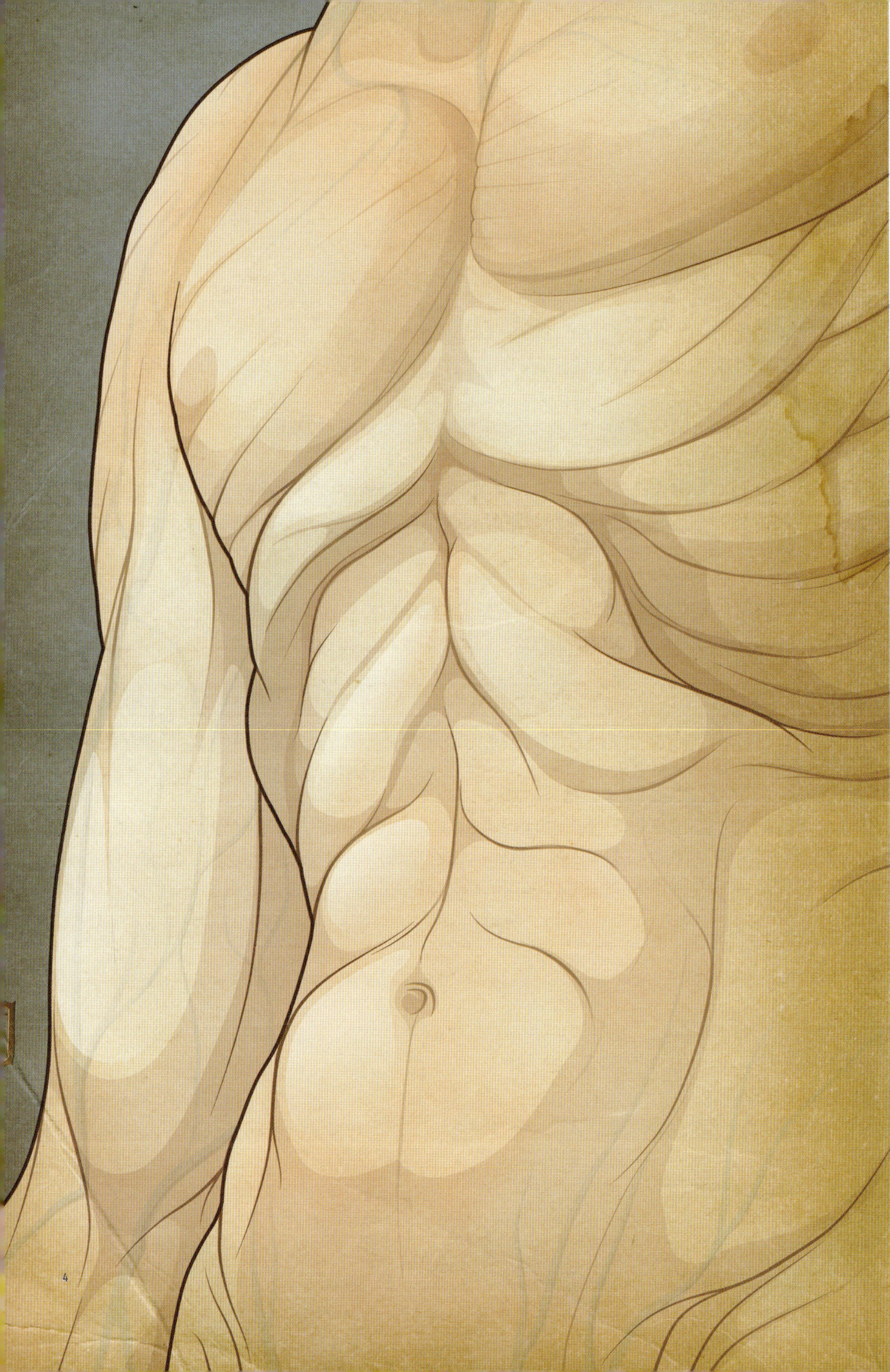

Richard Wilkinson
UK

www.richard-wilkinson.com

1. **He didn't suffer...** (2011). *Intelligent Life*. Digital

2. **Im so sorry...your son...** (2011). *Intelligent Life*. Digital

3. **We did all we could...** (2011). *Intelligent Life*. Digital

4. **David 2.0** (2009) *Telegraph Magazine*. Digital

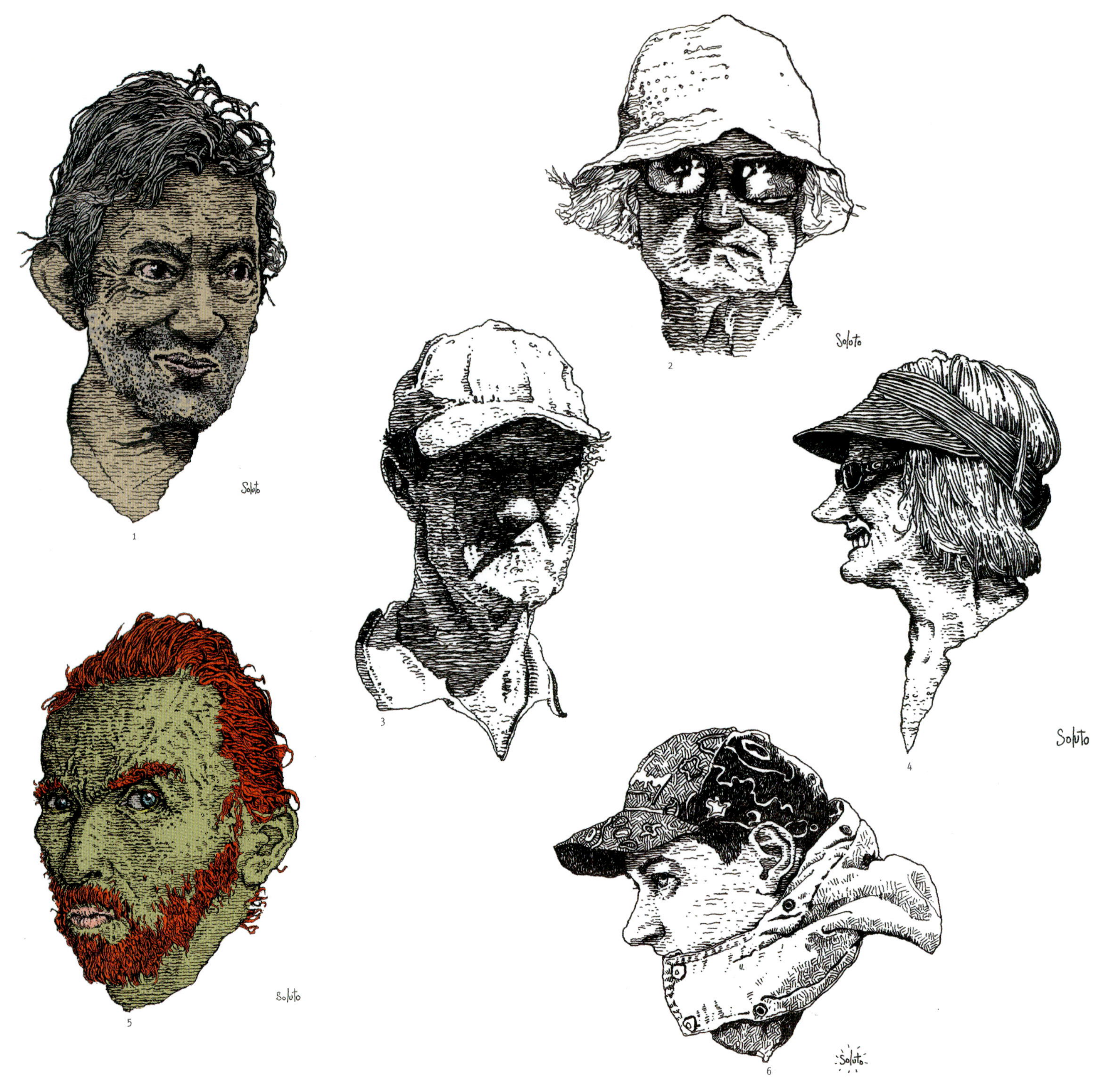

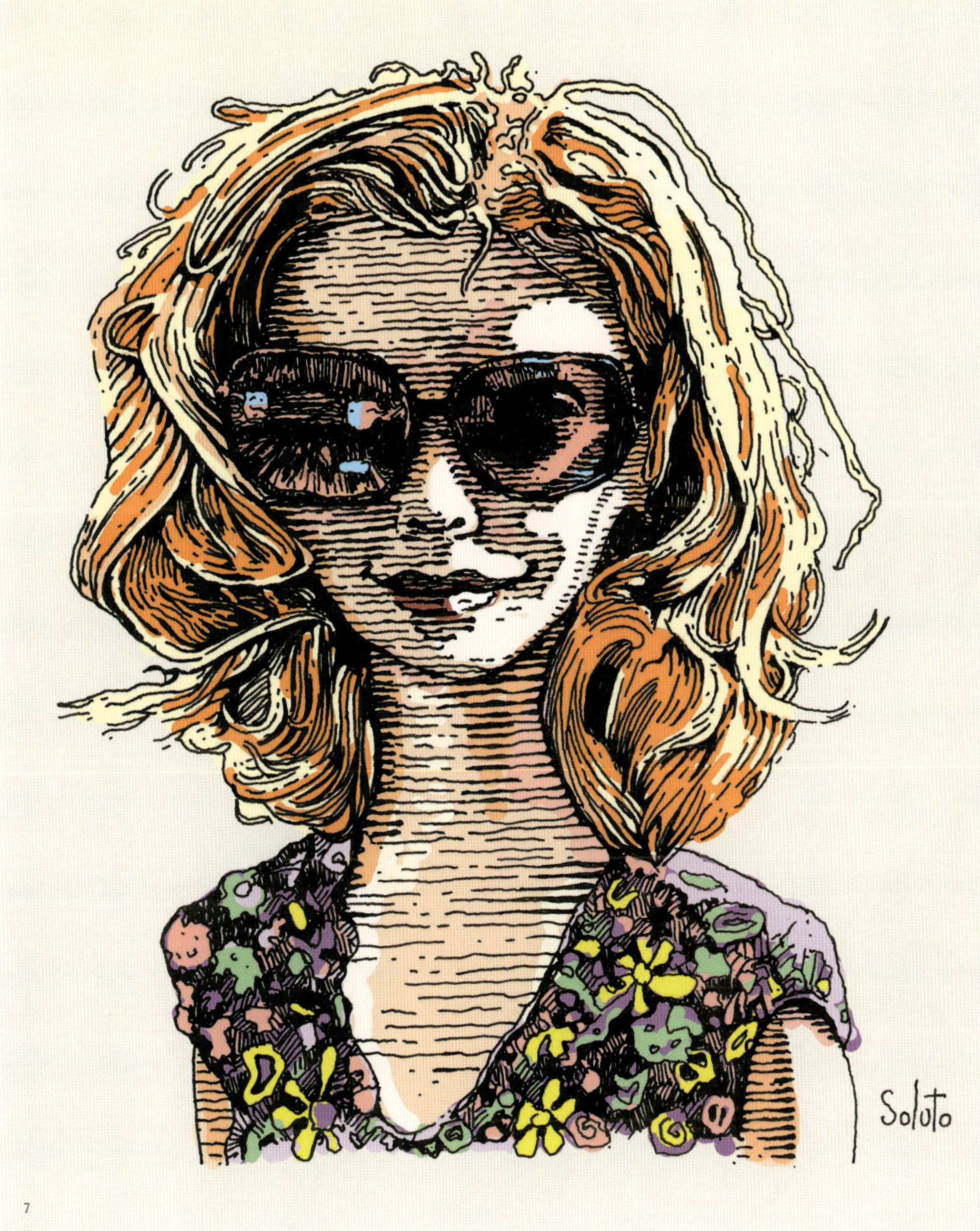

1. **Serge Gainsbourg** (2011). India ink, numeric colors

2. **Gaby** (2010). India ink

3. **Casquette** (2011). India ink

4. **Visière** (2011). India ink

5. **Vincent Van Gogh** (2011). India ink, numeric colors

6. **Autre Casquette** (2009). India ink

7. **Joss** (2011). India ink, numeric colors

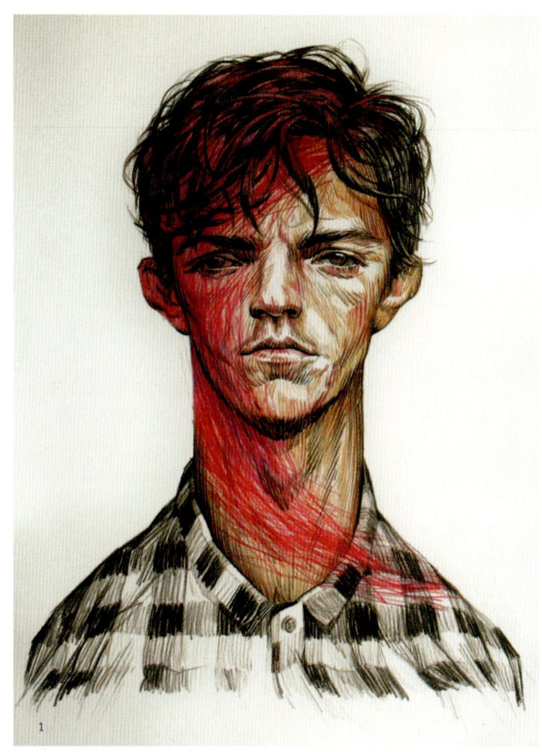

1

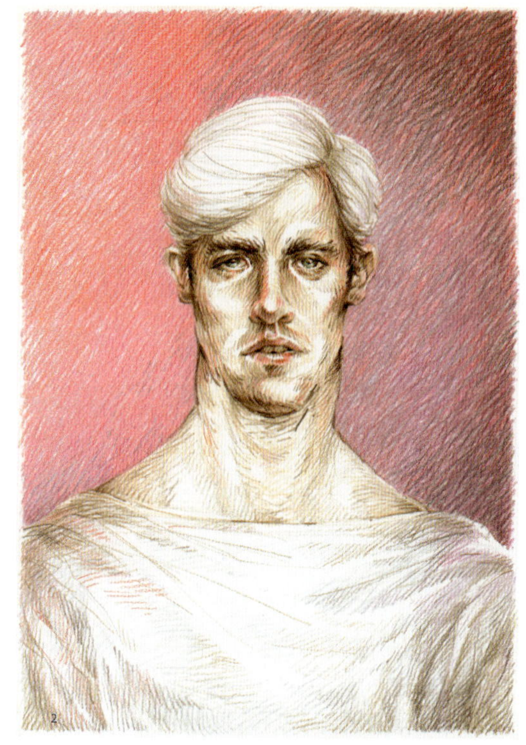

2

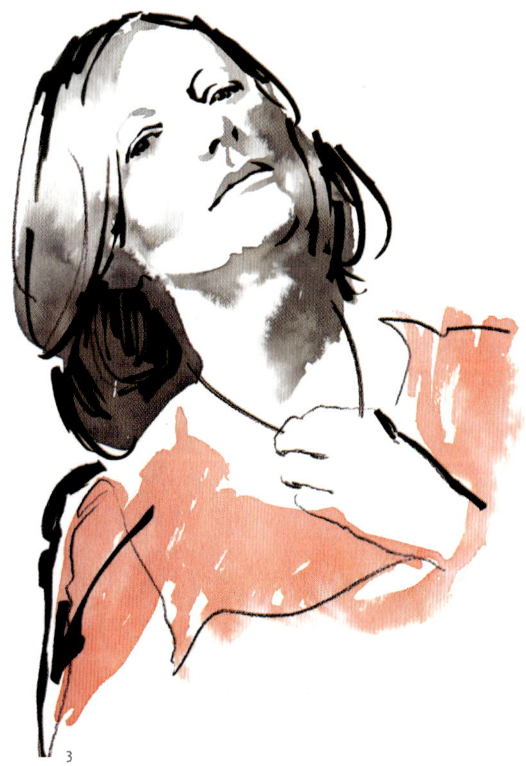

3

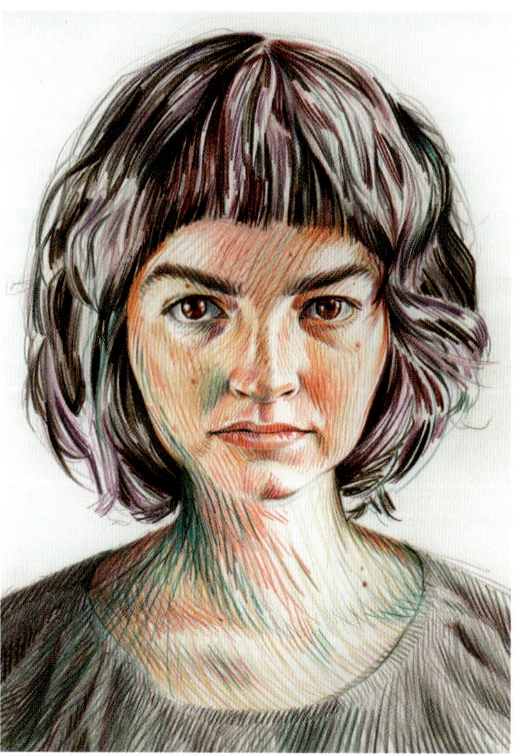

4

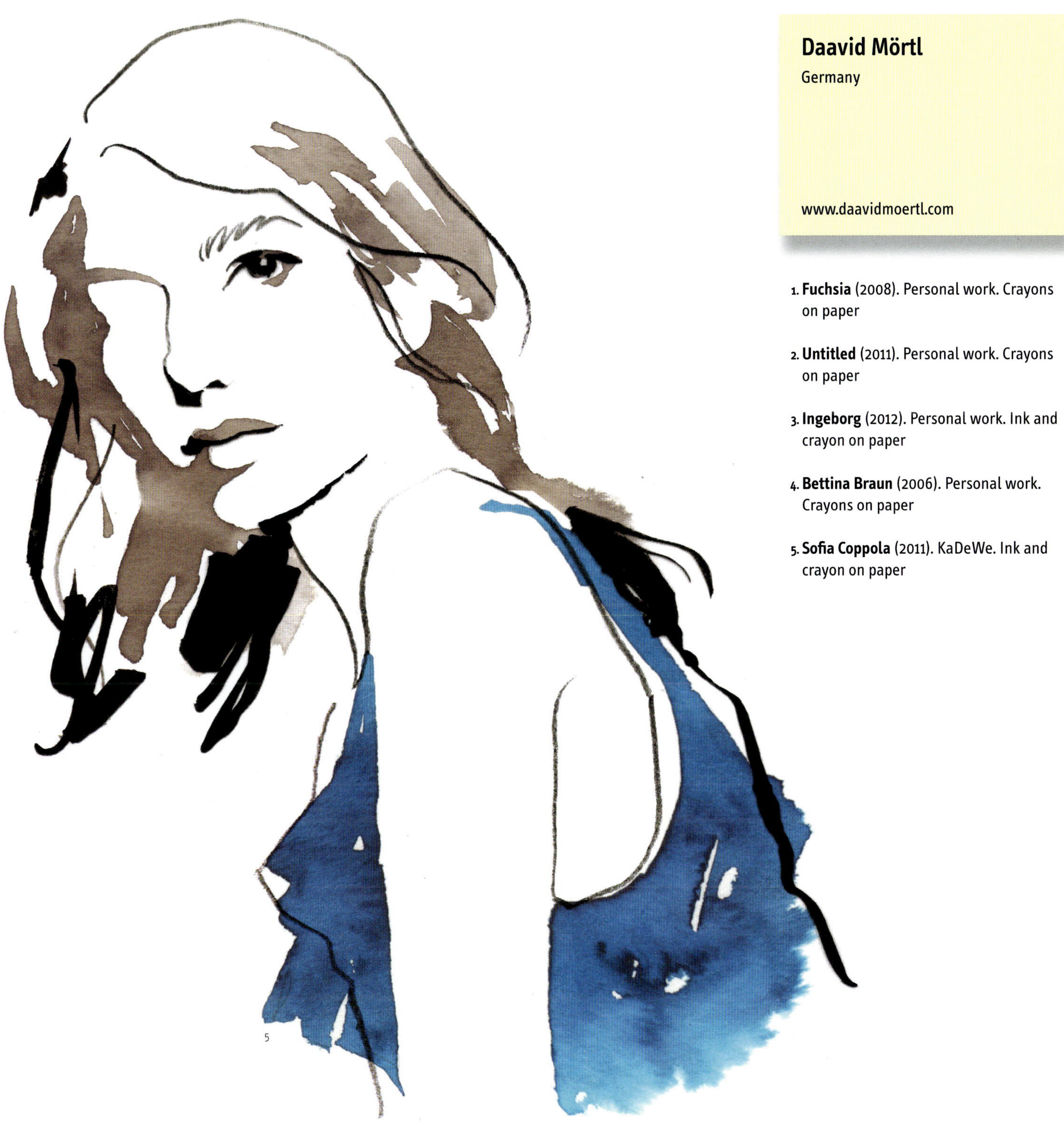

1. **Fuchsia** (2008). Personal work. Crayons on paper

2. **Untitled** (2011). Personal work. Crayons on paper

3. **Ingeborg** (2012). Personal work. Ink and crayon on paper

4. **Bettina Braun** (2006). Personal work. Crayons on paper

5. **Sofia Coppola** (2011). KaDeWe. Ink and crayon on paper

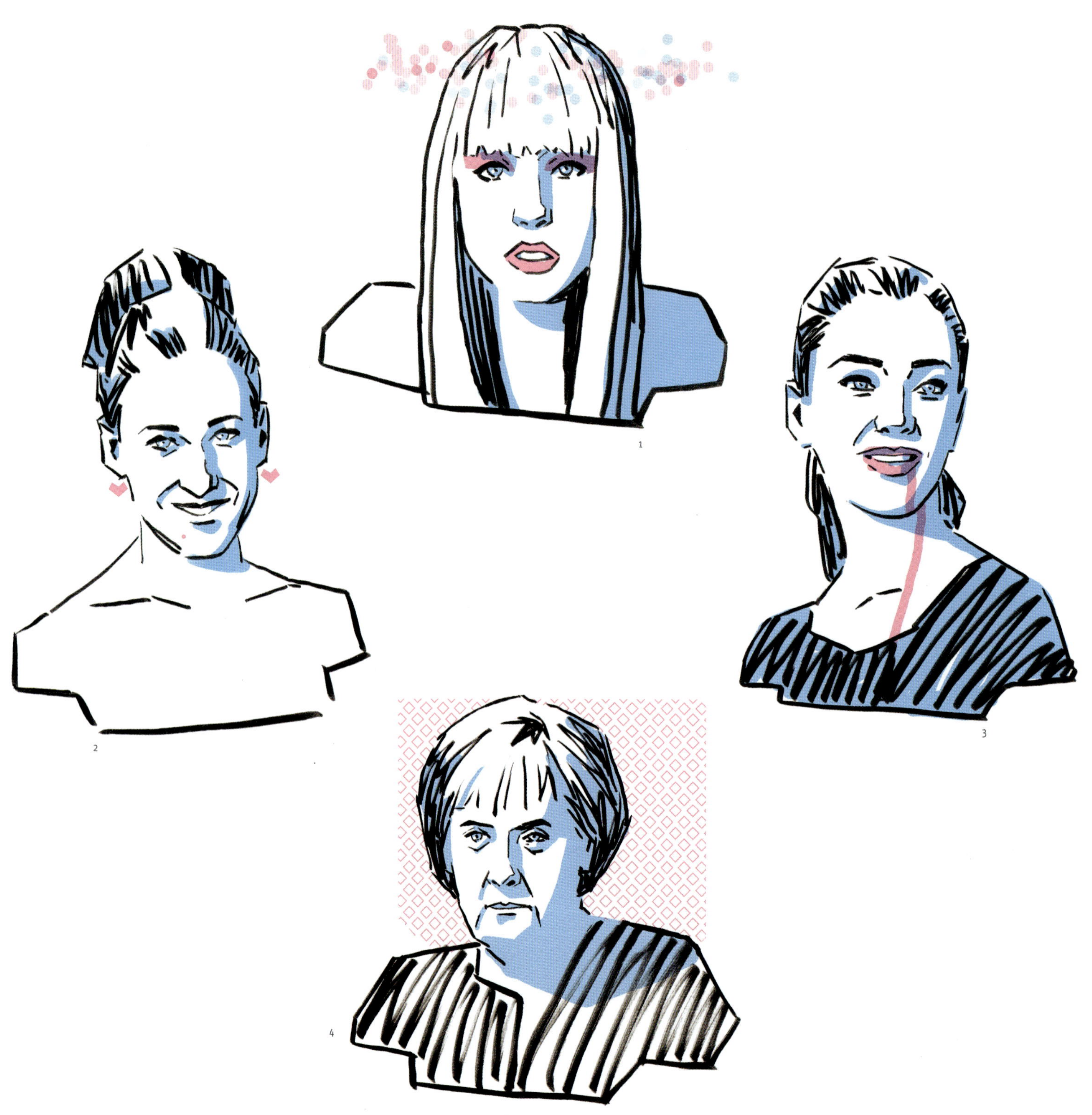

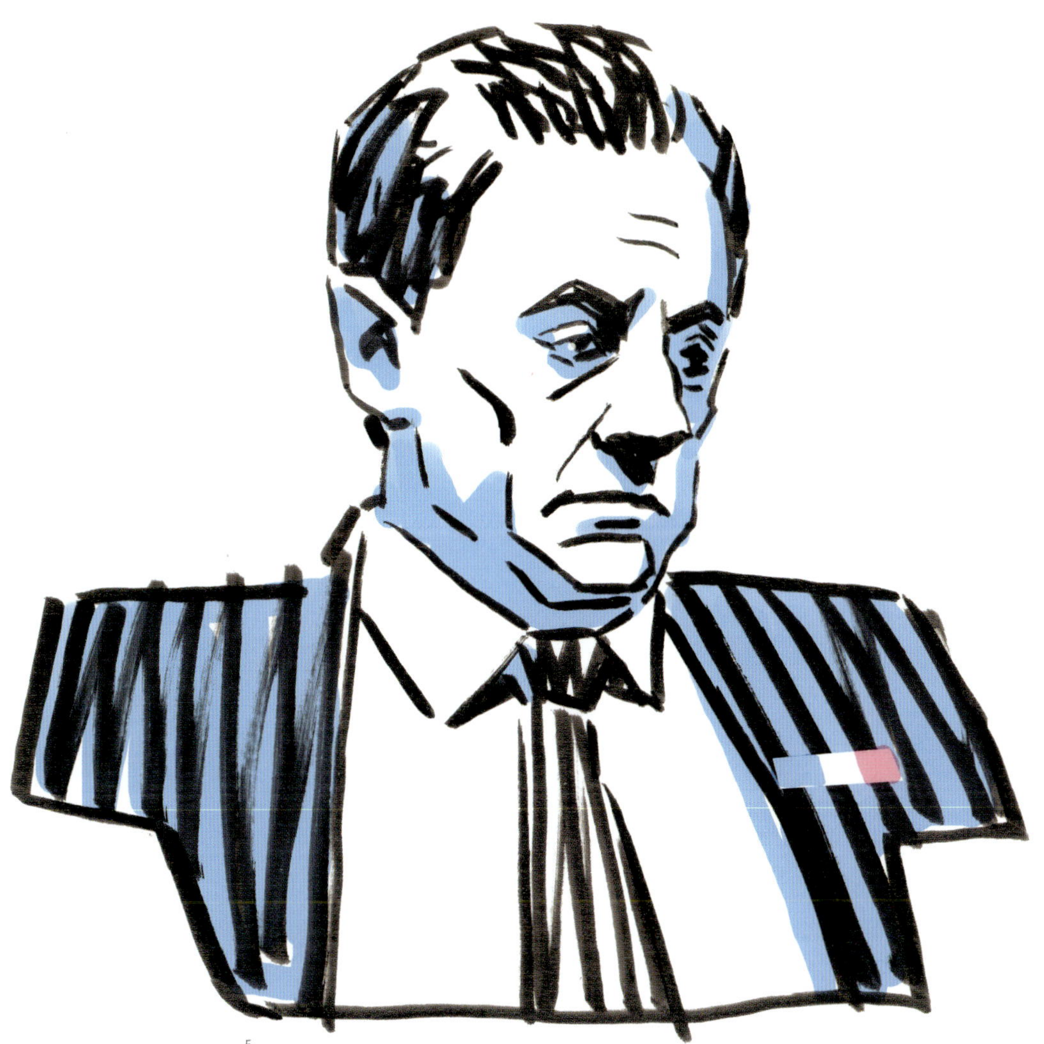

5

Sven Kalkschmidt
Germany

www.svenkalkschmidt.com

1. **Lady Gaga** (2010). Personal work.
   Brushpen, digital coloring in Photoshop

2. **Sarah Jessica Parker** (2010). Personal
   work. Brushpen, digital coloring in
   Photoshop

3. **Verona Feldbusch** (2010). Personal work.
   Brushpen, digital coloring in Photoshop

4. **Angela Merkel** (2010). Personal work.
   Brushpen, digital coloring in Photoshop

5. **Nicolas Sarkozy** (2010). Personal work.
   Brushpen, digital coloring in Photoshop

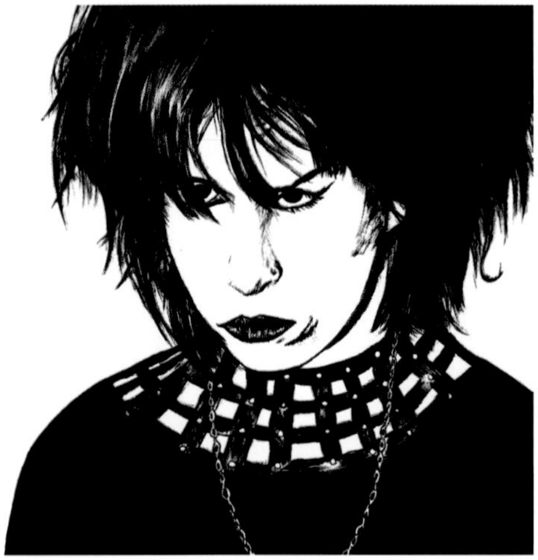

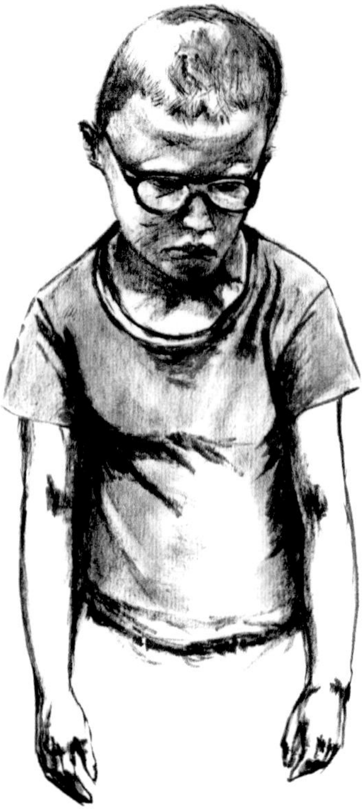

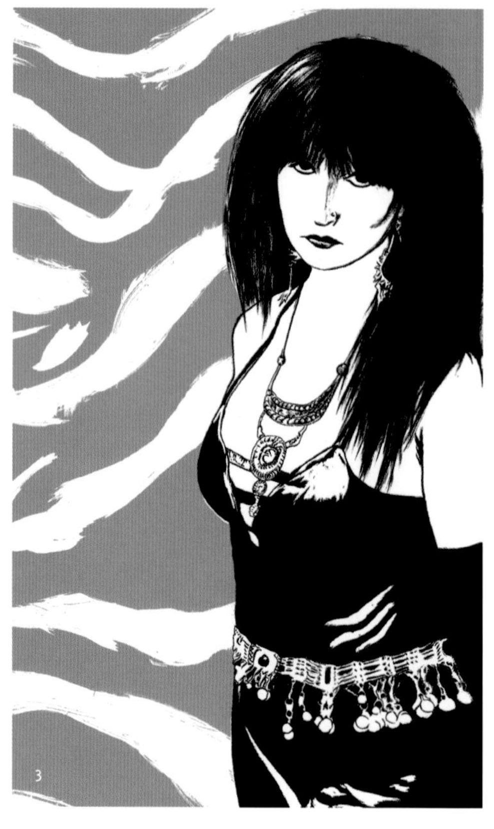

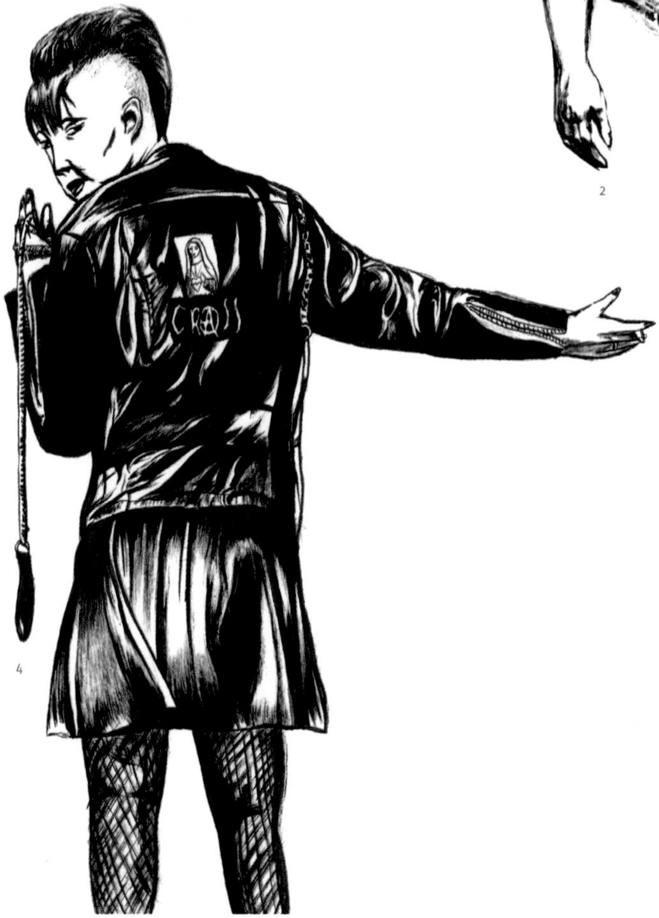

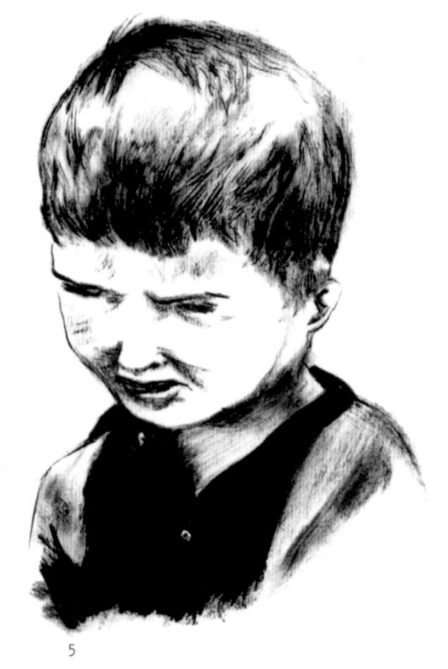

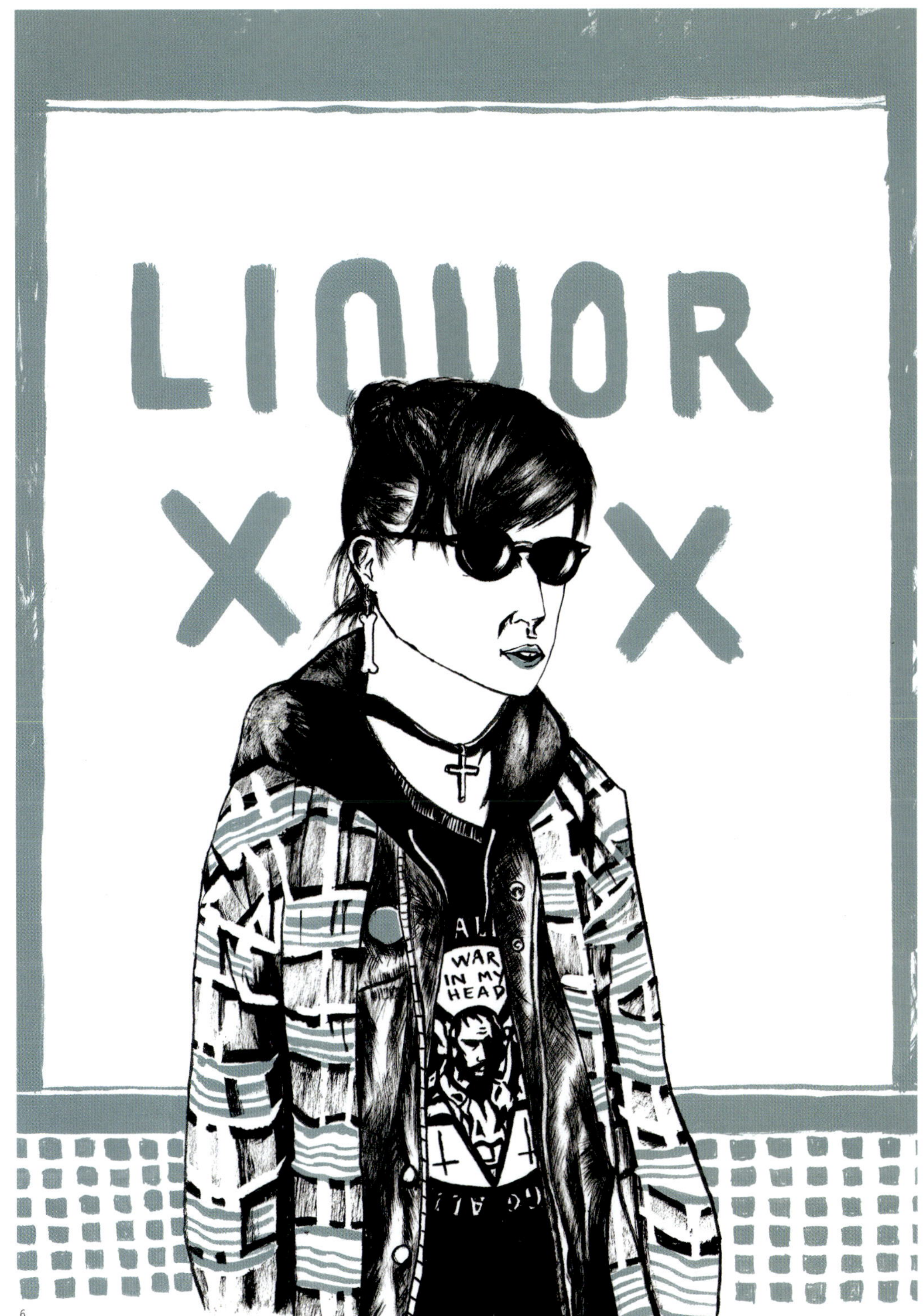

Joseph Gough
UK

www.josephgough.co.uk

1. **Trudi** (2011). Personal work. Ink

2. **Piggy** (2011). Personal work. Ink

3. **Lacrimosa** (2011). Personal work. Ink

4. **Crass** (2011). Personal work. Ink

5. **Simon** (2011). Personal work. Ink

6. **Pippa** (2011). Personal work. Ink

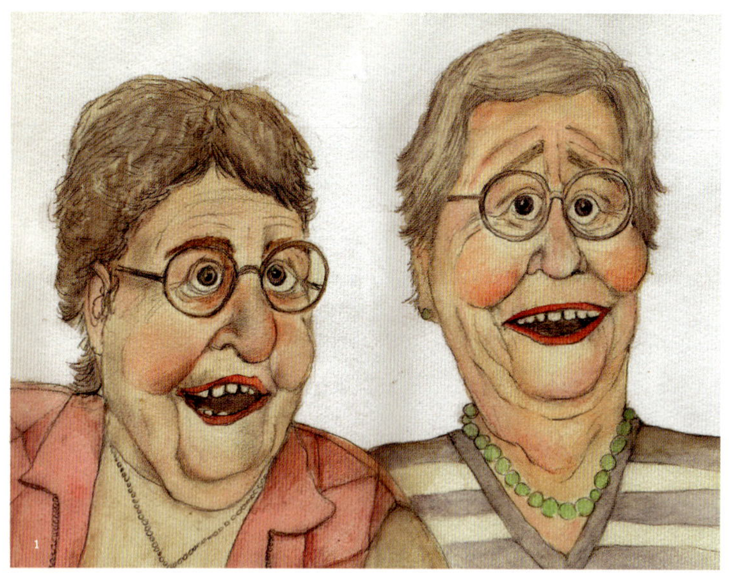

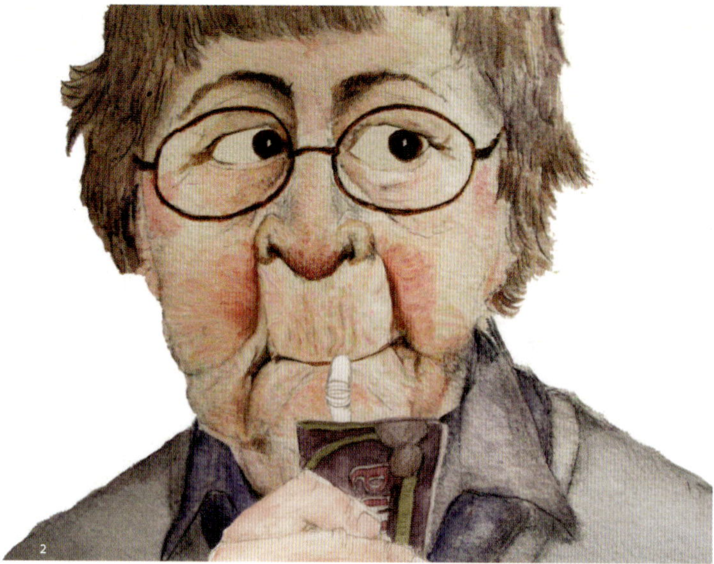

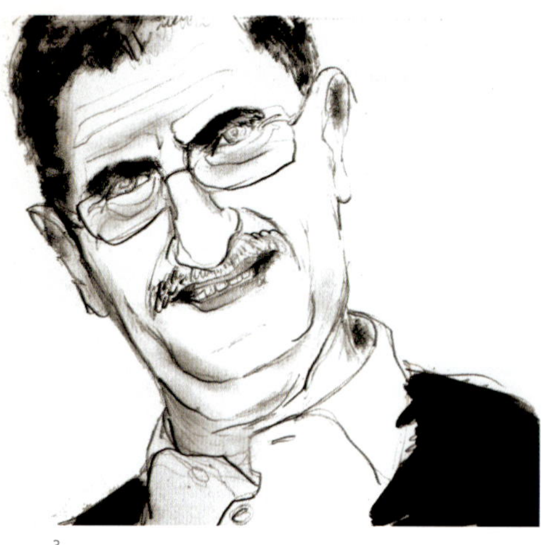

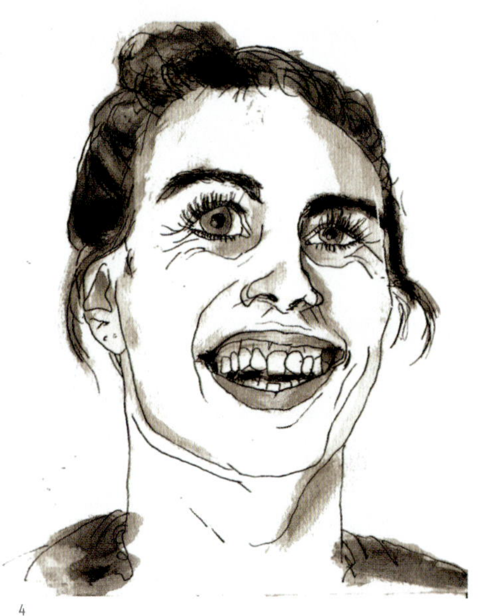

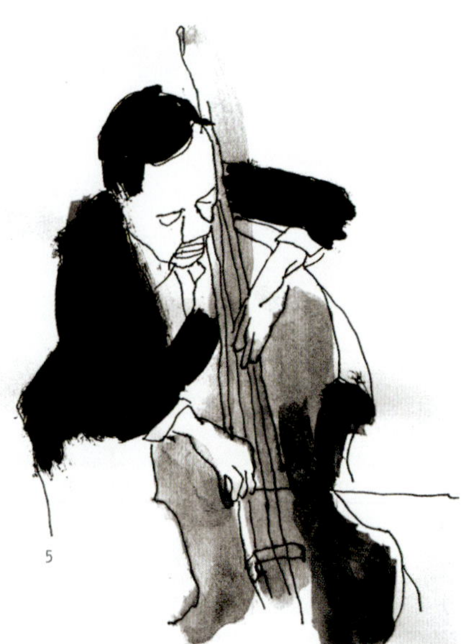

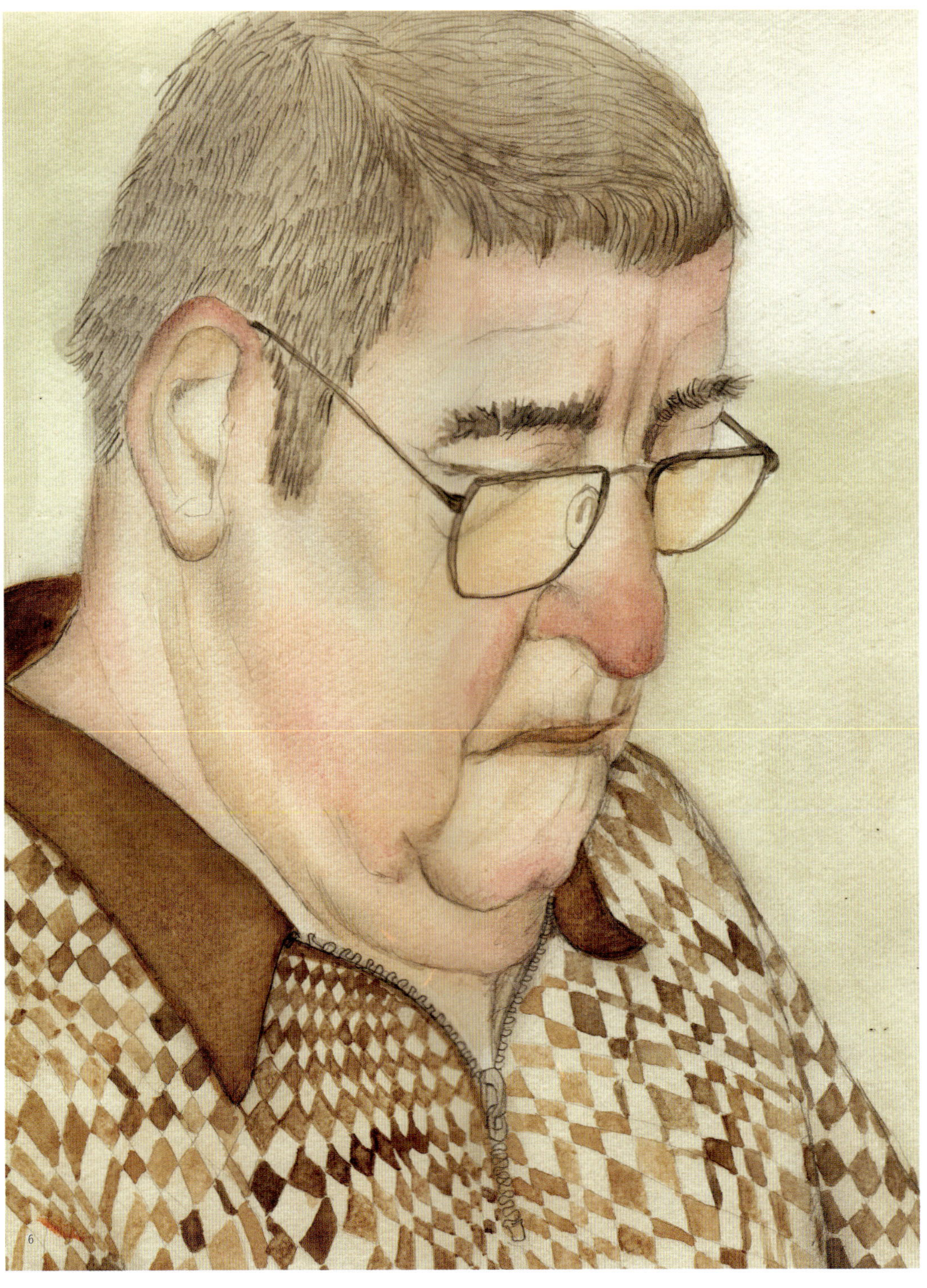

Marlene Rask
Denmark

www.marlenerask.dk

1. **Banko** (2009). Personal work. Pencil, watercolor, Photoshop

2. **Ellen Drinking Juice** (2009). Personal work. Pencil, watercolor, Photoshop

3. **Mogens Lykketoft** (2009). Personal work. Ink, pencil, Photoshop

4. **Sara** (2009). ArtRebels, Ink

5. **Miguel** (2008). Personal work. Ink, Photoshop

6. **Lars** (2009). Personal work. Pencil, watercolor

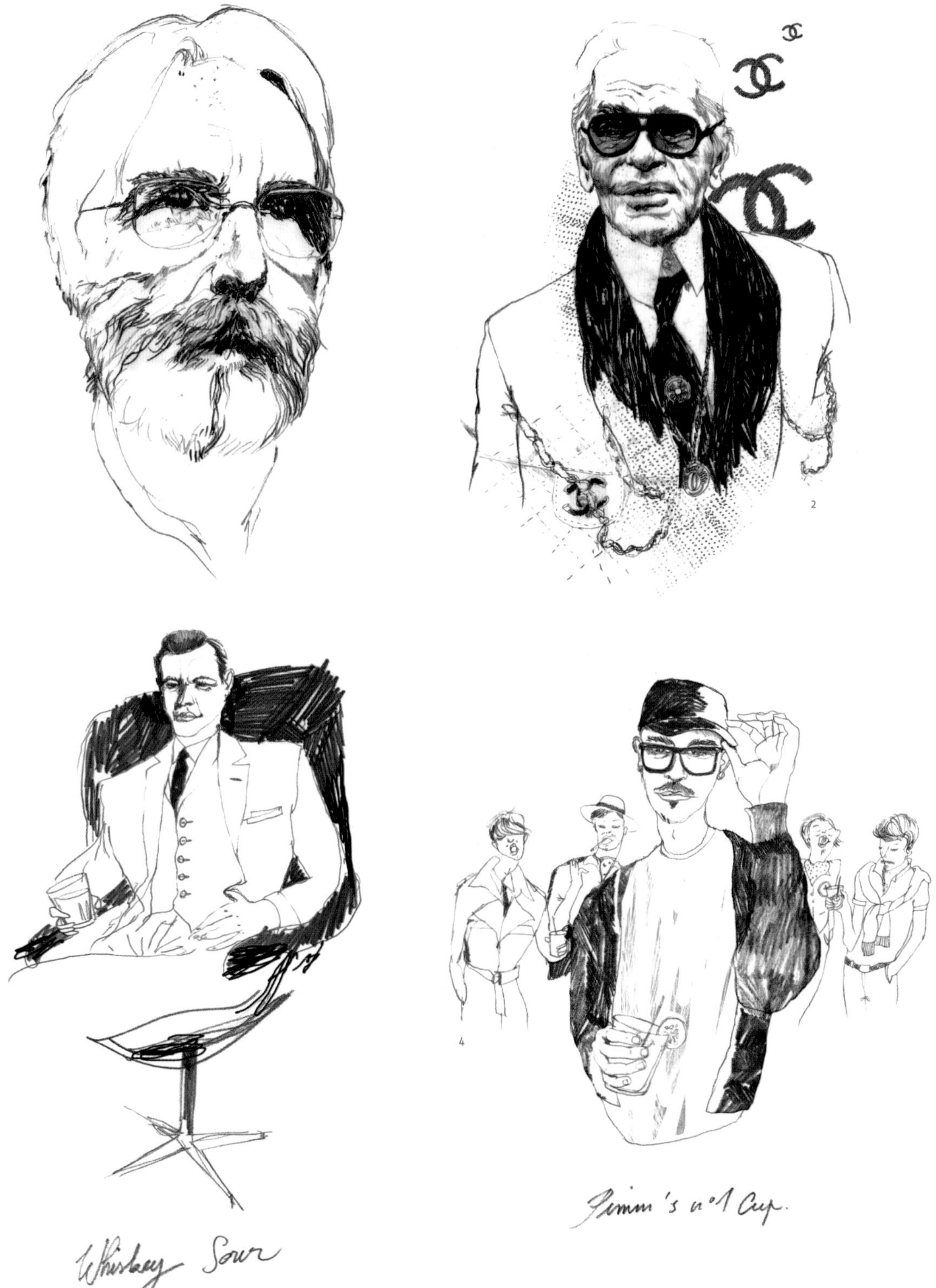

Whiskey Sour
Pimm's n°1 cup.

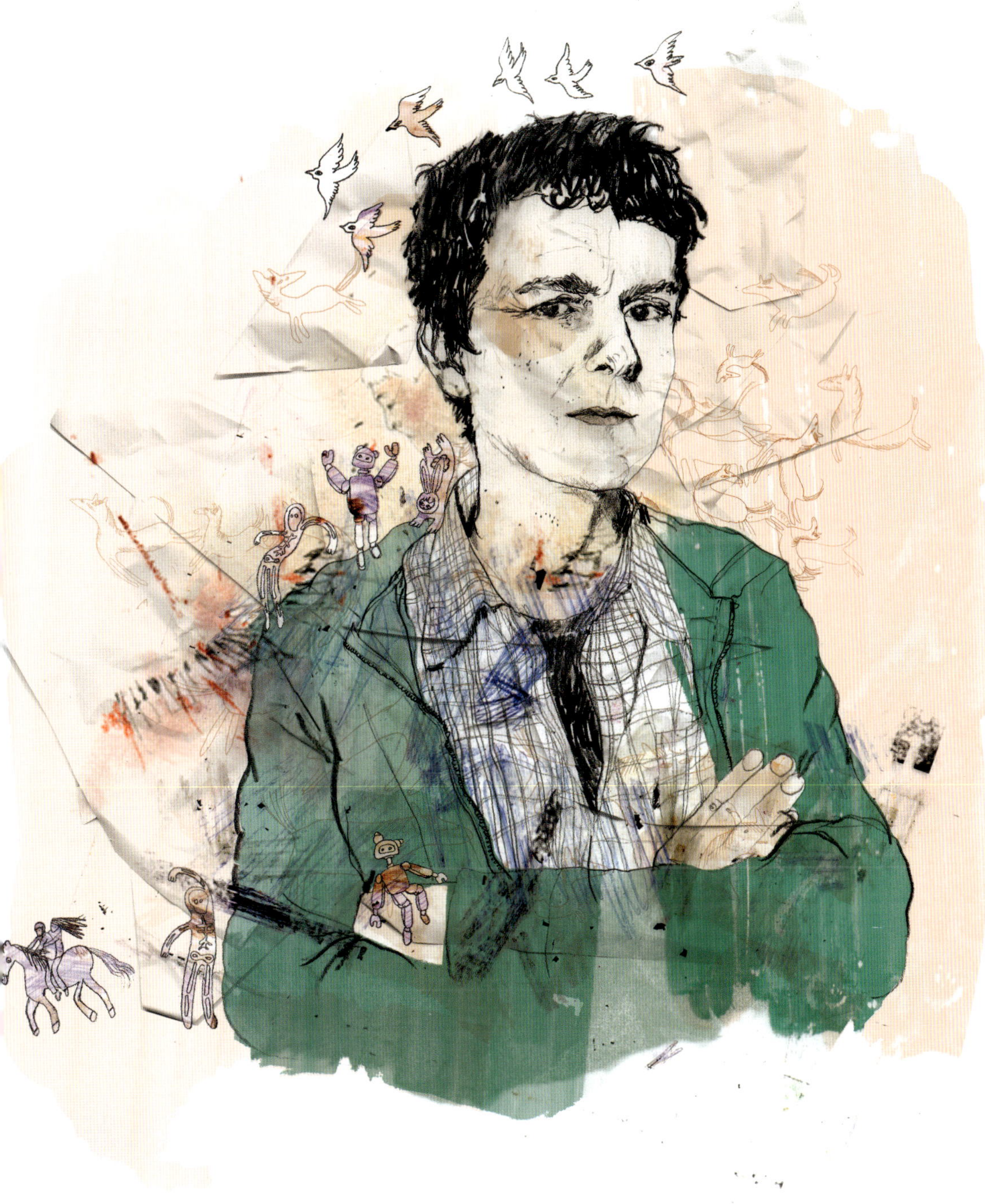

Myriam Heinzel

Germany

www.myri-a-berlin.blogspot.com
Agency: Caroline Seidler
www.carolineseidler.com

1. **Michael Haneke** (2010). Personal Work. Lead pencil

2. **Karl** (2010). Personal Work. Lead pencil

3. **Whisky Sour** (2011). *Zitty Essen und Trinken*. Lead pencil

4. **Pimm's N∞1** (2011). *Zitty Essen und Trinken*. Lead pencil

5. **Michel Gondry** (2010). Personal work. Mixed media

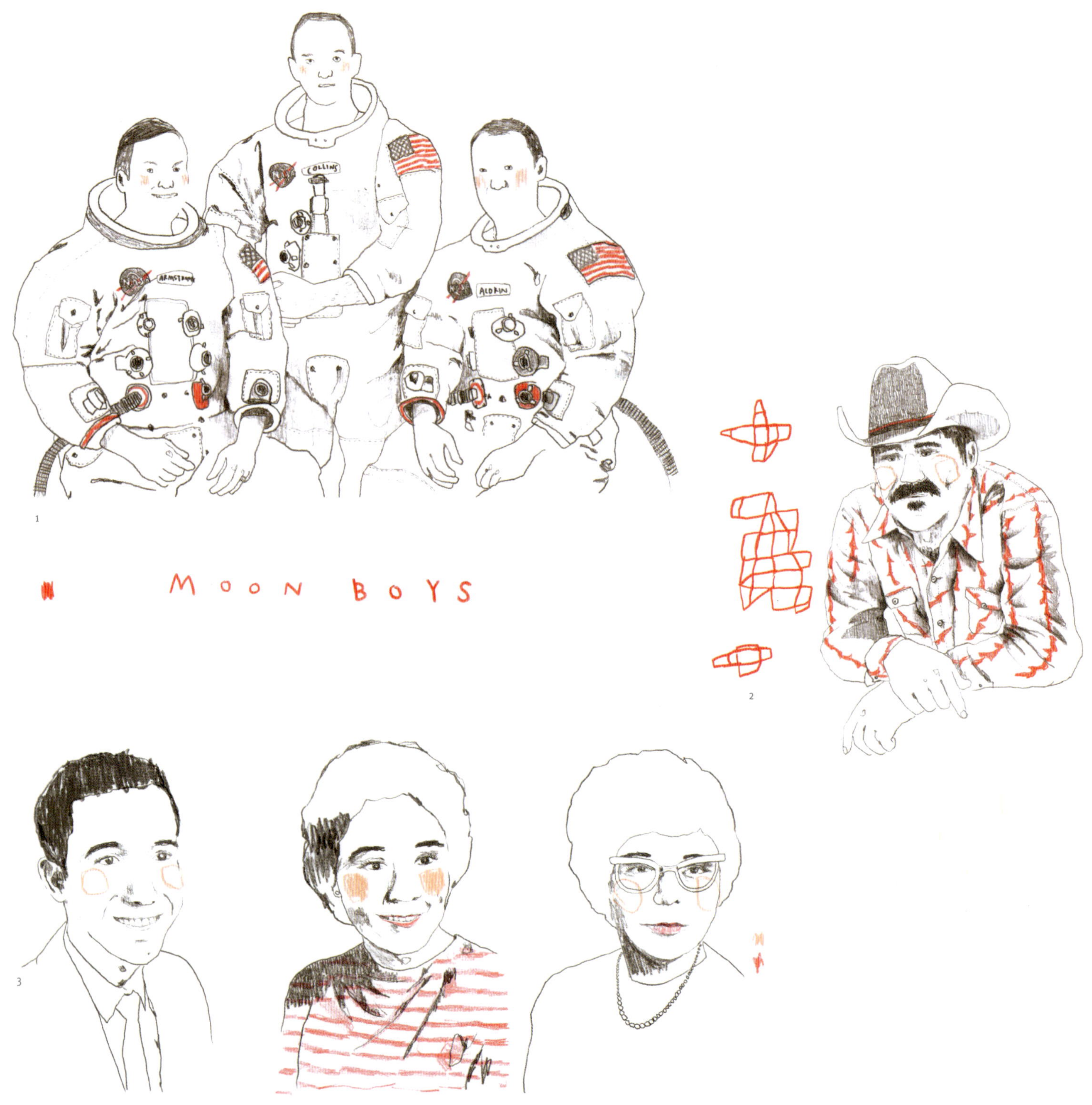
ARMSTRONG
COLLINS
ALDRIN
MOON BOYS

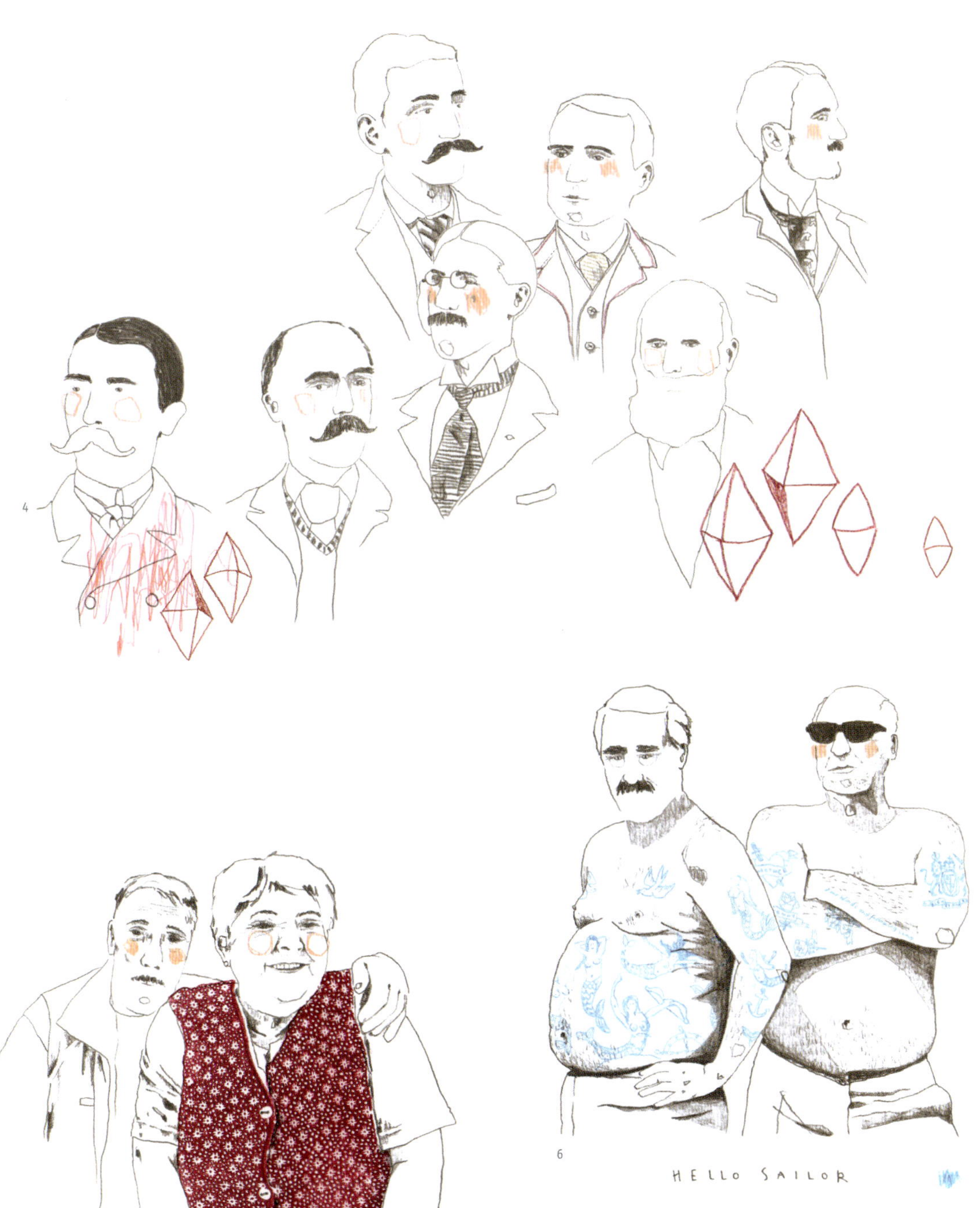

Pink Paper Circus

UK

www.pinkpapercircus.com

1. **Moonboys** (2010). Personal work. Pencil on paper

2. **Howdy** (2010). Personal work. Pencil on paper

3. **Class of '63** (2011). Personal work. Pencil on paper

4. **Chasing Prince Charming** (2010). Personal work. Pencil on paper

5. **Portrait in Red 3** (2011). Personal work. Pencil on paper

6. **Hello Sailor** (2011). Personal work. Pencil on paper

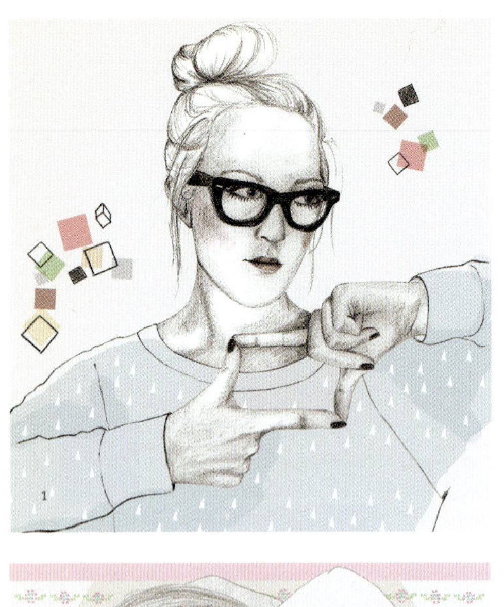

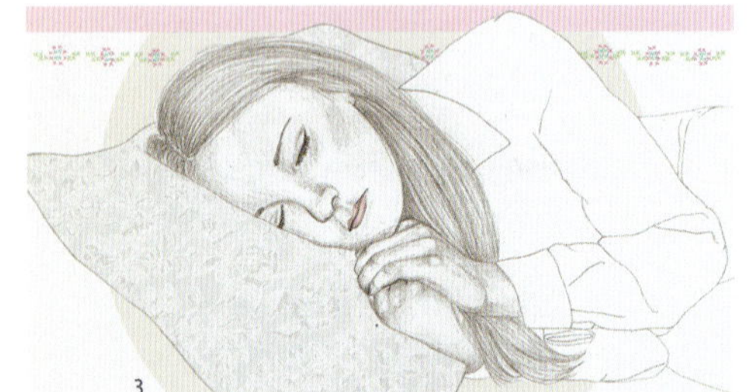

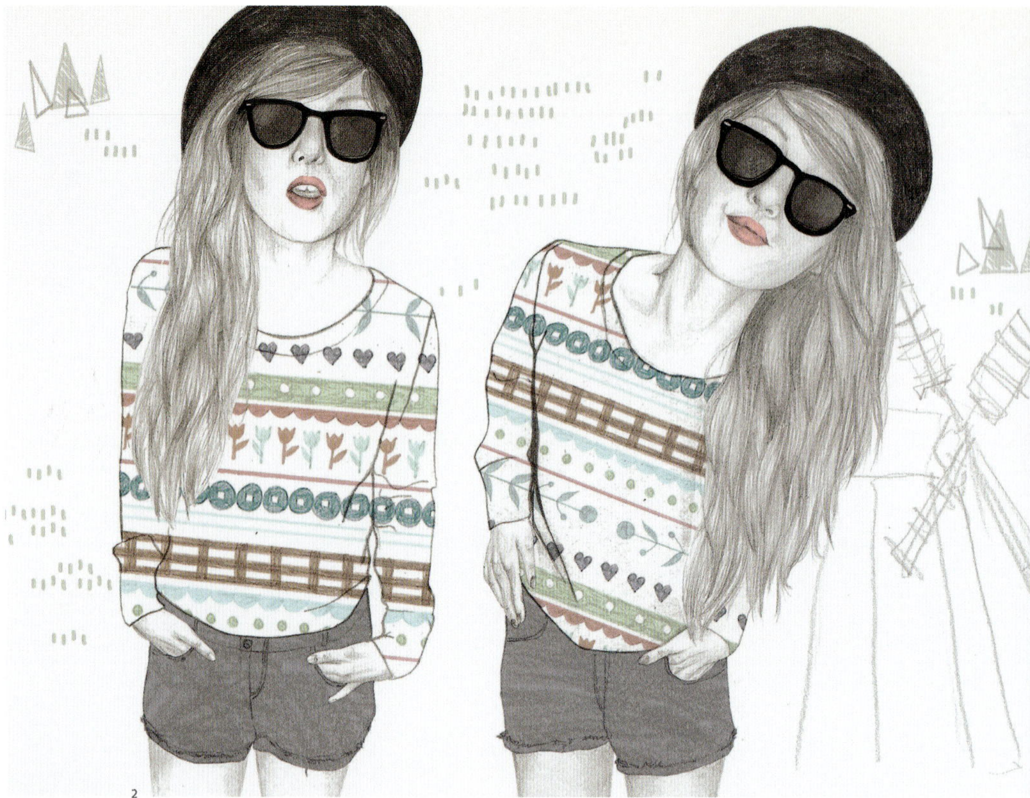

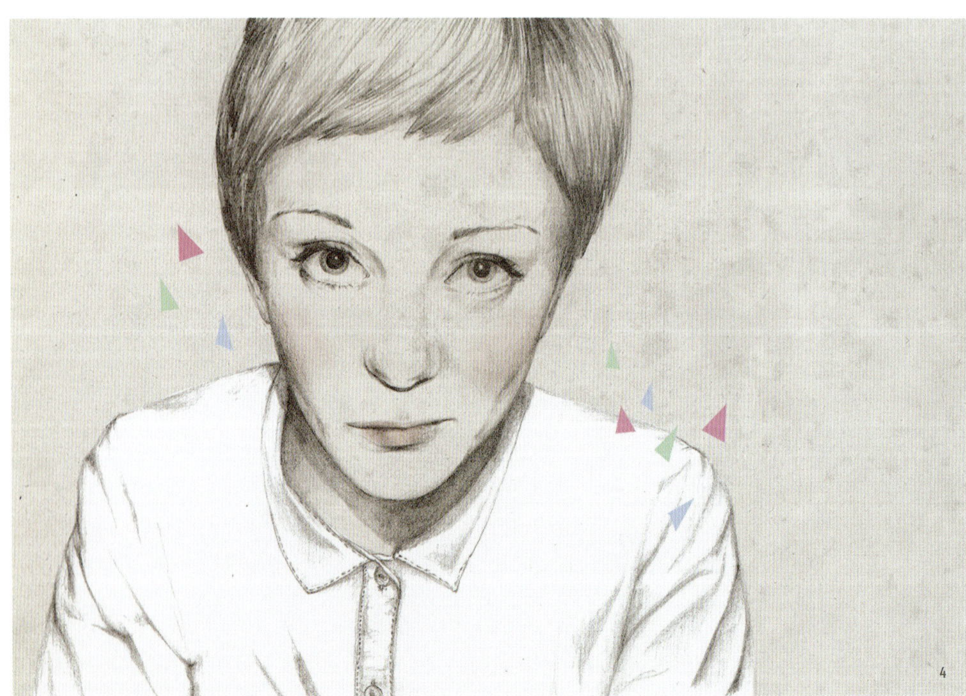

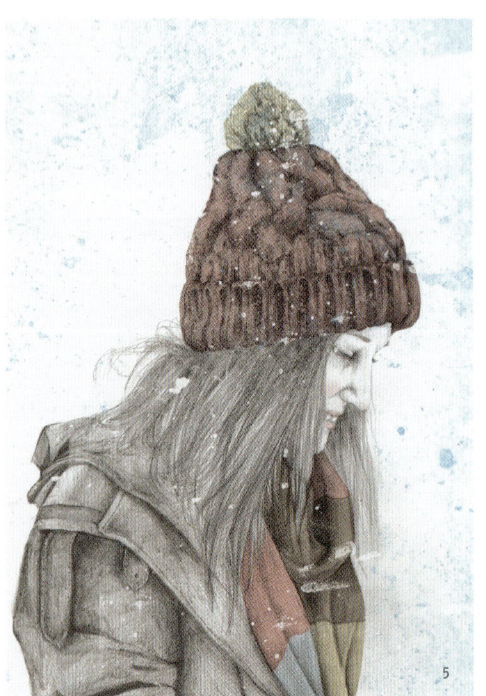

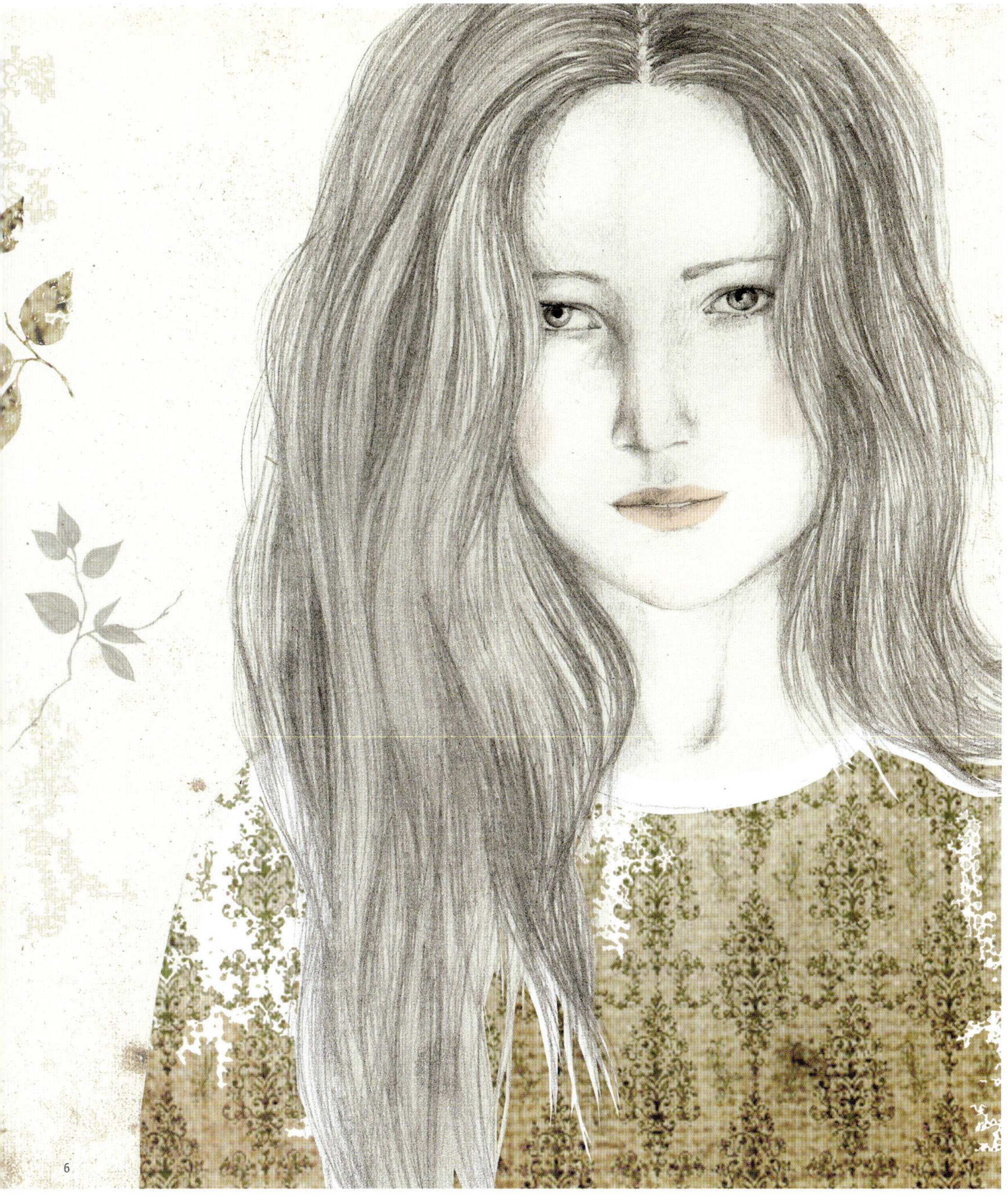

6

Rebecca Abell

UK

www.rebeccaabell.co.uk

1. **Clever Box** (2011)

2. **Double Dutch** (2011)

3. **The Best Advice Is Found on the Pillow** (2011)

4. **After the Rain** (2011)

5. **Winter** (2011)

6. **Ellie** (2011)

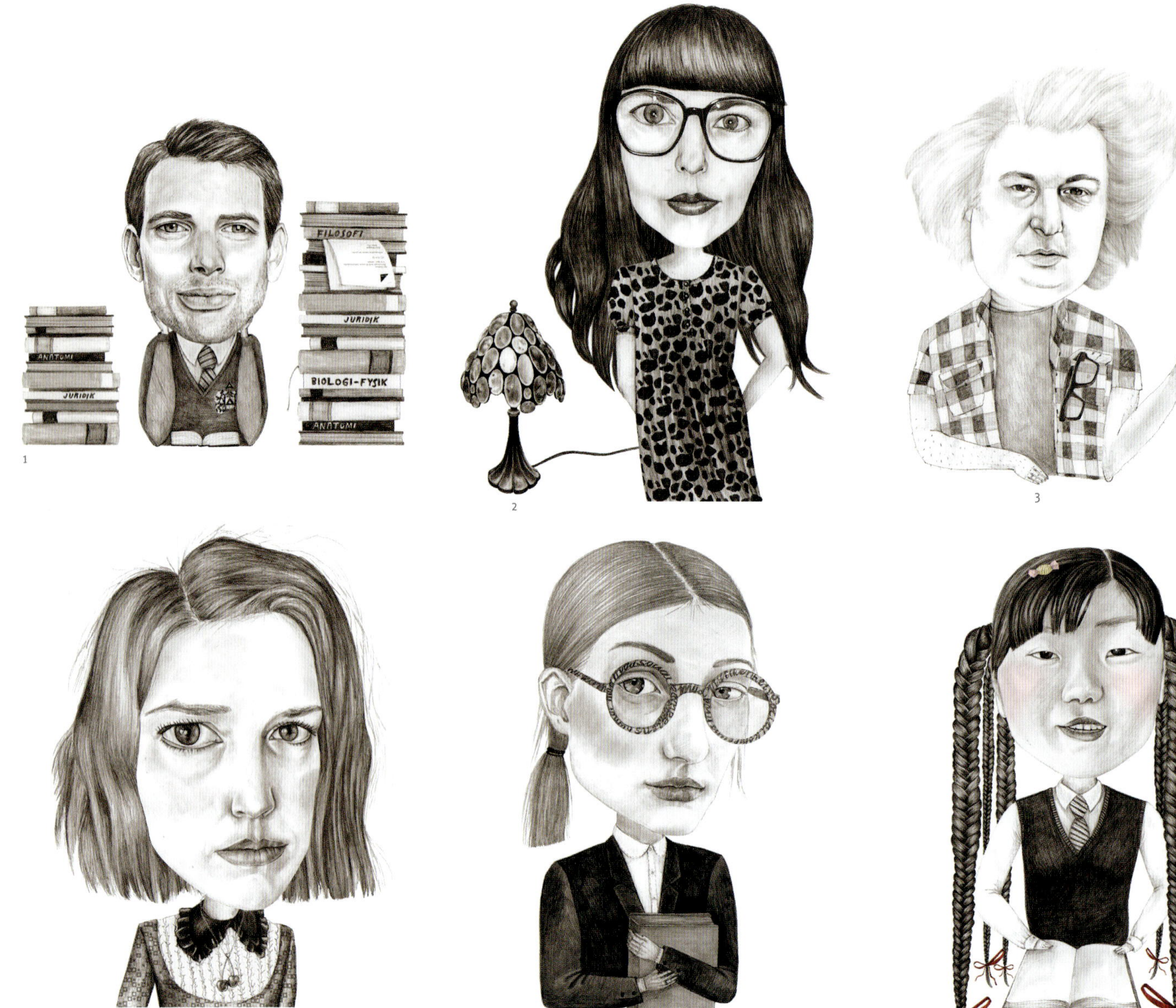

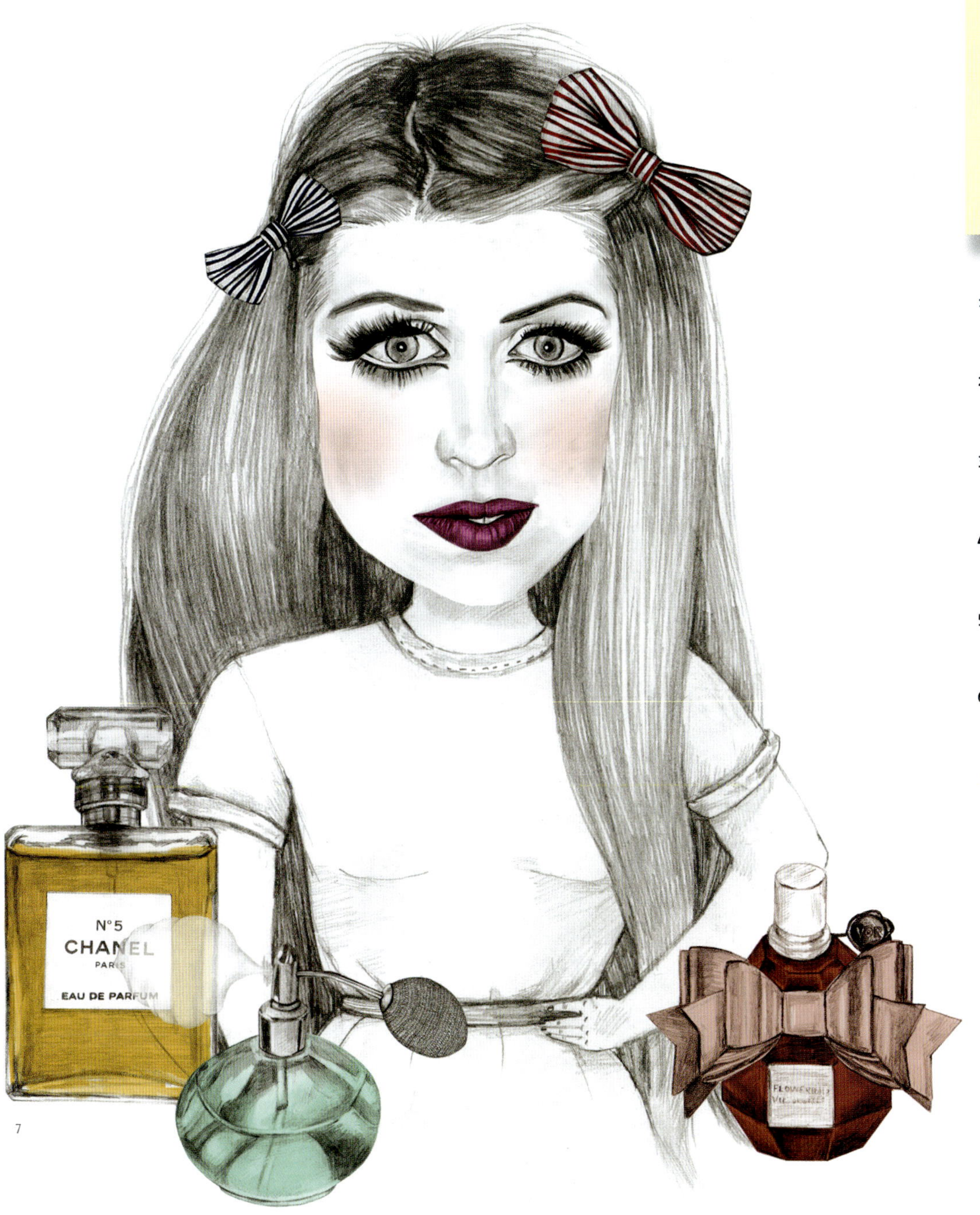

Annelie Carlström

Sweden

www.anneliecarlstrom.se

1. **Alex Schulman** (2010). *King Magazine.* Pencil, Photoshop

2. **Anna-Pi** (2009). Out of Office. Pencil, Photoshop

3. **Göran Geider** (2011) *Opus* magazine. Pencil, Photoshop

4. **Karolina** (2008). Personal work. Pencil, Photoshop

5. **Marion** (2011). Universum / Dagens Industri. Pencil, Photoshop

6. **Modern Psykologi** (2010). *Modern Psykologi.* Pencil, Photoshop

7 **Peaches** (2011). *Nylon* magazine. Pencil, Photoshop

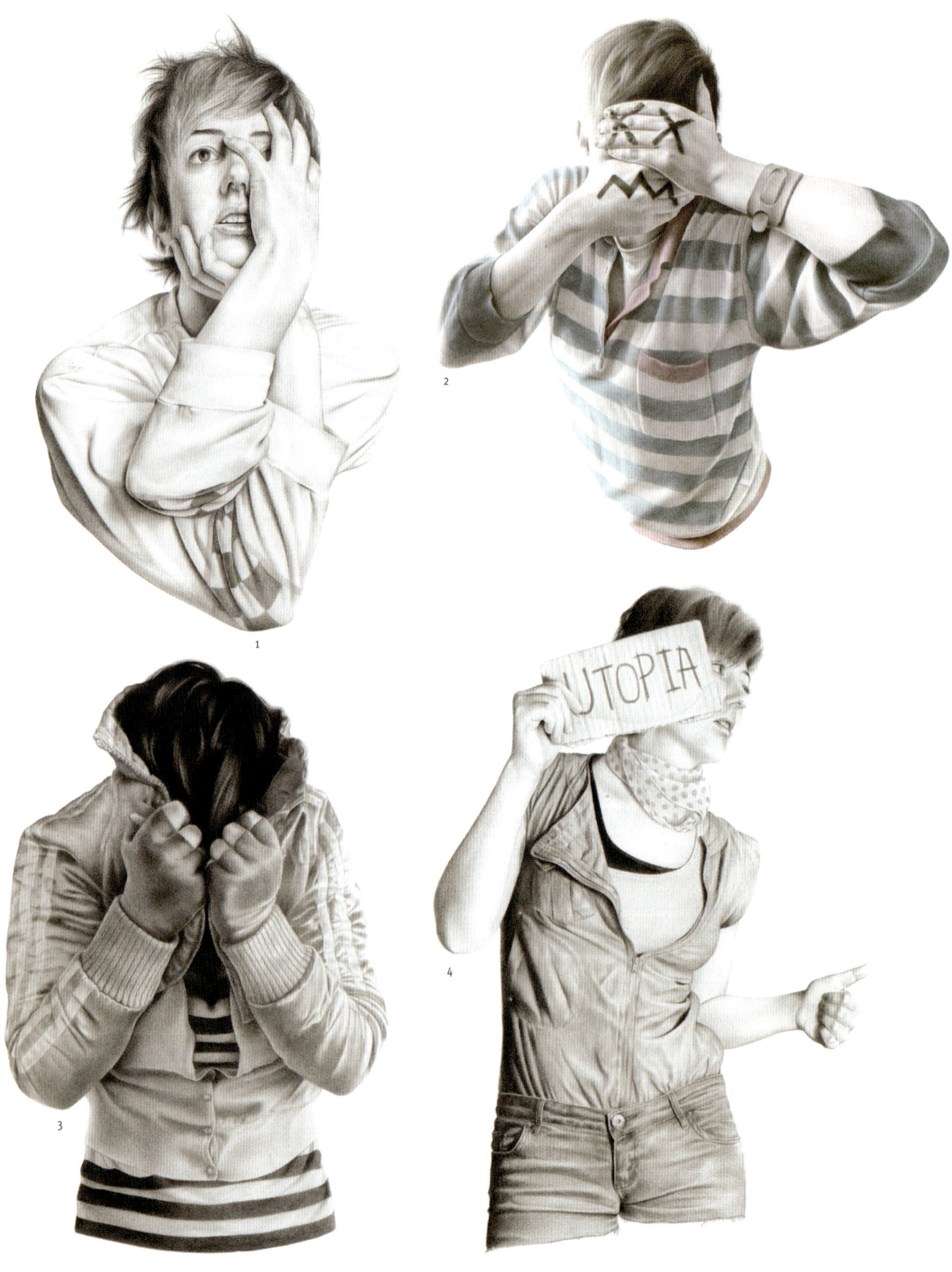

UTOPIA

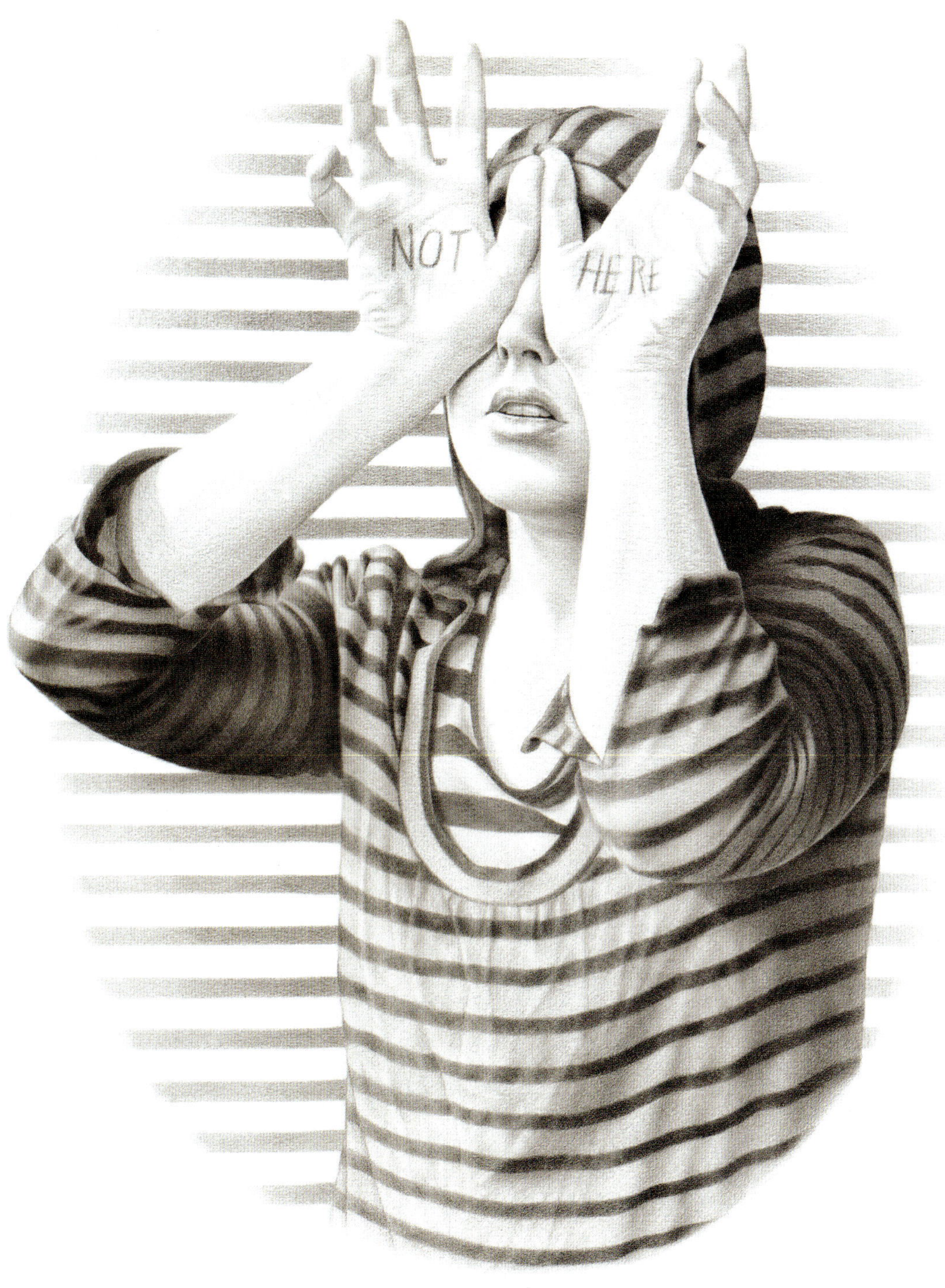

Rena Littleson
Australia

www.renalittleson.com

1. **Entwined** (2011). Pencil on paper

2. **Crosseyed** (2011). Pencil on paper

3. **Undercover** (2011). Pencil on paper

4. **Utopia** (2011). Pencil on paper

5. **Invisible** (2011). Pencil on paper

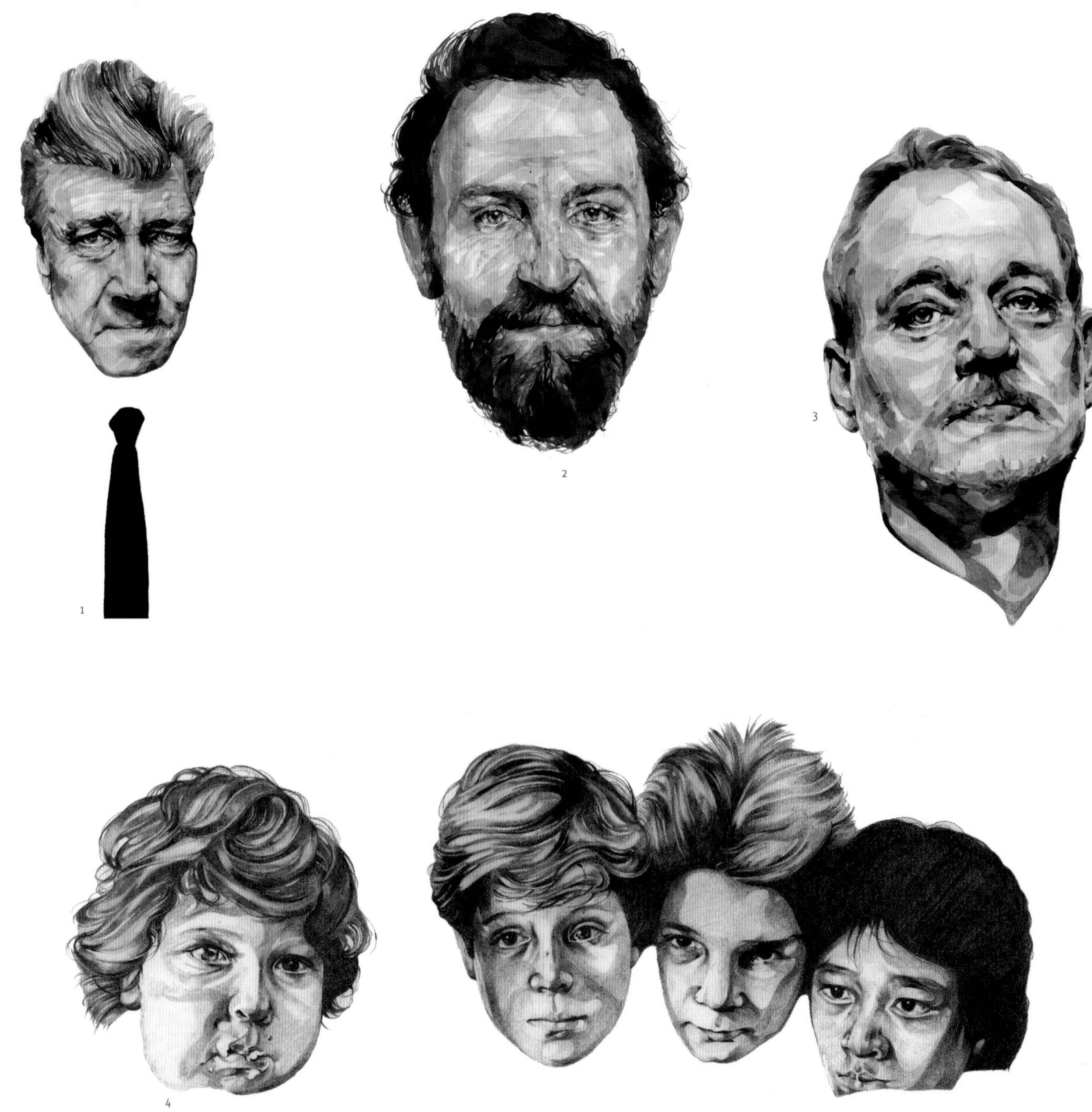

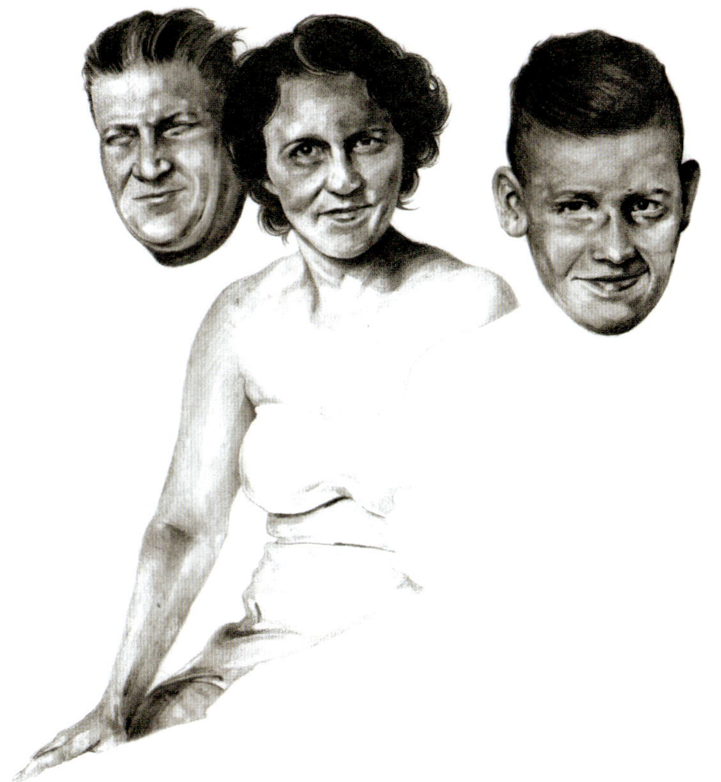

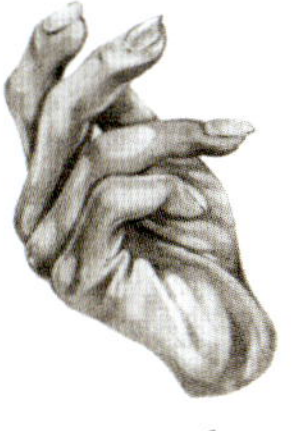

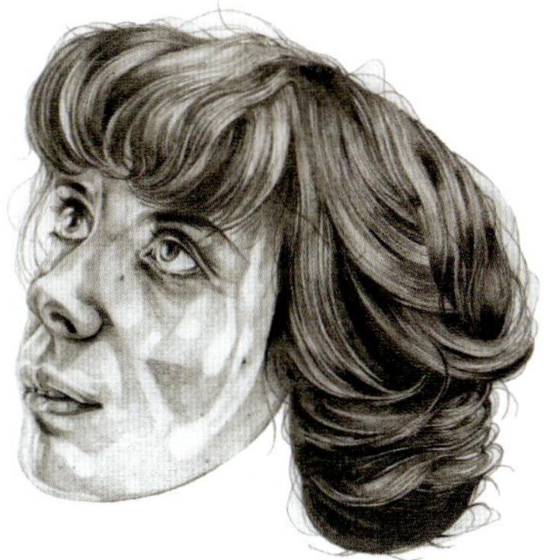

Kate Copeland

UK

www.katecopeland.co.uk

1. **David Lynch** (2011). Watercolor

2. **Phil Kay** (2011). Watercolor

3. **Bill Murray** (2011). Watercolor

4. **The Goonies, Film Stills** (2011). Pencil

5. **Fragments** (2011). Pencil

6. **Submarine, Film Stills** (2011). Pencil

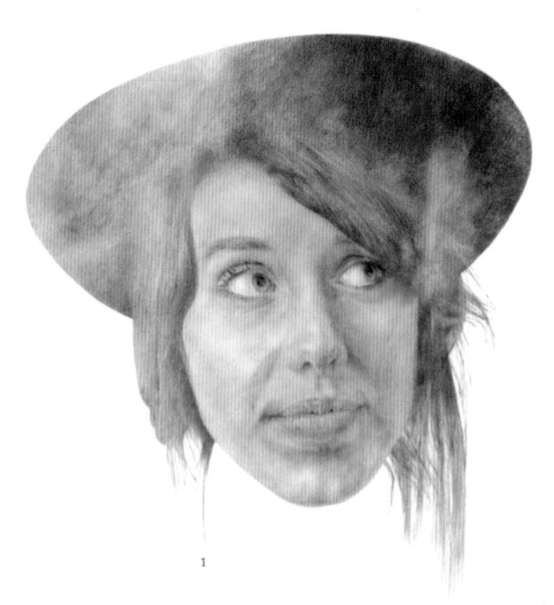

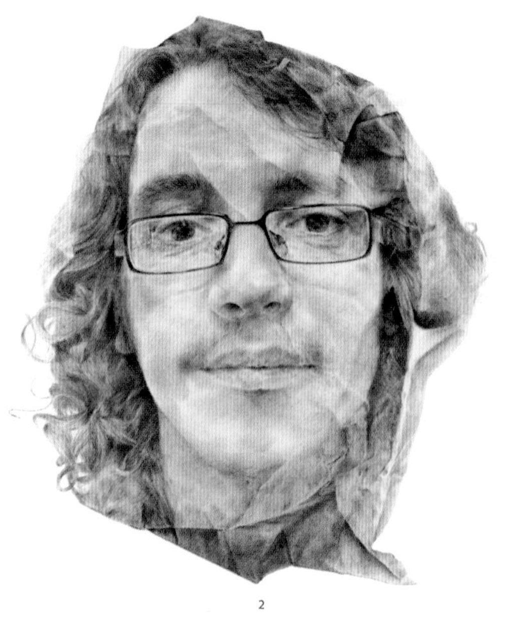

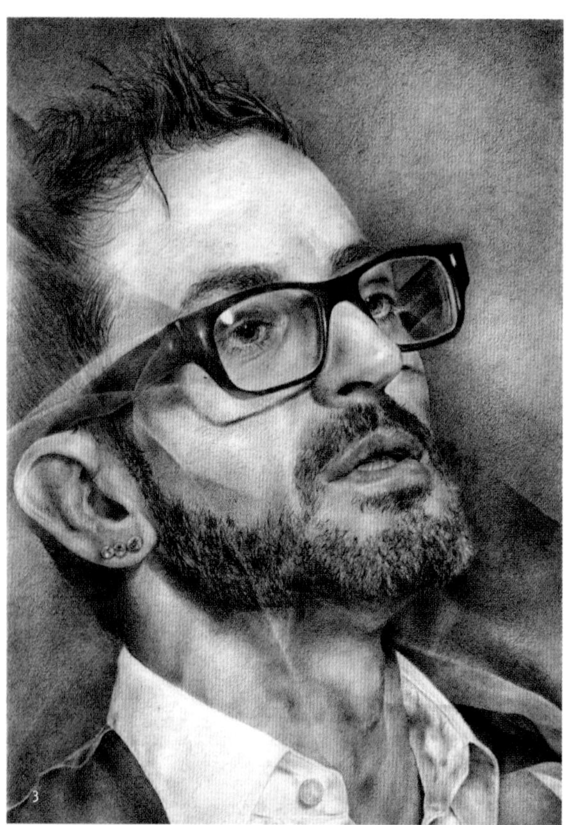

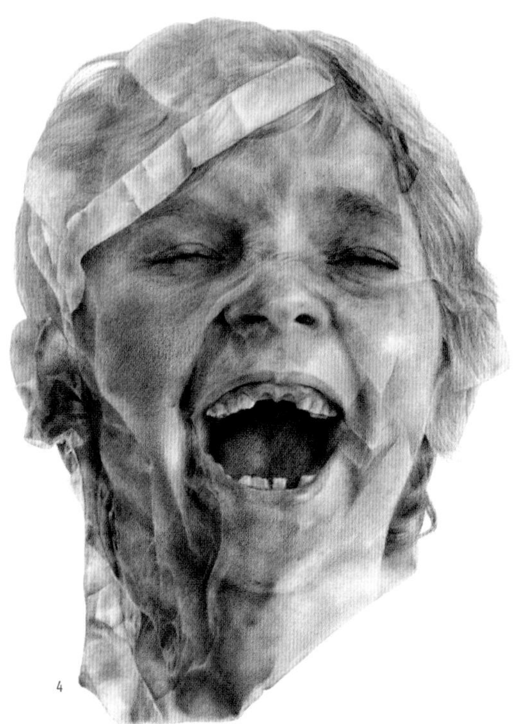

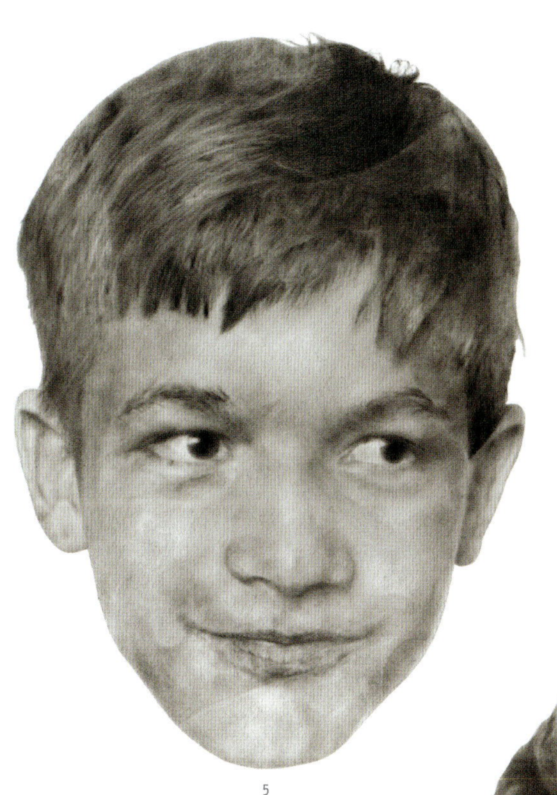

Stuart Whitton
UK

www.stuartwhitton.co.uk

1. **Beauty** (2011). Personal work. Pencil

2. **Brother** (2010). Personal work. Pencil

3. **Marc Jacobs** (2011). *Die Zeit*. Pencil

4. **Laughter** (2010). Personal work. Pencil

5. **Mischief** (2011). Personal work. Pencil

6. **Origin** (2011). Personal work. Pencil

5

6

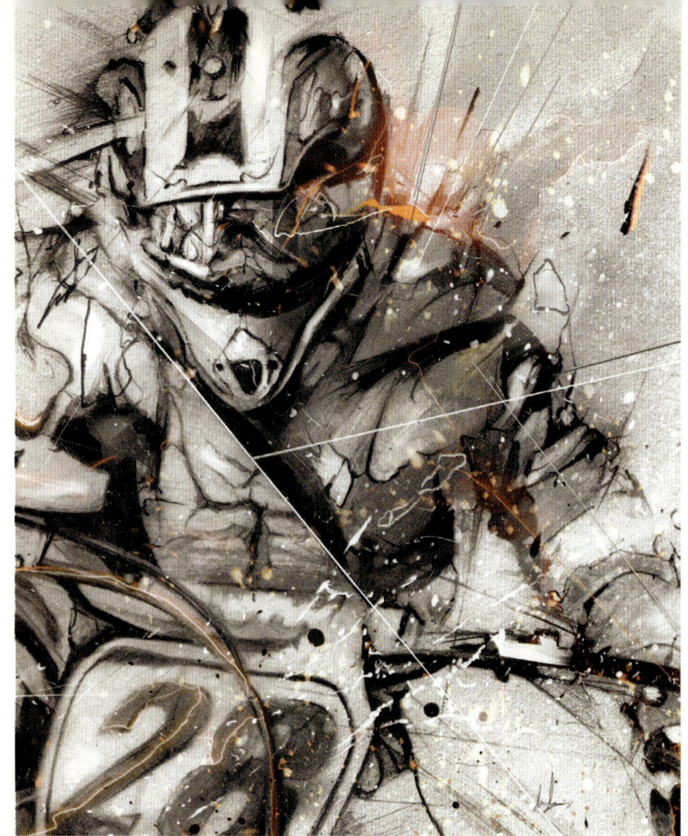

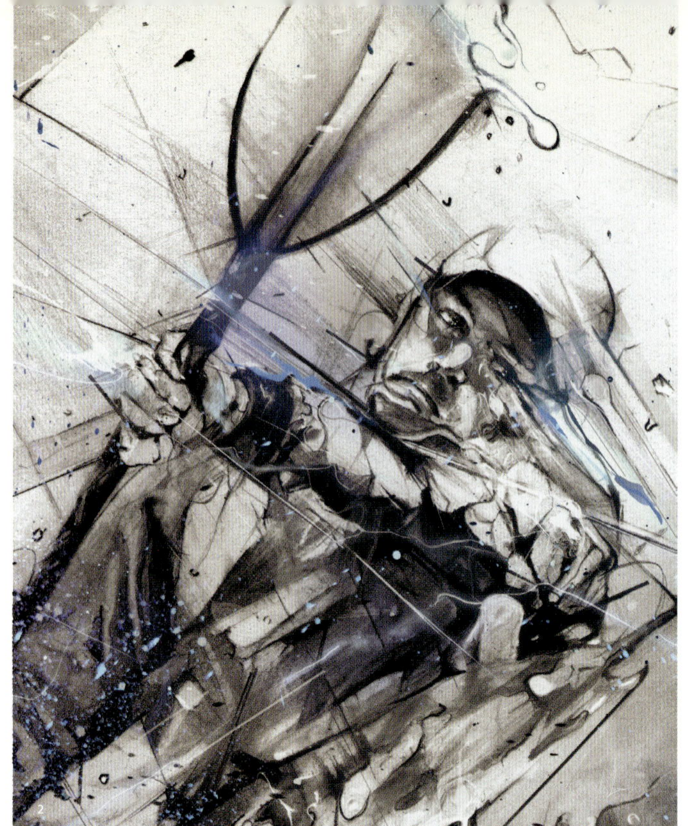

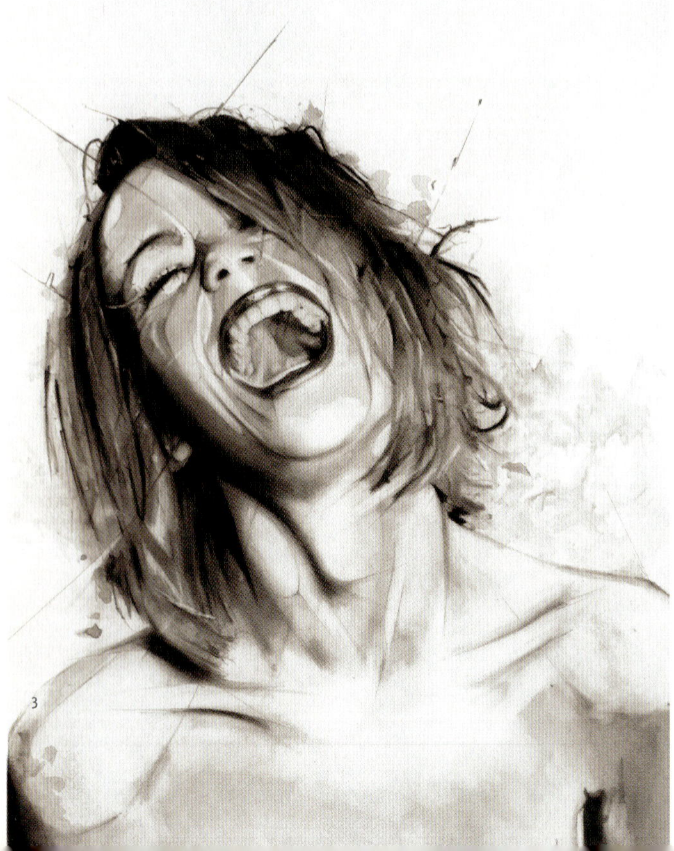

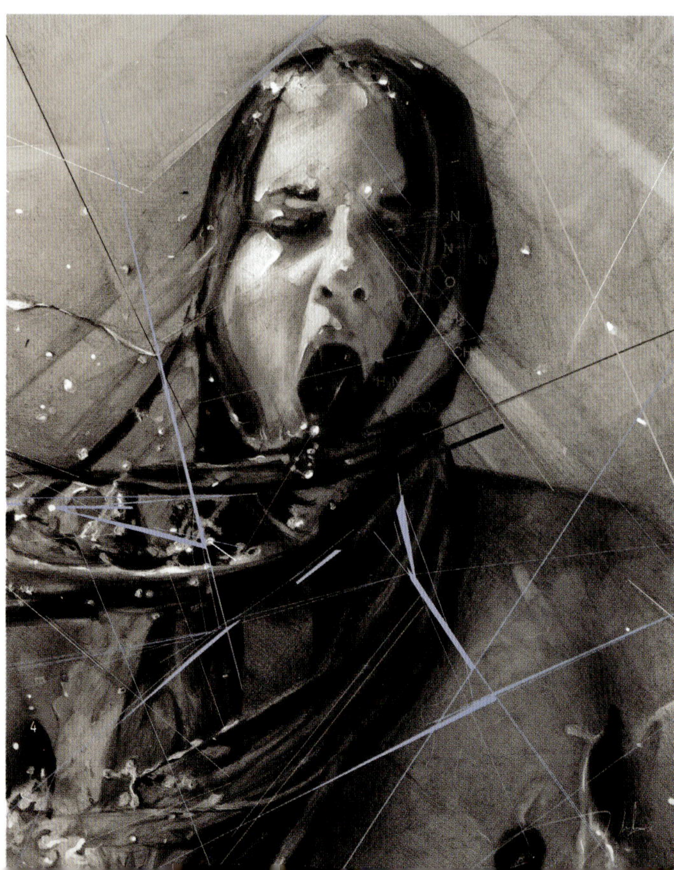

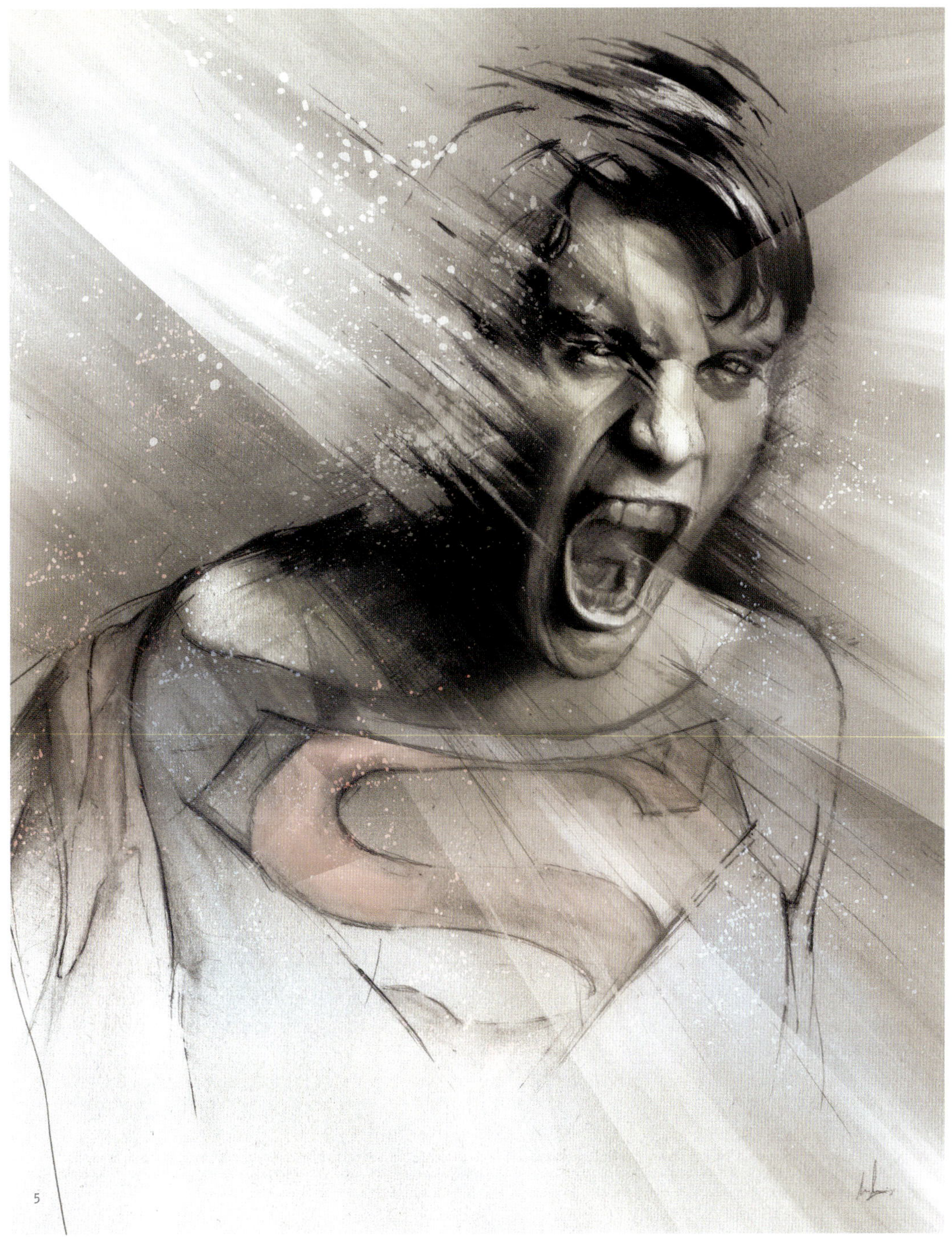

Alexis Marcou

Greece

www.alexismarcou.com

1. **Biker** (2011). Black Swan Life for Crusoe. Hand drawing and digital

2. **Kyaker** (2011). Black Swan Life for Crusoe. Hand drawing and digital

3. **Ms Antiqua** (2011). Insanity. Hand drawing and digital

4. **O2** (2011). Personal work. Hand drawing and digital

5 **Superheroes SF** (2011). Society 6. Hand drawing and digital

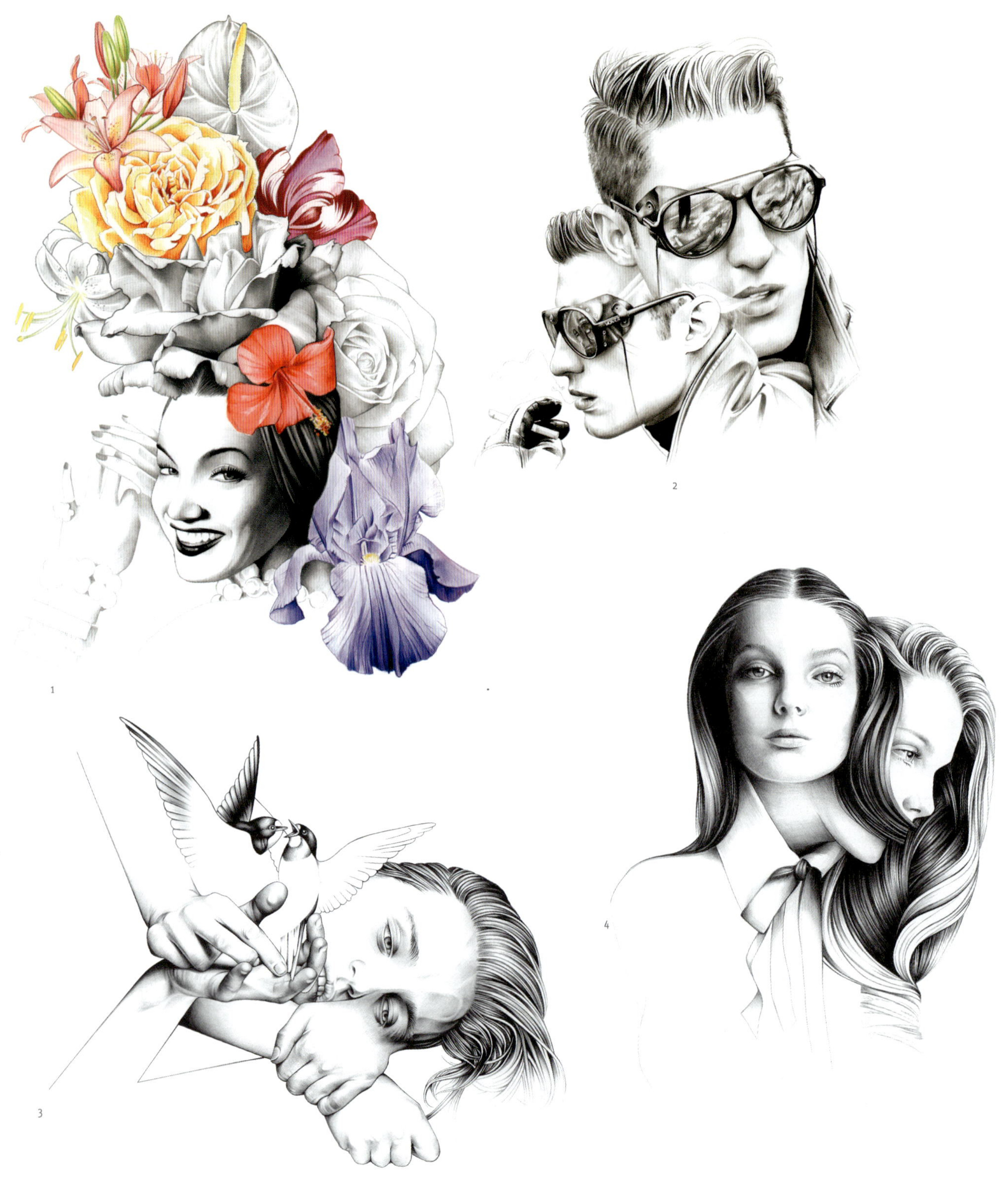

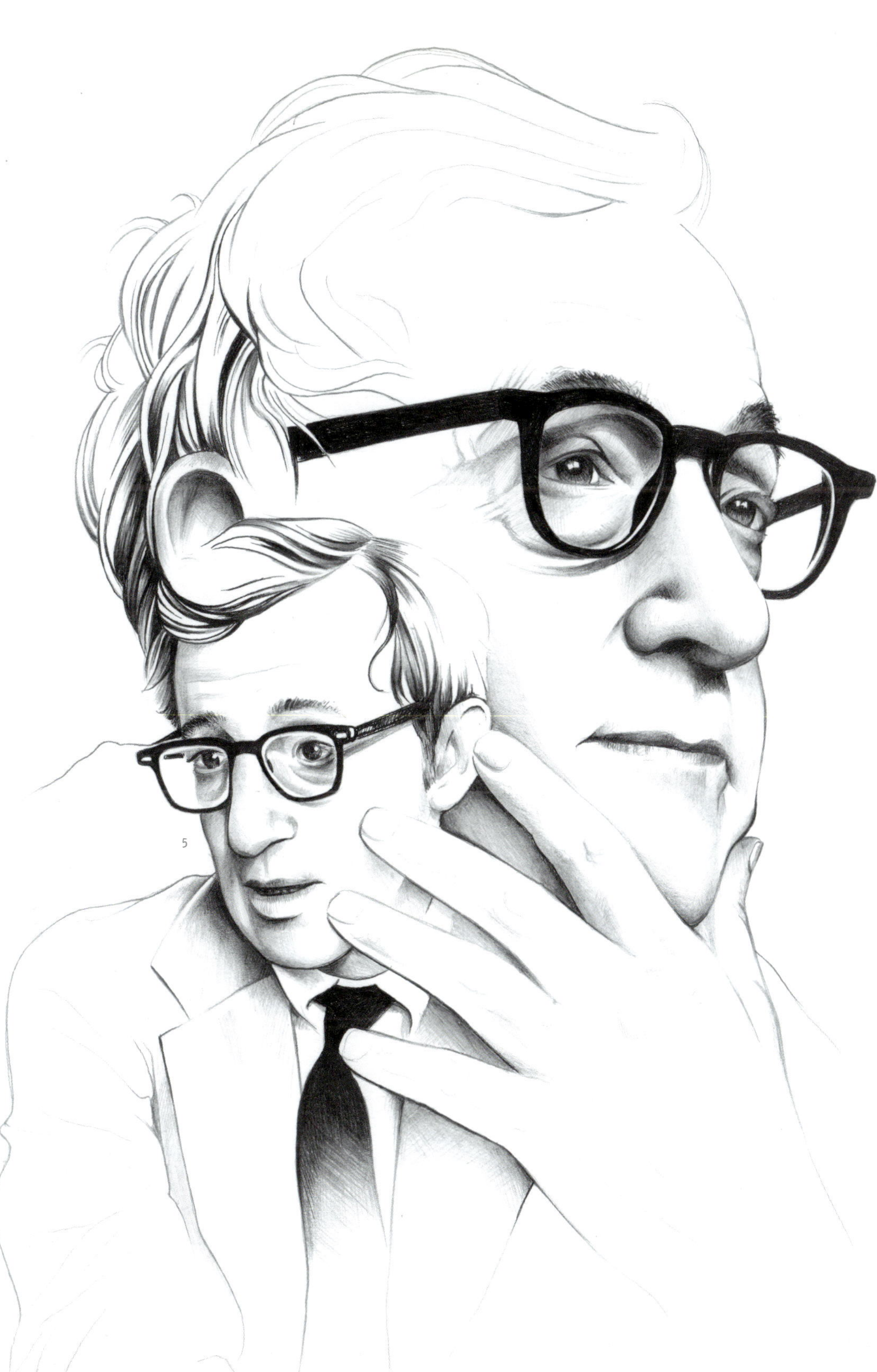

Ricardo Fumanal

Spain

www.ricardofumanal.com

1. **Carmen Miranda** (2010). *Hercules* magazine. Mixed media

2. **Automatic Lover** (2010). Ink, pencil

3. **Untitled** (2010). Lou Dalton. Ink, pencil

4. **Eniko Mihalik** (2009). *A Perfect Magazine*. Ink, pencil

5. **Woody Allen** (2009). *Madame Figaro*. Ink, pencil

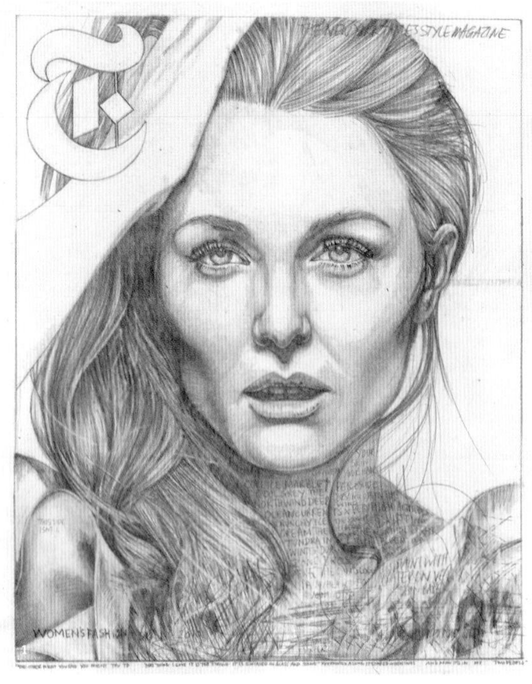
&
WOMENS FASHION

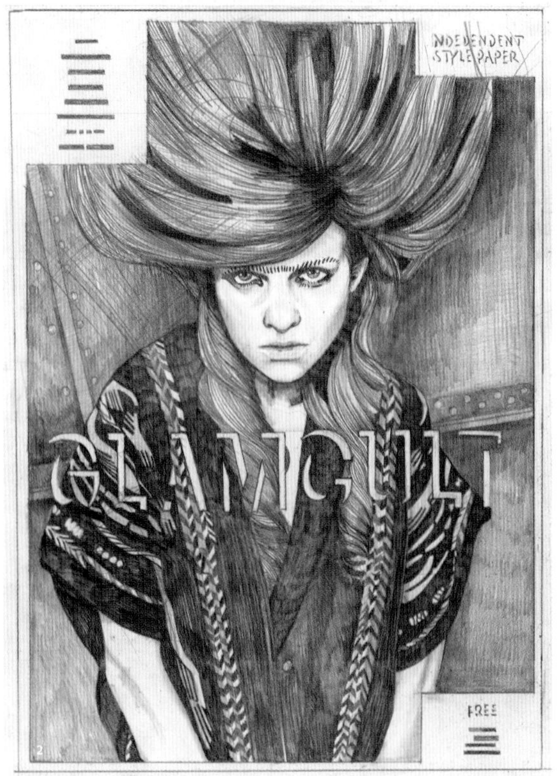
NDEPENDENT
STYLE PAPER
GLAMCULT
FREE

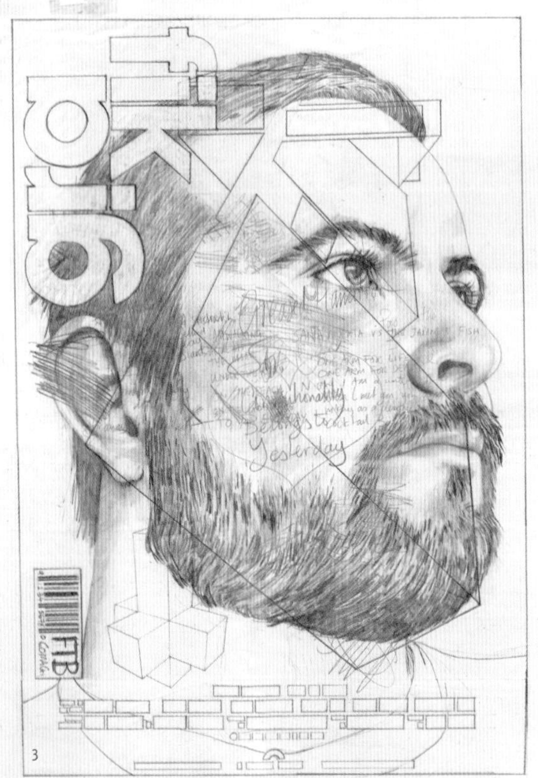
FIB

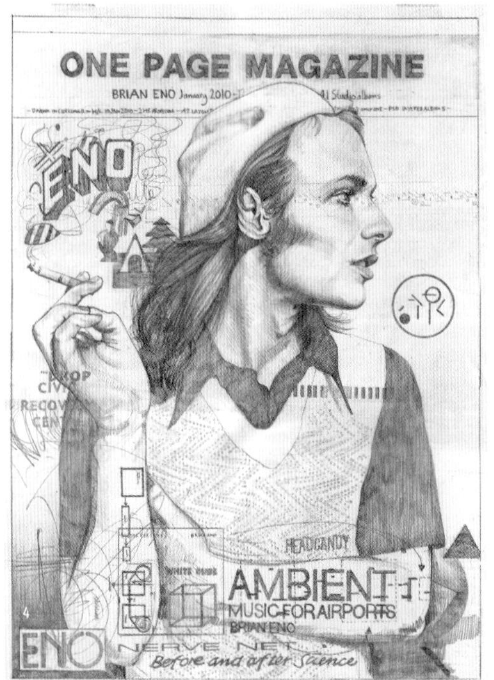
ONE PAGE MAGAZINE
BRIAN ENO January 2010
ENO
HEAD CANDY
AMBIENT
MUSIC FOR AIRPORTS
BRIAN ENO
ENO
NERVE NET
Before and after Science

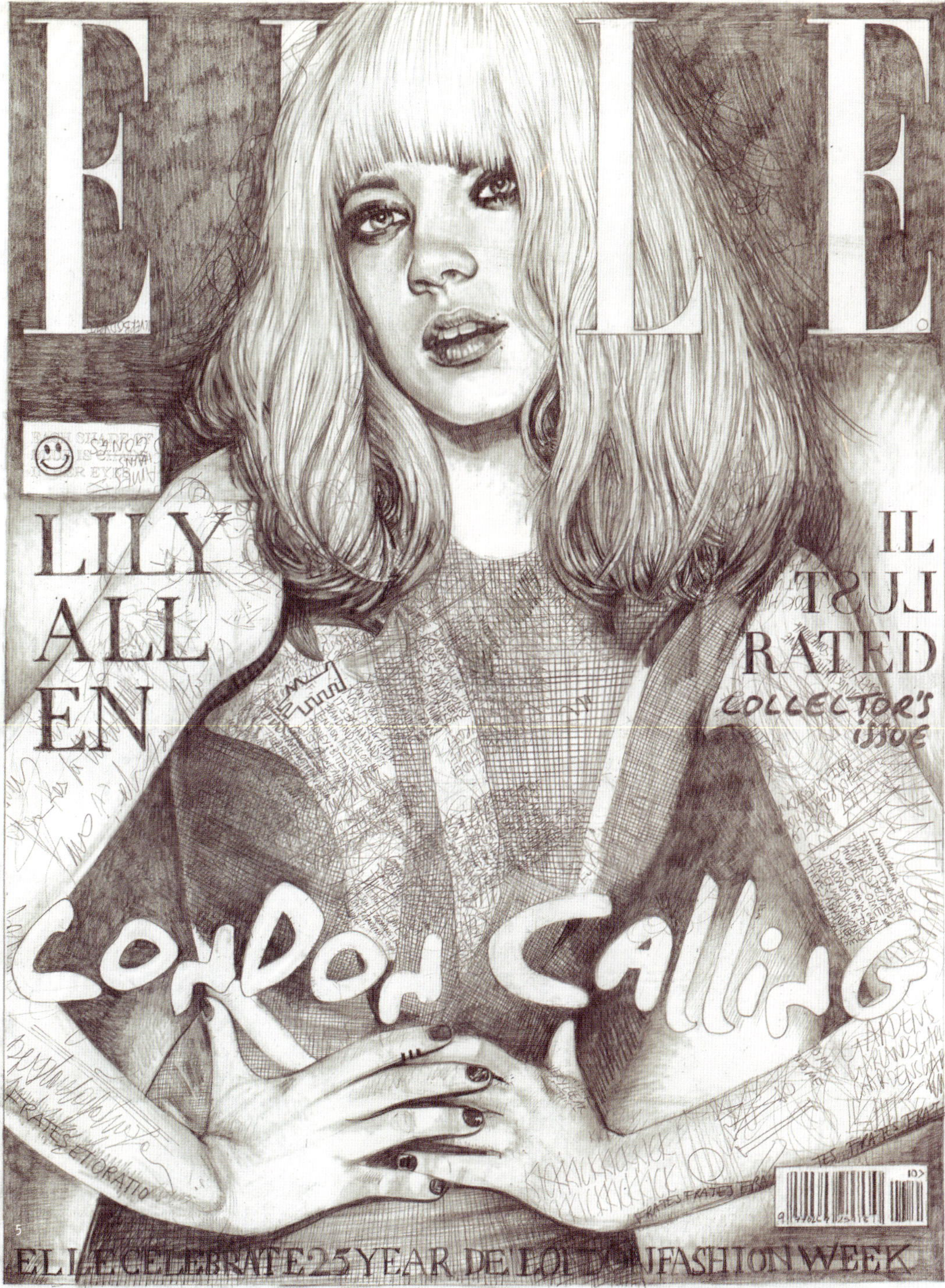

1. **Cover 72 - T** (2010). *Gym Class Magazine #06*. Pencil, layout paper, Photoshop

2. **Cover 82 - Glamcult** (2010). Personal work. Pencil, layout paper, Photoshop

3. **Cover 93 - Grafik/Film The Blanks** (2010). Personal work. pencil, layout paper, Photoshop

4. **Cover 96 - One Page Magazine** (2010). Personal work. pencil, layout paper, Photoshop

5. **Cover 92 - Elle** (2009). *Elle* UK. Pencil, layout paper, Photoshop

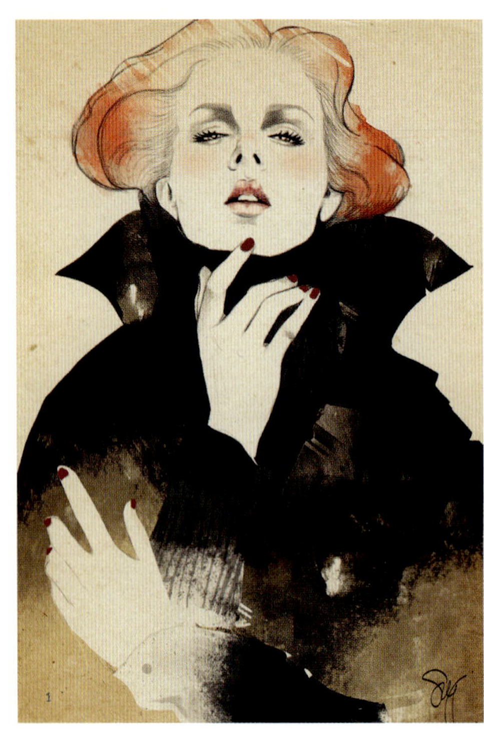

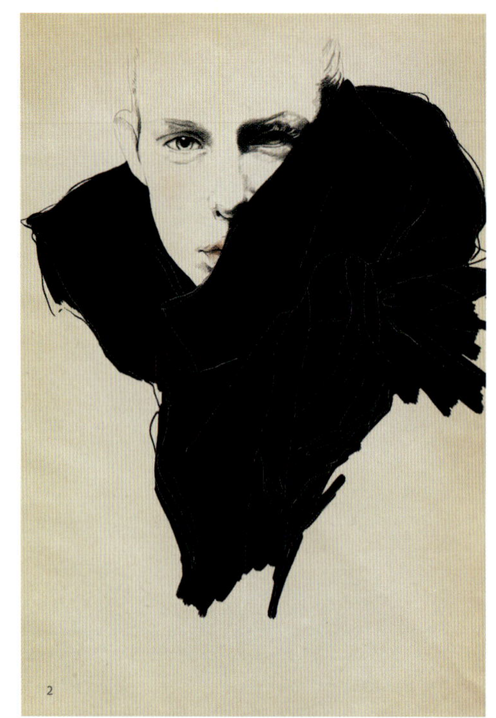

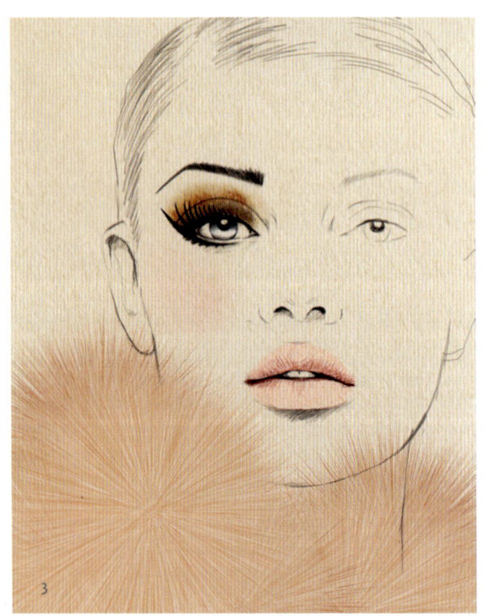

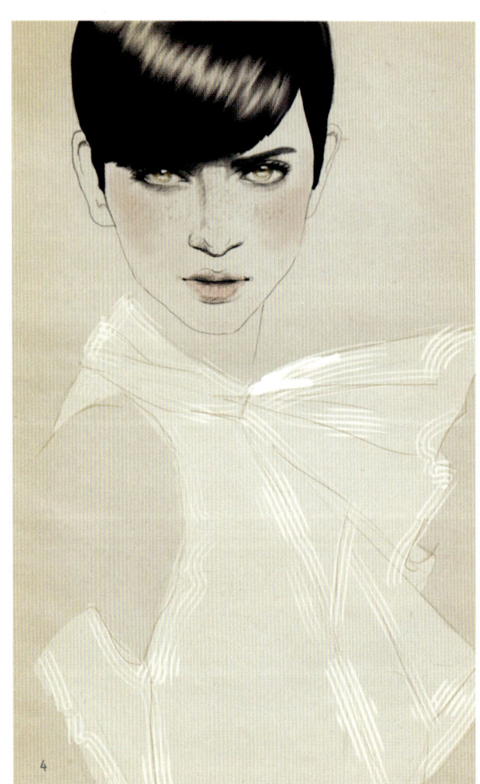

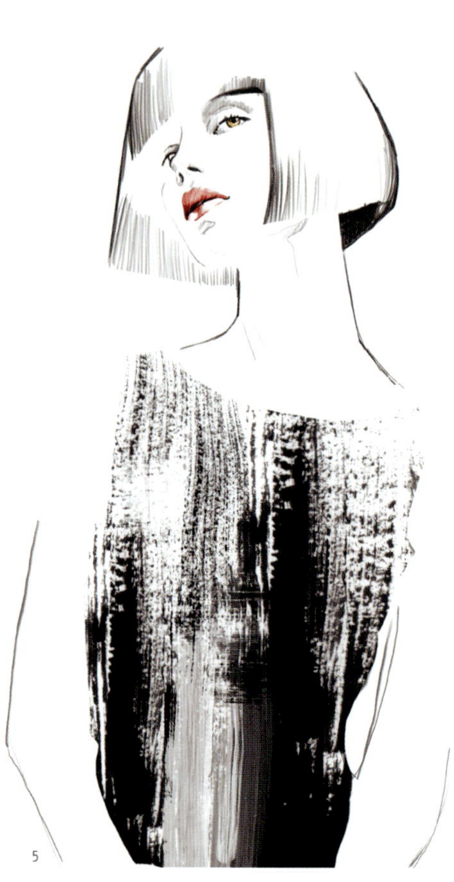

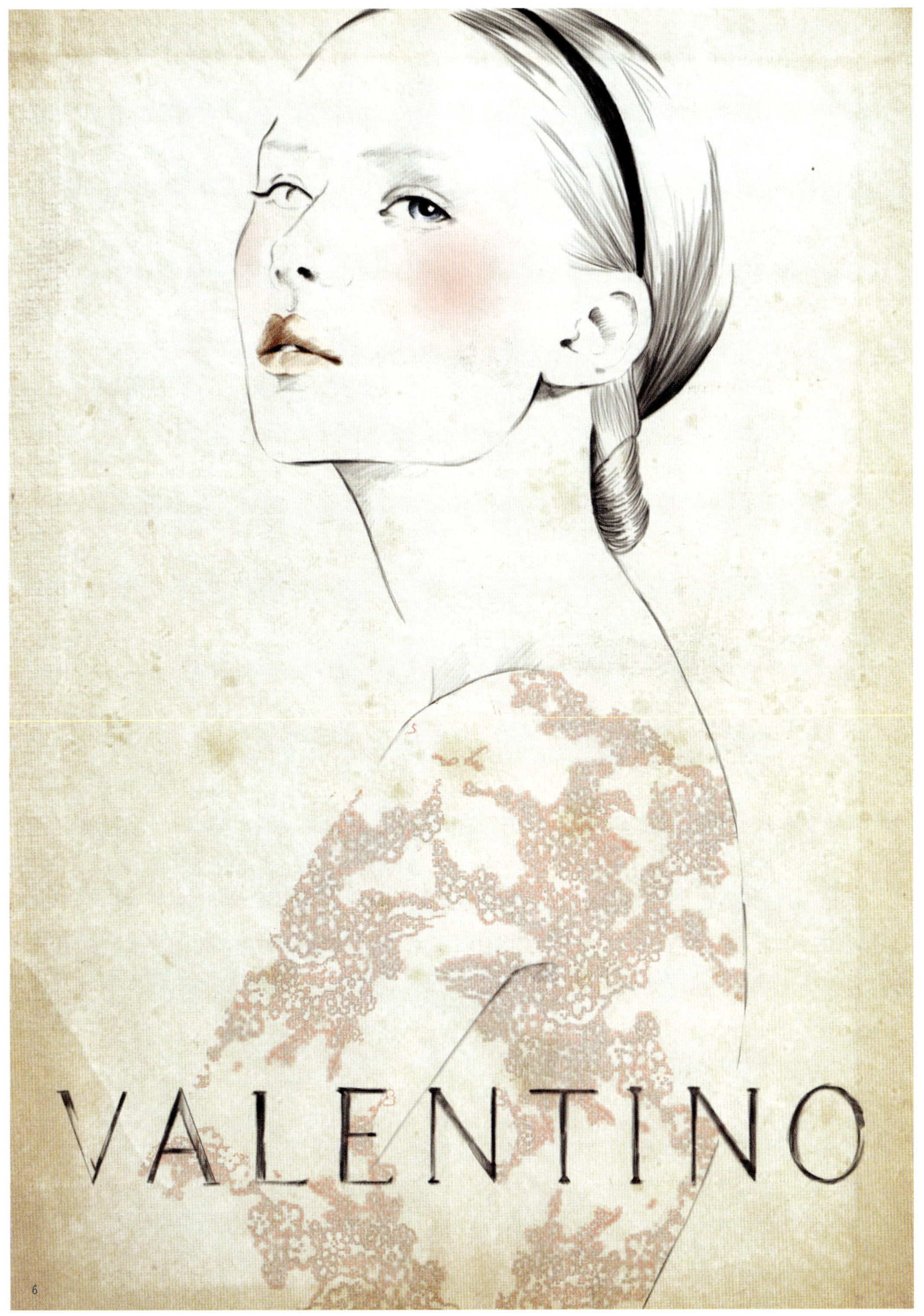

Sandra Suy

Spain

www.sandrasuy.com

1. **Berardi** (2009). *SO CHIC Magazine*. Mixed media

2. **Jeanne** (2008). Personal work. Mixed media

3. **Untitled** (2009). *Glamour* USA. Mixed media

4. **Lola** (2008). Personal work. Mixed media

5. *080* (2011). 55DSL. Mixed media

6. **Valentino** (2010). Personal work. Mixed media

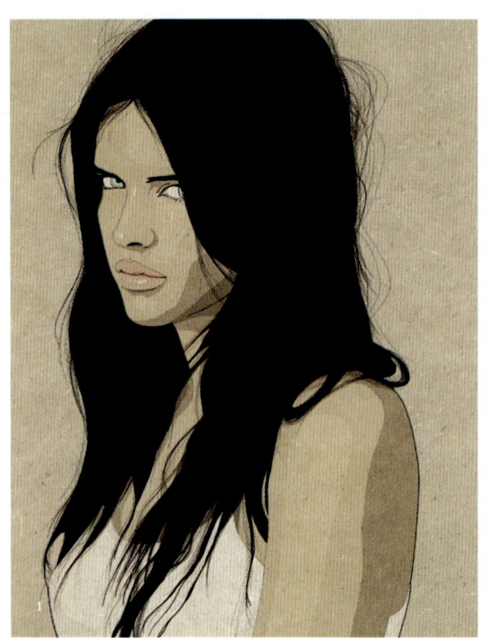

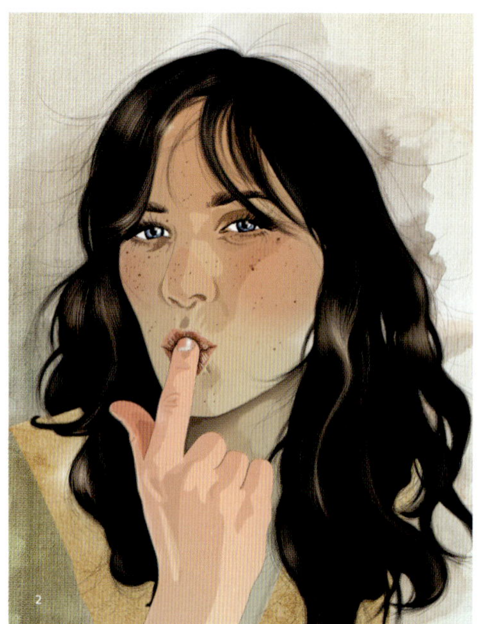

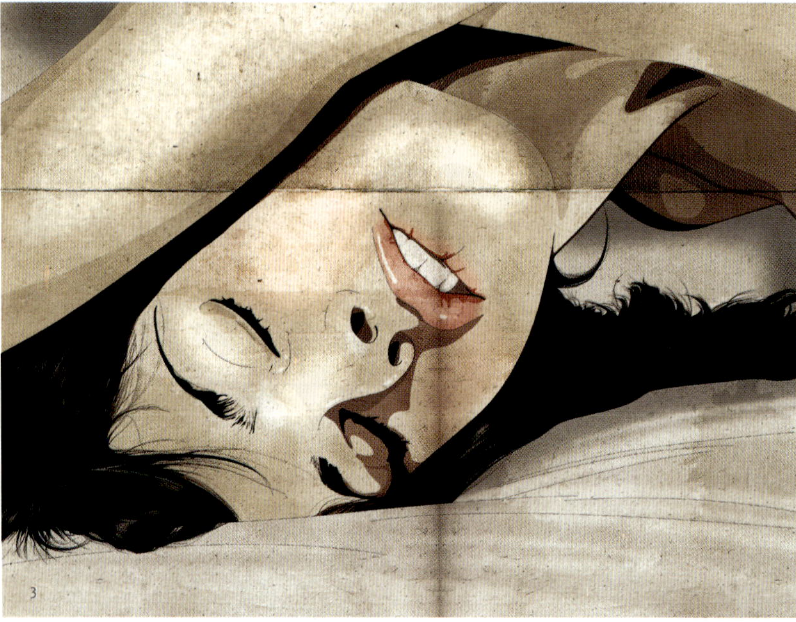

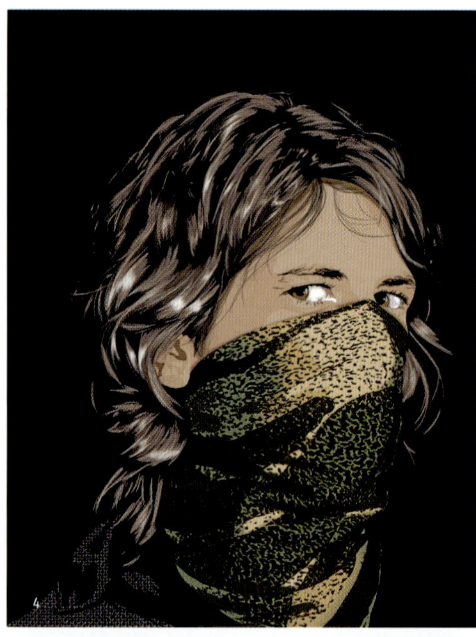

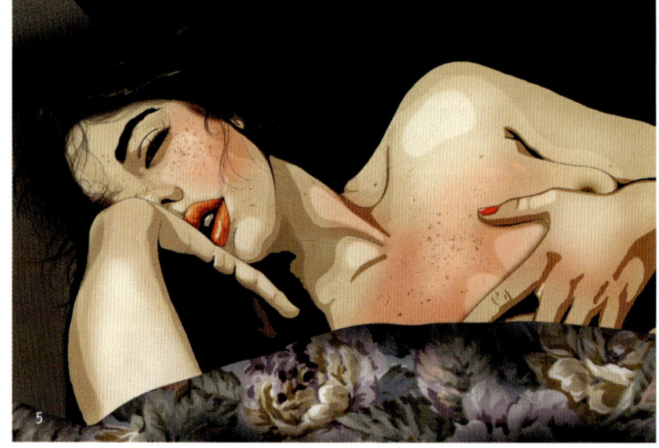

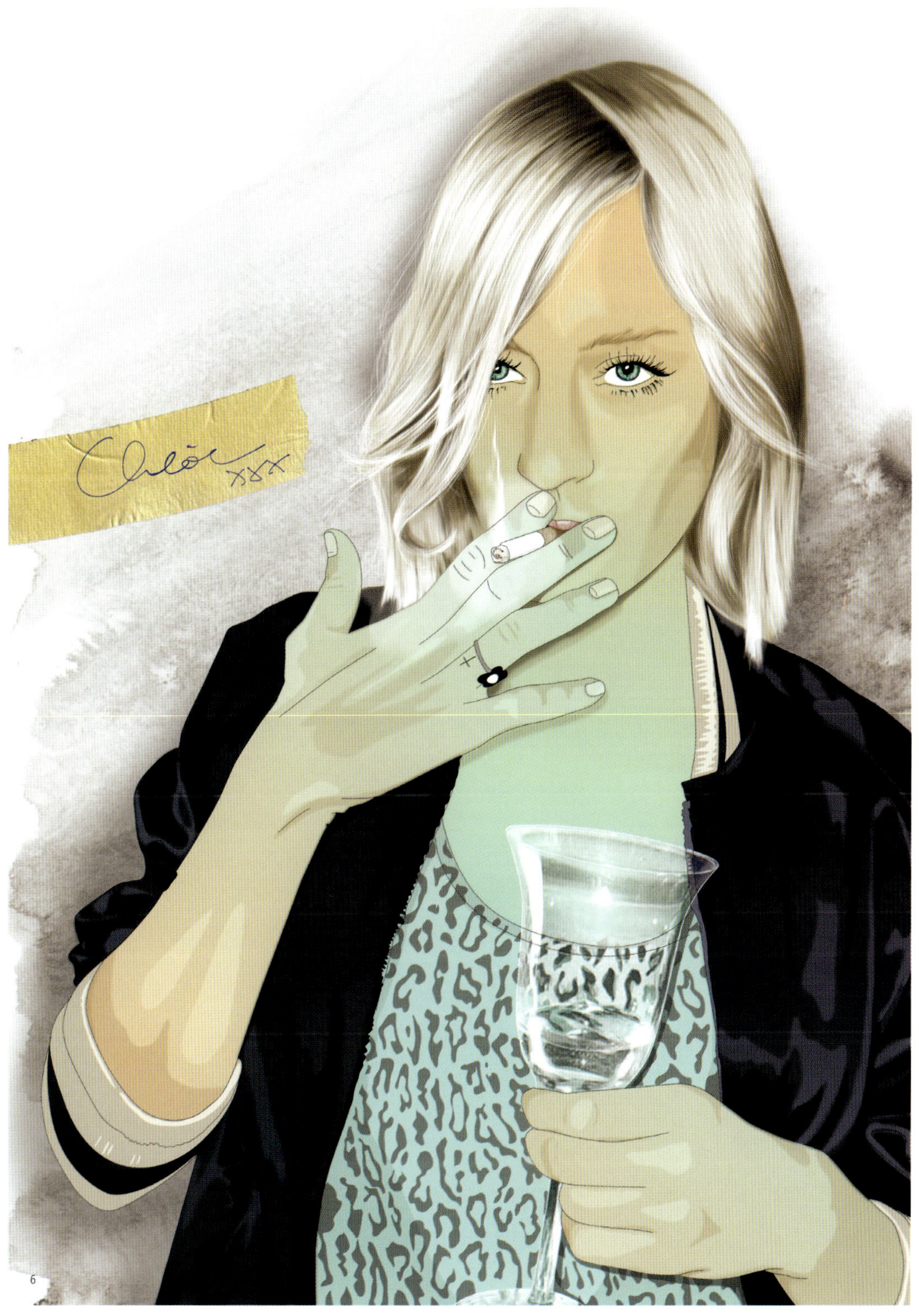

1. **Alicen** (2008). Personal work. Digital print

2. **Zooey** (2011). Personal work. Digital print

3. **Mieze** (2008). Personal work. Digital print

4. **Requiem** (2008). Personal work. Digital print

5. **Lea** (2010). *Cosmopolitan* magazine. Digital print

6. **Chloe** (2011). Personal work. Digital print

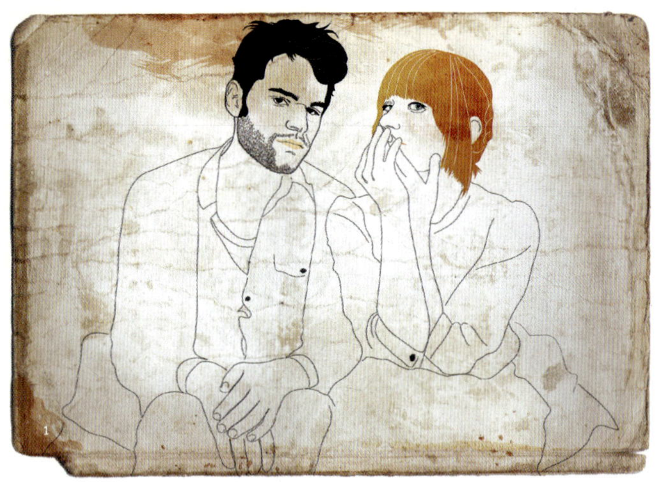

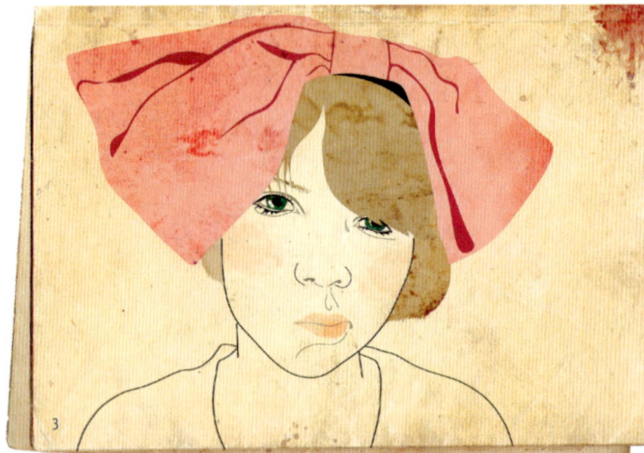
F U C K
B O Y S

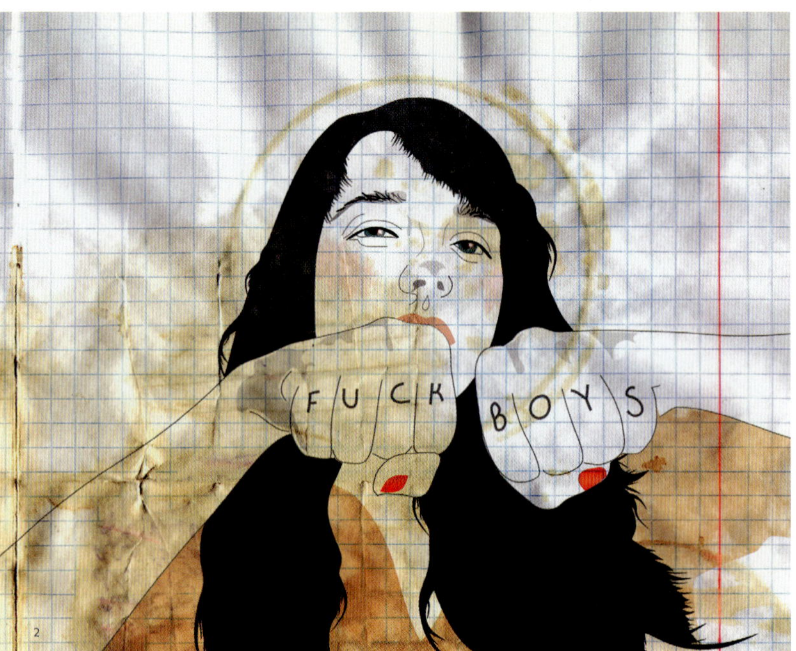

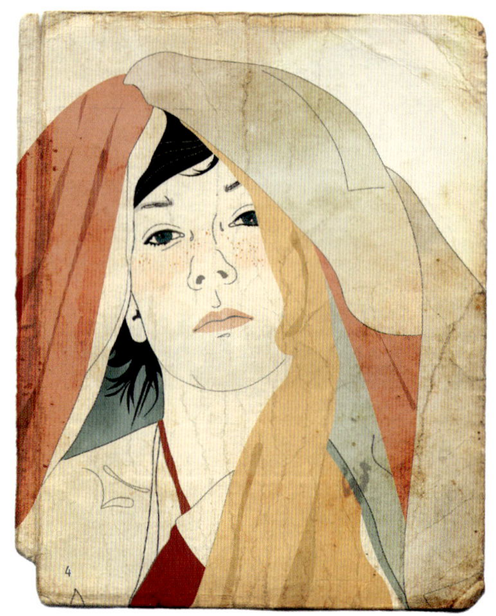

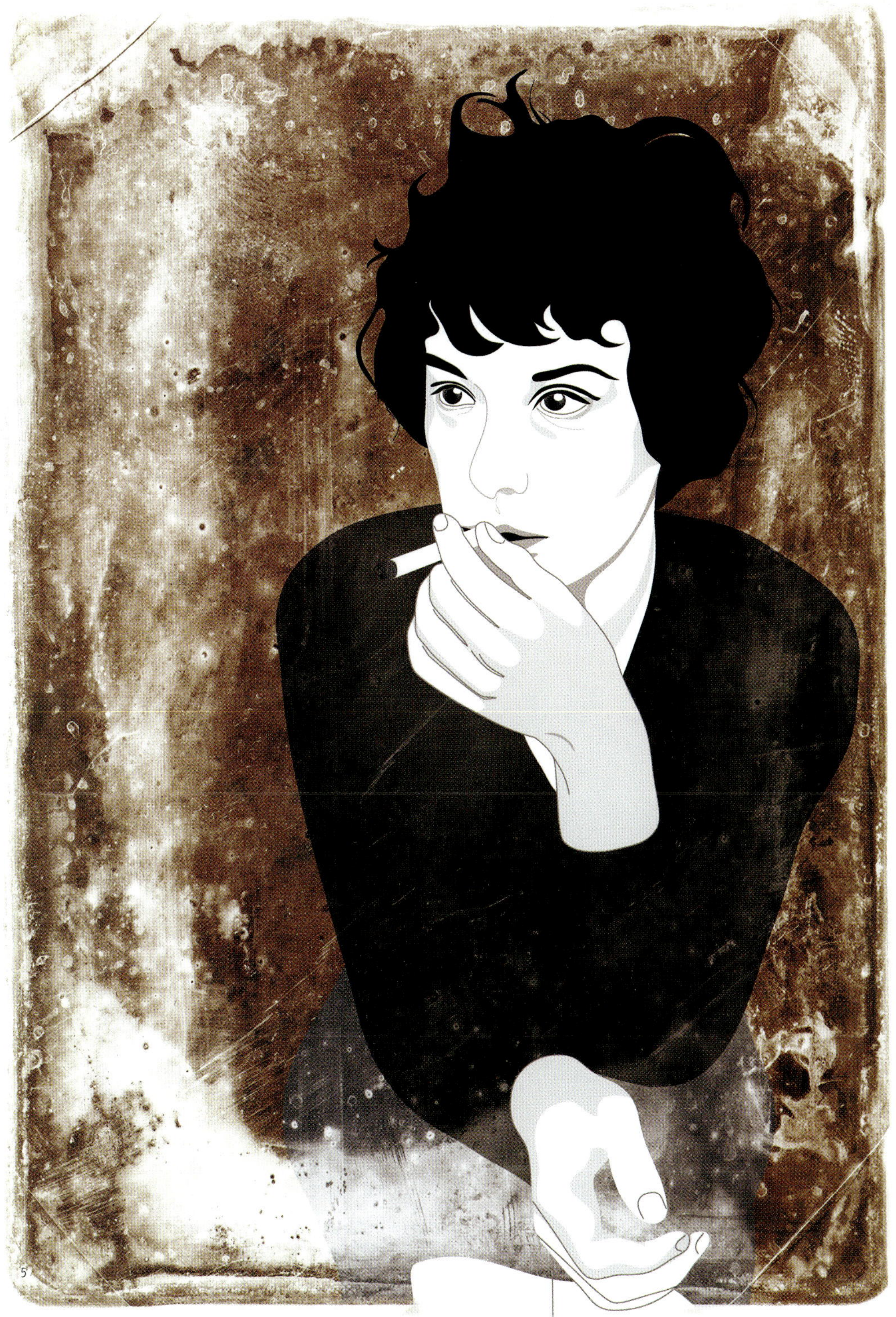

Bianca Heinrichs
aka la robotique

Germany

www.rbtq.de

1. **Sarah & Malte** (2009). Personal work. Freehand, Photoshop

2. **Boys** (2009). Personal work. Freehand, Photoshop

3. **Style Rookie** (2009). Tavi Gevinson. Freehand, Photoshop

4. **Sarah** (2009). *piaui #33* magazine. Freehand, Photoshop

5. **Silentness** (2009). Personal work. Freehand, Photoshop

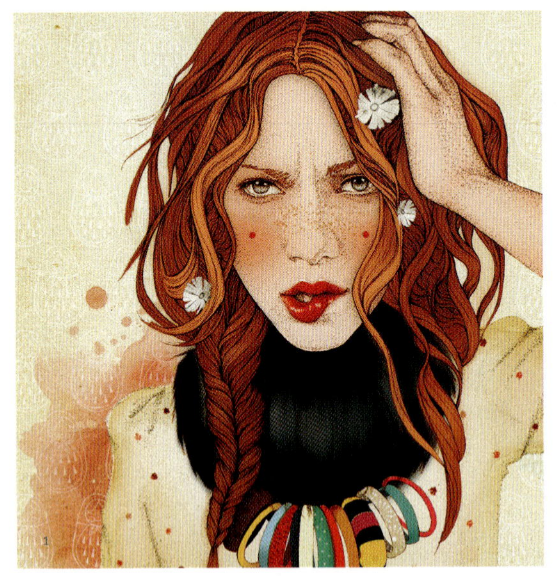

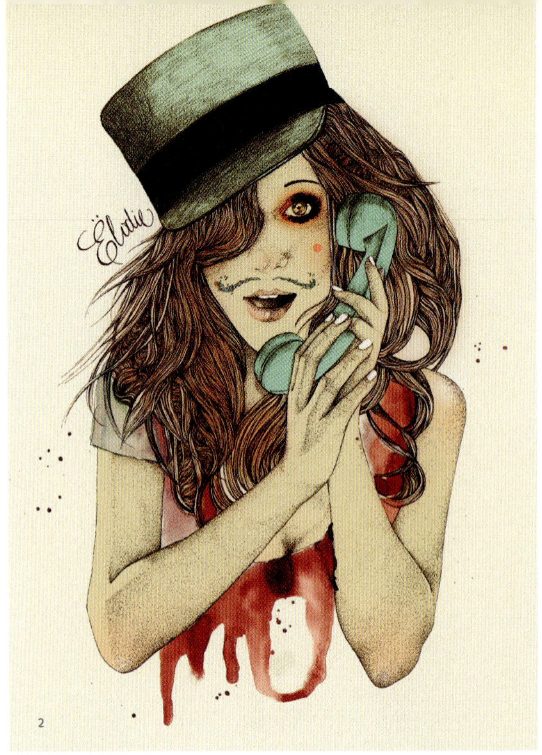

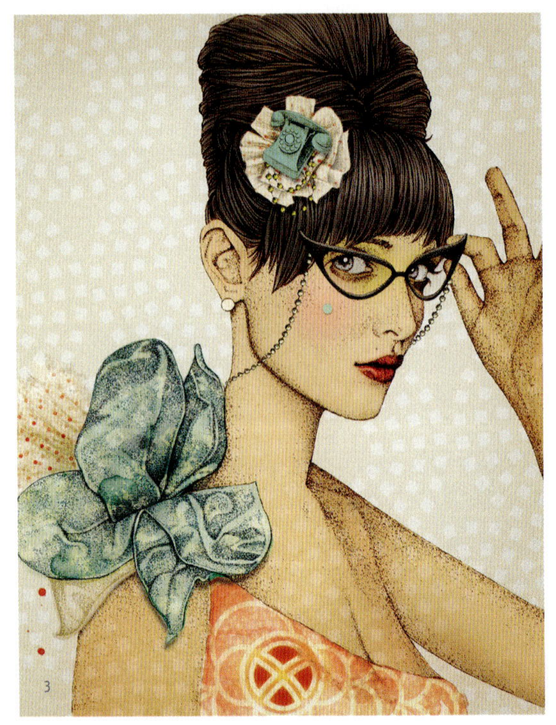

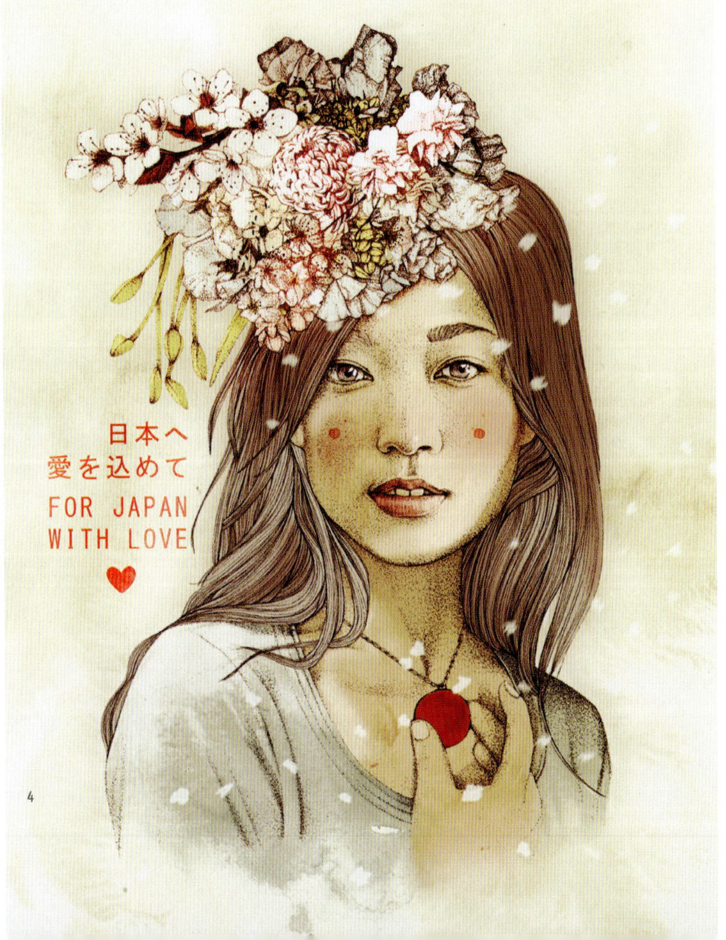
日本へ
愛を込めて
FOR JAPAN
WITH LOVE

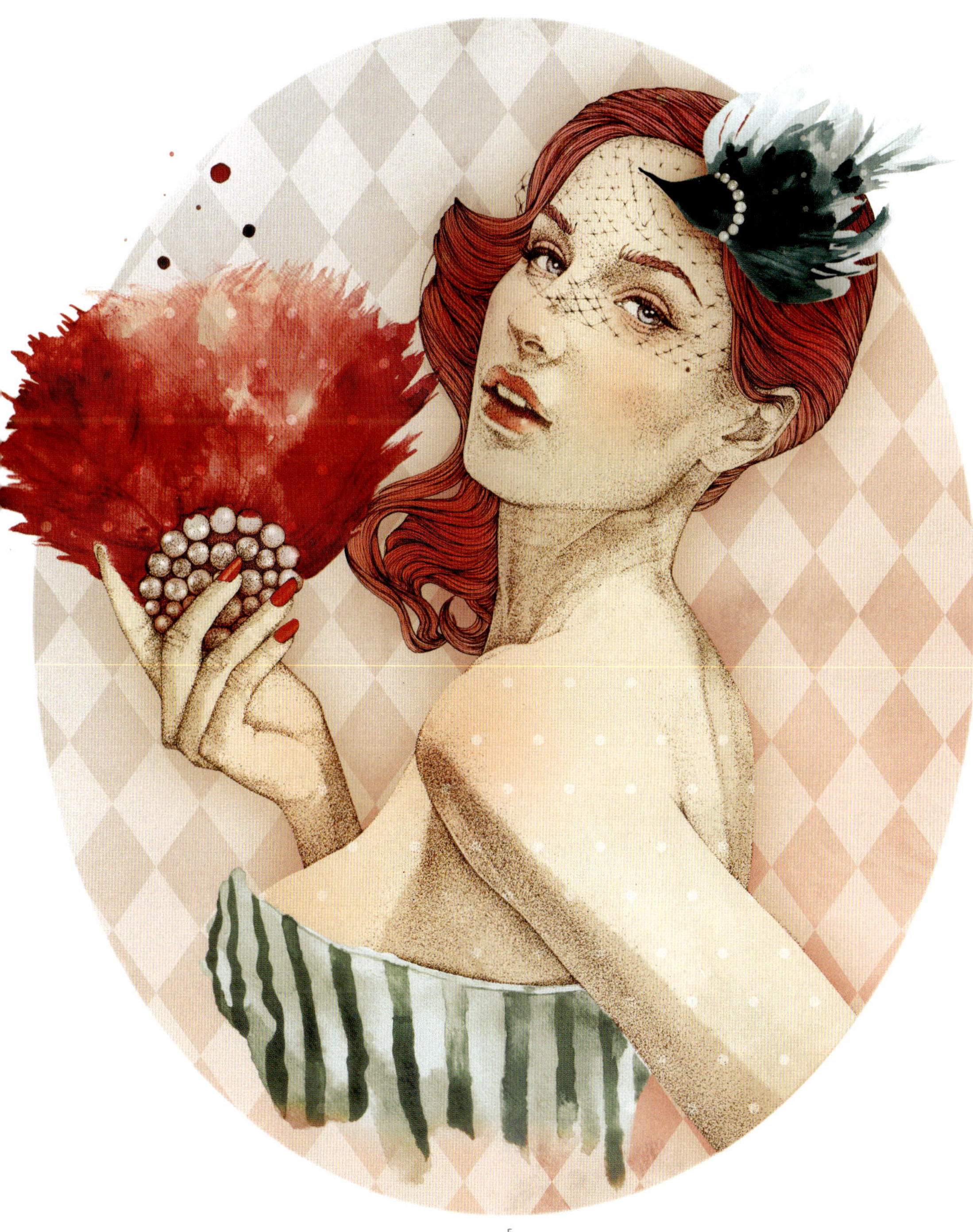

Ëlodie

France

Agency: Colagene, Illustration Clinic
www.colagene.com/fr/illustration/
elodie

1. **Poupée Russe** (2010). *La Marelle Editions.* Pencil, watercolor, Photoshop

2. **Sexy Mo** (2010). Personal work. Pencil, watercolor, Photoshop

3. **Charlotte** (2010). *La Marelle Editions.* Pencil, Photoshop

4. **For Japan with Love** (2011). Personal work. Pencil, watercolor, Photoshop

5. **Gorgeous** (2011). *La Marelle Editions.* Pencil, watercolor, Photoshop

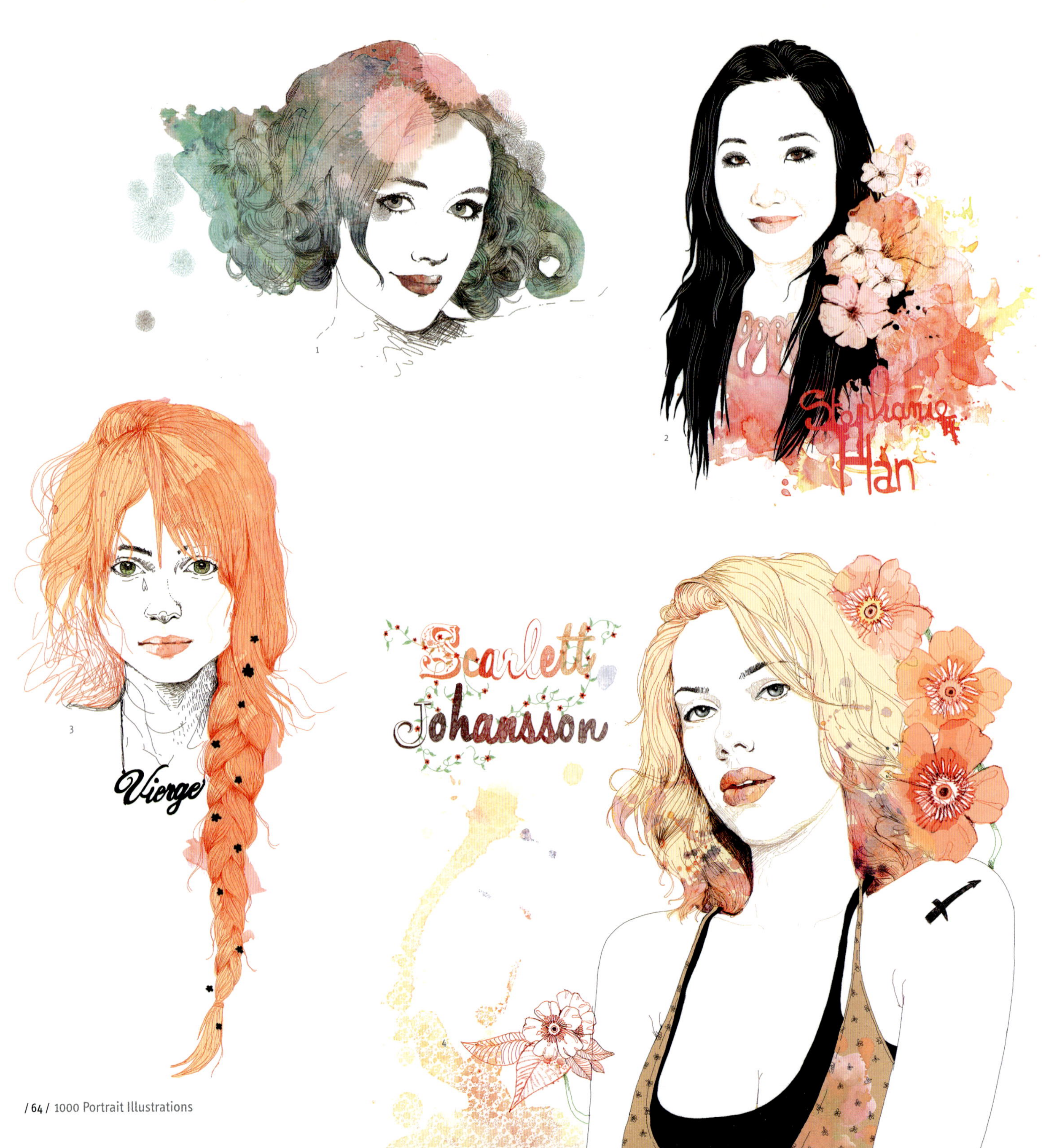
Stephanie Han
Vierge
Scarlett Johansson

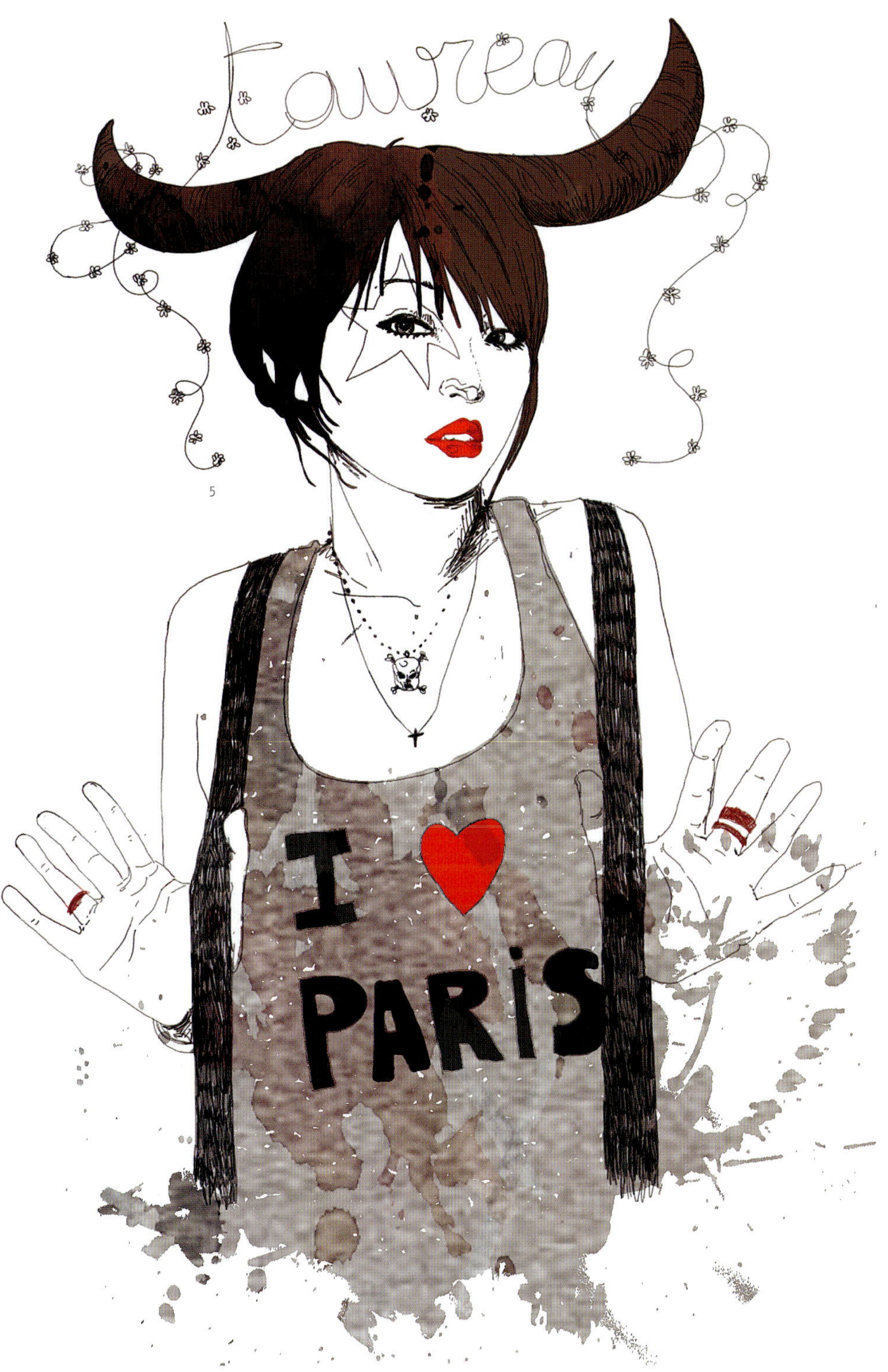

Anne Cresci

France

Agency: Colagene, Illustration Clinic
www.colagene.com/fr/illustration/
anne-cresci

1. **Blue girl** (2011). *Company Magazine.* Photoshop, watercolor

2. **Stephanie Han** (2011). *Best Health* magazine. Photoshop, watercolor

3. **Virgin Girl** (2011). *Be Magazine.* Photoshop, watercolor

4. **Scarlett Johansson** (2010). *Cosmopolitan* magazine. Photoshop, watercolor

5. **Taurus** (2011). *Be Magazine.* Photoshop, watercolor

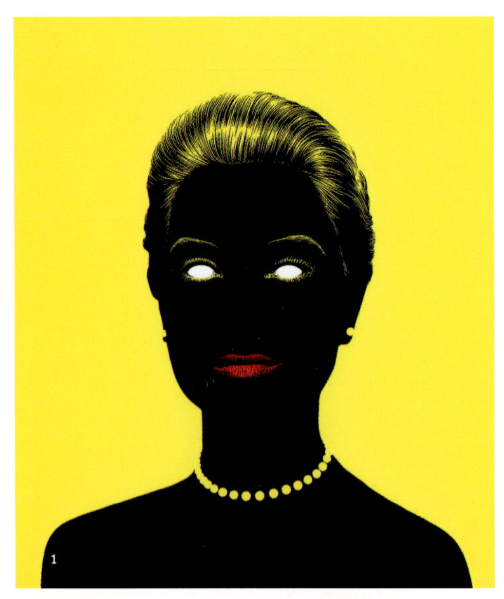

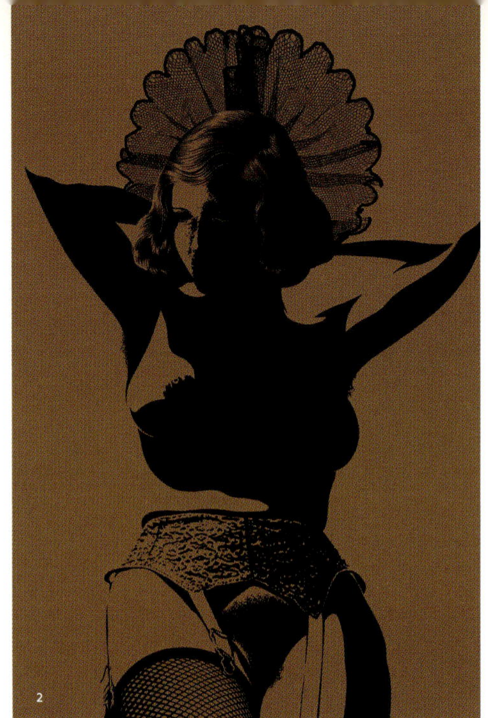

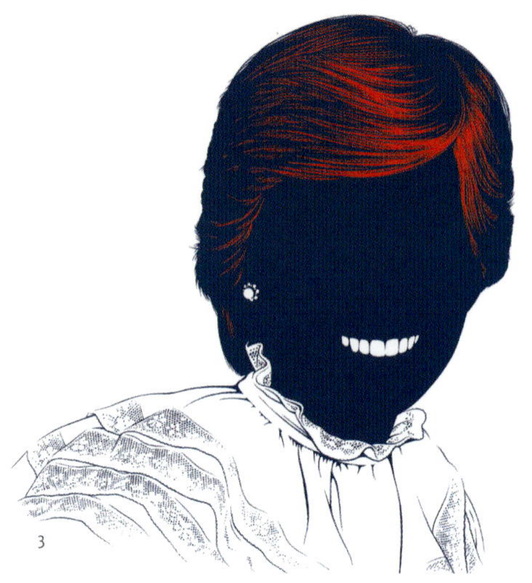

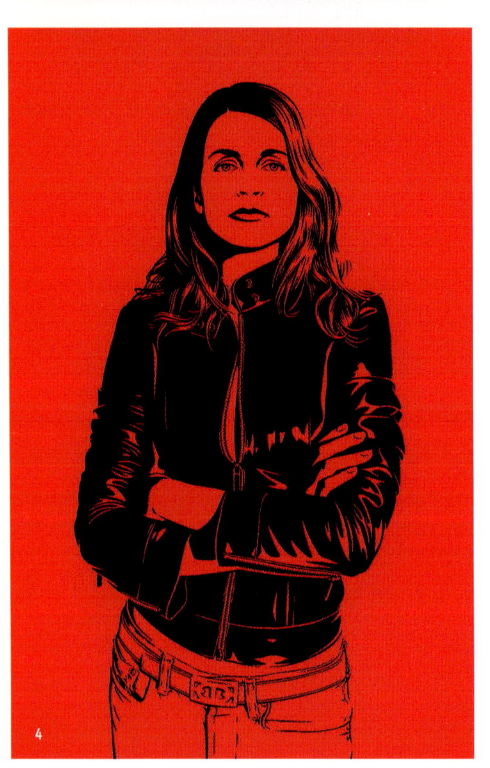

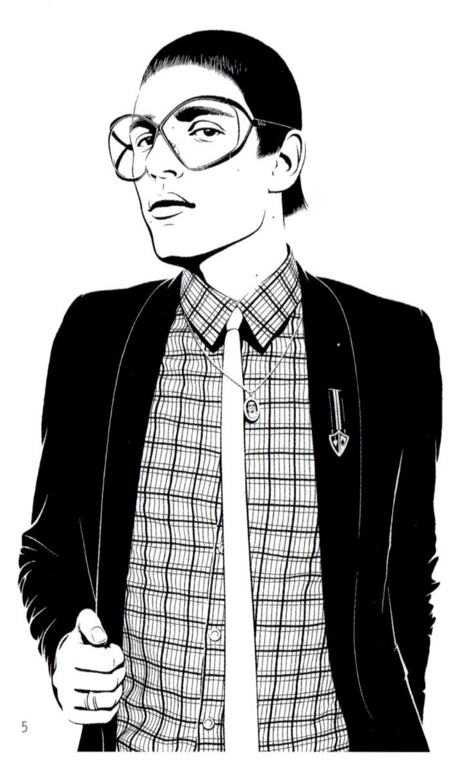

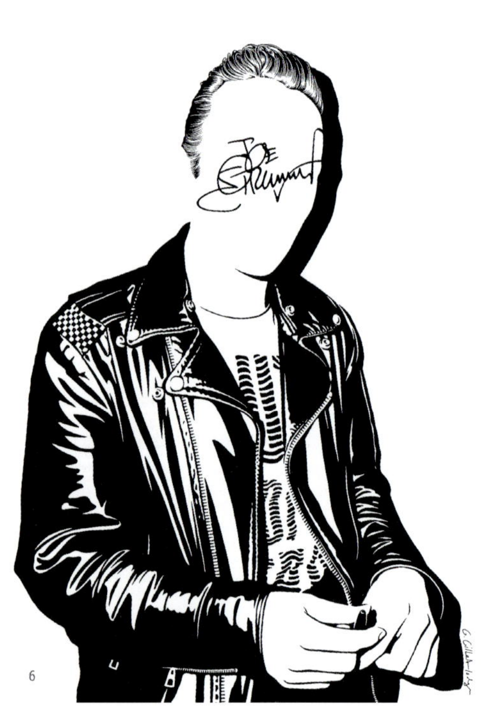

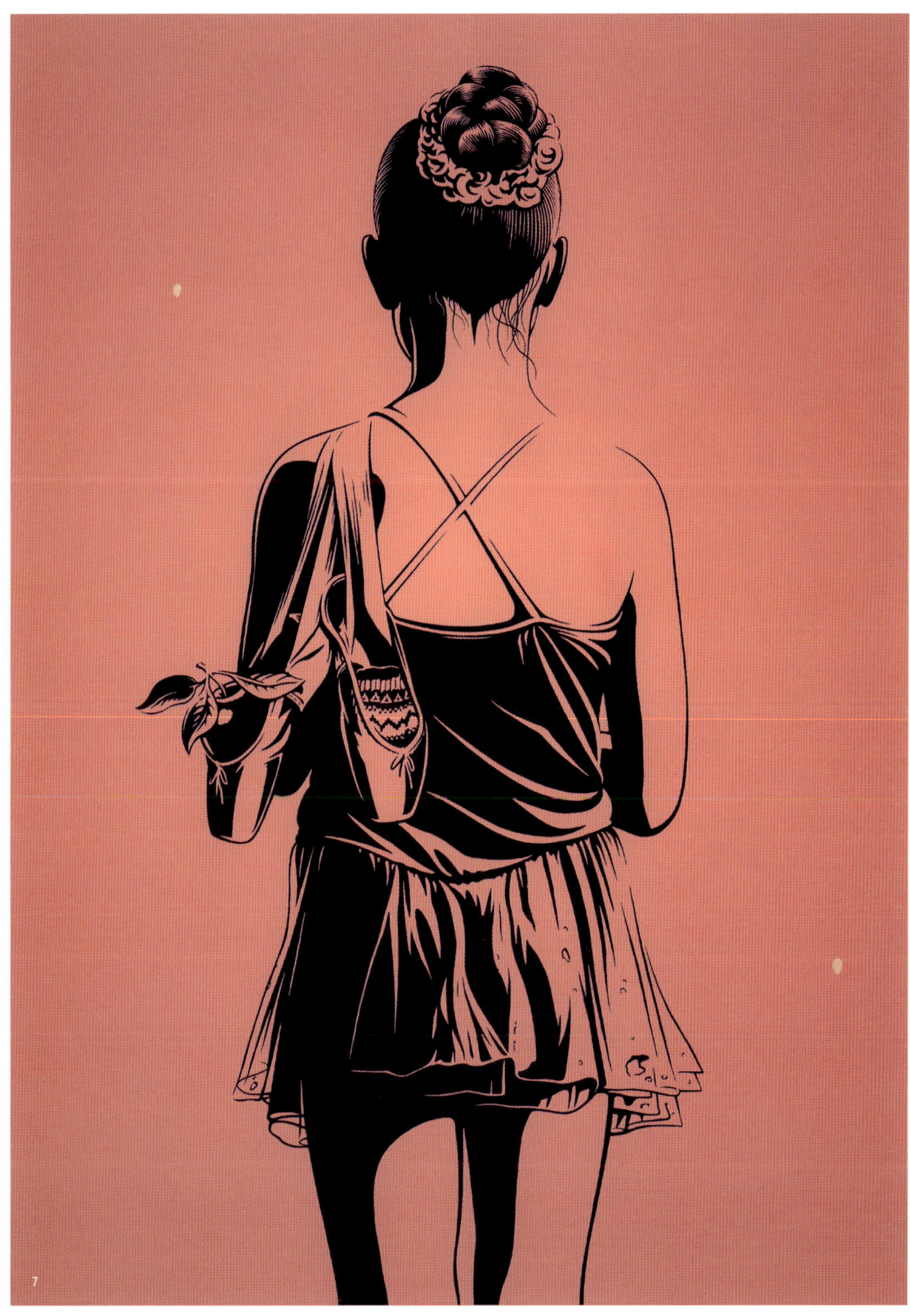

Gregory Gilbert-Lodge

Switzerland

www.gilbert-lodge.com

1. **Graciebird** (2010). Personal work. digital

2. **Fraeulein Braun** (2008). Personal work. Silkscreen print on paper

3. **Diana** (2005). Personal work. Silkscreen print on paper

4. **Karla Otto** (2008). *Die Weltwoche* Luxus/ Stil. Digital

5. **Hipster** (2011). *Das Magazin, Tages Anzeiger*. Digital

6. **Joe Strummer, The Clash** (2009). Museum Neu. Silkscreen print on cotton fabric

7. **Hartz IV Ballerina** (2011). *Die Zeit Magazin*. Digital

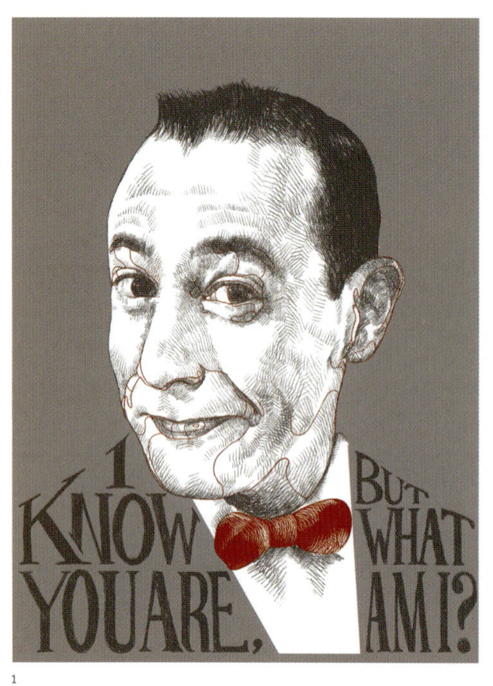
I KNOW
YOU ARE,
BUT
WHAT
AM I?

1

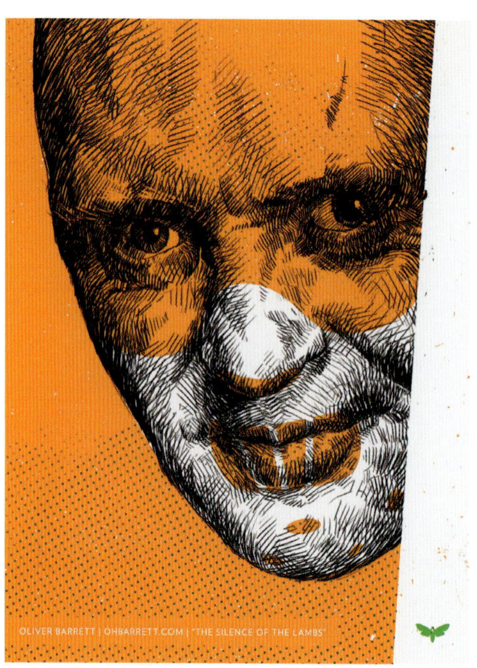
OLIVER BARRETT | OHBARRETT.COM | "THE SILENCE OF THE LAMBS"

2

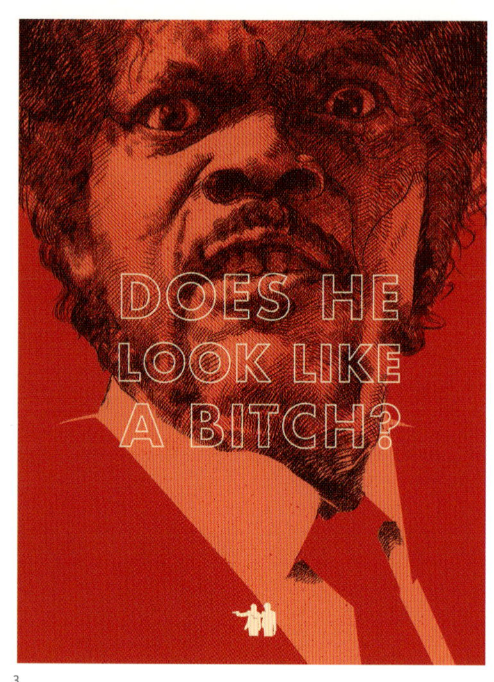
DOES HE
LOOK LIKE
A BITCH?

3

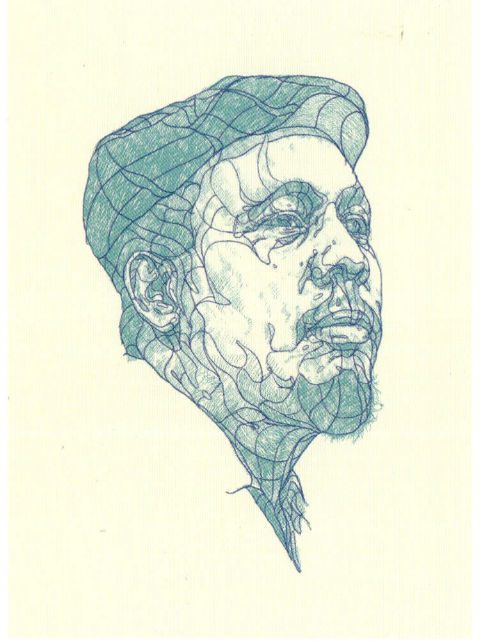

4

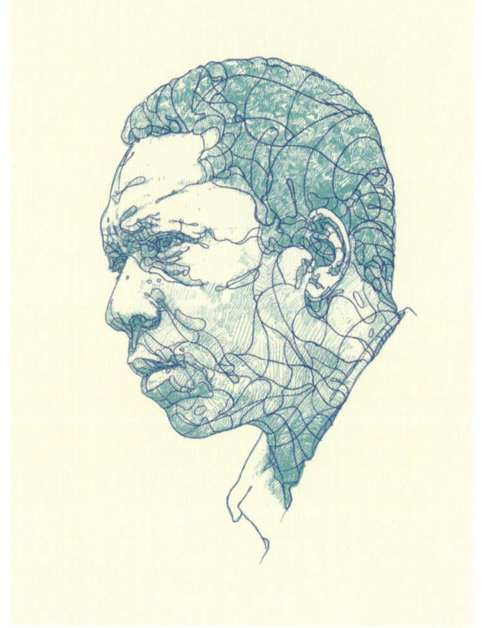

5

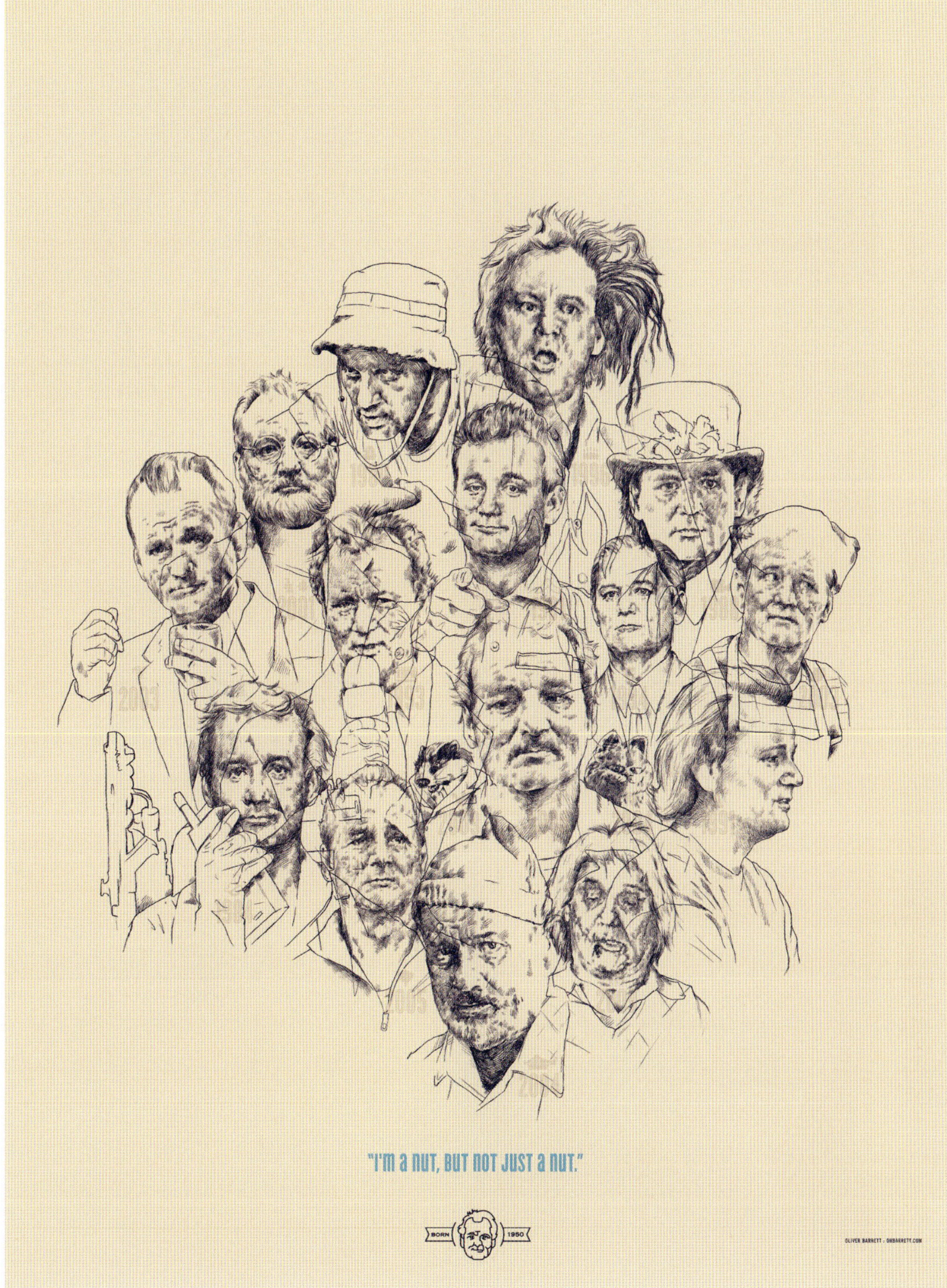

Oliver Barrett
USA

www.ohbarrett.com

1. **I know you are** (2011). G1988. Graphite, digital

2. **Lecter** (2011). Scream Prints. Mixed media

3. **What does Marcellus Wallace look like** (2011). Spoke Art. Mixed media

4. **Mingus** (2009). Personal work. Mixed media

5. **Coltrane** (2009). Personal work. Mixed media

6. **17 Bills** (2011). G1988

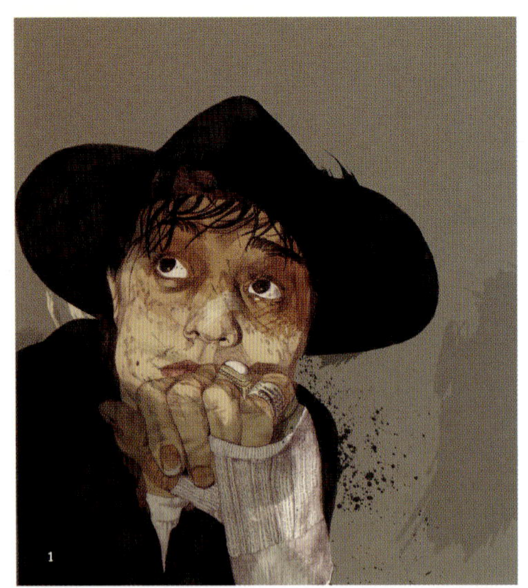

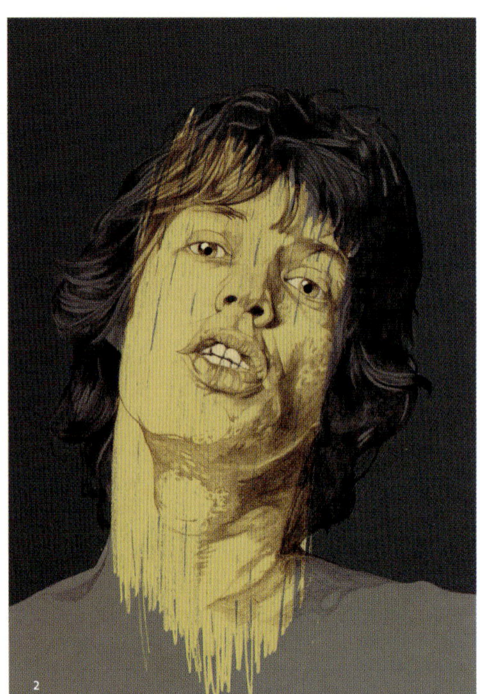

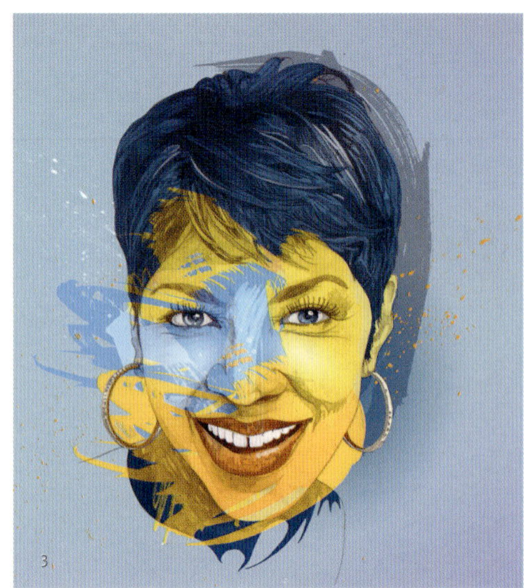

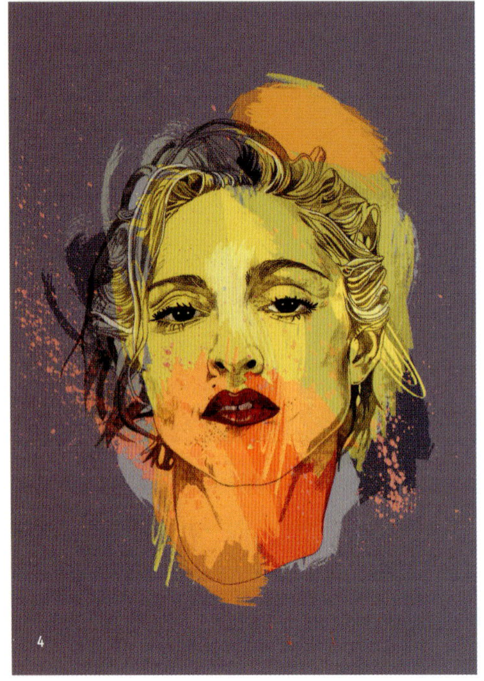

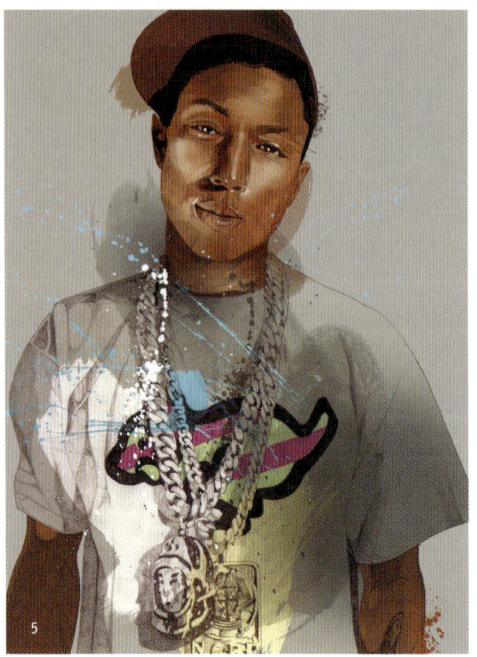

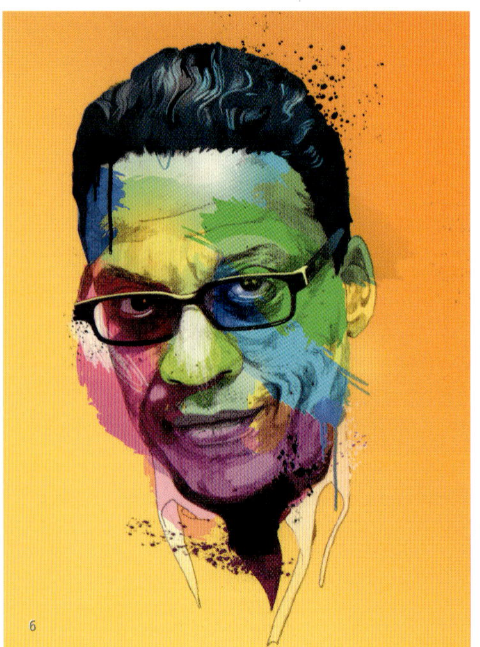

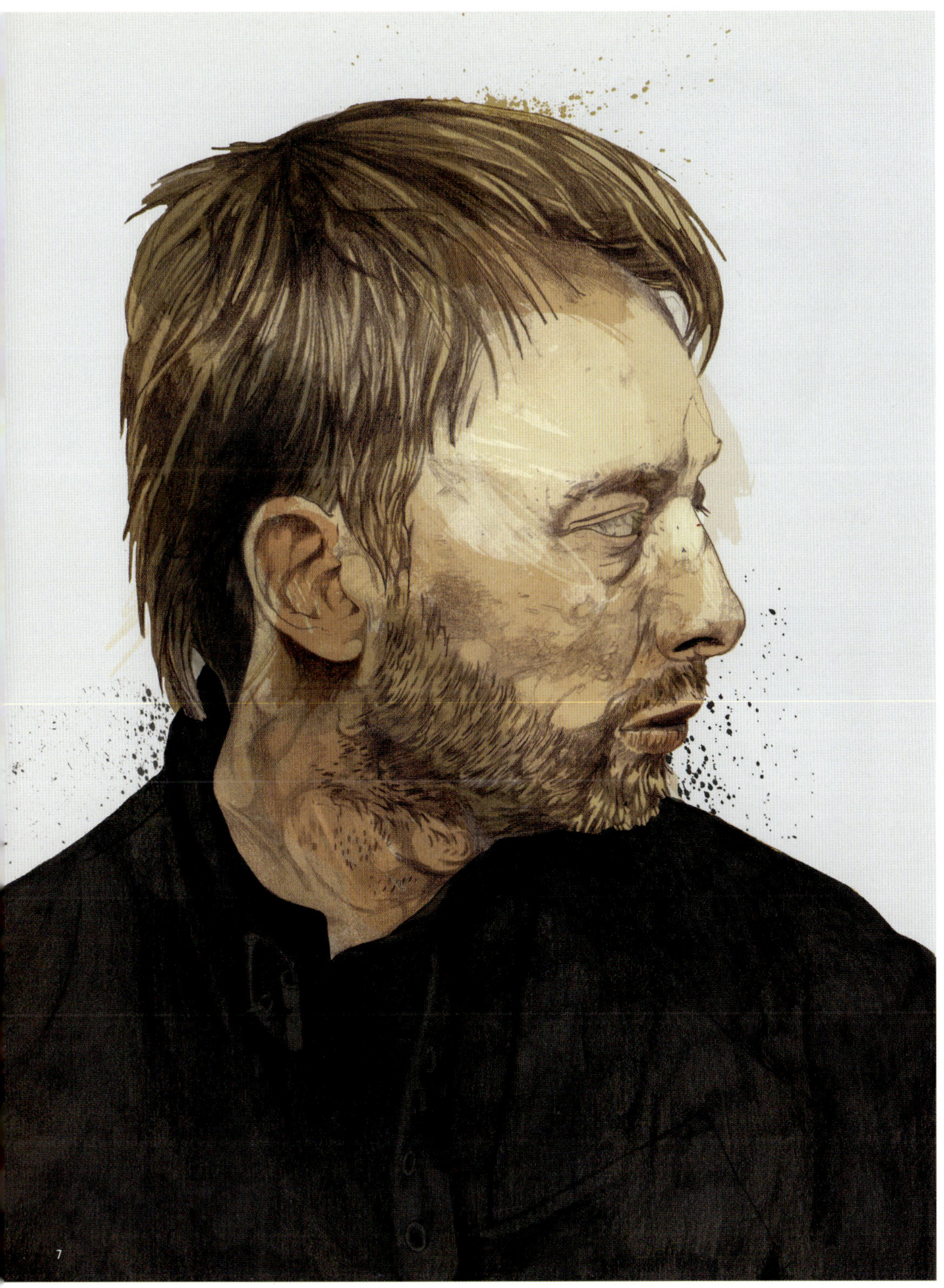

Matthew Hollings

UK

www.matthew-hollings.tumblr.com

1. **Pete Doherty** (2009). Personal work. Digital

2. **Mick Jagger** (2010). Private commission. Digital

3. **Natalie Cole** (2011). Rochester International Jazz Festival. Digital

4. **Madonna** (2009). Personal work. Digital

5. **Pharrell Williams** (2010). *Arise Magazine*. Digital

6. **Herbie Hancock** (2010). Personal work. Digital

7. **Thom Yorke** (2009). Personal work. Digital

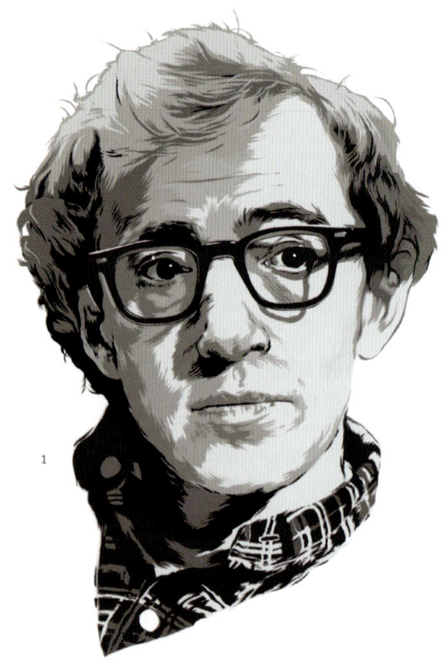

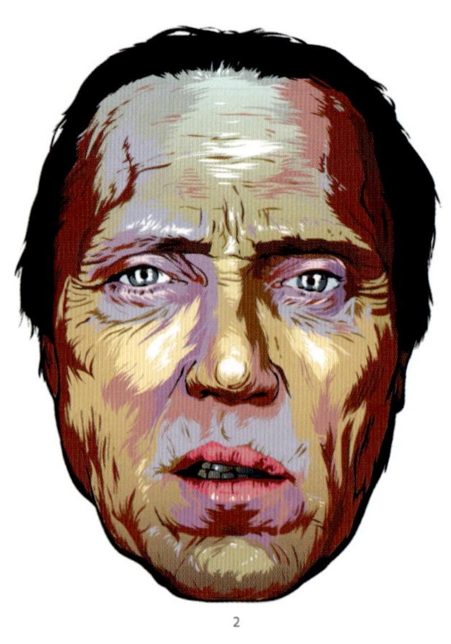

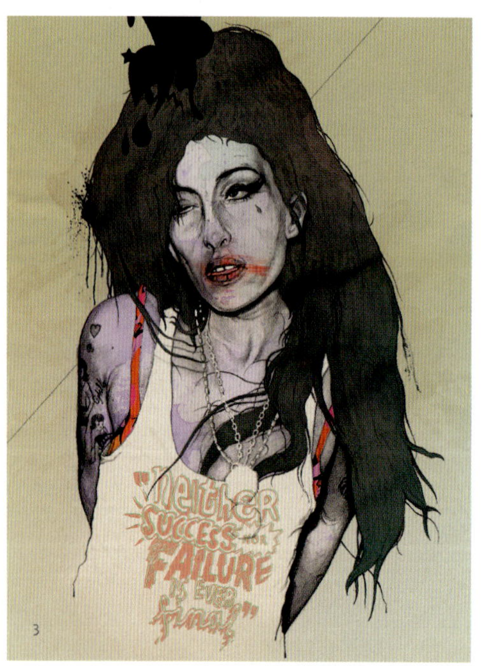
"neither
success
FAILURE
is ever final"

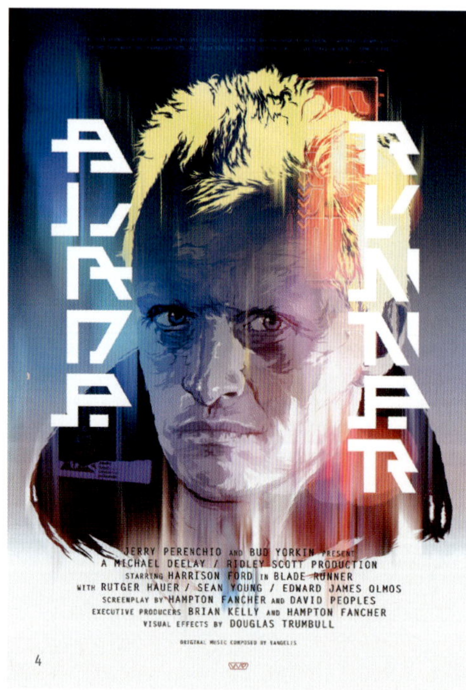
JERRY PERENCHIO AND BUD YORKIN PRESENT
A MICHAEL DEELAY / RIDLEY SCOTT PRODUCTION
STARRING HARRISON FORD IN BLADE RUNNER
WITH RUTGER HAUER / SEAN YOUNG / EDWARD JAMES OLMOS
SCREENPLAY BY HAMPTON FANCHER AND DAVID PEOPLES
EXECUTIVE PRODUCERS BRIAN KELLY AND HAMPTON FANCHER
VISUAL EFFECTS BY DOUGLAS TRUMBULL
ORIGINAL MUSIC COMPOSED BY VANGELIS

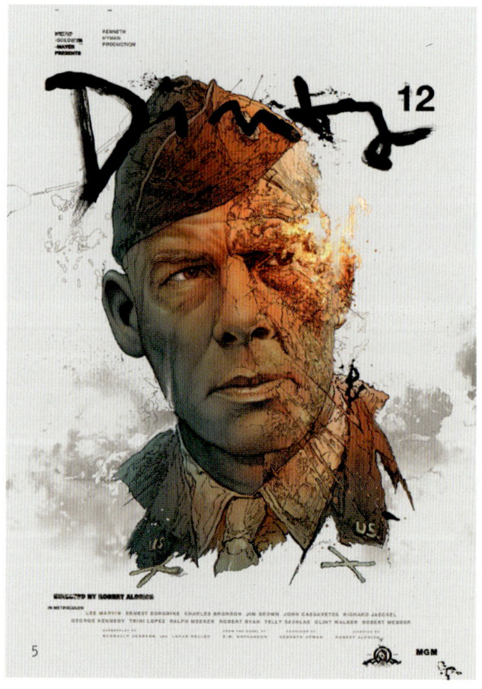
Dirty 12
METRO-GOLDWYN-MAYER PRESENTS
A KENNETH HYMAN PRODUCTION
DIRECTED BY ROBERT ALDRICH
LEE MARVIN ERNEST BORGNINE CHARLES BRONSON JIM BROWN JOHN CASSAVETES RICHARD JAECKEL
GEORGE KENNEDY TRINI LOPEZ RALPH MEEKER ROBERT RYAN TELLY SAVALAS CLINT WALKER ROBERT WEBBER
MGM

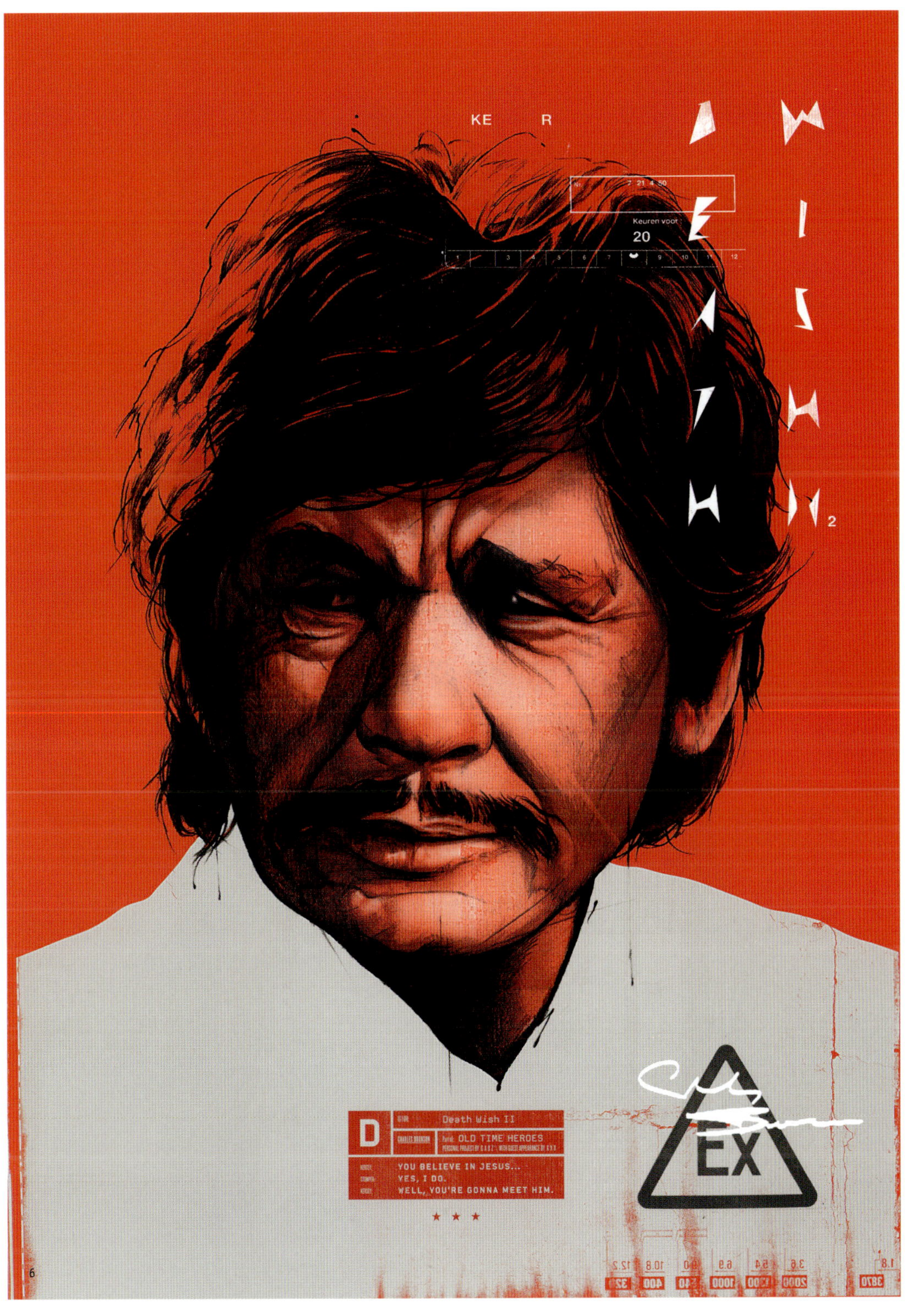

1. **Woody Allen** (2008). Personal work.
Illustrator

2. **Christopher Walken** (2008). Personal
work. Illustrator

3. **Amy** (2009). Personal work. Pencil,
Photoshop

4. **Blade Runner** (2010). Personal work.
Illustrator, Photoshop

5. **Dirty Dozen** (2011). Personal work.
Pencil, Photoshop

6. **Death Wish** (2011). Personal work.
Pencil, Photoshop

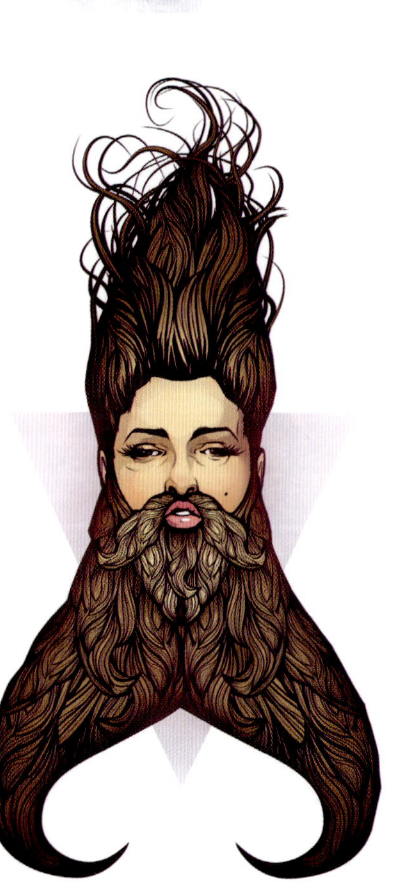
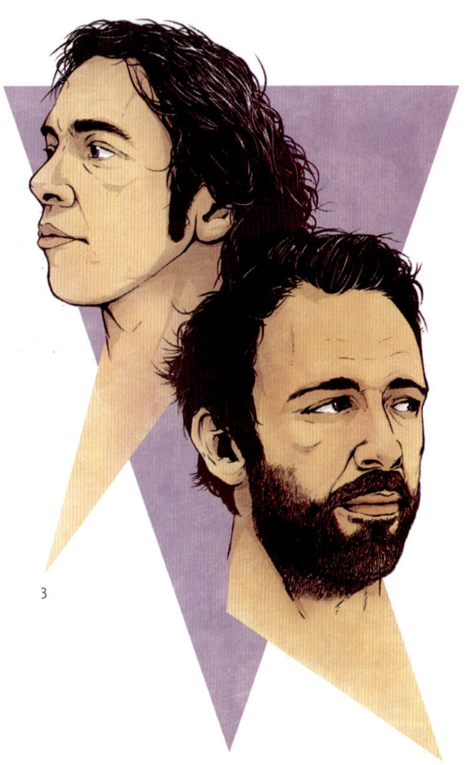

DEWAELE

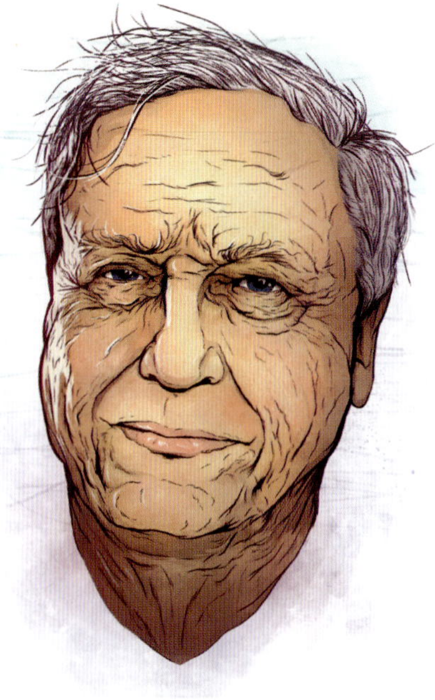

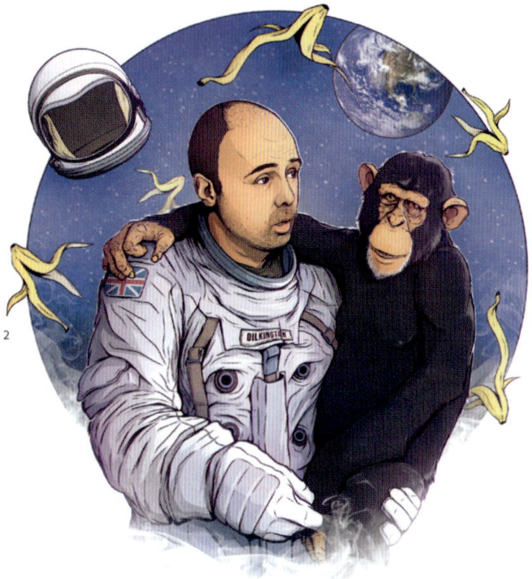

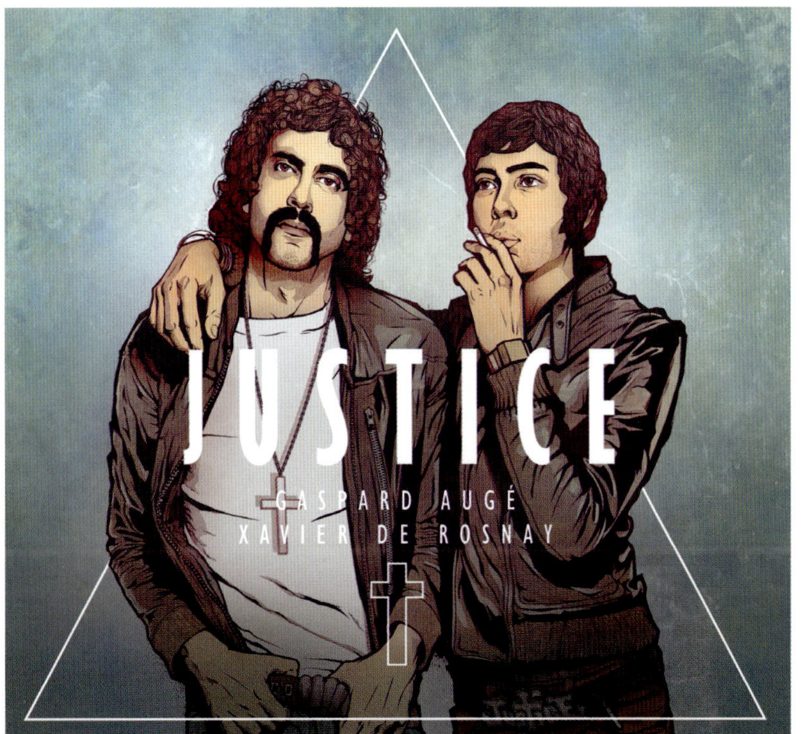

Matt Chinn
UK

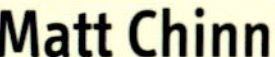
www.mattchinn.co.uk

1. **David Attenborough** (2011). Personal work. Digital

2. **Karl Pilkington - An Idiot in Space** (2011). Personal work. Digital

3. **2 Many Dj's** (2011). Personal work. Digital

4. **Bearded** (2011). Personal work. Digital

5. **Justice** (2011). Personal work. Digital

6. **Uffie** (2011). Personal work. Digital

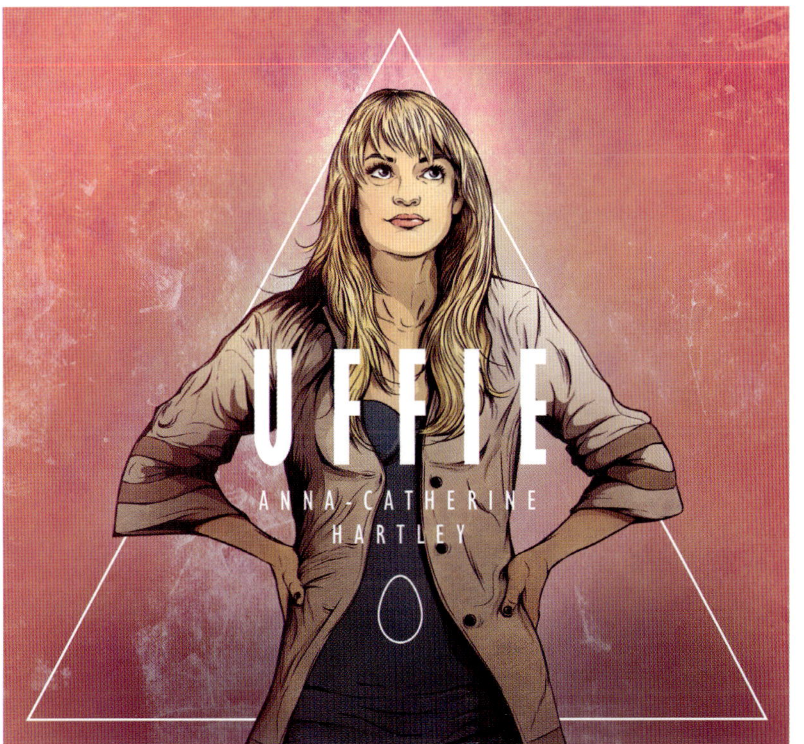

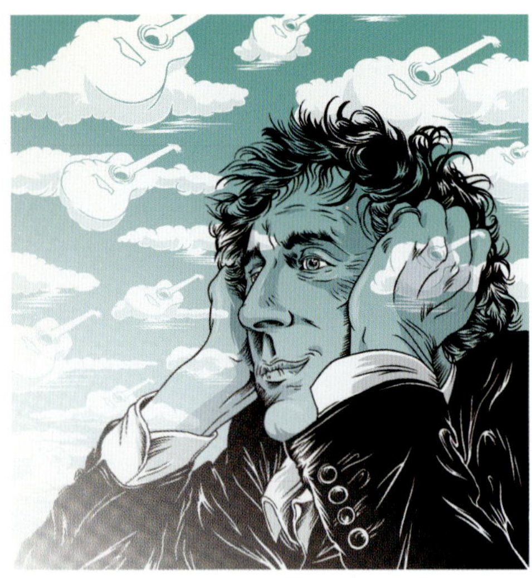

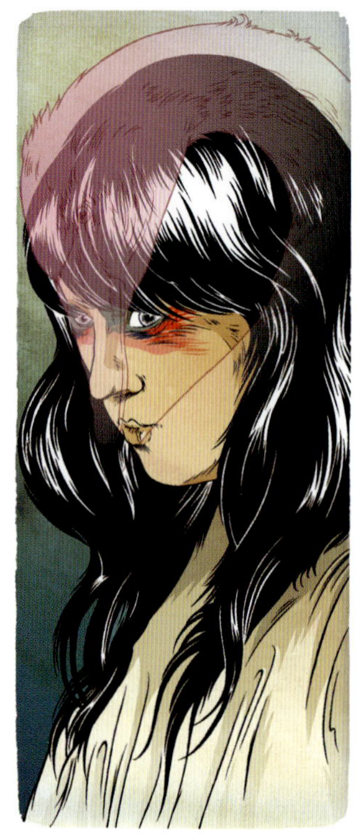

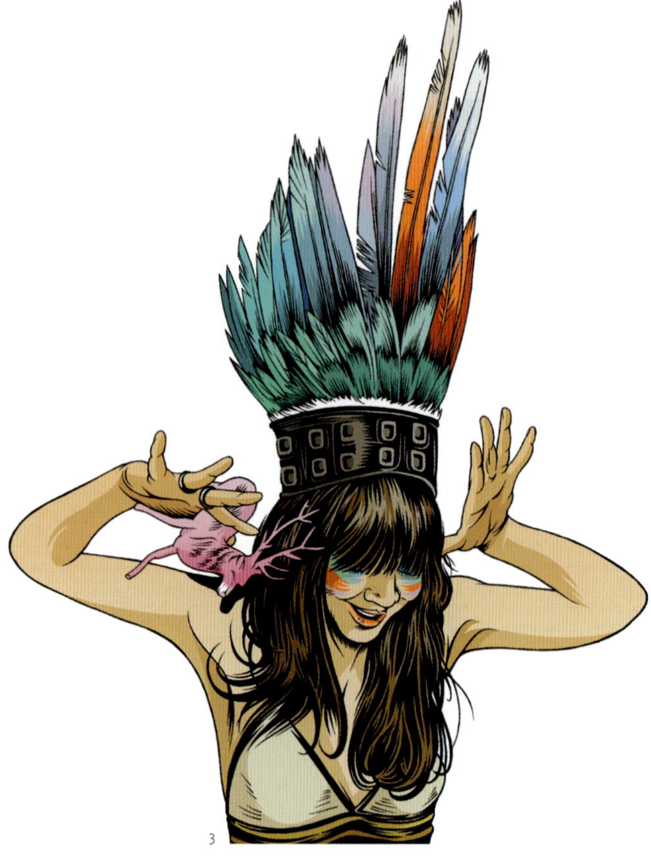

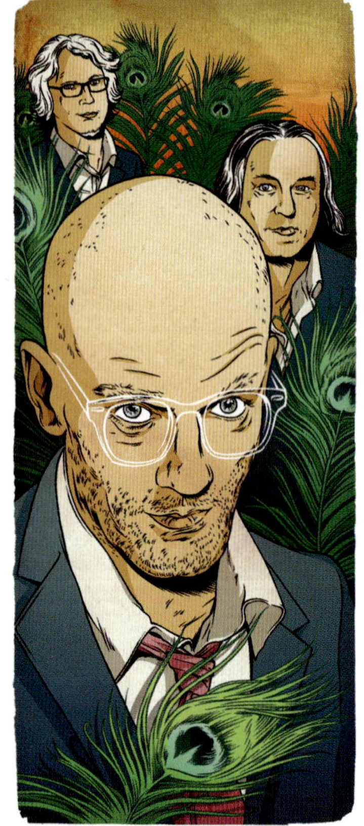

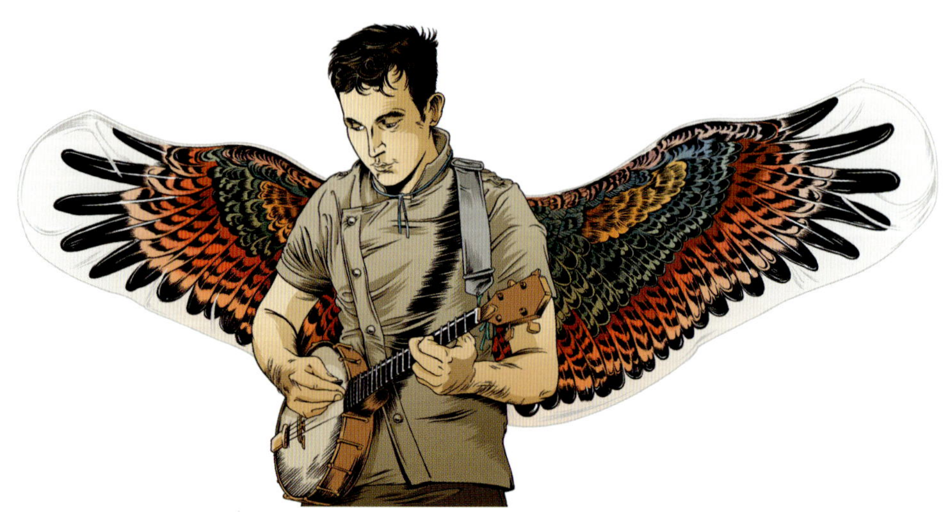

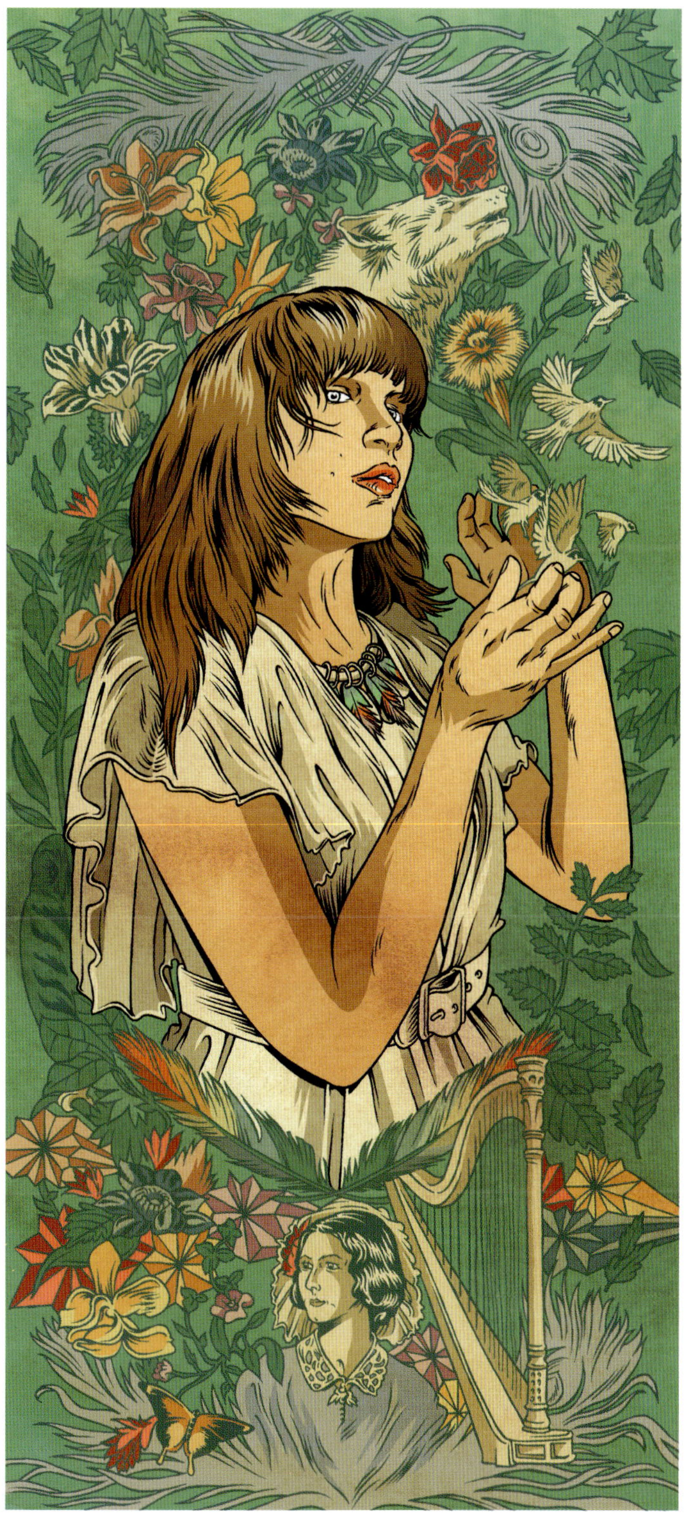

Jörn Kaspuhl

Germany

www.kaspuhl.com

1. **Alain Souchon** (2009). *GQ France.* Ink, Photoshop

2. **Anthony & The Johnsons** (2009). *Rolling Stone.* Ink, Photoshop

3. **Bat For Lashes** (2009). Personal work. Ink, Photoshop

4. **R.E.M** (2011). *Rolling Stone.* Ink, Photoshop

5. **Sufjan Stevens (2)** (2010). Personal work. Ink, Photoshop

6. **Joanna Newsom 2** (2009). *Rolling Stone.* Ink, Photoshop

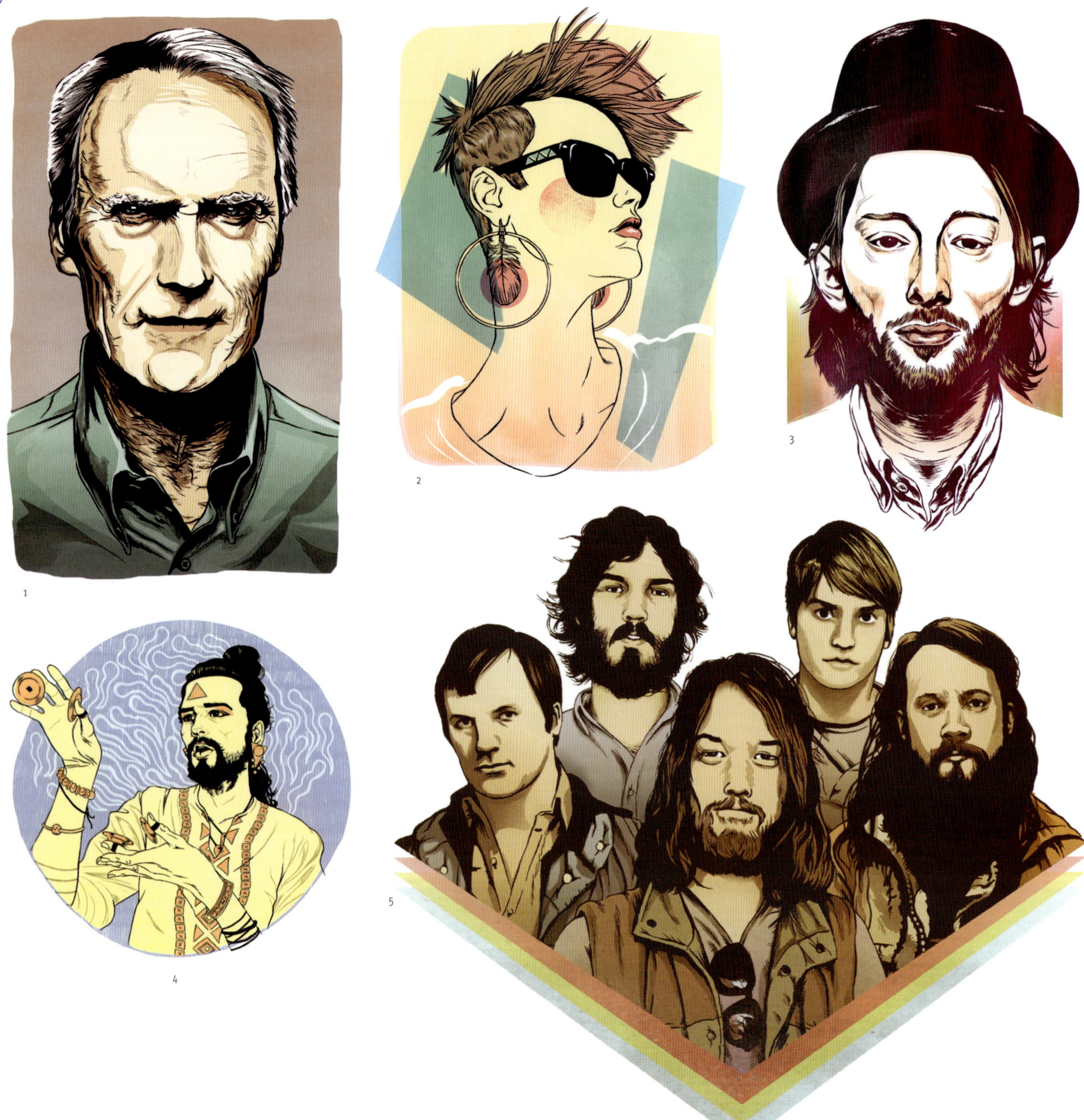

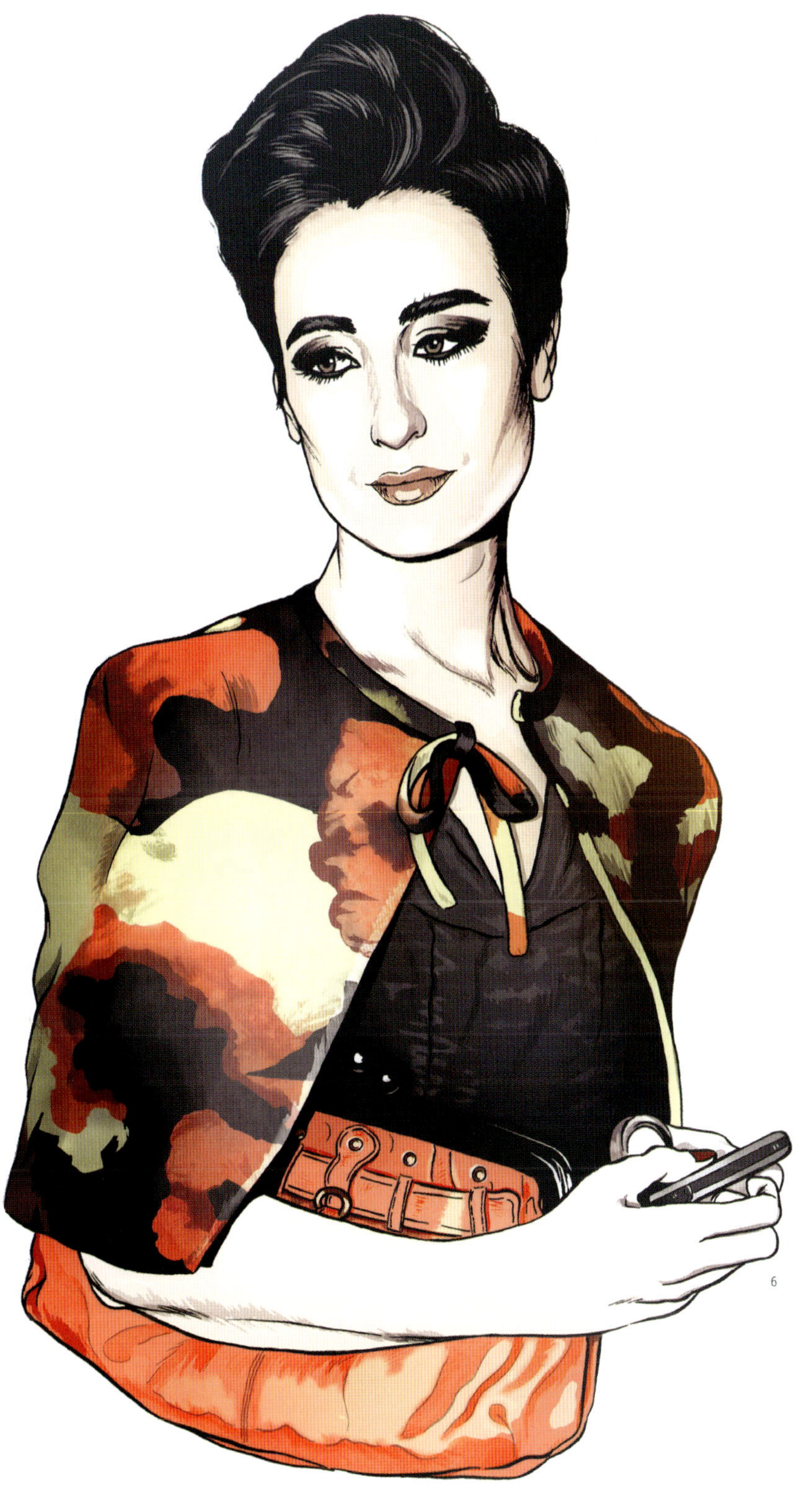

Joel Benjamin

UK

www.joelbenjamin.co.uk

1. **Clint Eastwood** (2011). Personal work. Indian ink, watercolor, Photoshop

2. **Shades** (2011). Personal work. Indian ink, watercolor, Photoshop

3. **Thom Yorke** (2011). Personal work. Indian ink, watercolor, Photoshop

4. **Devendra Banhart** (2011). Personal work. Indian ink, watercolor, Photoshop

5. **Fleet Foxes** (2011). Personal work. Indian ink, watercolor, Photoshop

6. **Erin O'Connor** (2011). Personal work. Indian ink, watercolor, Photoshop

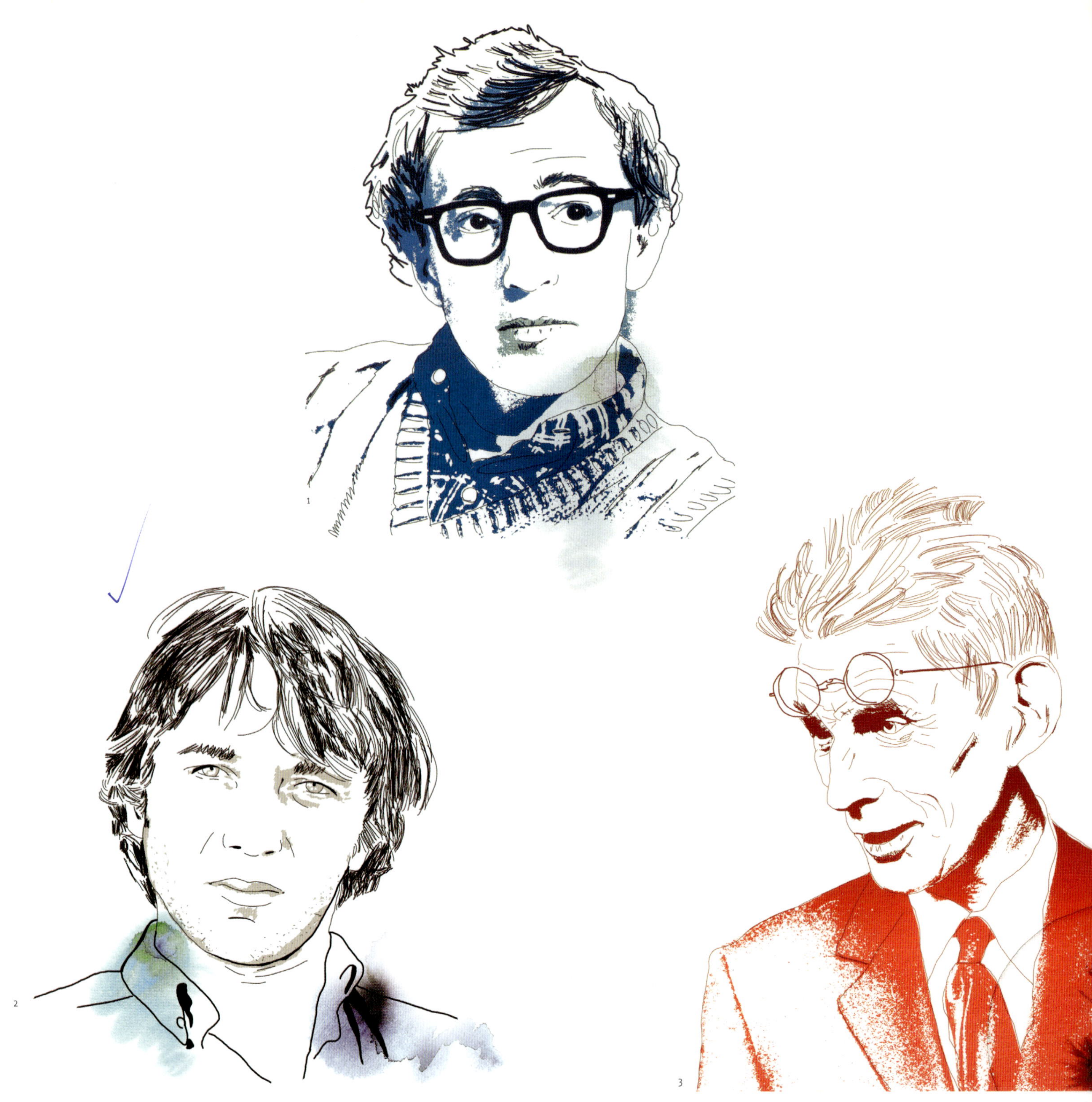

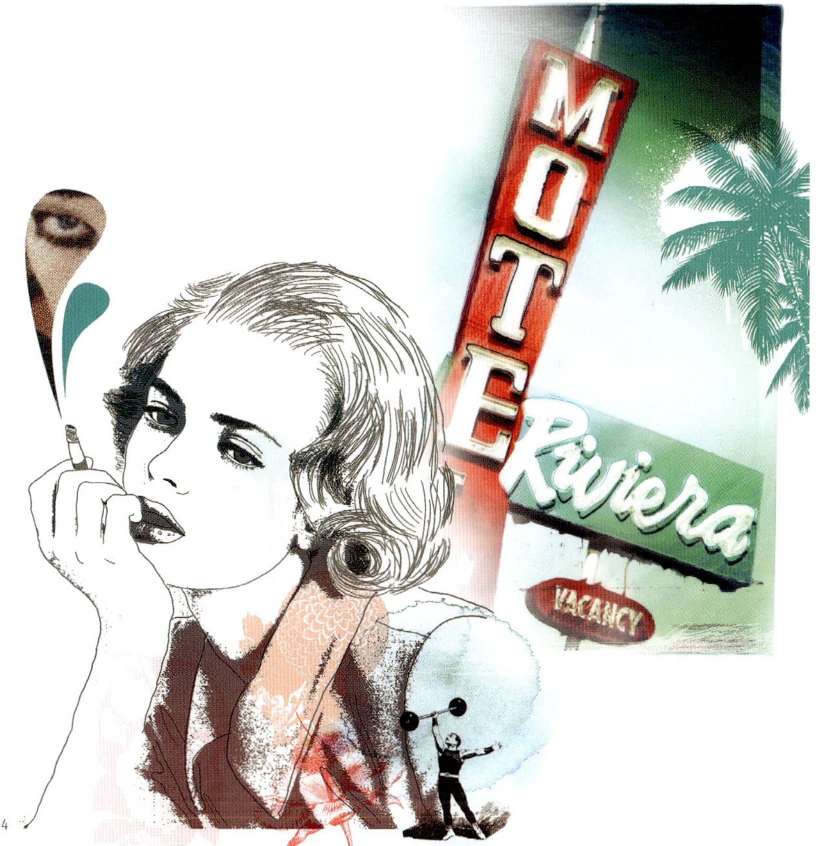

Flora Gressard

France

www.floradesign.fr

1. **Woody Allen** (2010). Personal work. Ink, watercolor, hand drawing

2. **Bernard Giraudeau** (2011) *Le Monde* Hors Série. Ink, watercolor, hand drawing

3. **Samuel Beckett** (2010). Personal work. Ink, watercolor, freehand drawing

4. **Mulholland Dr.** (2010). Personal work. Ink, watercolor, hand drawing, digital collage

5. **L'œil séduction** (2010). *Muteen* magazine. Ink, watercolor, hand drawing, digital collage

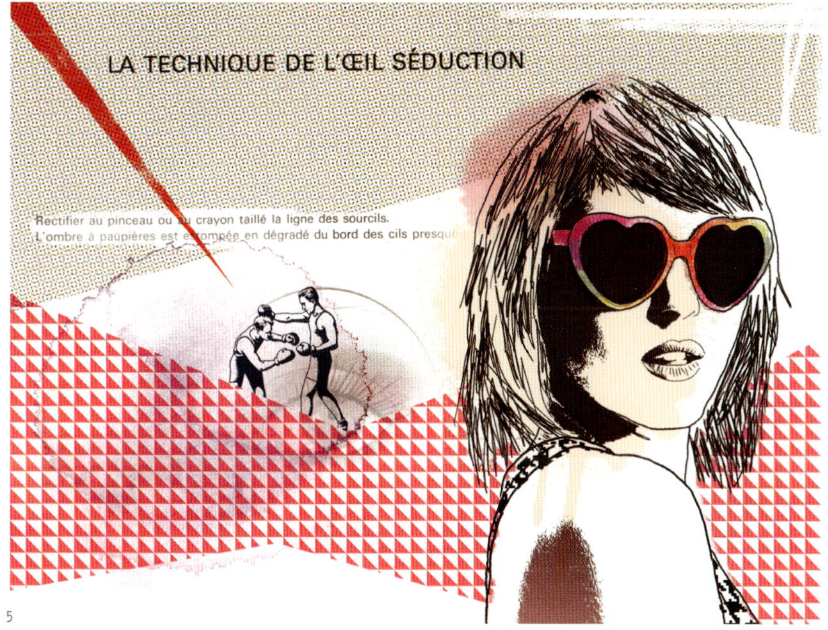

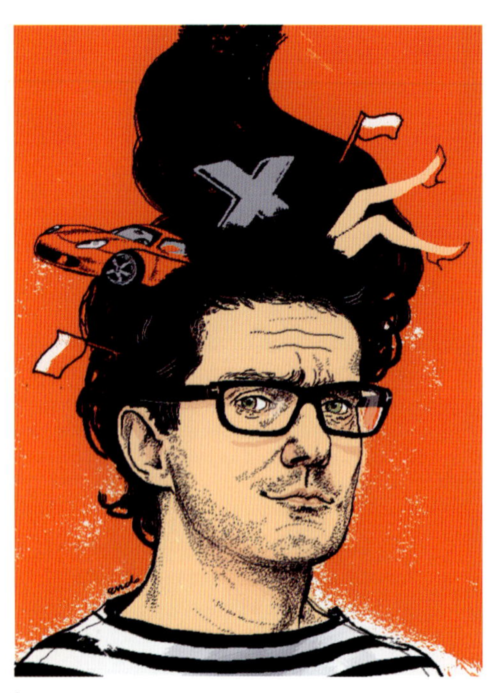

1

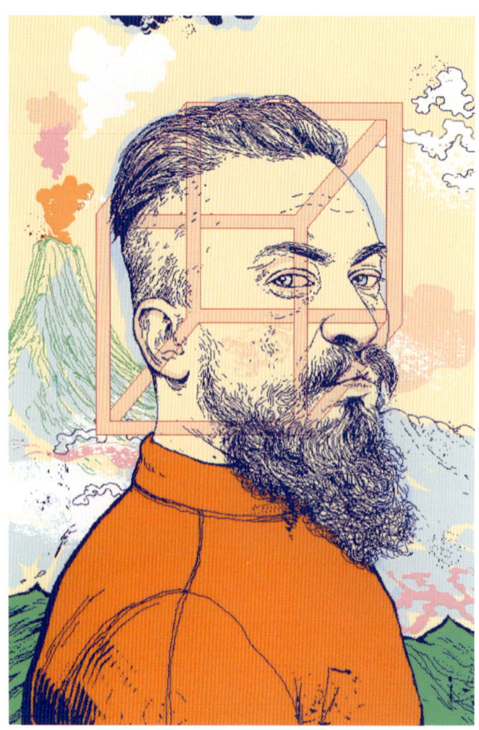

2

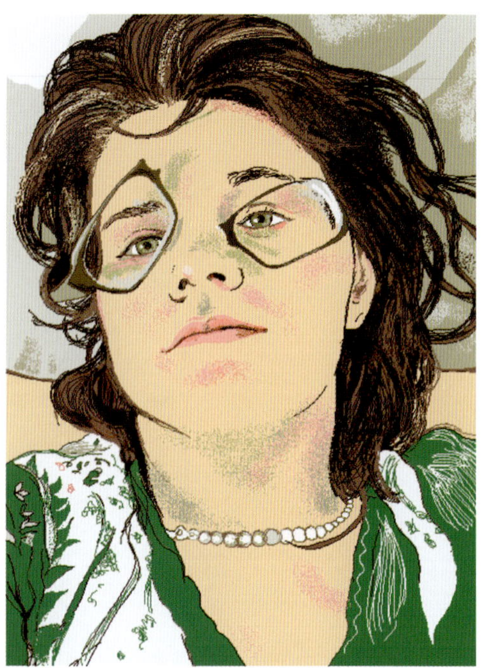

3

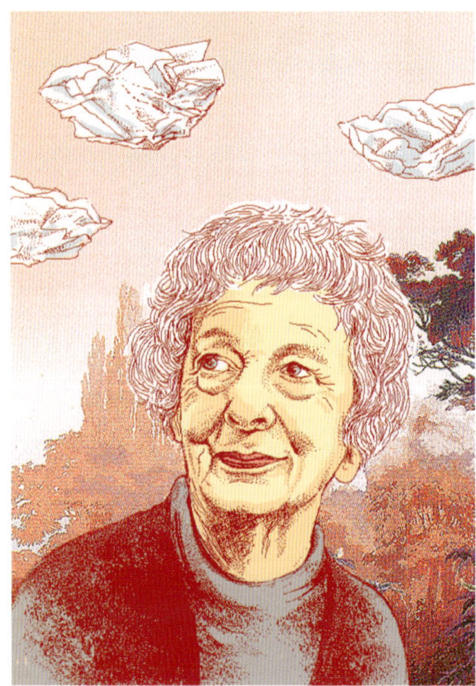

4

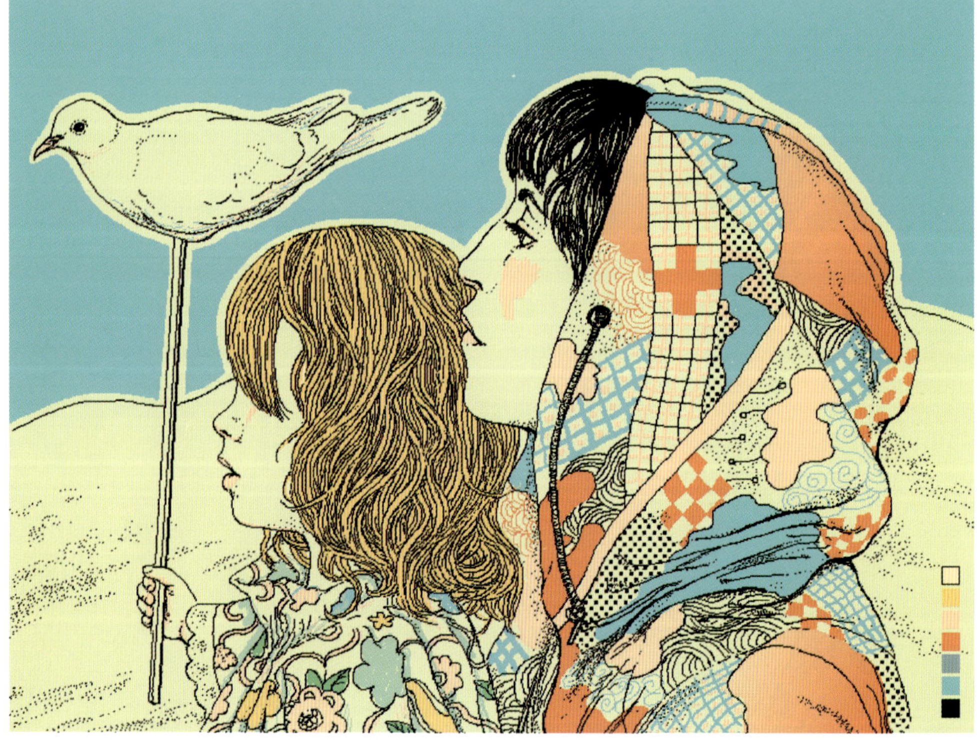

5

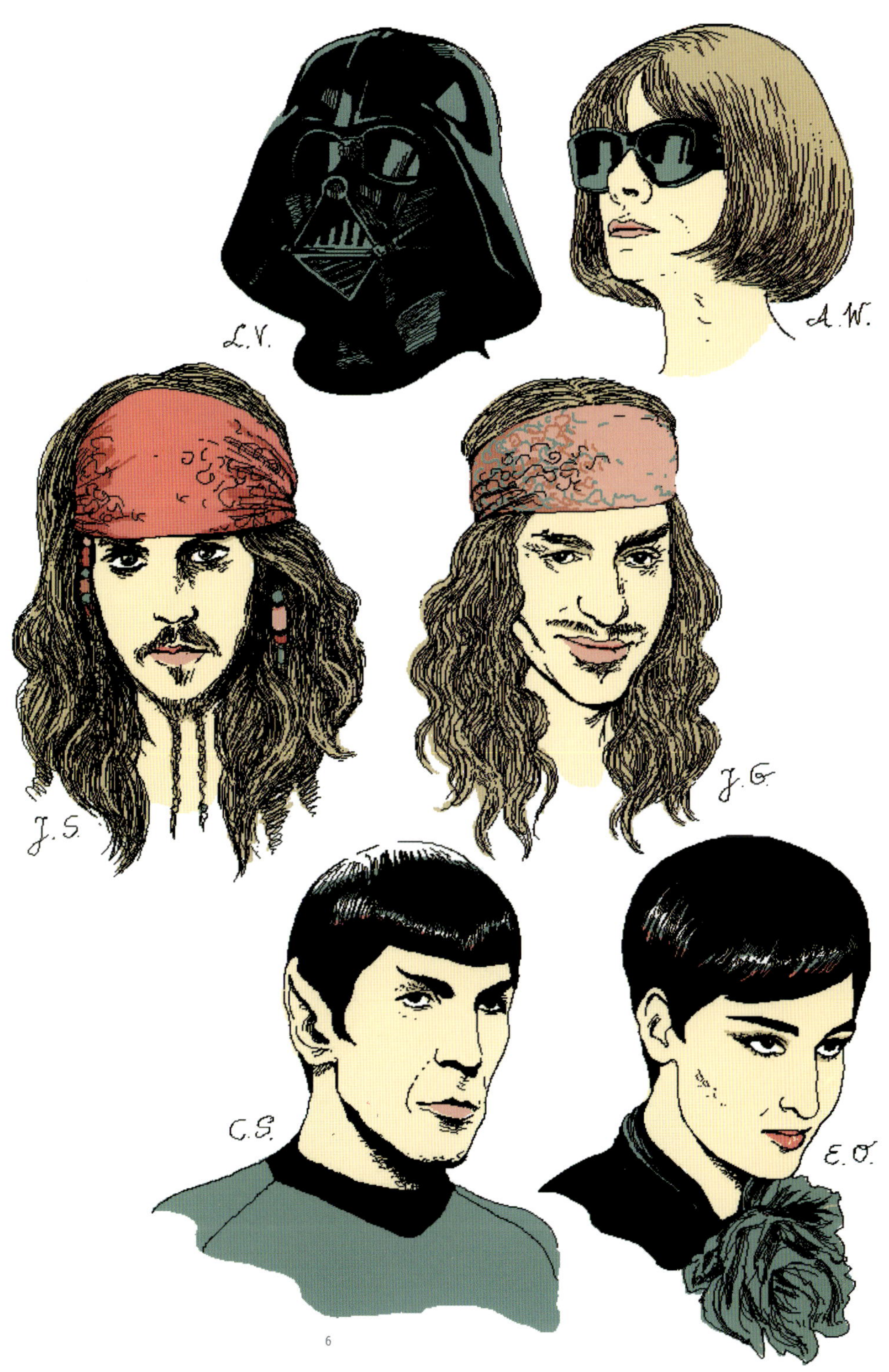

Agata Endo Nowicka

Poland

www.agatanowicka.com

1. **Kuba Wojewodzki, entertainer** (2011). *Bluszcz (Ivy)*

2. **Robert Kusmirowski, artist** (2009). *Lampa*

3. **Zuza Ziomecka 2** (2008). *ELLE*

4. **Wislawa Szymborska, poet** (2010). *GALA*

5. **Self-portrait with Mila** (2009). Fubon Art Foundation, Taipei

6. **Action Fashion** (2009). *ELLE*

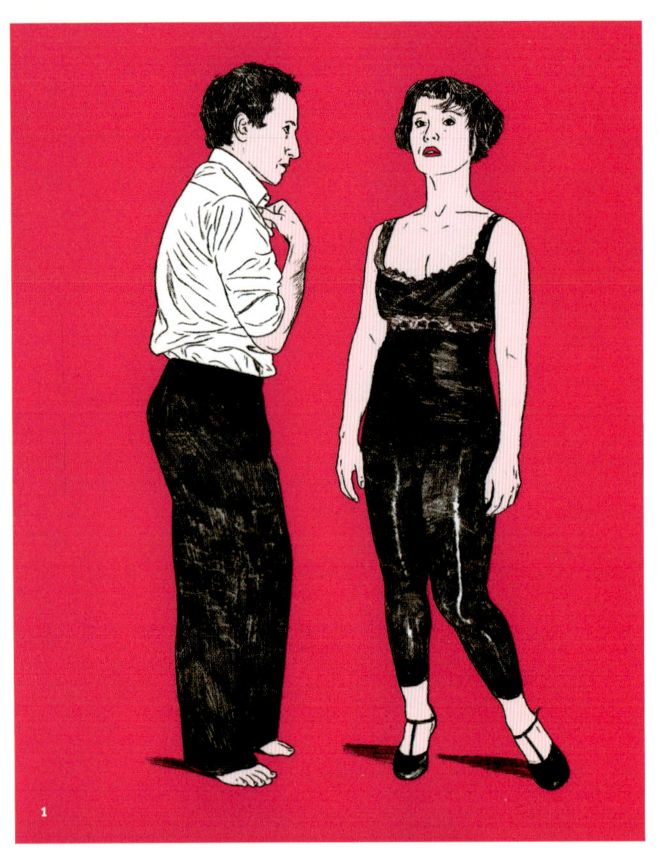

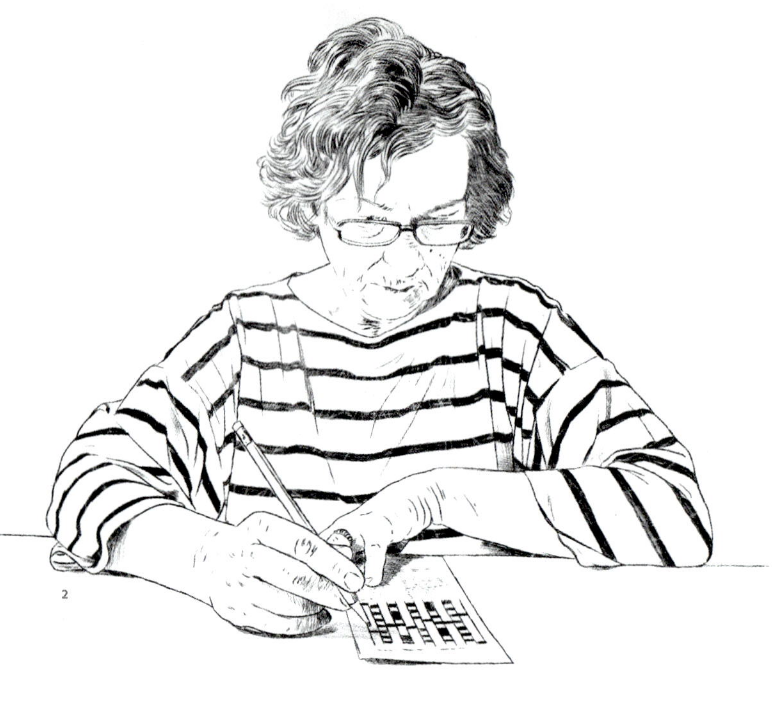

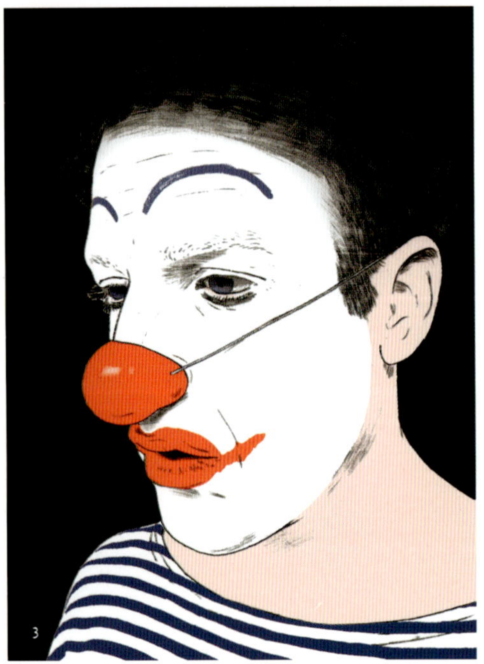

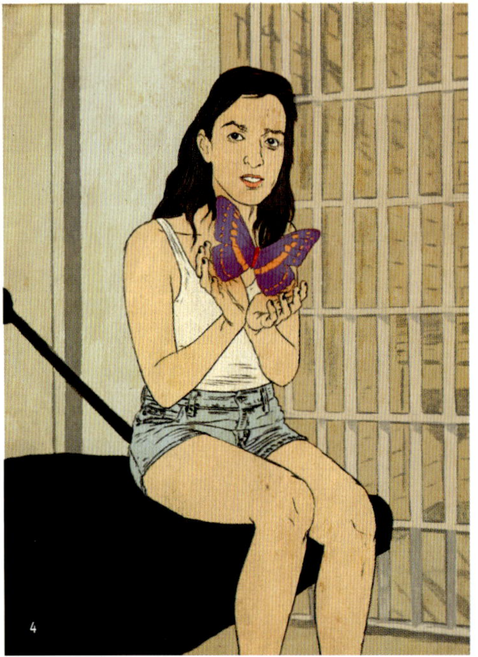

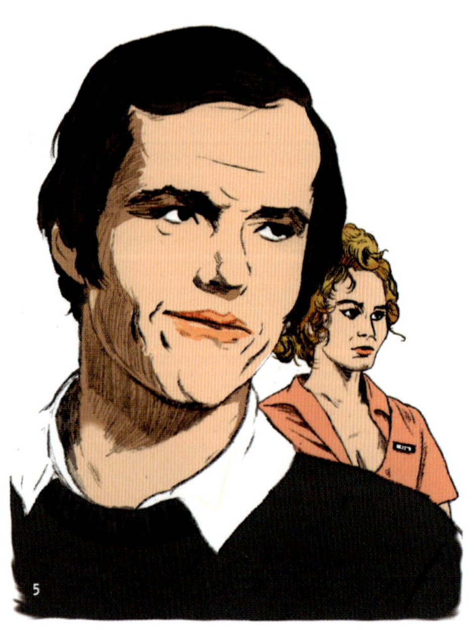

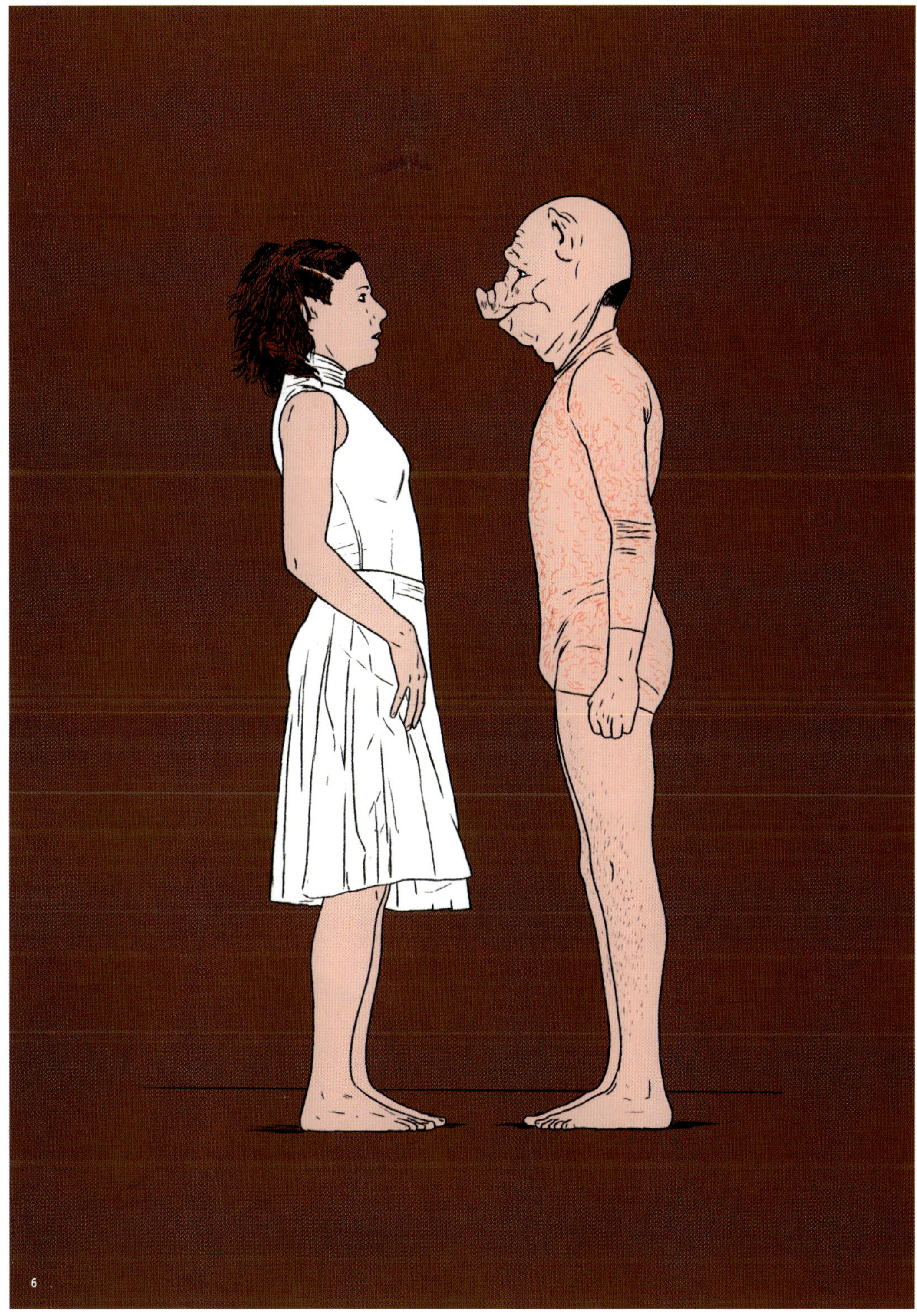

Ruth Gwily

Israel

www.ruthgwily.com

1. **No Title (2009).** Poster for a dance/theater evening *Martha* by Niv Sheinfeld and Oren Laor. Carbon paper on paper, digital coloring

2. **No Title (2010).** *The New York Times.* Carbon paper on paper, digital coloring

3. **No Title (2009).** Poster for Eldad Privas' clown show. Carbon paper on paper, digital coloring

4. **No Title (2009).** *Yediot Achronot.* Carbon paper on paper, digital coloring

5. **No Title (2009).** *The New Yorker.* Carbon paper on paper, digital coloring

6. **No Title (2005).** Poster for a dance evening *PIG* by Niv Sheinfeld. Carbon paper on paper, digital coloring

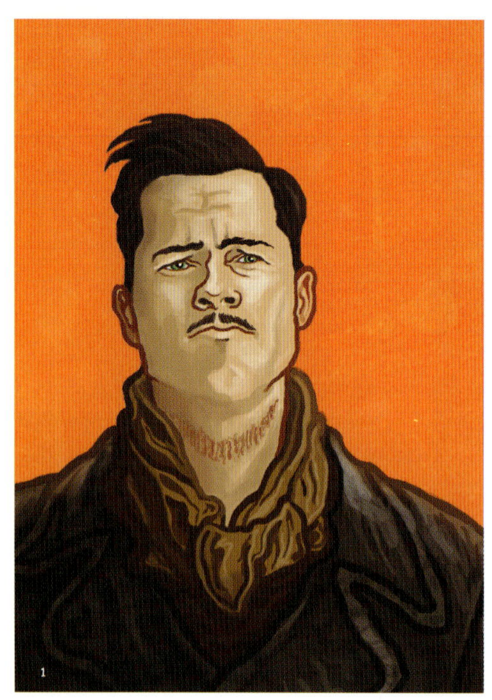

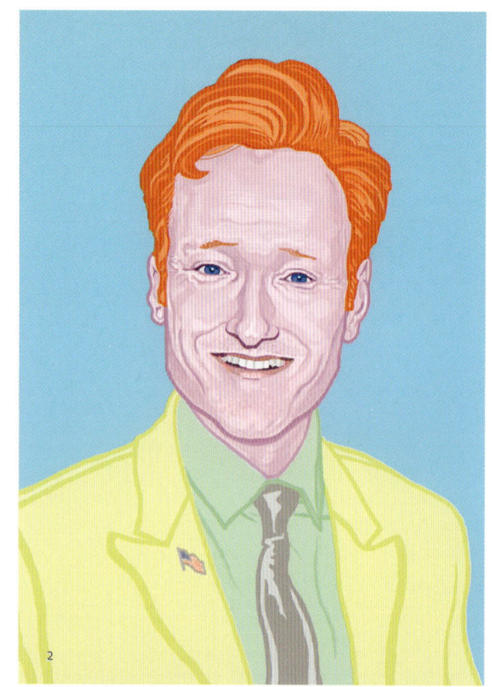

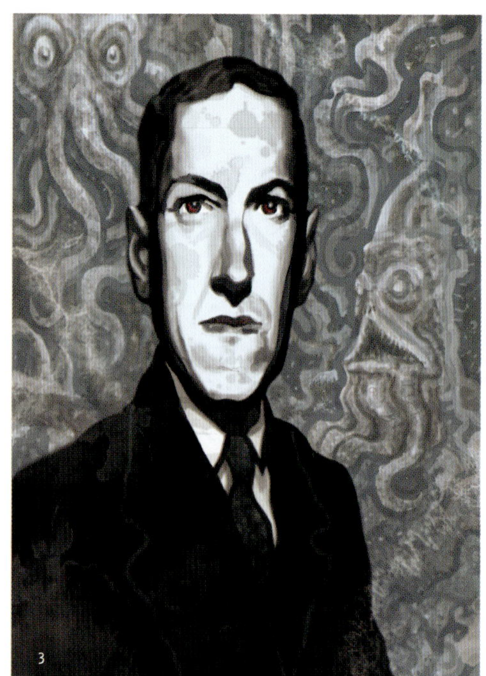

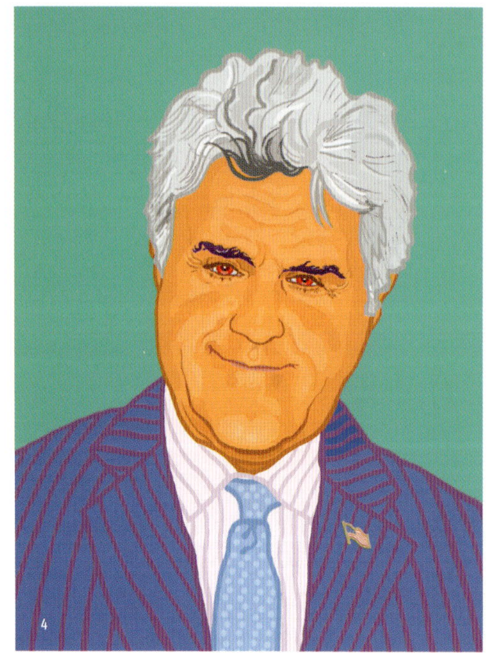

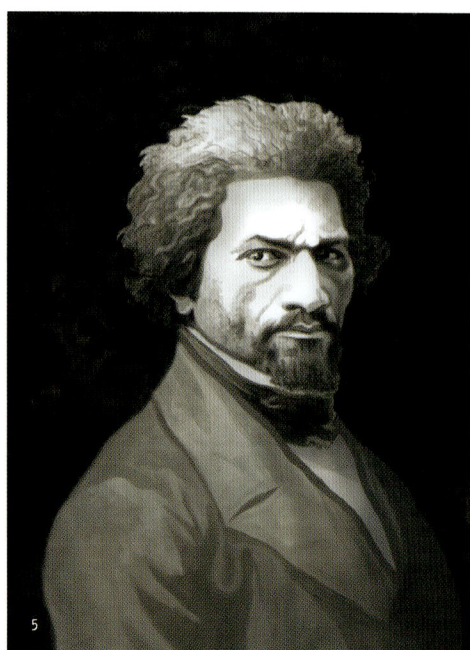

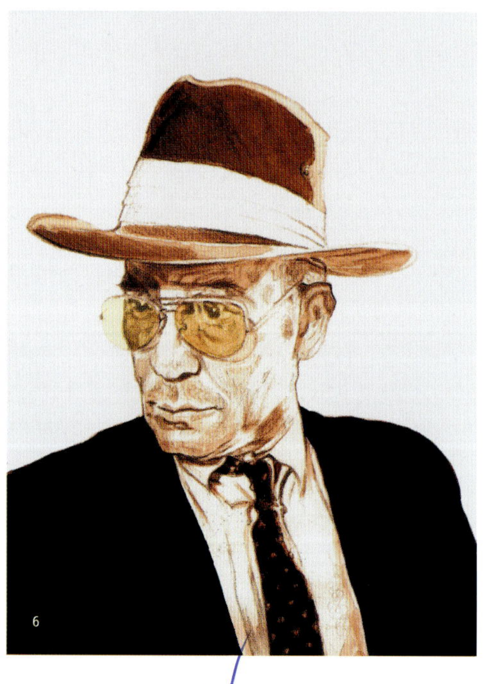

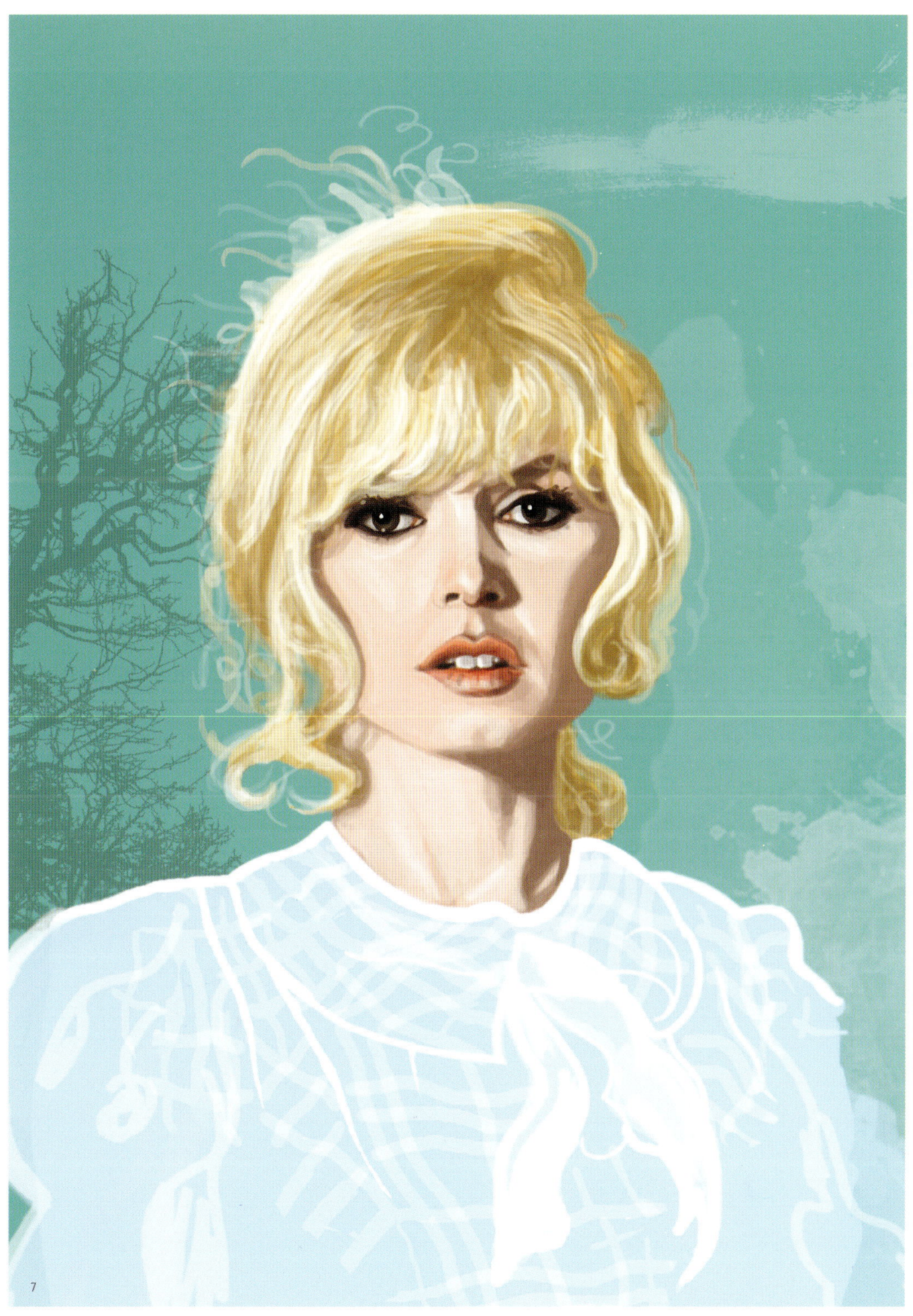

Patrick McQuade
USA

www.patrickmcquade.com

1. **Brad Pitt** (2010). *Royal Flush Magazine*. Digital

2. **Conan O'Brien** (2010). *Royal Flush Magazine*. Digital

3. **H.P. Lovecraft** (2010). Personal work. Traditional, digital

4. **Jay Leno** (2010). *Royal Flush Magazine*. Digital

5. **Frederick Douglass** (2010). Commission. Traditional, digital

6. **Hunter S. Thompson** (2010). Commission. Traditional, digital

7. **Brigitte Bardot** (2011). Personal work. Traditional, digital

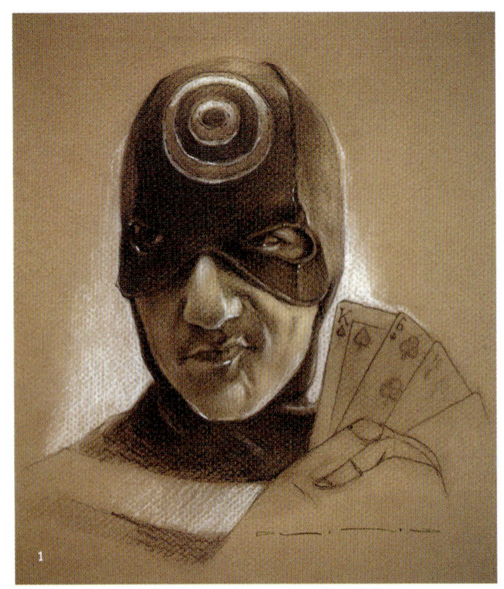

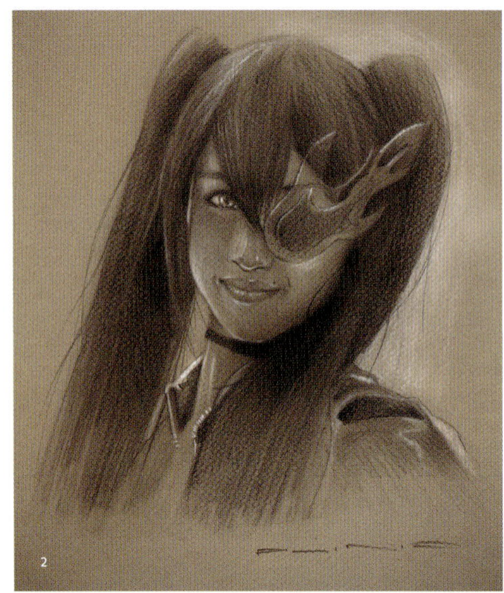

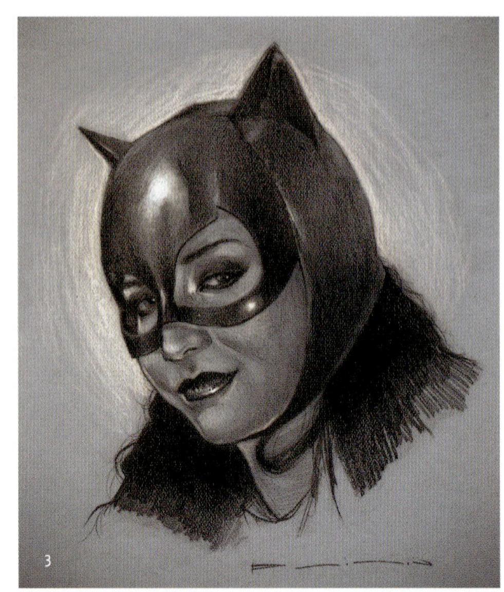

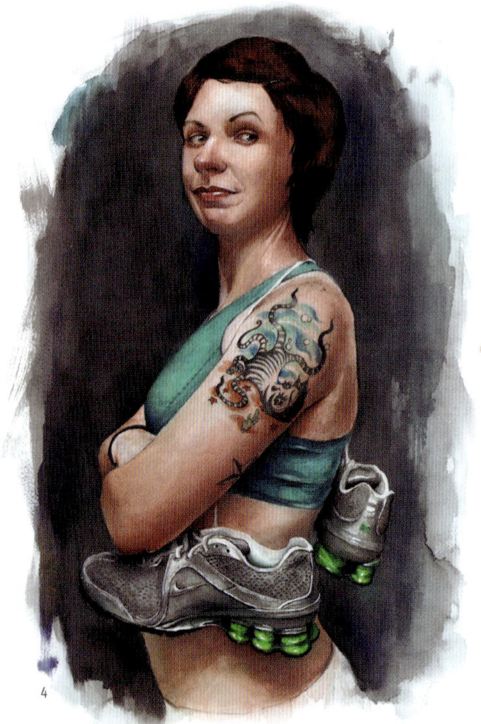

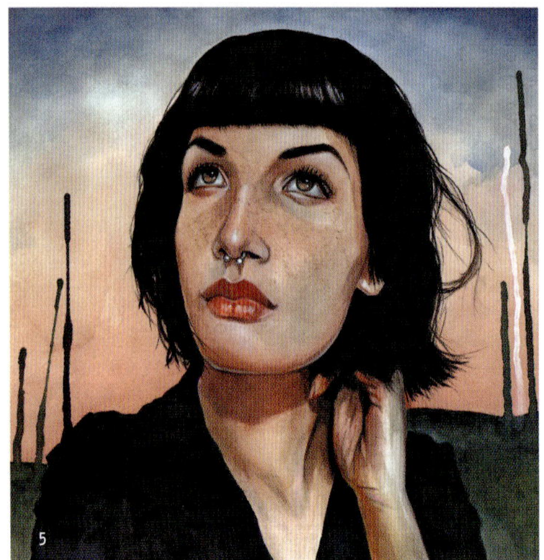

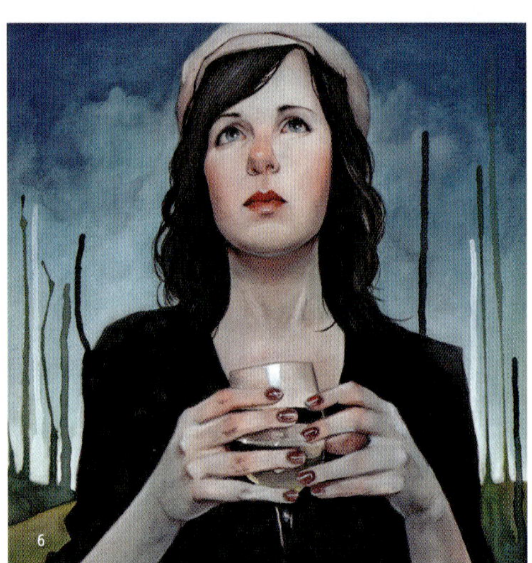

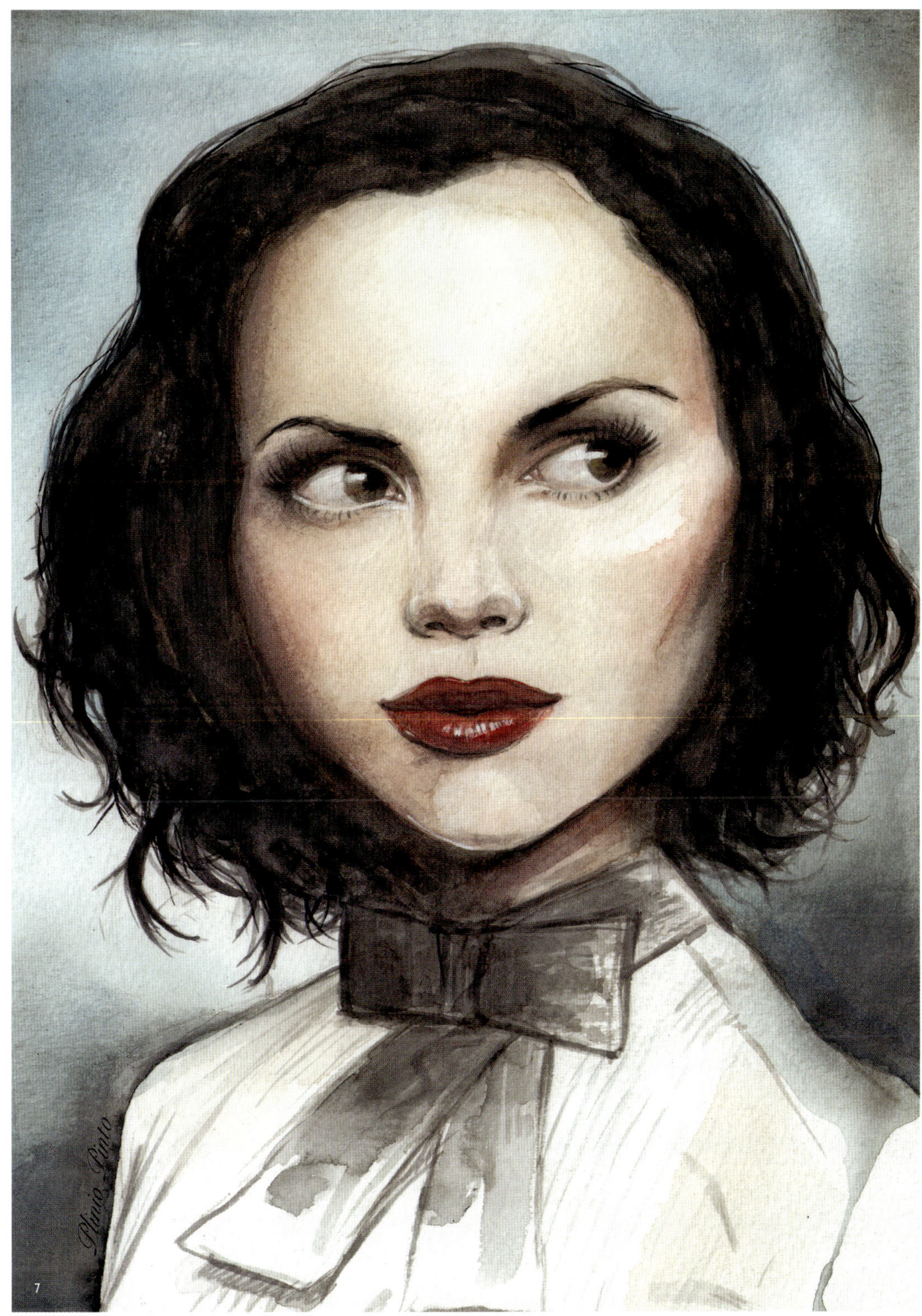

1. **Chris Burns as Bullseye** (2012). Personal work. Graphite, charcoal on toned paper

2. **Alouette Cosplay as Black Rock Shooter** (2012). Personal work. Graphite, charcoal on toned paper

3. **Tiffany Antrim as Catwoman** (2012). Personal work. Graphite, charcoal on toned paper

4. **Mrs. West-Pinto** (2009). Personal work. Watercolor on paper

5. **Eve** (2010). Personal work. Watercolor on paper

6. **Tia** (2010). Personal work. Watercolor on paper

7. **Mrs. Ricci** (2007). Personal work. Watercolor on paper

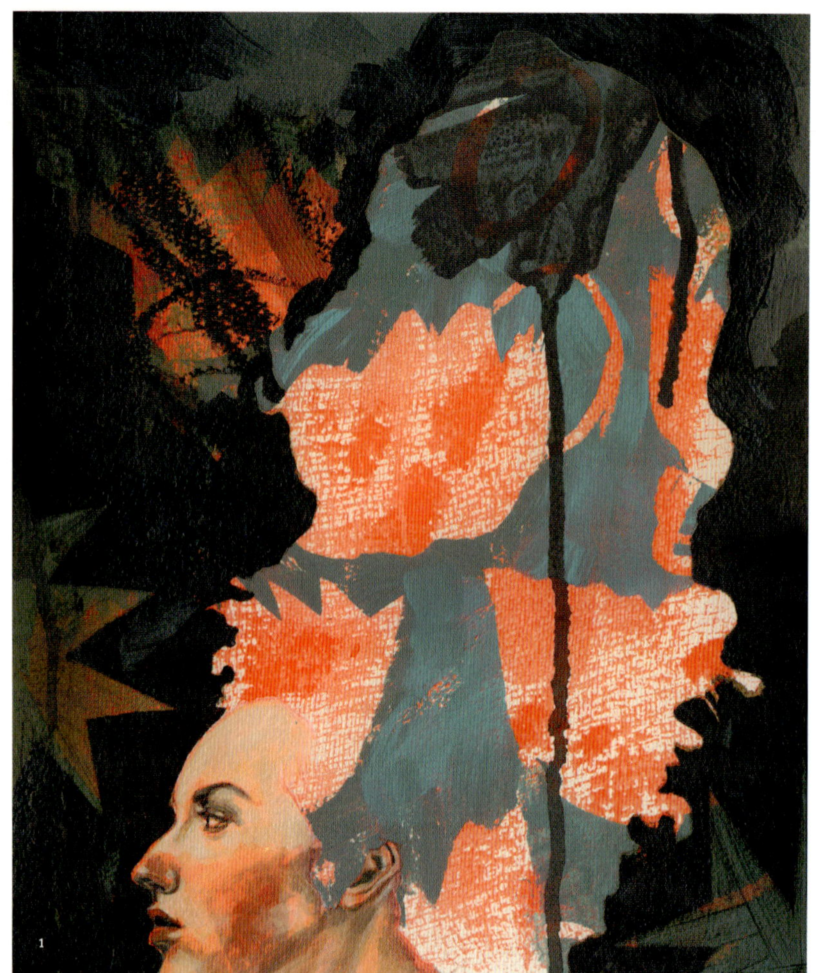

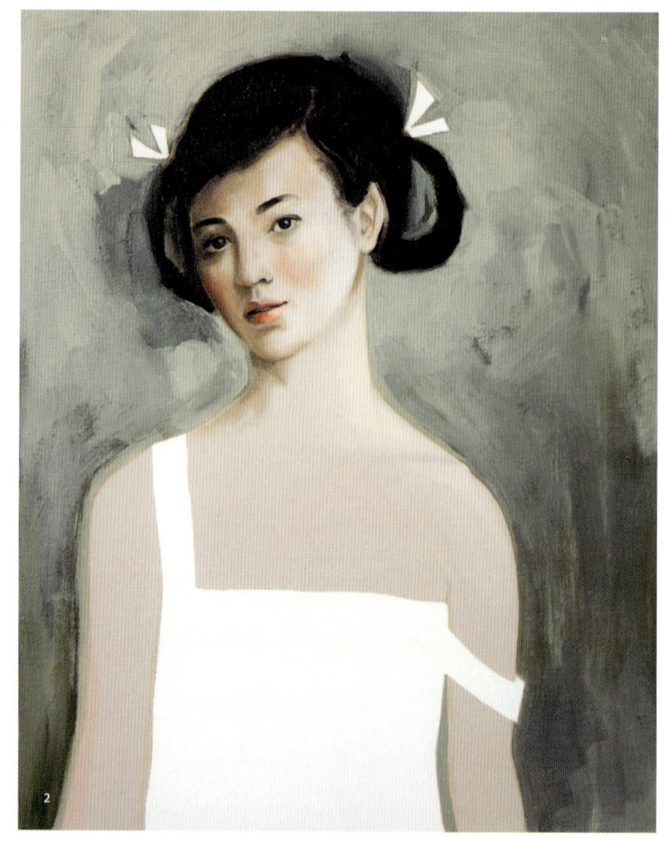

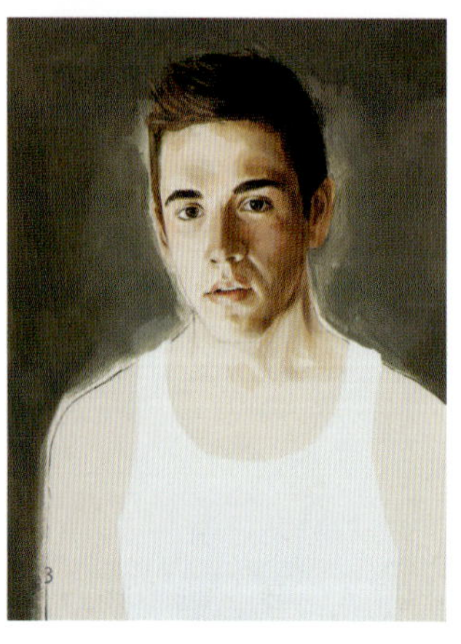

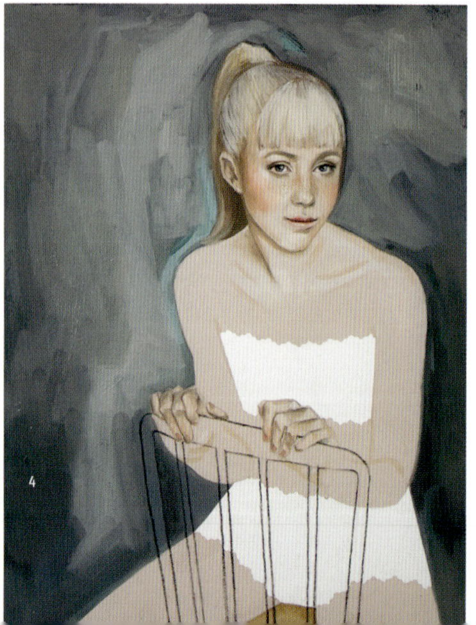

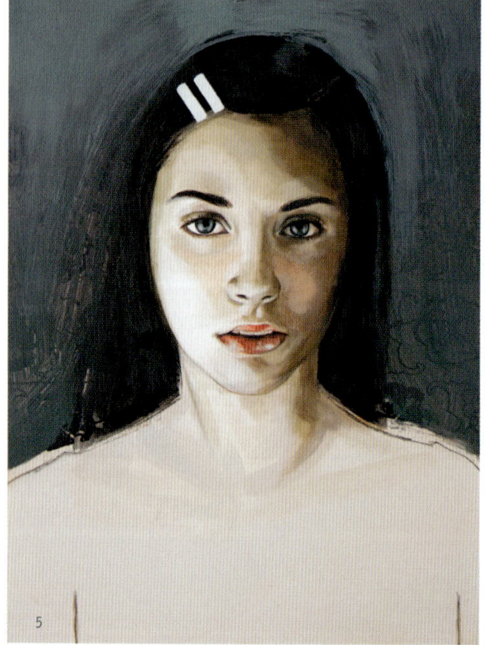

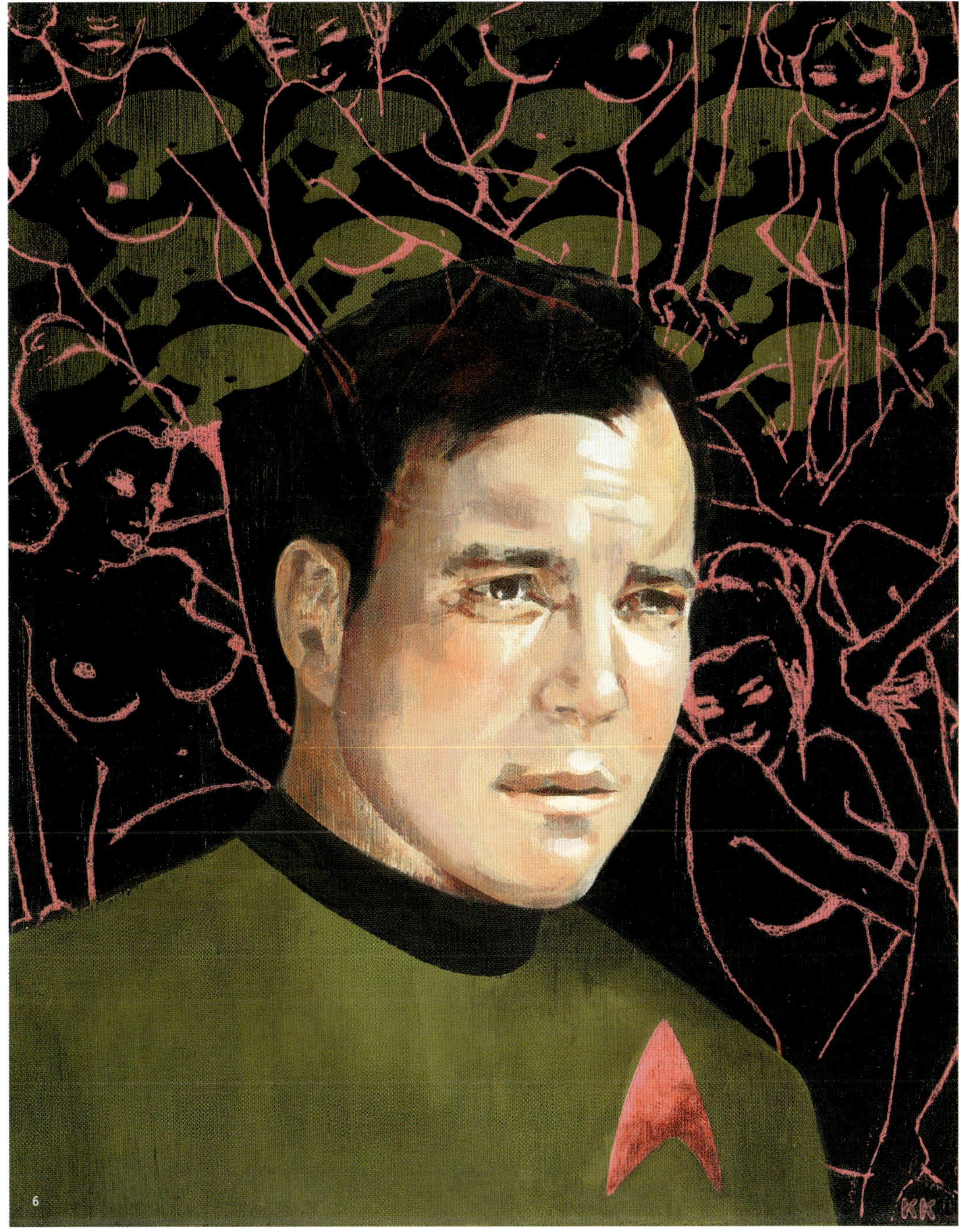

Karen Klassen

Canada

Agency: Colagene, Illustration Clinic
www.colagene.com/fr/illustration/
karen-klassen

1. **Beehive** (2010). Personal work. Acrylic, oil stick, oil paint

2. **Lolita Project: Amy** (2010). Personal work. Acrylic, oil

3. **Lolita Project: Chris** (2010). Personal work. Acrylic, oil

4. **Lolita Project: Jennifer** (2010). Personal work. Acrylic, oil

5. **Lolita Project: Lola** (2010). Personal work. Acrylic, oil

6. **William Shatner** (2007). Gallery Show. Mixed media

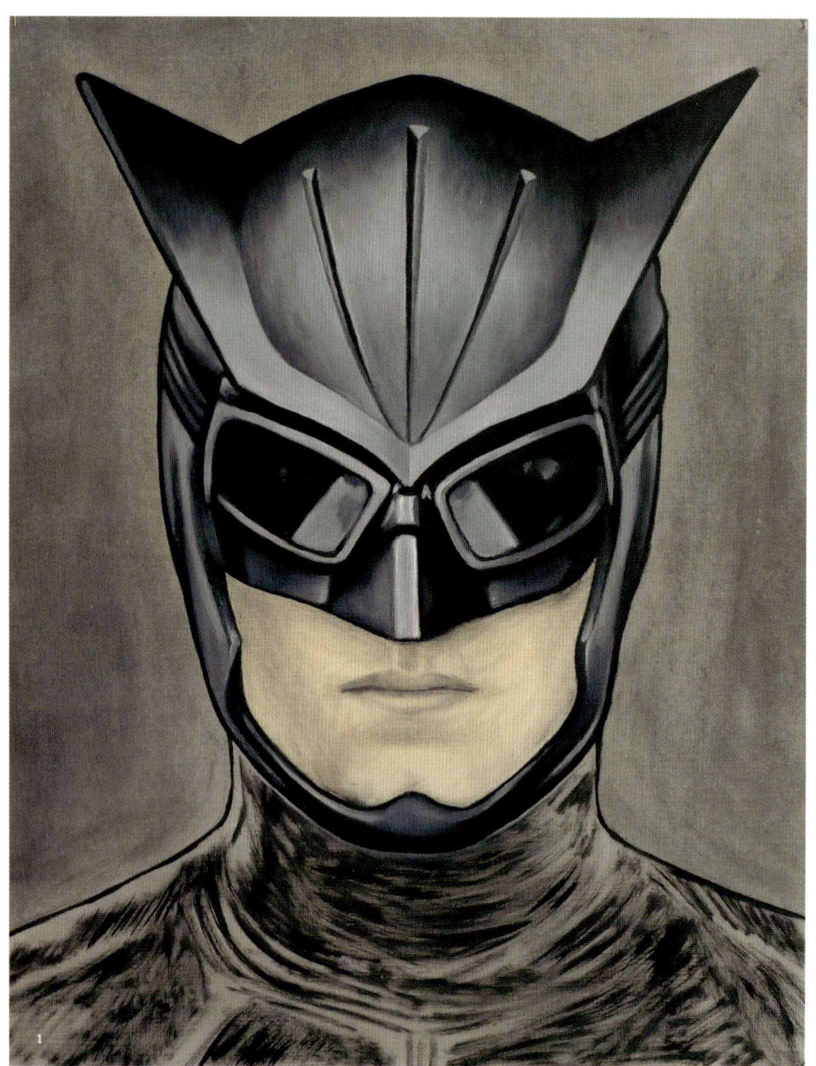

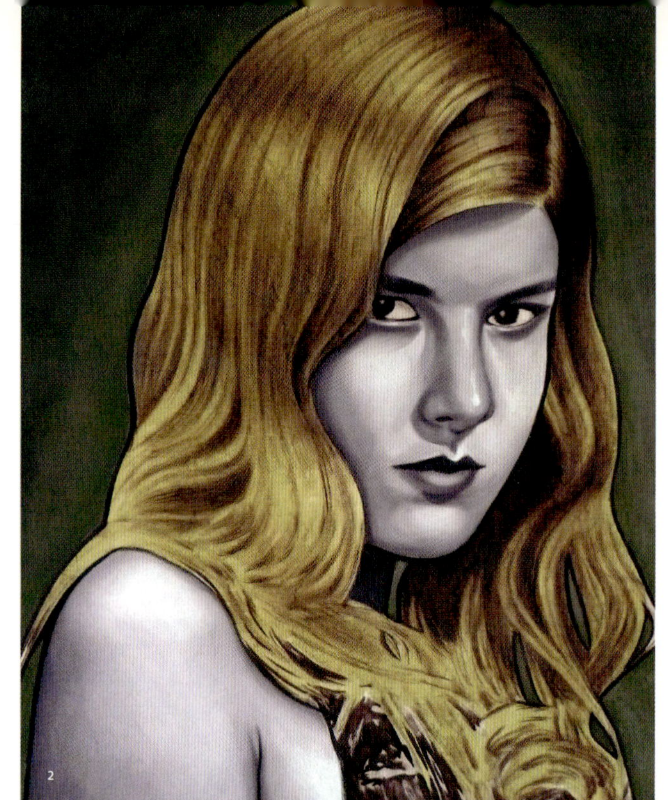

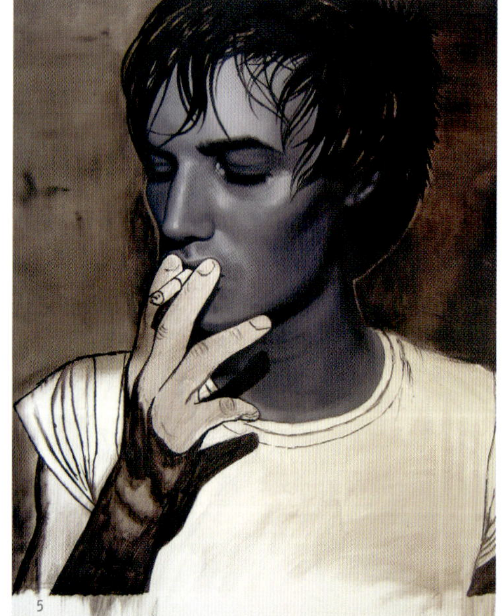

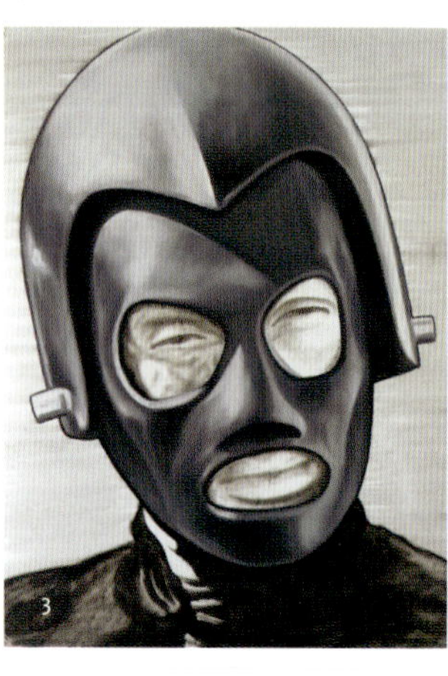

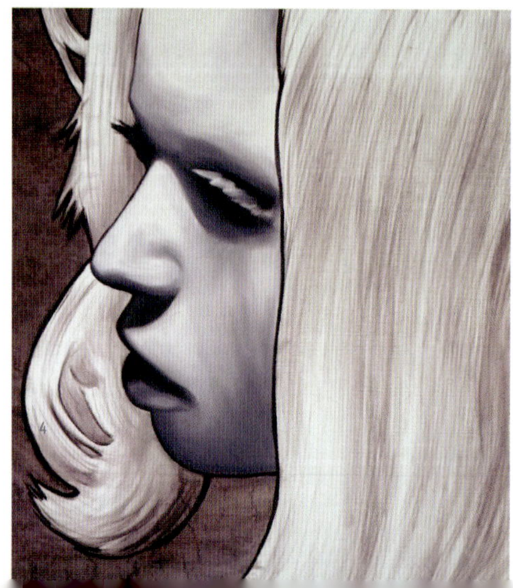

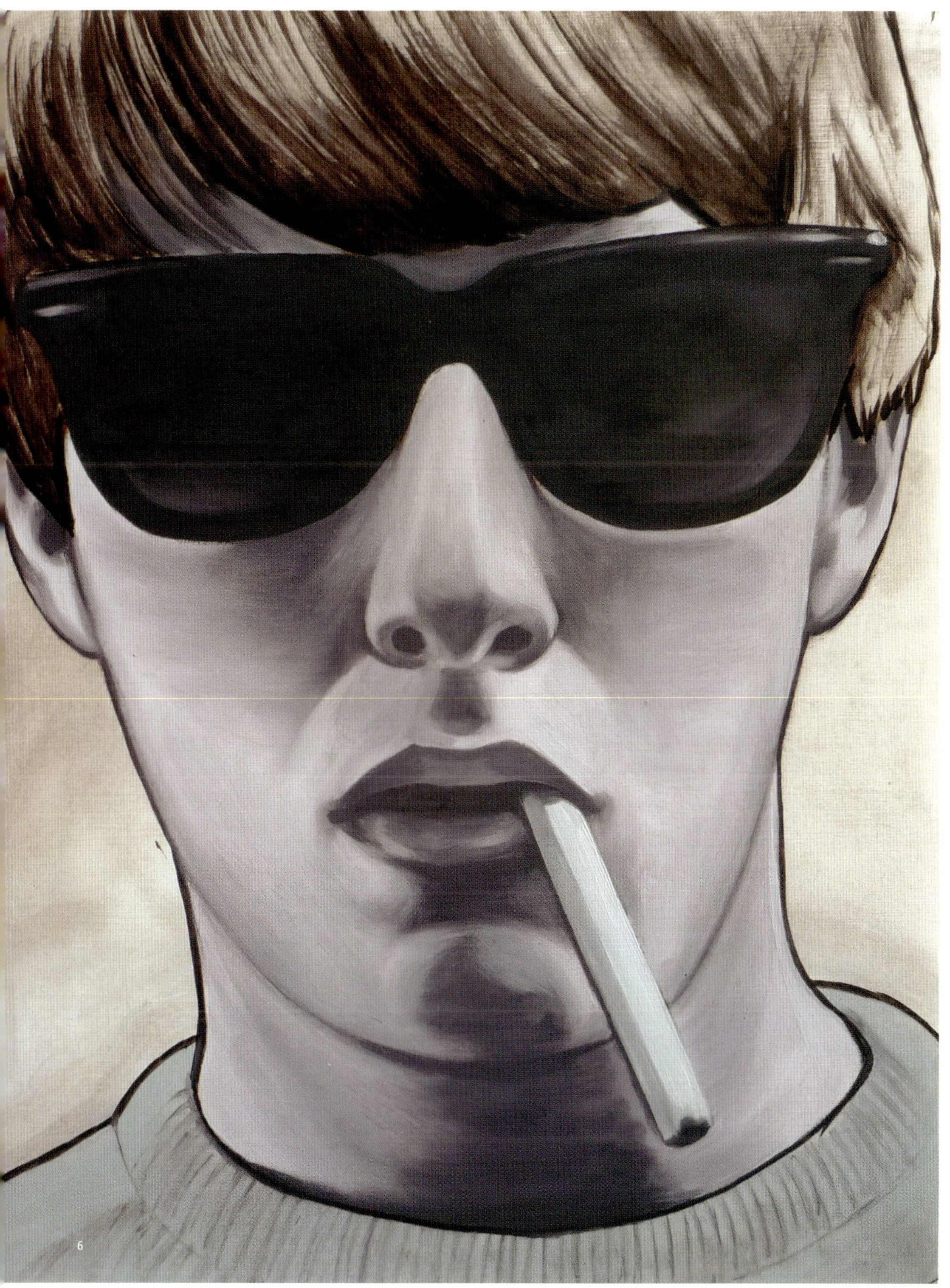

Jürgen Grewe
Germany

www.juergengrewe.com

1. **Nightowl** (2010). Personal work. Oil on paper

2. **Blond Girl** (2009). Personal work. Oil on paper

3. **Deathrace** (2010). Personal work. Oil on paper

4. **Dark Eyes** (2010). Personal work. Oil on paper

5. **Forever** (2006). Personal work. Oil on paper

6. **Tom** (2010). Personal work. Oil on paper

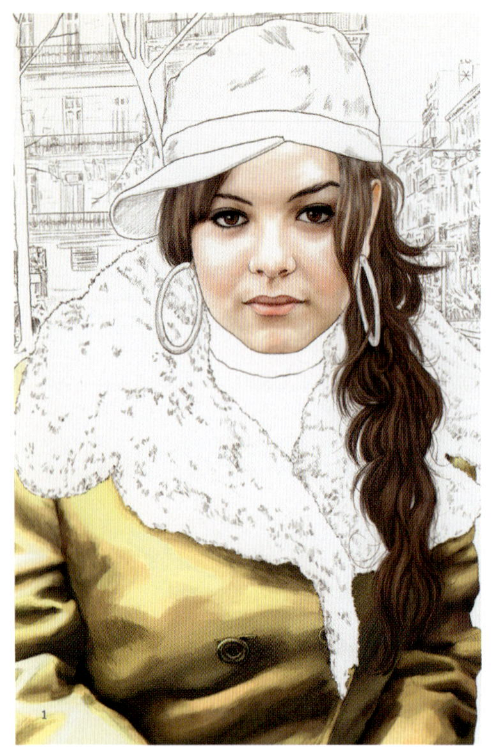

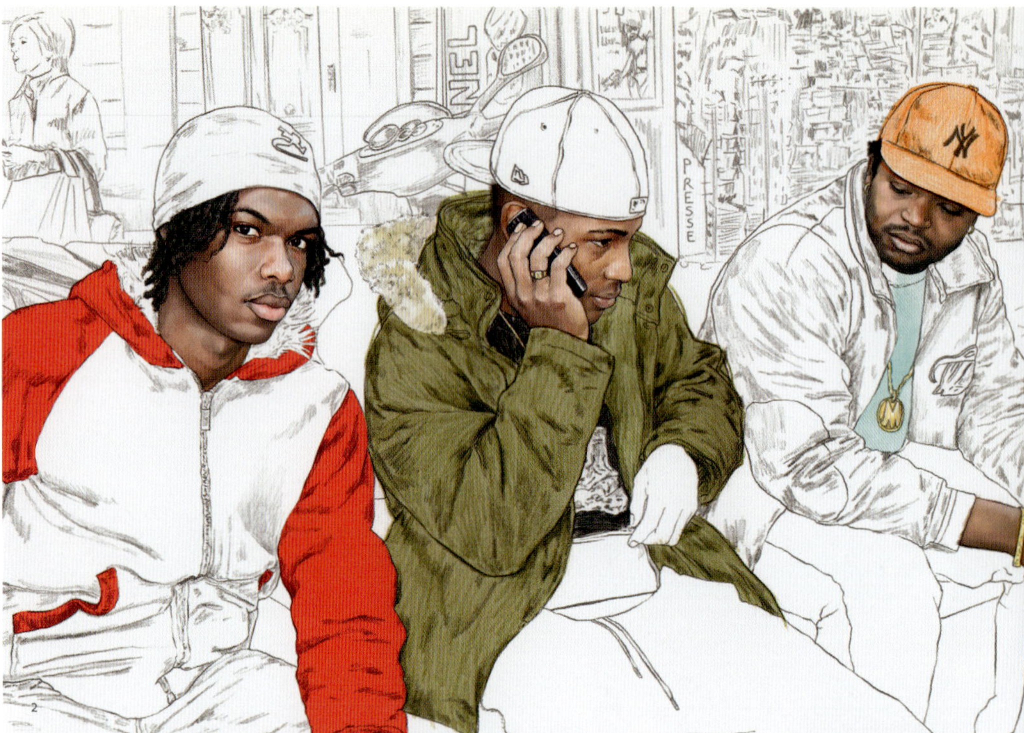

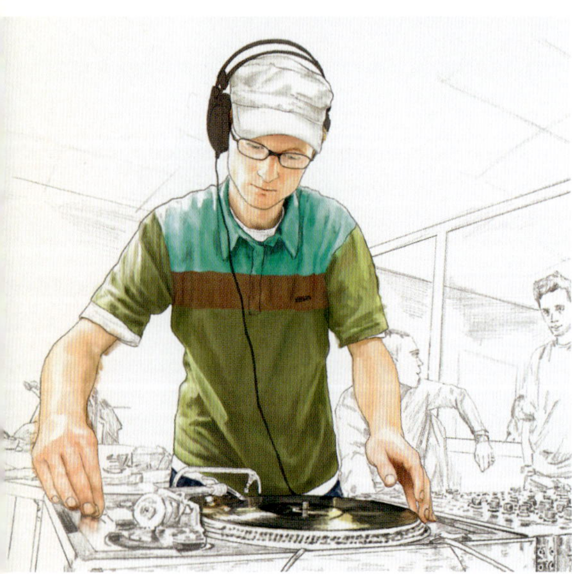

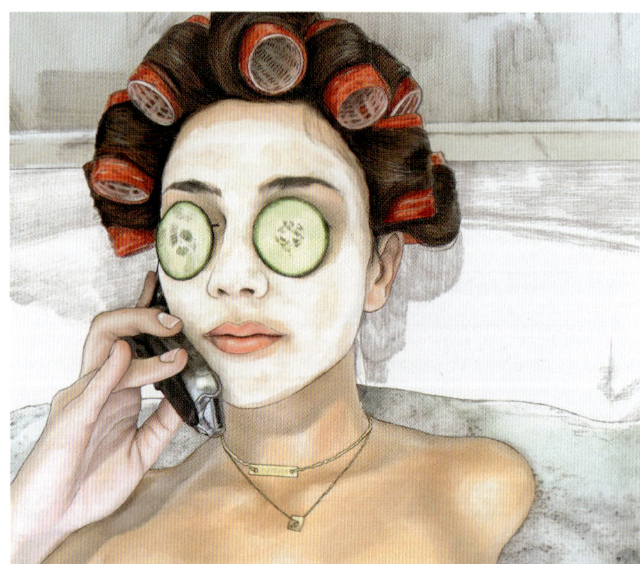

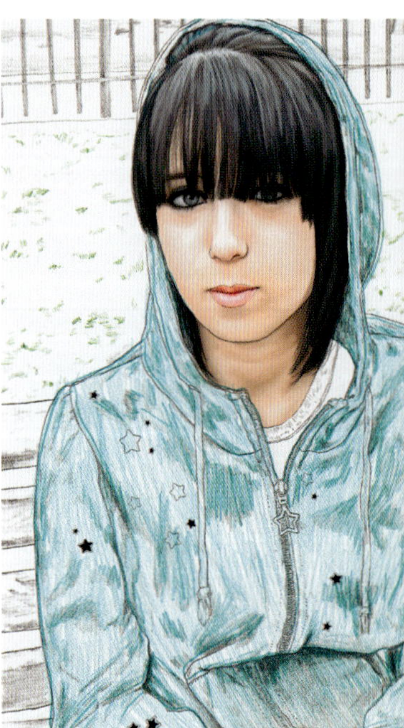

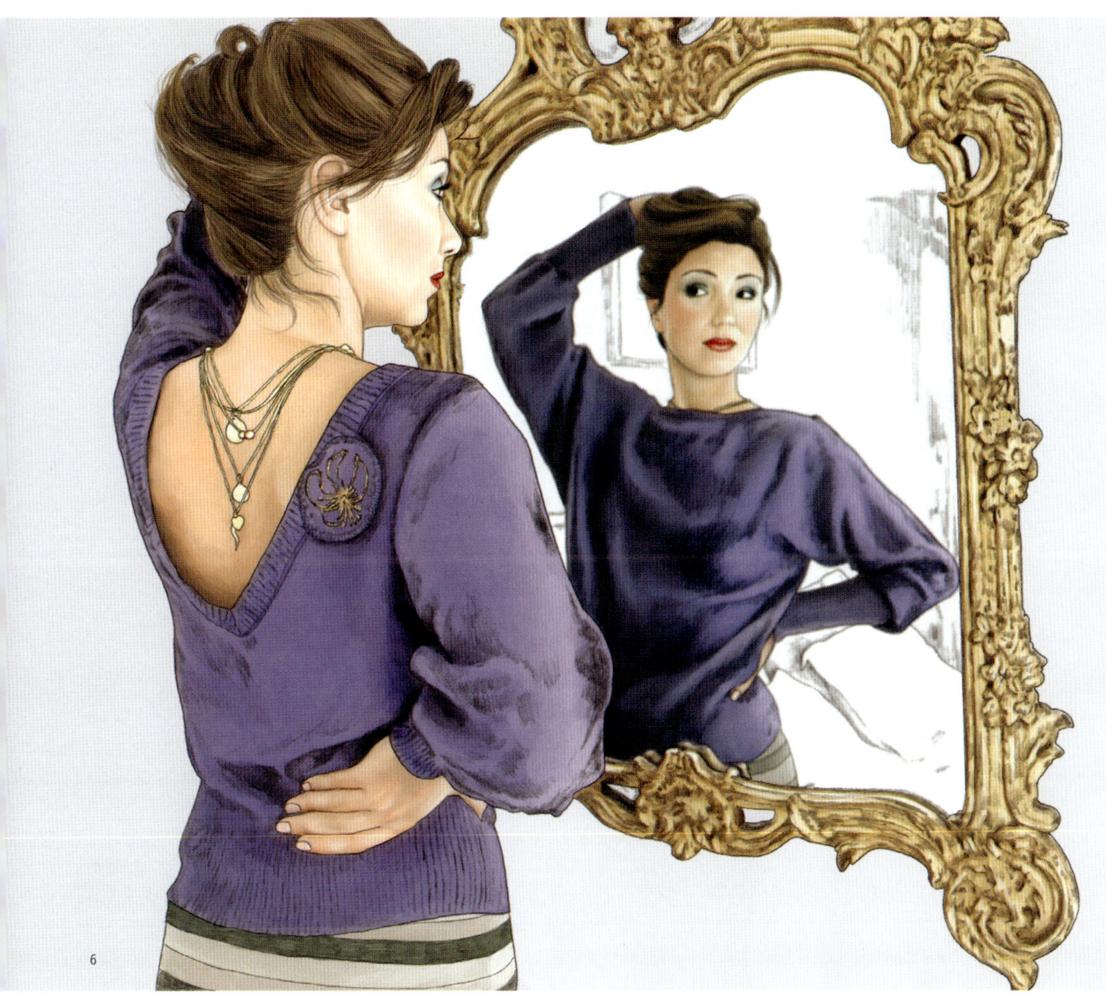

Kimi Kimoki

France

www.kimikimoki.blogspot.com

1. **New teenagers of Marseille 1** (2010). Personal work. Lead pencil, pencils, Photoshop

2. **New teenagers of Marseille 2** (2010). Personal work. Lead pencil, pencils, Photoshop

3. **DJ Anton Rotten** (2010). Personal work. Lead pencil, pencils, Photoshop

4. **No Title** (2005). FROJO Jewelry. Lead pencil, pencils, Photoshop

5. **New teenagers of Marseille 3** (2010). Personal work. Lead pencil, pencils, Photoshop

6. **No Title** (2005). FROJO Jewelry. Lead pencil, pencils, Photoshop

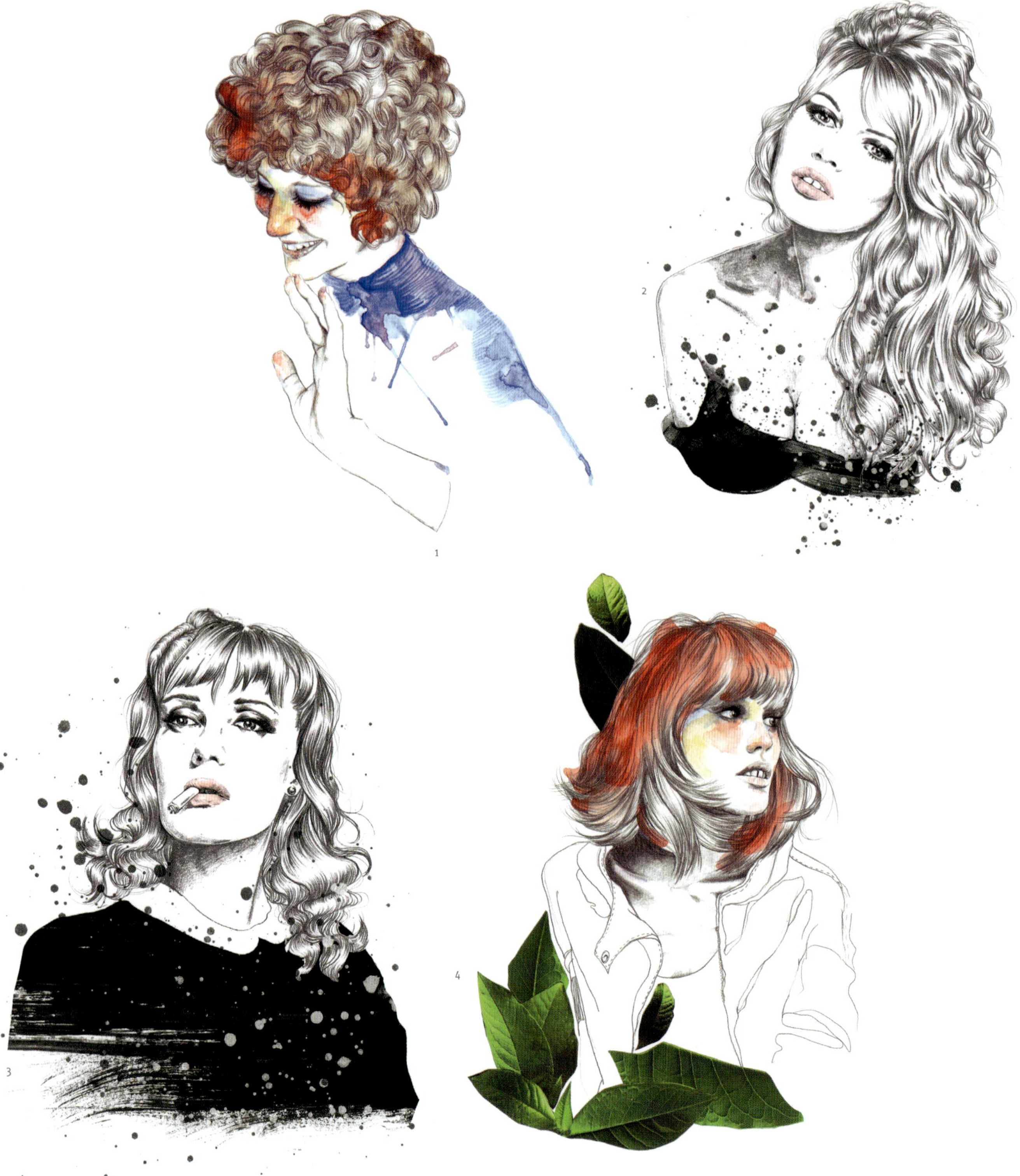

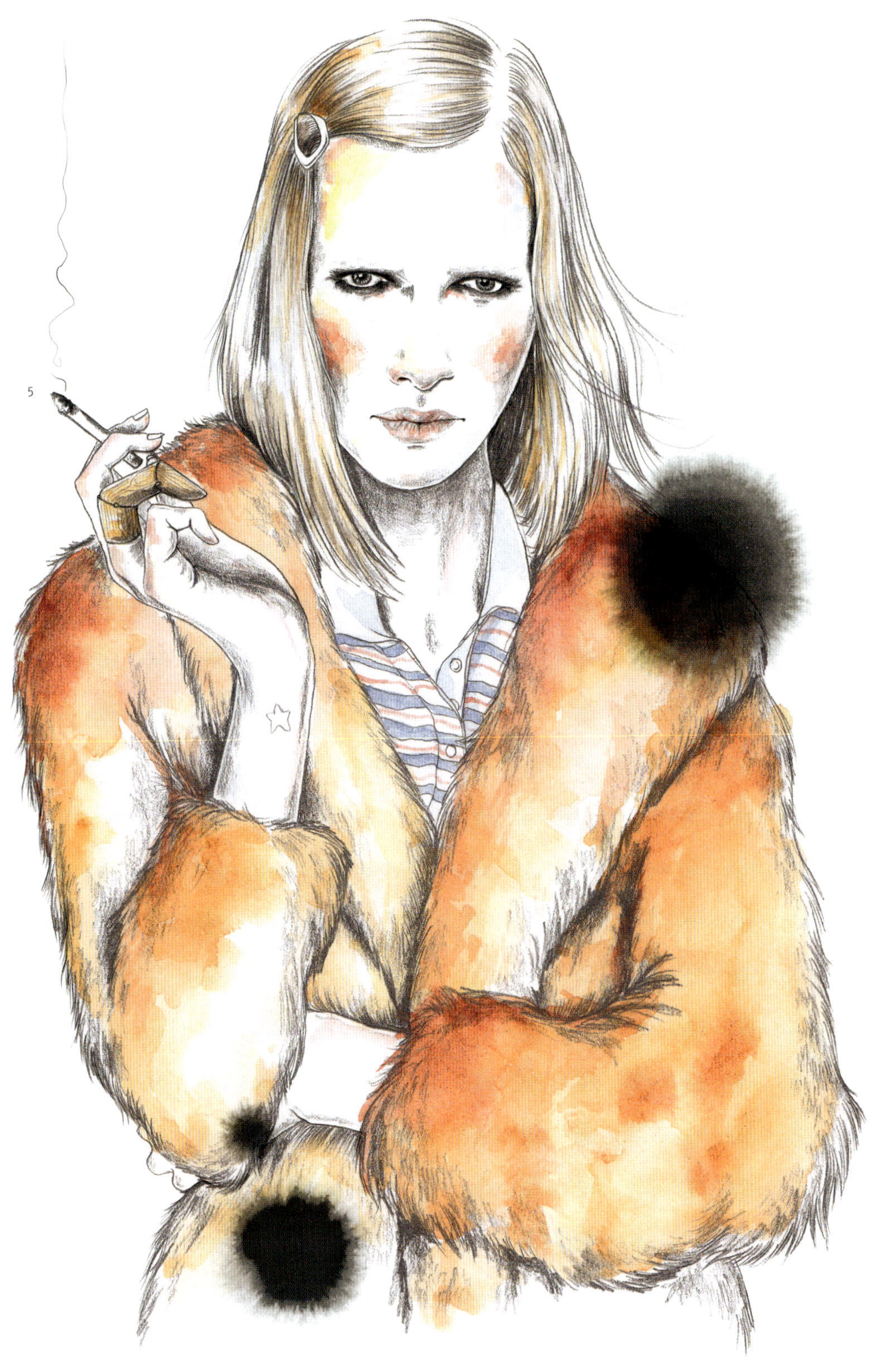

Esra Røise

Norway

www.esraroise.com

1. **Noone belongs here more than you** (2009). Personal work. Pencil, watercolor

2. **Birgitte** (2011). *MILK* magazine. Mixed media

3. **Jeanne** (2011). *MILK* magazine. Mixed media

4. **Lola** (2010). Personal work. Pencil, watercolor, collage

5. **Oh Margot!** (2011). Personal work. Pencil, watercolor

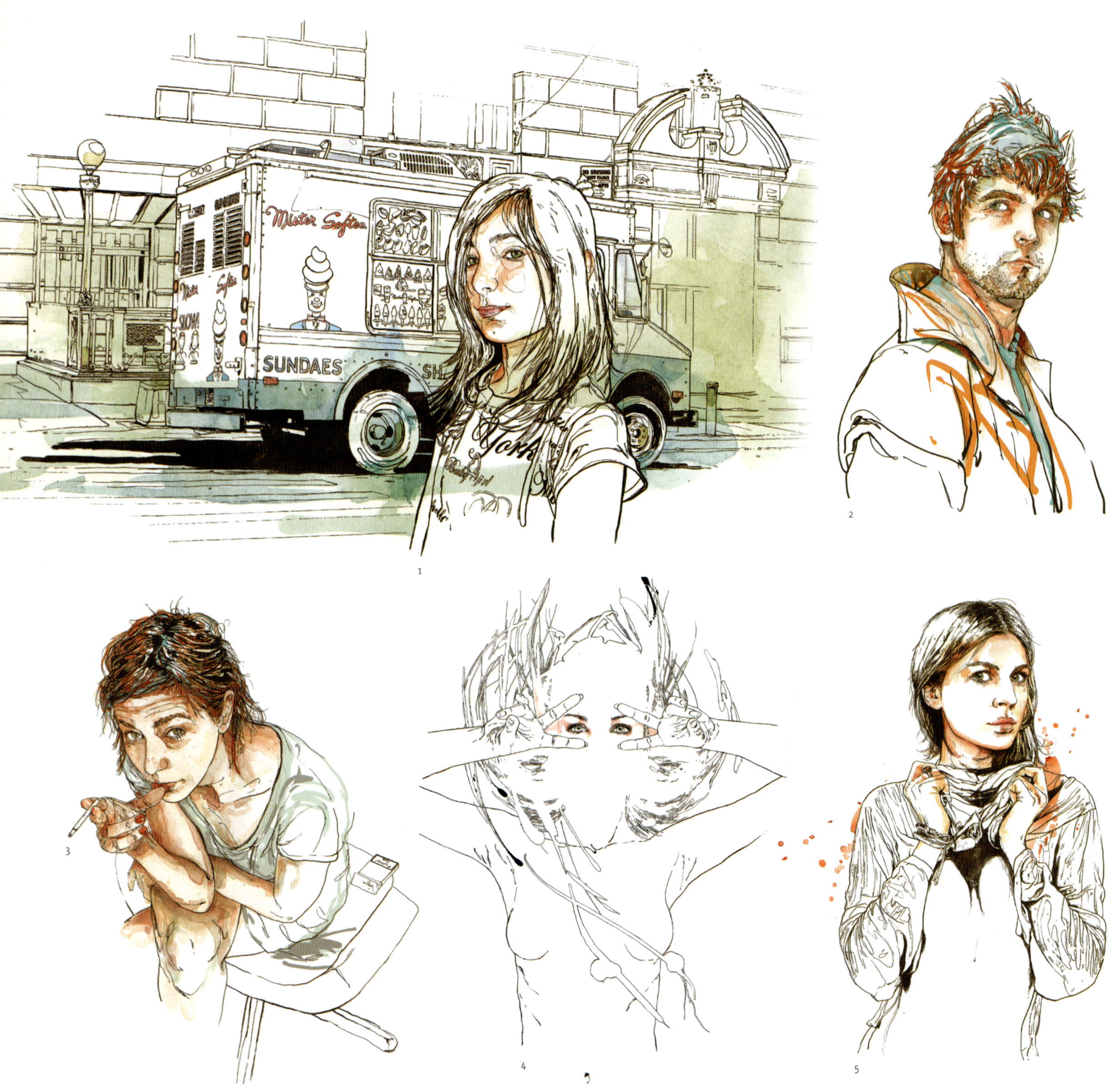

Mister Softee
SUNDAES

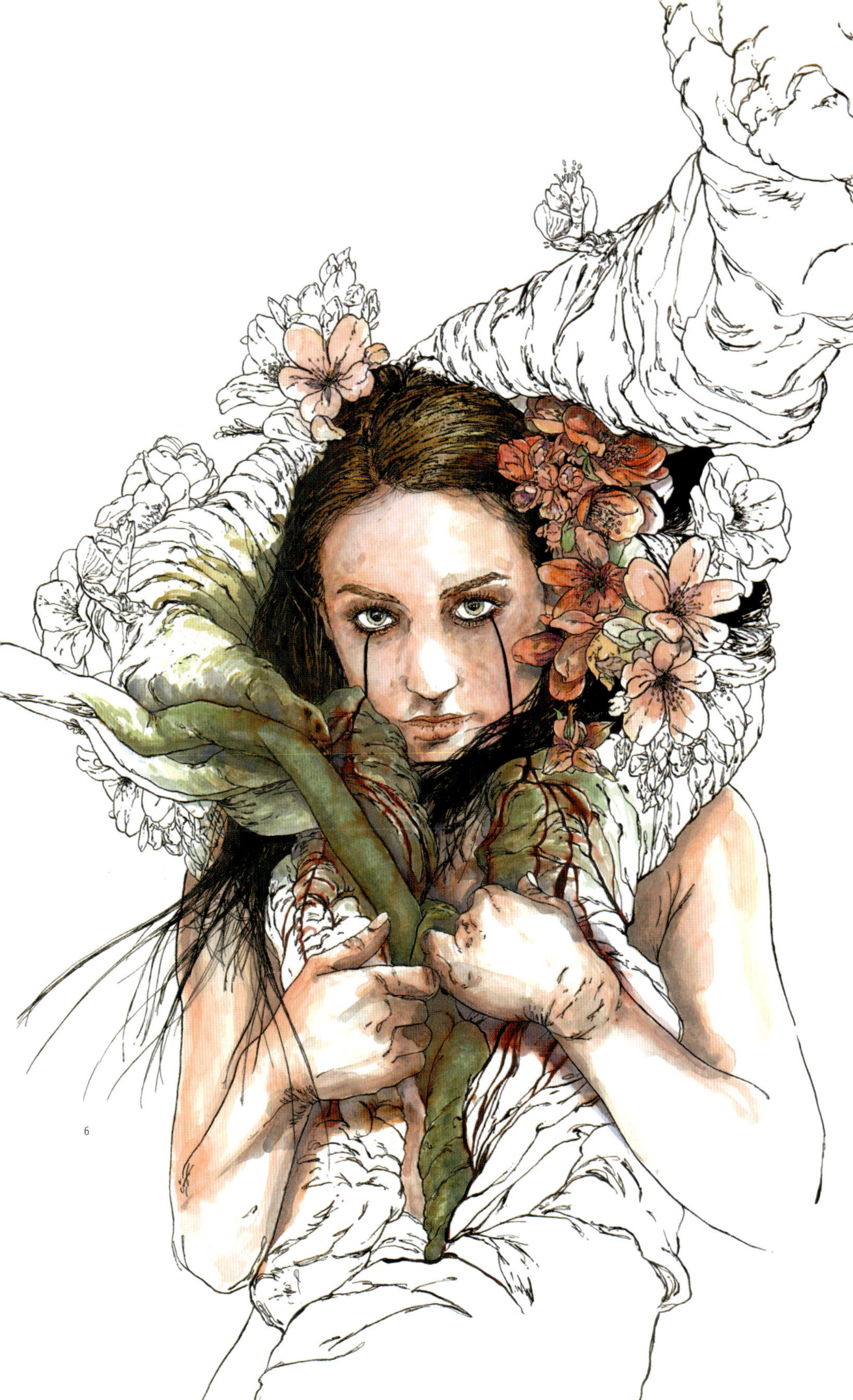

**Matthieu Appriou
aka Telmolindo**

France

www.telmolindo.net

1. **Childhood dream 3** (2009). Personal work. Digital drawing, watercolors

2. **Alex H.** (2010). Personal work. Digital drawing, watercolors

3. **Kiki** (2010). Personal work. Digital drawing, watercolors

4. **Untitled** (2011). Exhibition IP[01] _ Paris. Pencil, India ink, watercolors

5. **Lumi** (2011). Personal work. Digital drawing, watercolors

6. **Untitled** (2011). Exhibition IP[01] _ Paris. Pencil, India ink, watercolors

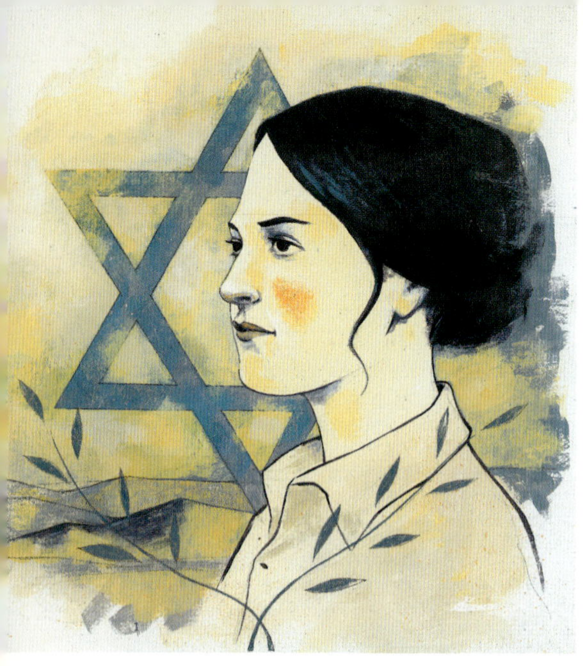

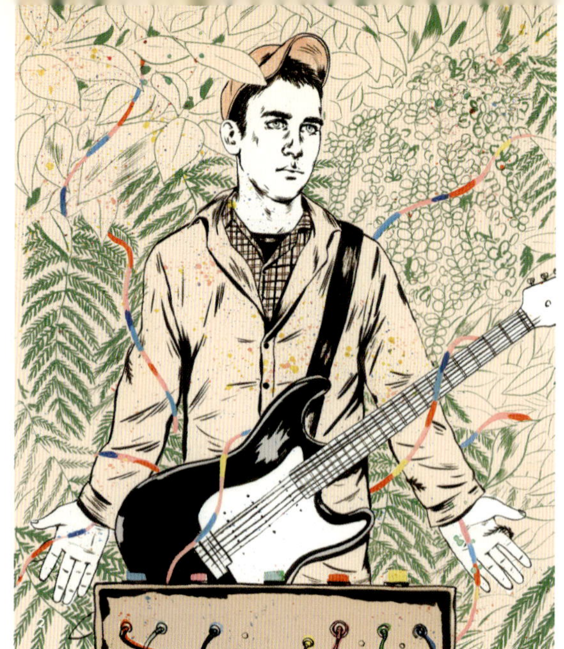

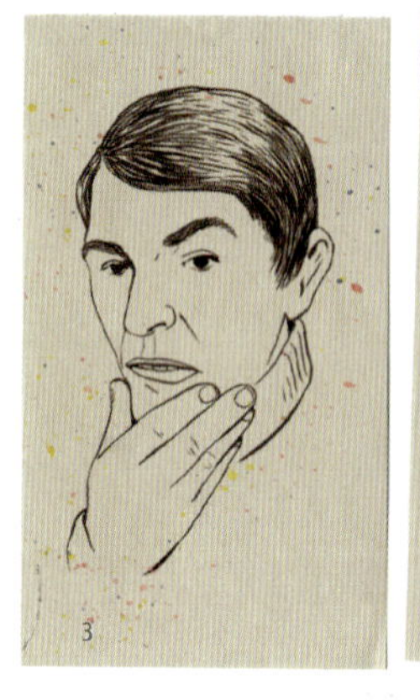

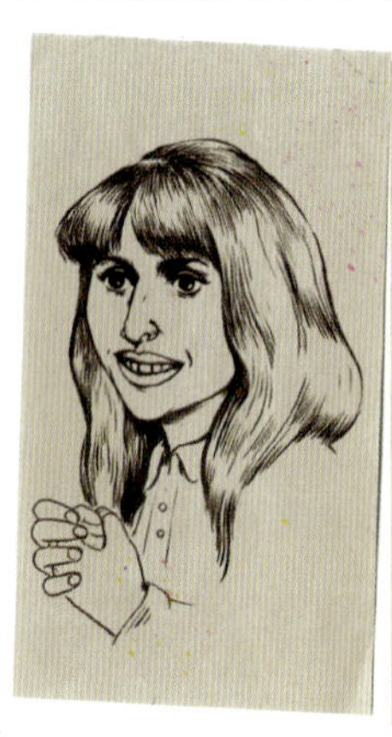

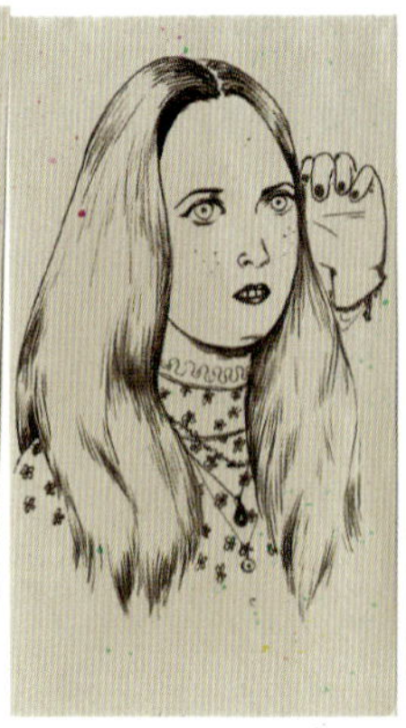

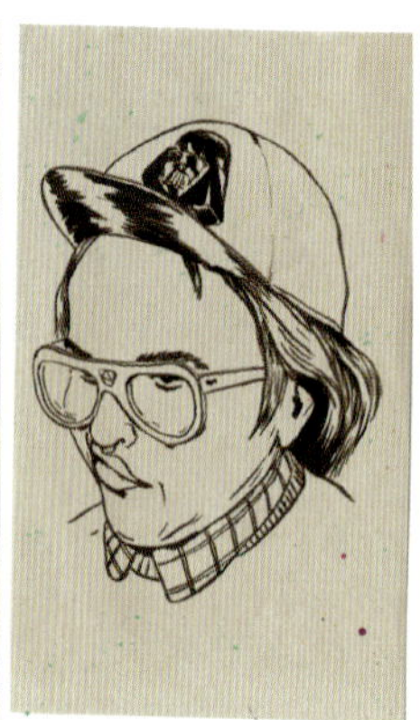

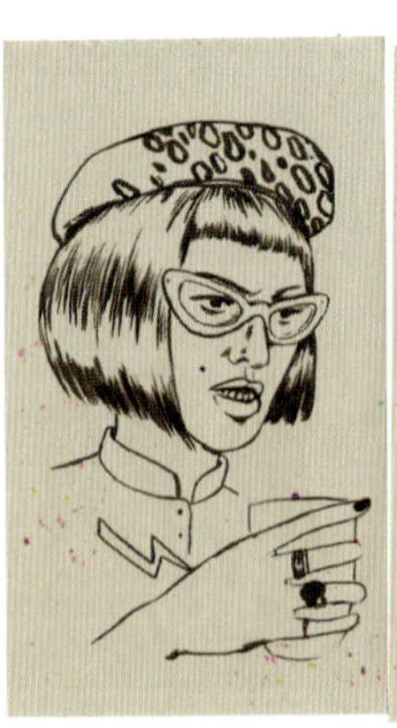

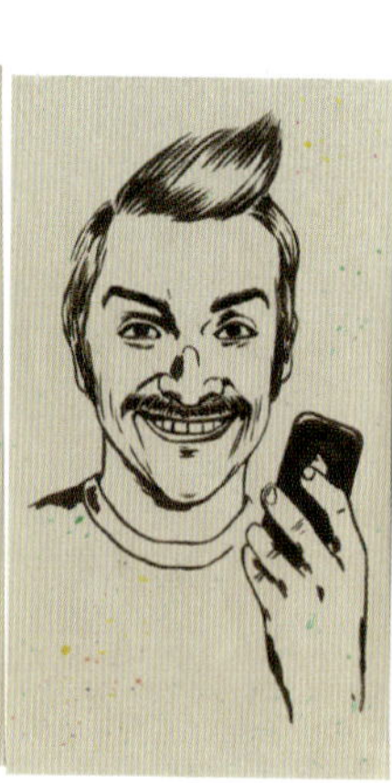

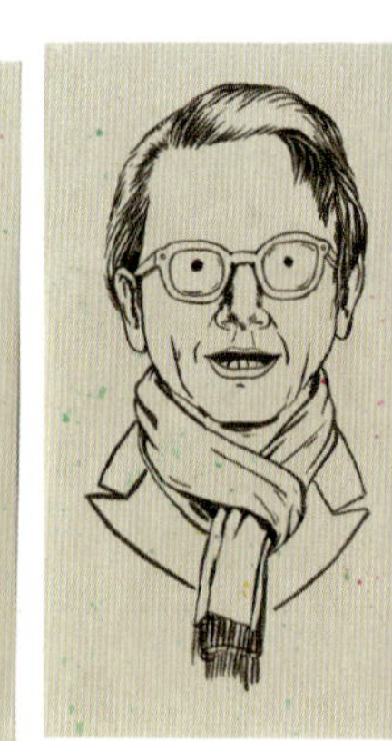

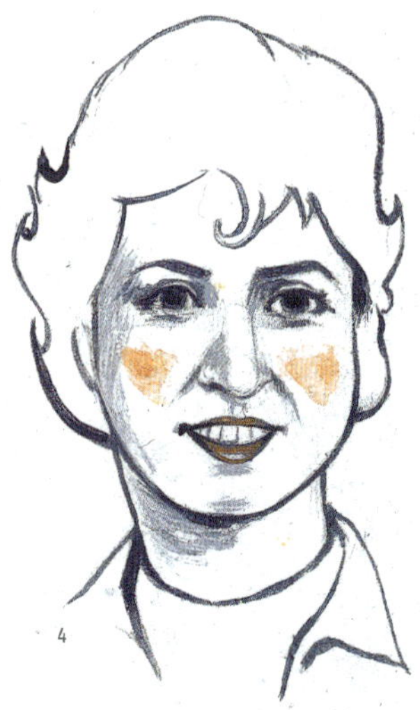

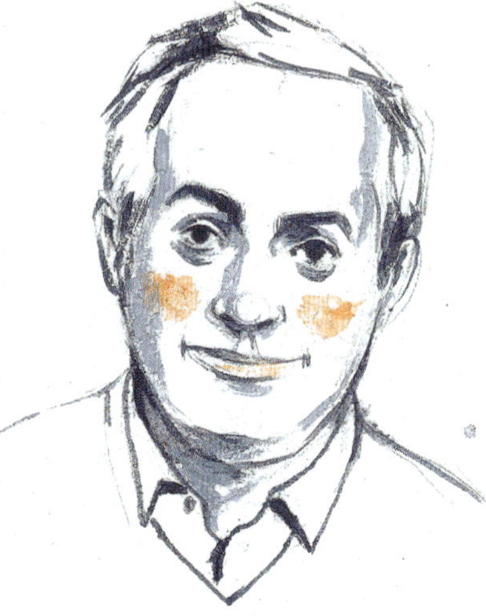

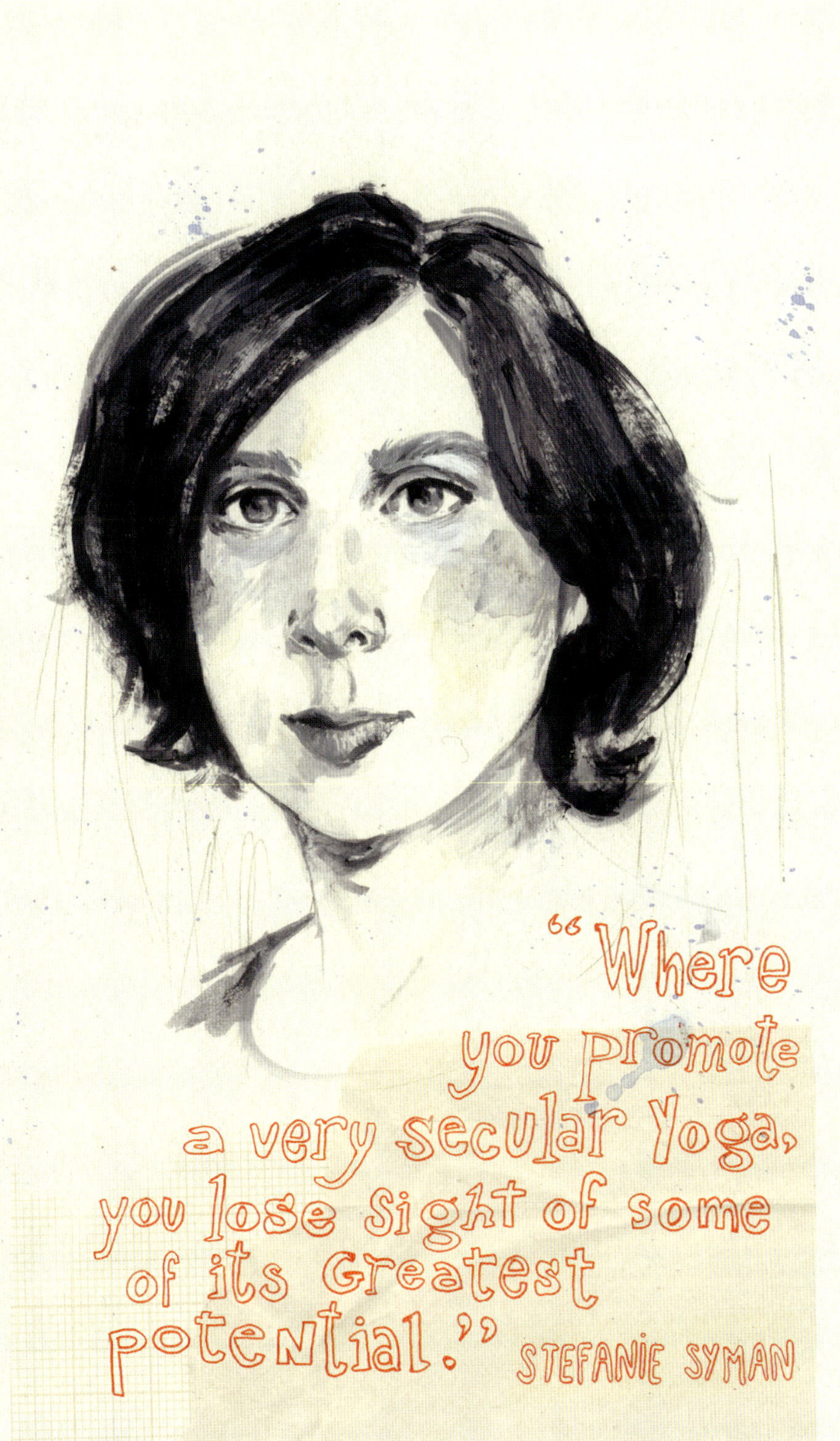

5

1. **Israel Cover** (2006). *La Vanguardia.*
   Acrylic

2. **Sufjan Stevens** (2010). *Spin Magazine.*
   Ink, digital

3. **Seven Types of Book Bored** (2010). *The National.* Ink, collage

4. **Israel Couple** (2006). *La Vanguardia.*
   Acrylic

5. **Yoga and Religion** (2011). *Yoga Journal.*
   Acrylic, collage, ink

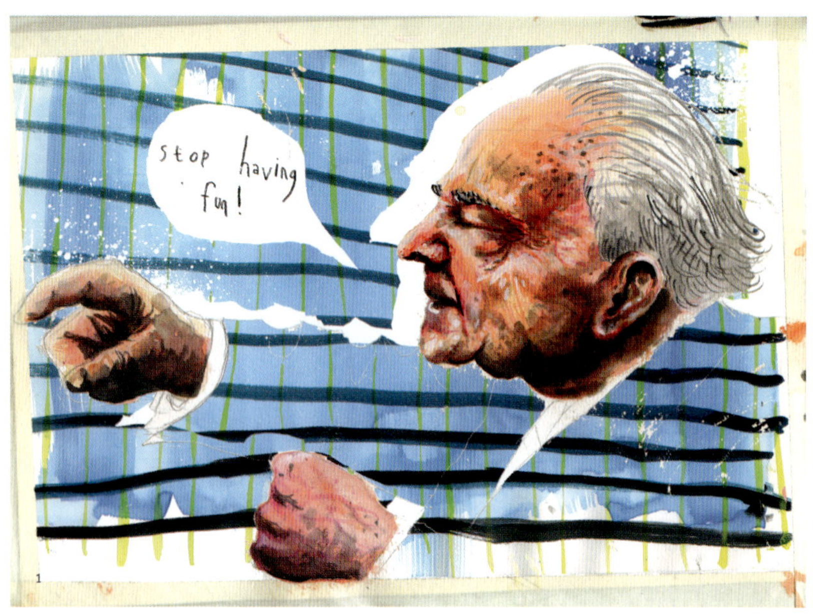
stop having
fun!

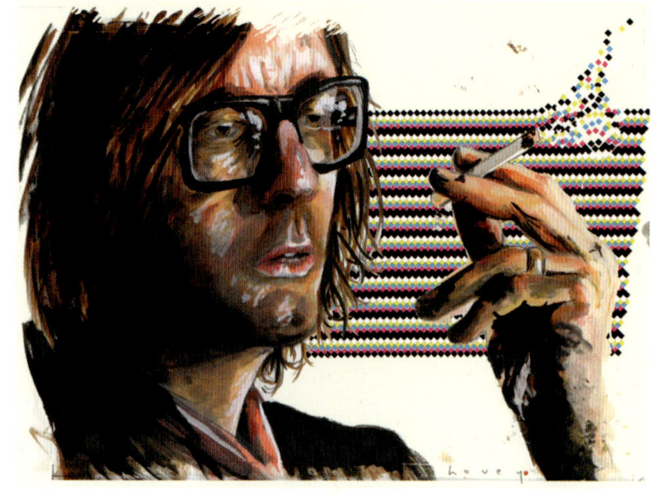

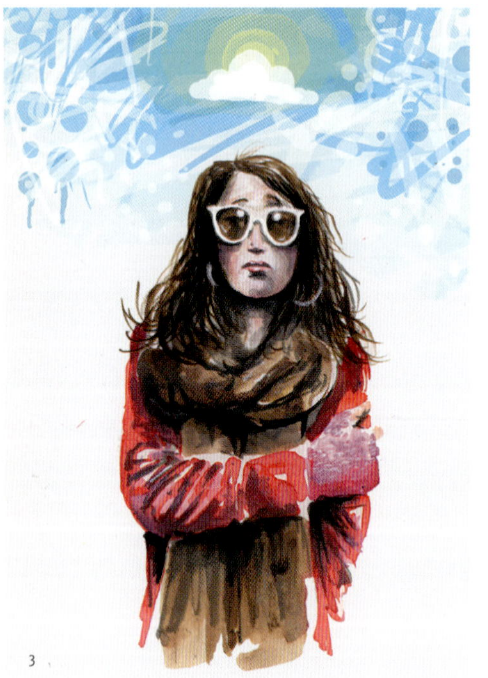

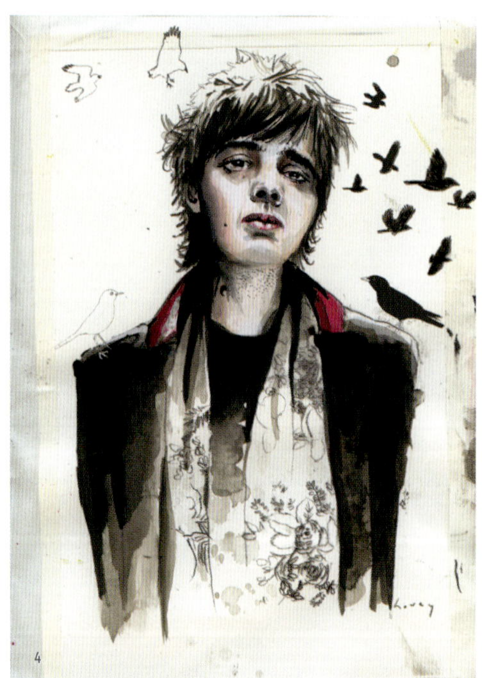

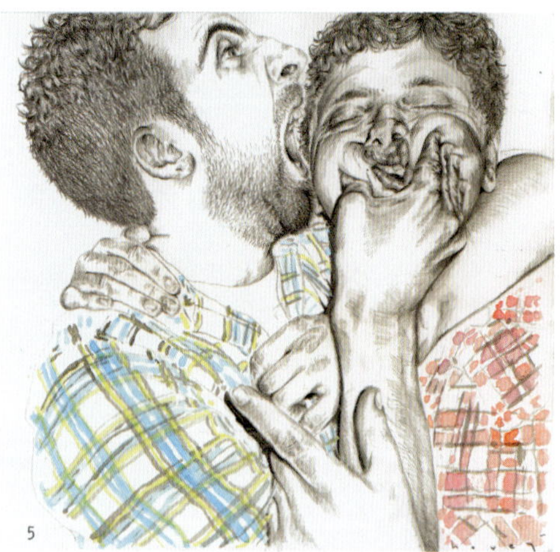

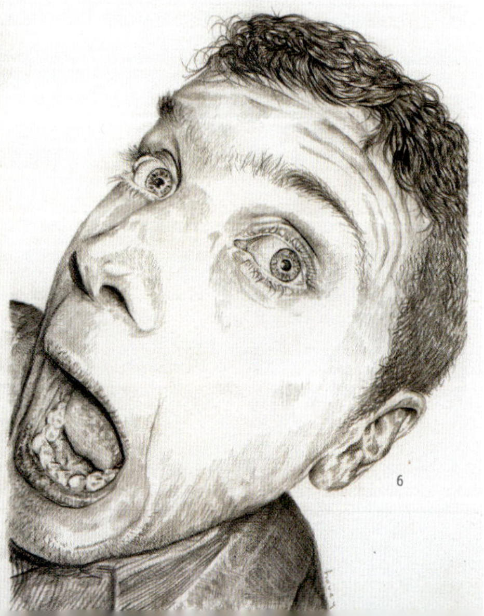

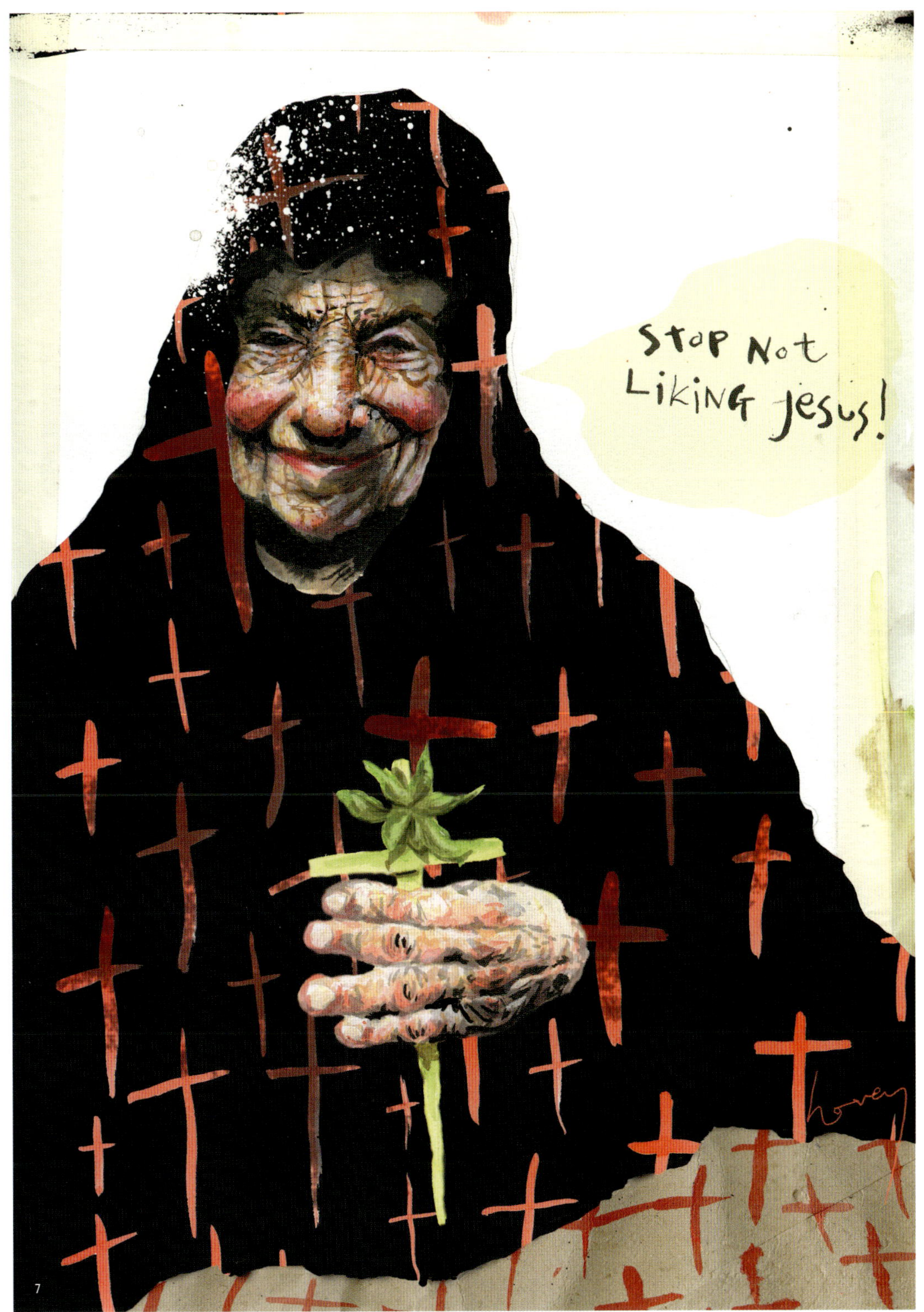

Tom Hovey
UK

www.tomhovey.co.uk

1. **Stop Having Fun** (2009). Personal work. Acrylic ink, Photoshop

2. **Jarvis Cocker** (2009). Personal work. Acrylic ink, acrylic paint

3. **Manda** (2010). Band Artwork Pitch. Acrylic ink

4. **Peter Docherty** (2009). Personal work. Acrylic ink, Photoshop

5. **Cheeky in Check** (2009). Tor Press. Acrylic ink

6. **Ree Ree** (2010). Personal work. Pencil

7. **Lets Get Religious** (2009). Personal work. Acrylic ink, Photoshop

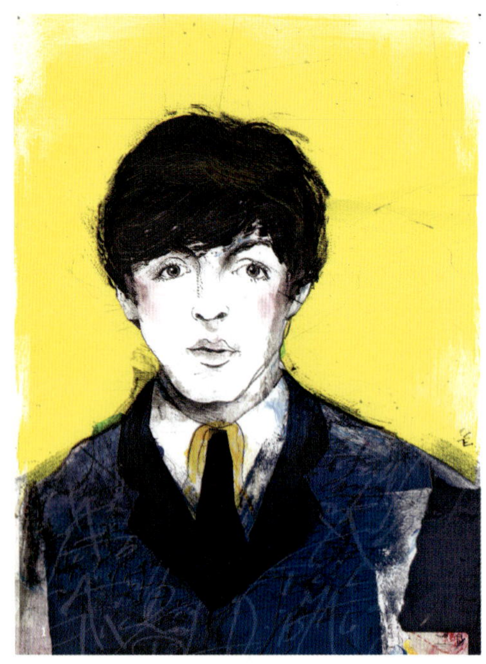

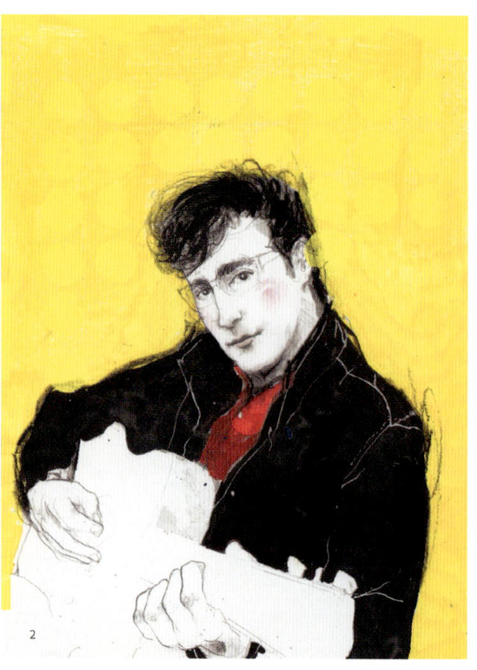

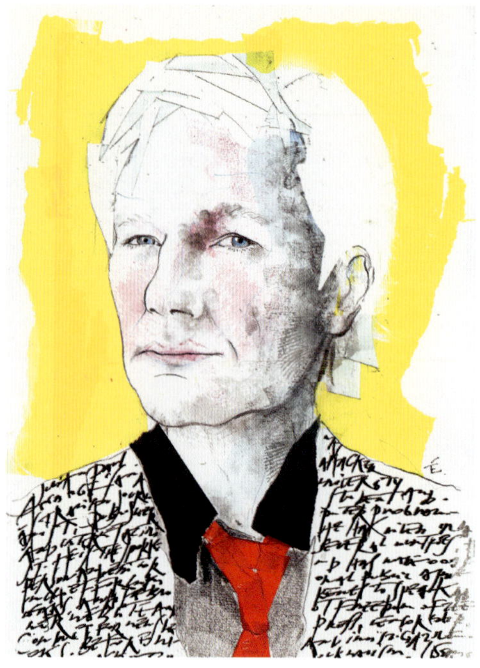

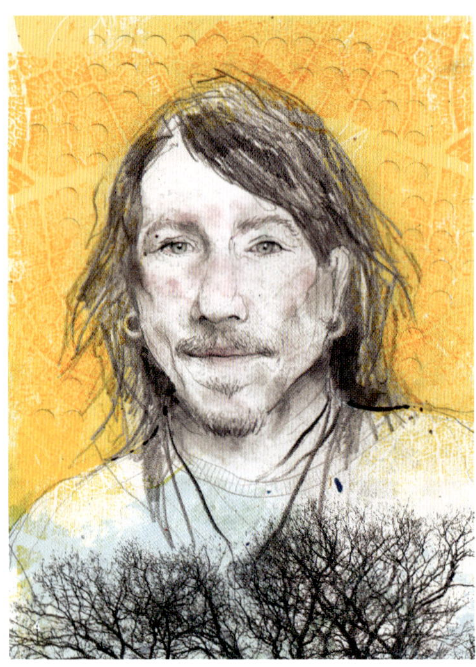

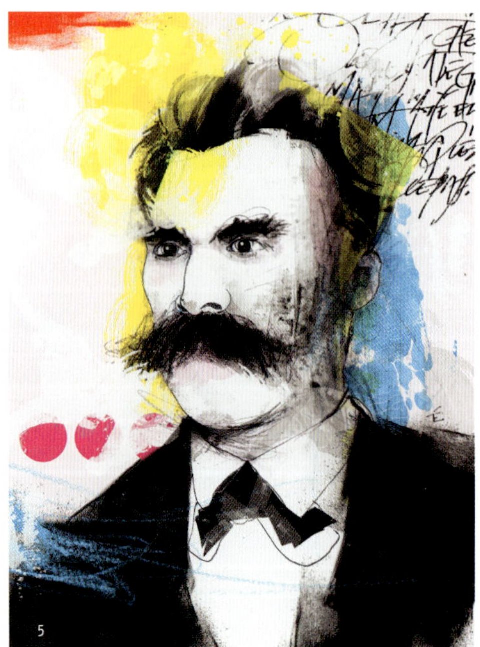

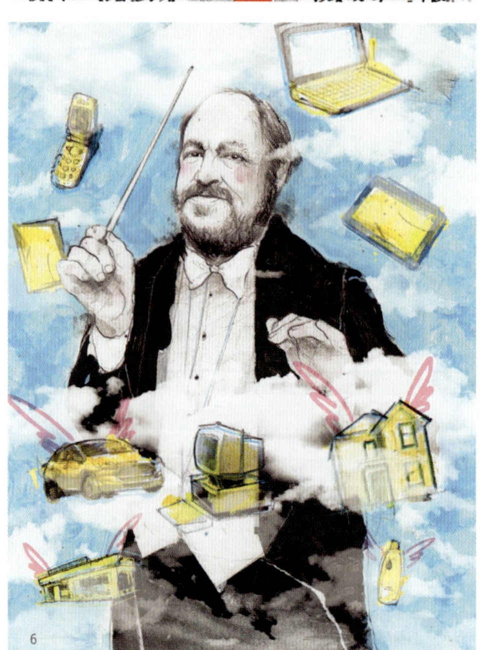

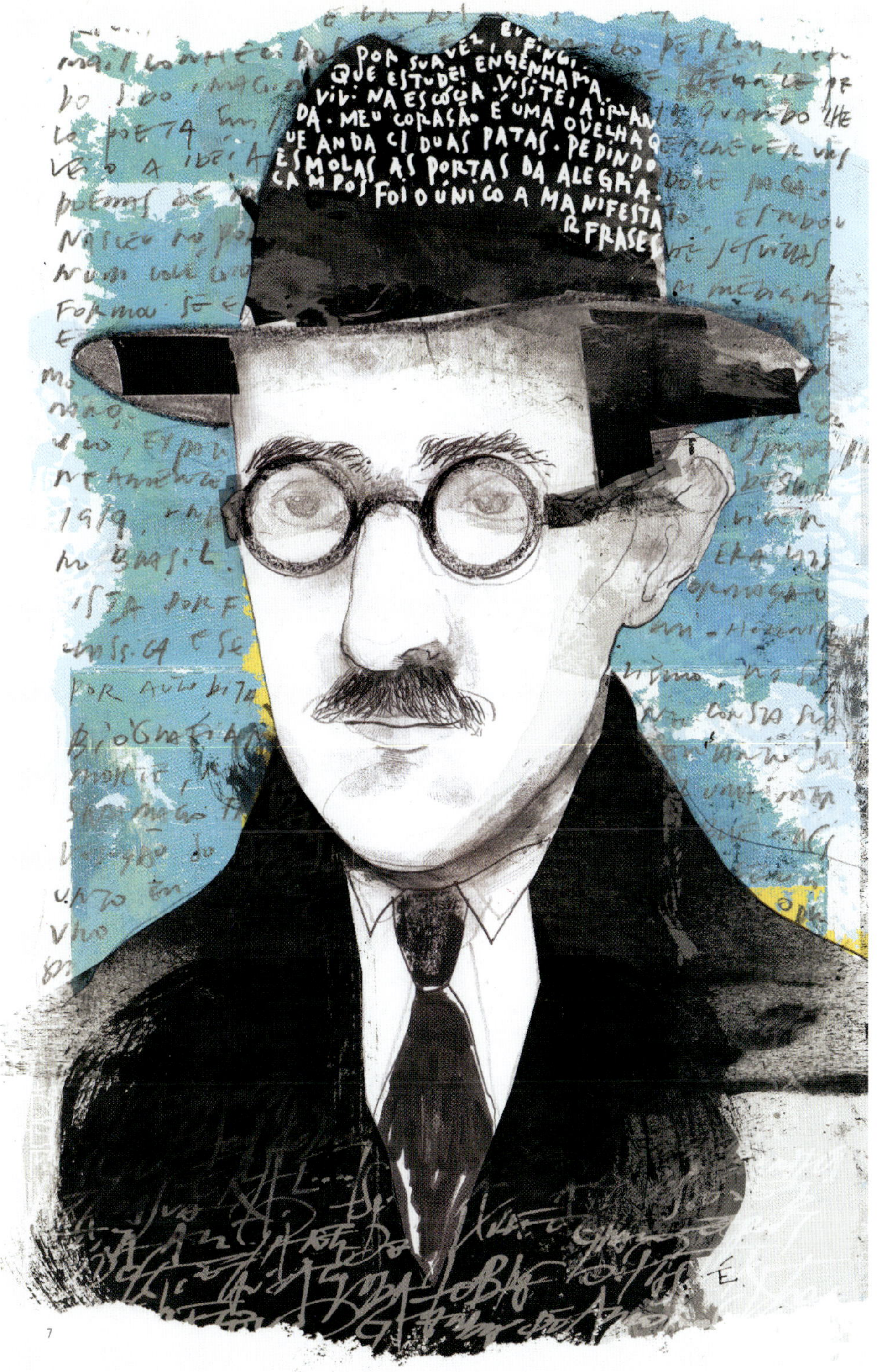

7

Zé Otavio

Brazil

www.zeotavio.com
Agency: Levy Creative Management

1. **Paul, The Early Years** (2011). Personal work. Mixed media

2. **John Lennon, The Early Years** (2011). Personal work. Mixed media

3. **Julian Assange** (2010). *O Estado de Sao Paulo*. Mixed media

4. **Lenine** (2011) *Rolling Stone* Brazil. Mixed media

5. **Nietzche is Pop** (2010). *Cult Magazine*. Mixed media

6. **The Man Behind the Cloud** (2011). The Korn/Ferry Institute magazine *Briefings on Talent & Leadership*. Mixed media

7. **Fernando Pessoa** (2011). *Cultura Magazine*. Mixed media

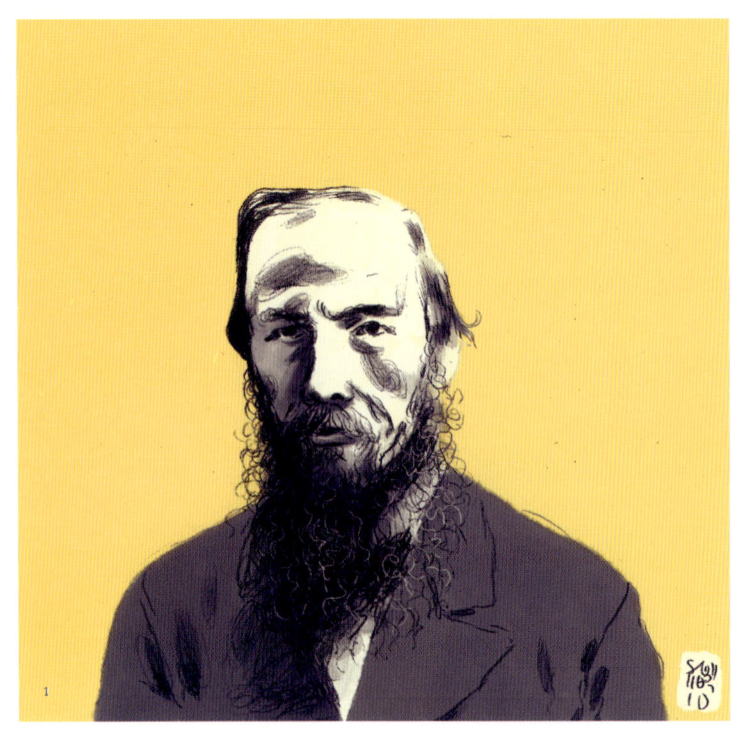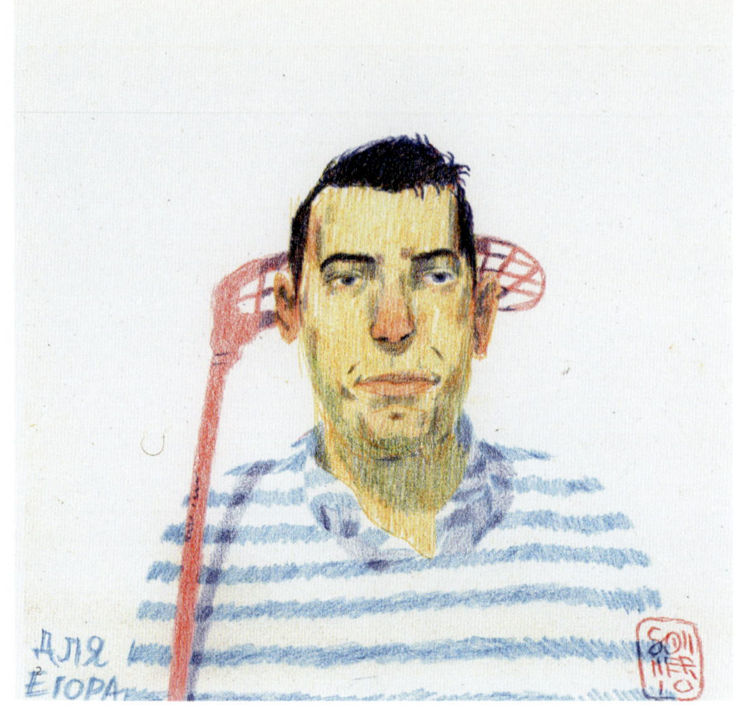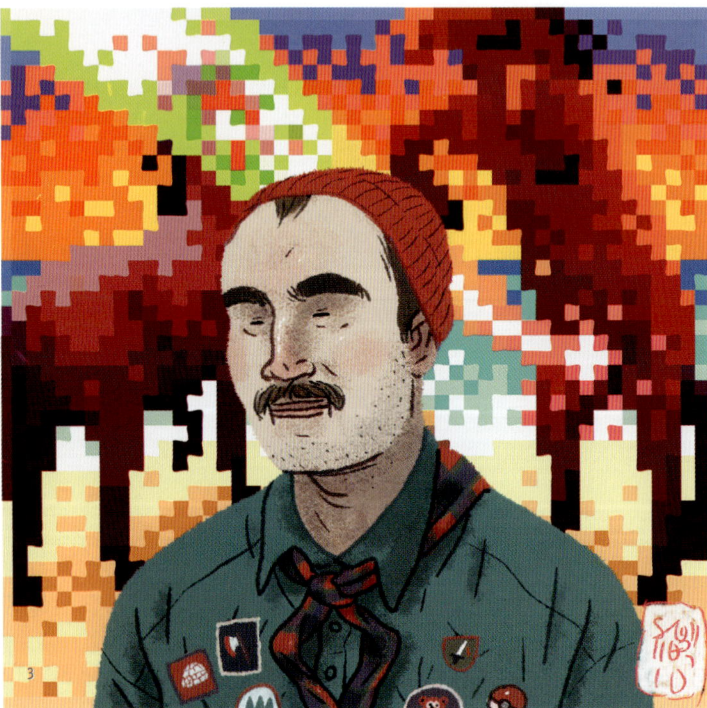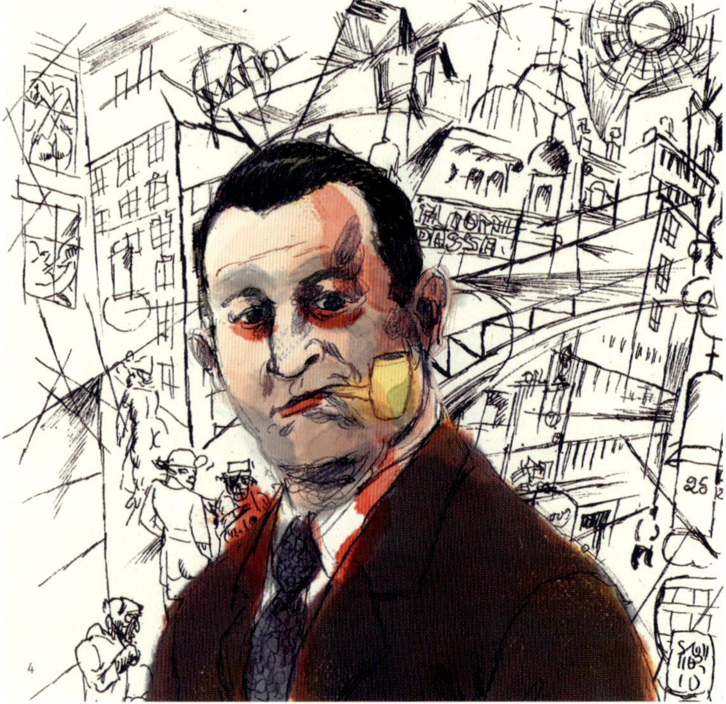

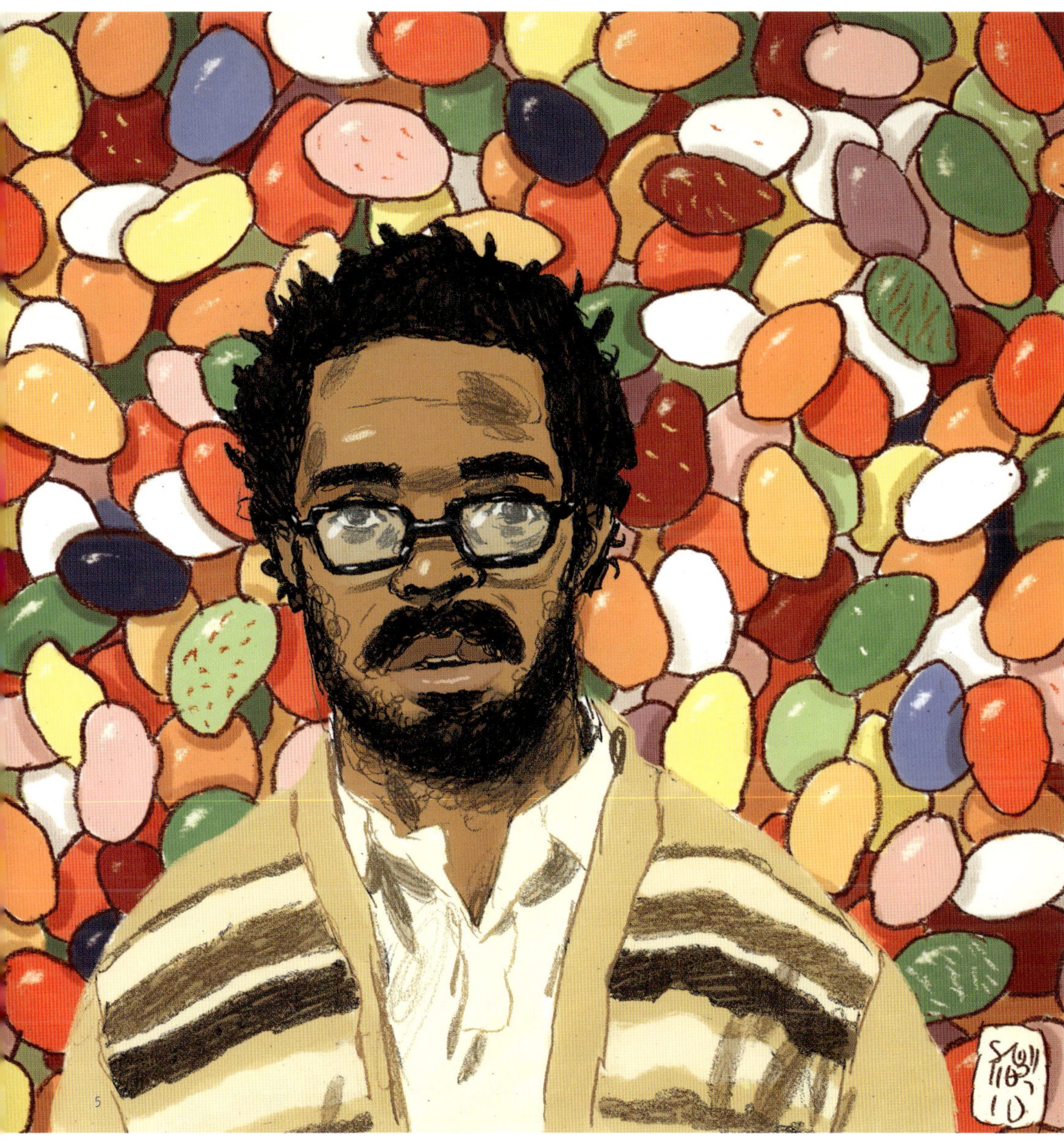

Mikkel Sommer

Denmark

www.mikkelsommer.com

1. **Dostoyevsky** (2011). Personal work. Pencil, Photoshop

2. **Egor** (2011). Personal work. Colored pencils

3. **Thomas** (2011). Personal work. Photoshop

4.
Grosz (2011). Personal work. Pencil, pen, Photoshop

5.
Busdriver (2011). Personal work. Pencil, Photoshop

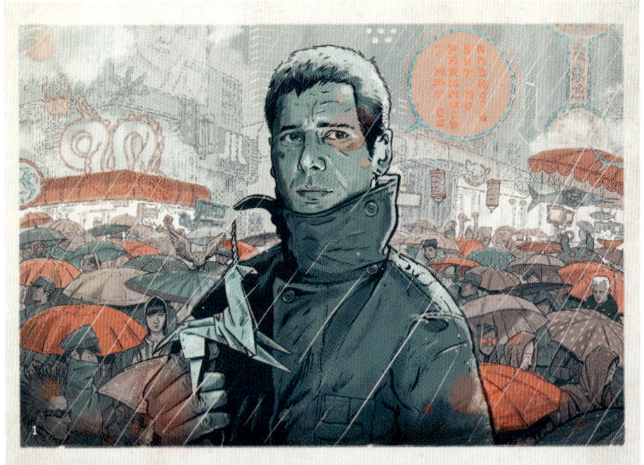

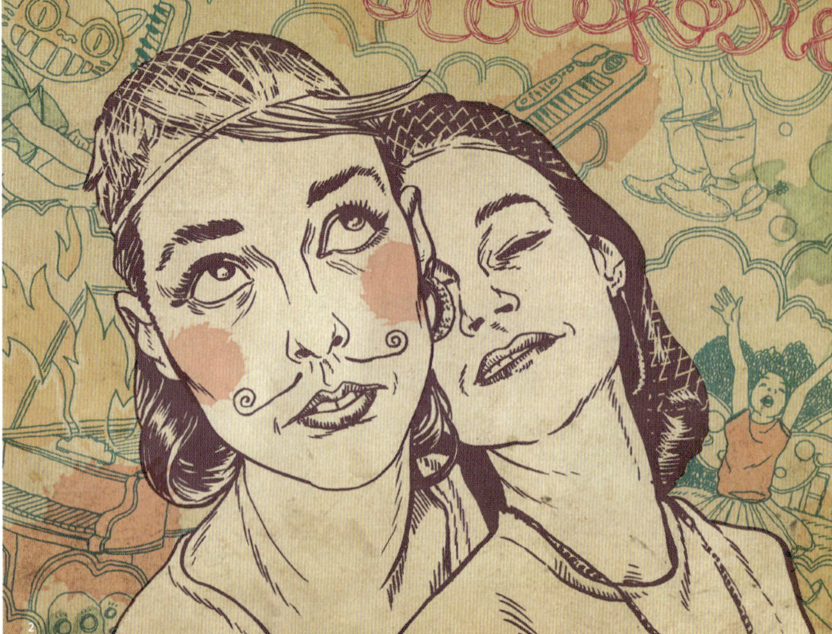

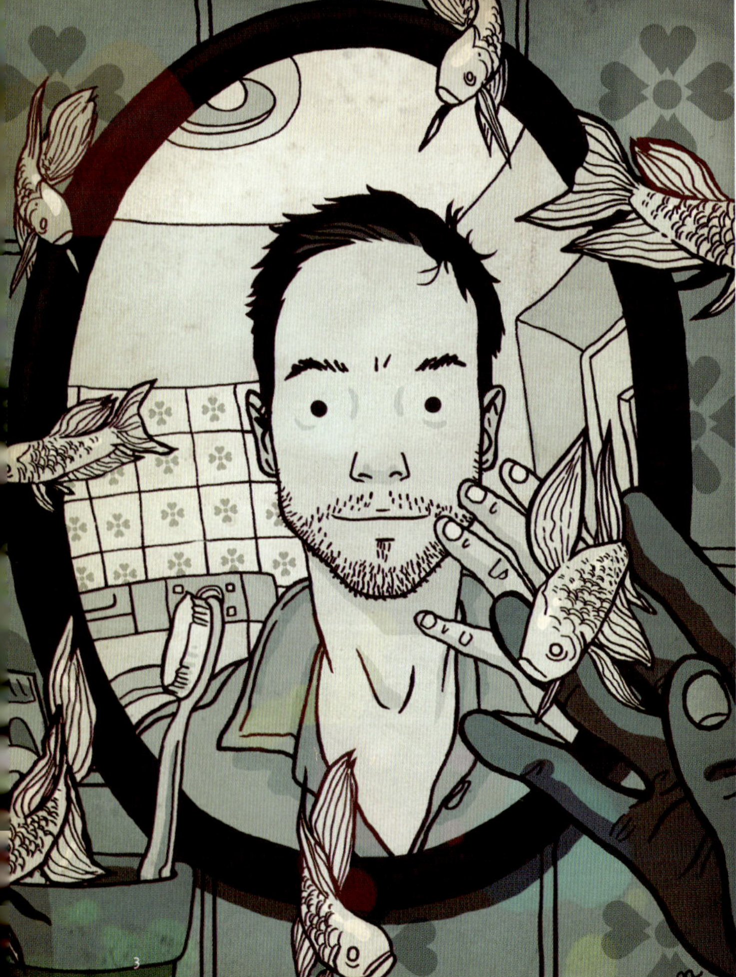

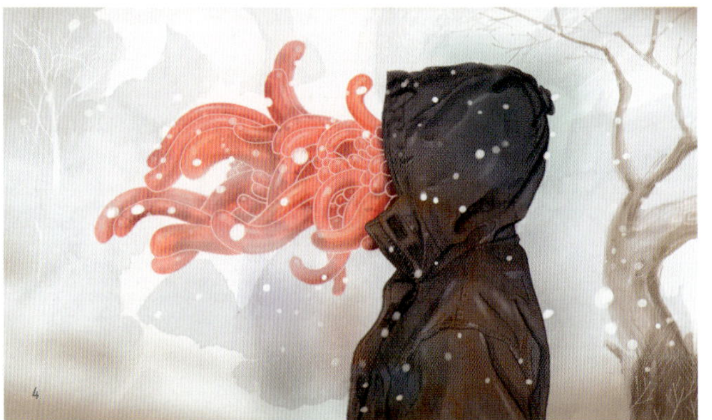

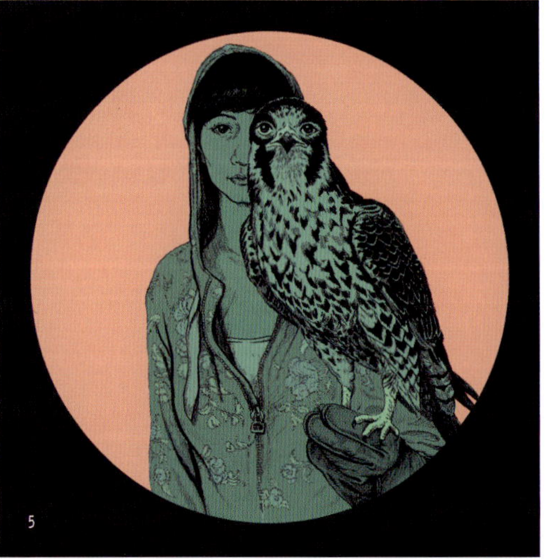

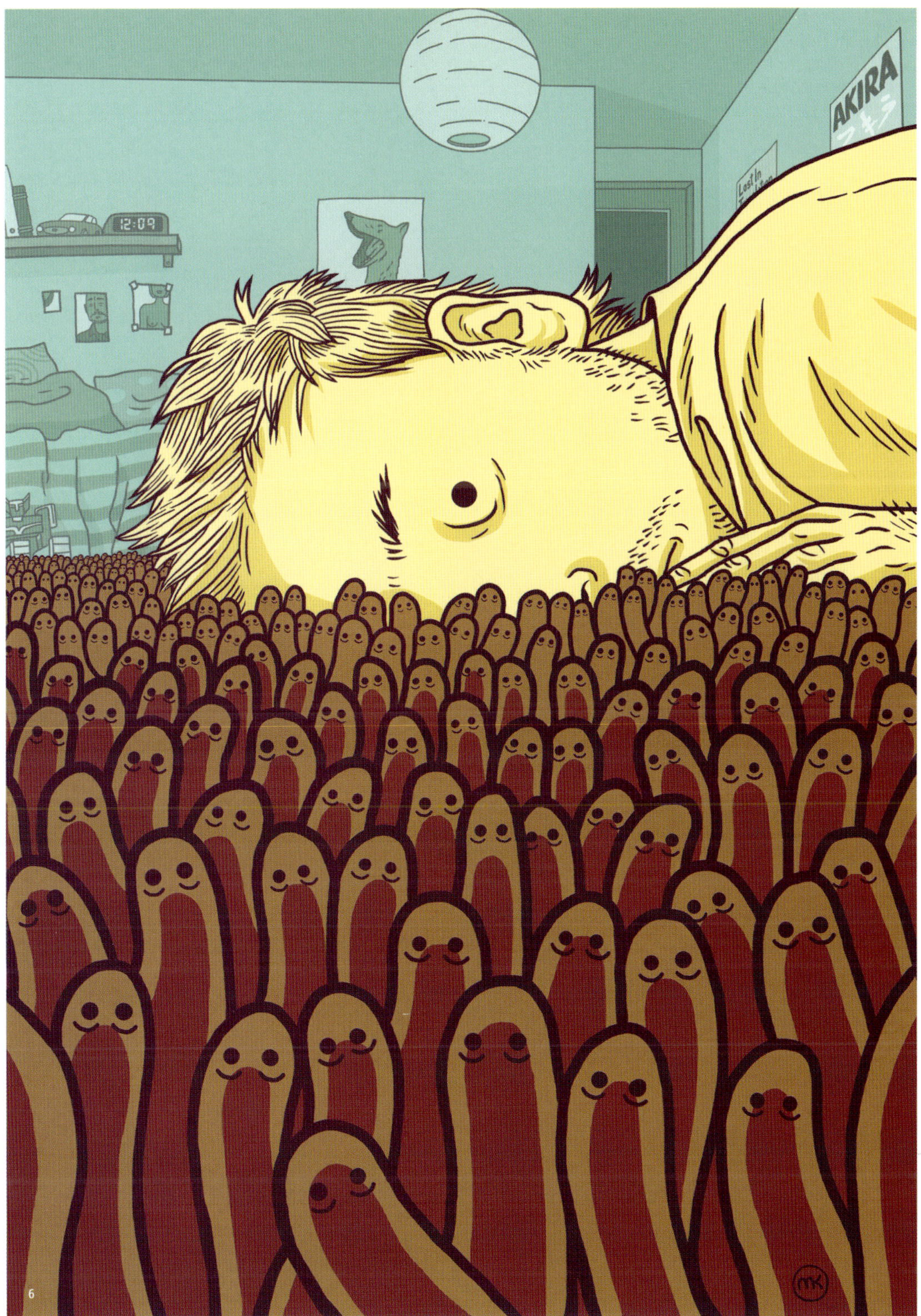

Mateusz Kołek
Polen

www.mateuszkolek.com

1. **Blade Runner** (2010). New Age Media. Ink drawing, digital color

2. **Cocorosie** (2008). Ink drawing, digital color

3. **Mirror** (2008). Ink drawing, digital color

4. **Jelly Demon** (2010). Ink drawing, watercolor, digital color

5. **Three eyes** (2011). Ink drawing, digital color

6. **Carpet** (2008). Personal work. Ink drawing, digital color

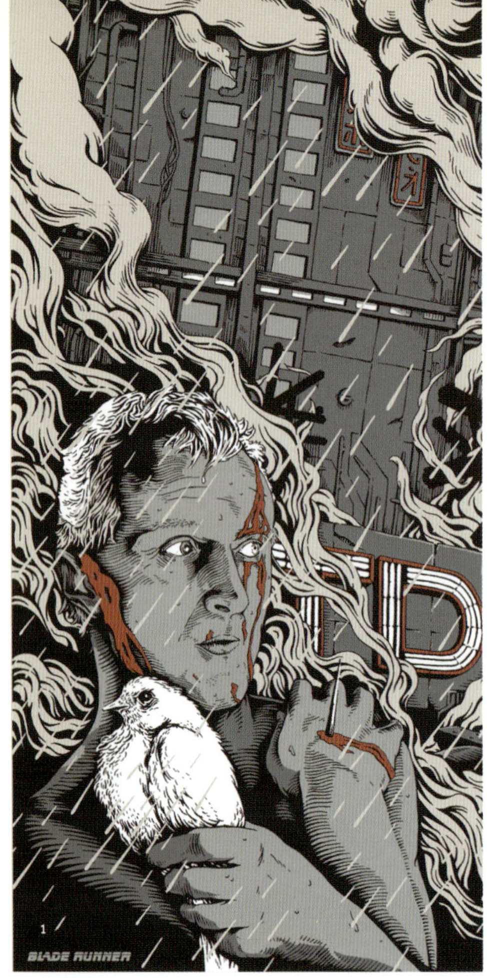
BLADE RUNNER

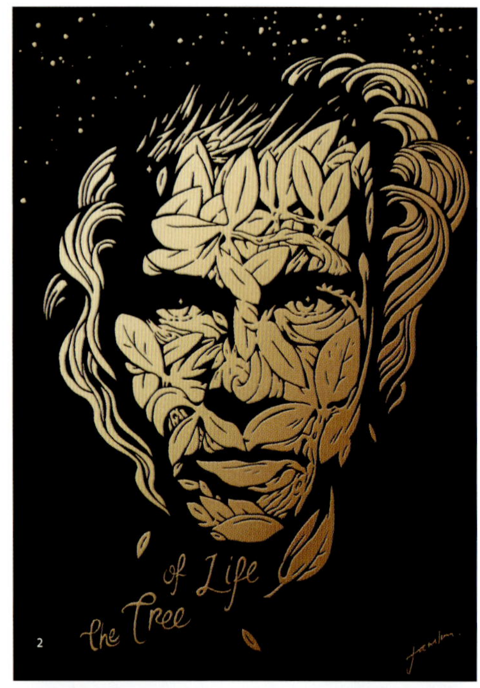
the Tree of Life

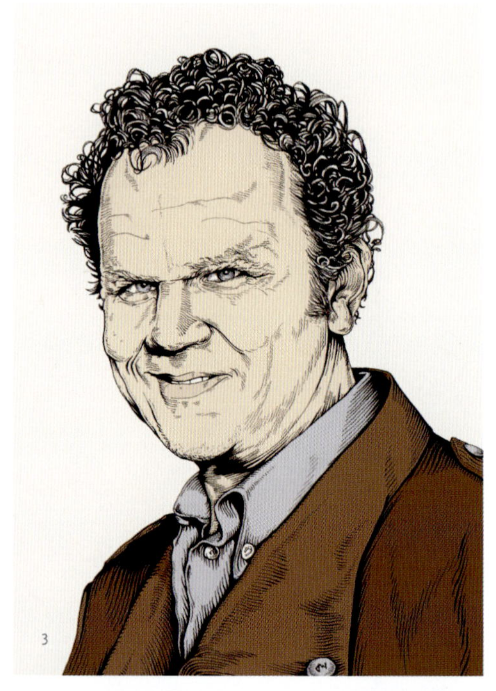

Little White Lies
Truth & Movies
the Attack Block

Little White Lies
Truth & Movies
ALIEN

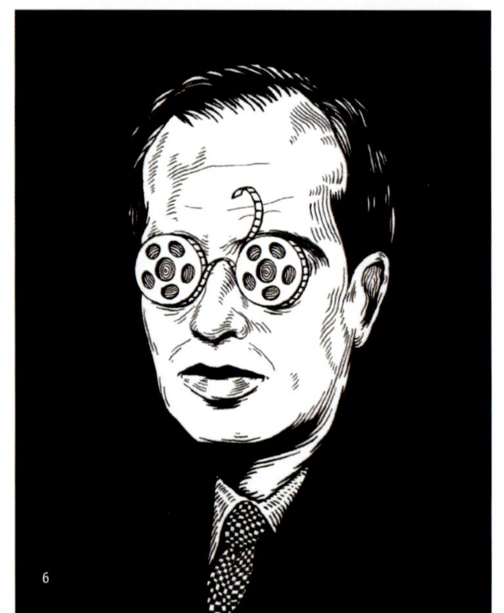

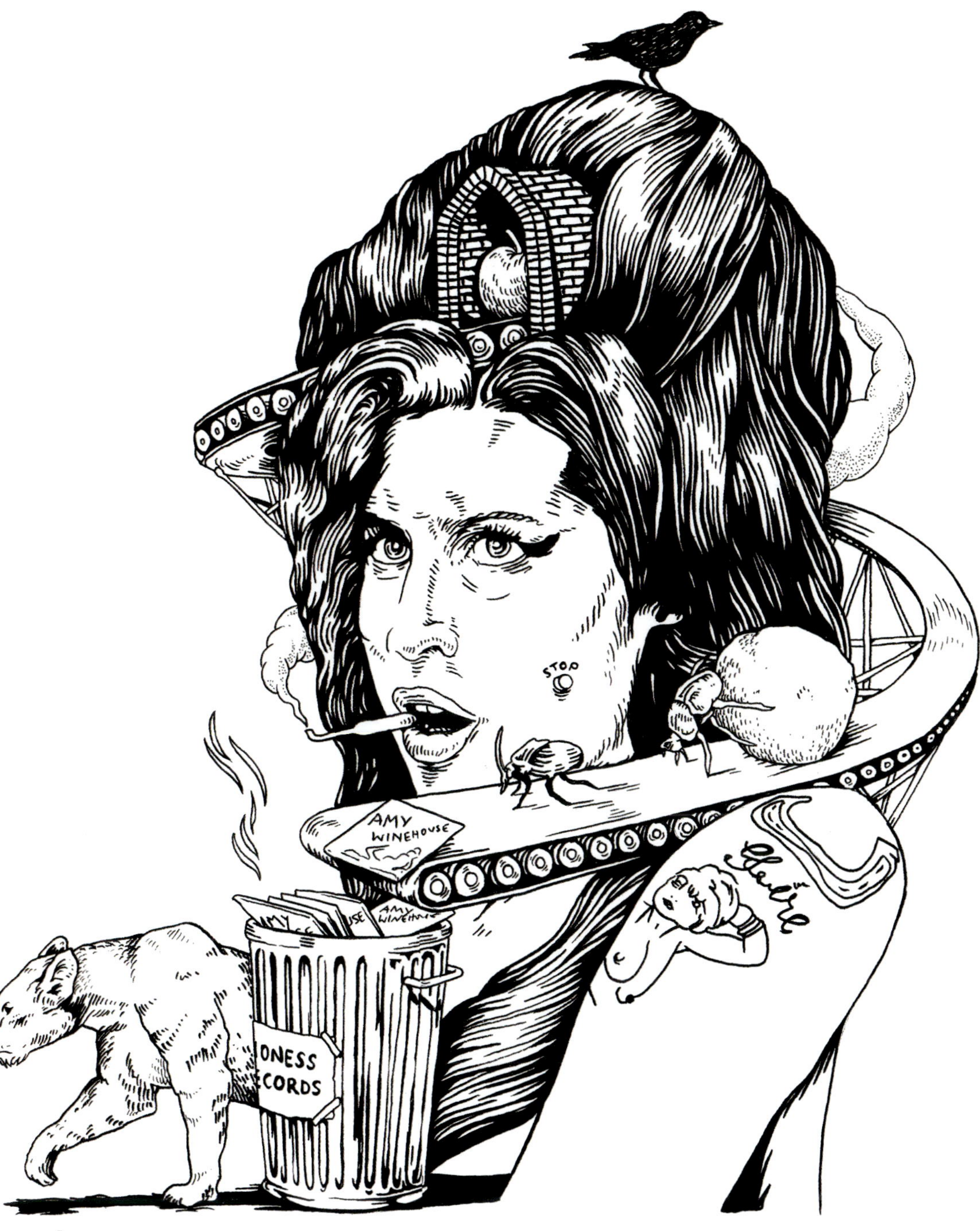

7

Joe Wilson
UK

www.joe-wilson.com

1. **Blade Runners Roy Baty** (2011). Personal work. Screenprint

2. **The Tree of Life** (2011). *Little White Lies* magazine. Gold foil block print

3. **John C Reilly** (2010). *Little White Lies* magazine. Ink and photoshop

4. **Attack The Block** (2011). *Little White Lies* magazine. Ink and photoshop

5. **Alien 1979** (2011). *Little White Lies* magazine. Ink and photoshop

6. **Cult Hero Thorold Dickinson** (2010). *Little White Lies Magazine*. Ink and photoshop

7. **Lioness Records** (2010). *GQ UK*. Ink

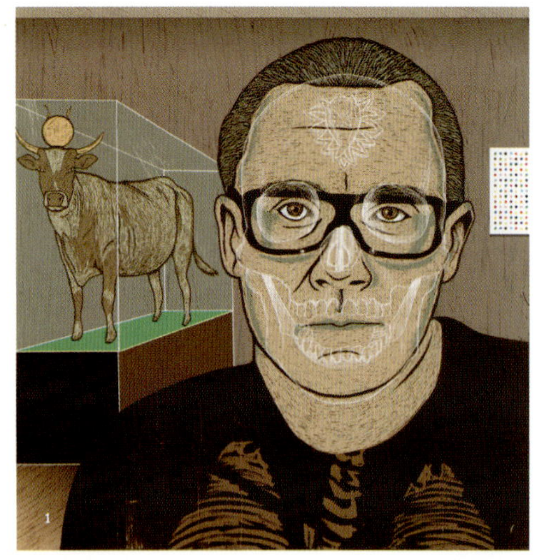

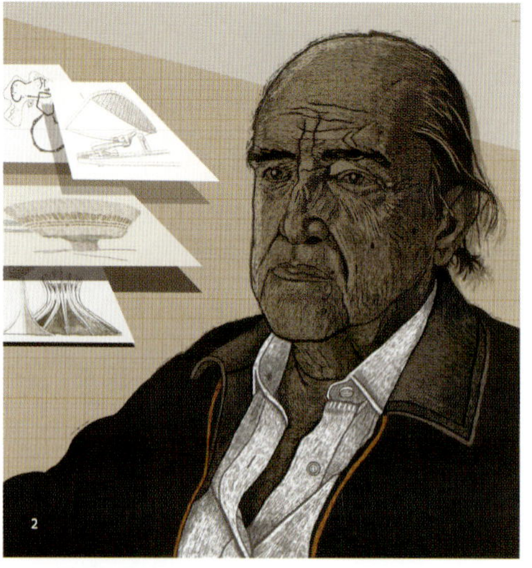

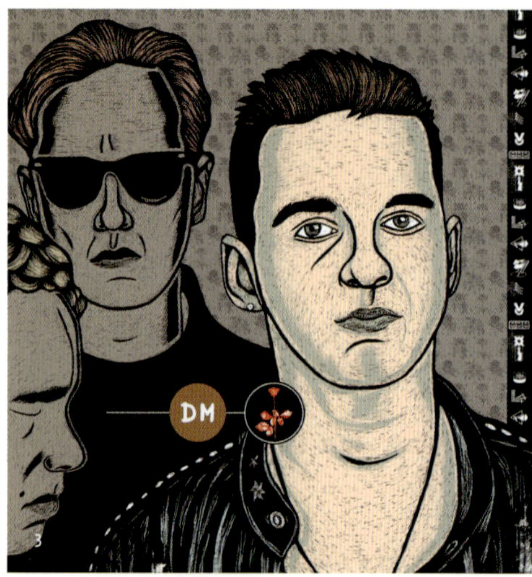

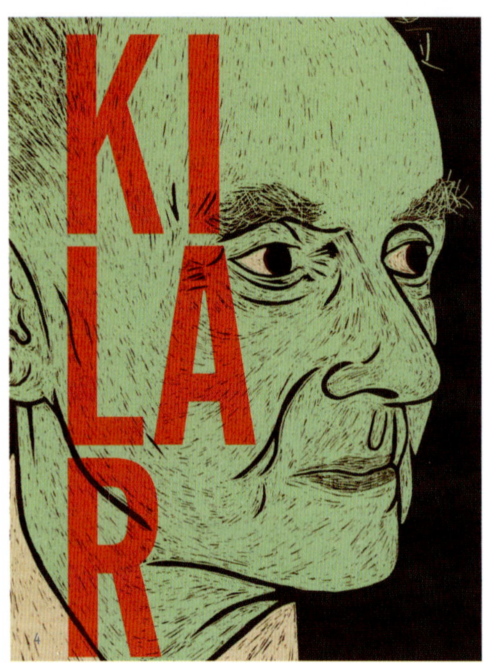
KI
LA
R

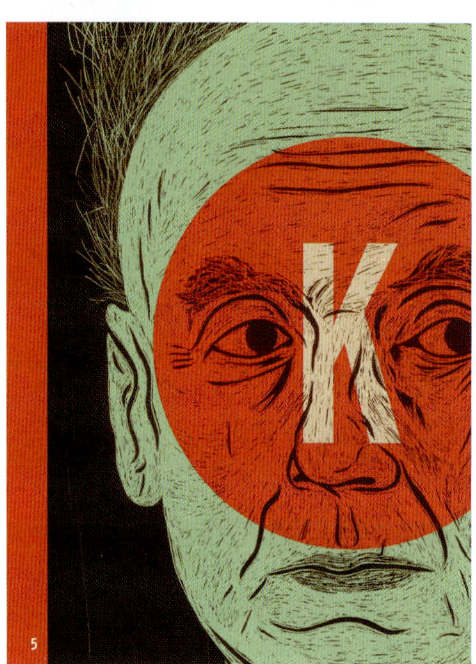
K

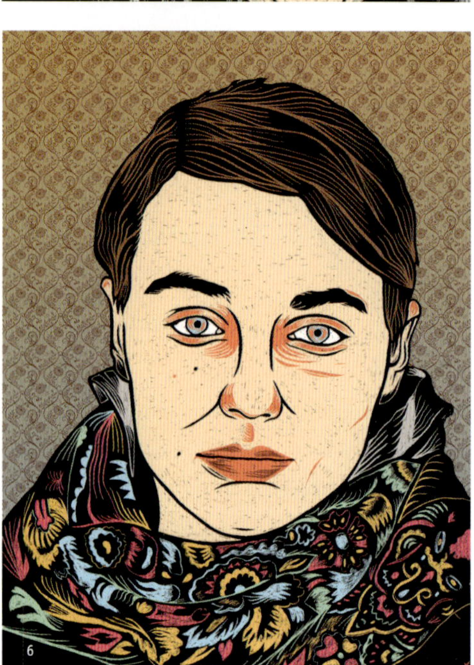

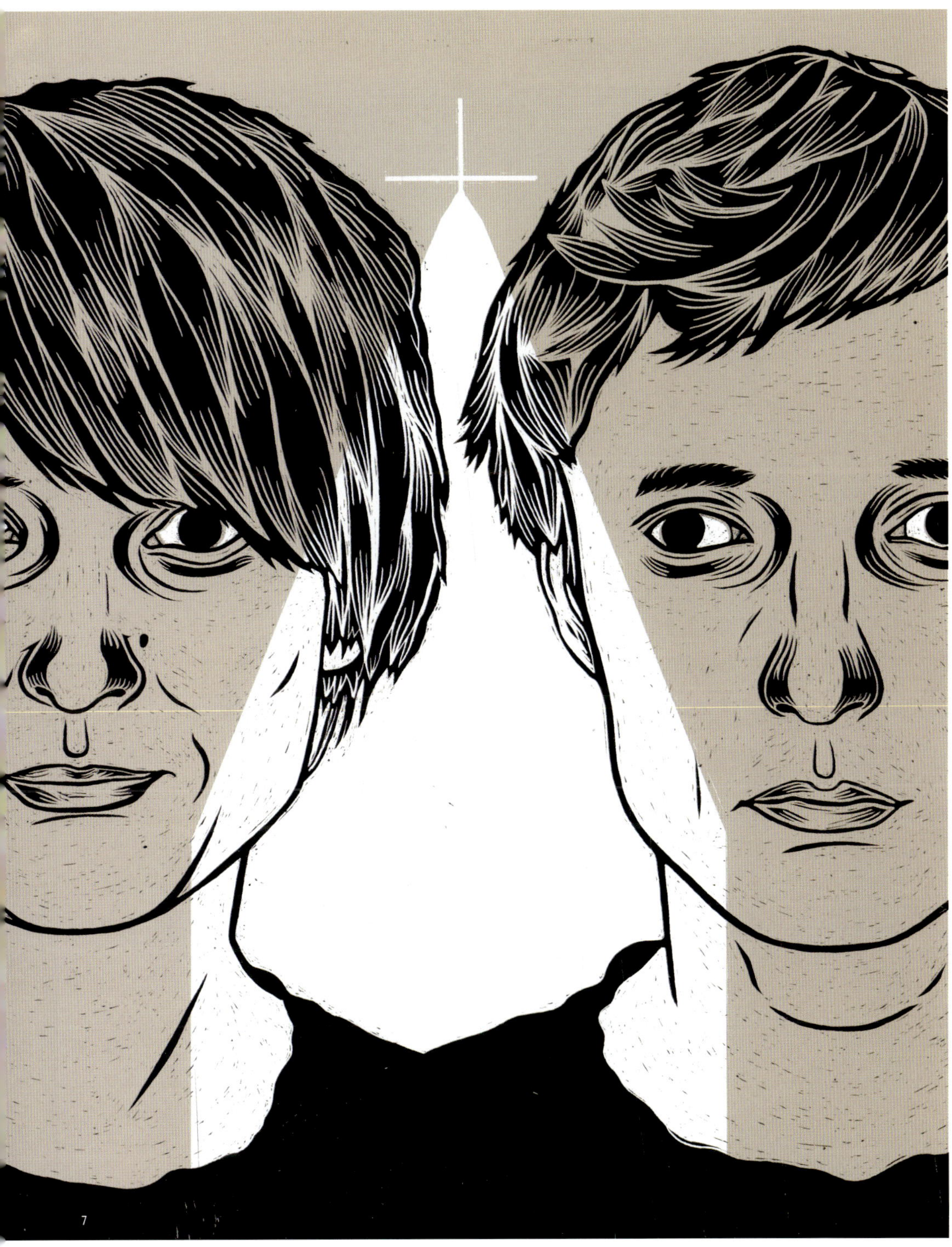

Patryk Mogilnicki

Poland

www.patrykmogilnicki.com

1. **Damien Hirst** (2008). *Playboy*. Own technique

2. **Oscar Niemeyer** (2007). *Playboy*. Own technique

3. **Dave Gahan** (2009). *Playboy*. Own technique

4. **Kilar 01** (2010). *K Mag*. Own technique

5. **Kilar 02** (2010). *K Mag*. Own technique

6. **Magda** (2011). Custom portrait. Own technique

7. **Marta i Lech Rowinscy** (2011). *Architektura*. Own technique

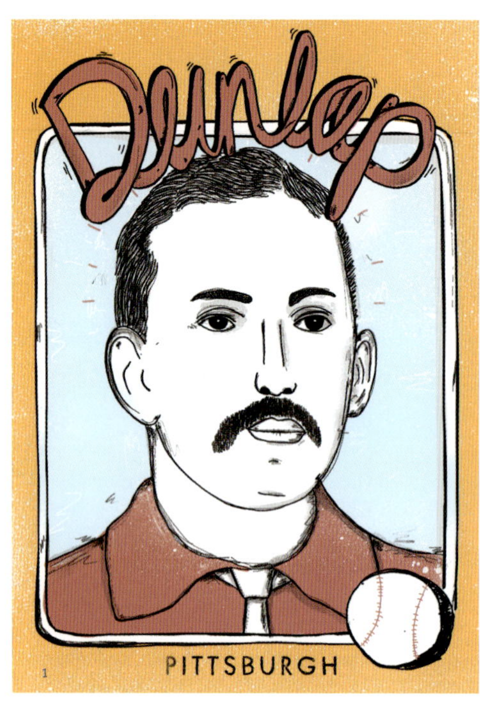

Dunlap
PITTSBURGH

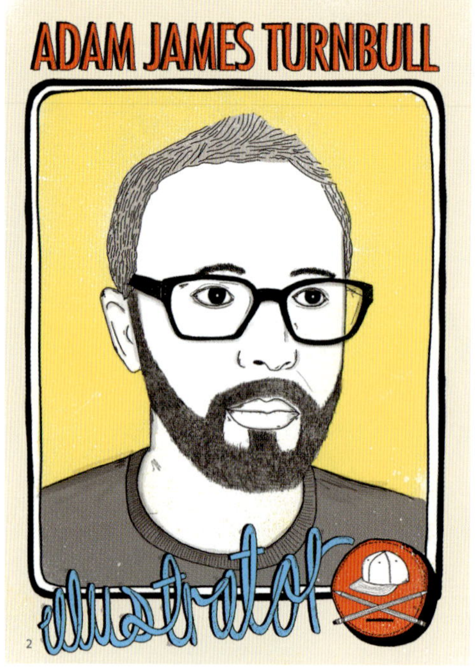

ADAM JAMES TURNBULL
illustrator

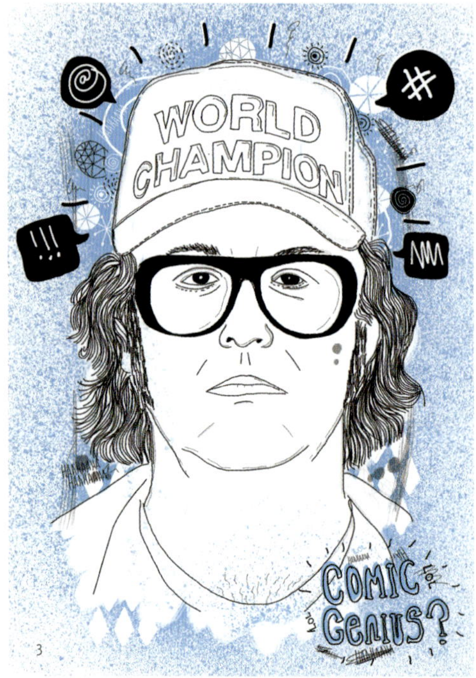

WORLD CHAMPION
COMIC Genius?

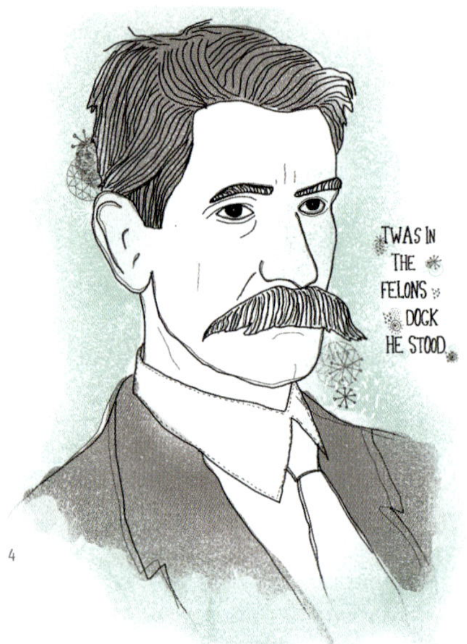

TWAS IN THE FELONS DOCK HE STOOD.

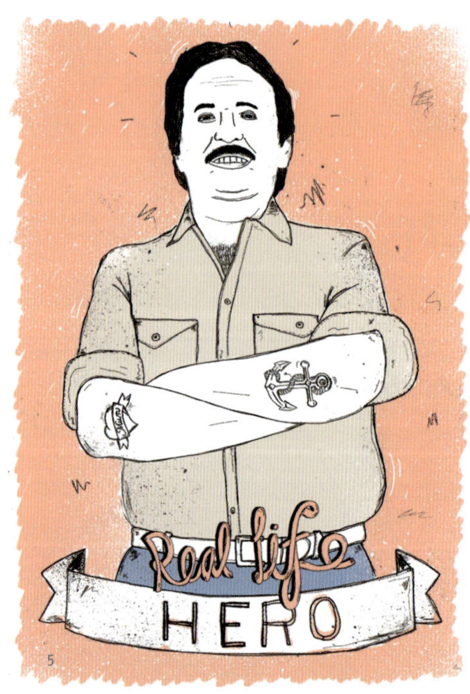

Real life HERO

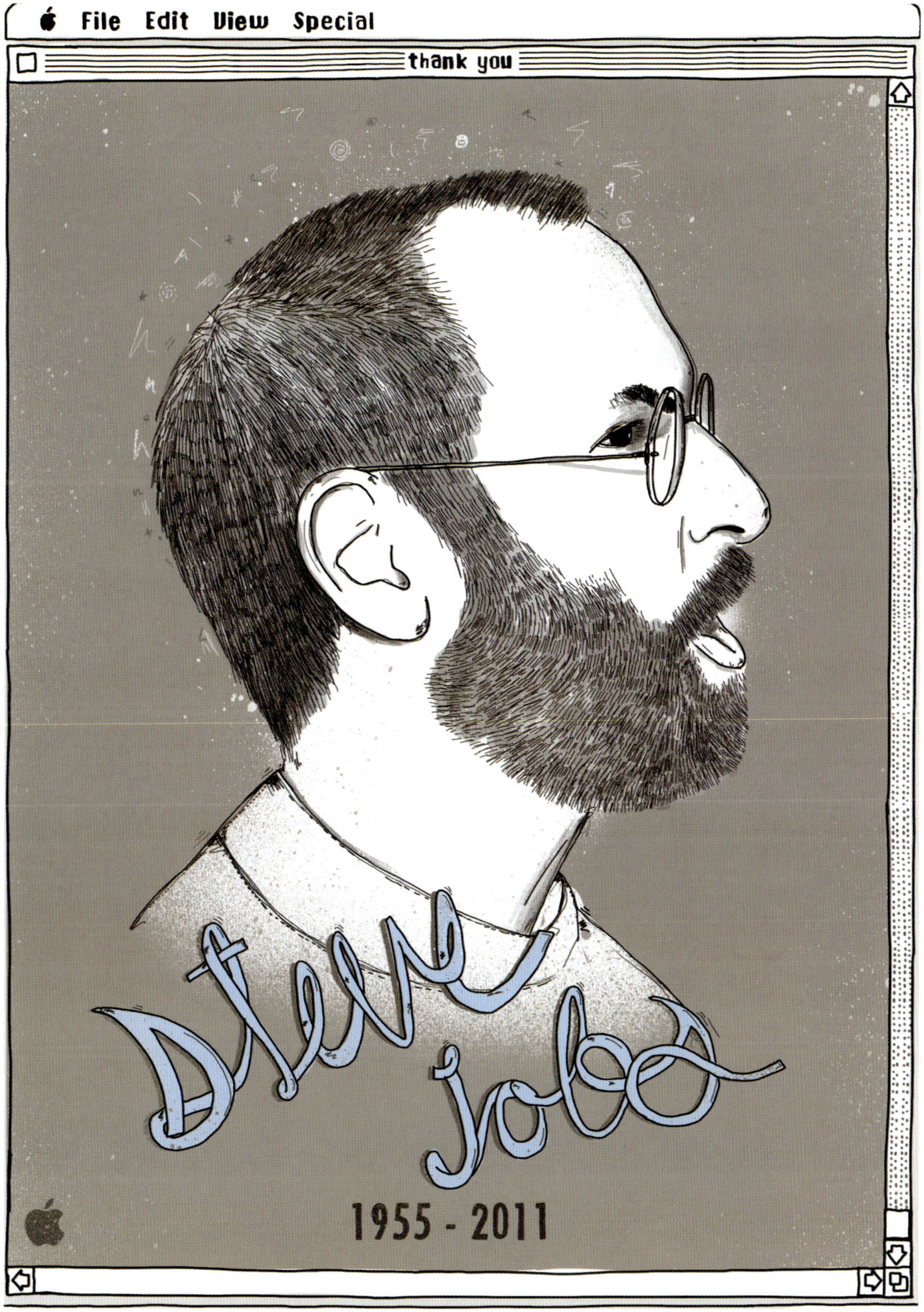

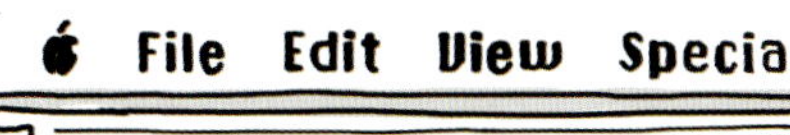

Adam James Turnbull
Australia

Agency: Colagene, Illustration Clinic
www.colagene.com/fr/illustration/
adam-james-turnbull

1. **Baseball Card** (2011). Personal work. Digital, mixed media

2. **Players Card** (2011). Personal work. Digital, mixed media

3. **Judah** (2011). Personal work. Digital, mixed media

4. **Twas in the Fellons Dock** (2011). Personal work. Digital, mixed media

5. **Real Life Hero** (2011). Personal work. Digital, mixed media

6. **Steve Jobs RIP** (2011). Colagene. Digital, mixed media

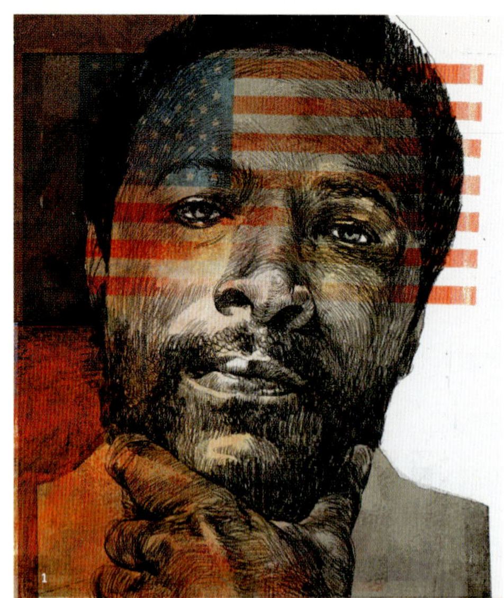

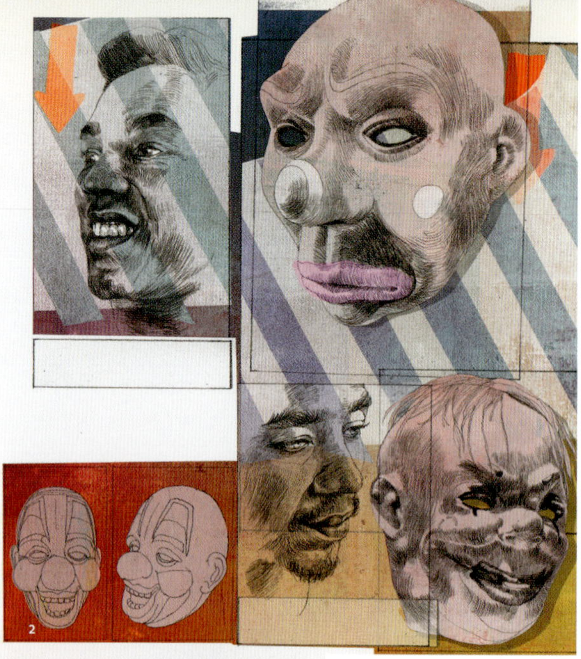

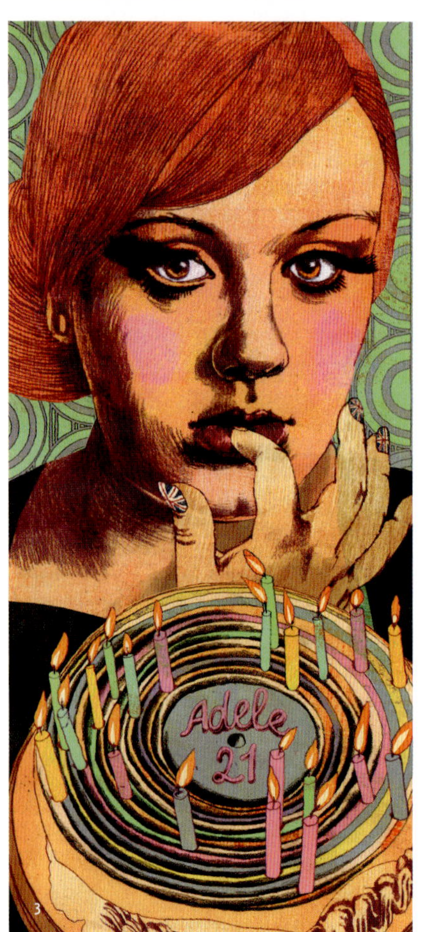

Adele
21

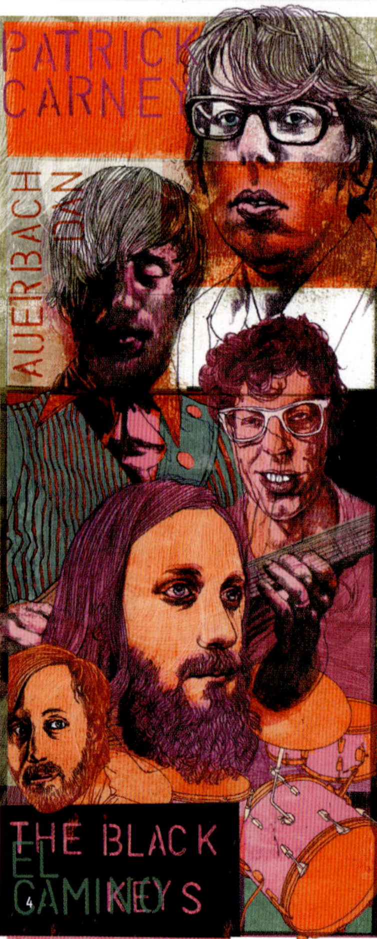

PATRICK CARNEY
DAN AUERBACH
THE BLACK KEYS
EL CAMINO

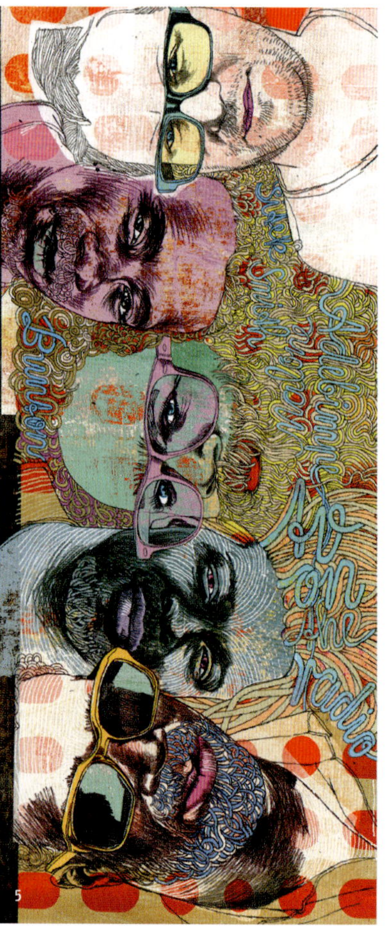

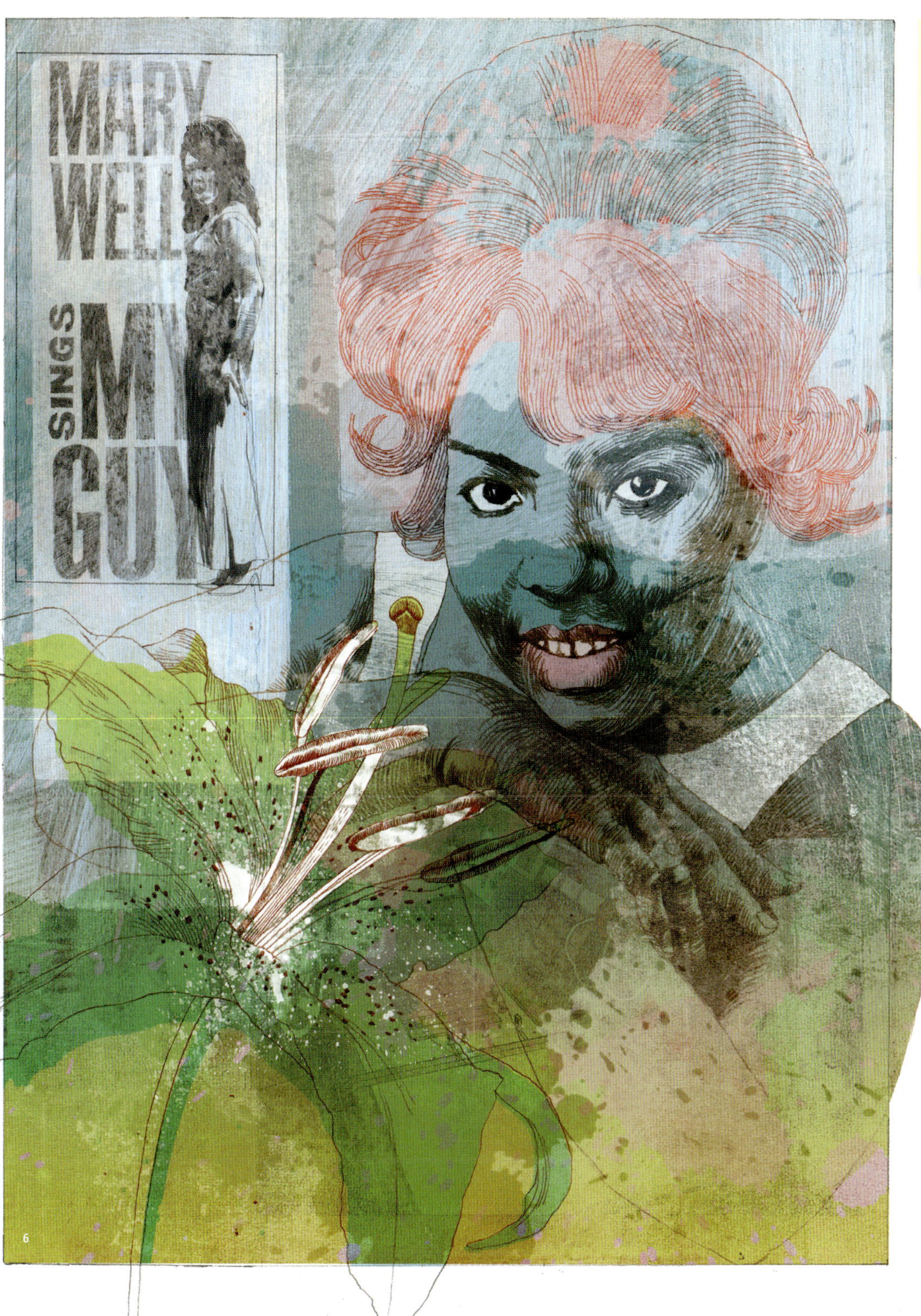

**Alexandra Kardinar
and Volker Schlecht
aka Drushba Pankow**

Germany

www.drushbapankow.de

1. **Marvin Gaye** (2009). edel Verlag + EMI. Pencil drawing, acrylic color, digital collage

2. **Smokey Robinson** (2009). edel Verlag + EMI. Pencil drawing, acrylic color, digital collage

3. **Adele *21*** (2010). *Rolling Stone*. Pencil drawing, acrylic color, digital collage

4. **The Black Keys** *El Camino* (2011). *Rolling Stone*. Pencil drawing, acrylic color, digital collage

5. **TV on the Radio** (2011). *Rolling Stone*. Pencil drawing, acrylic color, digital collage

6. **Mary Wells** (2009). edel Verlag + EMI. Pencil drawing, acrylic color, digital collage

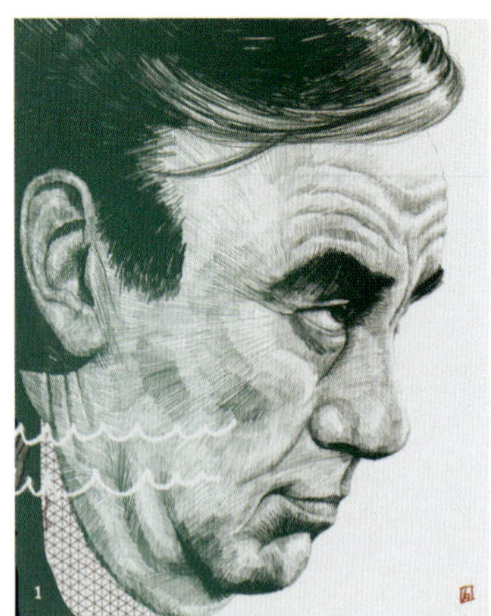

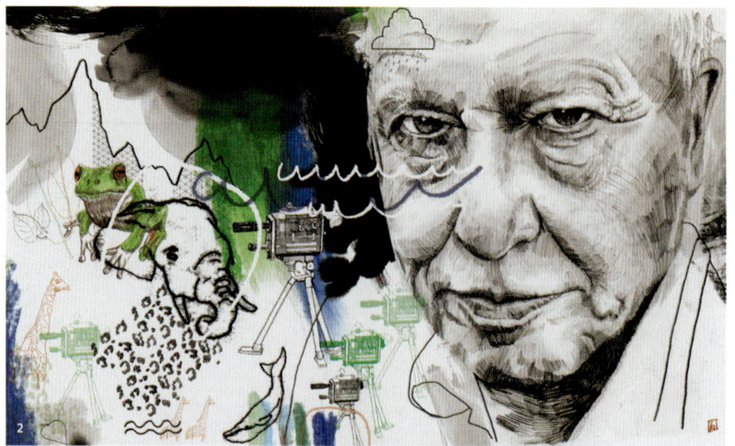

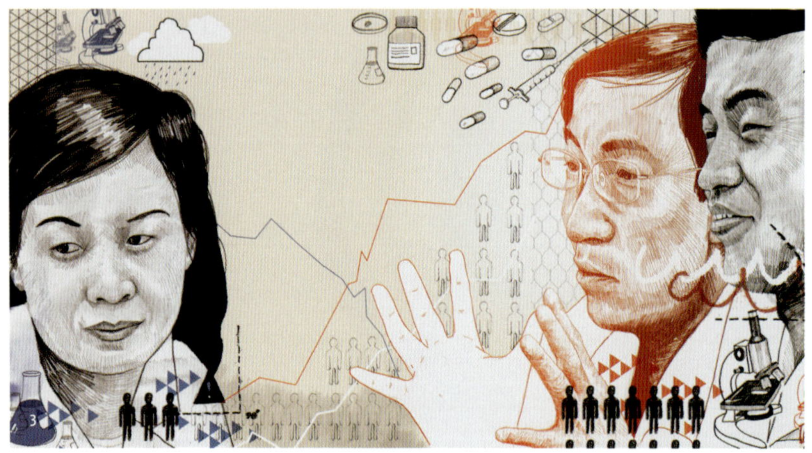

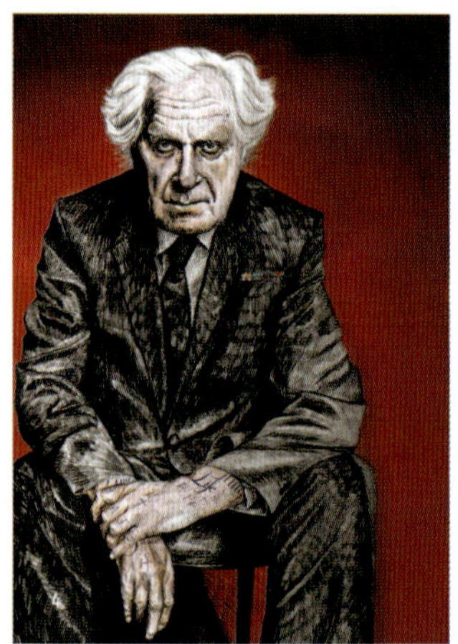

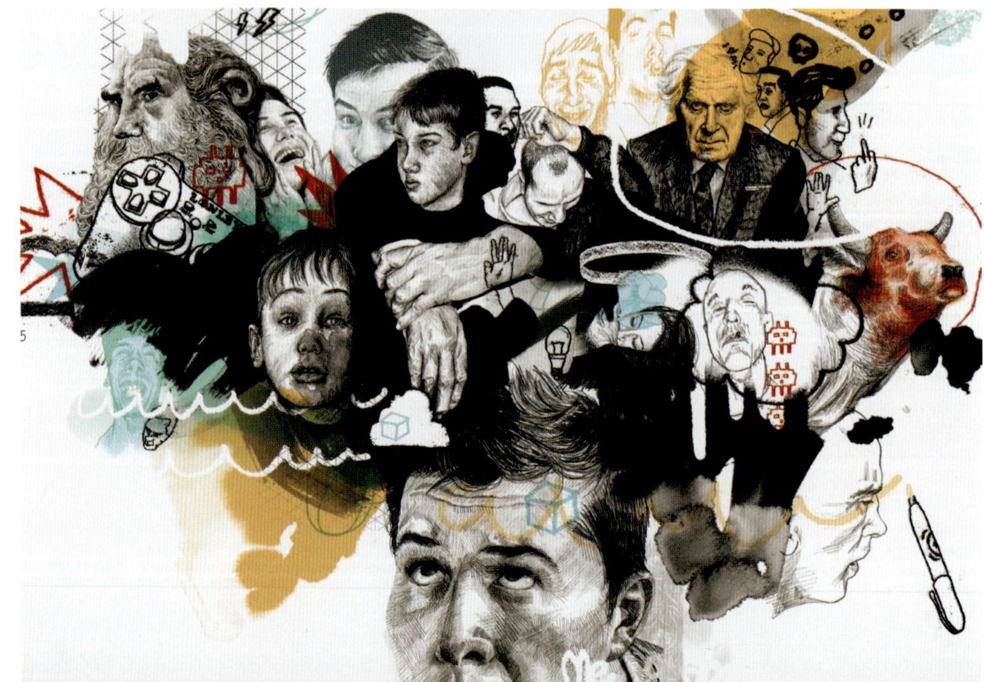

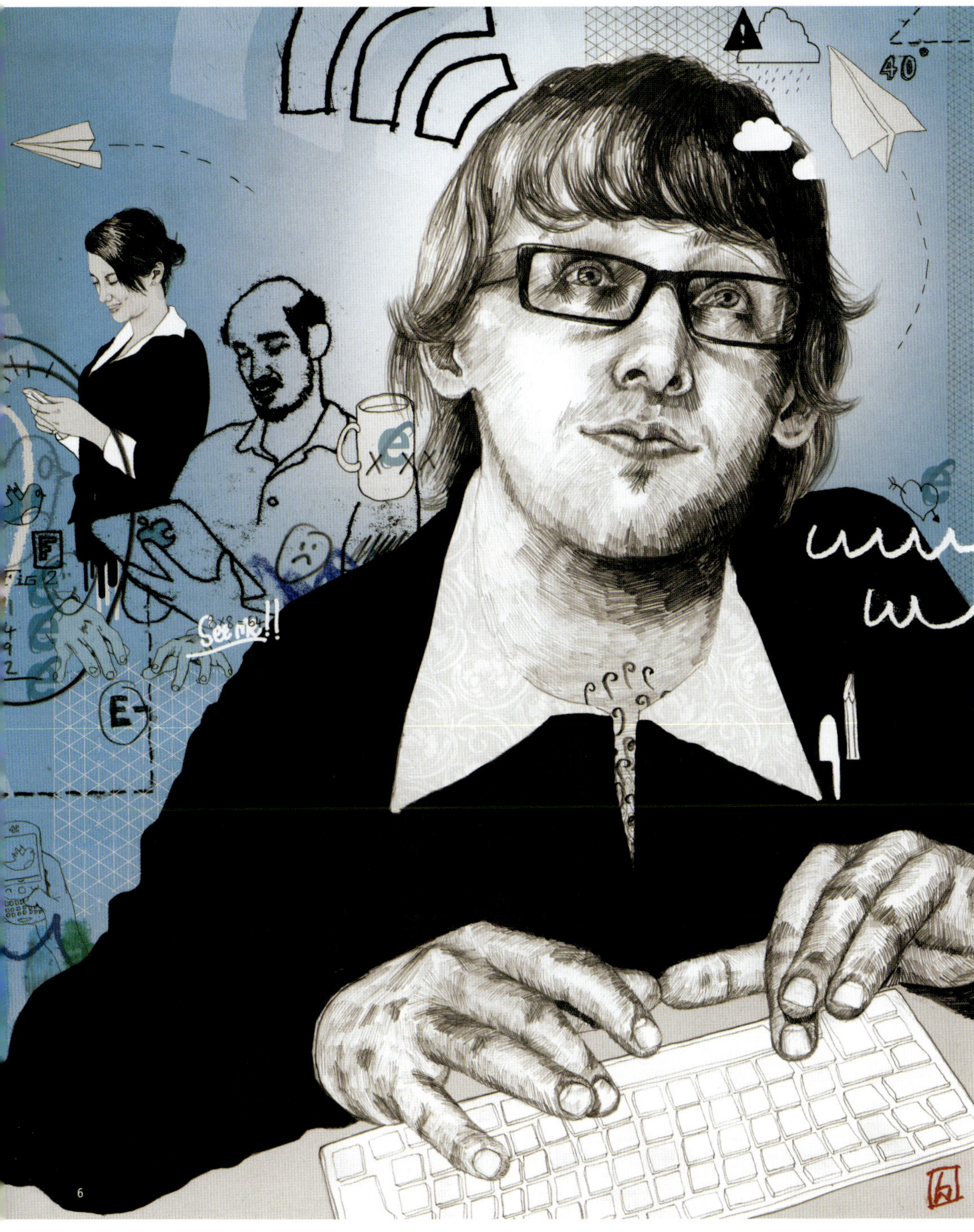

Luke Waller

UK

www.lukewaller.co.uk

1. **Spies** (2011). Personal work. Pencil, mono print, Photoshop

2. **Sir David Attenborough** (2011). Personal work. Pencil, mono print, oil pastel, watercolor, Photoshop

3. **Data From The East** (2011). *The British Medical Journal*. Pencil, mono print, Photoshop

4. **Perceptions** (2011). Promotional work. Pencil, oil pastel, watercolor, Photoshop

5. **Frolicsome Poster** (2011). Promotional work. Pencil, mono print, oil pastel, watercolor, Photoshop

6. **Personal Learning Networks** (2011). *The Times Educational Supplement*. Pencil, mono print, oil pastel, Photoshop

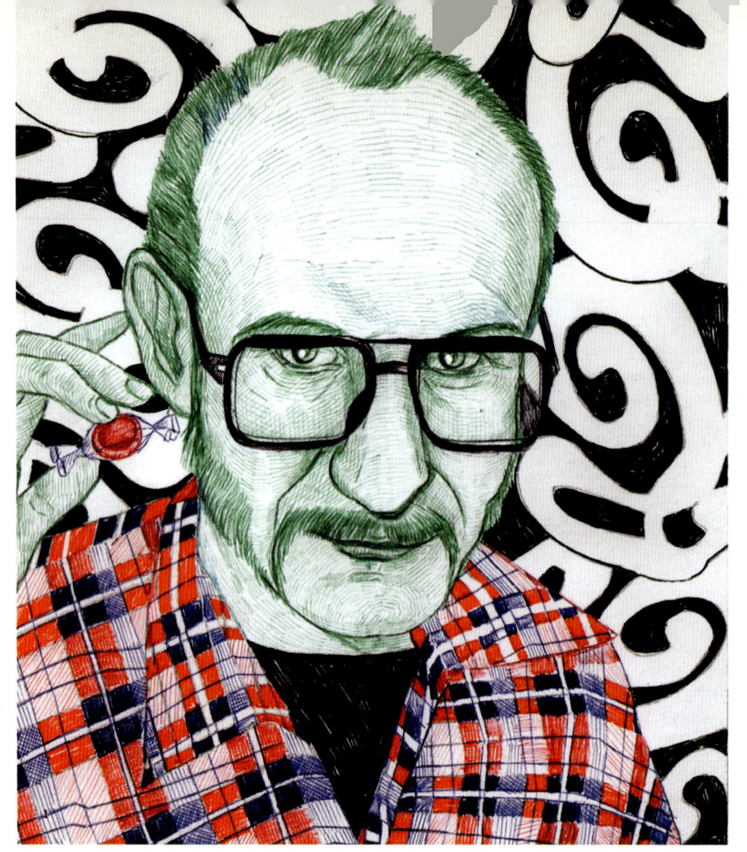
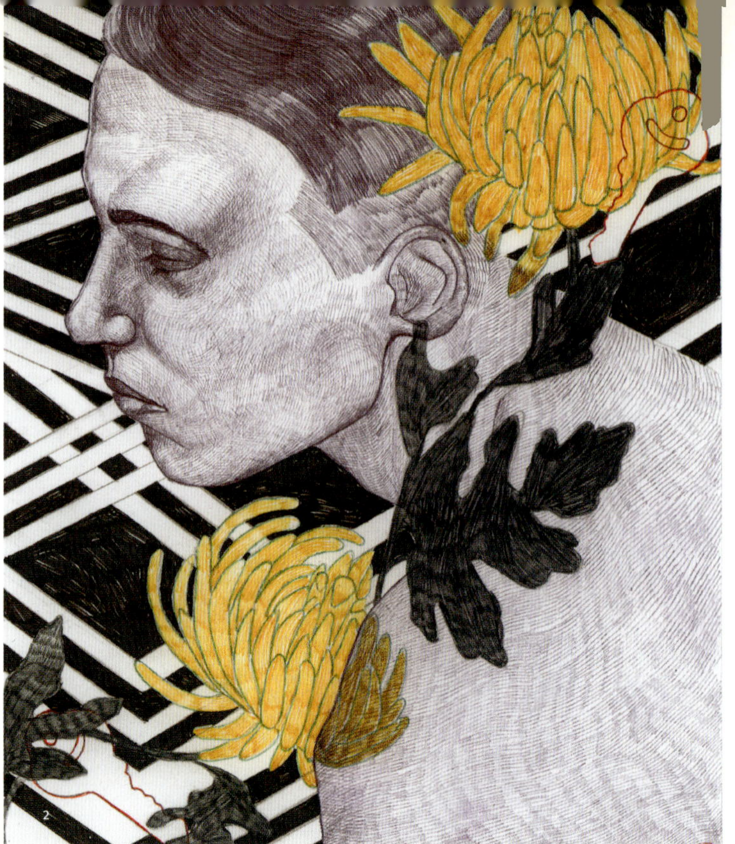
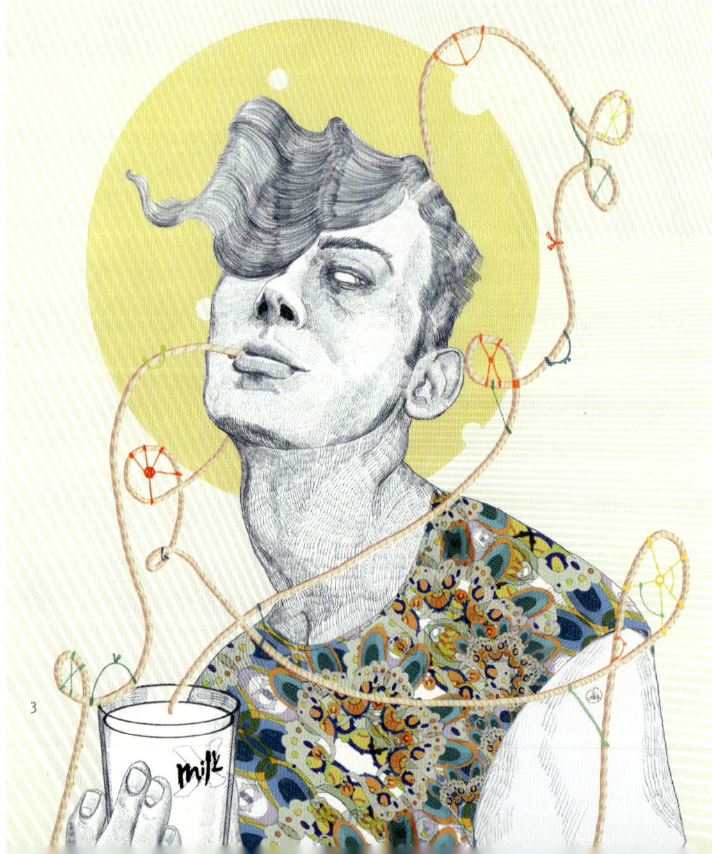
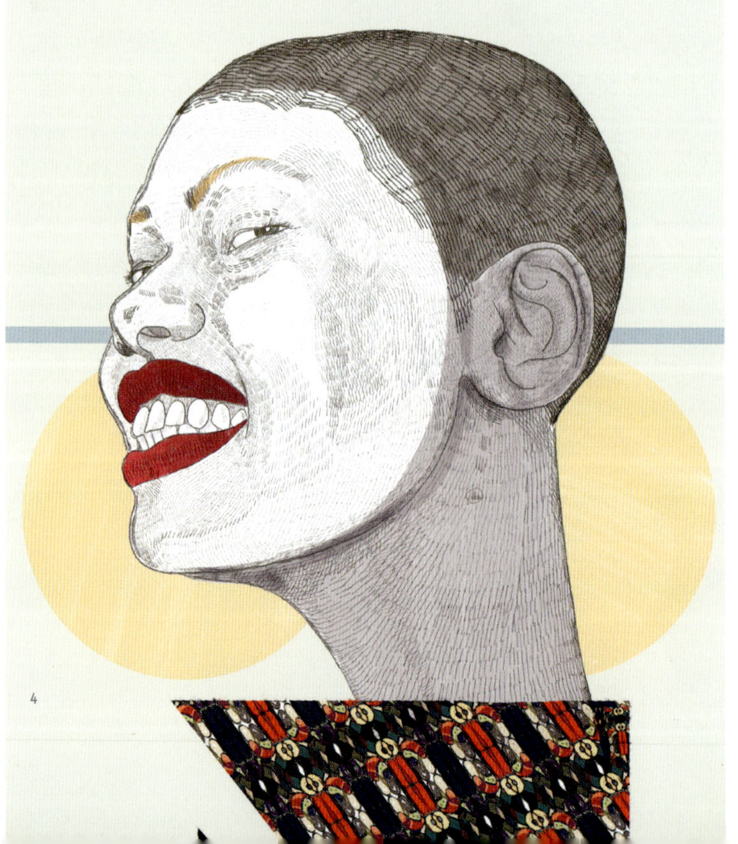

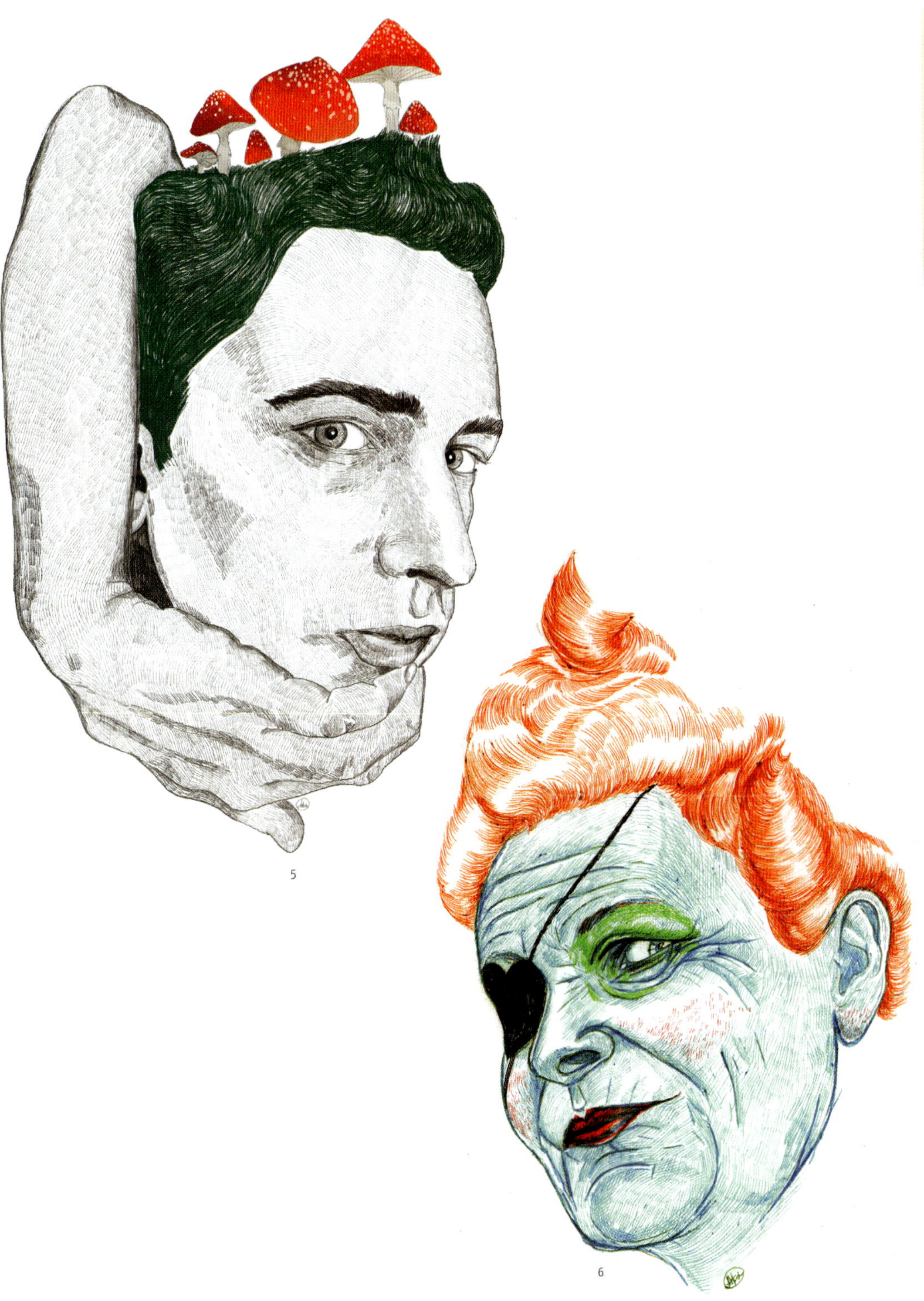

Artaksiniya

Russia

www.artaksiniya.com

1. **Terry** (2011). *Smart Guide*. Ball pen on paper

2. **Melancholy** (2011). Personal work. Ball pen on paper

3. **Untitled** (2010). *Milk X Magazine*. Ball pen, digital

4. **Smile** (2010). Personal work. Ball pen, pencil, collage

5. **Untitled** (2011). Fear Konstruktor promo. Ball pen, pencil

6. **Vivienne** (2011). *Smart Guide*. Ball pen on paper

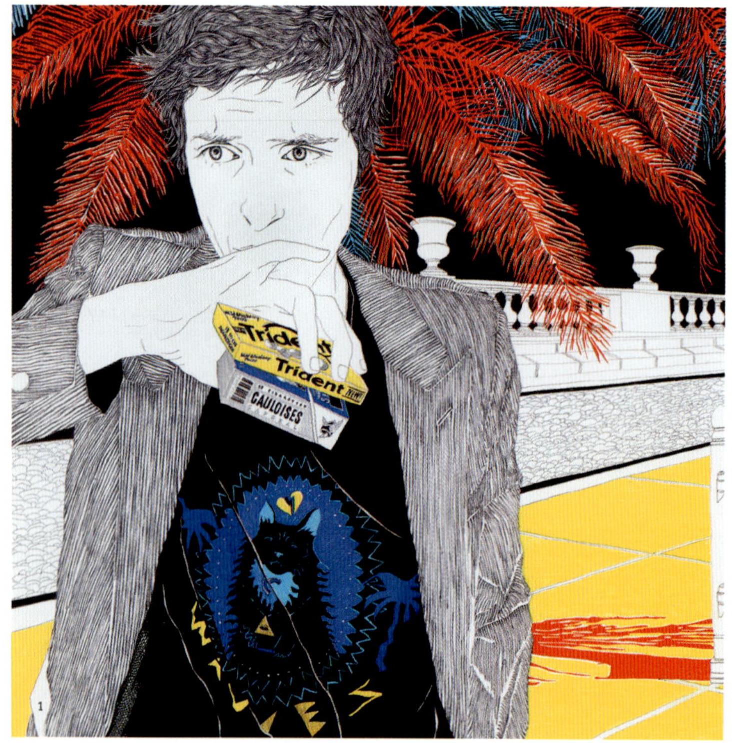
Trident
GAULOISES

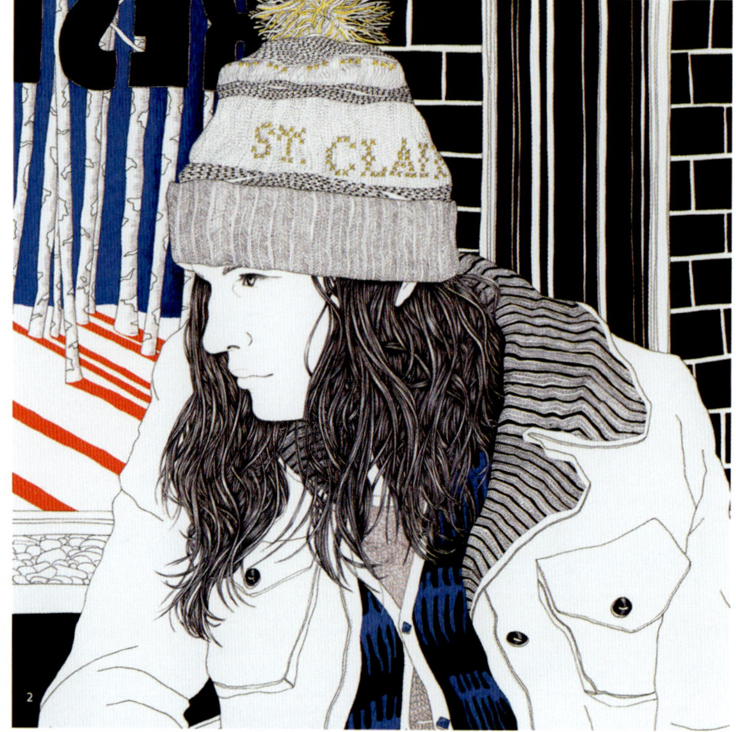
ST. CLAIR

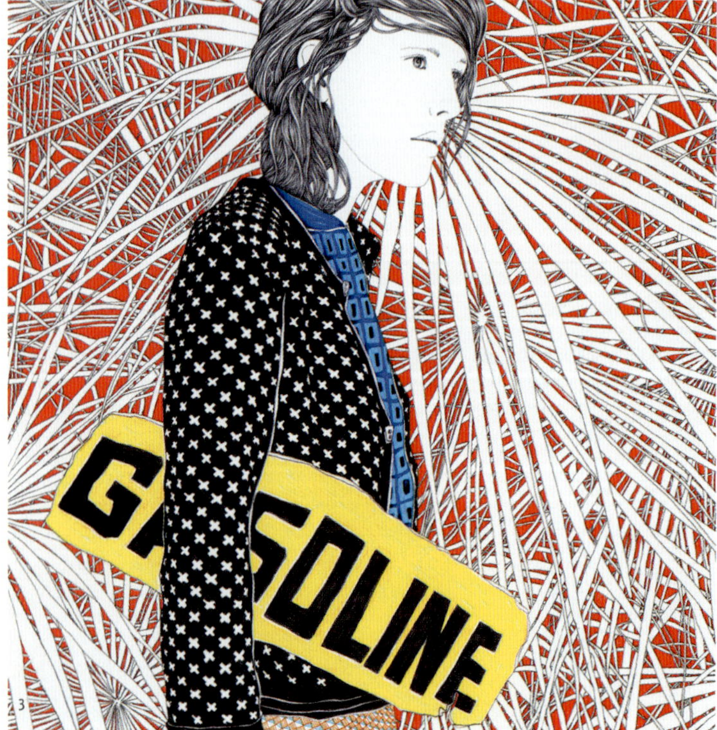
GASOLINE

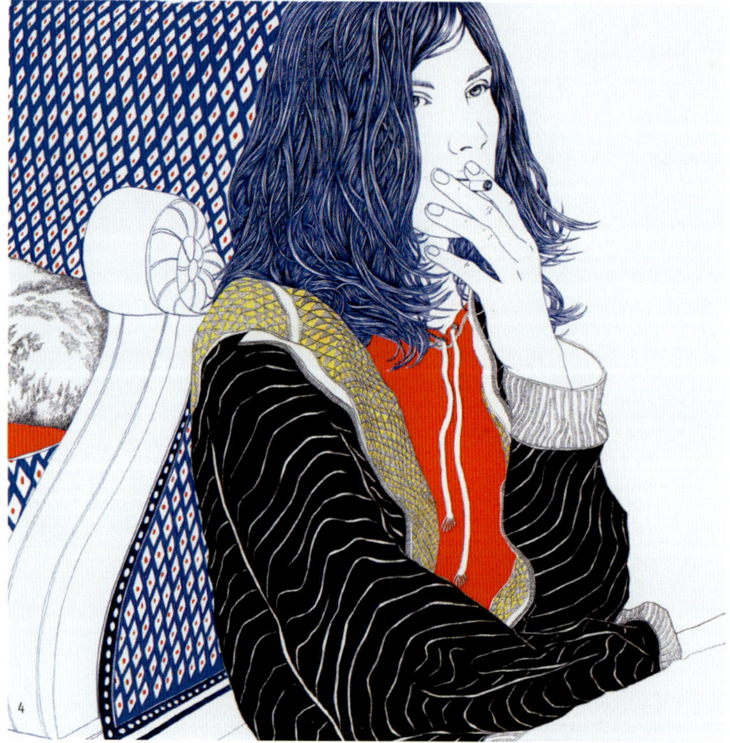

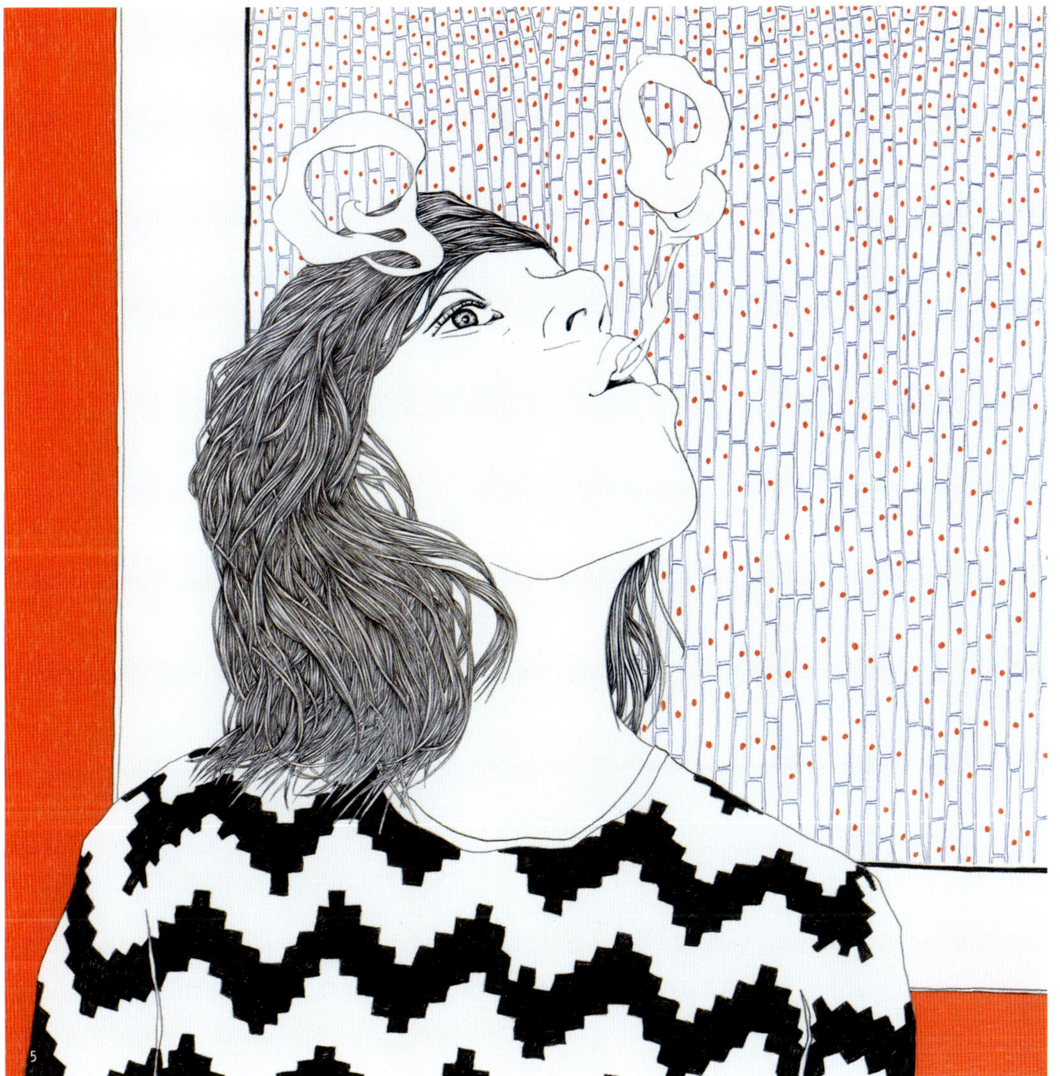

Carine Brancowitz

France

www.carinebrancowitz.com

1. **La Nouvelle Athènes** (2011). Personal work. Ballpoint, felt tip pens, pencil

2. **la Nuit du Doute** (2010). Personal work. Ballpoint, felt tip pens, pencil

3. **Le Cantique des Créatures** (2010). Personal work. Ballpoint, felt tip pens, pencil

4. **le Colloque Singulier** (2011). Personal work. Ballpoint, felt tip pens, pencil

5. **Smoke Rings** (2012). Personal work. Ballpoint, felt tip pens, pencil

Experimental

Experimentation is about pushing the boundaries of recognizability.
It can refer to the technique employed, which today ranges from
pencil drawings to digital image making. Other techniques such as
collage and the combination of image and text succeed in portraying
the multifaceted aspects of a personality. But experimentation
can also refer to a stylistic device whereby the portrait becomes
abstracted and the sitter is reduced to its essential characteristics.

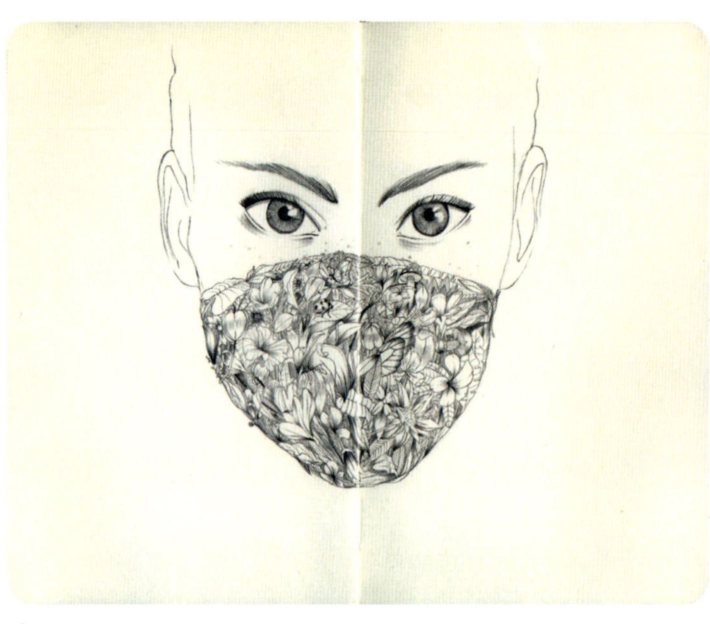

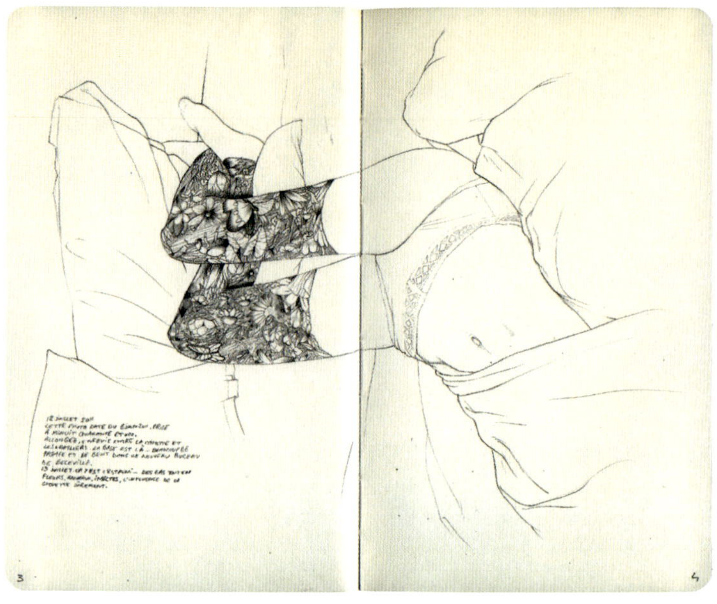

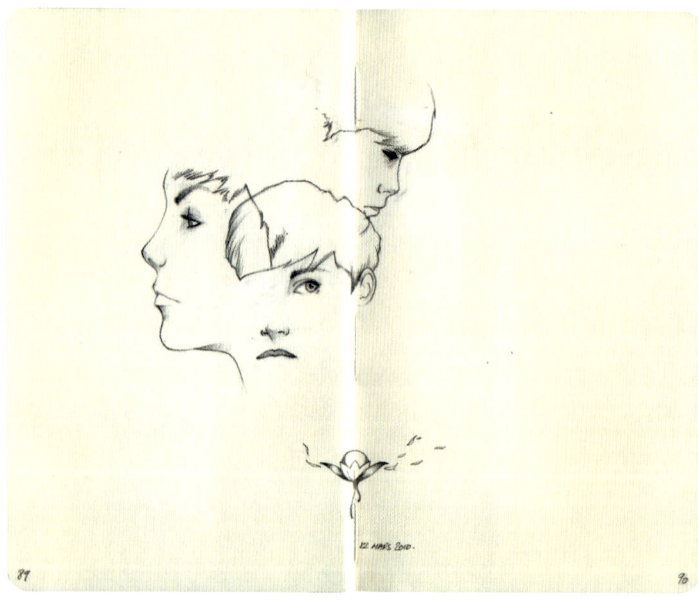

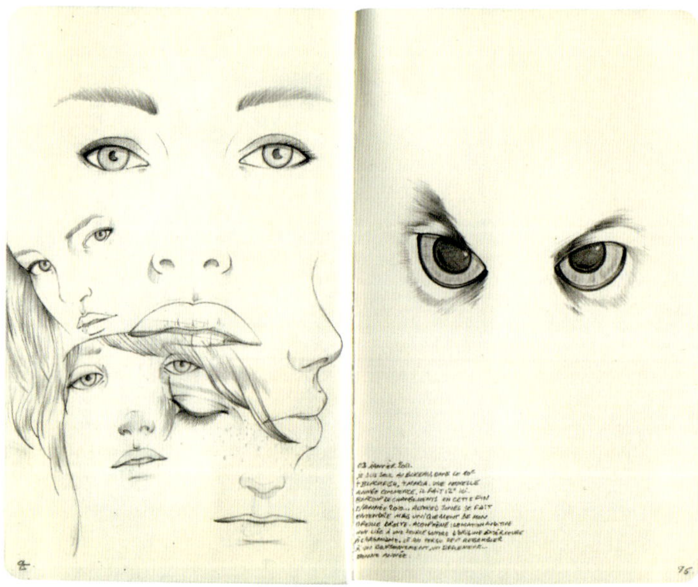

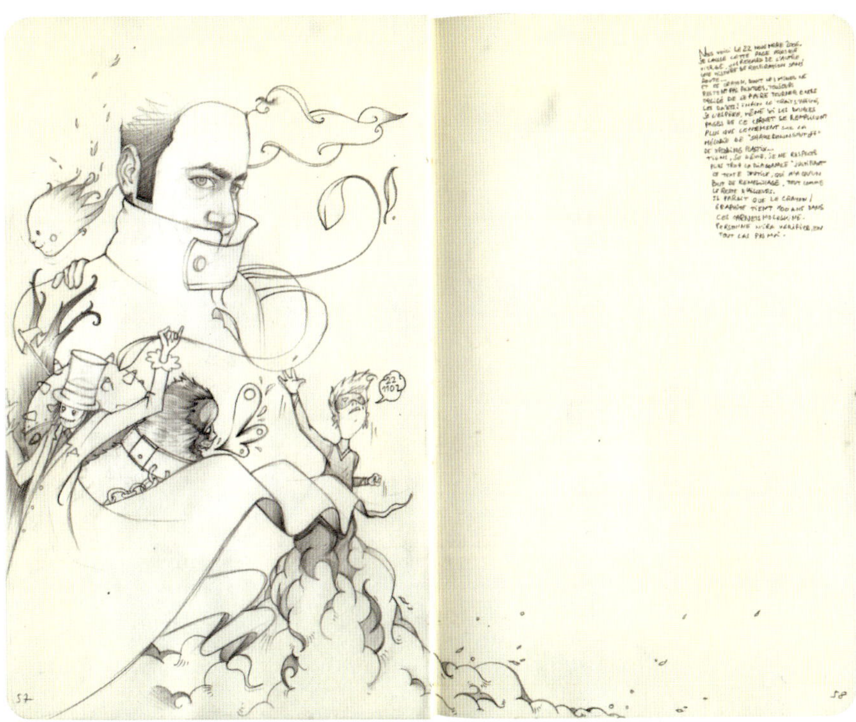

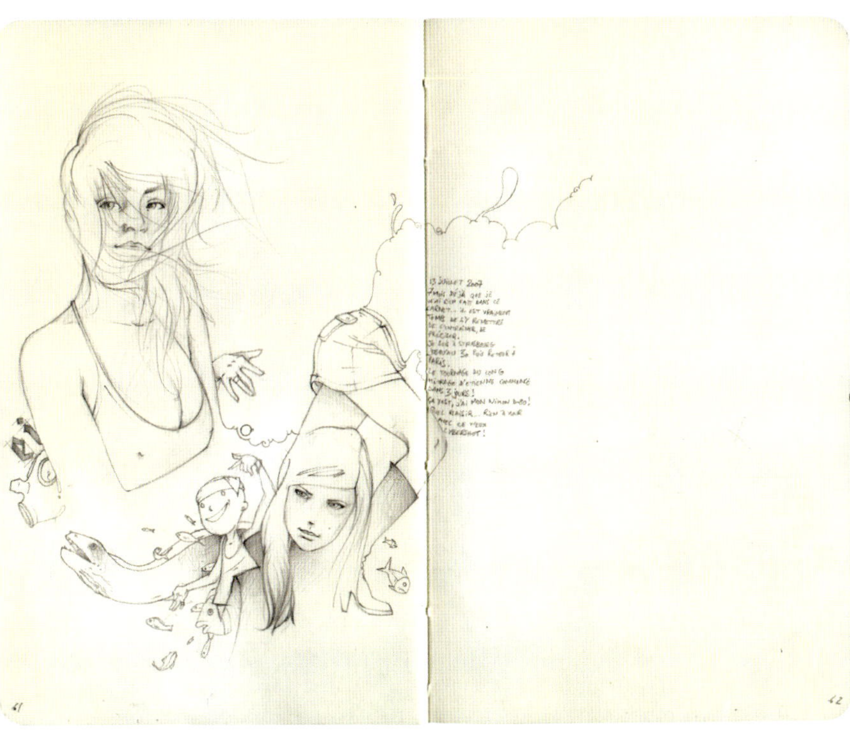

Philippe Constantinesco
aka Faunesque

France

www.faunesque.com

1. **No Title** (2009 to 2011). Pencil

2. **No Title** (2009 to 2011). Pencil

3. **No Title** (2009 to 2011). Pencil

4. **No Title** (2009 to 2011). Pencil

5. **No Title** (2009 to 2011). Pencil

6. **No Title** (2009 to 2011). Pencil

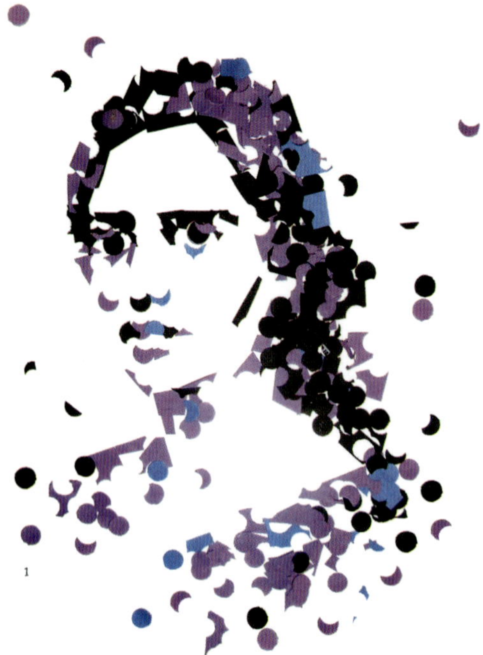

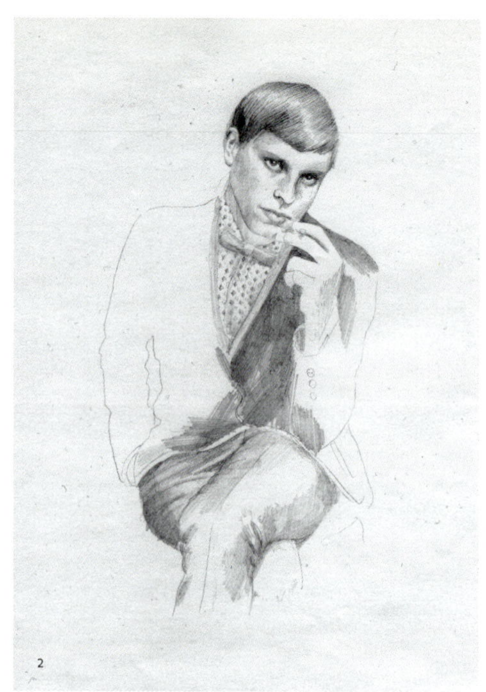

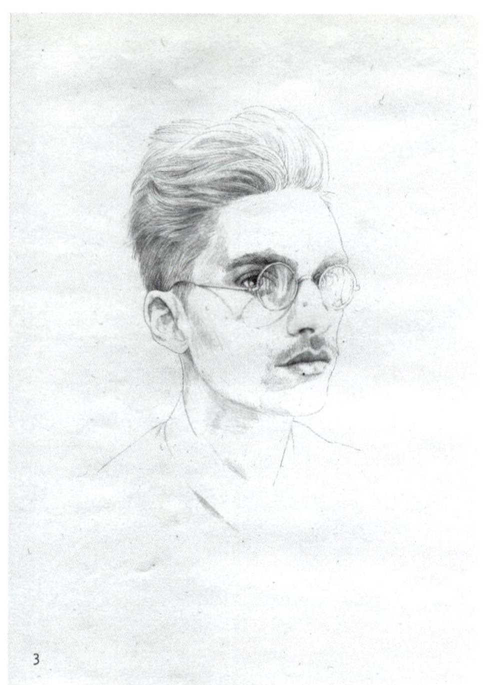

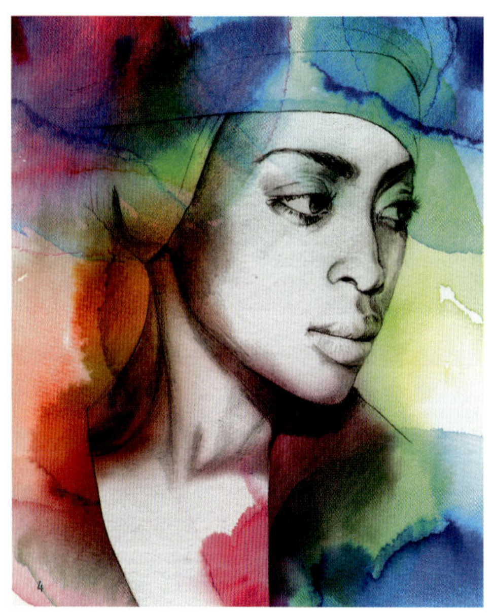

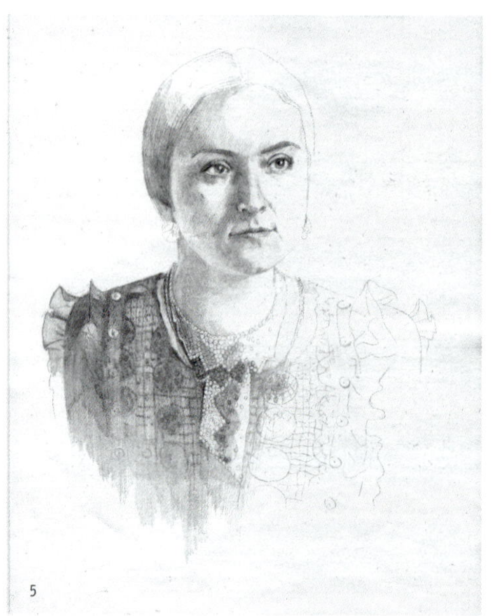

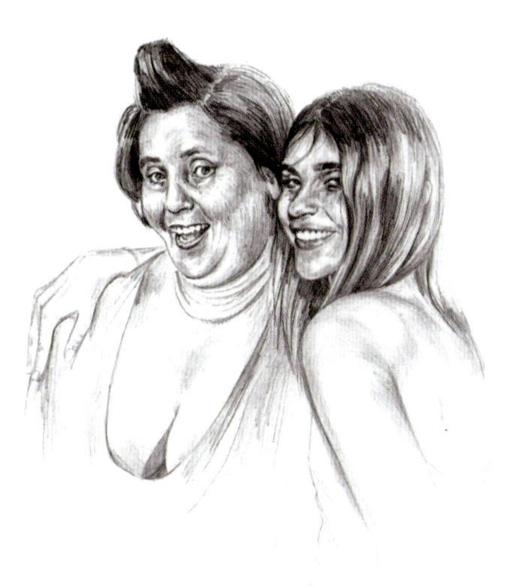

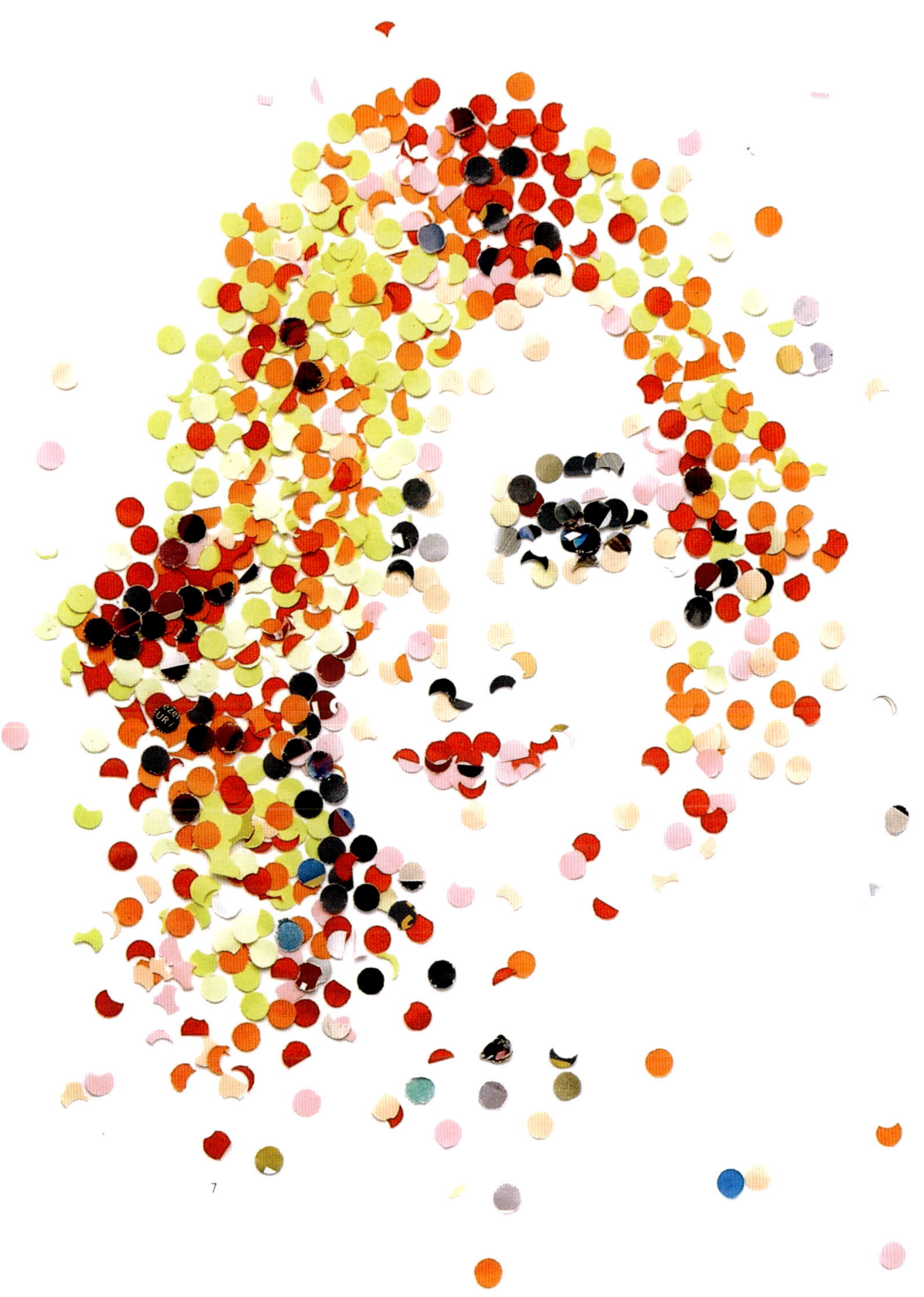

Elisabeth Moch

Germany

www.elisabethmoch.com

1. **Taryn** (2010). *Esquire Russia*. Colored confetti

2. **August Sander** (2008). *Fashiontale Magazine*. Pencil

3. **August Sander** (2008). *Fashiontale Magazine*. Pencil

4. **Erykah Badu** (2010). Uptown Strut magazine. Pencil, watercolor, Photoshop

5. **August Sander** (2008). *Fashiontale Magazine*. Pencil

6. **Suzy and Carine** (2010). Fashion label VIER5. Pencil

7. **Madonna** (2007). *Zeit Magazin*. Colored confetti

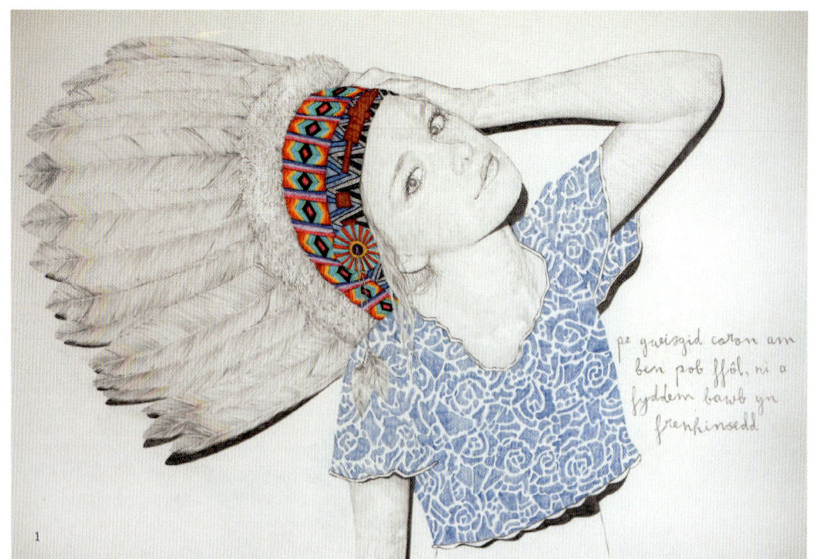

pe gwisgid coron am
ben pob ffôl, ni a
fyddem bawb yn
frenhinedd

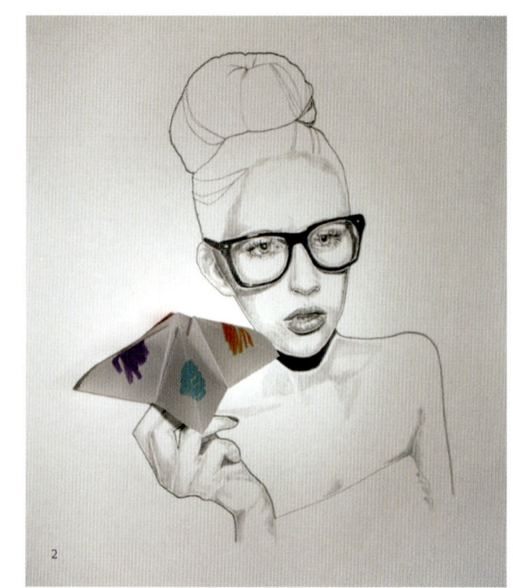

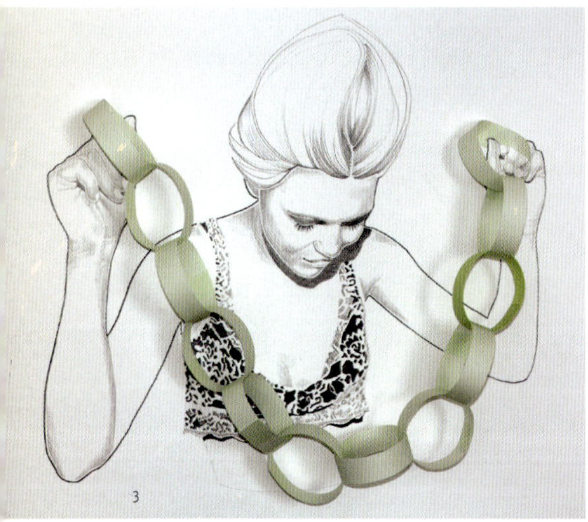

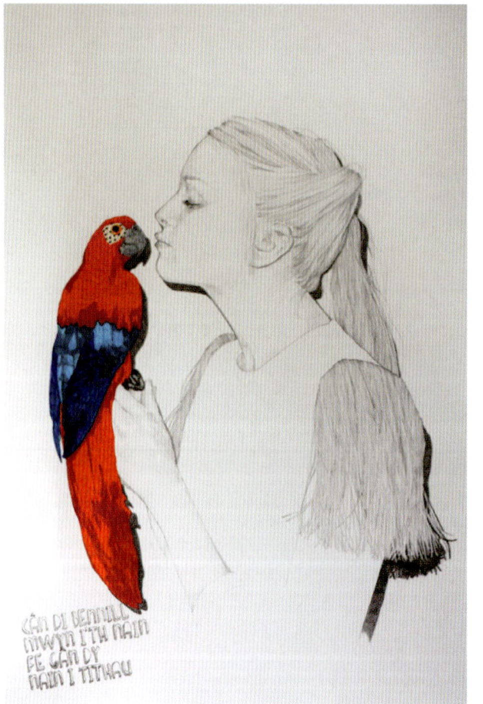

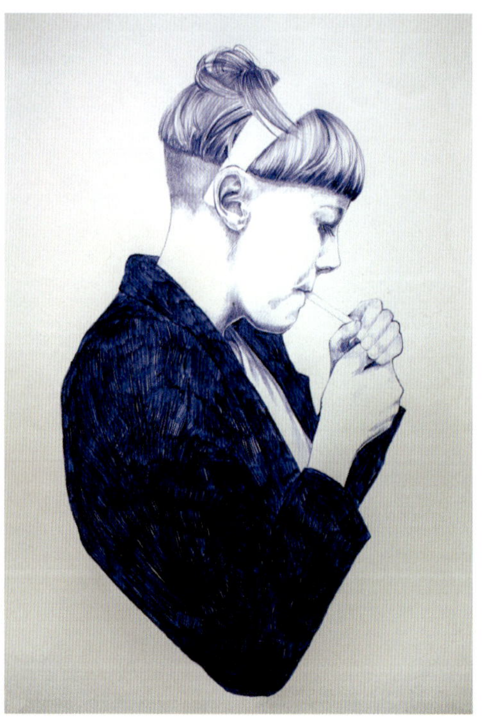

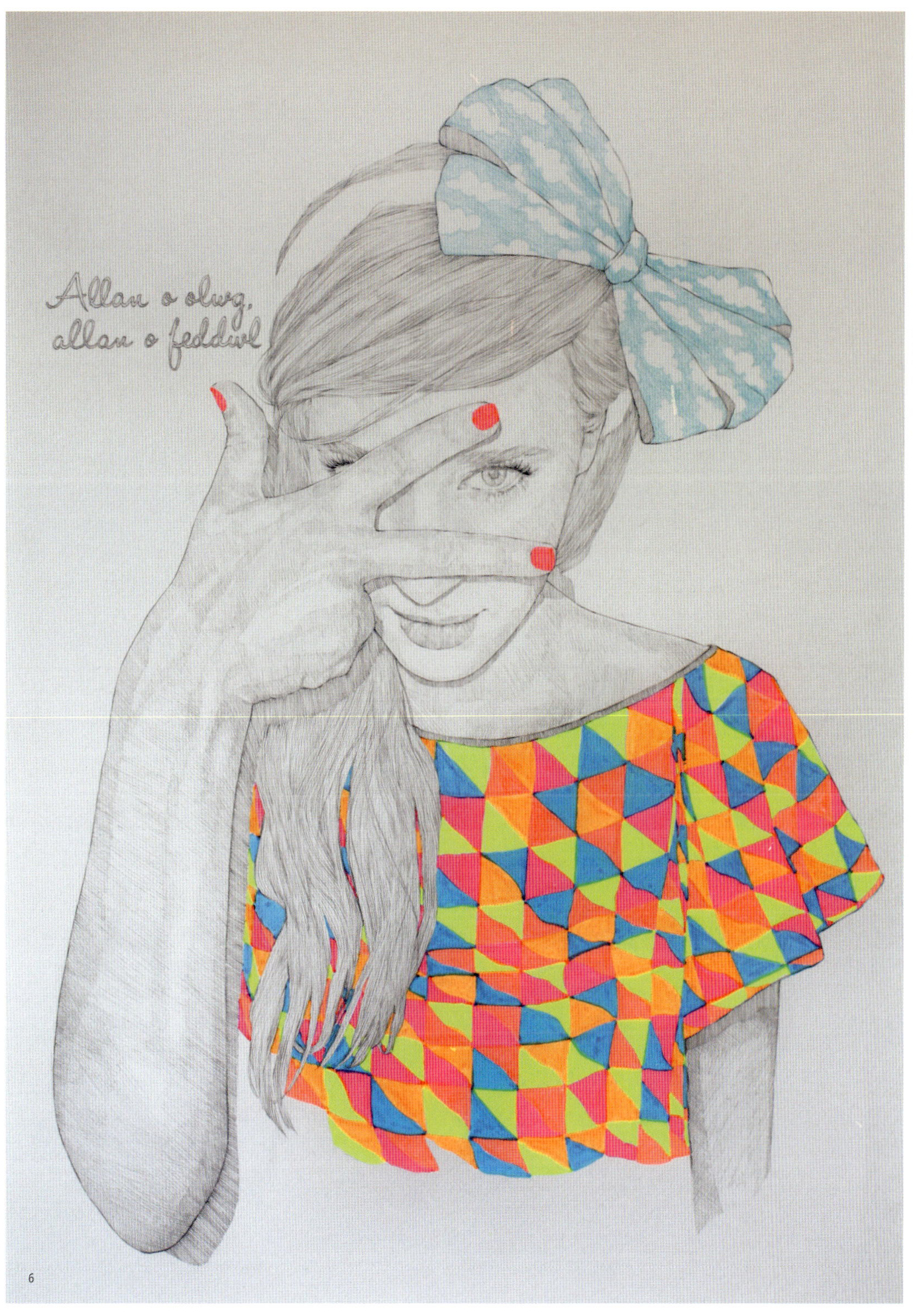

Niki Pilkington
UK

www.nikipilkington.com

1. **We would all be kings...** (2011). Exhibition piece. Mixed media

2. **Fortune Teller** (2010). Personal work. Mixed media, collage

3. **Paper chains** (2010). Personal work. Mixed media, collage

4. **Sing to your grandmother a sweet song...** (2010). Exhibition piece. Mixed media

5. **Too much is never enough** (2010). Exhibition piece. Ball pen

6. **Out of sight out of mind** (2011). Exhibition piece. Mixed media

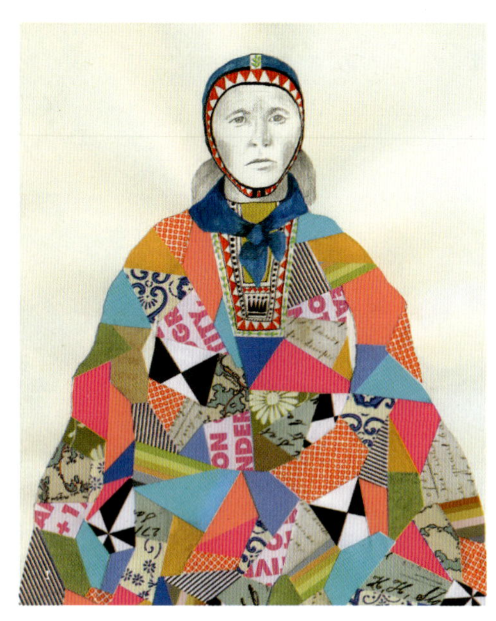

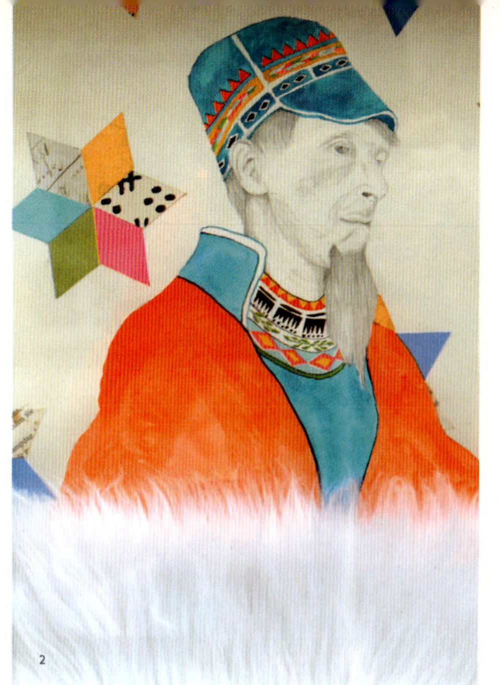

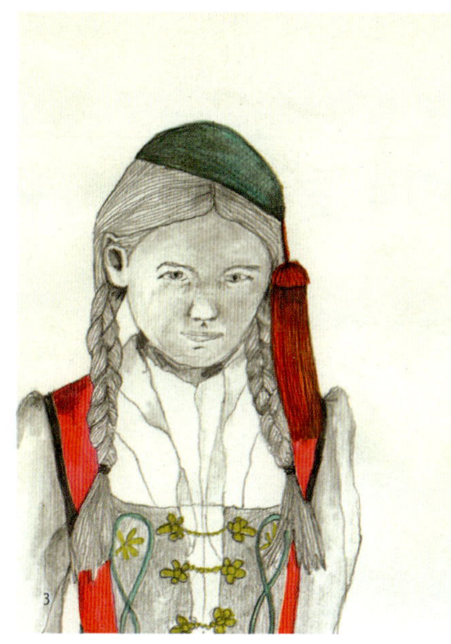

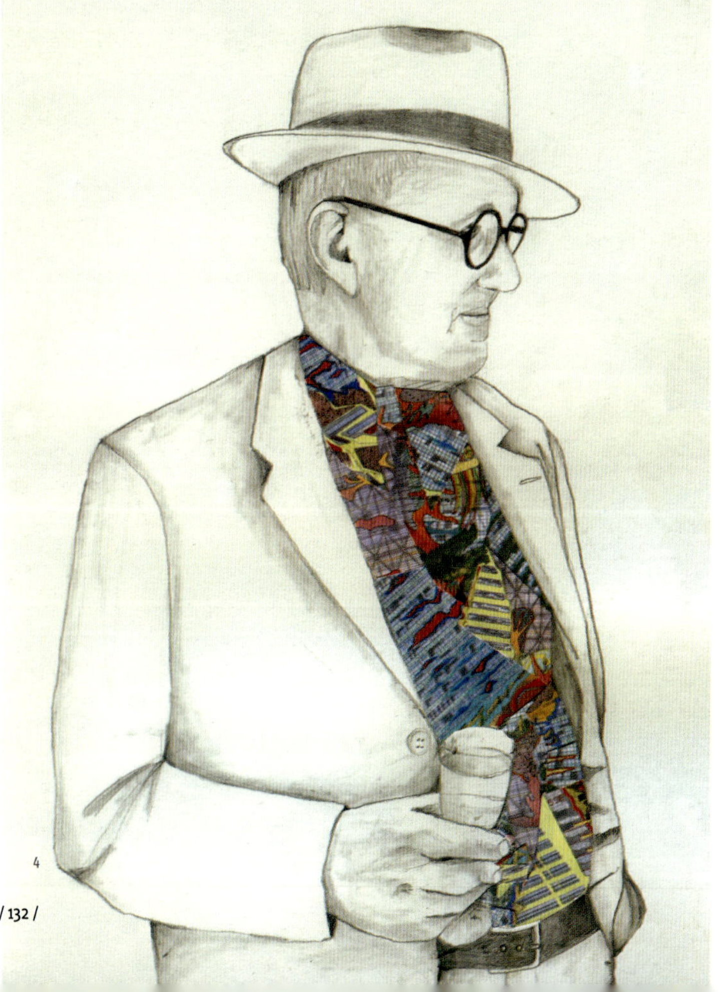

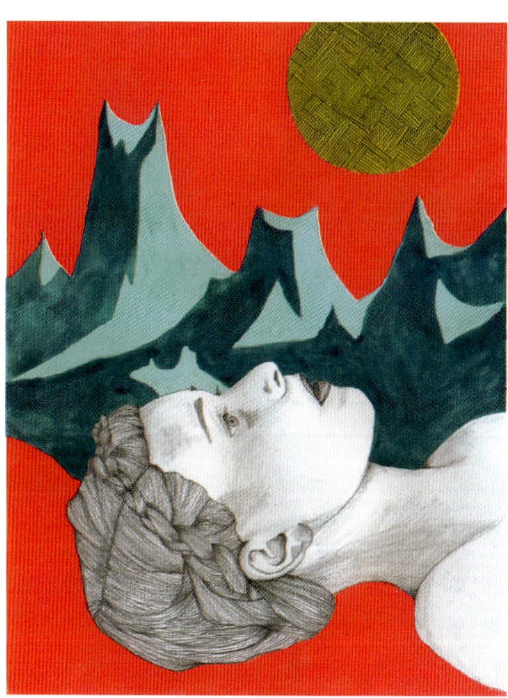

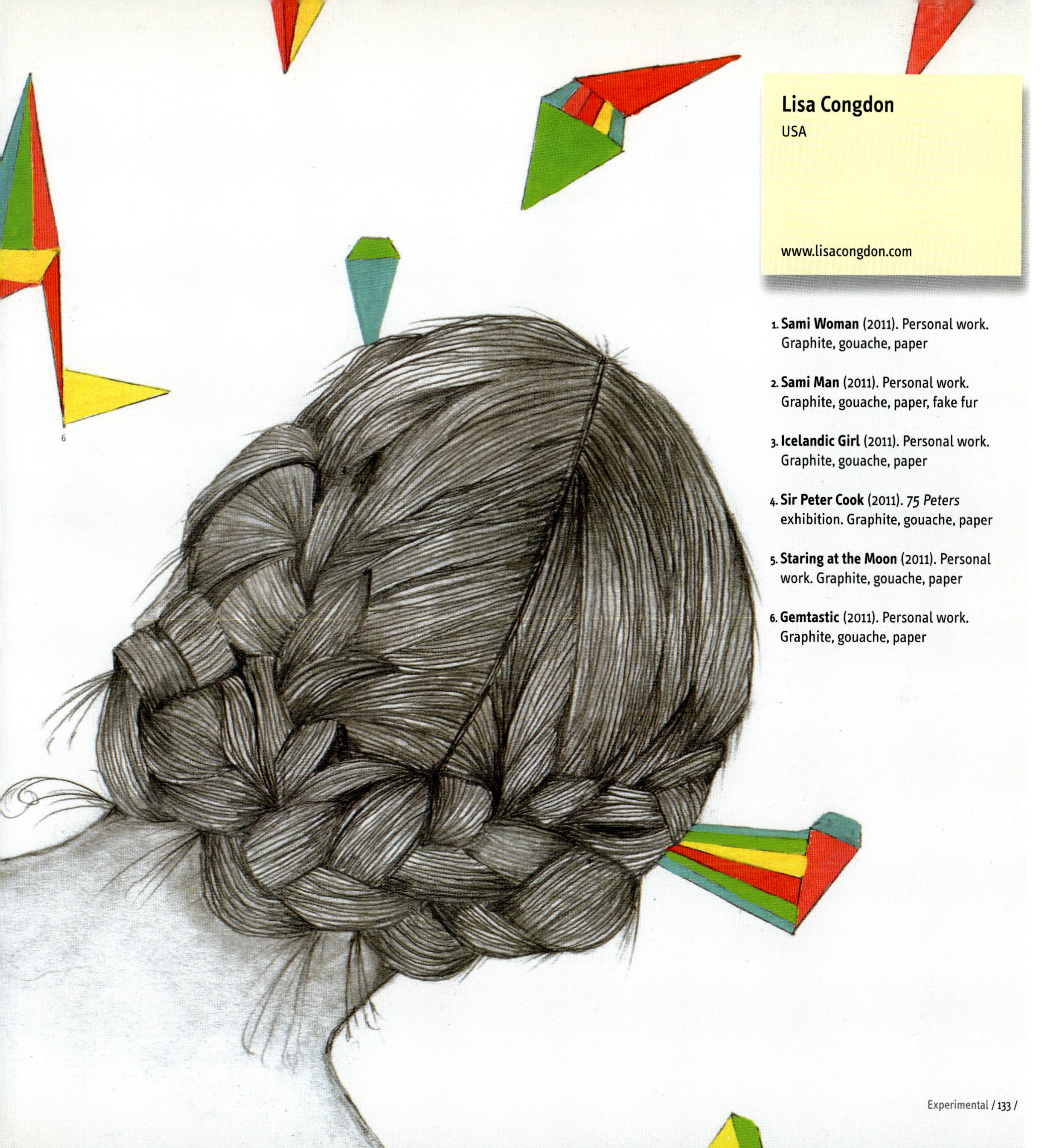

Lisa Congdon
USA

www.lisacongdon.com

1. **Sami Woman** (2011). Personal work. Graphite, gouache, paper

2. **Sami Man** (2011). Personal work. Graphite, gouache, paper, fake fur

3. **Icelandic Girl** (2011). Personal work. Graphite, gouache, paper

4. **Sir Peter Cook** (2011). *75 Peters* exhibition. Graphite, gouache, paper

5. **Staring at the Moon** (2011). Personal work. Graphite, gouache, paper

6. **Gemtastic** (2011). Personal work. Graphite, gouache, paper

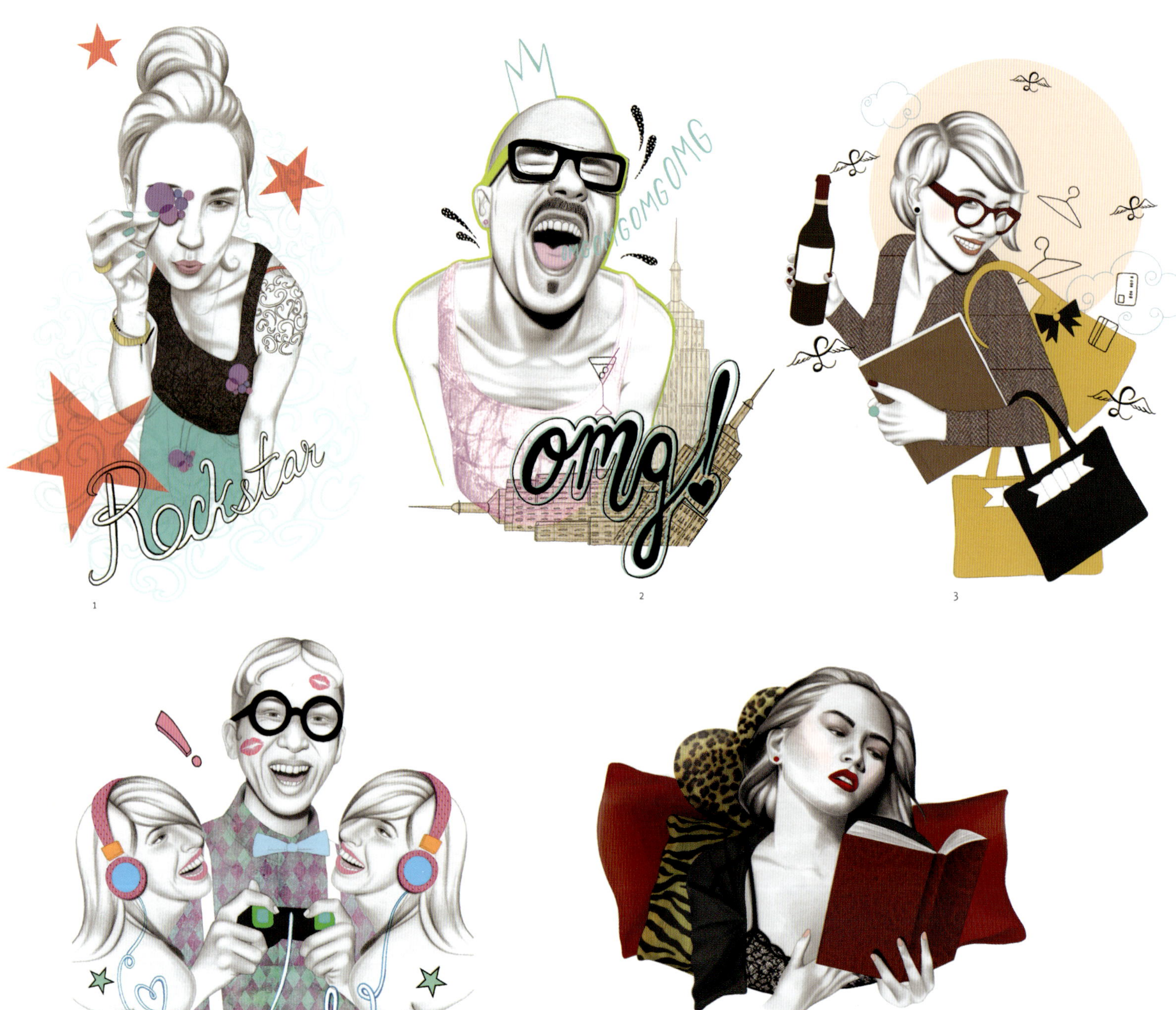

Rockstar
omg!
OMGOMGOMG
geek

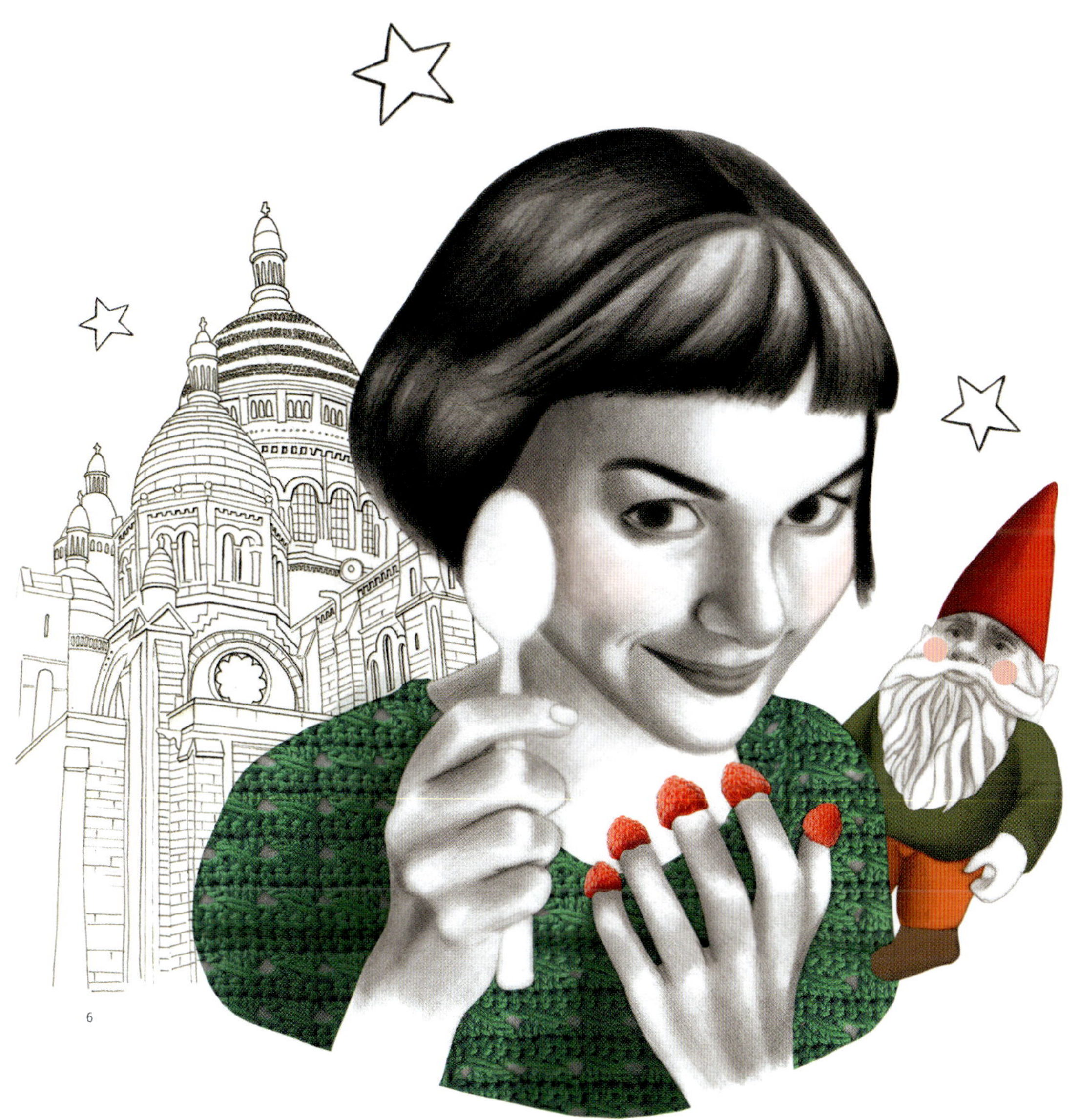

6

Nicole Jarecz
France

Agency: Colagene, Illustration Clinic
www.colagene.com/fr/illustration/
nicole-jarecz

1. **Rockstar** (2011). Personal work. Pencil, pen, found texture, Photoshop

2. **OMG** (2011). Personal work. Pencil, pen, found texture, Photoshop

3. **Untitled** (2011). *Company Magazine.* Pencil, pen, found texture, Photoshop

4. **Untitled** (2011). *Elle girl* Japan. Pencil, pen, found texture, Photoshop

5. **Untitled** (2010). *Be Magazine.* Pencil, pen, found texture, Photoshop

6- **Untitled** (2010). *Glamour Magazine* Germany. Pencil, pen, found texture, Photoshop

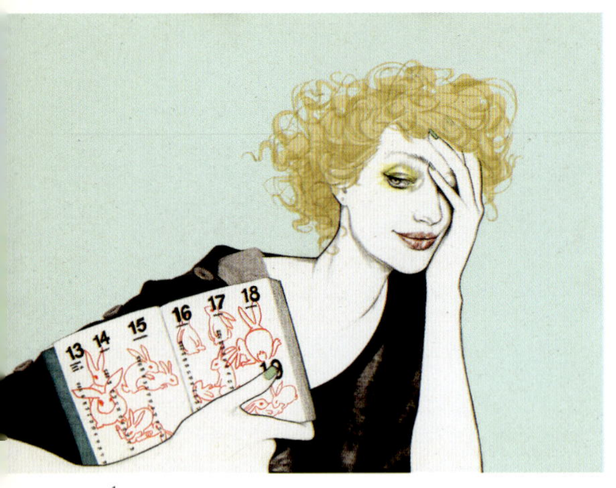

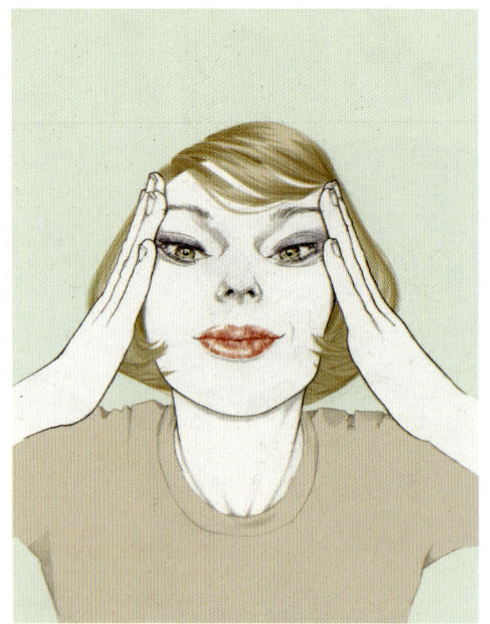

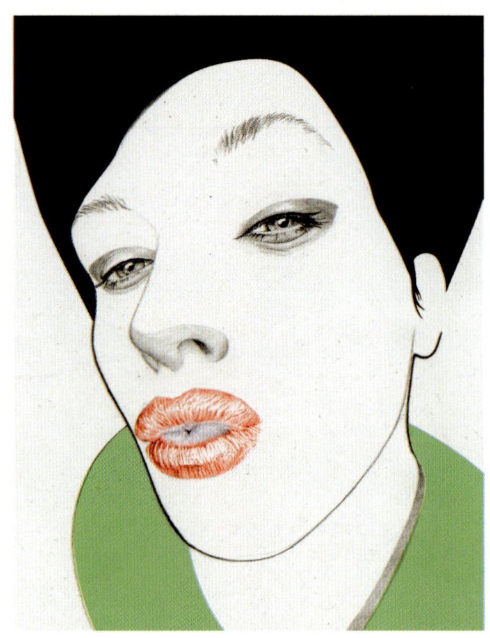

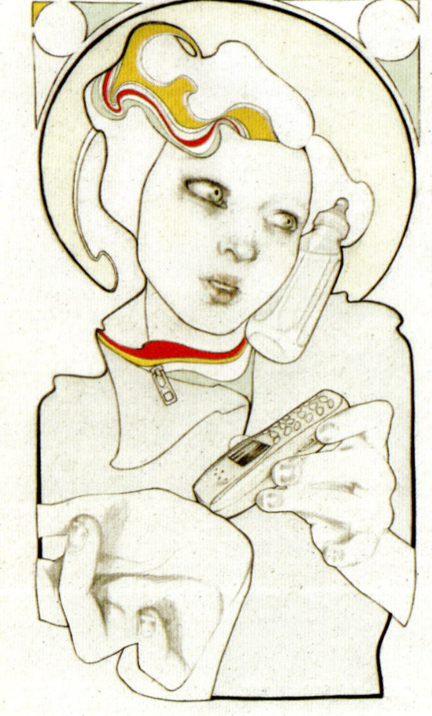

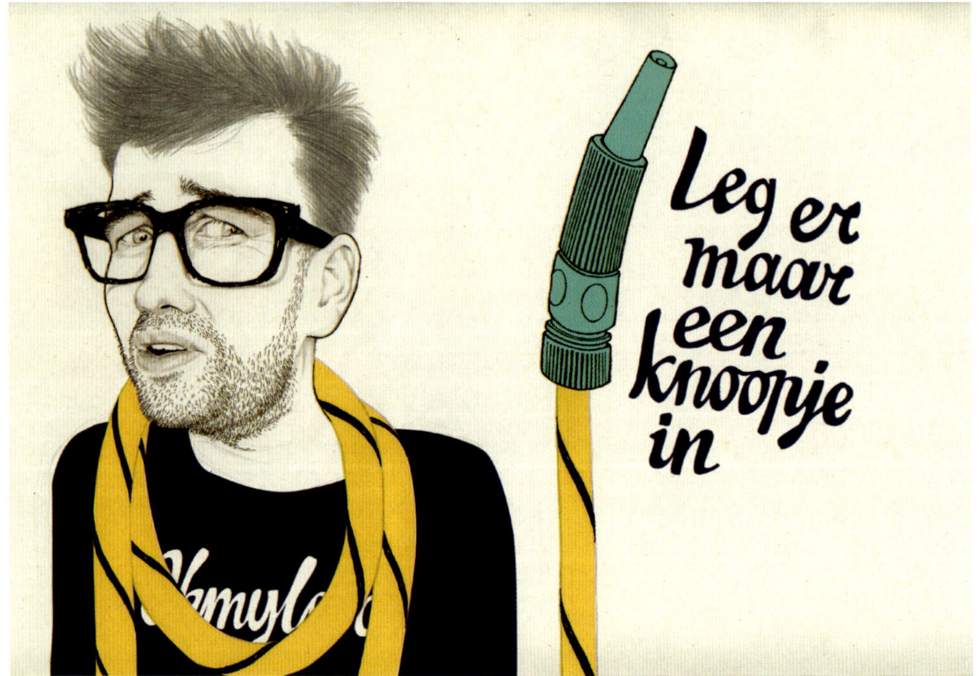

Leg er
maar
een
knoopje
in

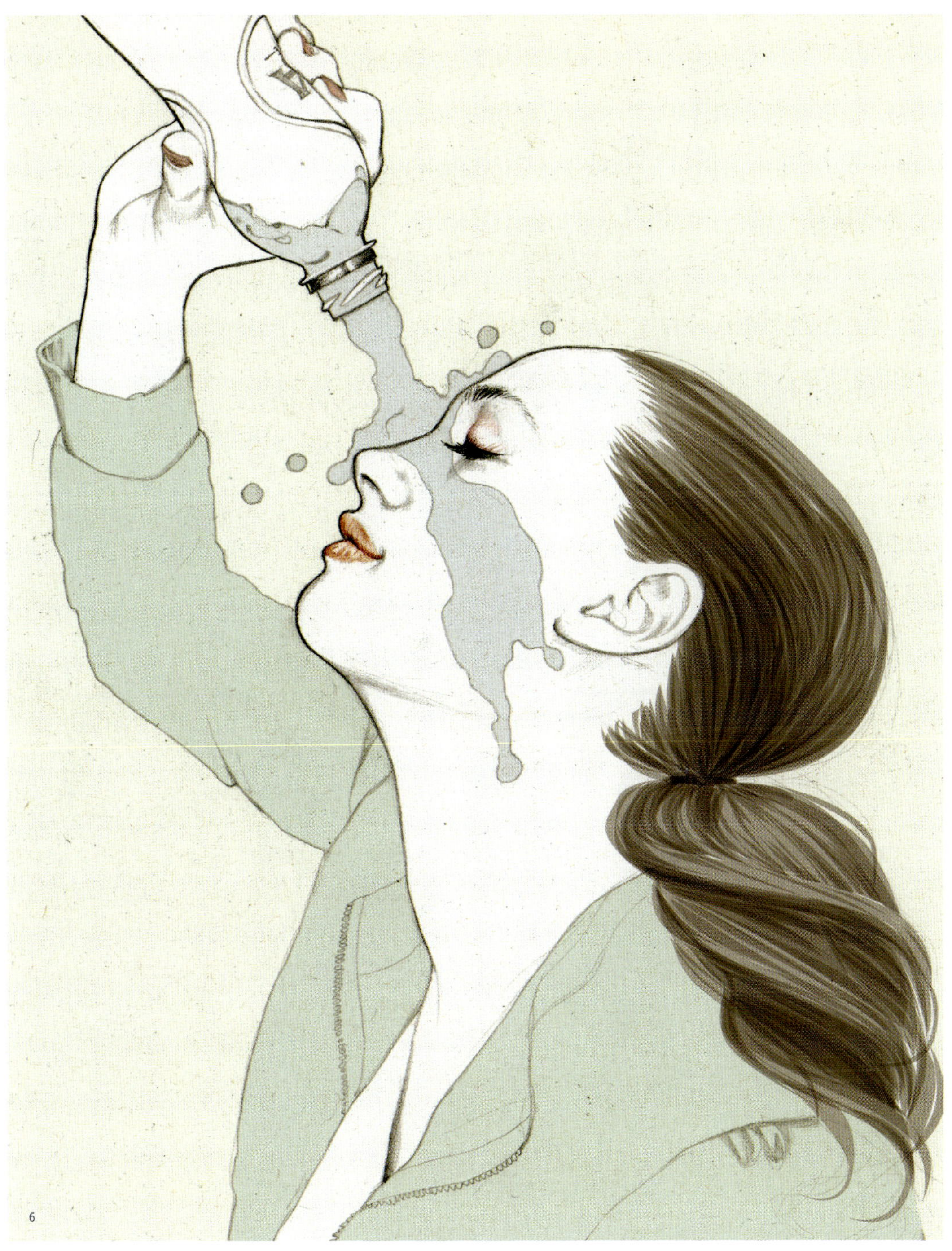

Denise van Leeuwen

Netherlands

www.denisevanleeuwen.com

1. **Elke Dag Seks** (2011). *Viva.* Pen, pencil on paper, colored in Photoshop

2. **Pulling Skin** (2011). *Annabelle.* Pen, pencil on paper, colored in Photoshop

3. **Kusetiquette** (2011). *ELLE* NL. Pen, pencil on paper, colored in Photoshop

4. **Moederschapsideologie** (2007). *Lof.* Pen, pencil on paper, colored in Photoshop

5. **Sterilisatie** (2011). *Lof.* Pen, pencil on paper, colored in Photoshop

6. **Water** (2011). *Annabelle.* Pen, pencil on paper, colored in Photoshop

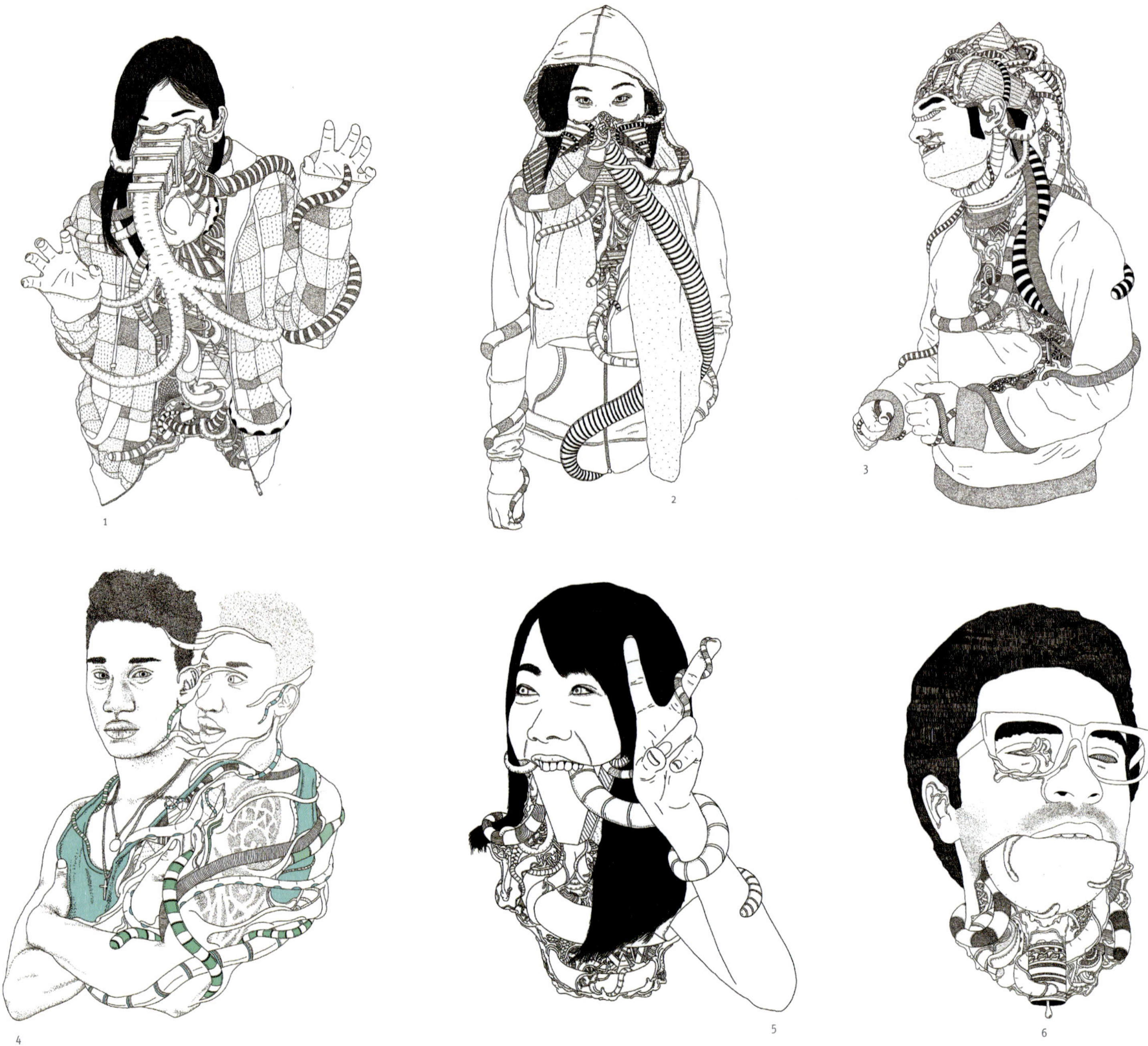

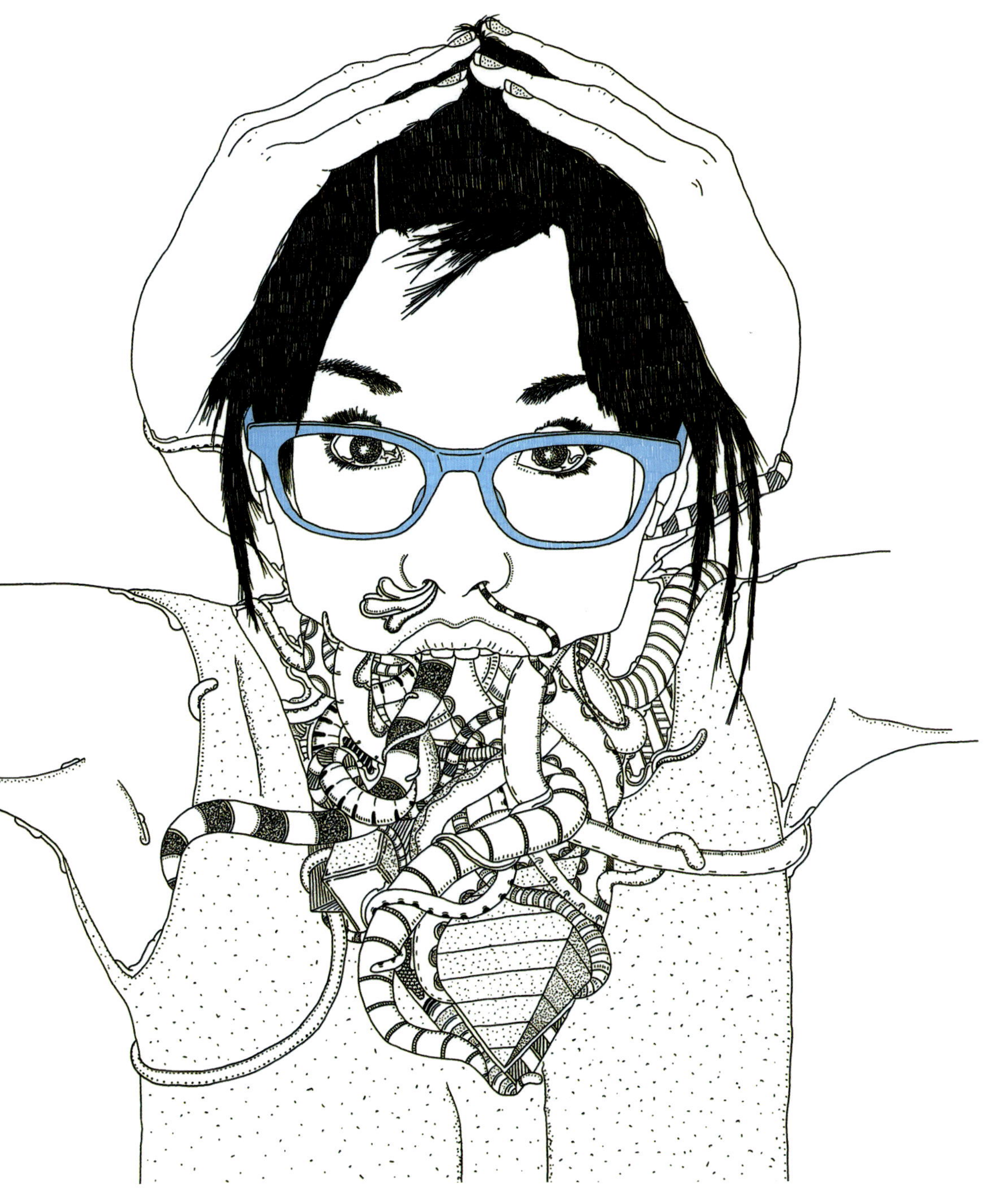

Ant Hayes
Australia

www.antisant.com

1. **Taylor** (2009). Personal work. Digital

2. **Shirley** (2009). Personal work. Digital

3. **Cory** (2010). Personal work. Digital

4. **Misfit** (2011). BBC Worldwide. digital

5. **Mieko** (2010). Personal work. Digital

6. **Cs Rucker** (2009). Cs Rucker. Digital

7. **Lantian** (2009). Personal work. Digital

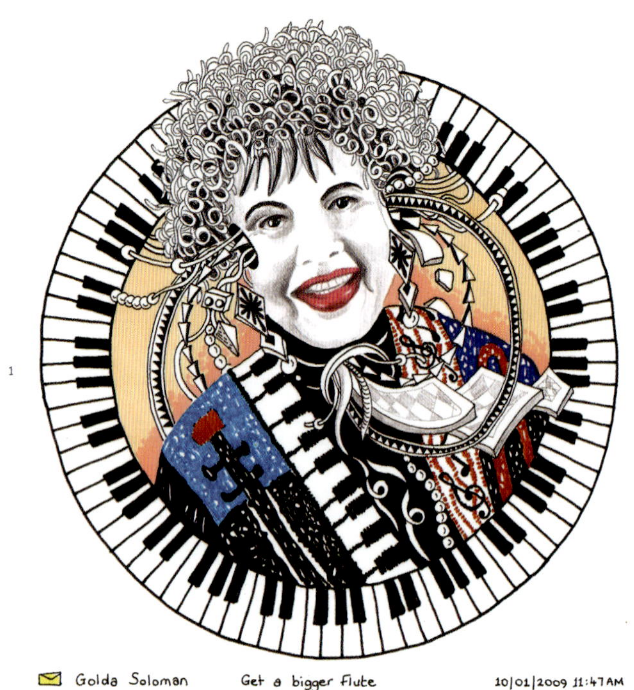

✉ Golda Soloman   Get a bigger flute   10|01|2009 11:47AM

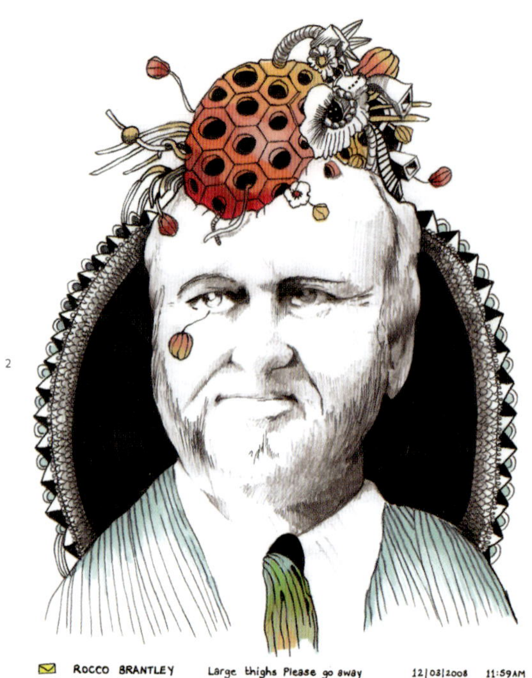

✉ ROCCO BRANTLEY   Large thighs Please go away   12|03|2008 11:59AM

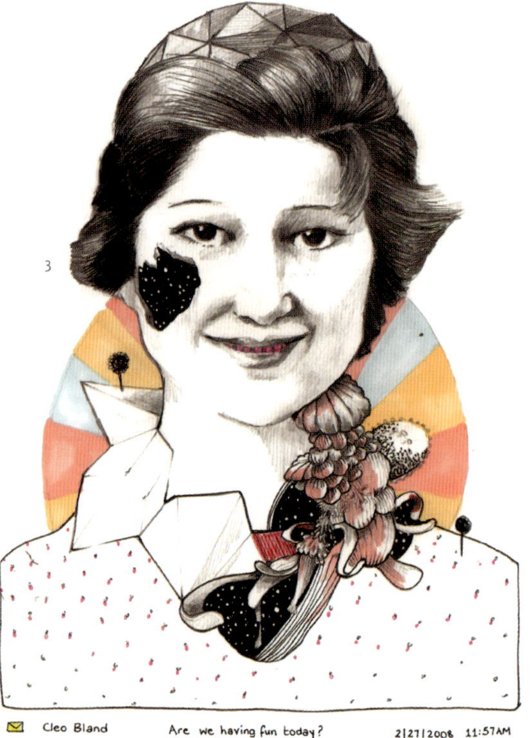

✉ Cleo Bland   Are we having fun today?   2|27|2008 11:57AM

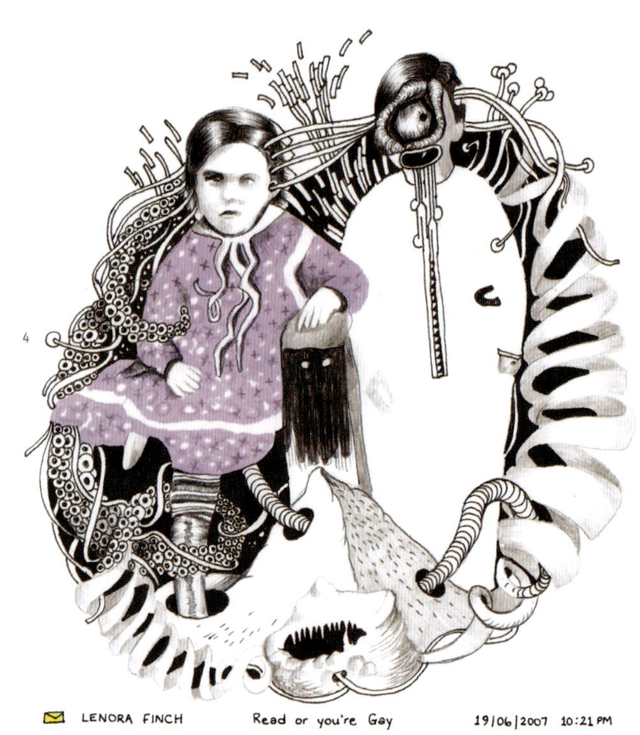

✉ LENORA FINCH   Read or you're Gay   19|06|2007 10:21PM

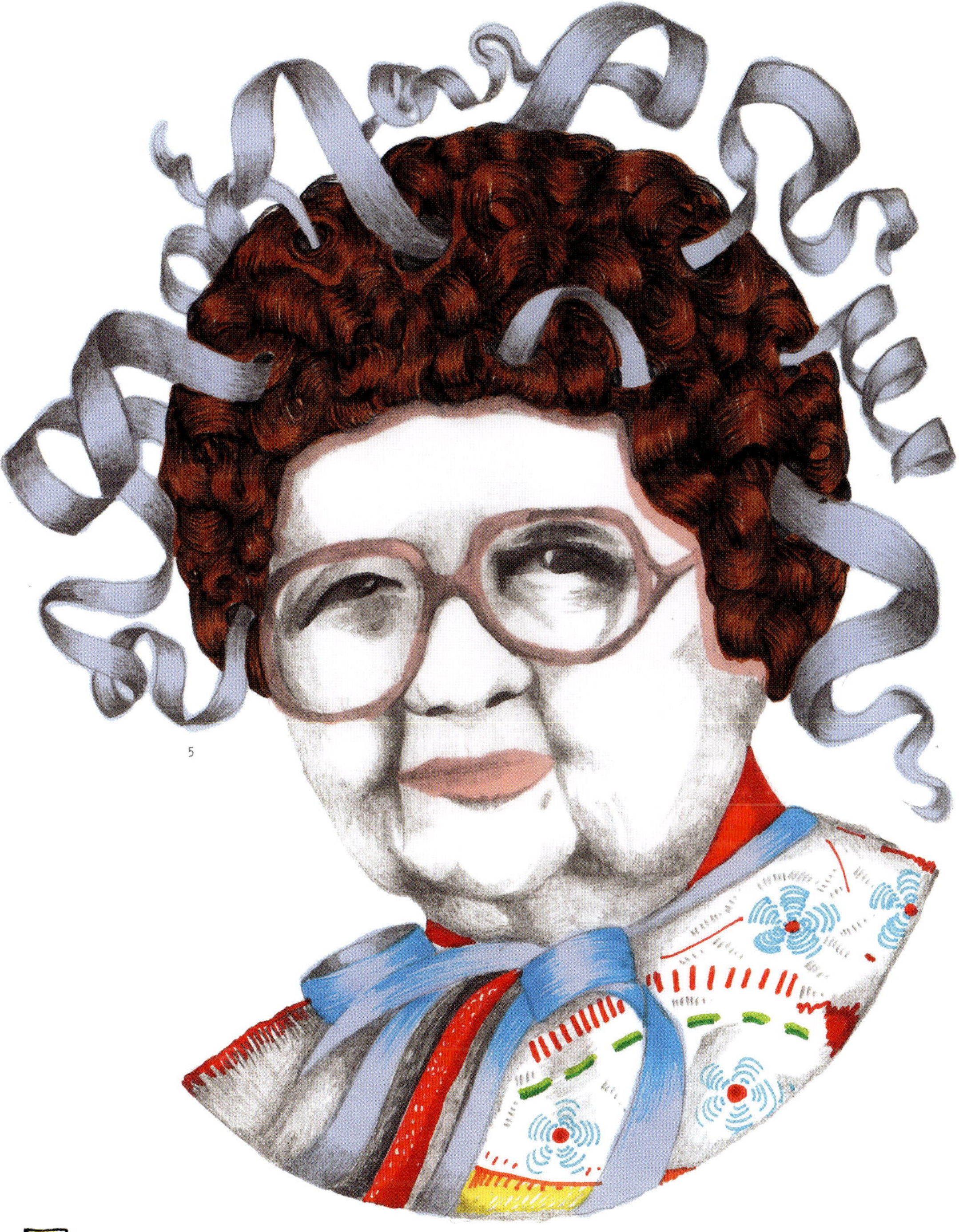

Good Wives and Warriors
UK

www.goodwivesandwarriors.co.uk

1. **Golda Soloman** (2010). Personal project: *Spam Senders Volume 4*. Fine liner, ball pen, pencil, colored pen

2. **Rocco Brantley** (2010). Personal project: *Spam Senders Volume 4*. Fine liner, ball pen, pencil, colored pen

3. **Cleo Bland** (2010). Personal project: *Spam Senders Volume 4*. Fine liner, ball pen, pencil, colored pen

4. **Lenora Finch** (2010). Personal project: *Spam Senders Volume 4*. Fine liner, ball pen, pencil, colored pen

5. **Bertha Suggs** (2010). Personal project: *Spam Senders Volume 4*. Fine liner, ball pen, pencil, colored pen

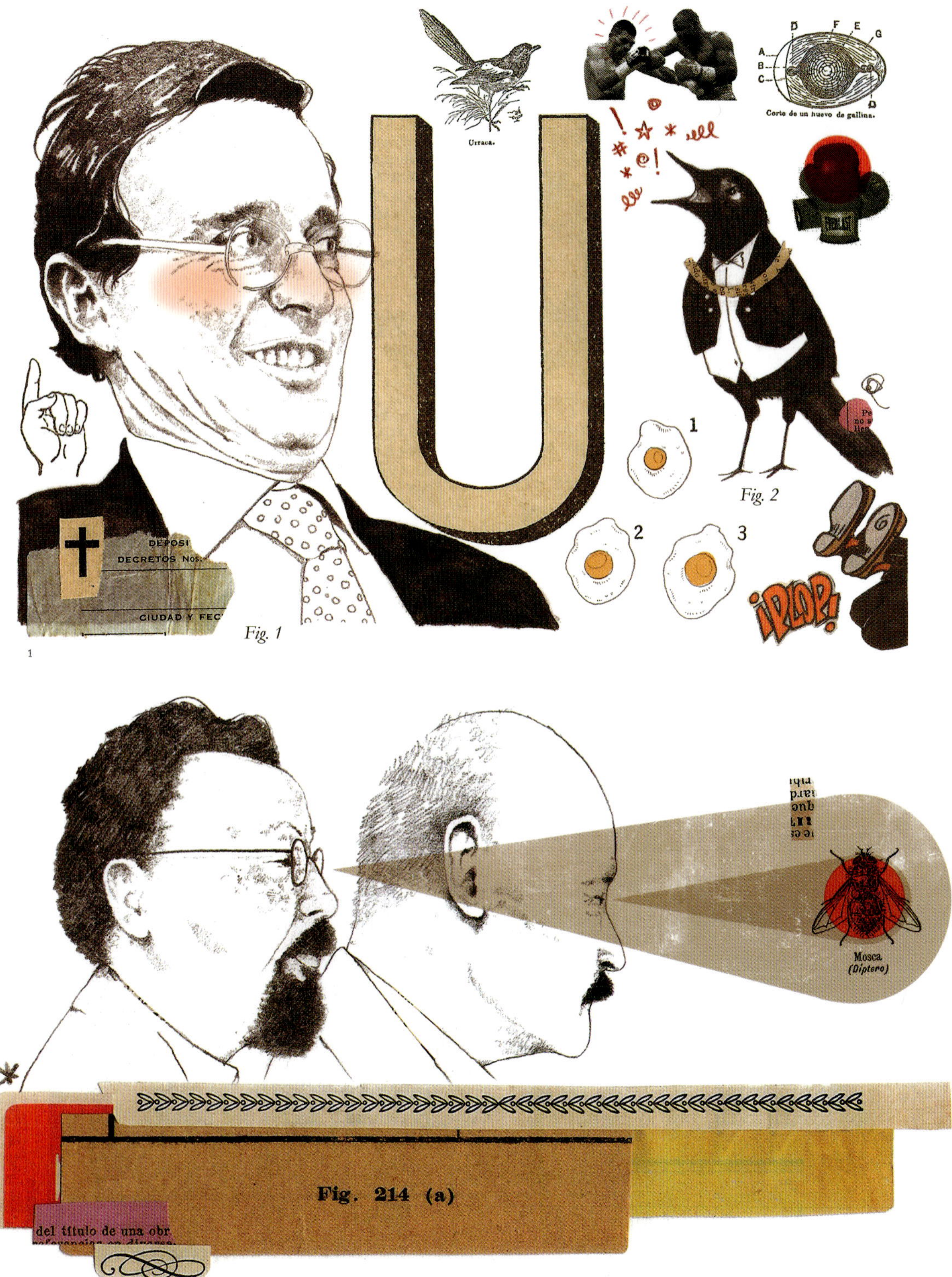
Urraca.
Corte de un huevo de gallina.
Fig. 1
Fig. 2
1
2
3
¡PLOP!
DEPOSI
DECRETOS Nos.
CIUDAD Y FEC
Mosca
(Díptero)
Fig. 214 (a)
del título de una obr

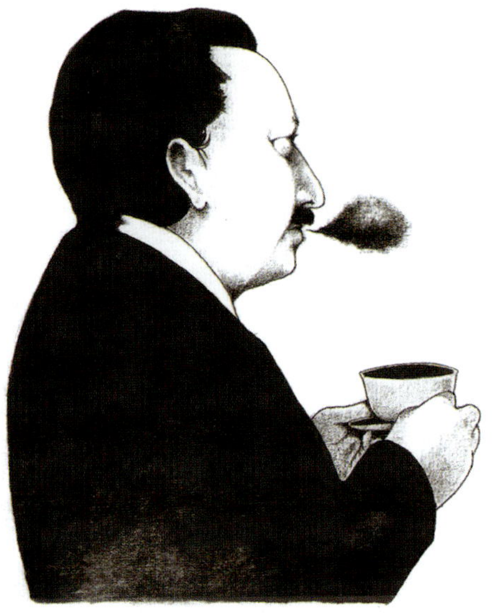

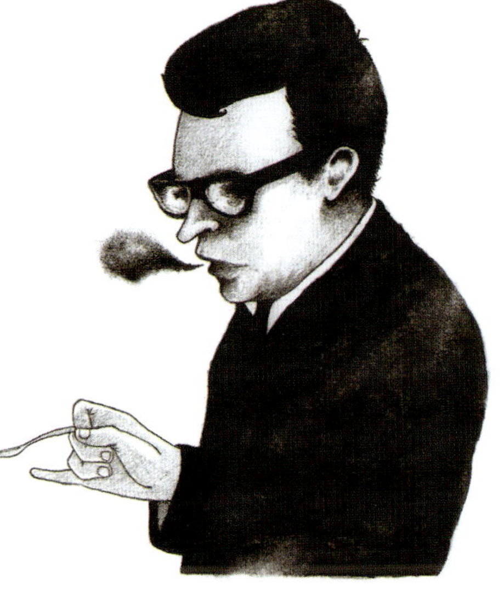

3

Situación 004
Entre los sujetos A y B.

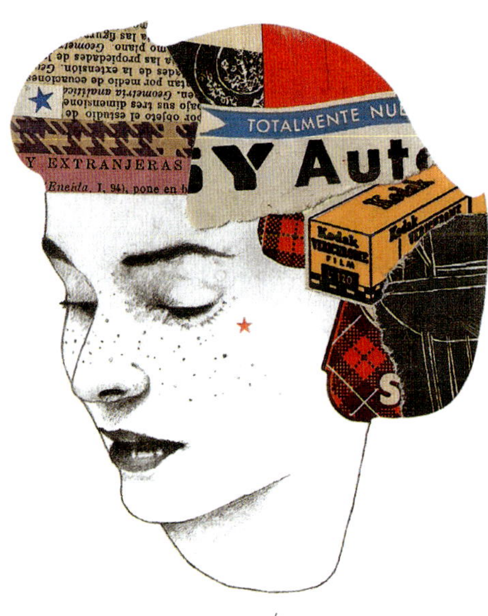

4

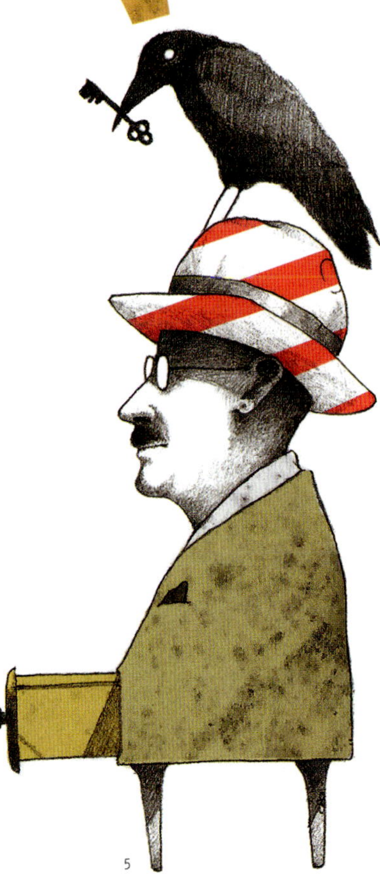

5

1. **Álvaro Uribe** (2011). *Bacanika Magazine.* Mixed media

2. **Poquer de Descuentos** (2011). *El Malpensante* Magazine. Collage, graphite, digital

3. **Coffee** (2011). Personal work. Graphite

4. **Woman's Head** (2010). Personal work. Collage, graphite

5. **Rising Crows** (2010). Personal work. Hand drawing, digital coloring

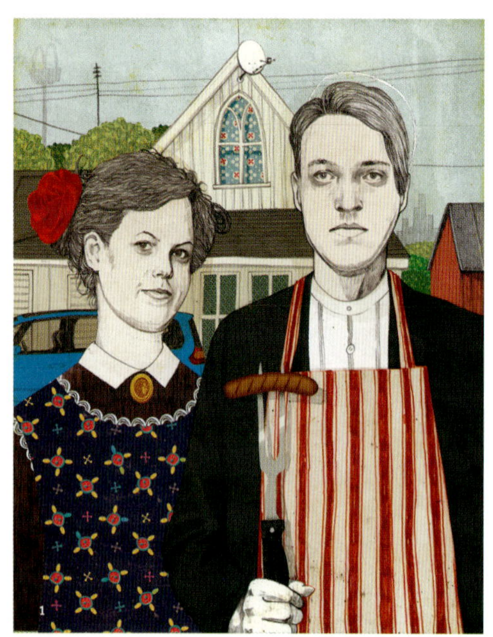

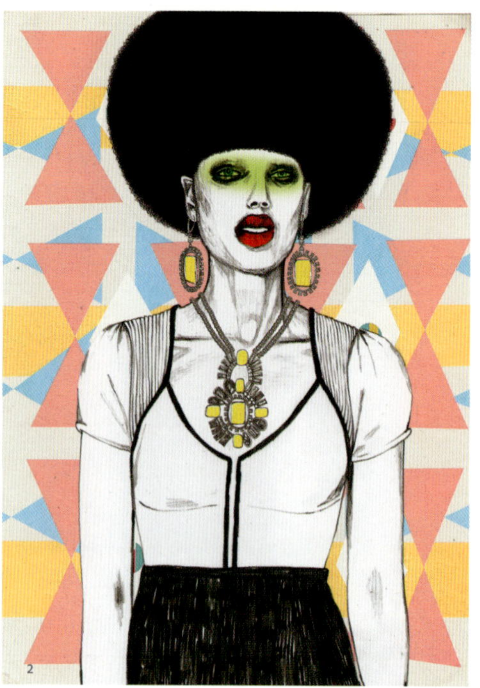

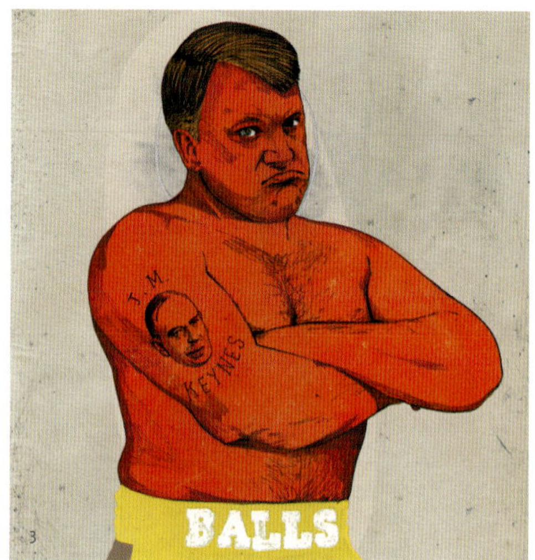

J M
KEYNES
BALLS

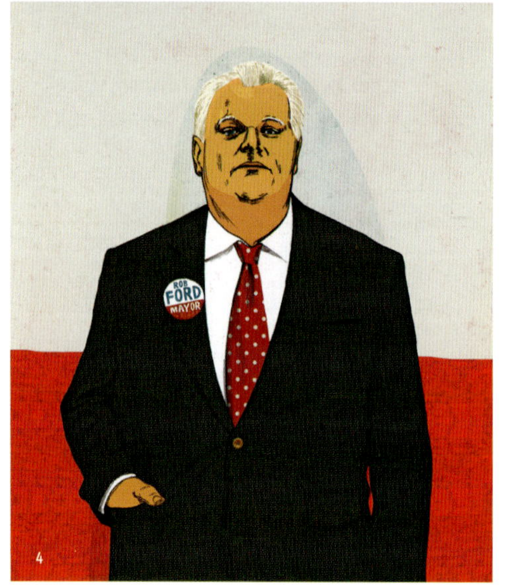

FORD
MAYOR

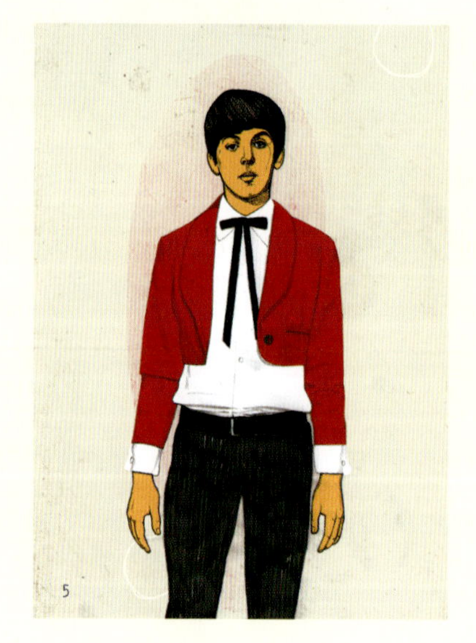

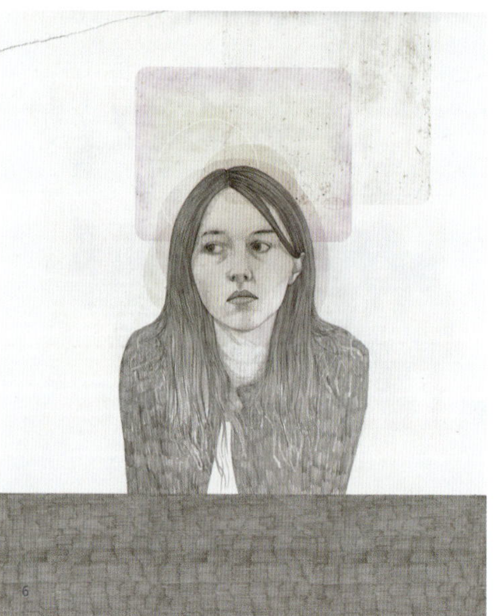

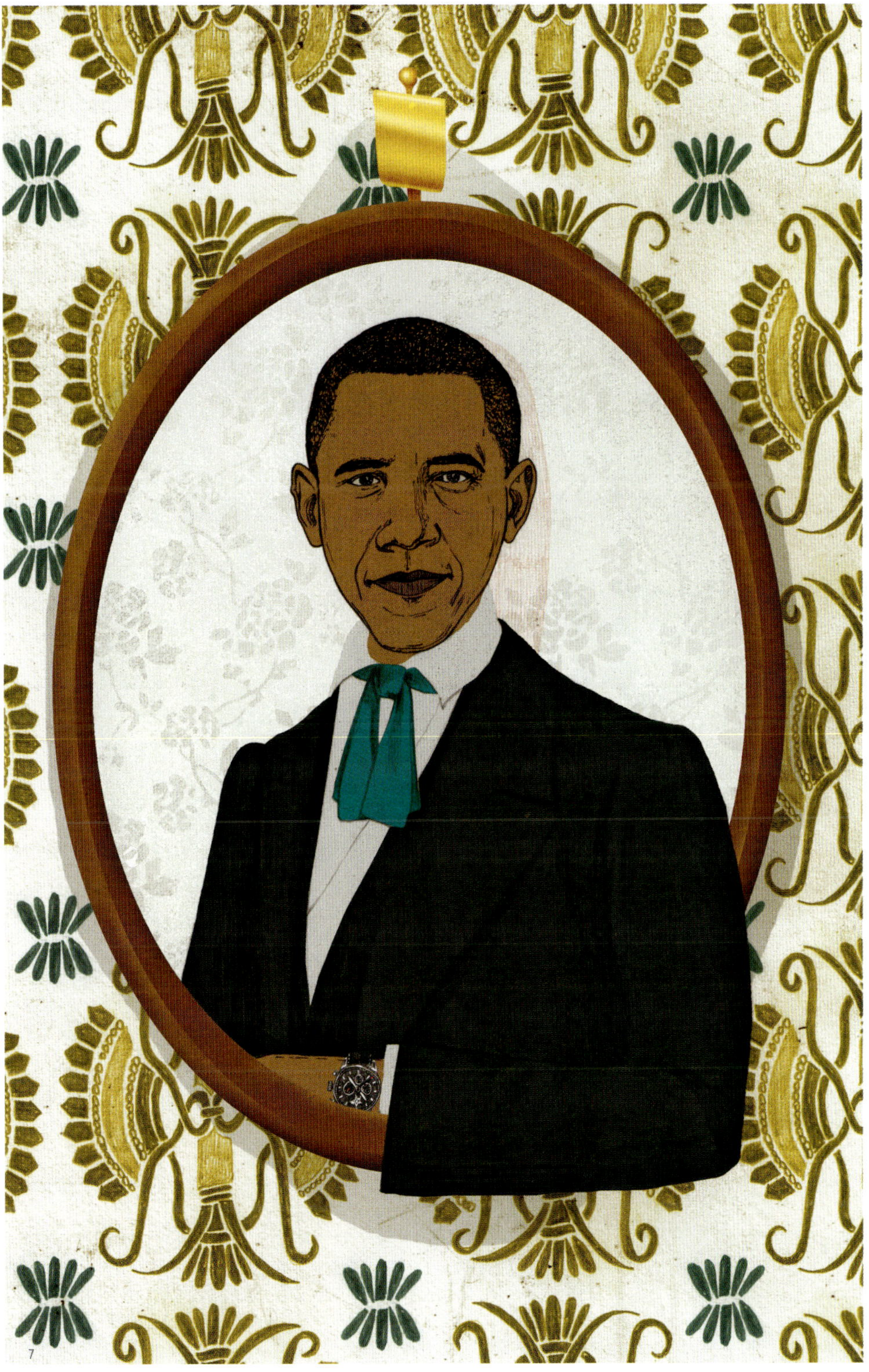

Barry Falls

Ireland

www.barryfalls.com

1. **The Arcade Fire** (2012). Personal work

2. **Woman with necklace** (2012). Personal work

3. **Ed Balls** (2012). *Financial Times*

4. **Rob Ford** (2012). *Eye Weekly Magazine*

5. **Paul** (2012). Personal work

6. **Cath** (2012). Personal work

7. **Barack Obama** (2012). *Spectator*

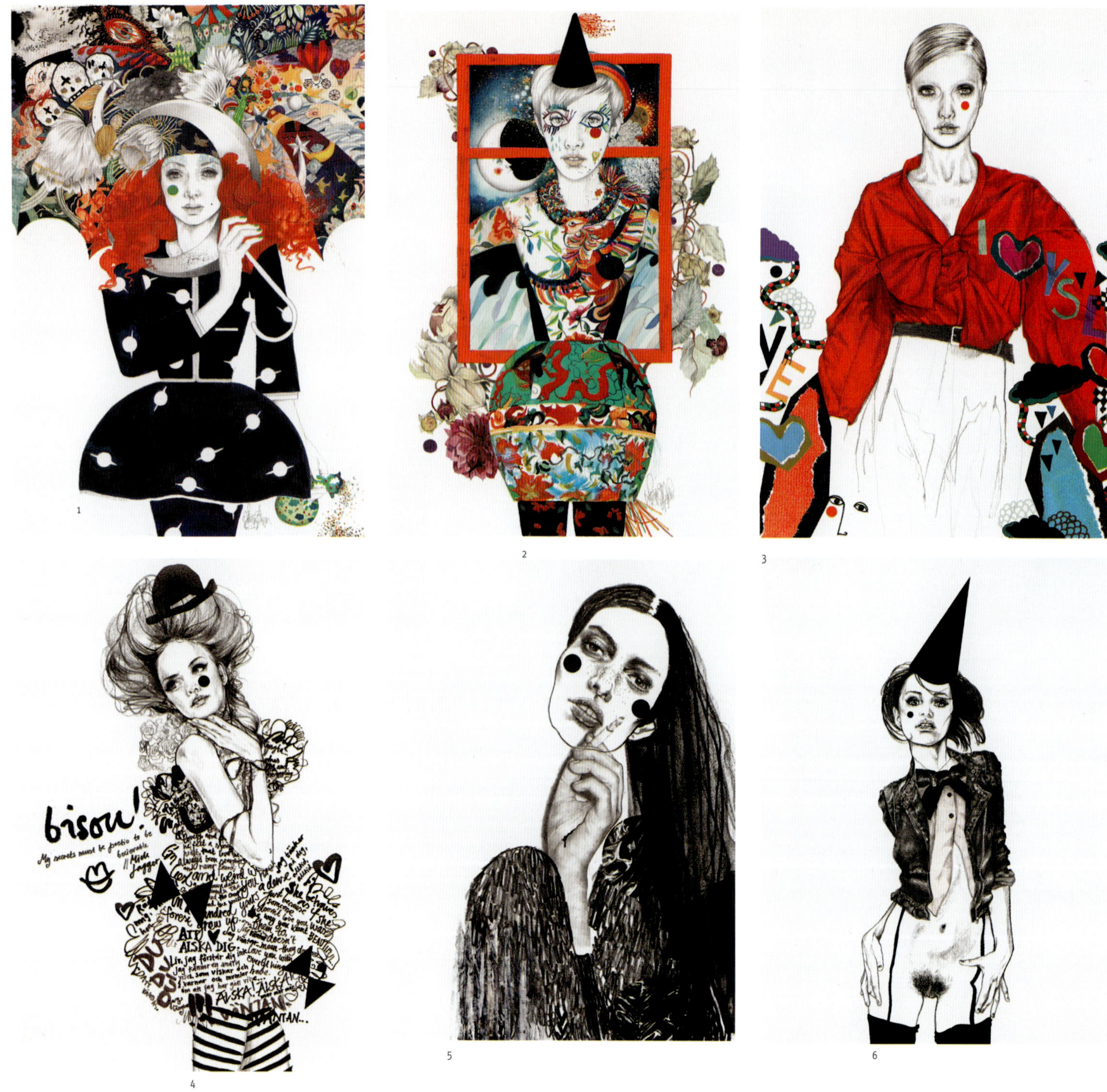

Lina Ekstrand

Sweden

www.linaekstrand.se

1. **Magic boys: John Blund** (2011). Personal work. Pencil, ink, watercolor

2. **Magic boys: Peter Pan** (2011). Personal work. Pencil, ink, watercolor, acrylic

3. **YSL fever** (2011). *Damernas Värld*. Pencil, ink, ripped paper

4. **Bisou** (2011). Hansacompagniet. Pencil, ink

5. **Future form** (2010). *Future Form* exhibition arranged by Jotta. Acrylic paint, pencil, ink, charcoal

6. **Tender is the Night** (2010). Personal work. Pencil, ink

7. **Forestlove** (2010). Monki. Pencil, ink, watercolor

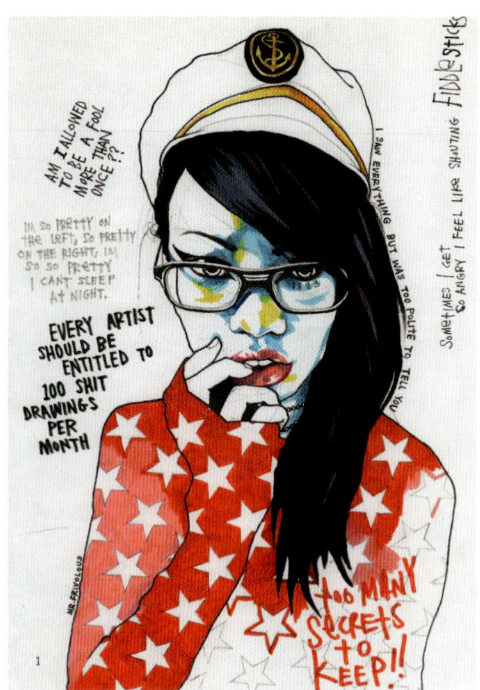
AM I ALLOWED TO BE A FOOL MORE THAN ONCE ??
IM SO PRETTY ON THE LEFT, SO PRETTY ON THE RIGHT, IM SO SO PRETTY I CANT SLEEP AT NIGHT.
EVERY ARTIST SHOULD BE ENTITLED TO 100 SHIT DRAWINGS PER MONTH
I SAW EVERYTHING BUT WAS TOO POLITE TO TELL YOU
SOMETIMES I GET SO ANGRY I FEEL LIKE SHOUTING
FIDDLESTICKS
TOO MANY SECRETS TO KEEP!!
MR.PRINCE1002

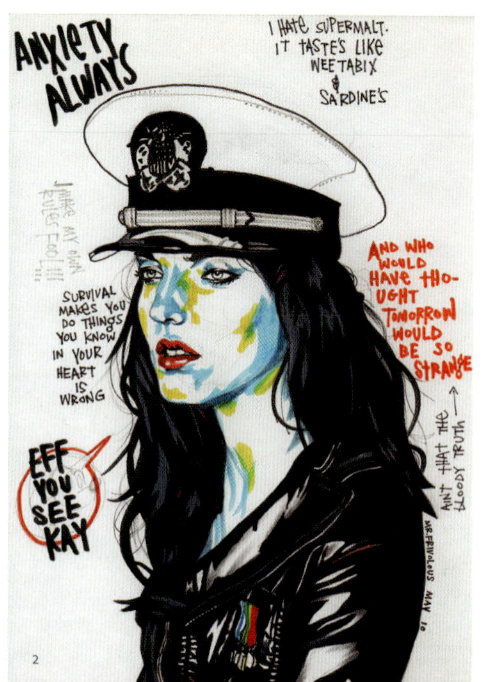
ANXIETY ALWAYS
I HATE SUPERMALT. IT TASTE'S LIKE WEETABIX & SARDINE'S
MAKE MY OWN RULES FOOL!!!
SURVIVAL MAKES YOU DO THINGS YOU KNOW IN YOUR HEART IS WRONG
AND WHO WOULD HAVE THOUGHT TOMORROW WOULD BE SO STRANGE
AINT THAT THE BLOODY TRUTH
EFF YOU SEE KAY
MR.PRINCE1002, MAY 10

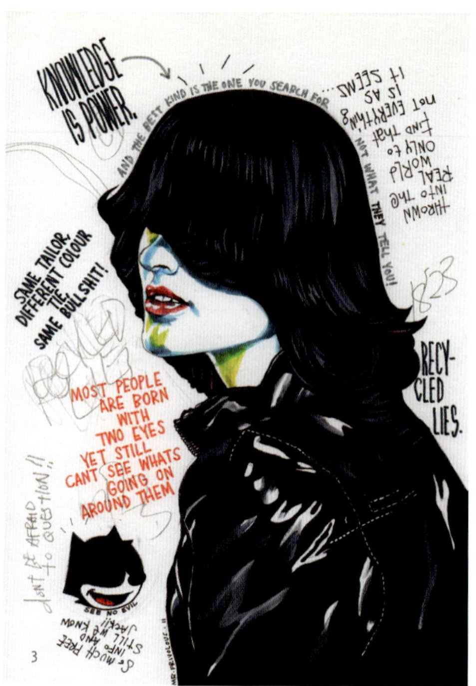
KNOWLEDGE IS POWER.
AND THE BEST KIND IS THE ONE YOU SEARCH FOR
NOT EVERYTHING IS AS IT SEEMS
THROWN INTO THE REAL WORLD ONLY TO FIND THAT NOT WHAT THEY TELL YOU
SAME TAILOR, DIFFERENT COLOUR SAME TIE, SAME BULLSHIT!
MOST PEOPLE ARE BORN WITH TWO EYES YET STILL CANT SEE WHATS GOING ON AROUND THEM
DONT BE AFRAID TO QUESTION!!
SO MUCH FREE INFO AND STILL WE KNOW JACK!!
SEE NO EVIL
RECYCLED LIES.

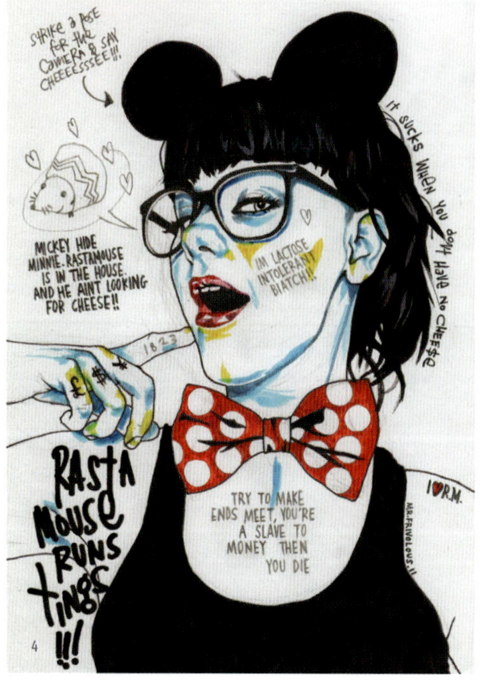
STRIKE A POSE FOR THE CAMERA & SAY CHEEESSSEE!!!
MICKEY HIDE MINNIE. RASTAMOUSE IS IN THE HOUSE. AND HE AINT LOOKING FOR CHEESE!!
IM LACTOSE INTOLERANT BIATCH!!
IT SUCKS WHEN YOU DONT HAVE NO CHEESE
RASTA MOUSE RUNS TINGS !!!
TRY TO MAKE ENDS MEET, YOU'RE A SLAVE TO MONEY THEN YOU DIE
I ♥ R.M.
MR.PRINCE1002 !!

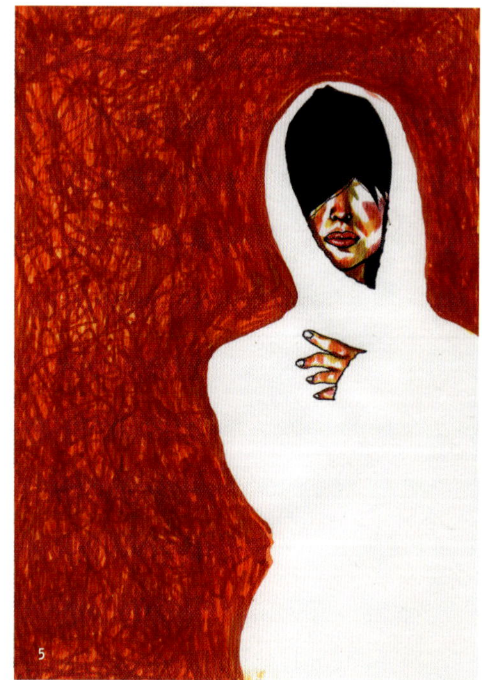

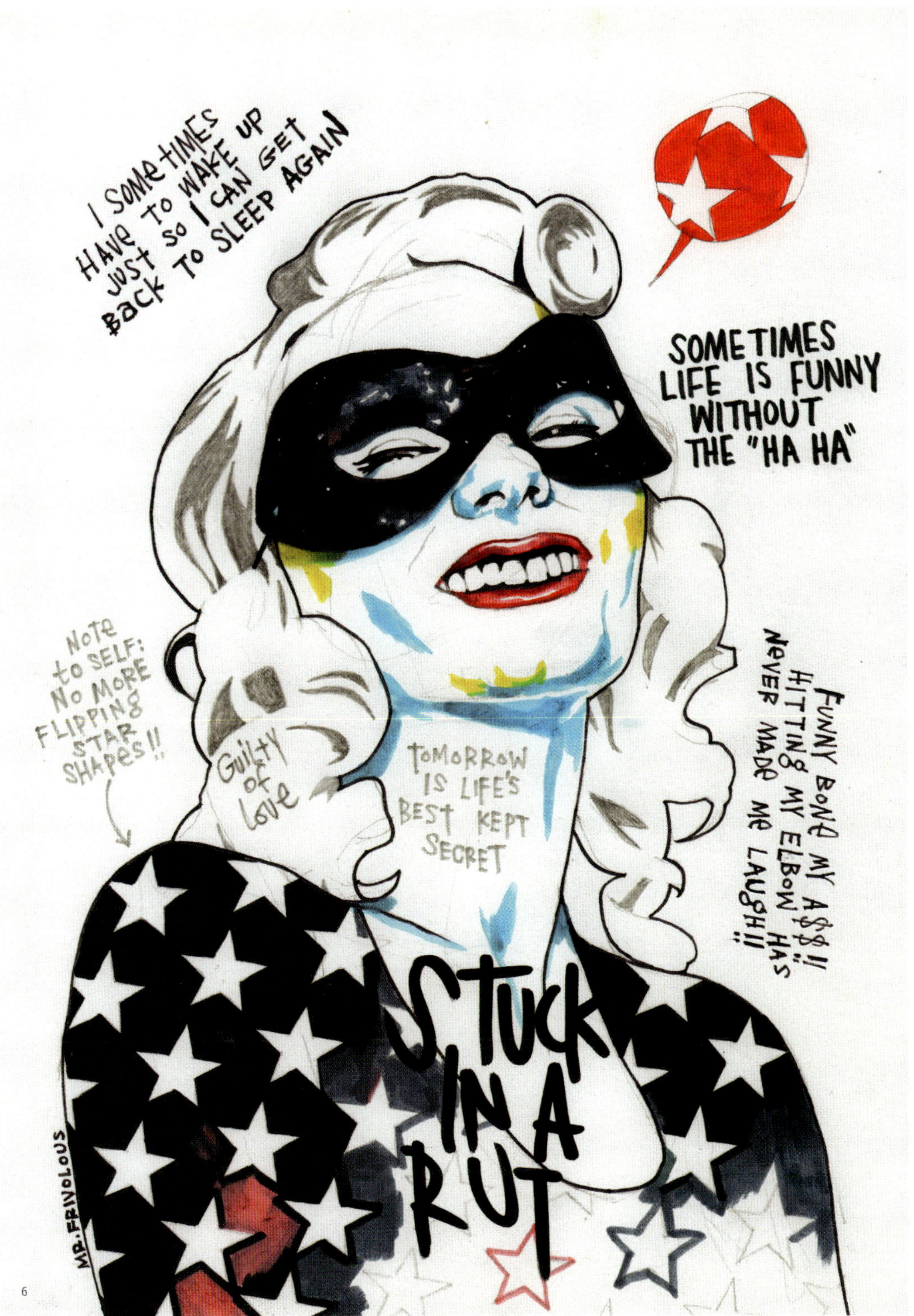

Mr. Frivolous

UK

www.mrfrivolous.com

1. **It Ain't Easy Playing Dumb** (2011). Personal work. Felt tip pens

2. **Anxiety Always** (2011). Personal work. Felt tip pens

3. **See No Evil** (2011). Personal work. Felt tip pens

4. **Don't Take the Mickey Mate I'm Lactose Intolerant** (2011). Personal work. Felt tip pens

5. **Lonely** (2008). Personal work. Felt tip pens

6. **Sometimes Life is Funny Without the HA HA** (2011). Personal work. Felt tip pens

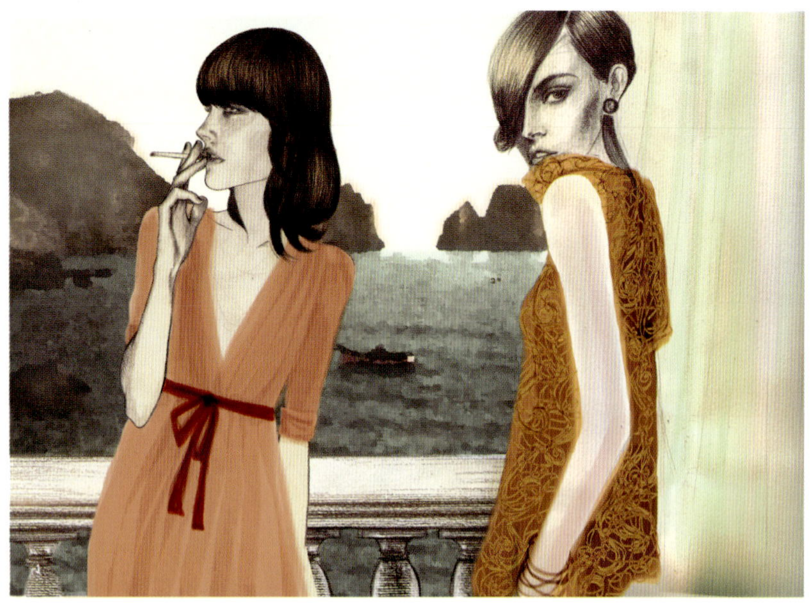

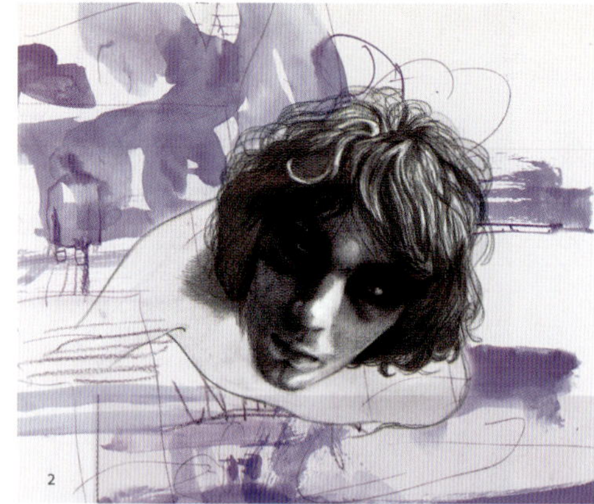

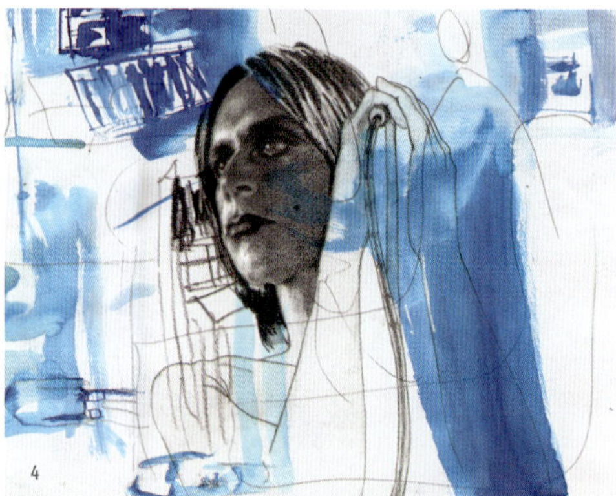

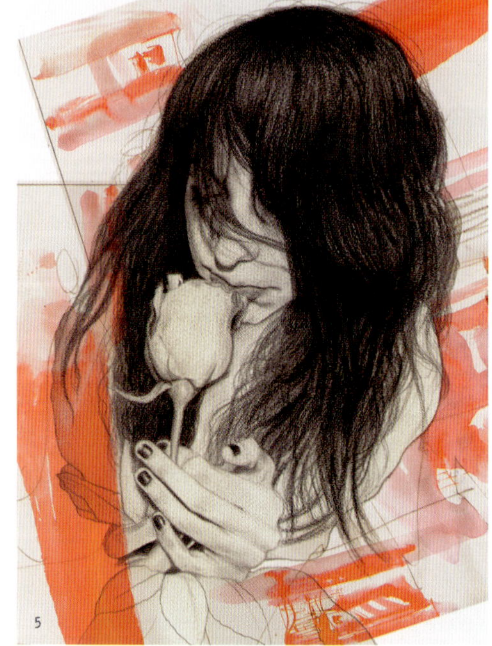

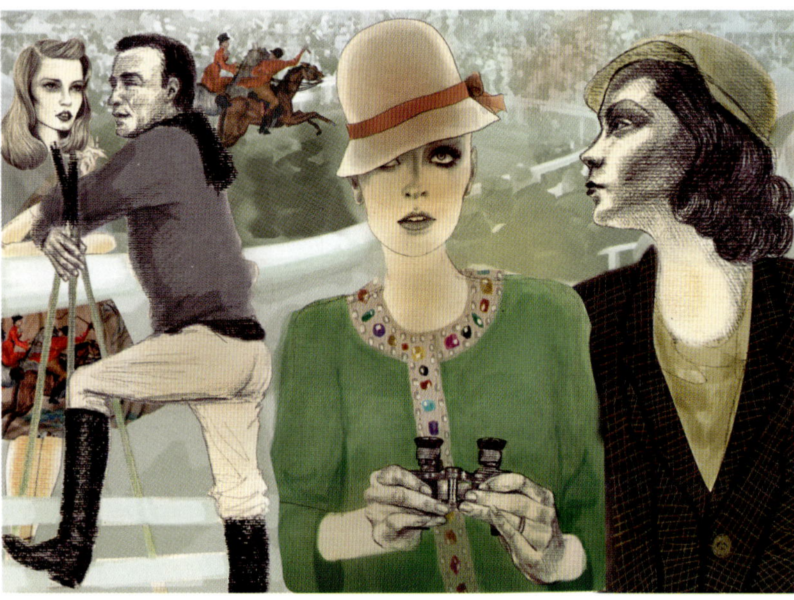

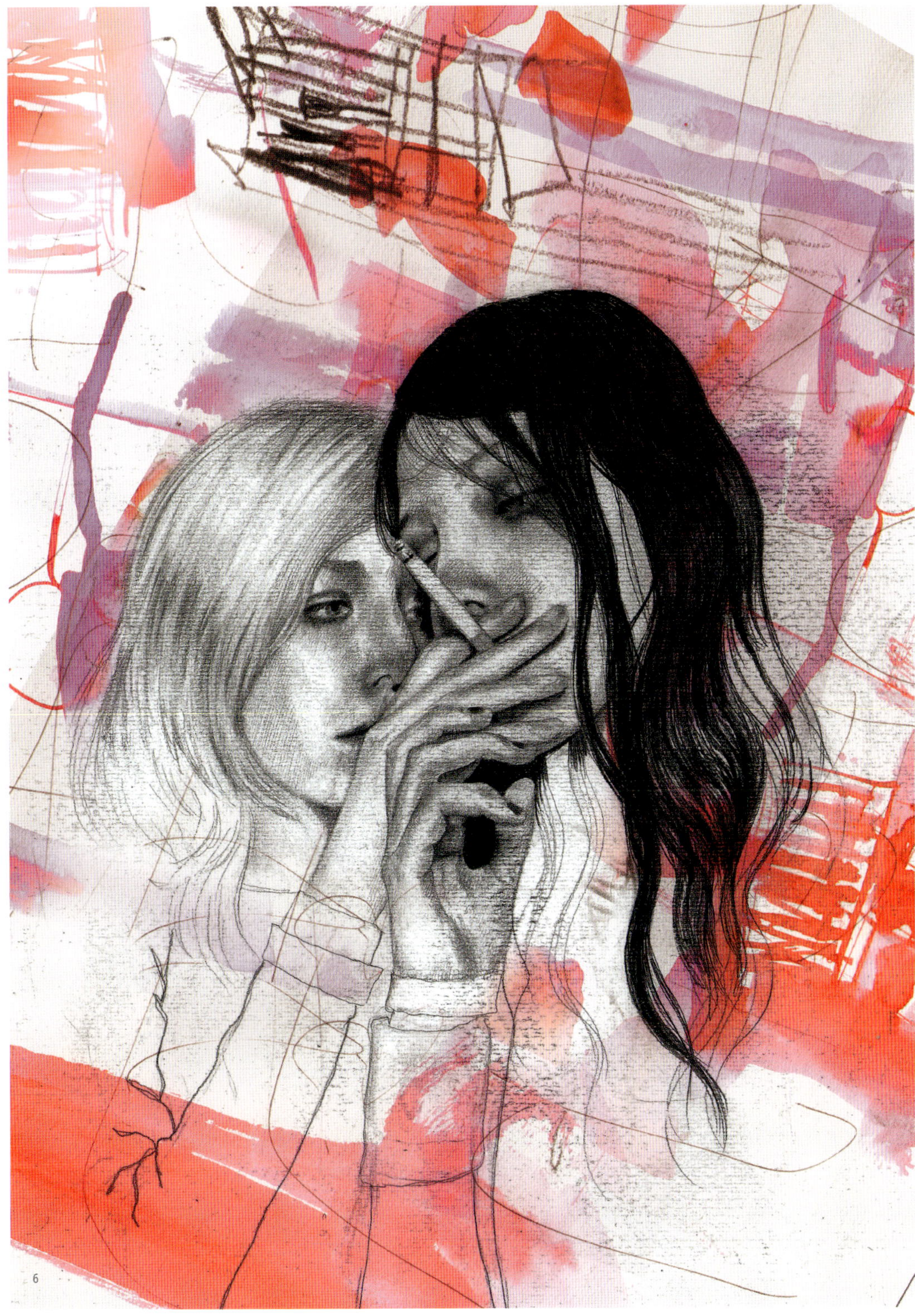

Roberta Zeta

Italy

www.robertazeta.com

1. **Capri** (2011). On The Table for Semi Couture

2. **Barrett** (2009). Personal work

3. **Horse Racing** (2011). On The Table for Semi Couture

4. **Iggy** (2009). Personal work

5. **A Rose** (2009). Personal work

6. **Smokers** (2009). Personal work

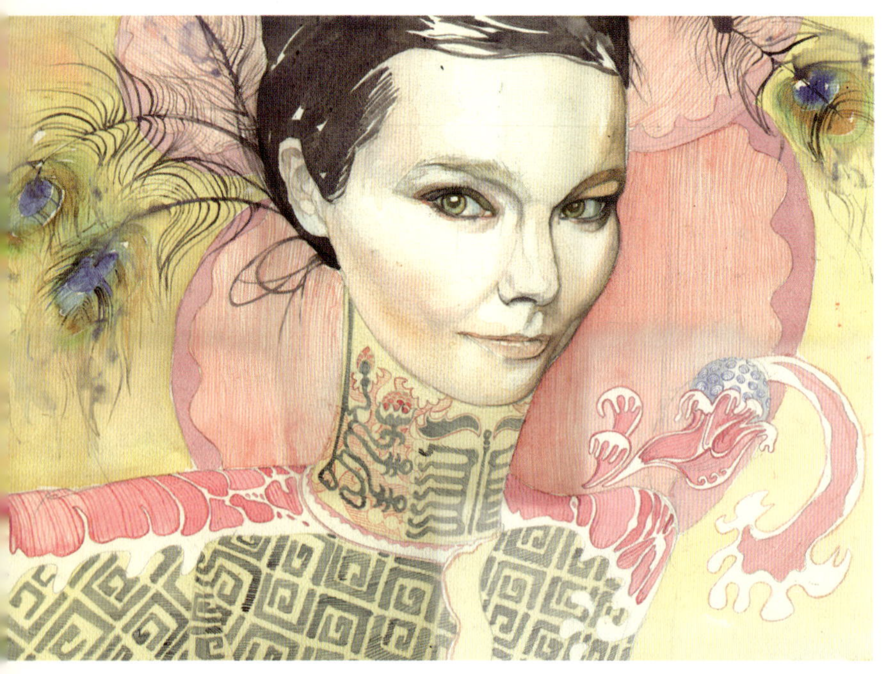

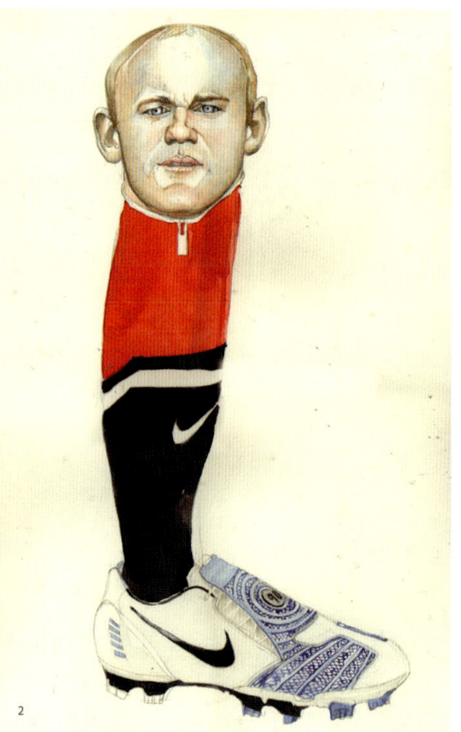

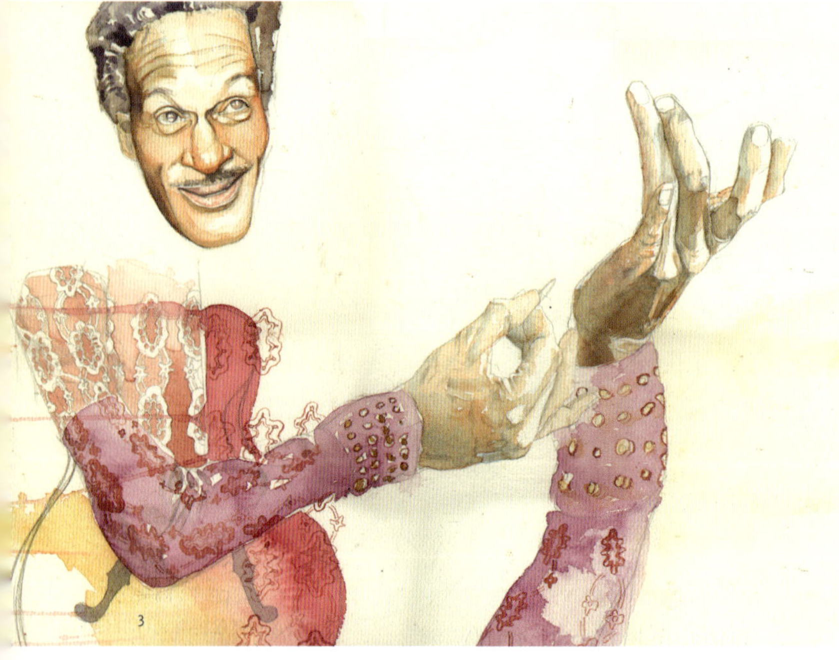

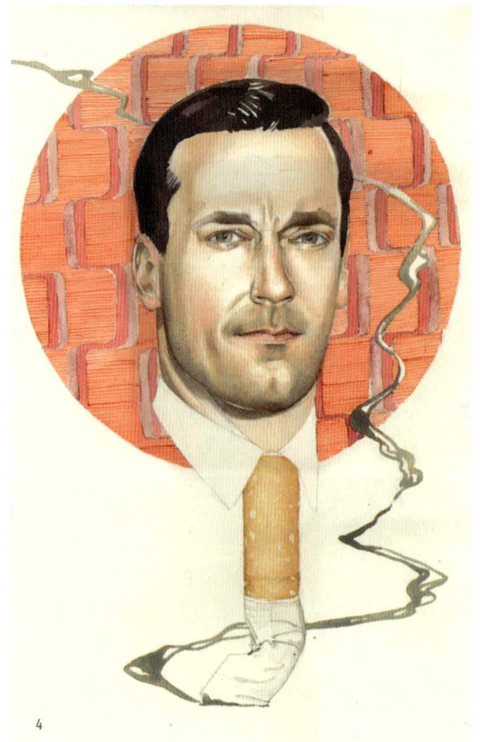

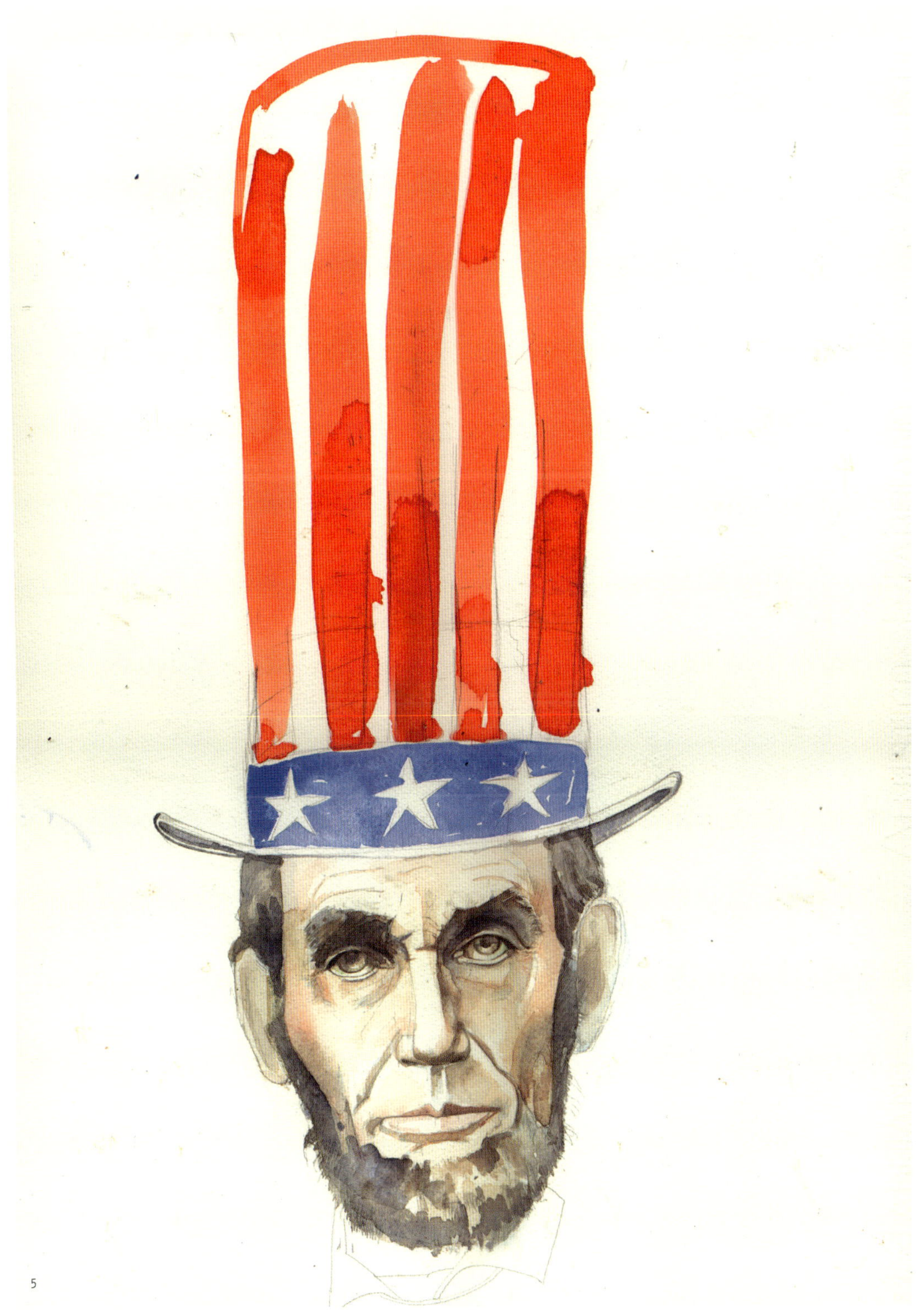

Daniel Mackie
UK

www.danielmackie.com

1. **Bjork** (2010). Personal work. Watercolor

2. **Wayne Rooney** (2011). Personal work. Watercolor

3. **Chuck Berry** (2011). Personal work. Watercolor

4. **Don Draper from Mad Men** (2011). Personal work. Watercolor

5. **Abraham Lincoln** (2010). Personal work. Watercolor

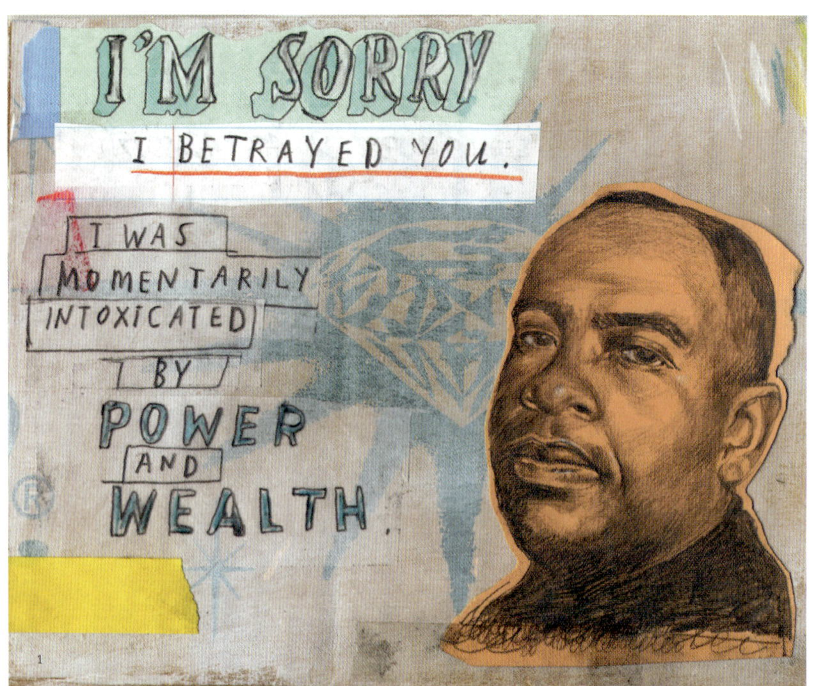
I'M SORRY
I BETRAYED YOU.
I WAS MOMENTARILY INTOXICATED
BY
POWER
AND
WEALTH.
1

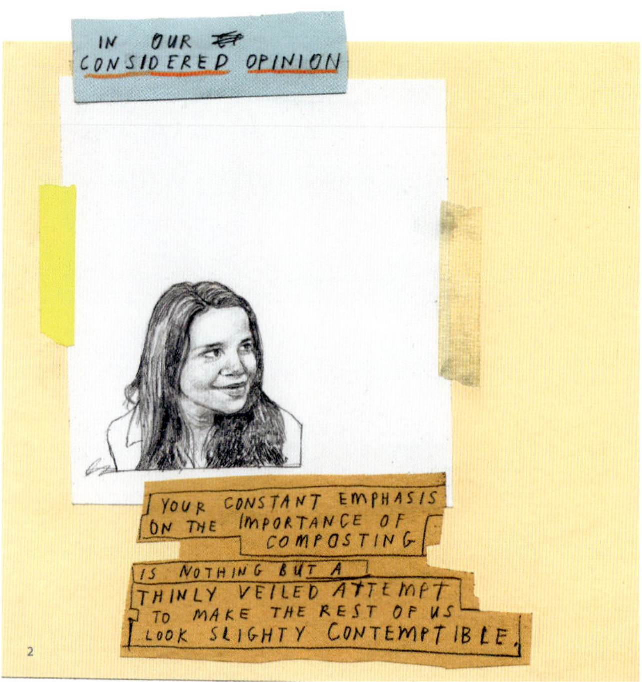
IN OUR CONSIDERED OPINION
YOUR CONSTANT EMPHASIS ON THE IMPORTANCE OF COMPOSTING
IS NOTHING BUT A THINLY VEILED ATTEMPT TO MAKE THE REST OF US LOOK SLIGHTY CONTEMPTIBLE.
2

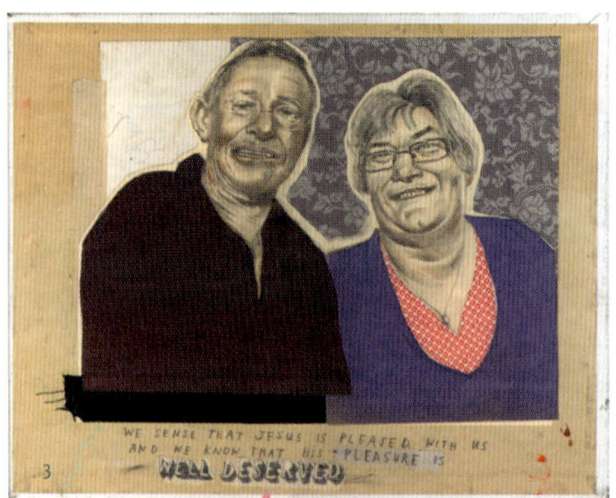
WE SENSE THAT JESUS IS PLEASED WITH US AND WE KNOW THAT HIS PLEASURE IS
WELL DESERVED
3

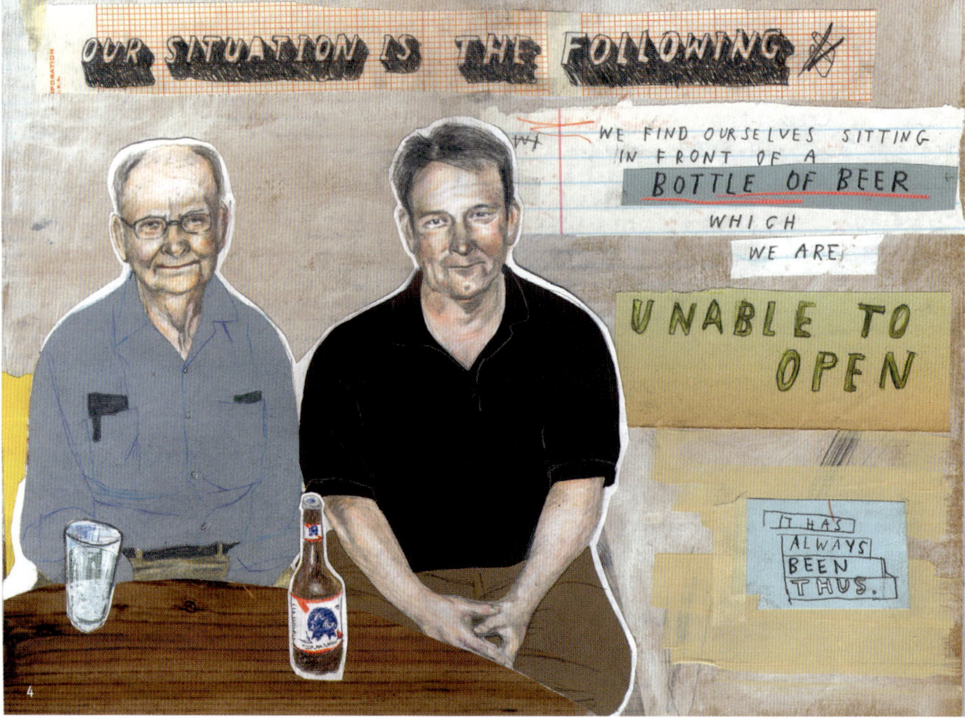
OUR SITUATION IS THE FOLLOWING
WE FIND OURSELVES SITTING IN FRONT OF A
BOTTLE OF BEER
WHICH
WE ARE
UNABLE TO OPEN
IT HAS ALWAYS BEEN THUS.
4

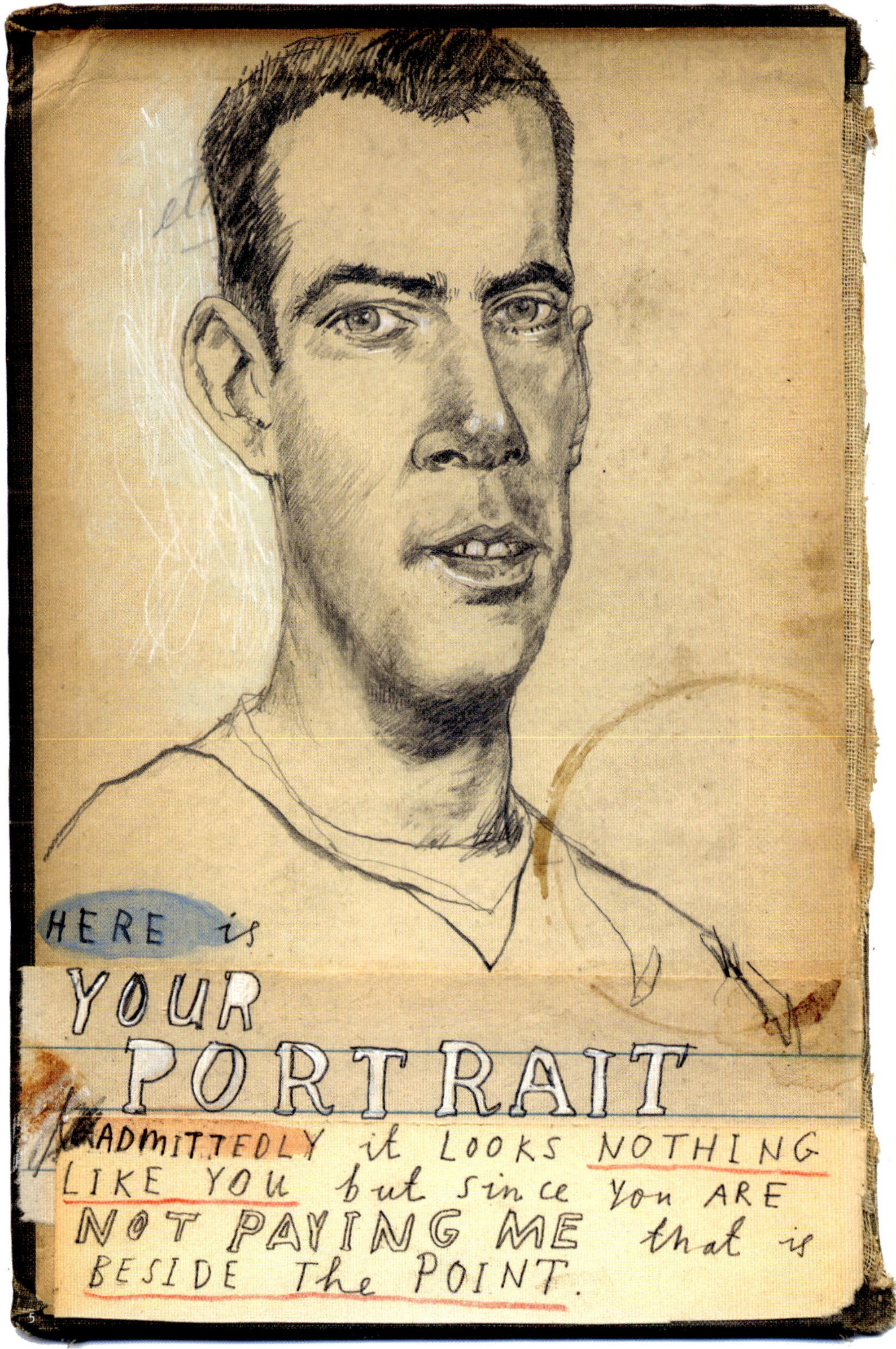

David Fullarton
USA

www.davidfullarton.com

1. **Apology No.3** (2011). Personal work. Mixed media on cardboard

2. **Ulterior Motives** (2010). Personal work. Mixed media on paper

3. **Heaven Awaits** (2011). Personal work. Mixed media on found canvas board

4. **The Ponderers** (2010). Personal work. Mixed media on cardboard

5. **Artistic License** (2009). Personal work. Mixed media, found book cover

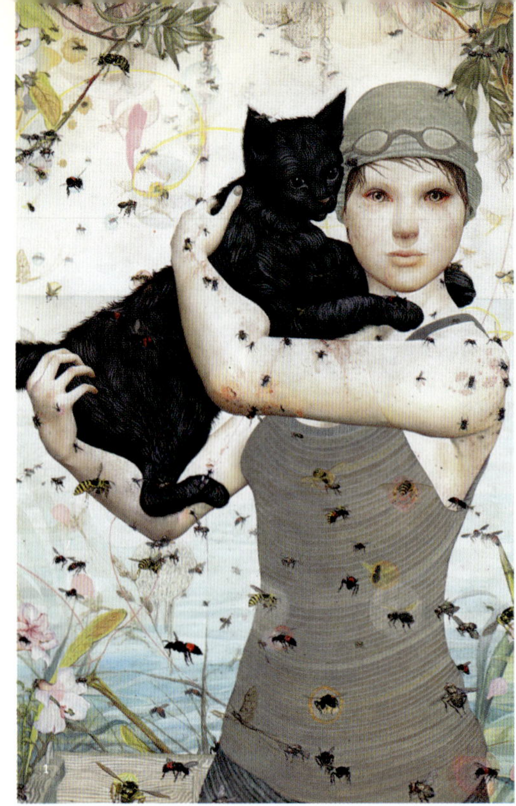

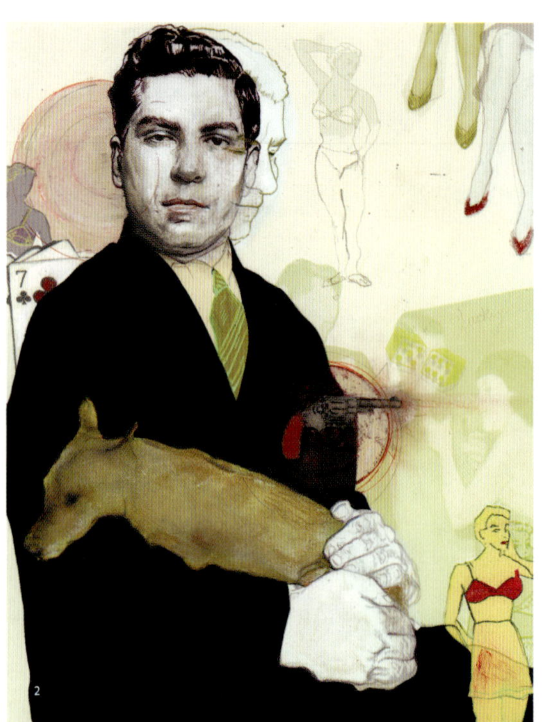

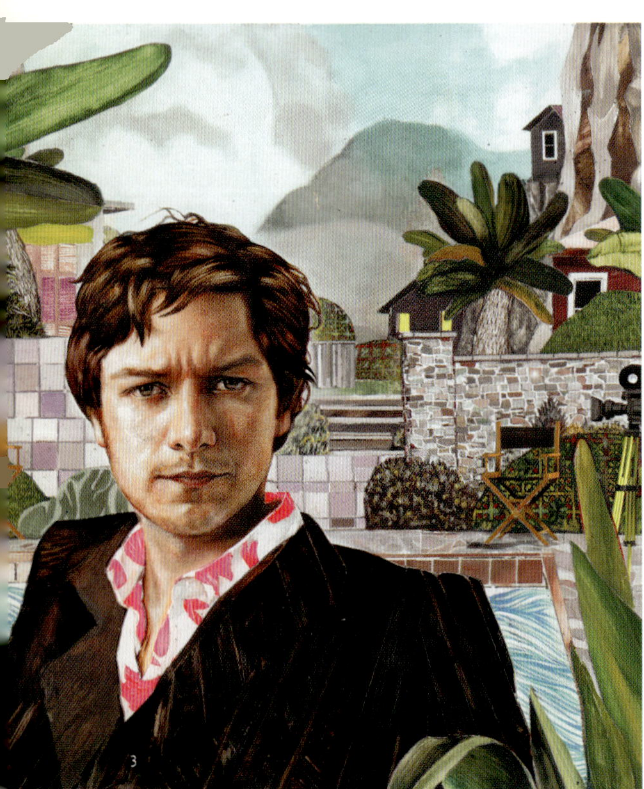

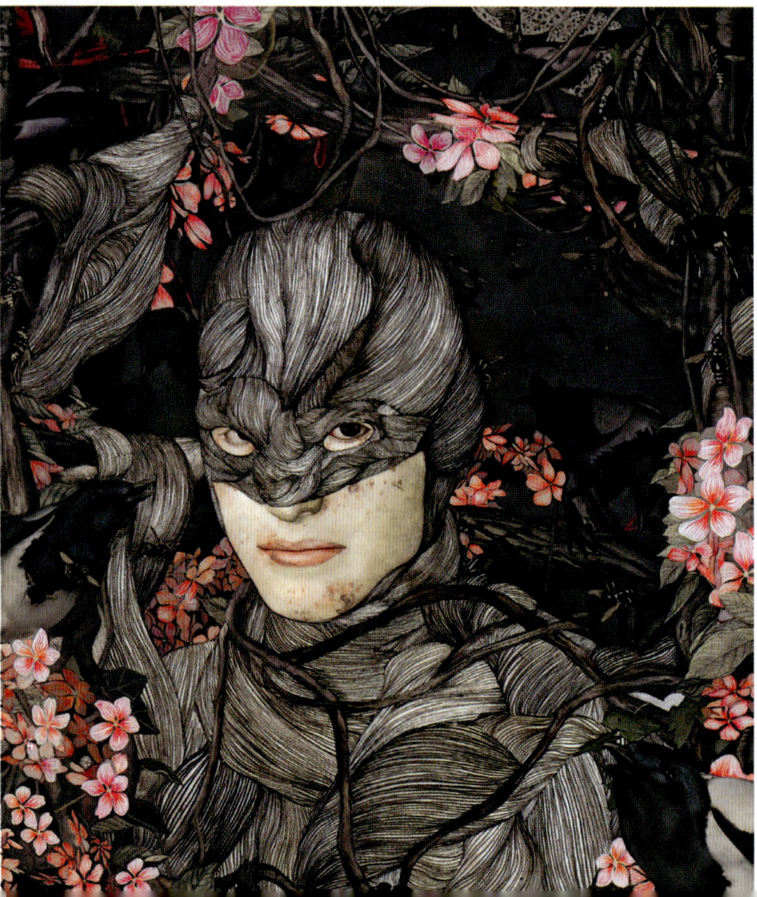

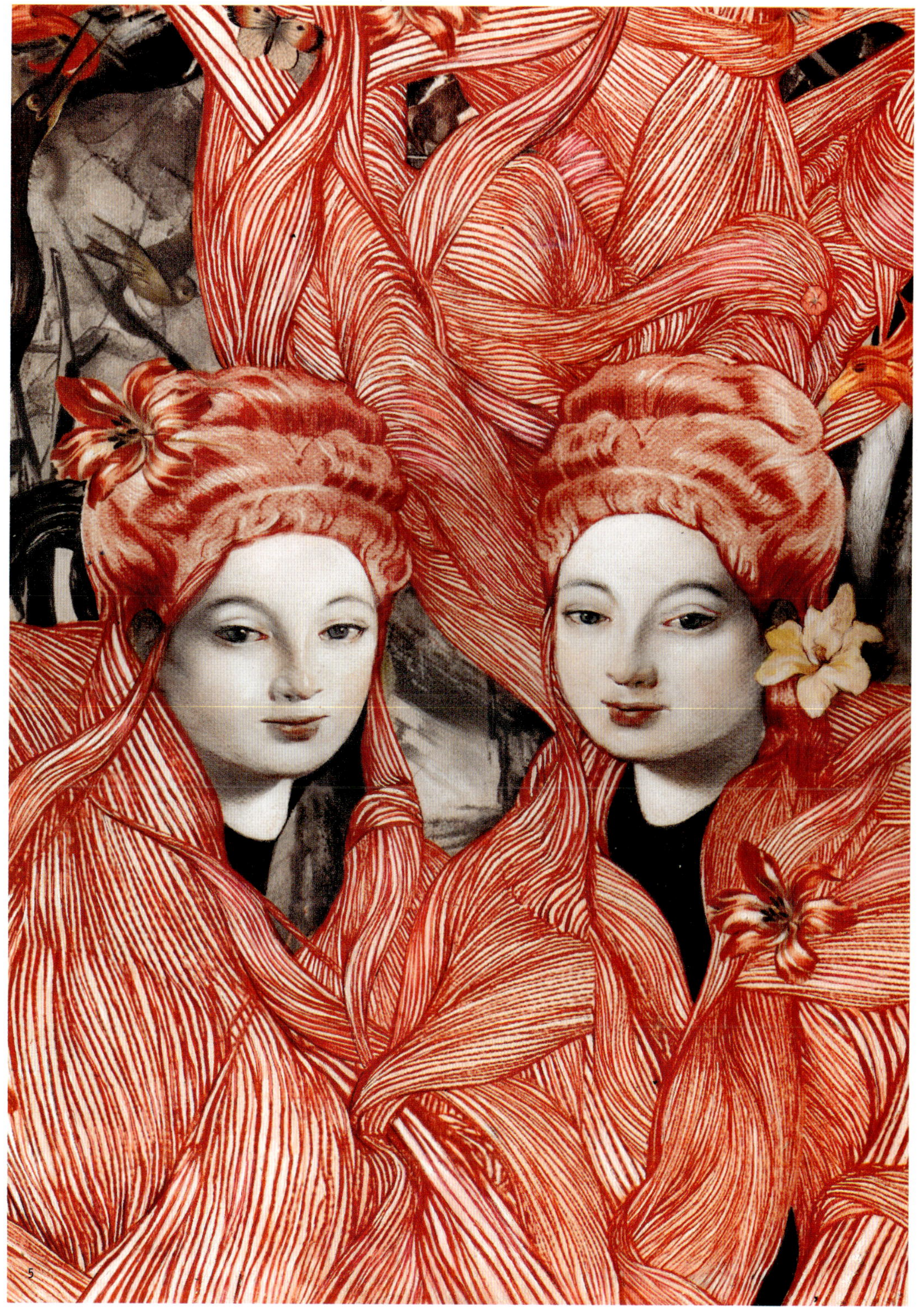

Steven Tabbutt

USA

www.steventabbutt.com

1. **Infest** (2011). Personal work. Acrylic on paper

2. **Lucky Luciano** (2007). Personal work. Acrylic on paper

3. **James McAvoy** (2008). Personal work. Acrylic on paper

4. **Subcreation** (2011). Personal work. Acrylic on paper

5. **Oracles** (2007). Personal work. Acrylic, ink, pencil on watercolor paper

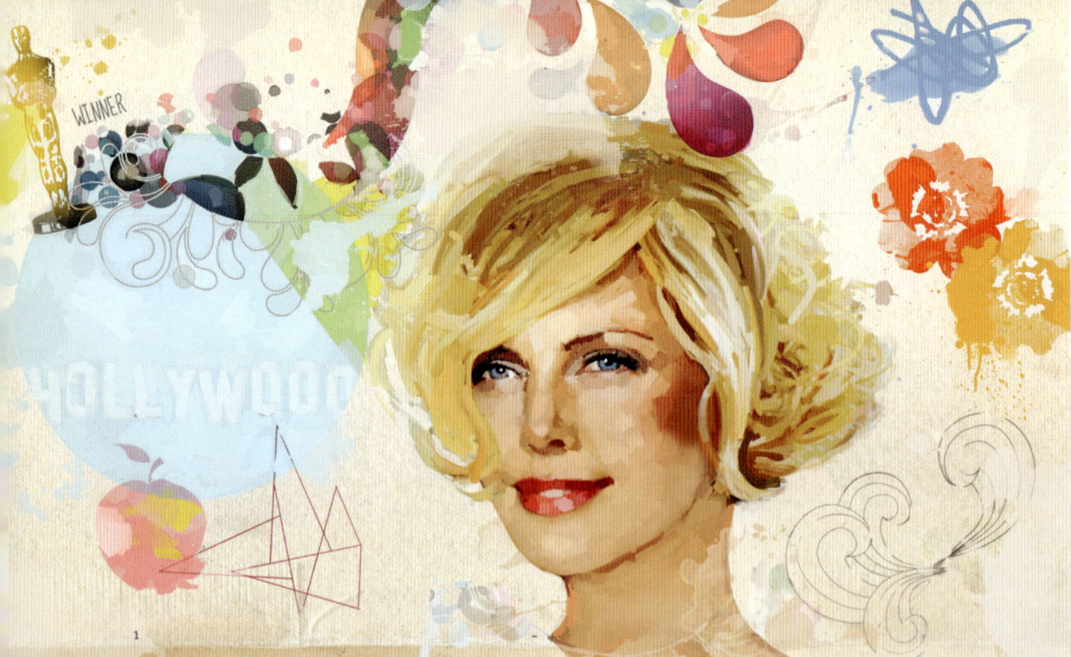

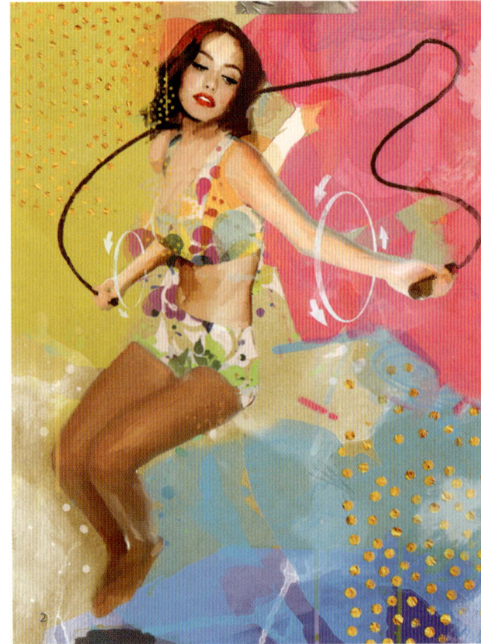

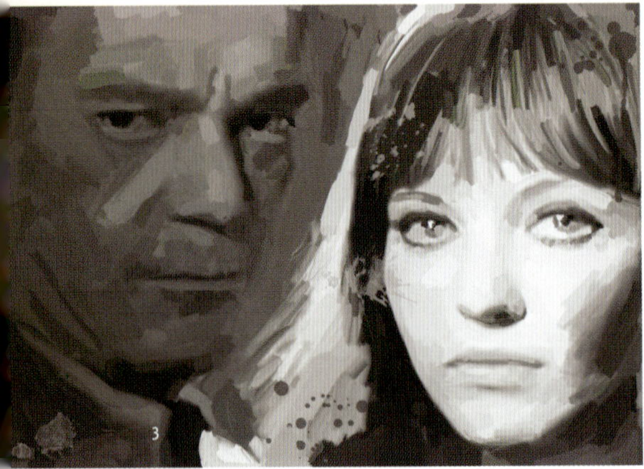

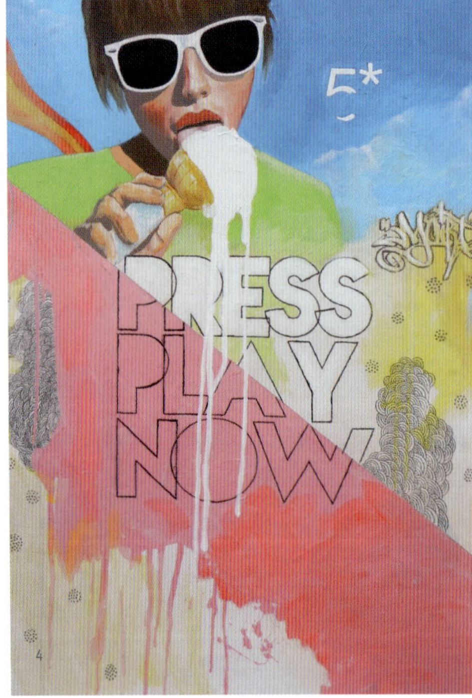
5*
PRESS
PLAY
NOW

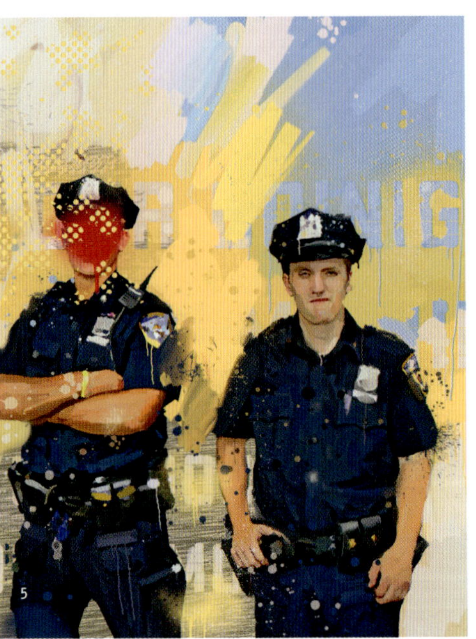

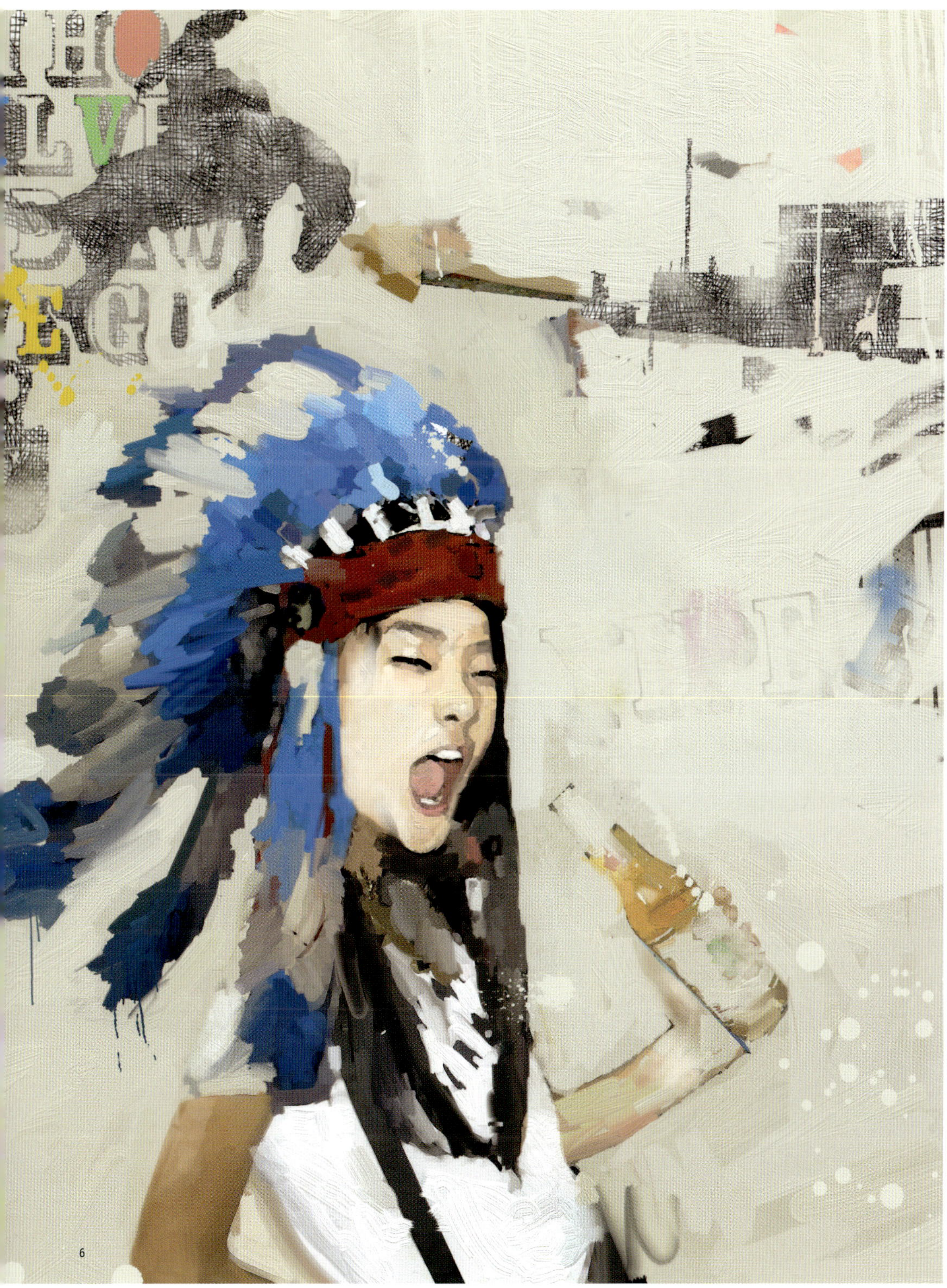

Chris Arran

UK

Agency: Colagene, Illustration Clinic
www.colagene.com/fr/illustration/
chris-arran

1. **Charleze Theron** (2011). *Glamour*. Digital media, paint

2. **Skipping** (2011). *Votre Beute*. Digital media, paint

3. **Film Star Portrait** (2010). *Next Magazine - La Libération*. Digital media, paint, pencil

4. **Press Play Now** (2011). Personal work. Acrylic

5. **Cops** (2009). Personal work. Digital media, paint, pencil

6. **Yippee** (2009). Personal work. Digital media, paint

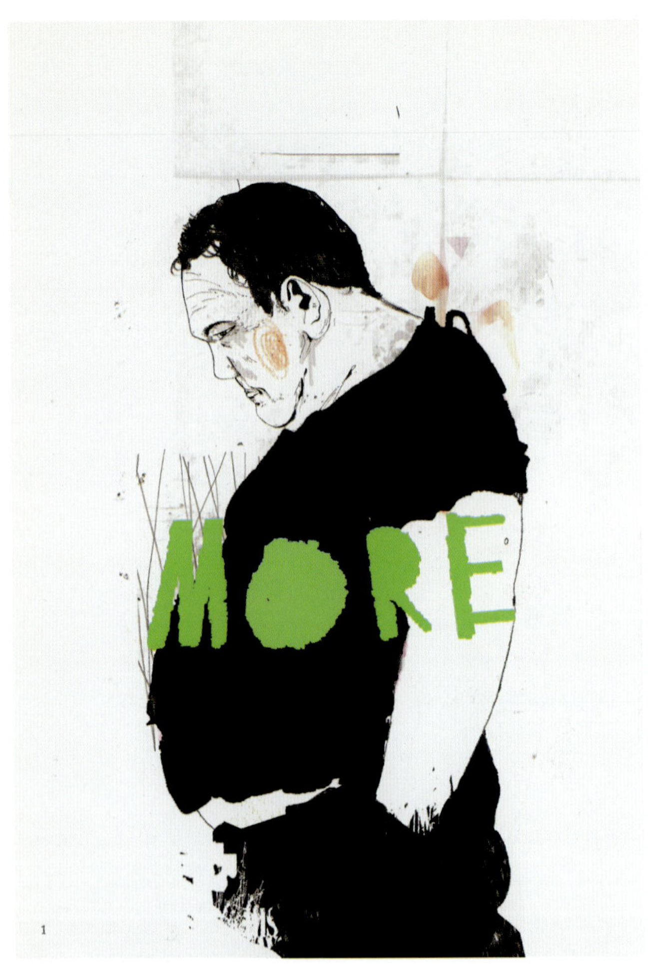

MORE

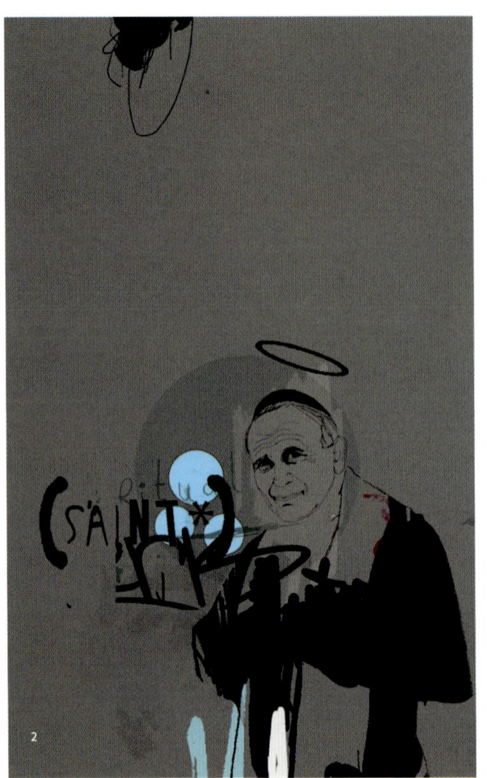

(SAINT)

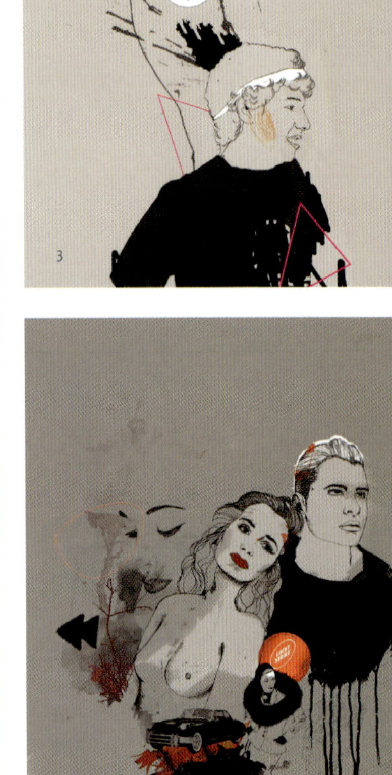

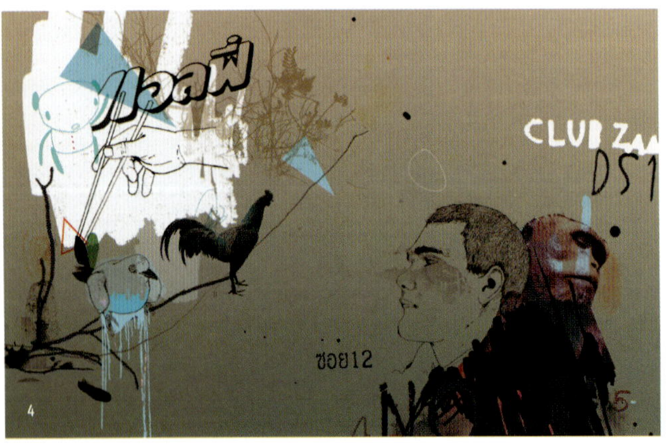

CLUB Z
D51
ขอย12

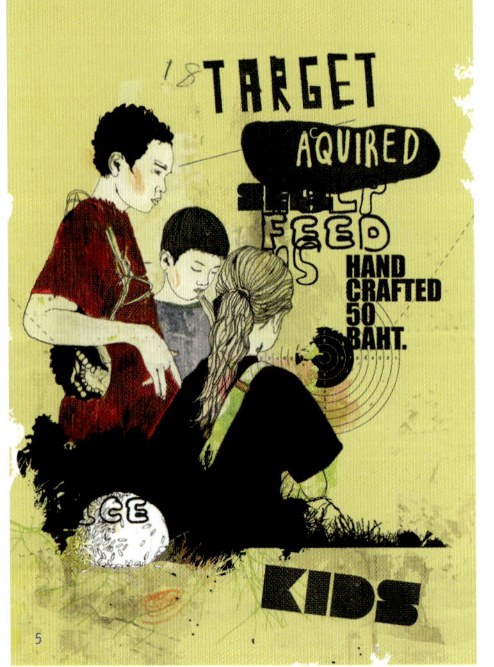

18
TARGET
AQUIRED
FEED
HAND
CRAFTED
50
BAHT.
KIDS

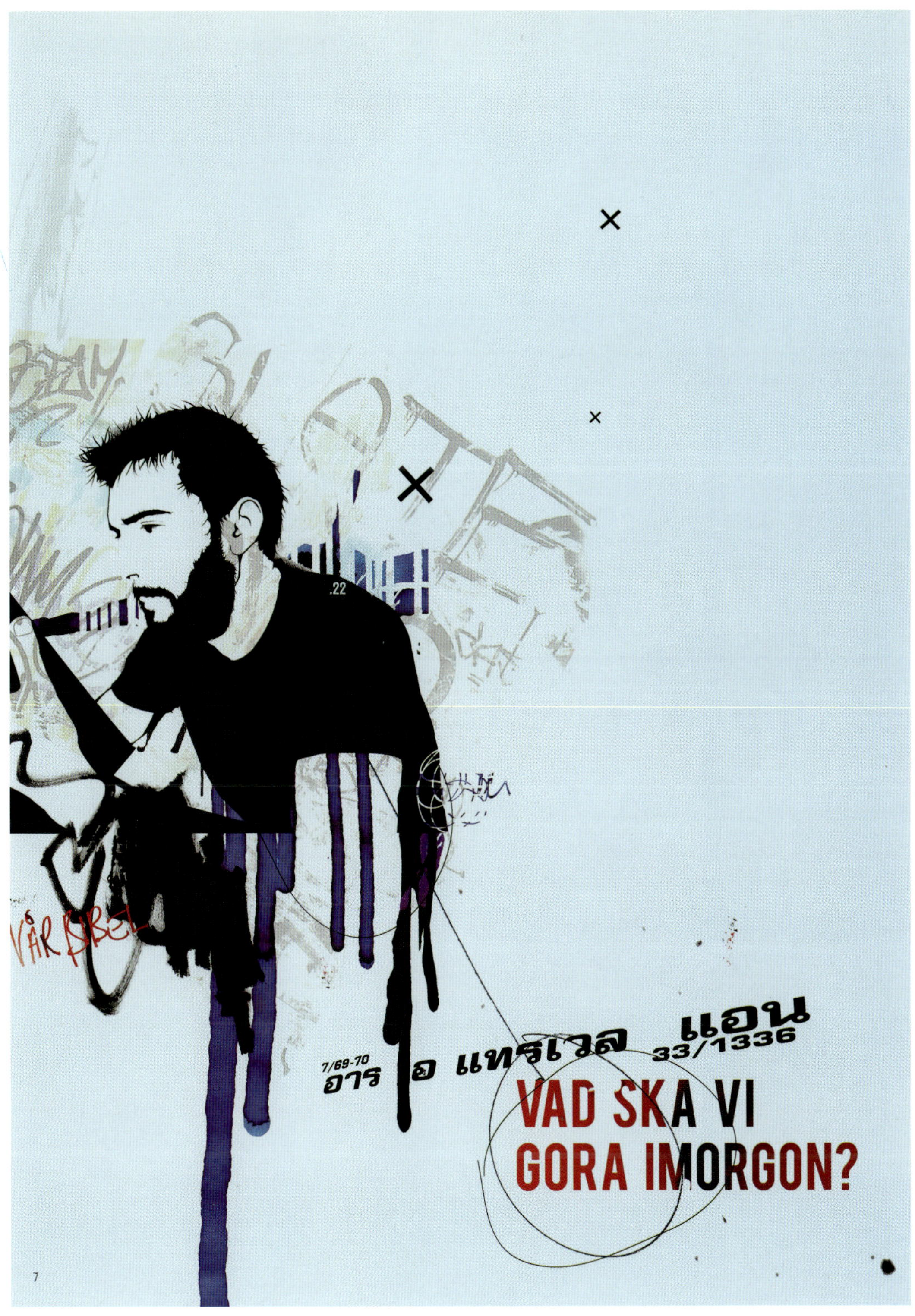

Steven Jarvis
UK

www.stevenjarvisdesign2.4ormat.
com

1. **More** (2011). *CREATUREMAG*. Hand drawing, Photoshop

2. **Pope** (2012). *The Crack Magazine*. Hand drawing, Photoshop

3. **Blow My Mind** (2010). *CREATUREMAG*. Hand drawing, Photoshop

4. **Nostalgia** (2011). *AMMO Magazine*. Hand drawing, Photoshop

5. **Kids** (2010). Personal work. Hand drawing, Photoshop

6. **Monaco** (2011). *CREATUREMAG*. Hand drawing, Photoshop

7. **Imorgon** (2009). Personal work. Hand drawing, Photoshop

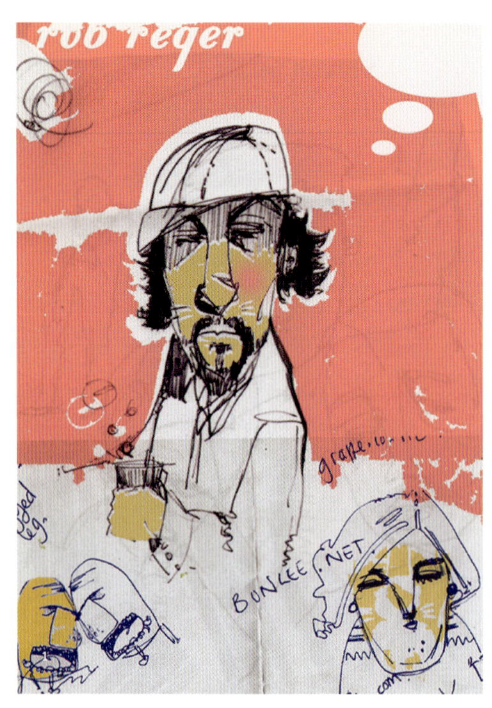
rob reger
BONLEE.NET

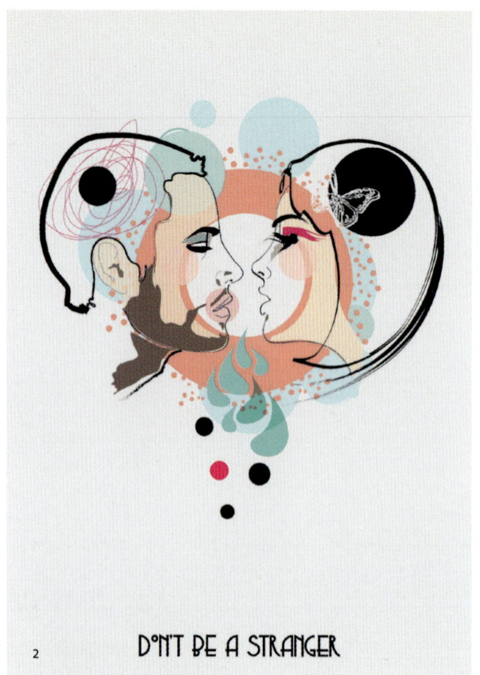
DON'T BE A STRANGER

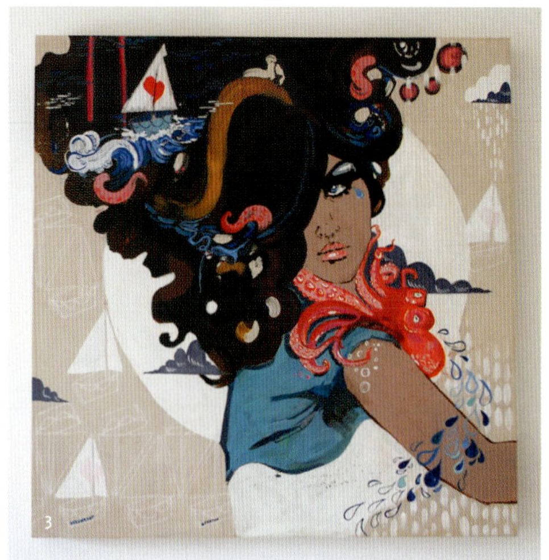

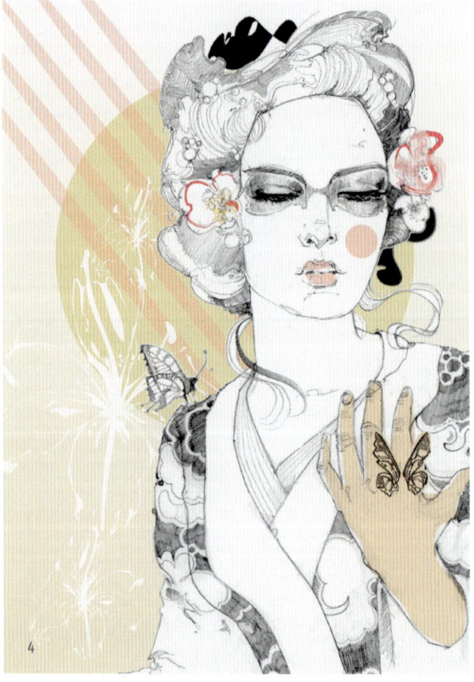

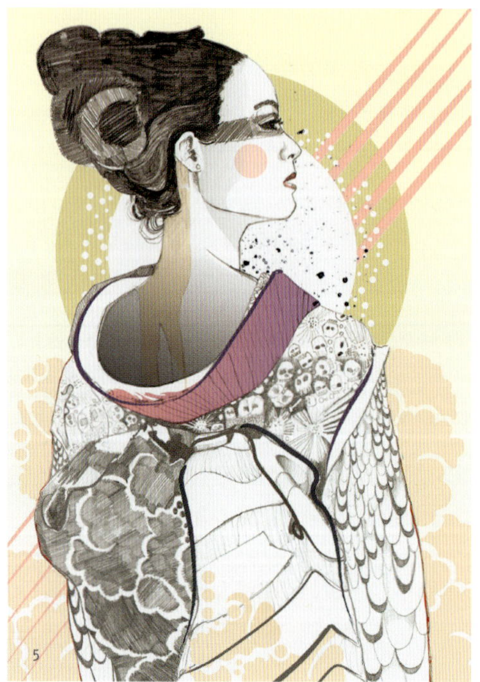

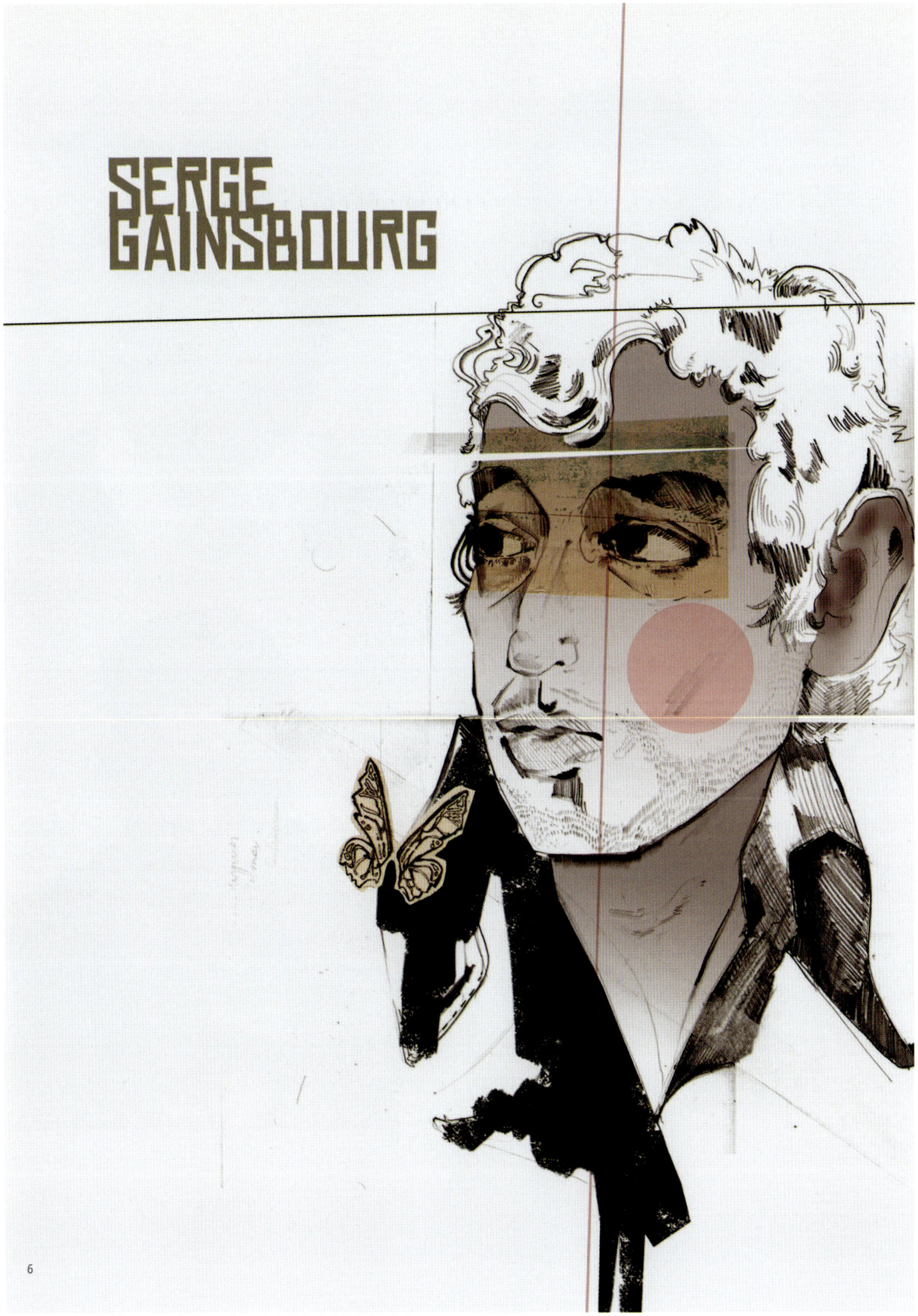

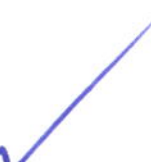

SERGE
GAINSBOURG

Michelle Turton
UK

michelleturton.com

1. **Rob Reger** (2005). Personal work. Pencil, pen, ink, digital

2. **Don't Be A Stranger** (2007). DBAS. Digital

3.
   Dreamboat (2010). Inkygoodness. Acrylic, gouache on canvas

4.
   Hope (2009). Inkygoodness. Pencil, digital

5.
   Fear (2009). Inkygoodness. Pencil, digital

6.
   Serge Gainsbourg (2009). Draw Serge. Pencil, digital

6

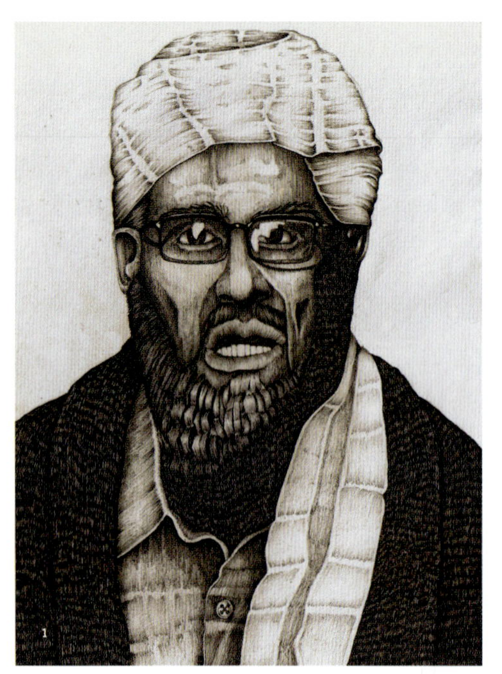

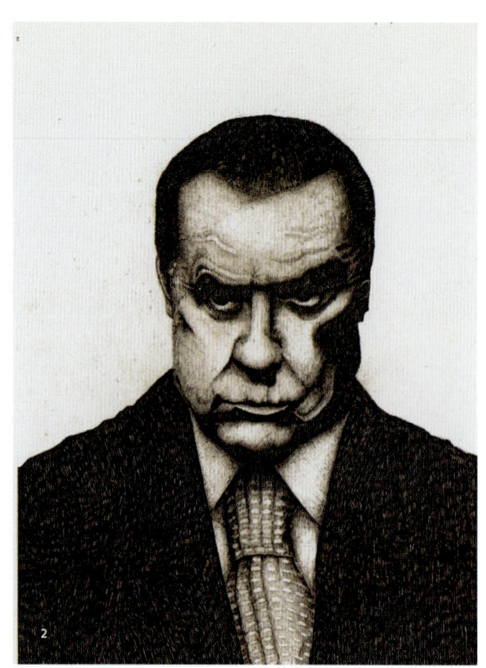

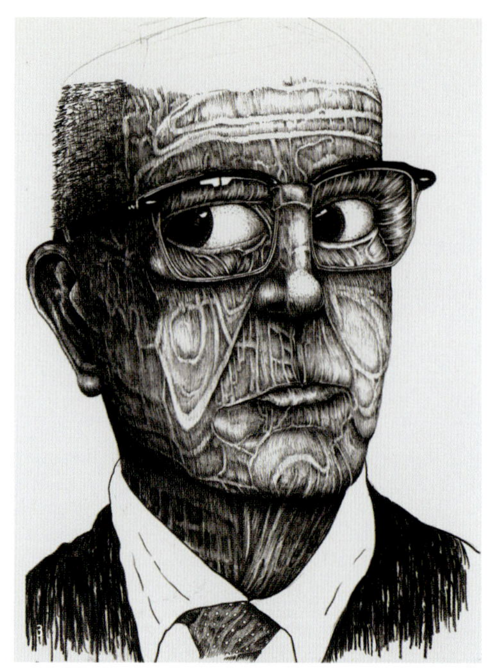

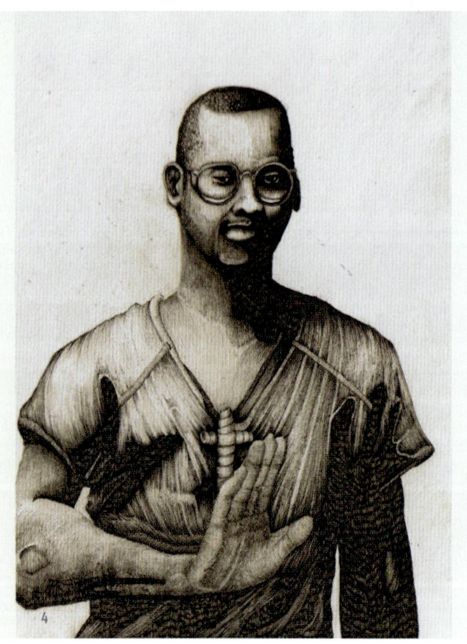

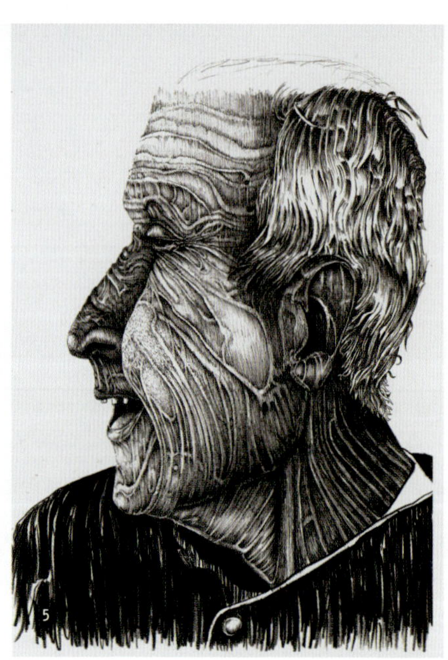

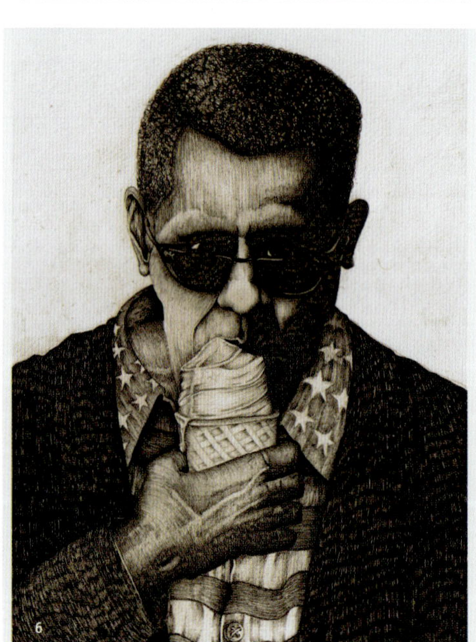

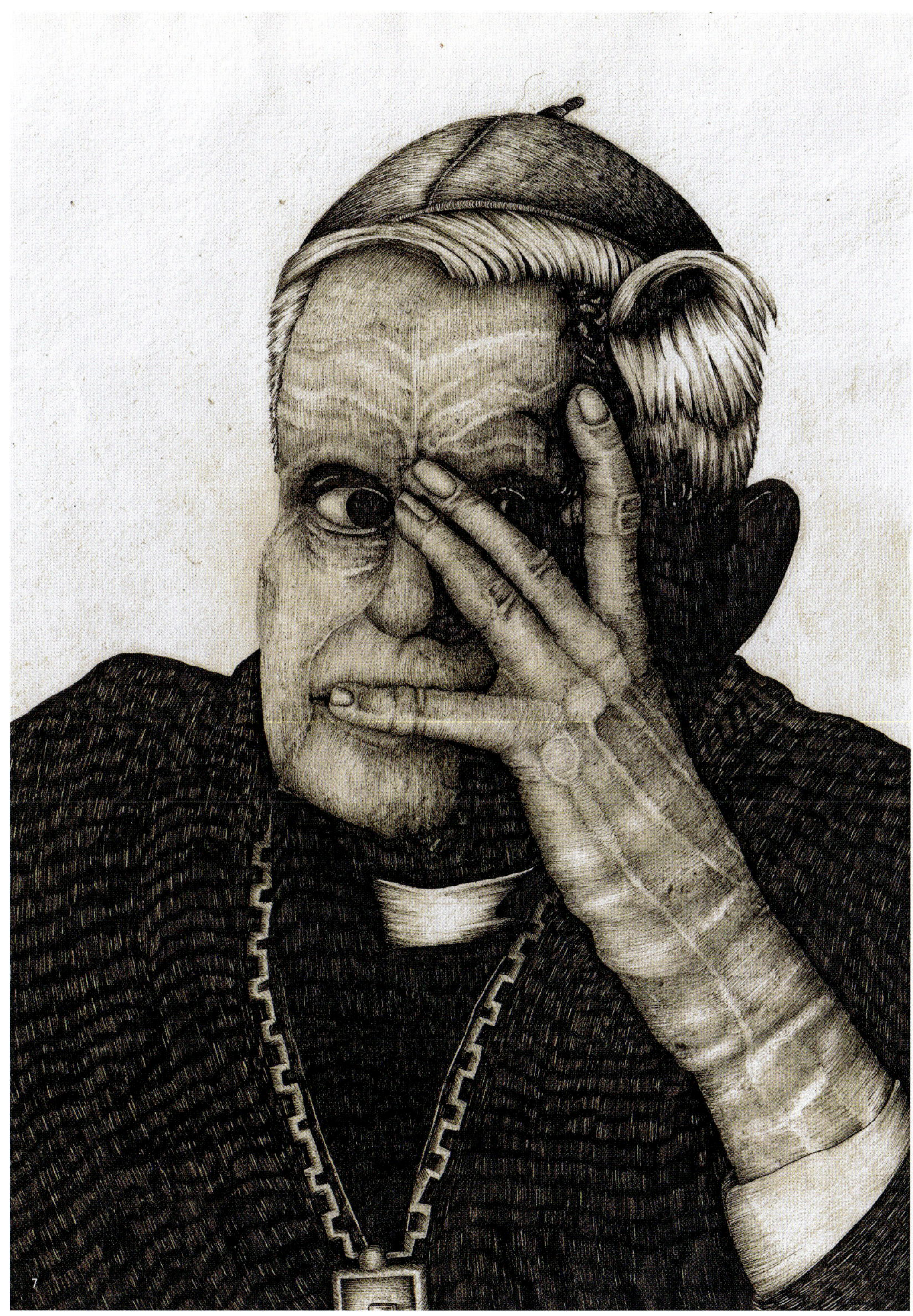

Bastian Preussger

Germany

www.bastianpreussger.com

1. **Mustafa Abu Al-Yazid** (2011). Personal work. India ink

2. **Silvio Berlusconi** (2011). Personal work. India ink

3. **Bruno** (2010). Personal work. India ink, wooden peg

4. **Troy Davis** (2011). Personal work. India ink

5. **Matteo** (2010). Personal work. India ink, wooden peg

6. **Barack Obama** (2011). Personal work. India ink

7. **Pope Benedikt XVI** (2011). Personal work. India ink

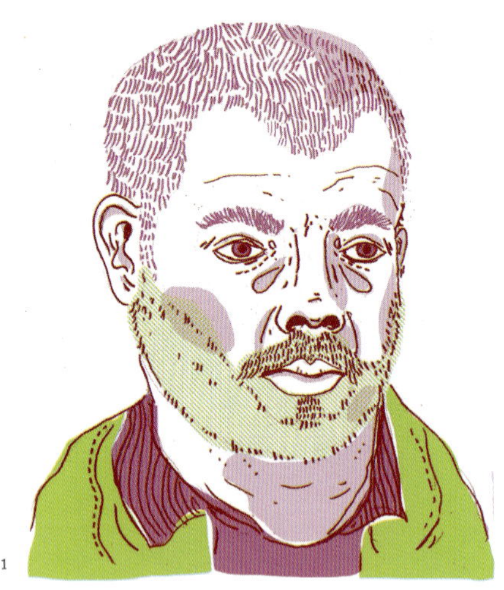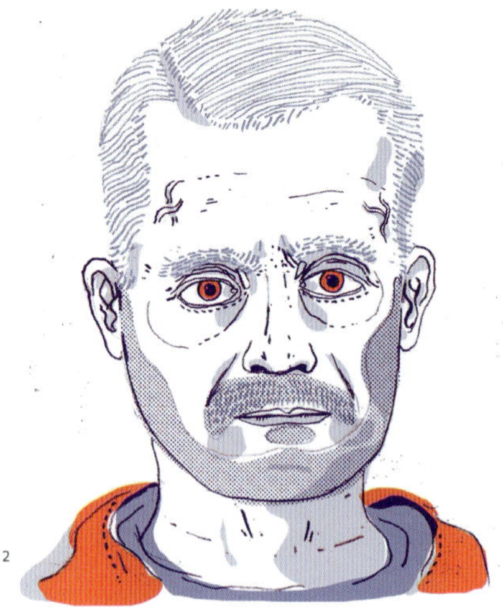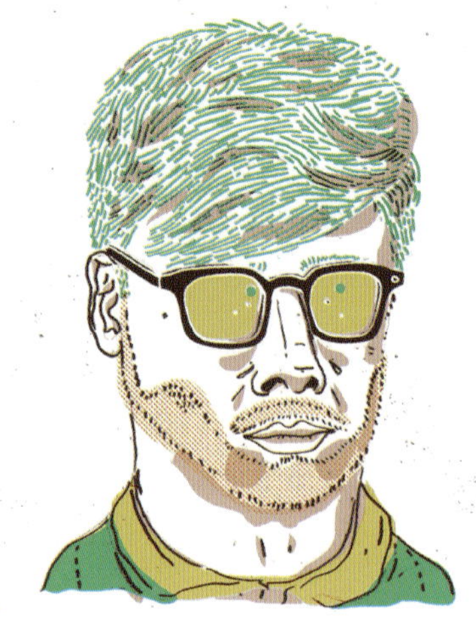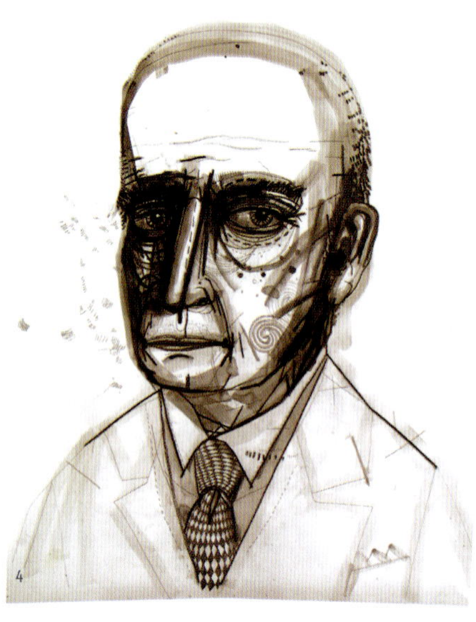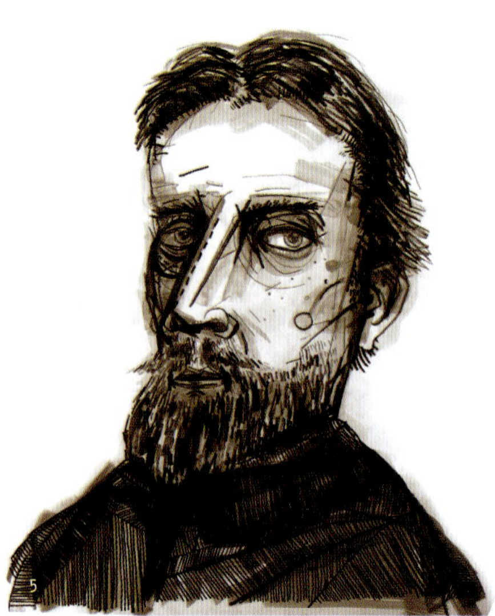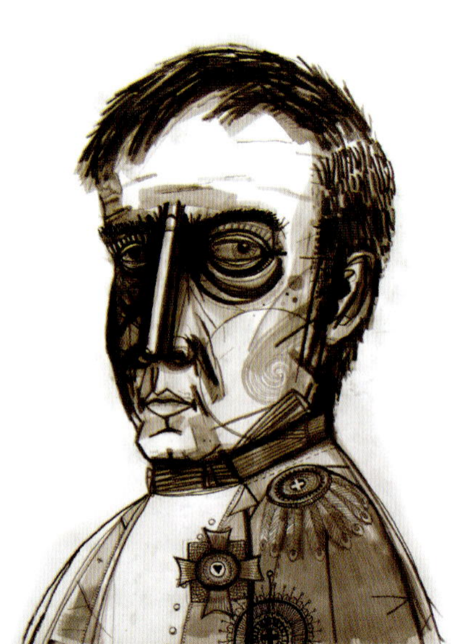

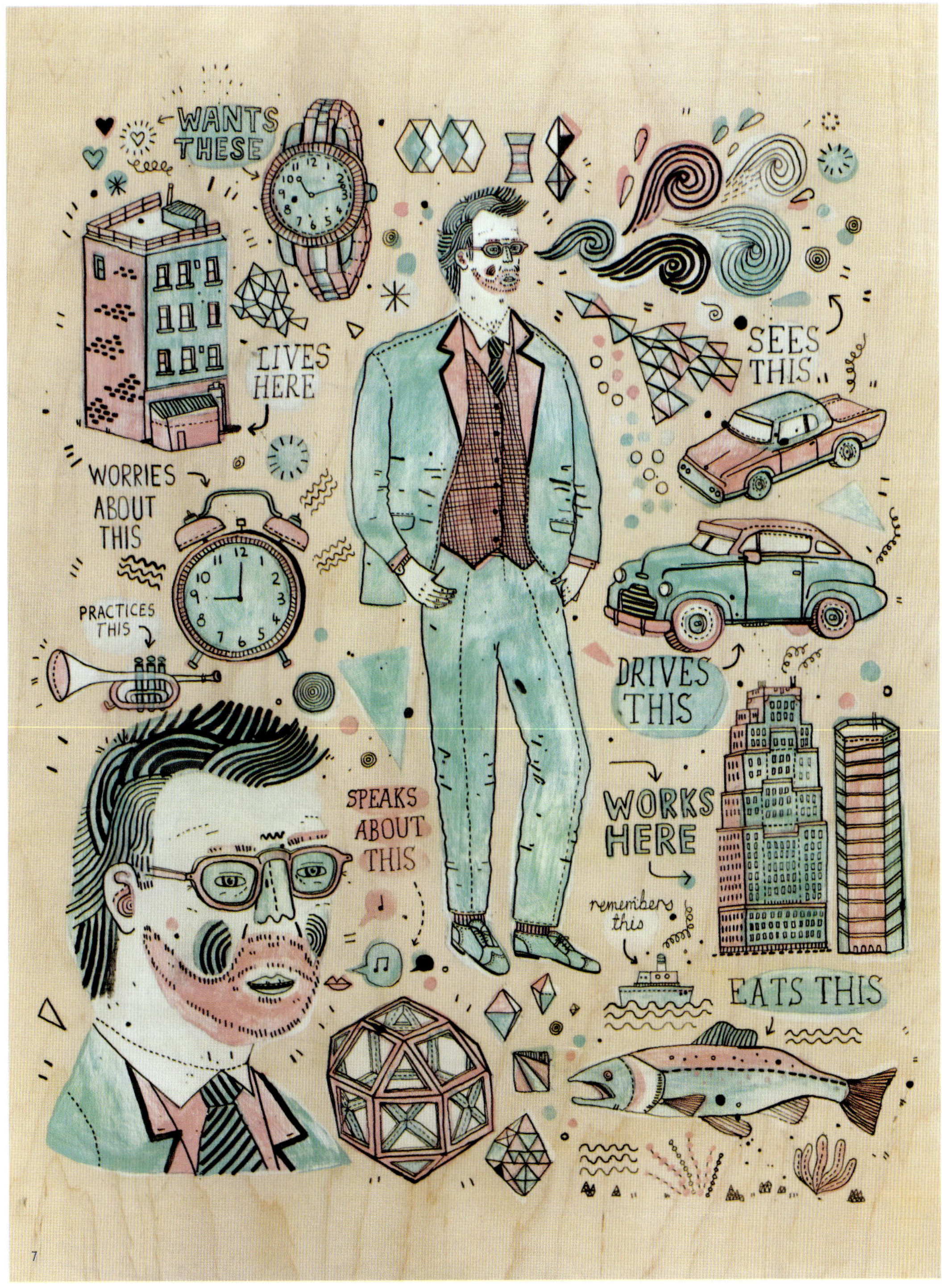

James Gulliver Hancock
Australia

www.jamesgulliverhancock.com

1. **Subway Man** (2010). Personal work. Silkscreen

2. **Subway Man** (2010). Personal work. Silkscreen

3. **Subway Man** (2010). Personal work. Silkscreen

4. **Eisenhower** (2009). Personal work. Pen, ink on paper

5. **Goldmund** (2009). Personal work. Pen, ink on paper

6. **Napoleon** (2009). Personal work. Pen, ink on paper

7. **Manhattan Man** (2011). Personal work. Acrylic, pen, ink, lacquer on board

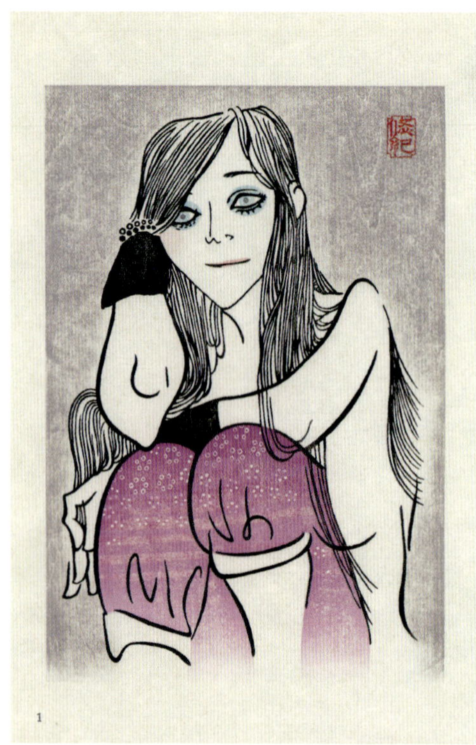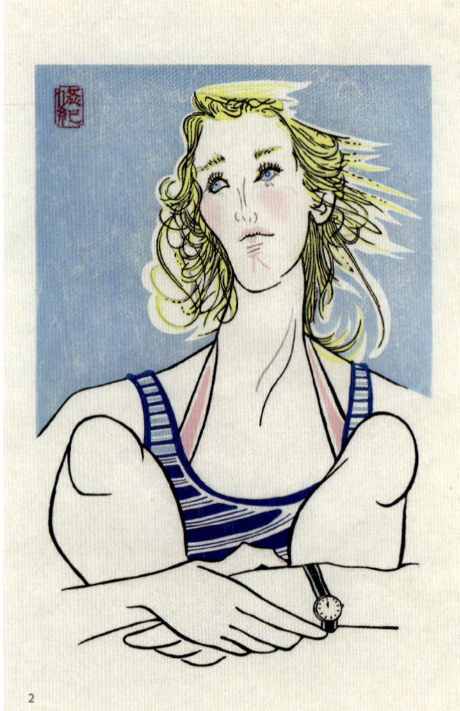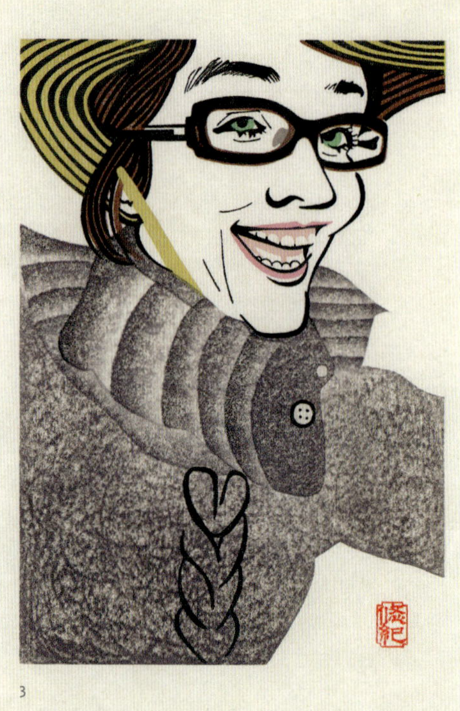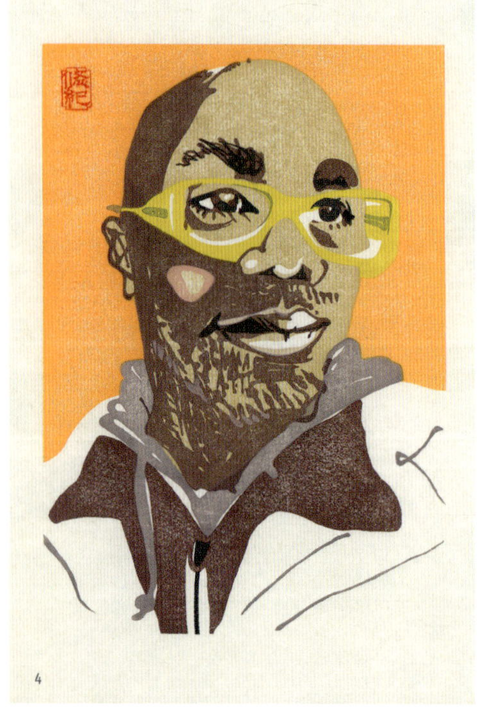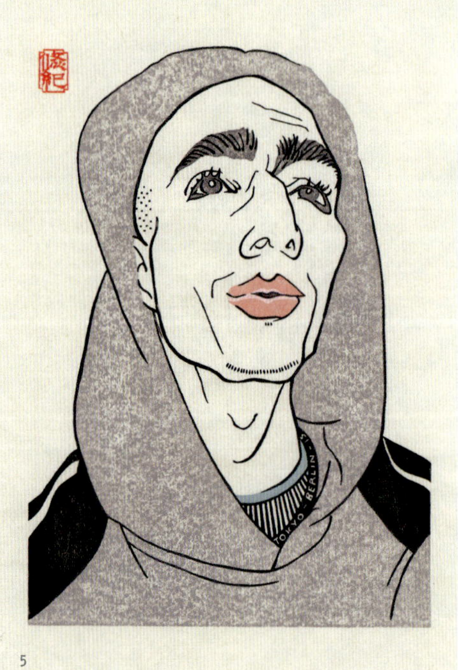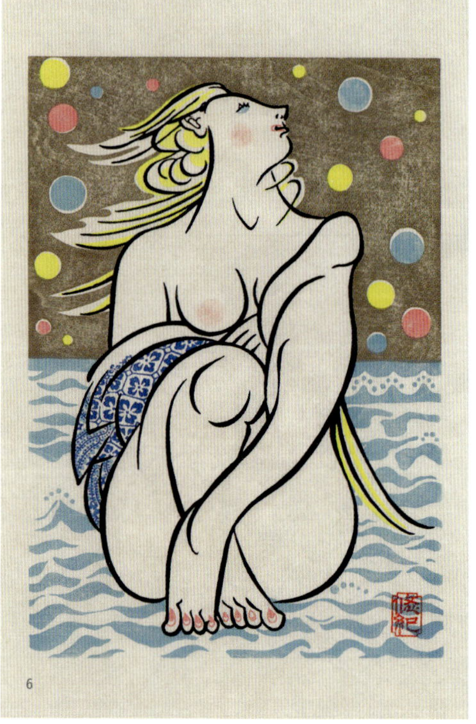

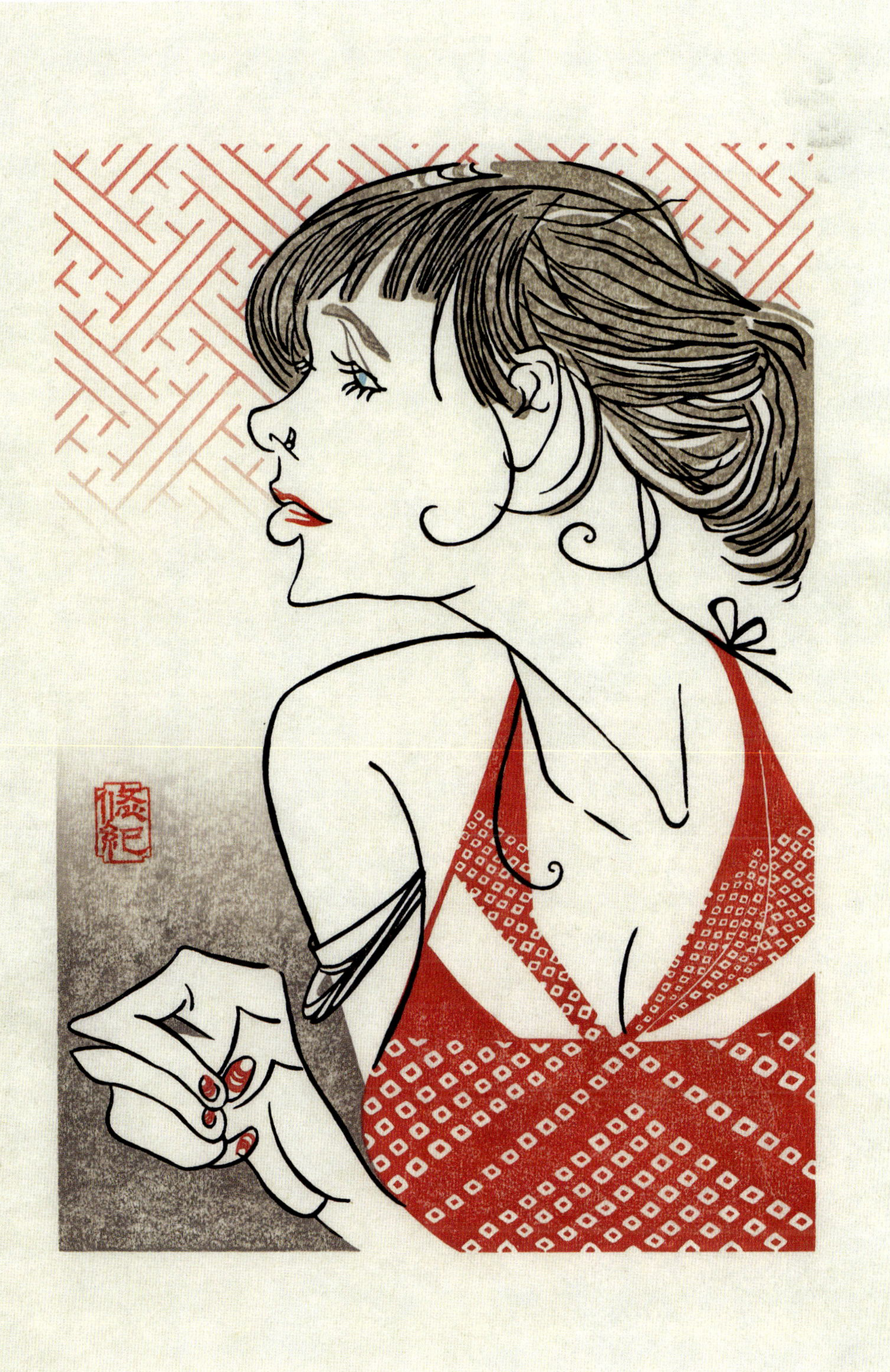

7

Yuko Chikazawa & Maki Shimizu

Japan

www.blockingwood.com
www.makishimizu.de

1. **Anna** (2011). Personal work. Japanese woodcut printing

2. **Sanne** (2011). Personal work. Japanese woodcut printing

3. **Annette** (2011). Personal work. Japanese woodcut printing

4. **Daniel** (2011). Personal work. Japanese woodcut printing

5. **Ferhat** (2011). Personal work. Japanese woodcut printing

6. **Sanne 2** (2011). Personal work. Japanese woodcut printing

7. **Elena** (2011). Personal work. Japanese woodcut printing

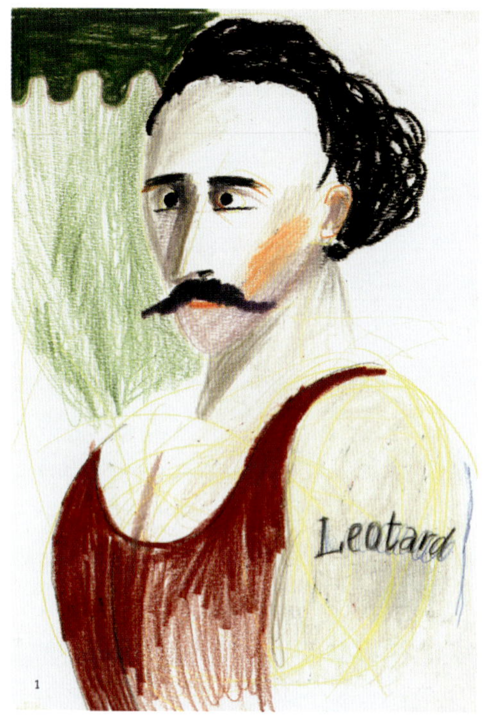

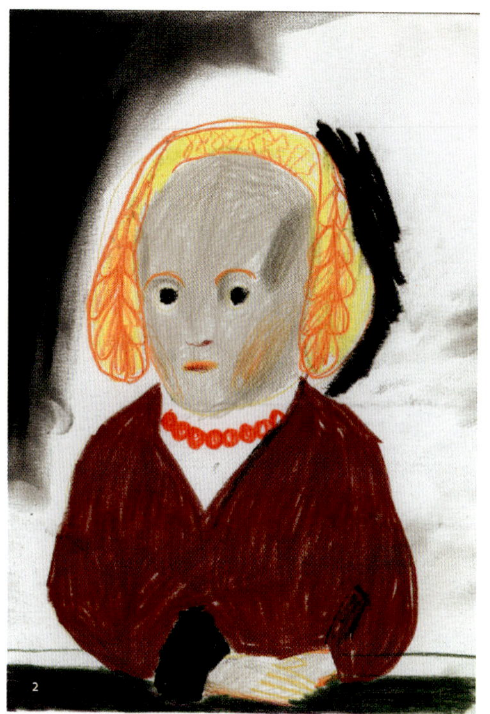

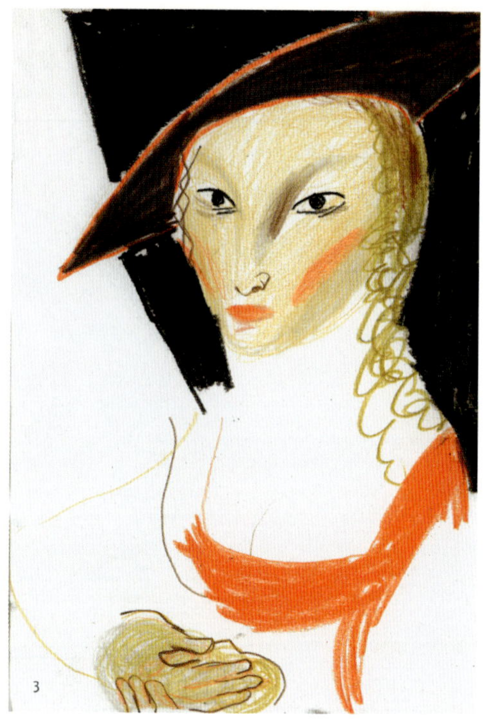

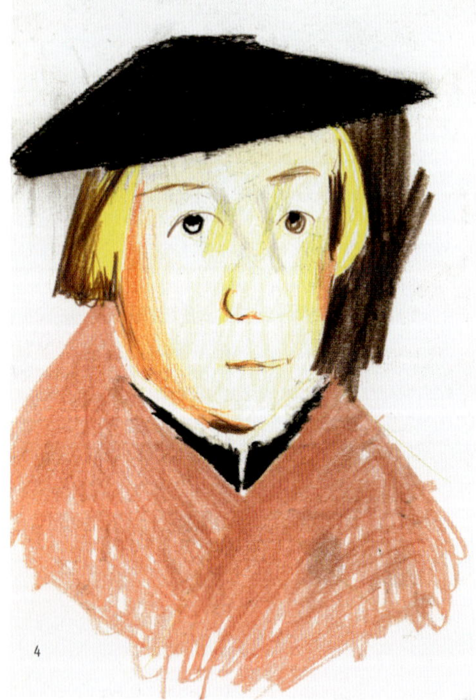

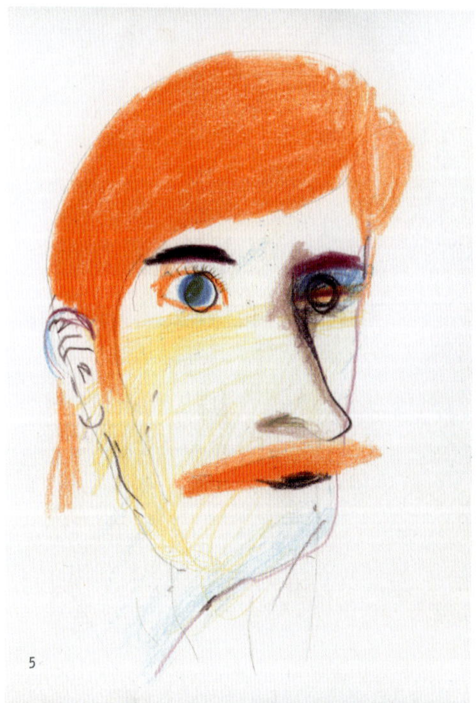

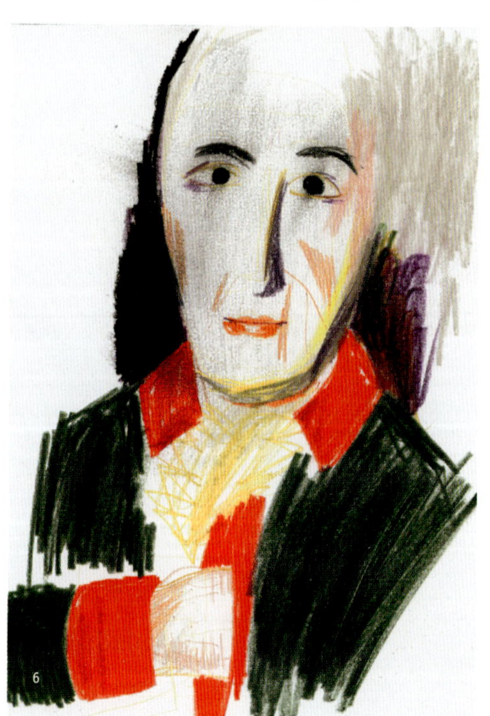

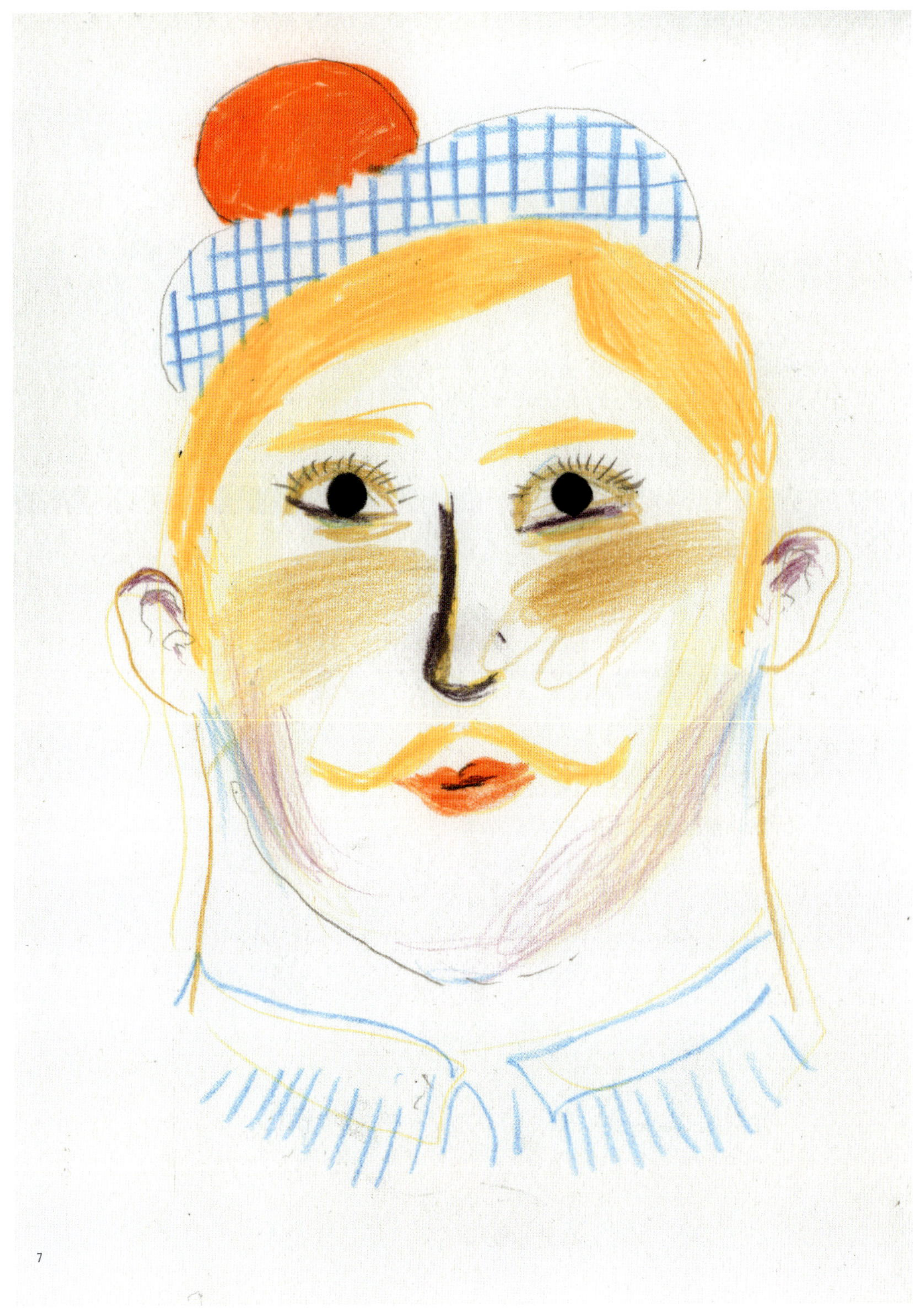

7

Inga Dorofeeva

Germany

www.dorofeeva.de

1. **Leotard** (2010). Elefant Art Space Gallery. Colored crayon

2. **Kind** (2010). Elefant Art Space Gallery. Colored crayon

3. **Frau** (2010). Elefant Art Space Gallery. Colored crayon

4. **Kaufmann** (2010). Elefant Art Space Gallery. Colored crayon

5. **Hermann** (2011). Personal work. Colored crayon

6. **General** (2010). Elefant Art Space Gallery. Colored crayon

7. **Matrose** (2011). Personal work. Colored crayon

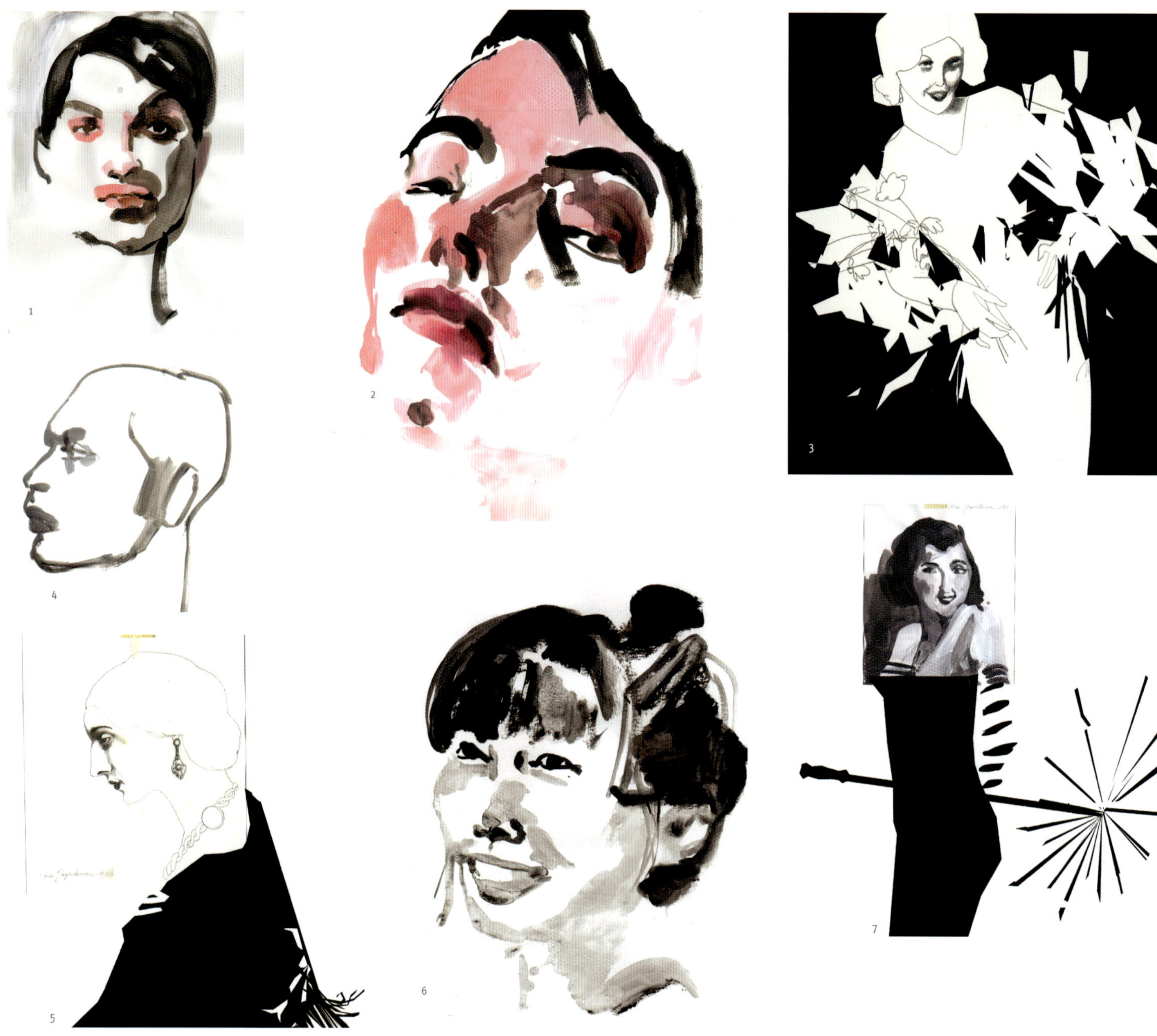

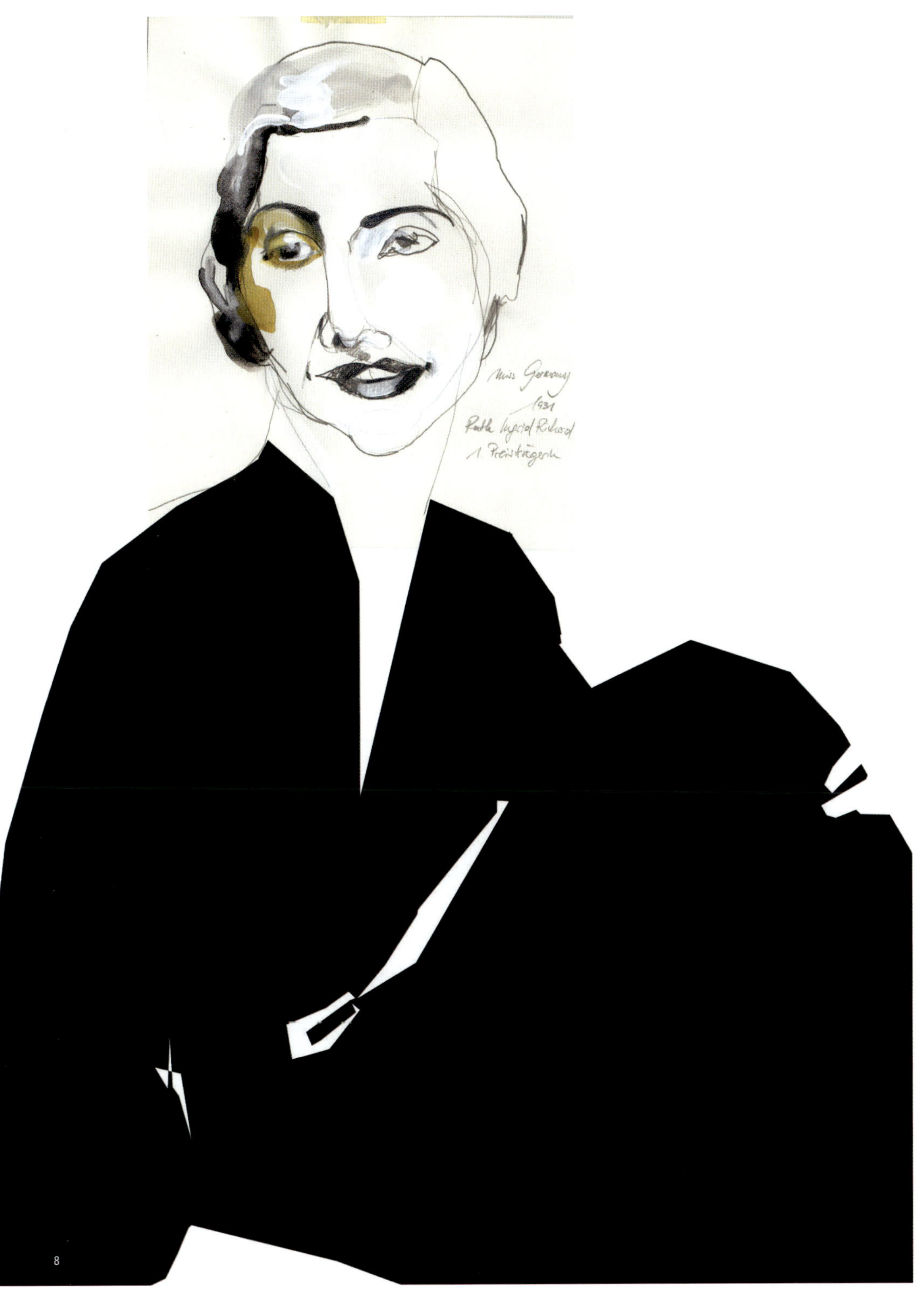

Katrin Funcke
Germany

www.katrinfuncke.de

1. **Earnest** (2007). Personal work. Gouache
2. **Manon** (2007). Personal work. Gouache
3. **Miss Hungary 1930** (2011). Personal work. Pencil, black paper

4. **Martin** (2008). Personal work. Acrylic
5. **Miss Yugoslavia 1930** (2011). Personal work. Pencil, black paper

6. **Sue** (2011). Susanne Hu / Suhu Fashion. Acrylic

7. **Miss Yugoslavia 1932** (2011). Personal work. Acrylic, black paper

8. **Miss Germany 1931** (2011). Personal work. Pencil, gouache, acrylic, black paper

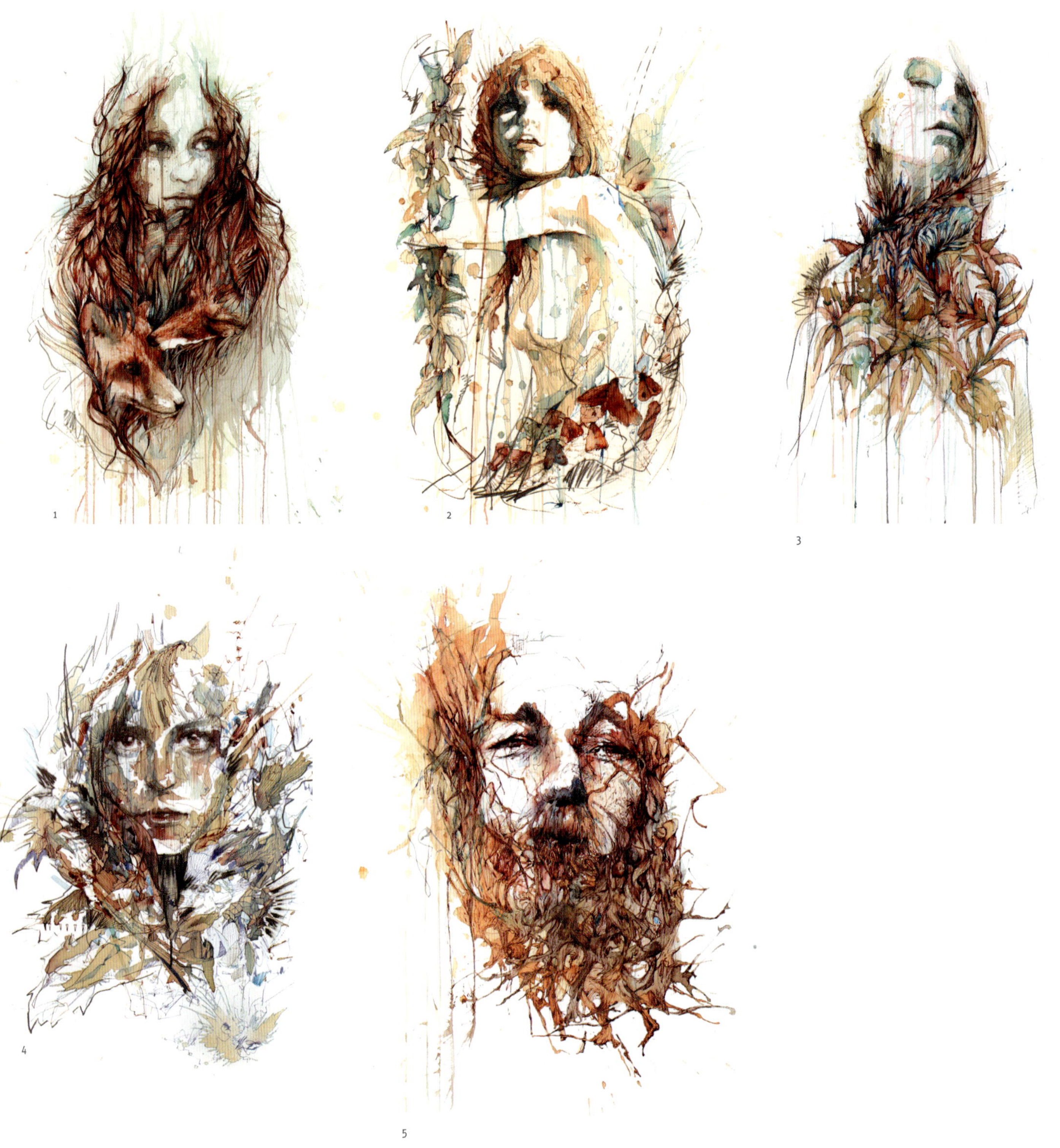

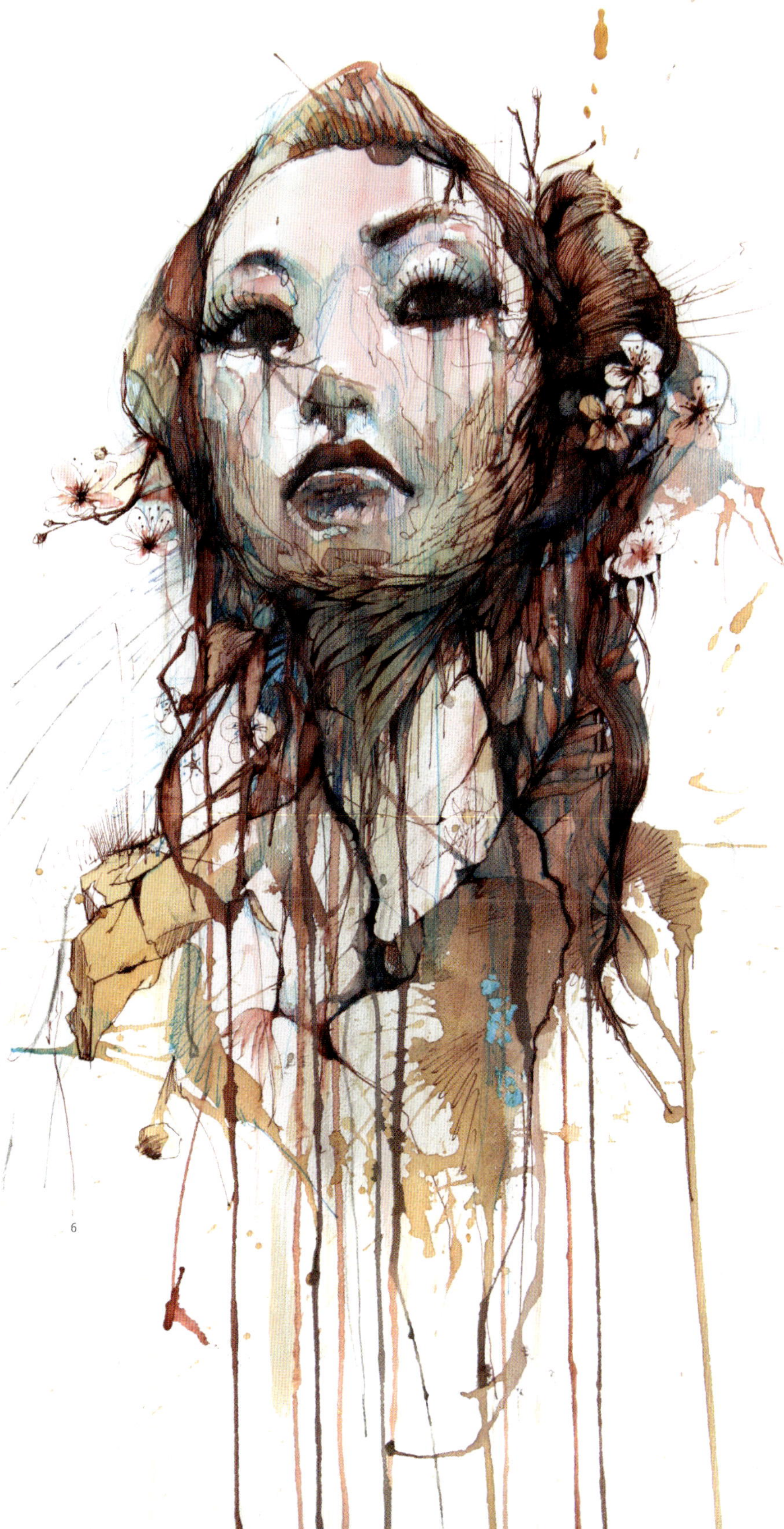

Carne Griffiths

UK

www.carnegriffiths.com

1. **Comfort** (2011). Personal work. Ink, tea on watercolor paper

2. **Metamorphosis** (2011). Personal work. Ink, tea on watercolor paper

3. **Parassita** (2011). Personal work. Ink, tea on watercolor paper

4. **Take Cover** (2011). Personal work. Ink, tea on watercolor paper

5. **Roots 2011** (2011). Personal work. Ink, tea on watercolor paper

6. **Strength** (2011). Personal work. Ink, tea on watercolor paper

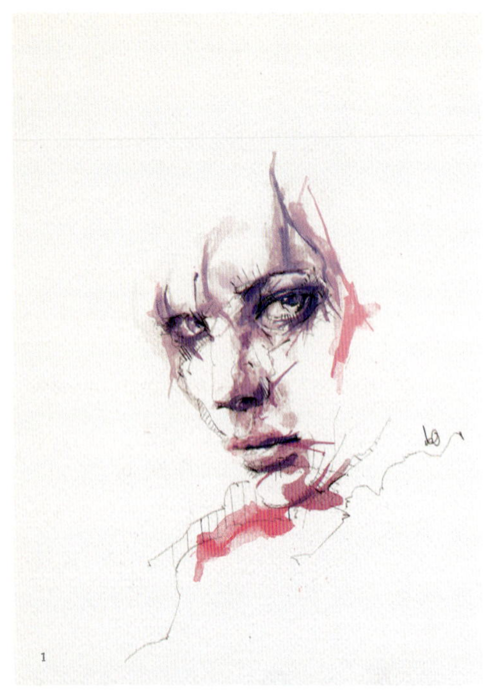
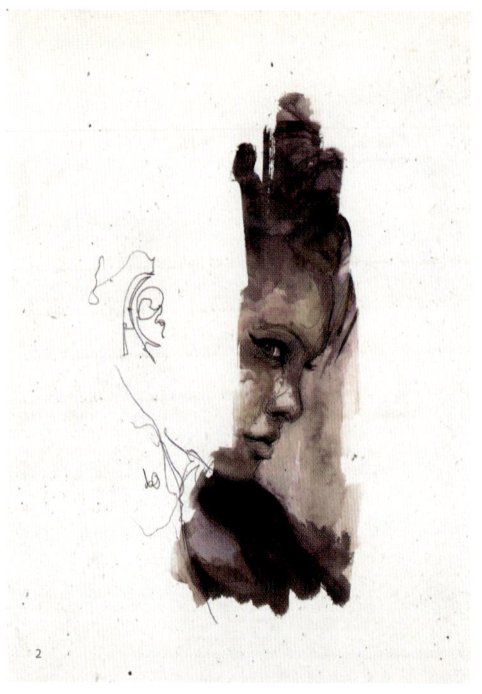
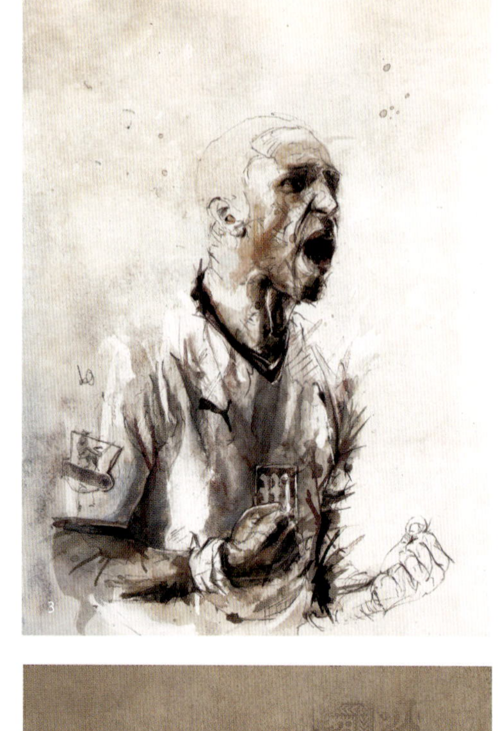
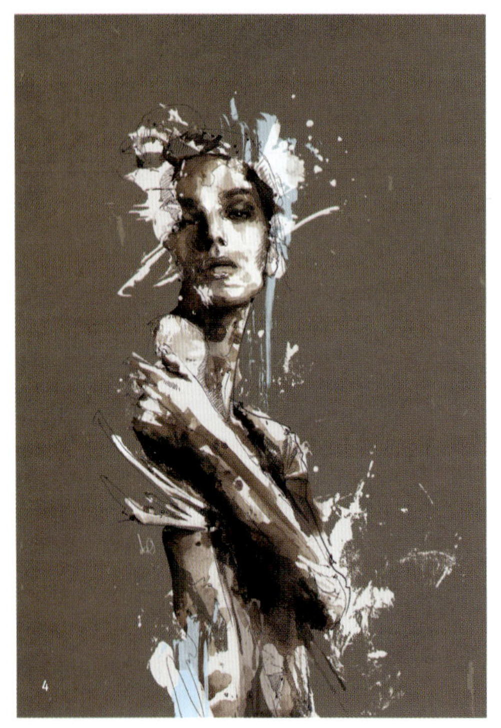
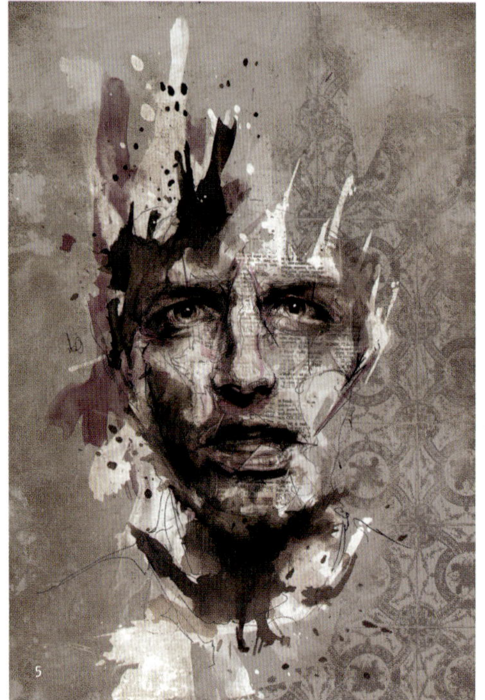
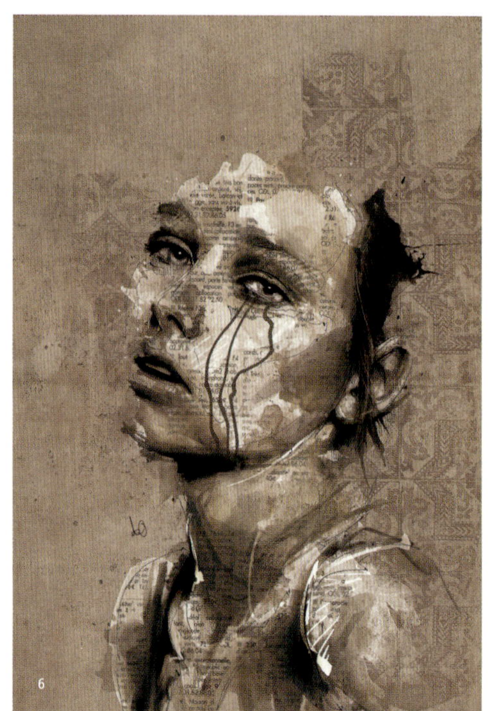

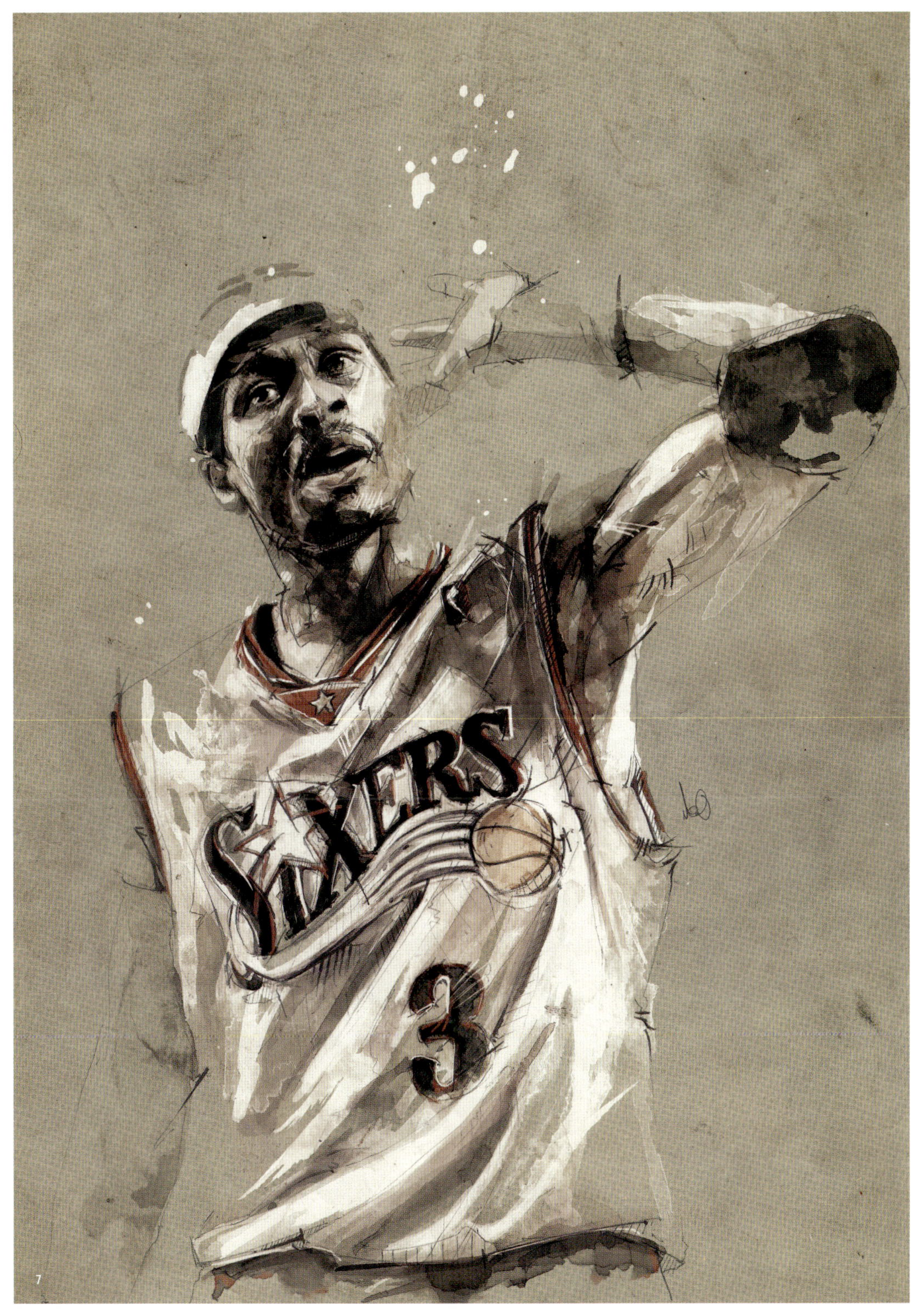

Florian Nicolle
aka neo

France

www.neo-innov.fr

1. **Acacia** (2011). Personal work. Tradigital

2. **Angelina Jolie** (2009). Personal work. Tradigital

3. **Jermain Defoe** (2011). Personal work. Tradigital

4. **Lize** (2009). Personal work. Tradigital

5. **Y** (2010). Personal work. Tradigital

6. **Iris** (2010). Personal work. Tradigital

7. **Allen Iverson** (2011). Personal work. Tradigital

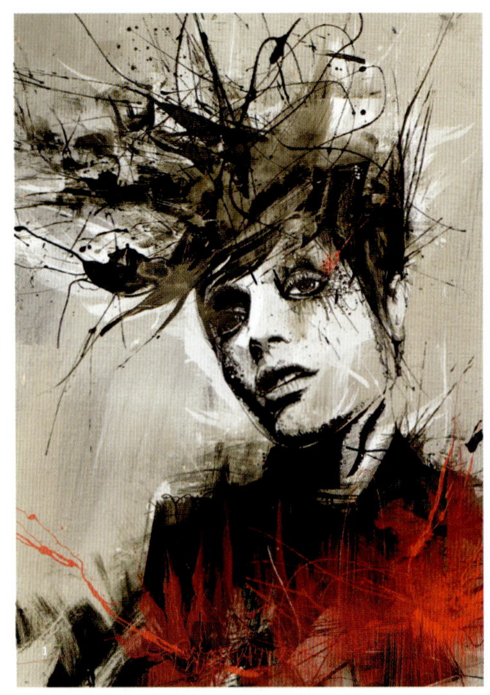
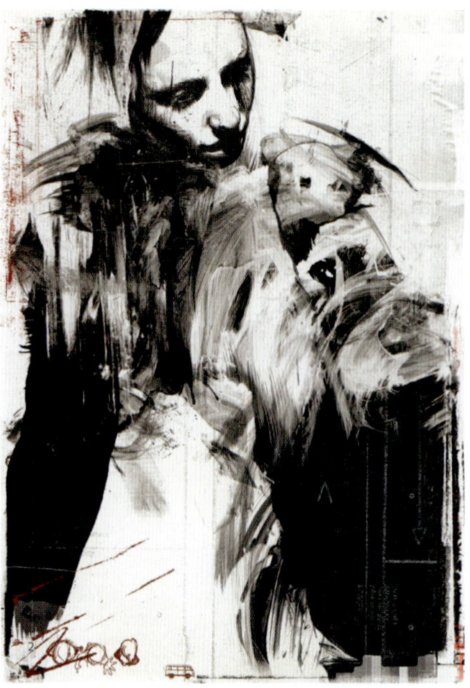
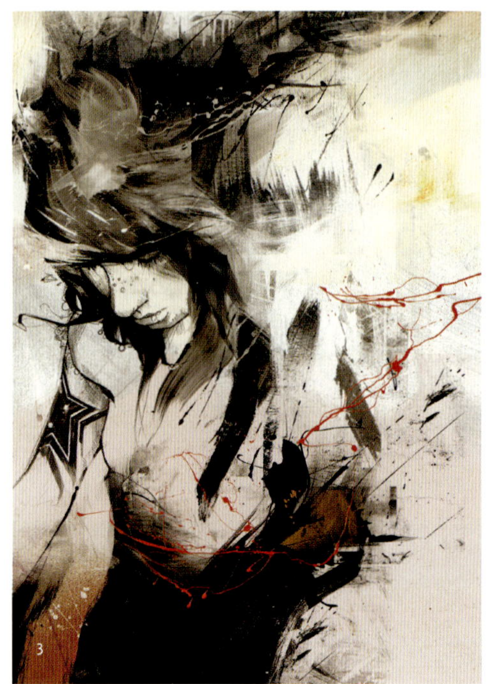
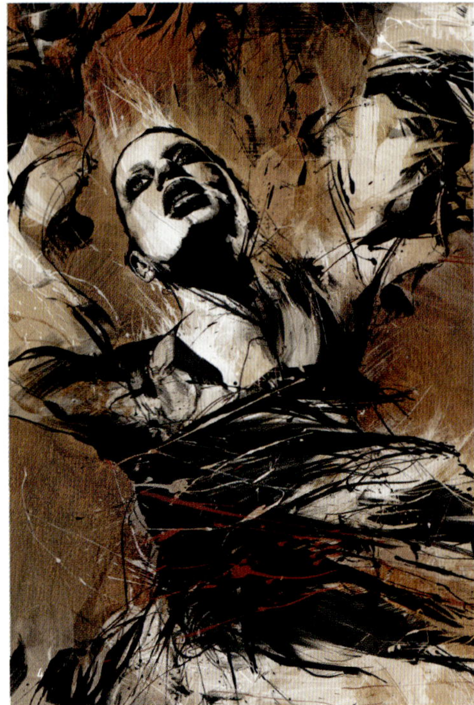
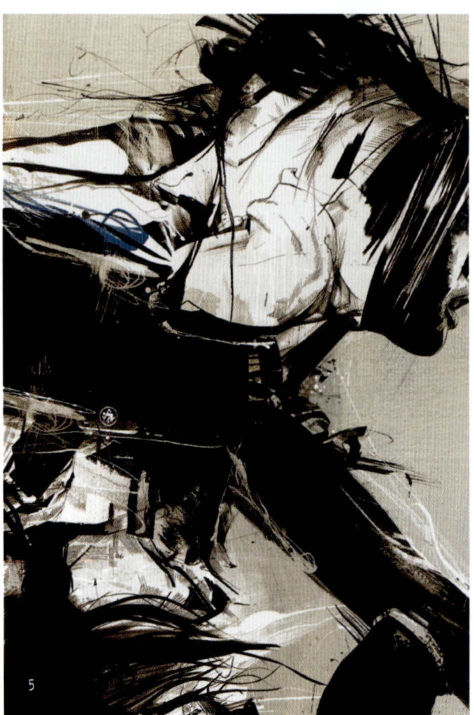

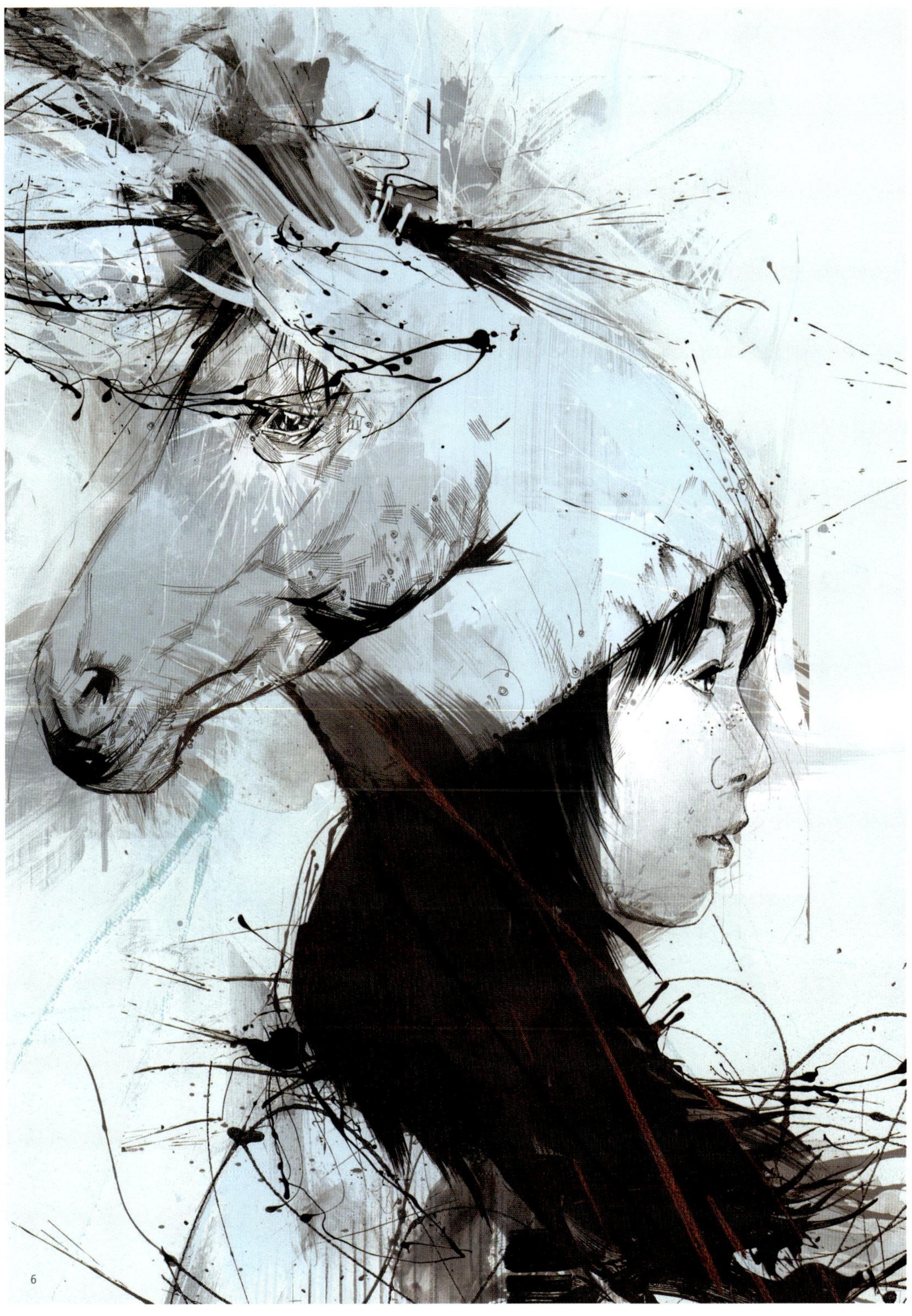

Russ Mills
UK

www.byroglyphics.com

1. **Astrophytum** (2008). Personal work. Digital composite

2. **Asphyxsia** (2010). Personal work. Digital composite

3. **Delphinium** (2008). Personal work. Digital composite

4. **Gethsemane** (2009). *Domestic Science.* Show at Signal Gallery. Digital composite

5. **Tyderium** (2009). Personal work. Digital composite

6. **Equinopsis** (2008). Personal work. Digital composite

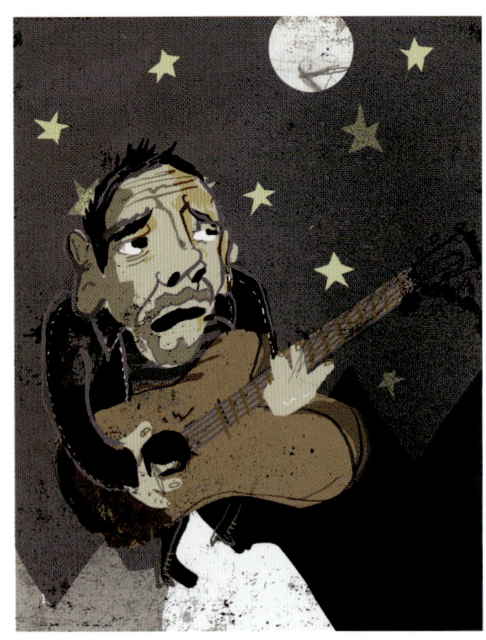

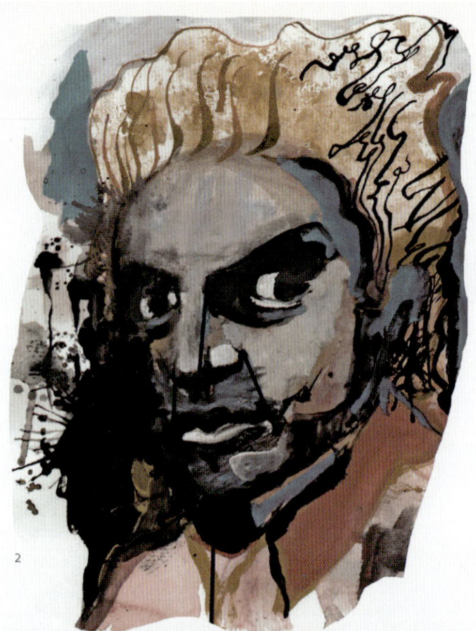

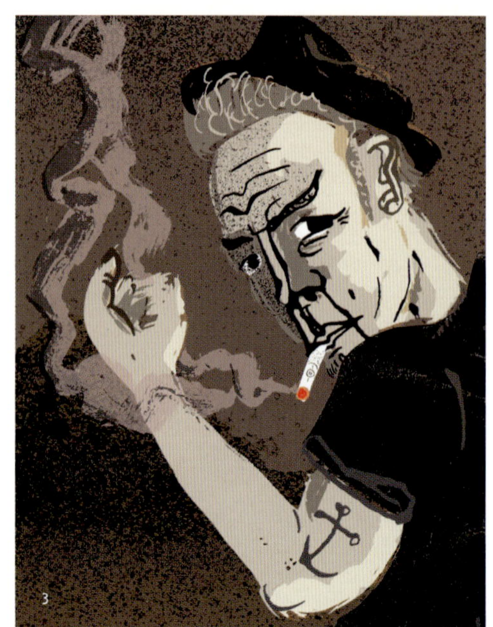

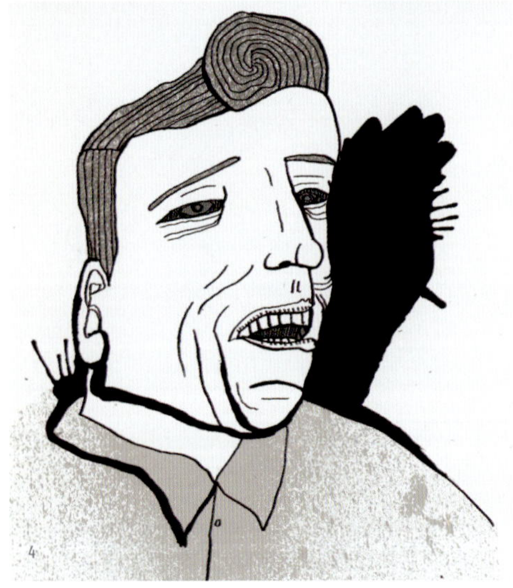

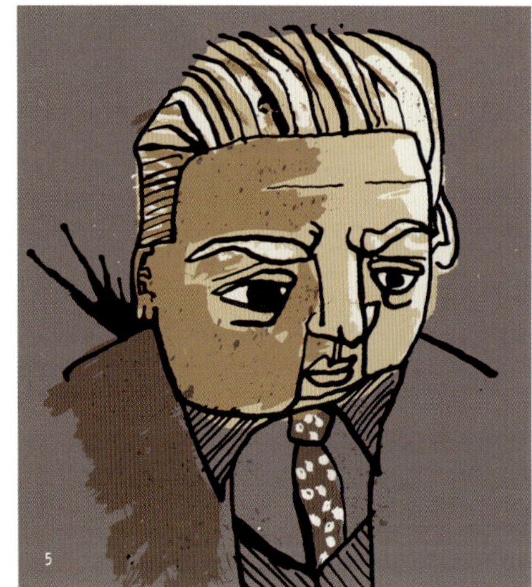

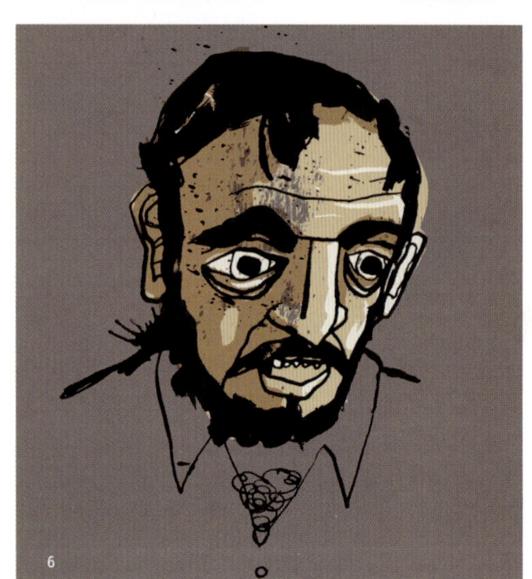

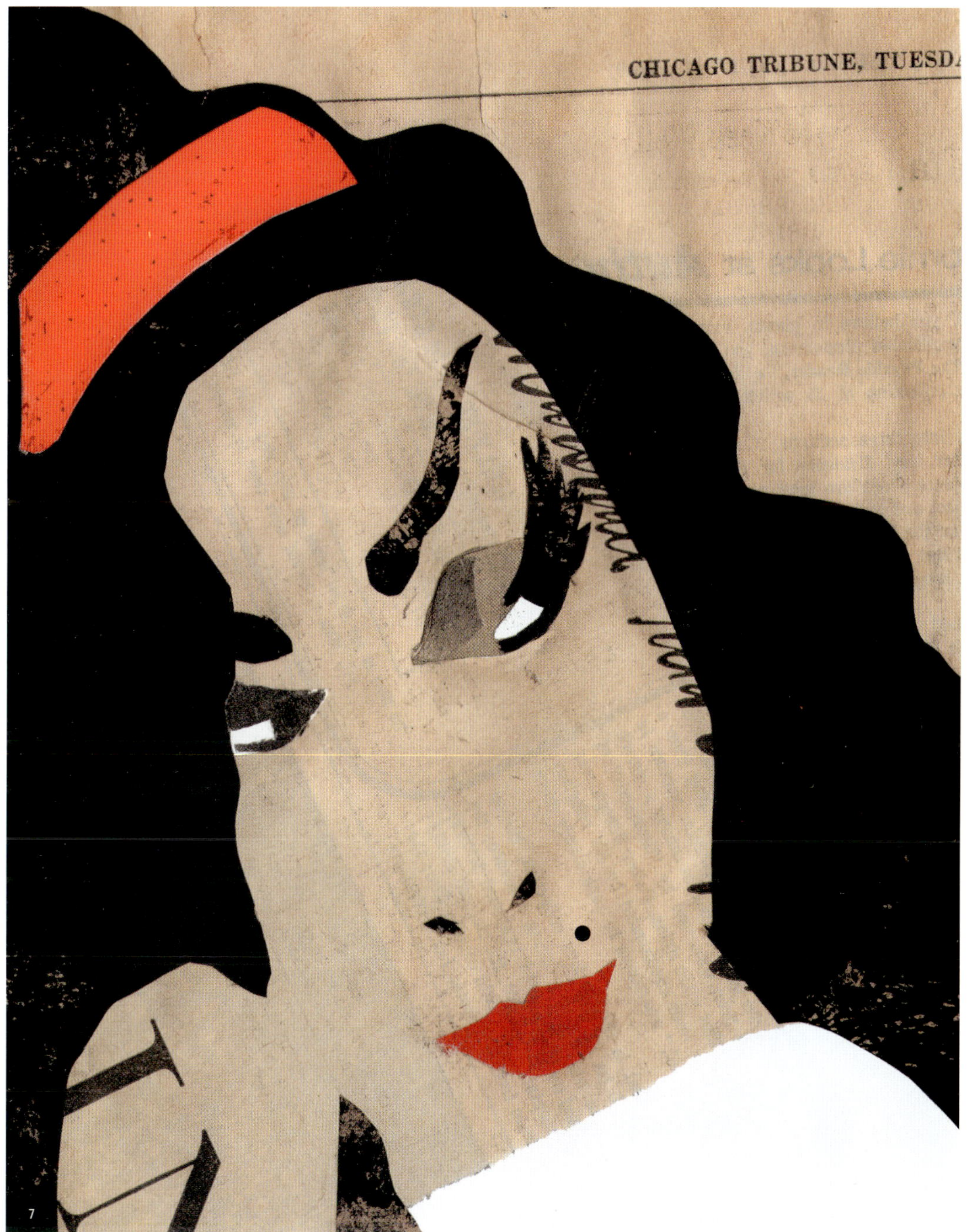

Daniel Zender
USA

www.danielzender.com

1. **Jonathan Richman** (2011). Personal work. Mixed media, digital

2. **M. Ward** (2011). Personal work. Ink, gouache

3. **Tom Waits** (2011). Personal work. Mixed media, digital

4. **Conan** (2011). SSLBYl. Ink

5. **Fredrico** (2011). Personal work. Mixed media, digital

6. **Stanley** (2011). Personal work. Mixed media, digital

7. **Amy Winehouse** (2011). Personal work. Cut paper collage

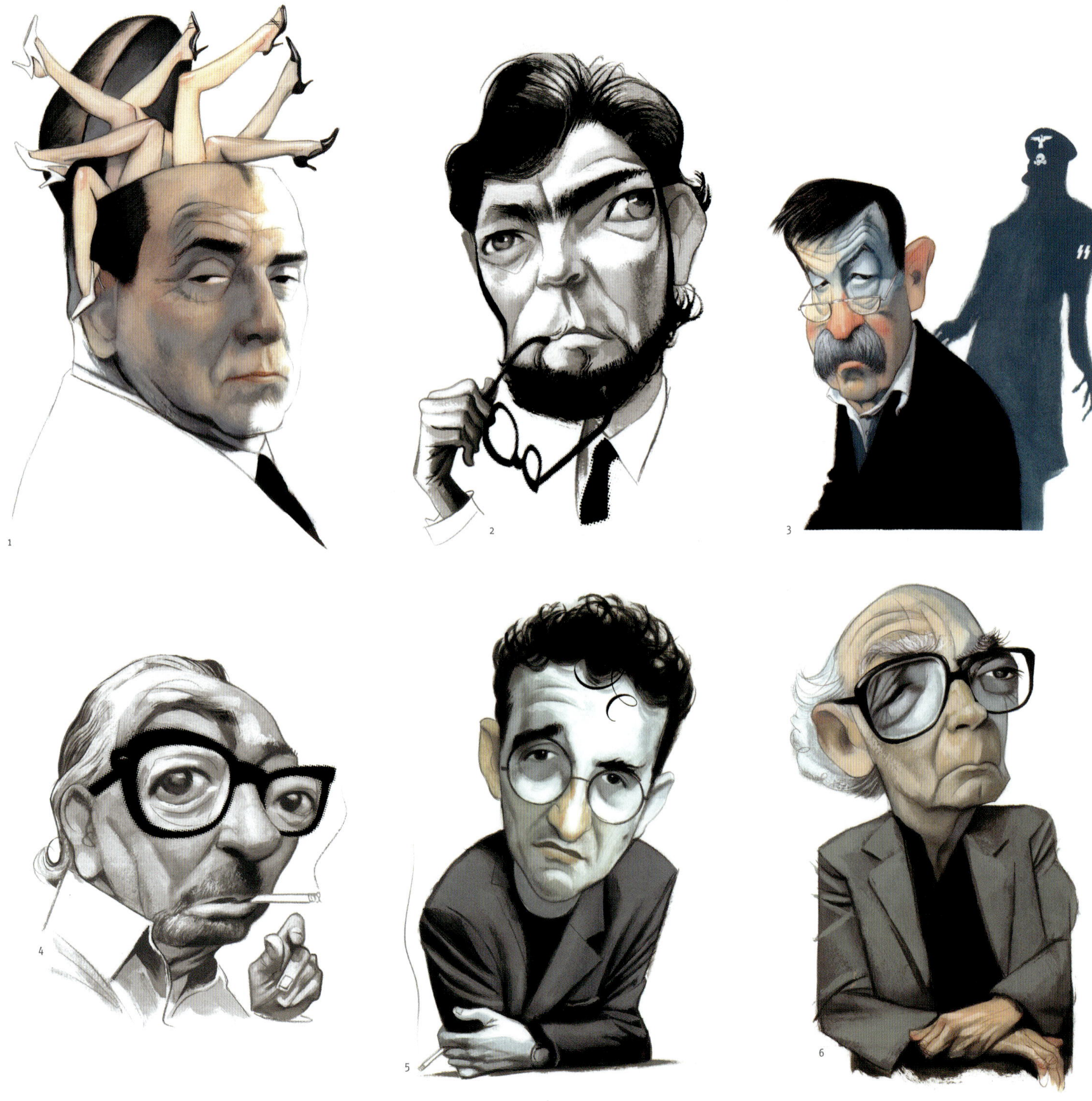

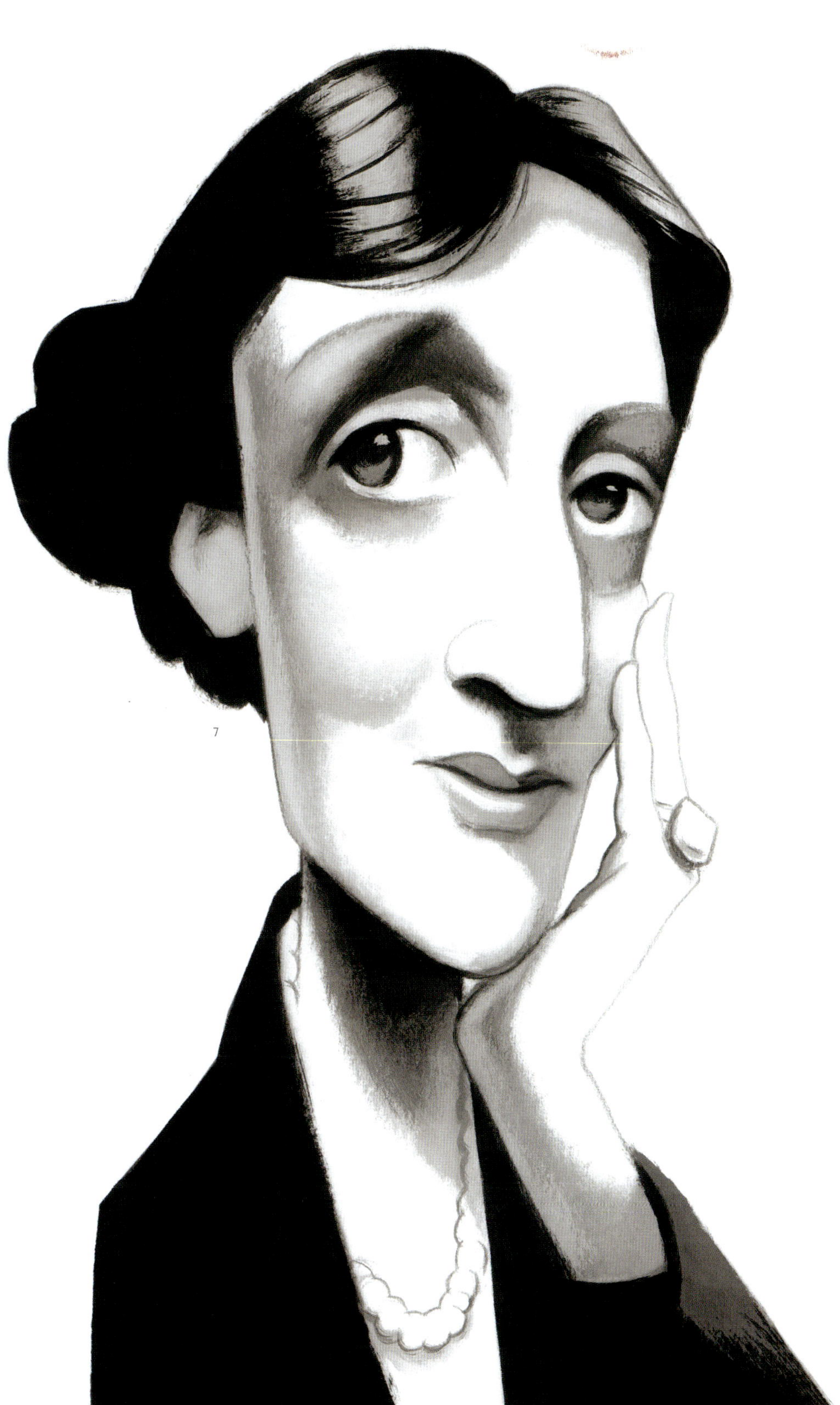

Fernando Vicente
Spain

www.fernandovicente.es

1. **Berlusconi** (2011). *Discover Magazine NY*

2. **Julio Cortazar** (2009). *Editorial Alfaguara*

3. **Günter Grass** (2006). *Letras Libres*

4. **Juan Carlos Onetti** (2009). *Editorial Alfaguara*

5. **Roberto Bolaño**

6. **RJosé Saramago** (2010). *Blur Ediciones*

7. **Virginia Woolf** (2009). *Editorial Alfaguara*

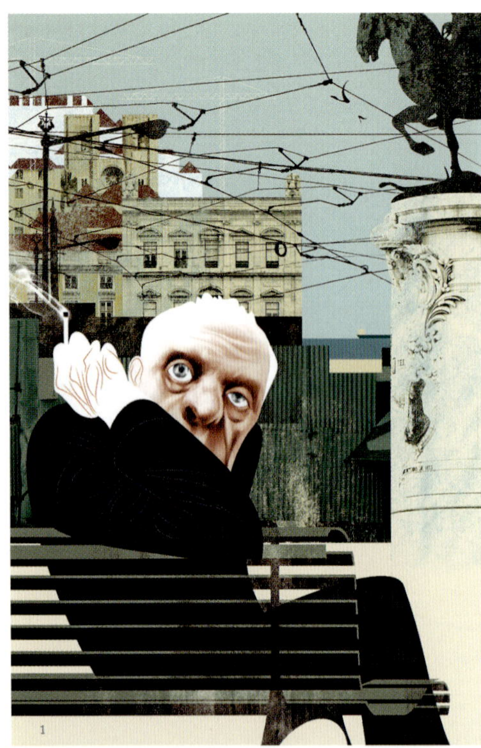

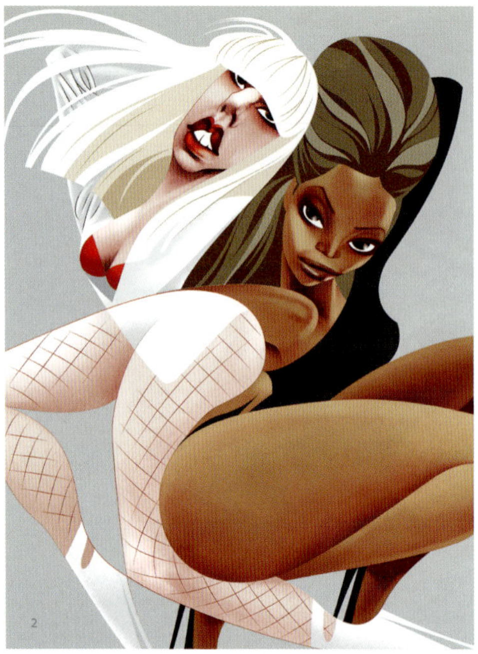

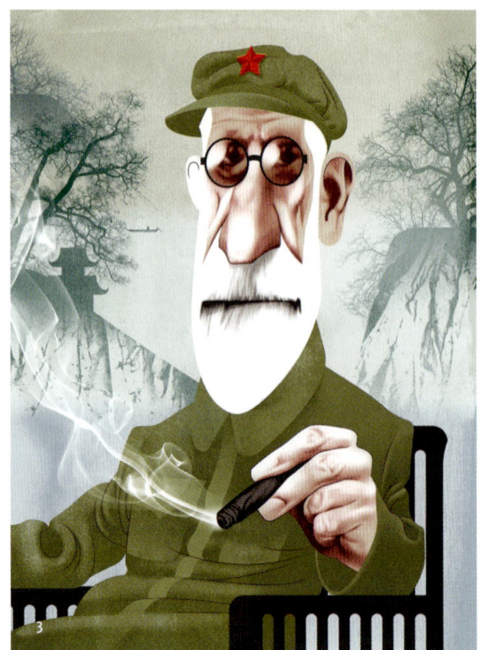

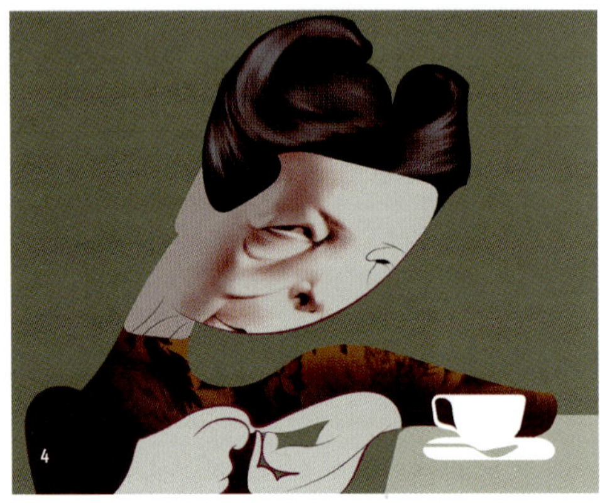

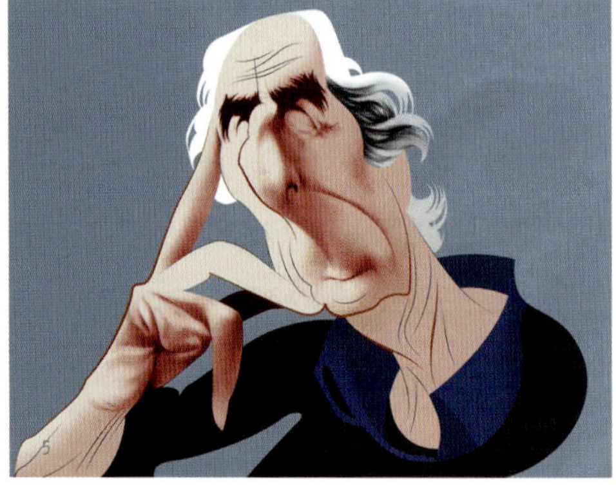

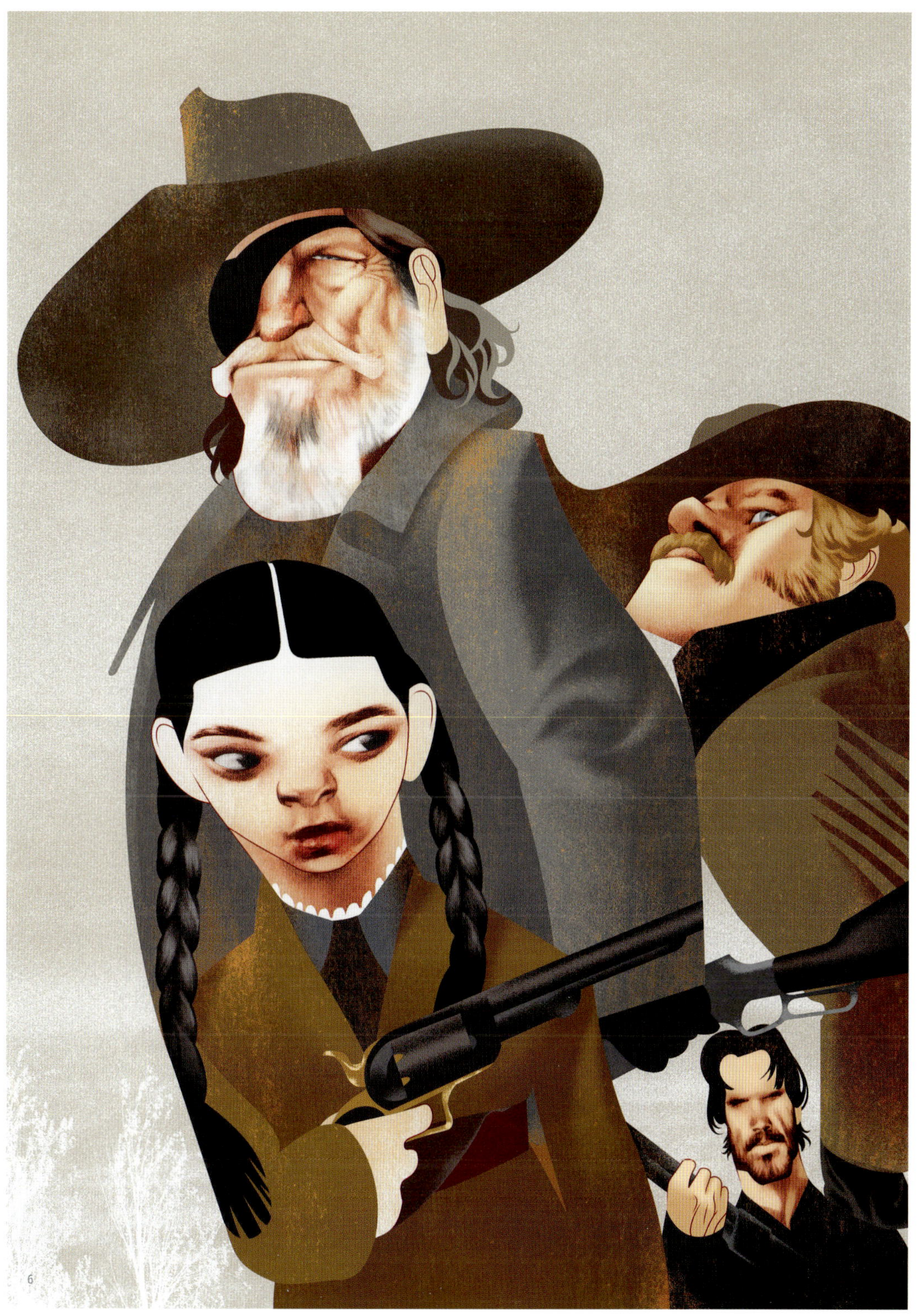

André Carrilho

Portugal

www.andrecarrilho.com

1. **Antonio Lobo Antunes** (2009). *The New Yorker*. Graphite on paper, Photoshop
2. **Beyonce & Lady Gaga** (2011). *The New Yorker*. Graphite on paper, Photoshop
3. **Freud in China** (2010). *The New Yorker*. Graphite on paper, Photoshop
4. **Simone Beauvoir** (2007). *NZZ am Sonntag*. Graphite on paper, Photoshop
5. **Philip Roth** (2008). *NZZ am Sonntag*. Graphite on paper, Photoshop
6. **True Grit** (2010). *The New Yorker*. Graphite on paper, Photoshop

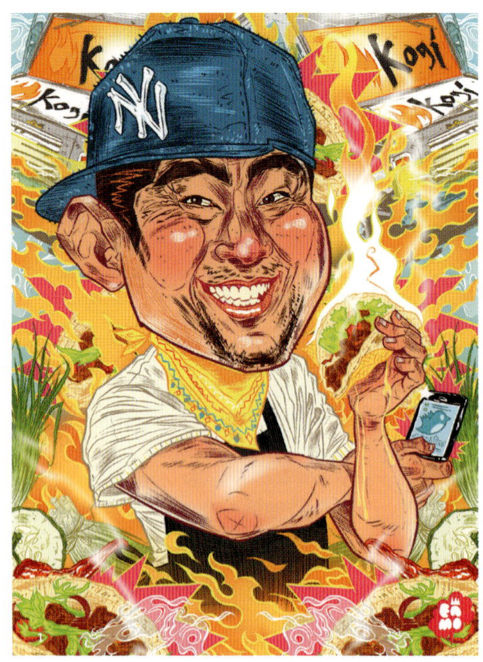 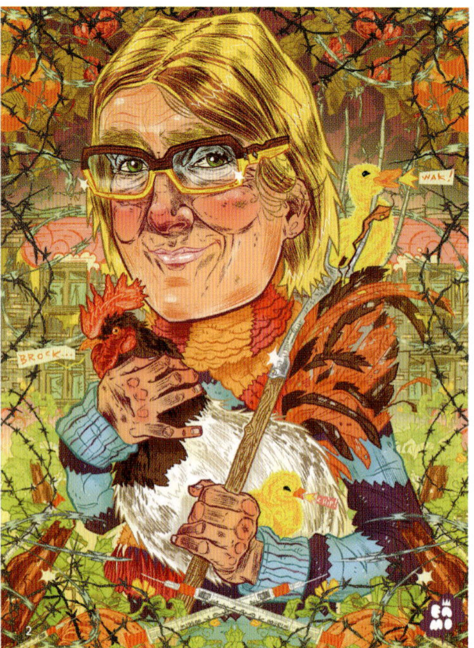 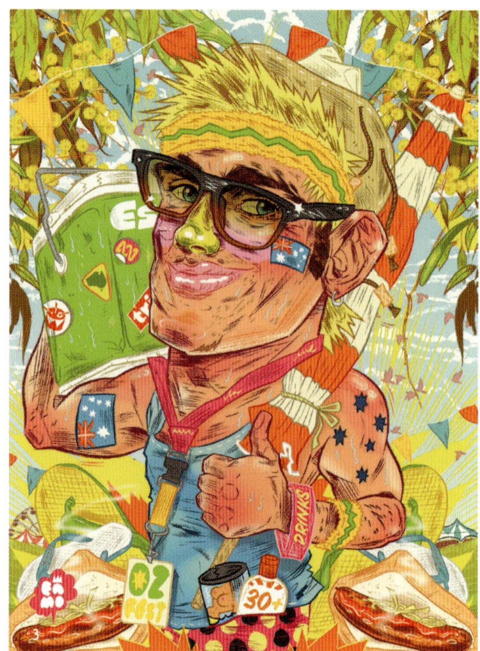

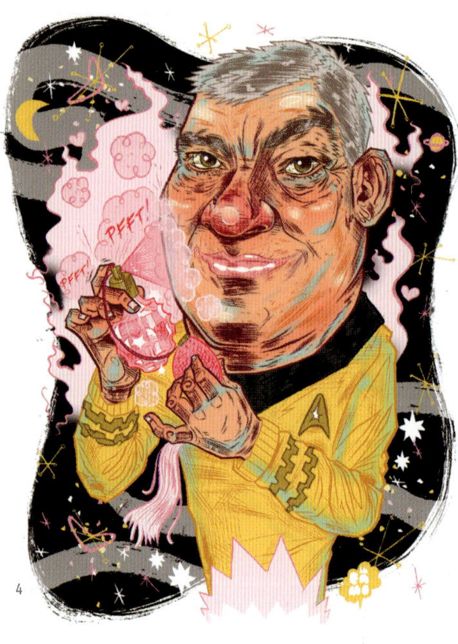 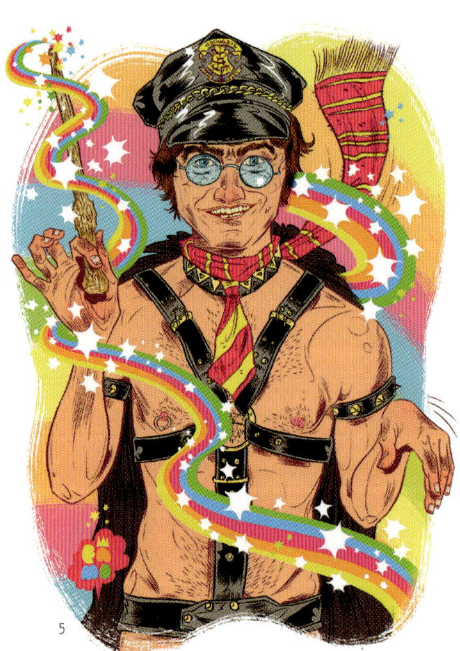

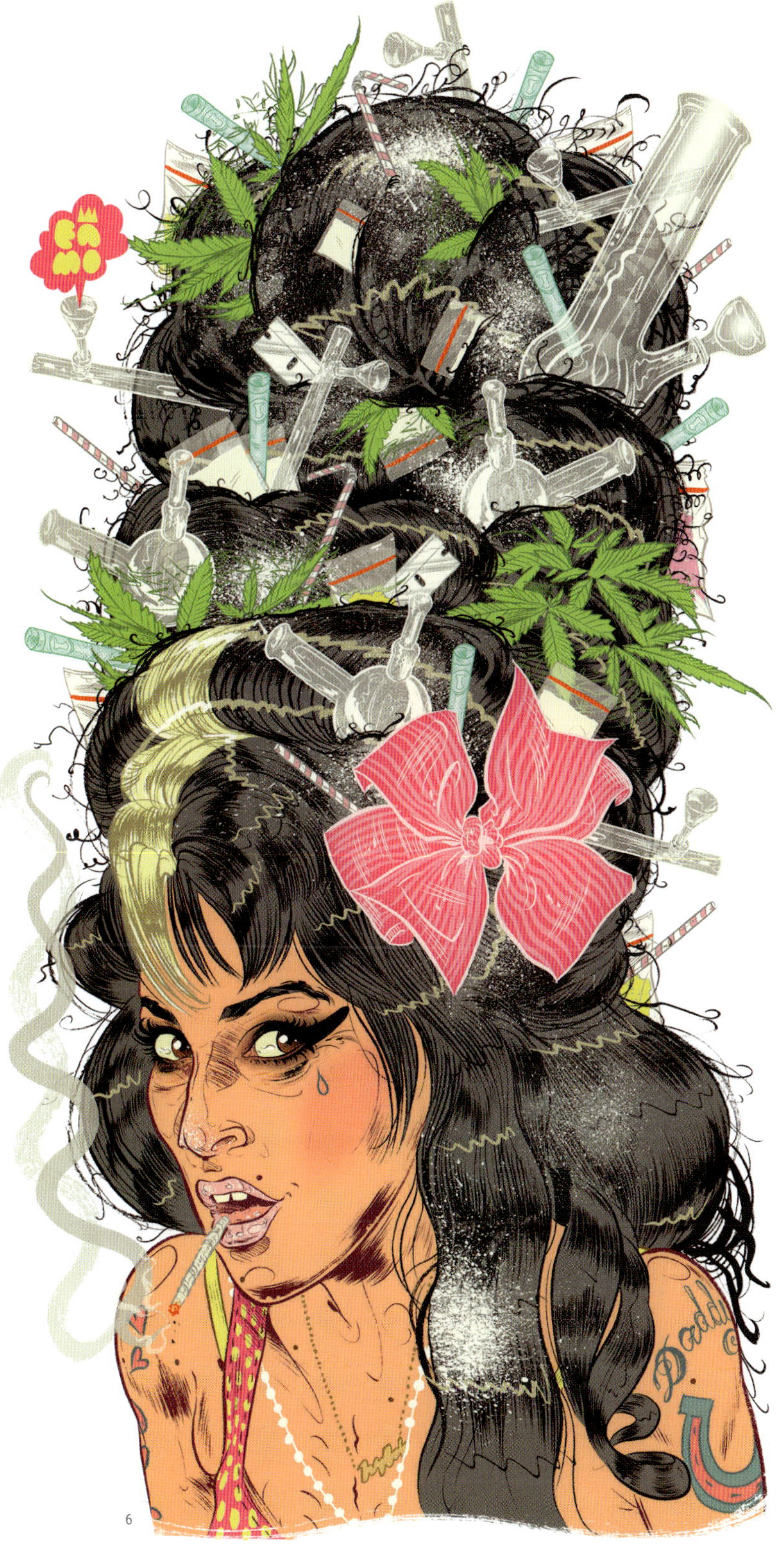

Eamo Donnelly
Australia

www.eamo.com.au

1. **Chef Roy Choi CHOW 13 Food Awards** (2009). CBS Interactive USA. Ink and brush, digital coloring

2. **Novella Carpenter CHOW 13 Food Awards** (2009). CBS Interactive USA. Ink and brush, digital coloring

3. **20 Bands You Must See This Summer** (2010). *Triple J Magazine* Australia. Ink and brush, digital coloring

4. **SHAT ON THAT!** (2010). *Maxim Magazine* USA. Ink and brush, digital coloring

5. **Sexily Ever After** (2009). *Maxim Magazine* USA. Ink and brush, digital coloring

6. **Amy Winehouse** (2009). *Blender Magazine* USA. Ink and brush, digital coloring

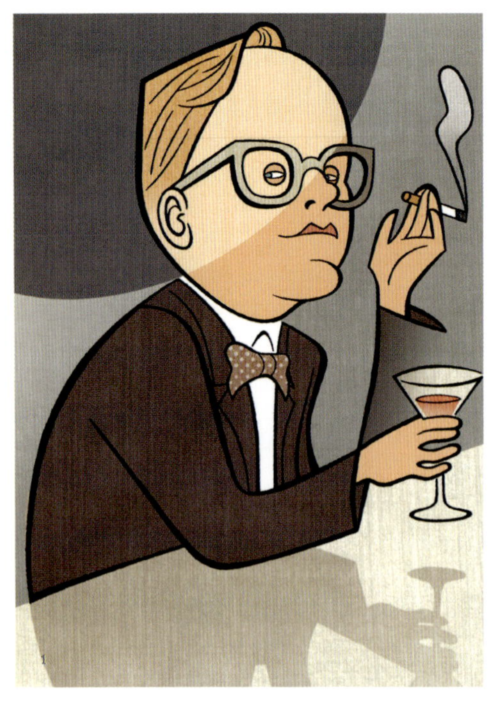

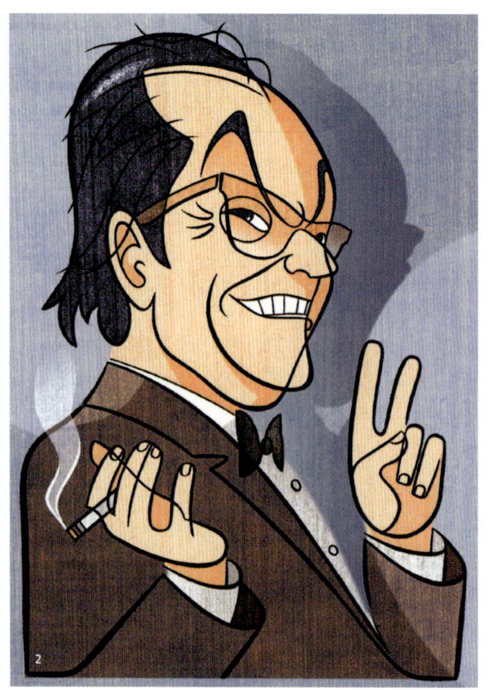

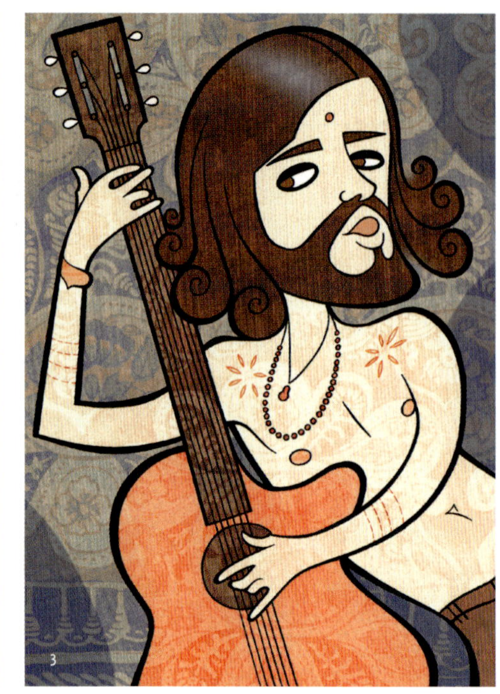

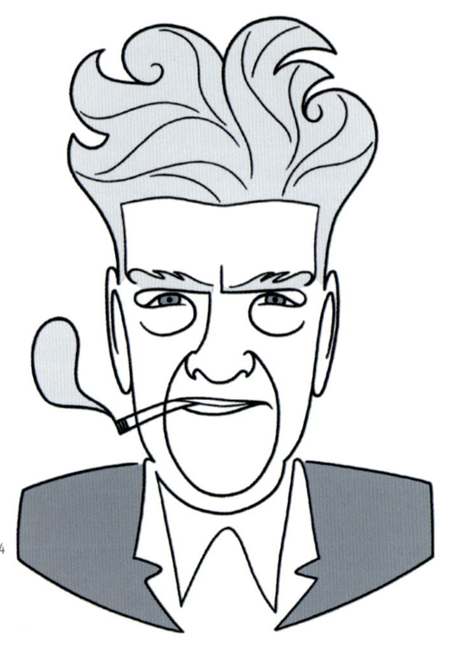

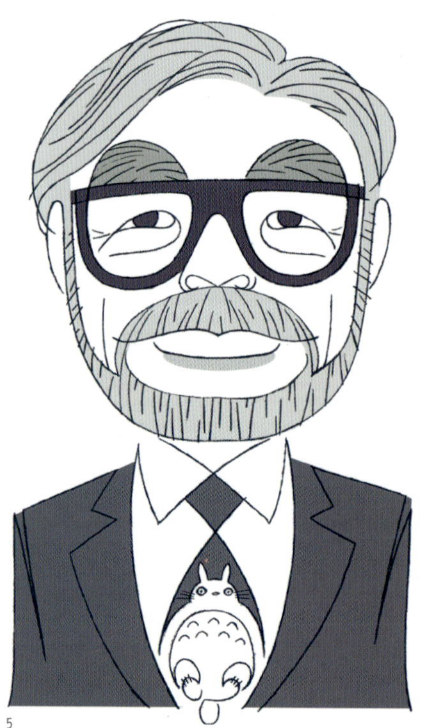

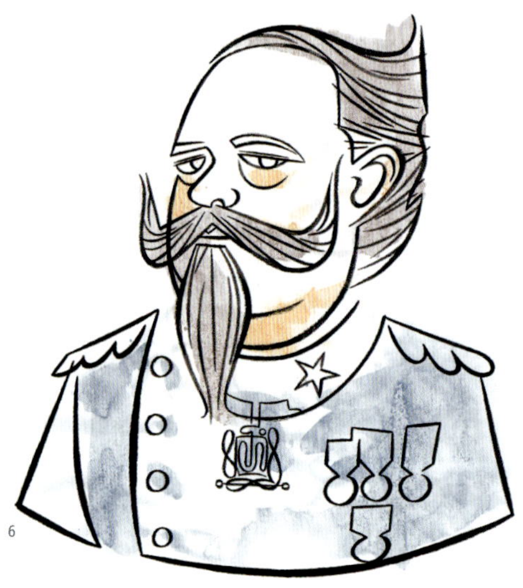

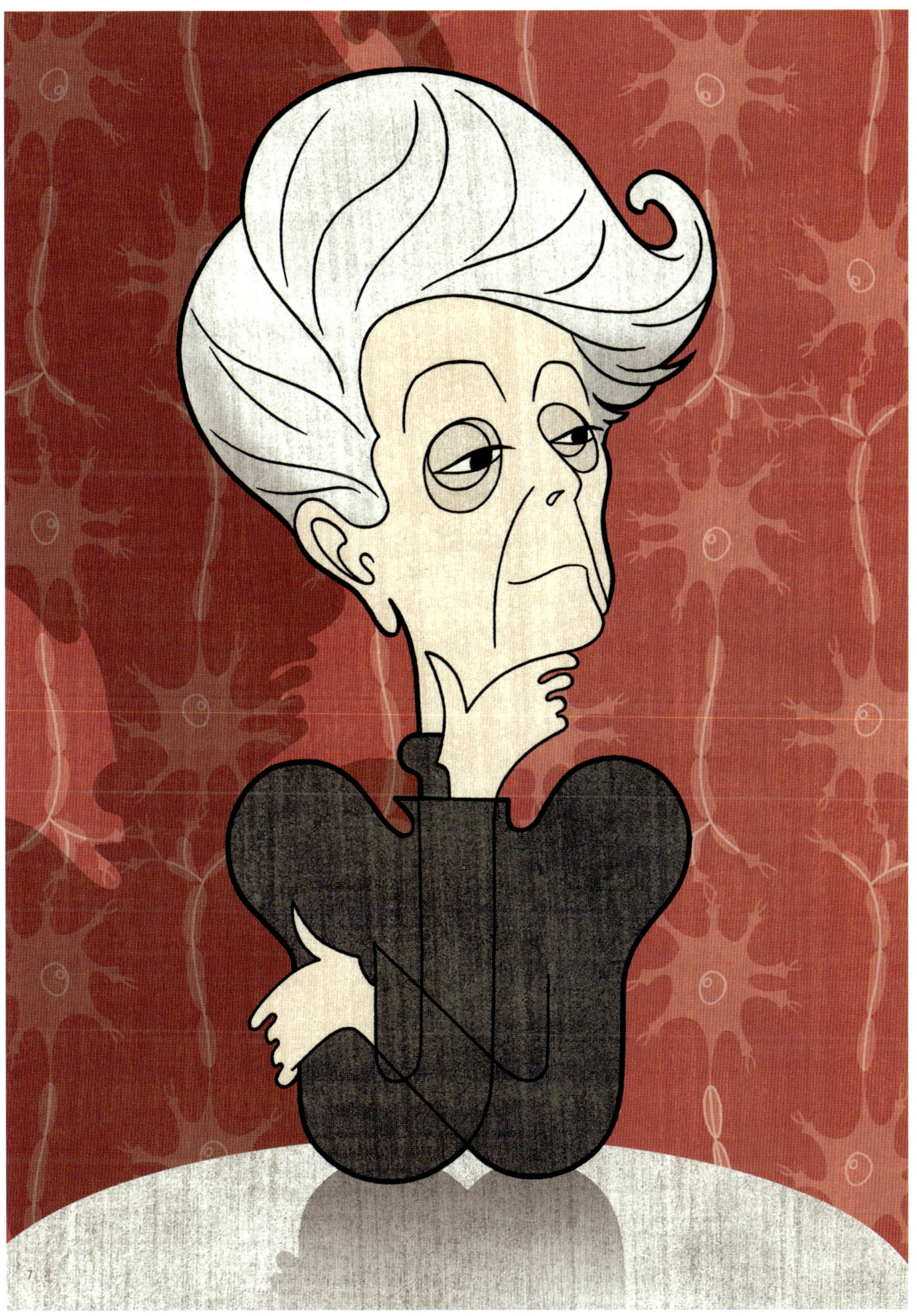

Massimo Basili
Italy

www.illustratori.it/MassimoBasili

1. **Philip Seymour Hoffman in Capote** (2007). Self-promotion. Marker on paper, digital

2. **Jack Nicholson** (2007). Universitiy.it. Marker on paper, digital

3. **Devendra Banhart** (2007). *Rolling Stone* Italia. Marker on paper, digitaL

4. **David Lynch** (2008). Self-promotion. Marker on paper, digital

5. **Hayao Miyazaki** (2009). Self-promotion. Marker on paper, digital

6. **Vittorio Emanuele II** (2010). Self-promotion. Ink on paper

7. **Rita Levi Montalcini** (2007). *Marie Claire*. Marker on paper, digital

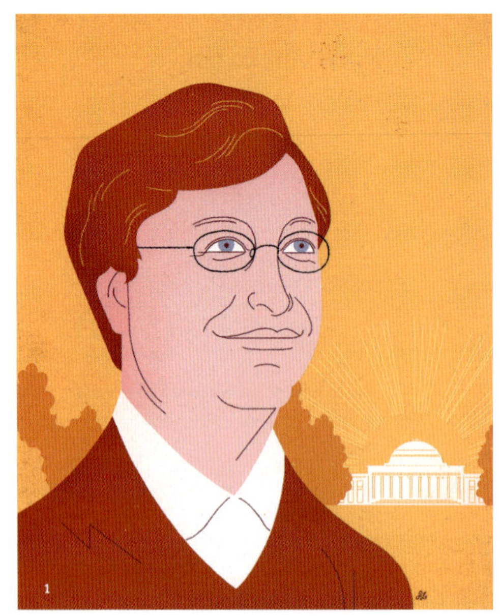

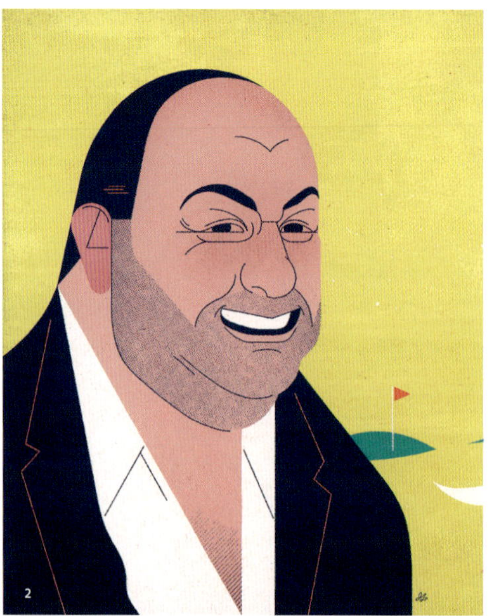

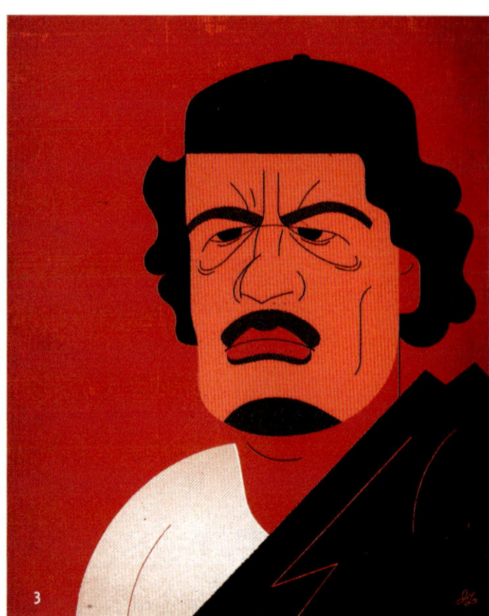

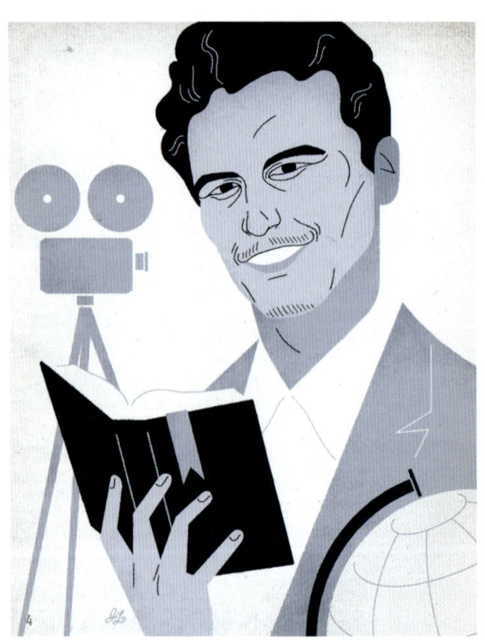

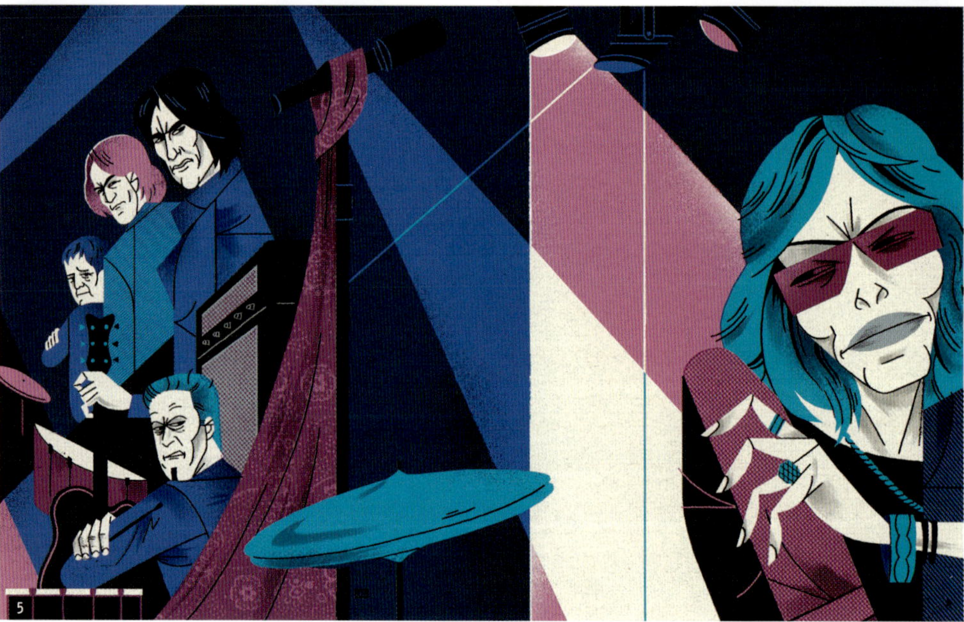

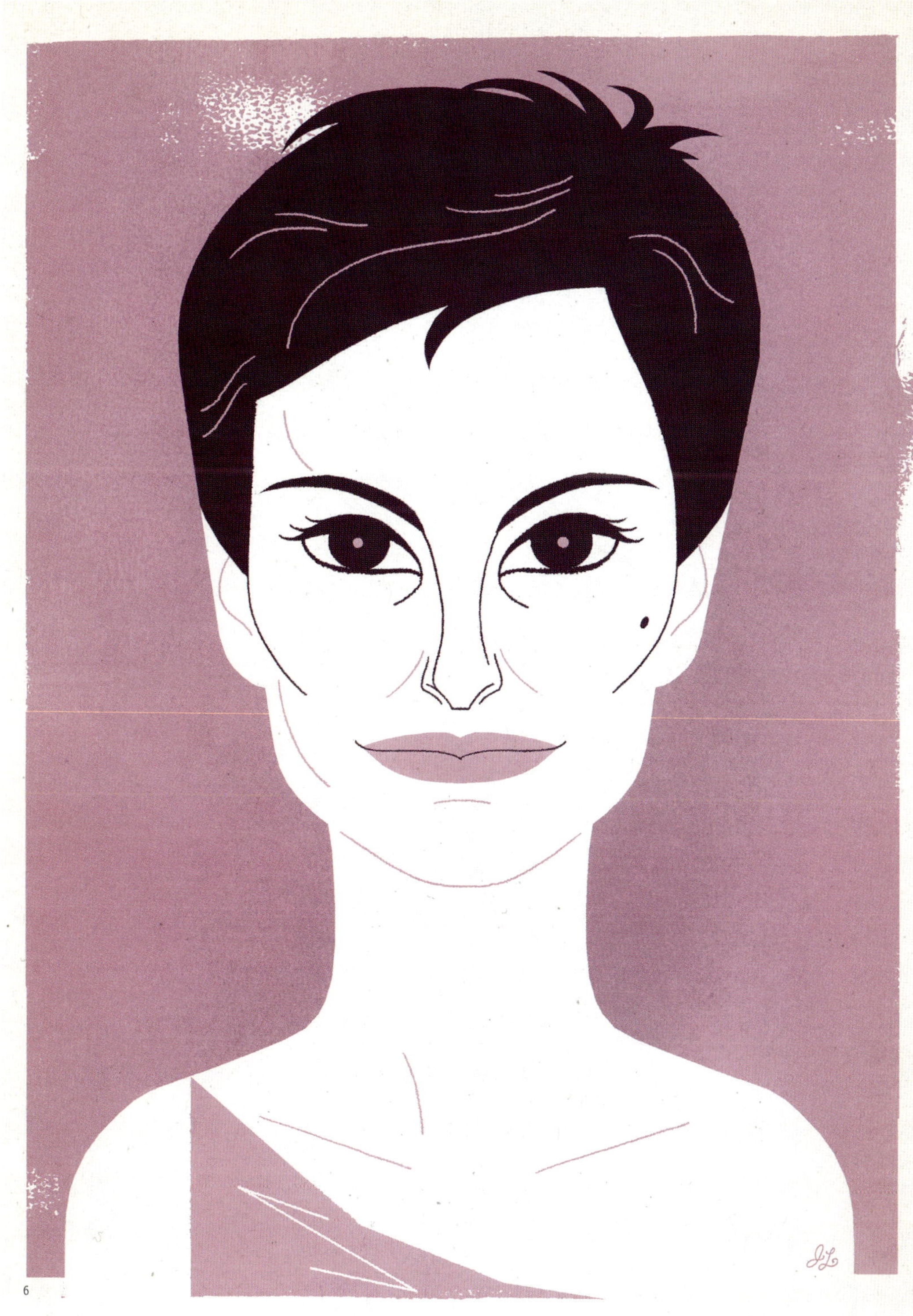

Jesse Lefkowitz
USA

www.jesse-lefkowitz.com

1. **Bill Gates** (2011). *Boston Globe*

2. **Chubby Chandler** (2011). *Golf World*

3. **Muammar al-Qaddafi** (2011). Personal work

4. **James Franco** (2011). Personal work

5. **Aerosmith** (2010). *Boston Magazine*

6. **Natalie Portman** (2011). Personal work

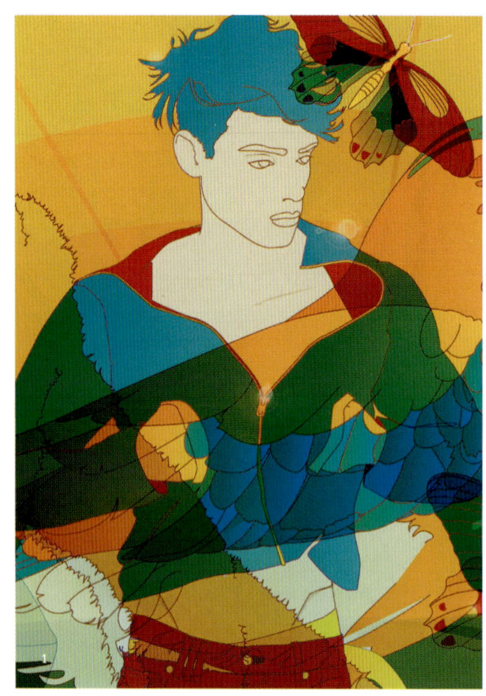
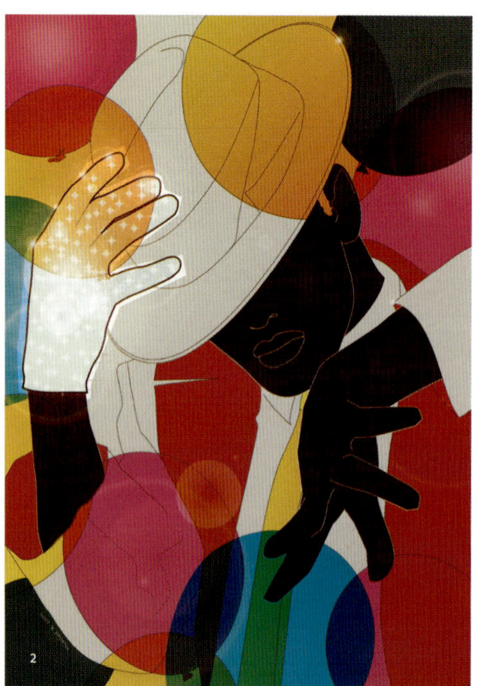
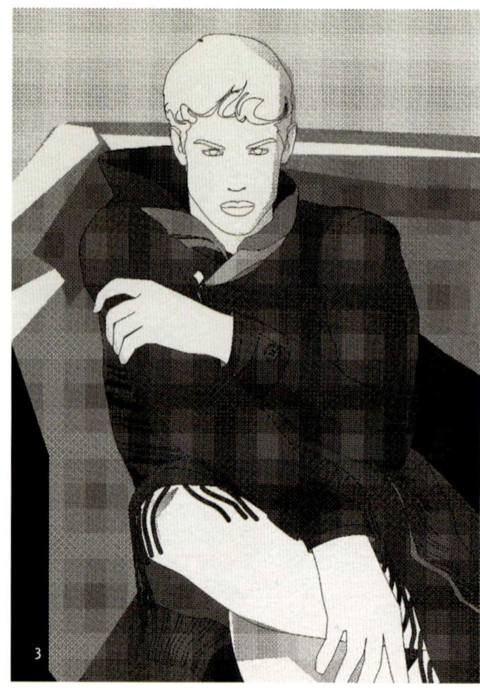
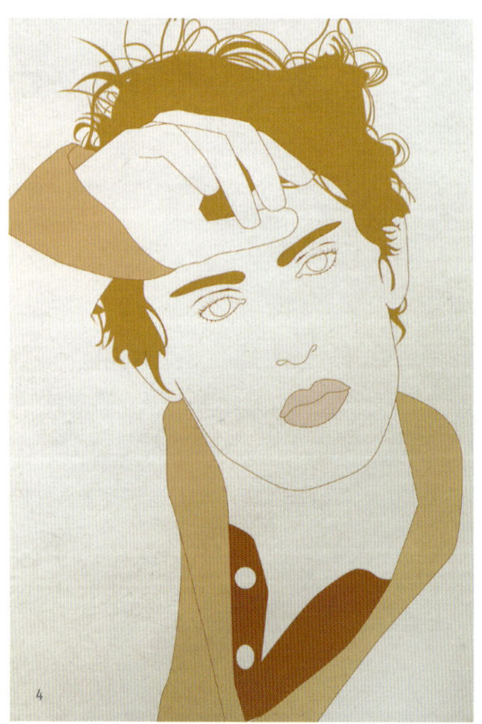
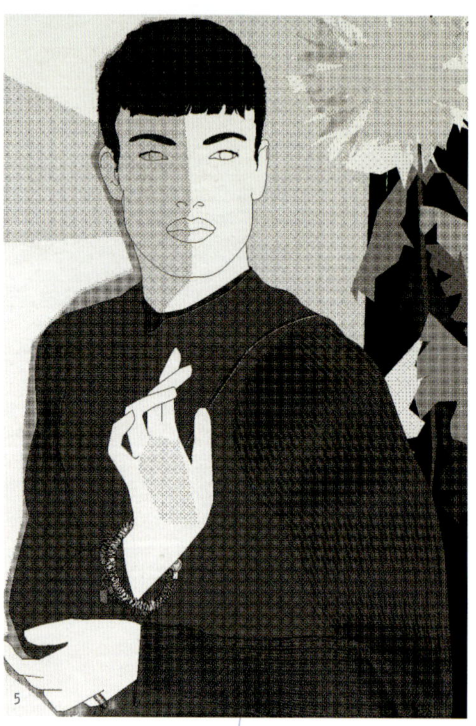
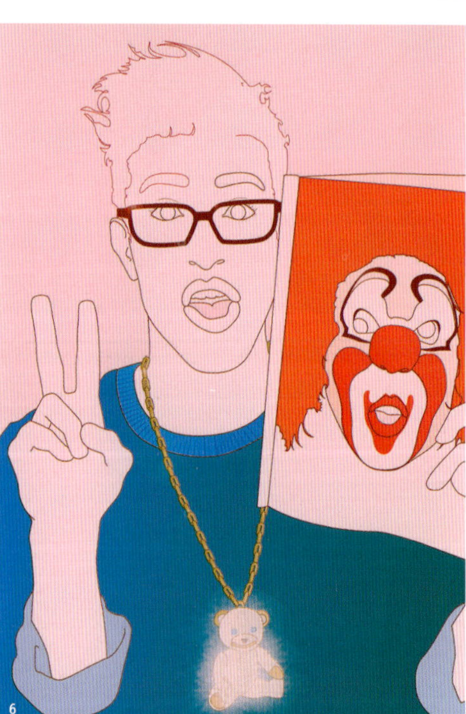

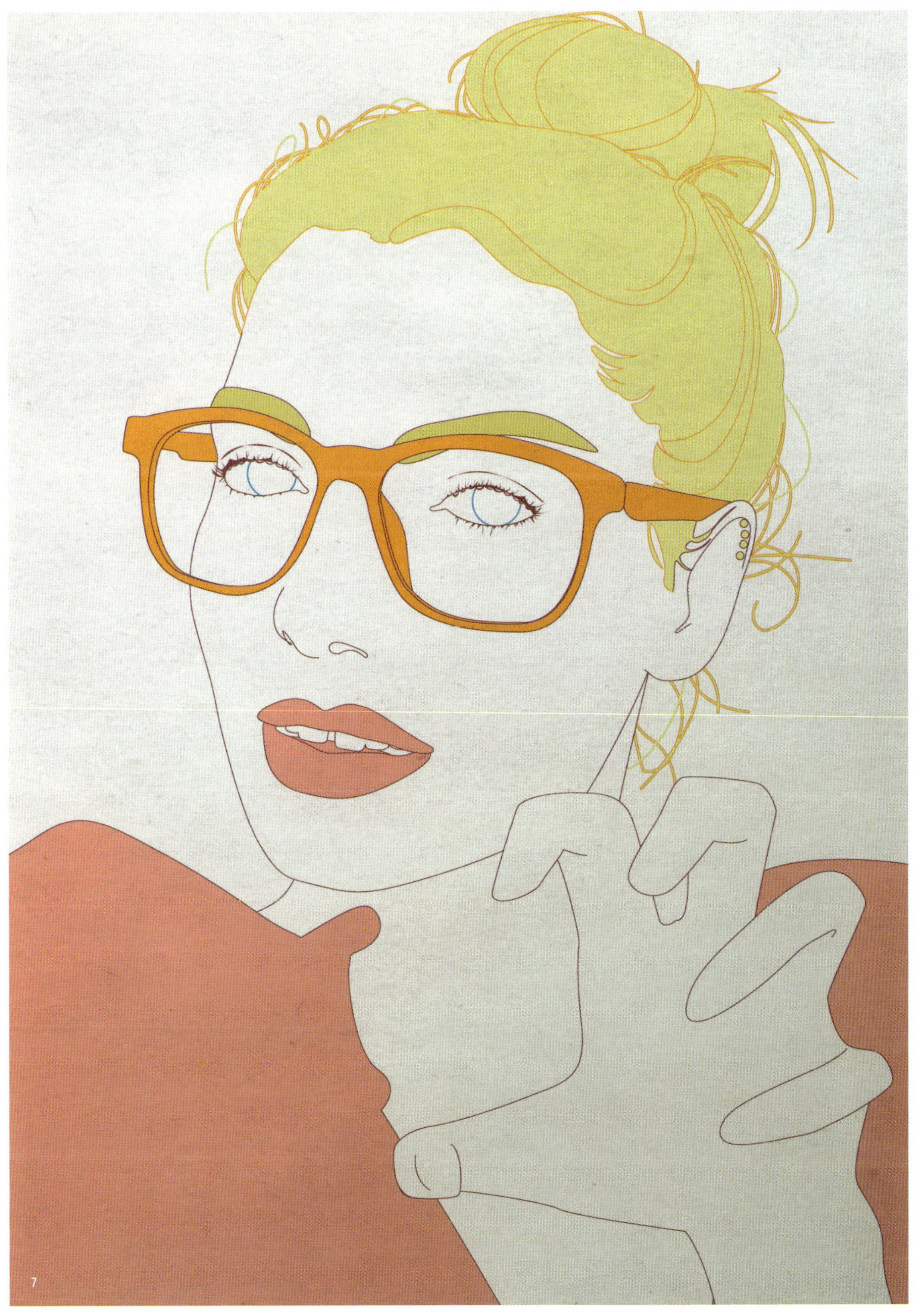

Mikael Kangas

Sweden

www.mikaelkangas.com

1. **Boy Blue** (2010). Personal work. Digital

2. **Prince of Pop** (2009). *Love the Glove* benefit party. Digital

3. **Lupevelez** (2009). Edward Streichen Tribute. Digital

4. **Mathias** (2009). Personal work. Digital

5. **Wong** (2009). Edward Streichen Tribute. digital

6. **Roberto** (2009). *Rosebud Magazine.* Digital

7. **Jessica** (2009). Personal work. Digital

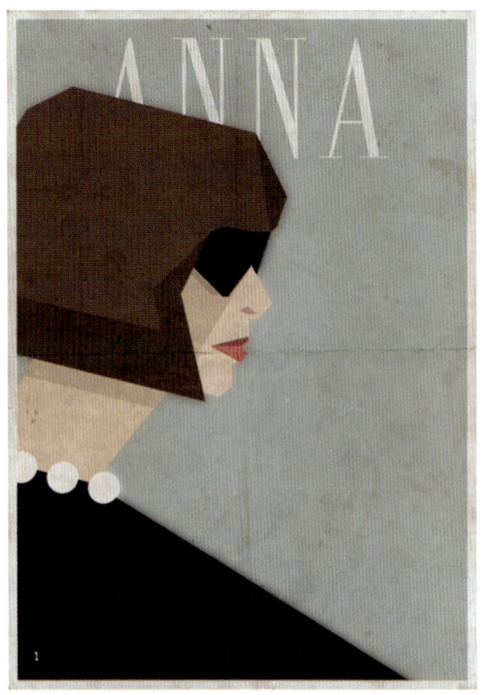

ANNA

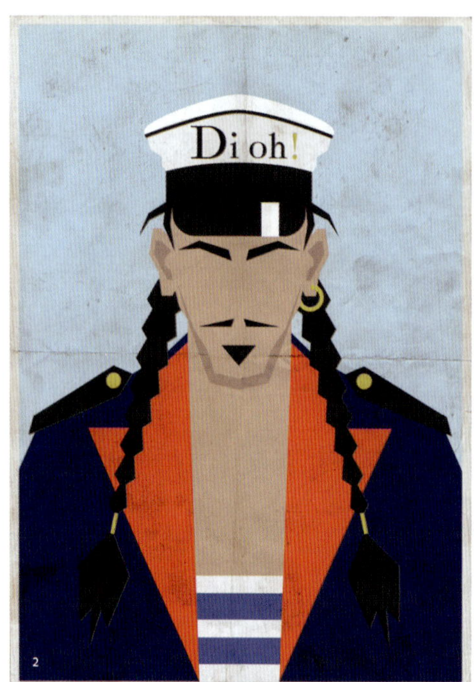

Di oh!

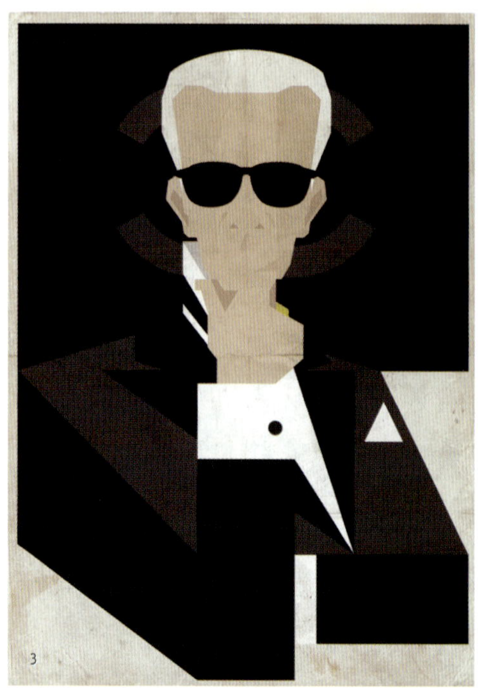

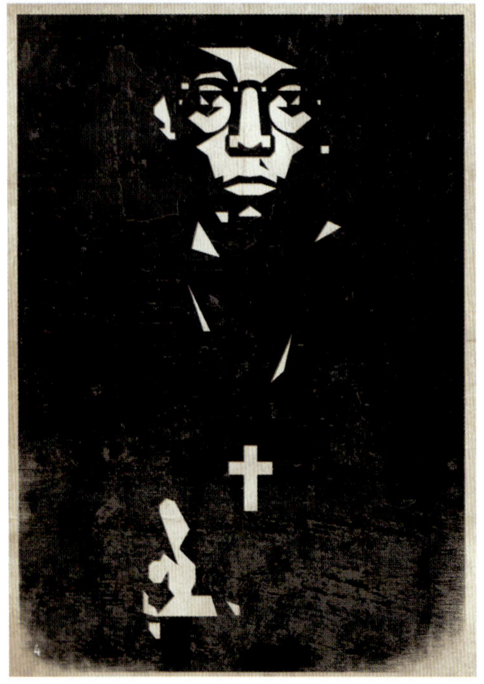

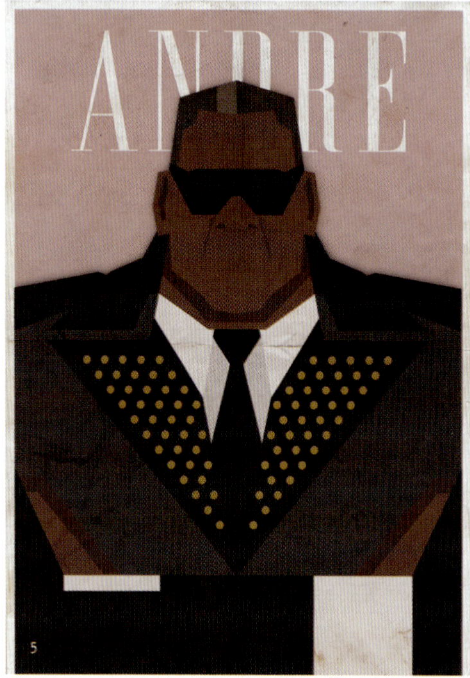

ANDRE

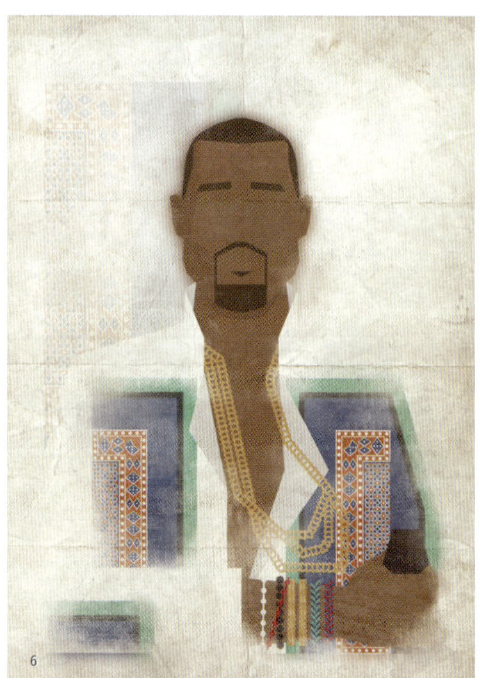

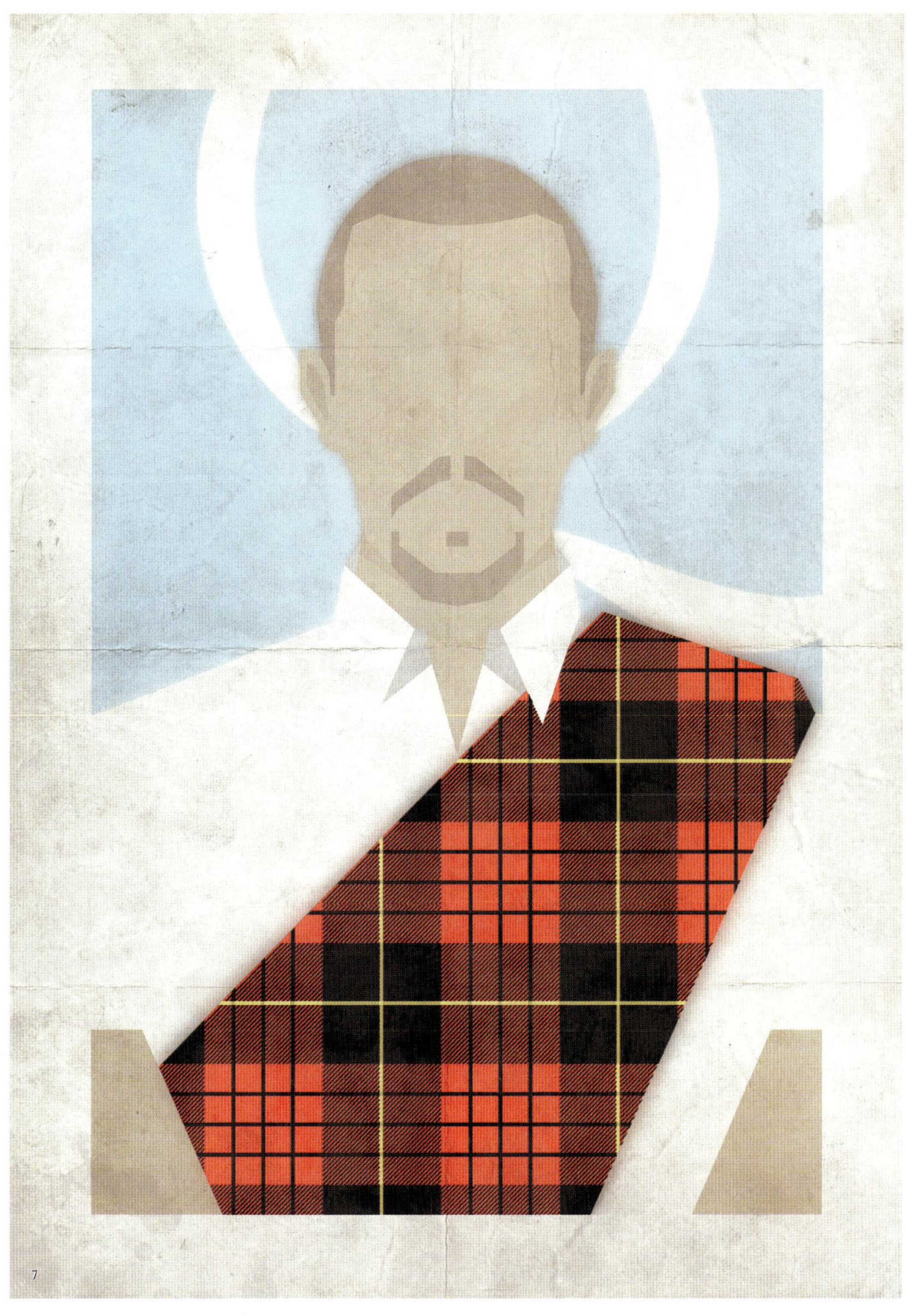

1. **From the series *Andre – The Fashion Crowd*** (2011). *Highsnobiety*. Photoshop

2. **From the series *Andre – The Fashion Crowd*** (2011). *Highsnobiety*. Photoshop

3. **From the series *Andre – The Fashion Crowd*** (2011). *Highsnobiety*. Photoshop

4. **BIG L** (2011). Acht Amsterdam. Screenprint

5. **From the series *Andre – The Fashion Crowd*** (2011). *Highsnobiety*. Photoshop

6. **Kanye** (2011). *Highsnobiety*. Photoshop

7. **McQueen** (2011). Fancy x Mr Burt Collaboration. Photoshop

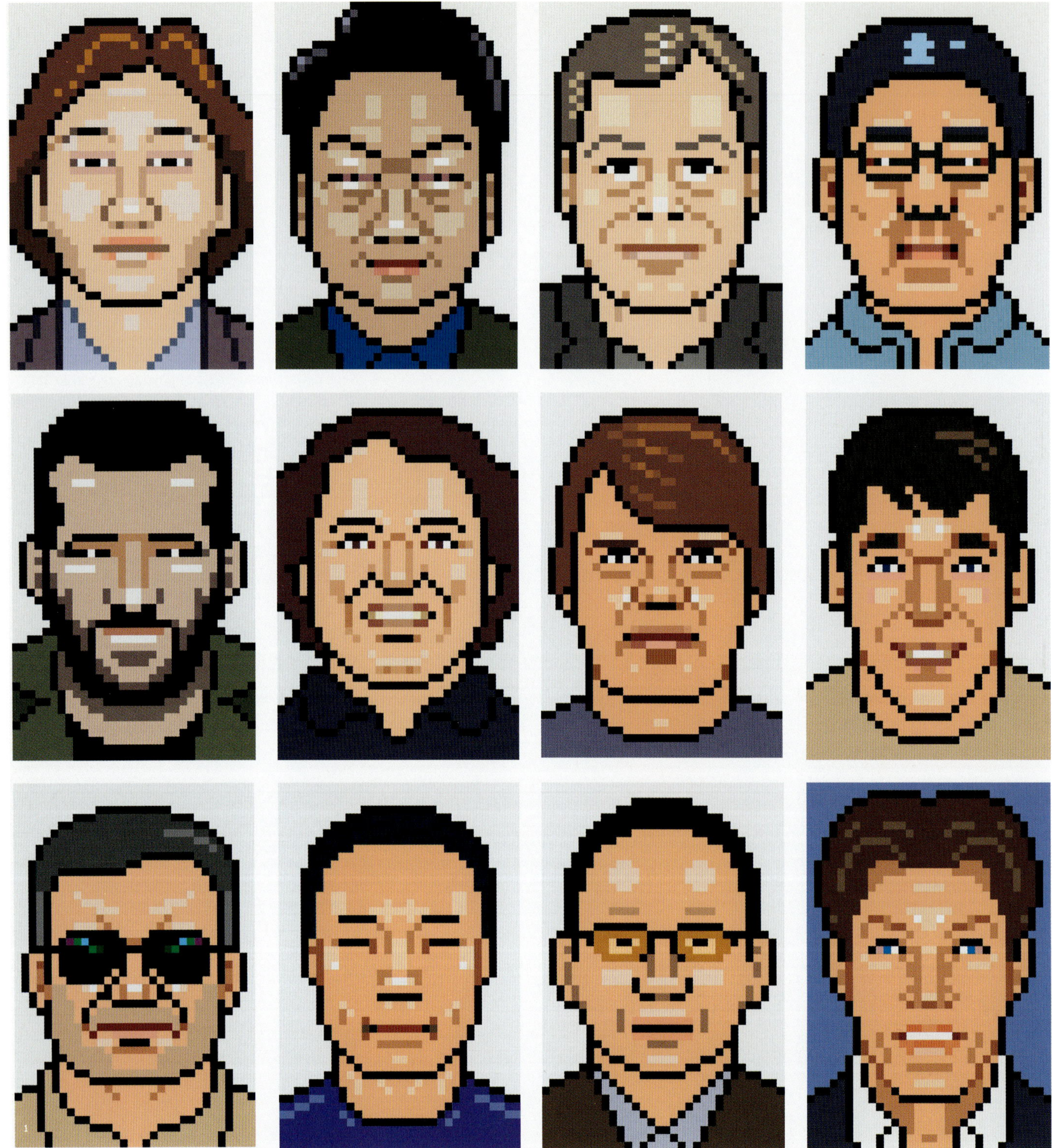

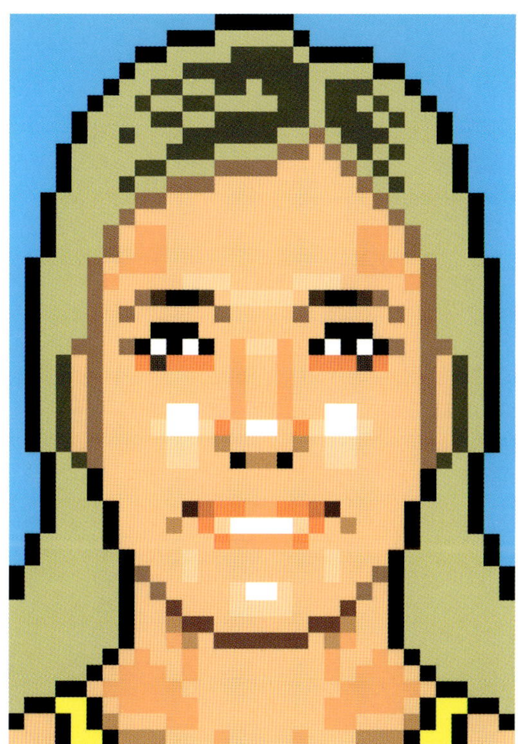

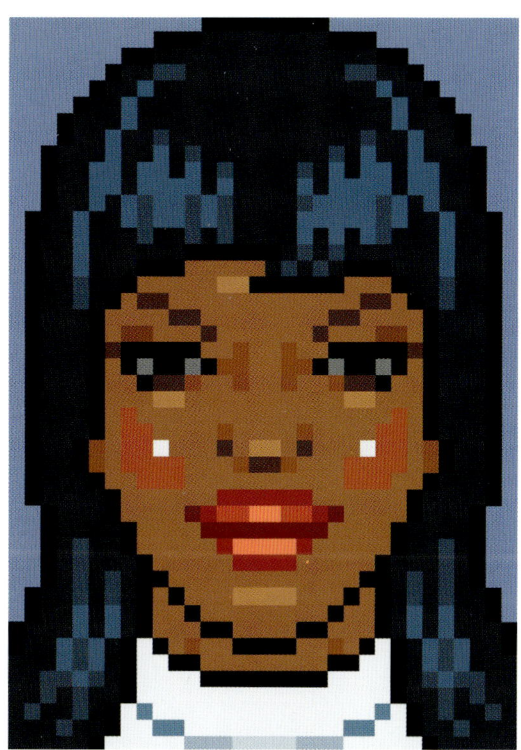

EBoy

Germany

www.hello.eboy.com

1. **Fumito Ueda, Ken Kutaragi, Larry Probst, Masachatani, Sam Houser, Seth Luisi, Stephen White, Ted Price, Tom Clancy, Yamauchi, Yuji Horii** and **Hugh Grant** (2005). *Official US Playstation Magazine.* Digital

2. **Francesca Versace, Naomi Campbell, Harvey Weinstein** and **Paul Allen** (2006). *Wirtschafts Woche.* Digital

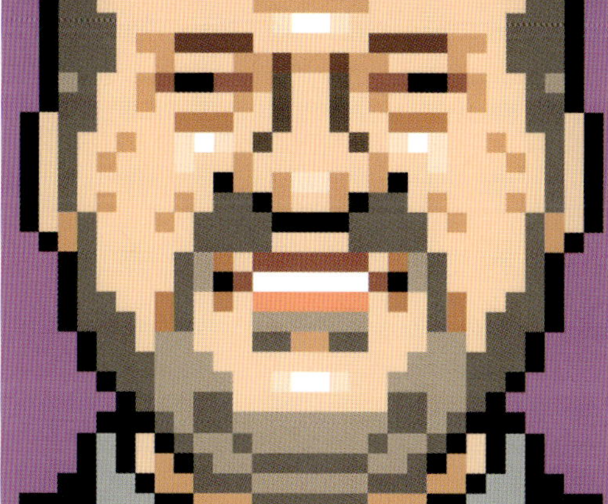

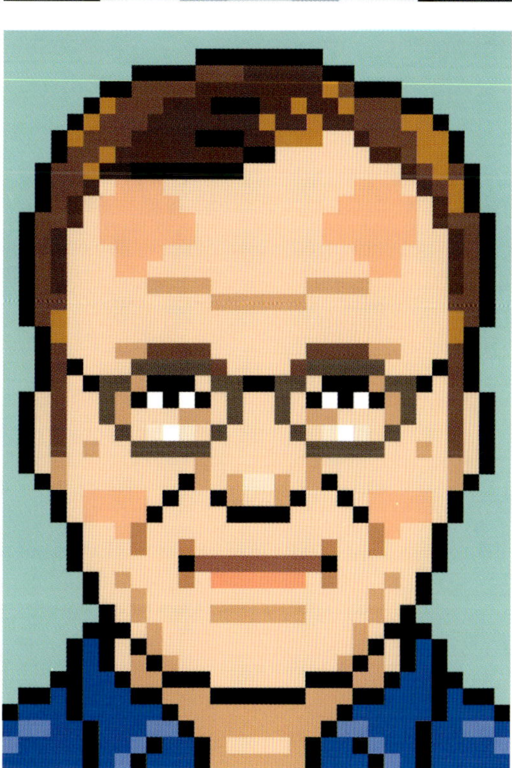

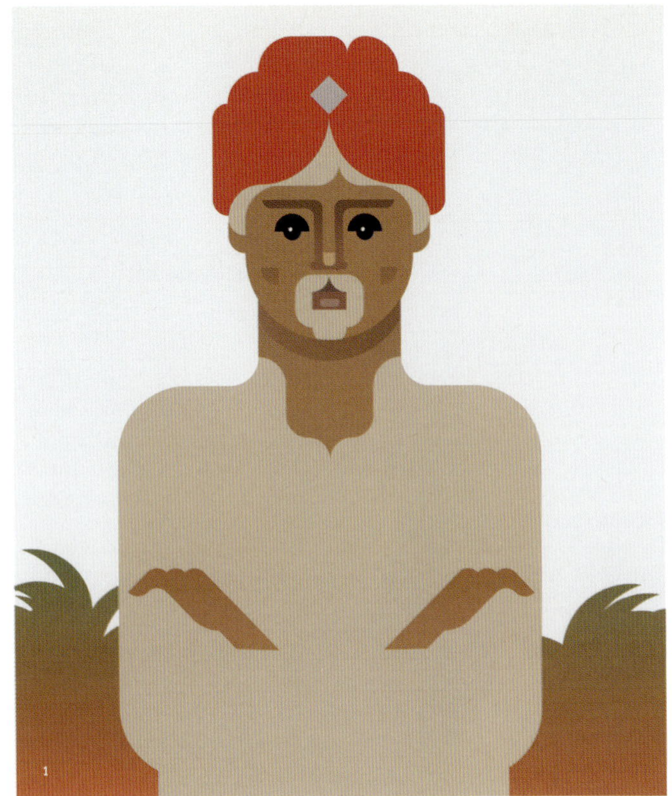

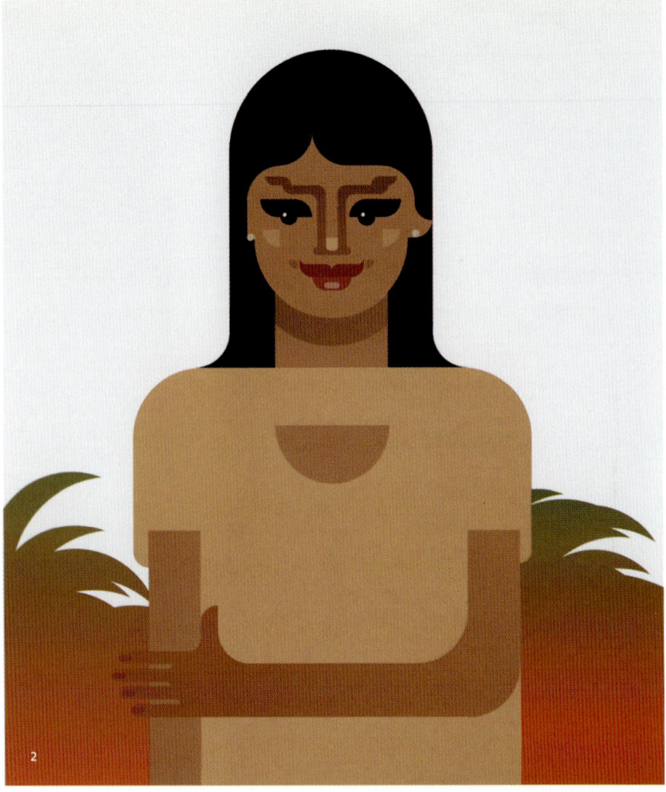

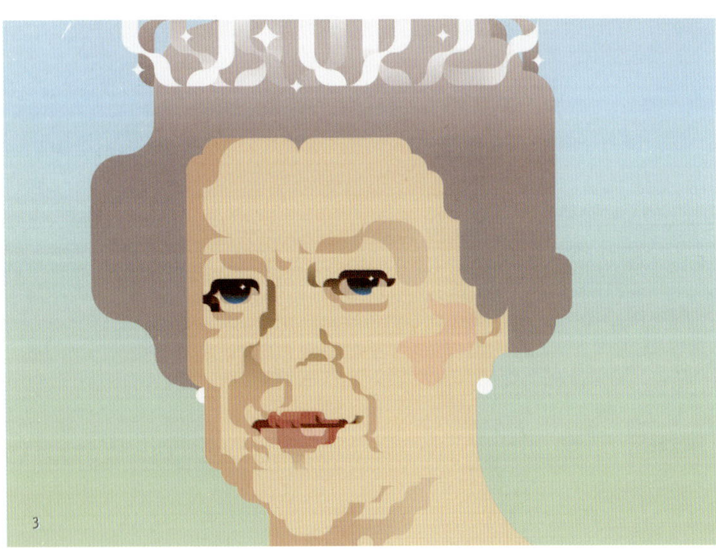

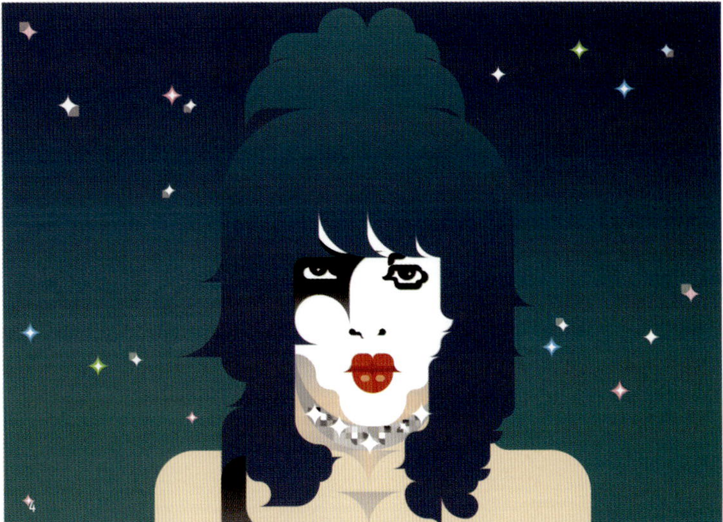

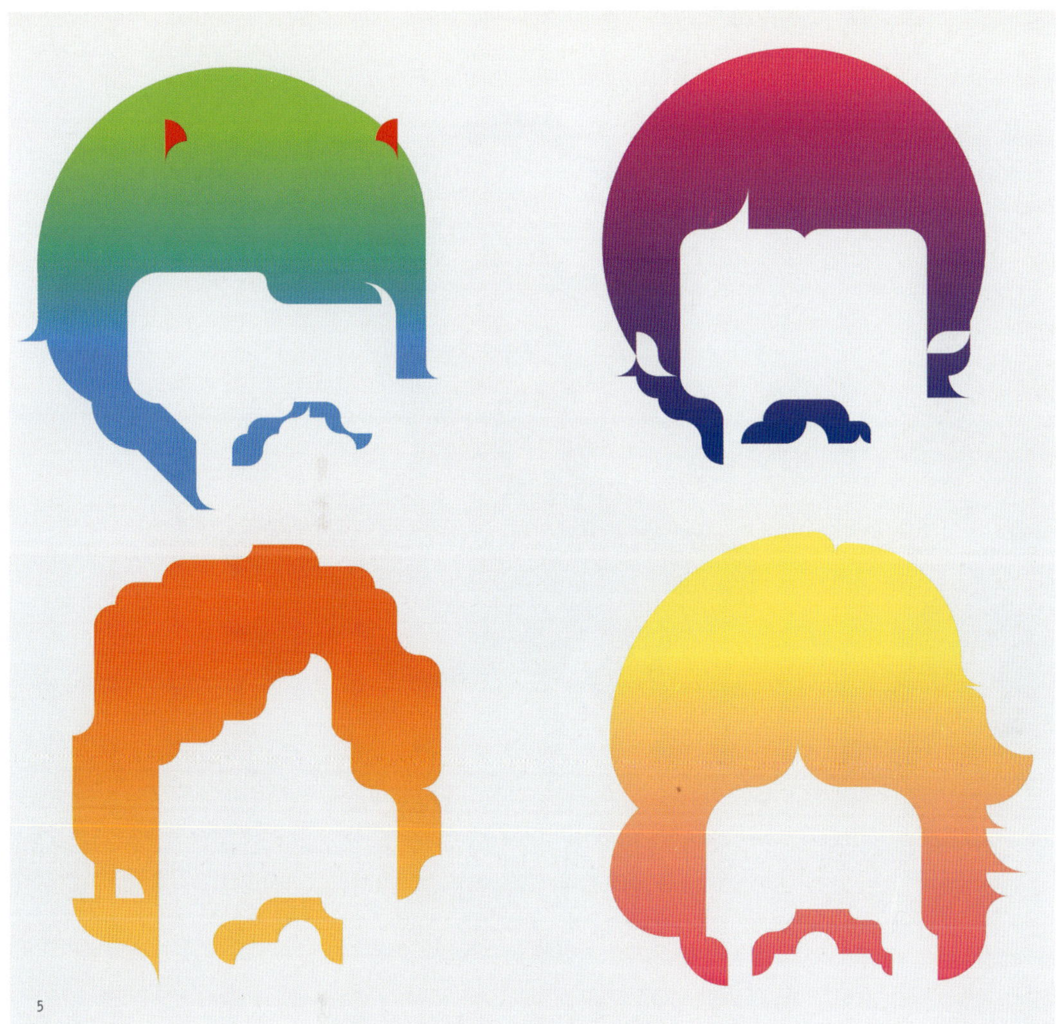

José Lozano
France

www.jose-lozano.com

1. **Prakash** (2011). Personal work. Digital

2. **Shyamala** (2011). Personal work. Digital

3. **The Queen** (2010). Personal work. Digital

4. **Paul Stanley** (2010). Personal work. Digital

5. **The Beatles** (2011). Personal work. Digital

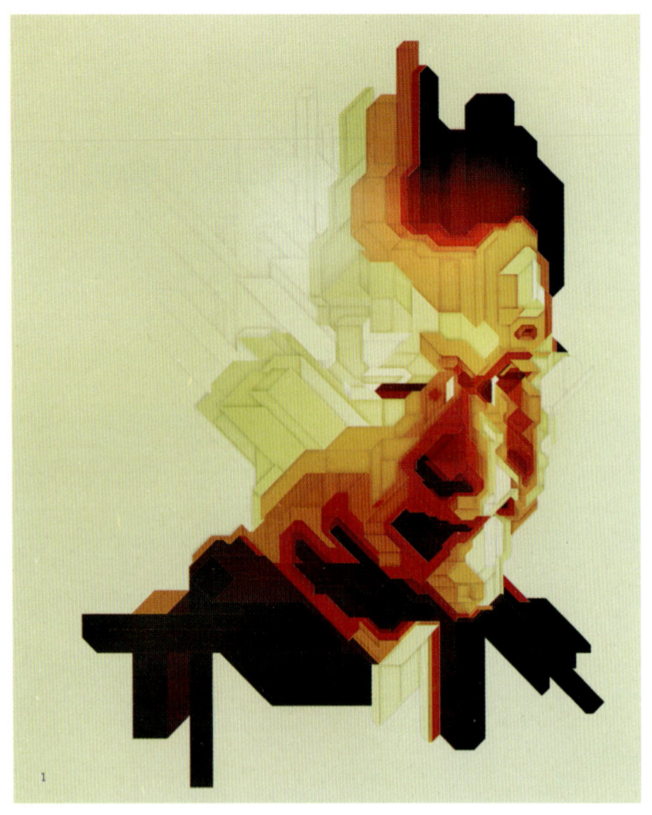

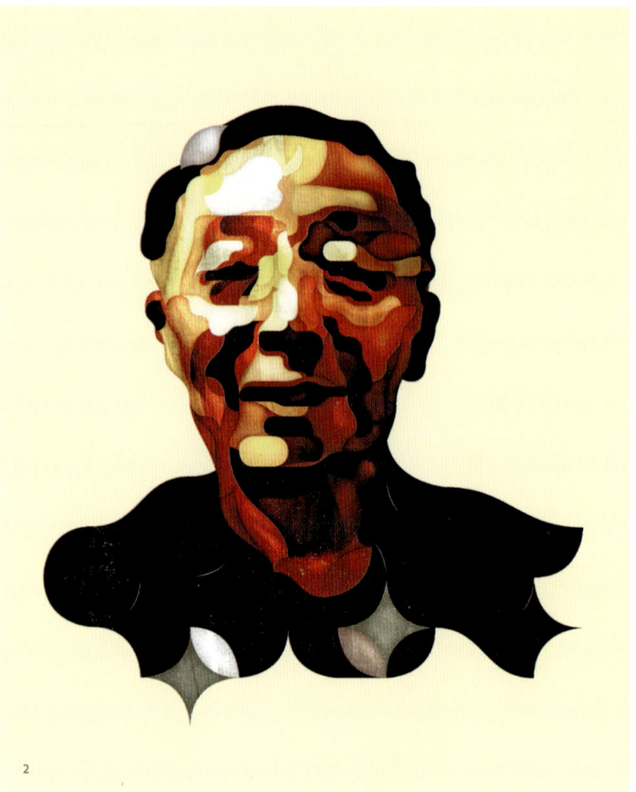

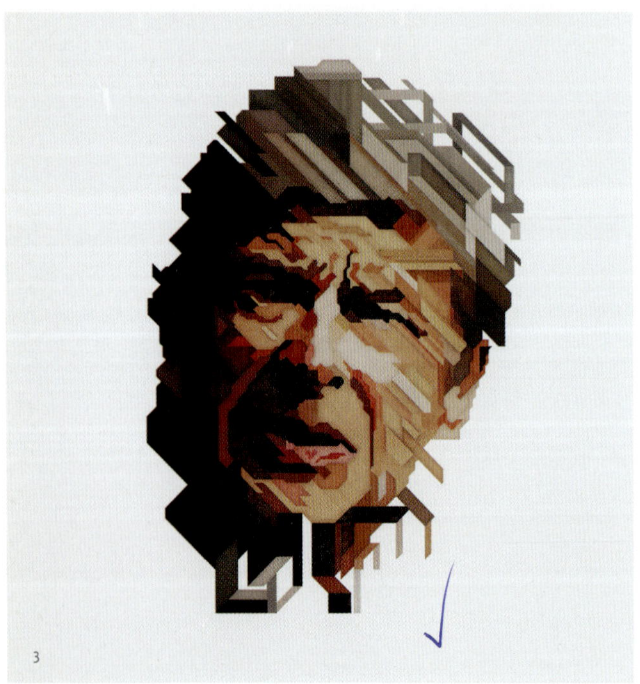

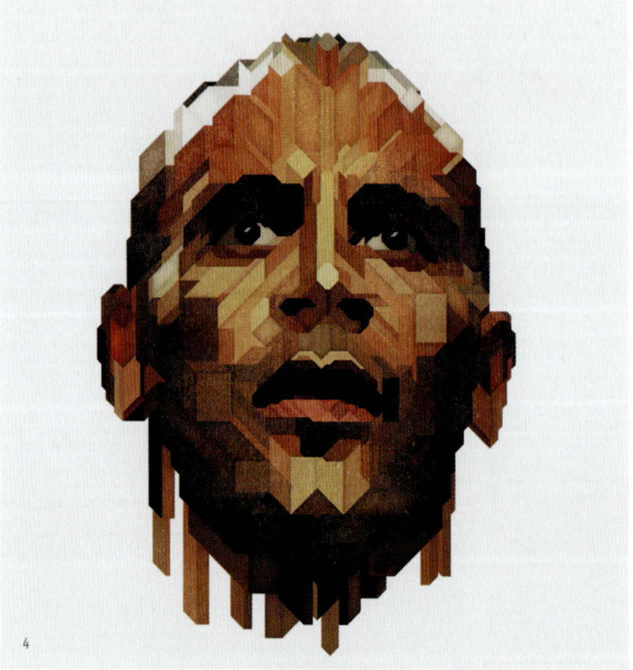

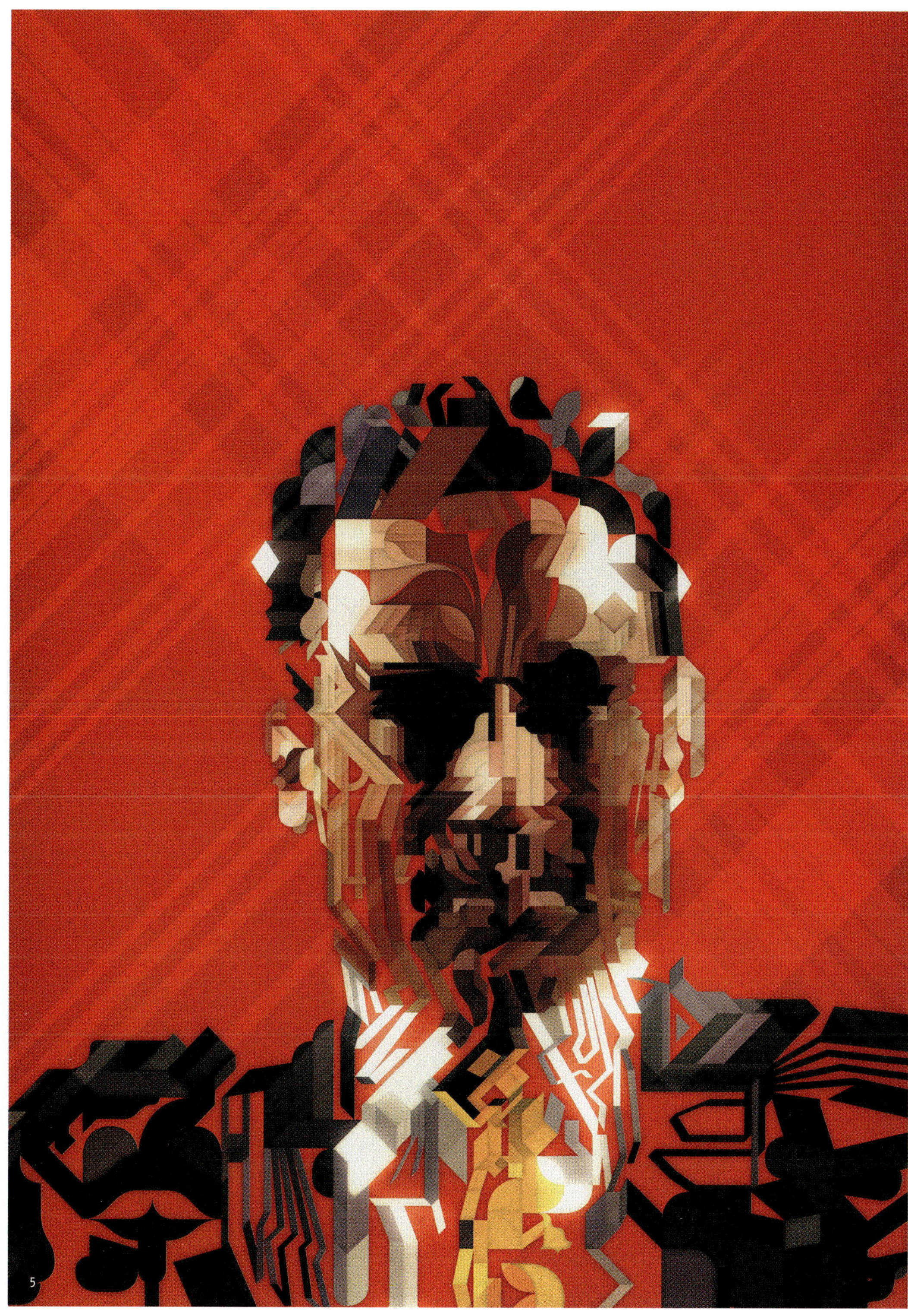

Charles Williams

UK

www.madeup.org

1. **Bom Kim** (2011). *Google - Think Quarterly.* Digital

2. **Takumi Asano** (2011). Uniqlo. Digital

3. **Arsene Wenger** (2011). *GQ Magazine.* Digital

4. **Rio Ferdinand** (2010). *GQ Magazine.* Digital

5. **Madness** (2010). The Association Of Illustrators. Digital

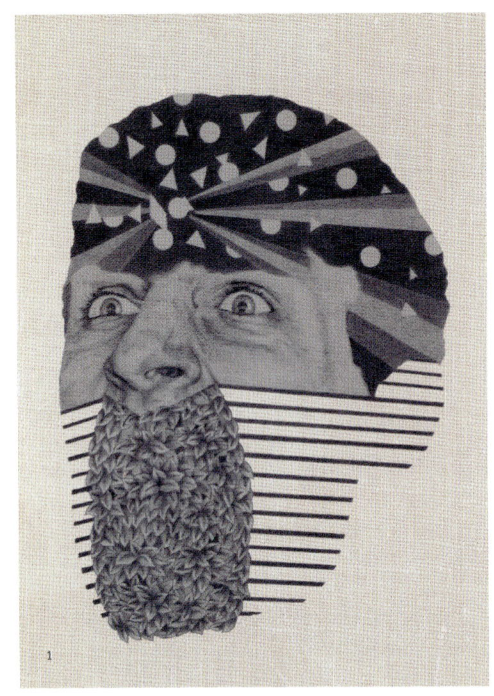
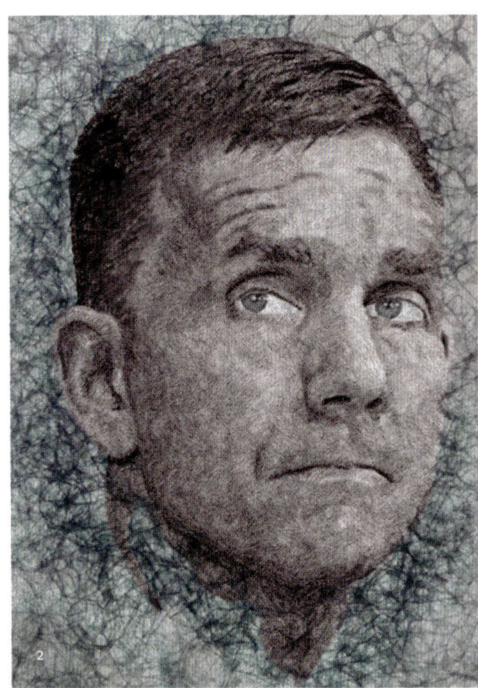
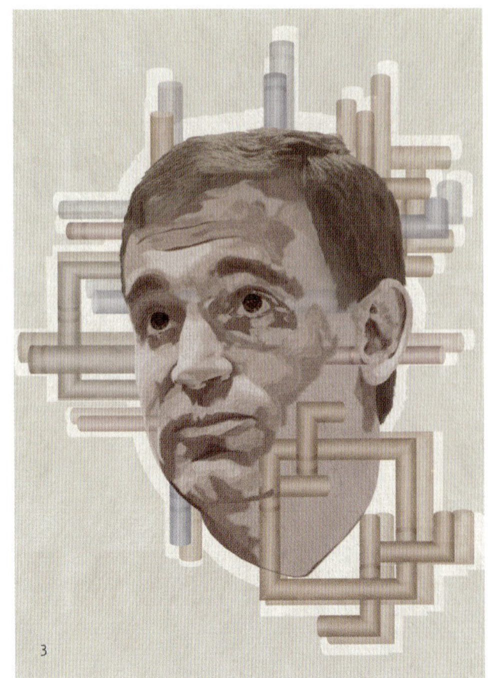
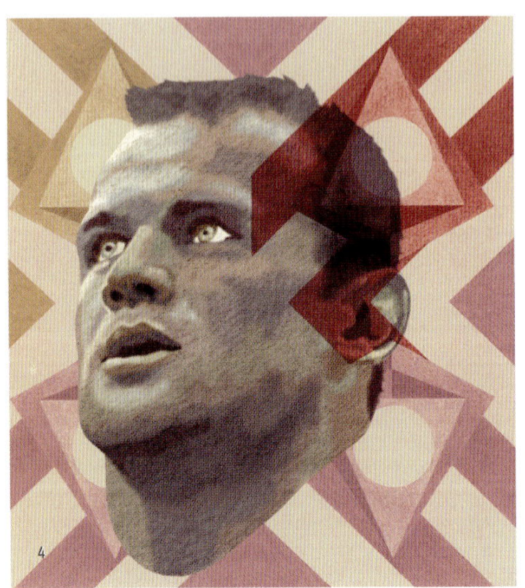
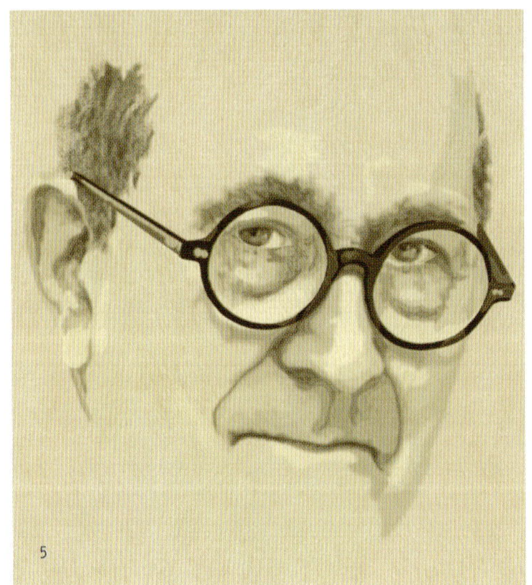

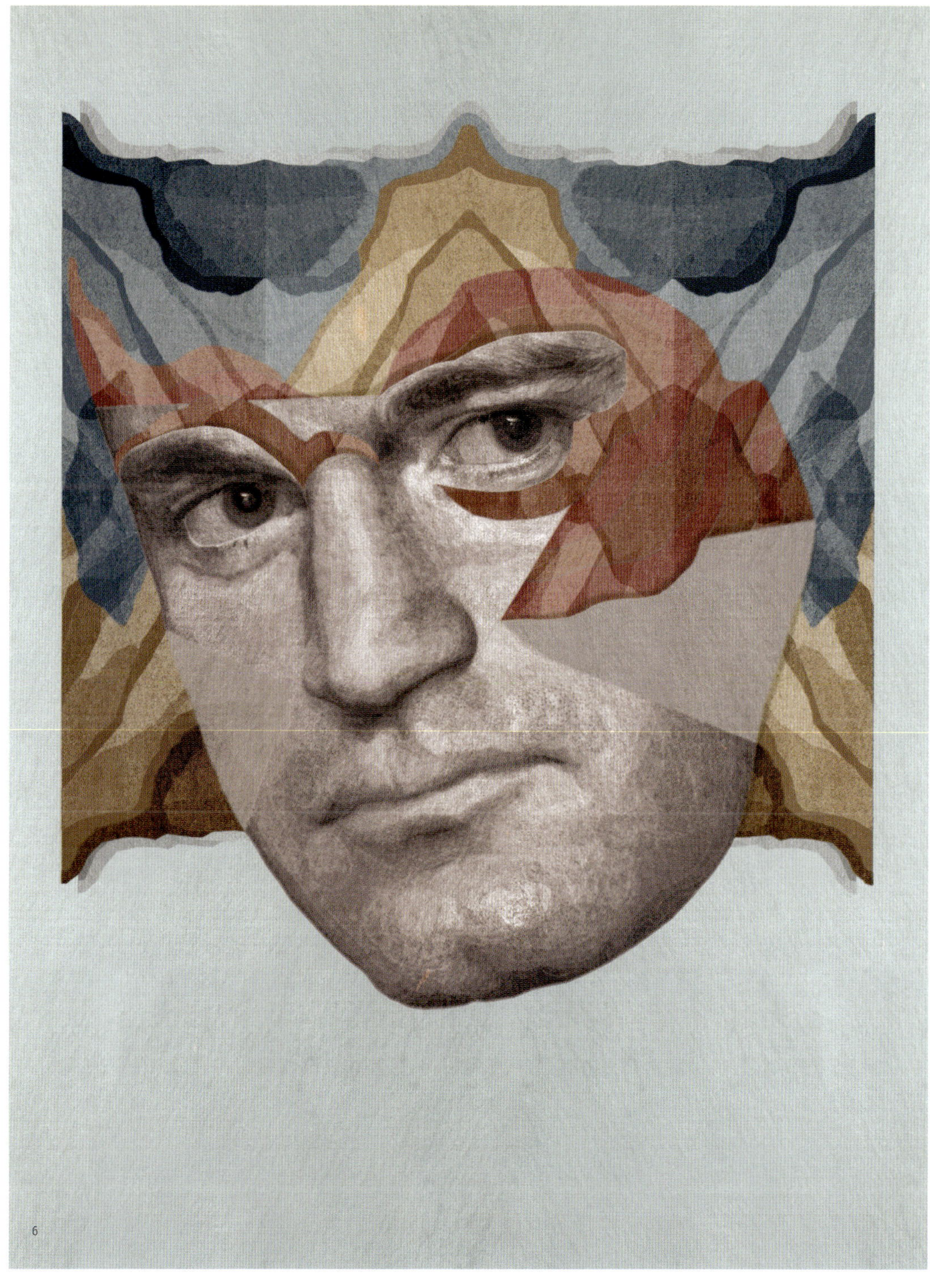

Andrew Clark
UK

www.thisisandrewclark.com

1. **A Face** (2010). KK Outlet. Pencil, Photoshop

2. **General Caldwell** (2011). *Revue Feuilleton*. Photoshop

3. **John Arnold Two** (2011). *AR Magazine*. Photoshop

4. **Rooney** (2010). Personal work. Pencil, Photoshop

5. **Sir Peter Cook** (2011). Adam and Eve Project. Photoshop

6. **John Arnold** (2011). *AR Magazine*. Photoshop

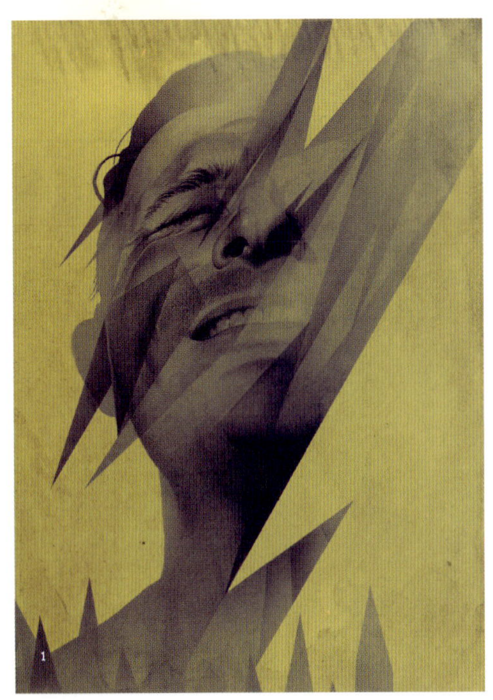

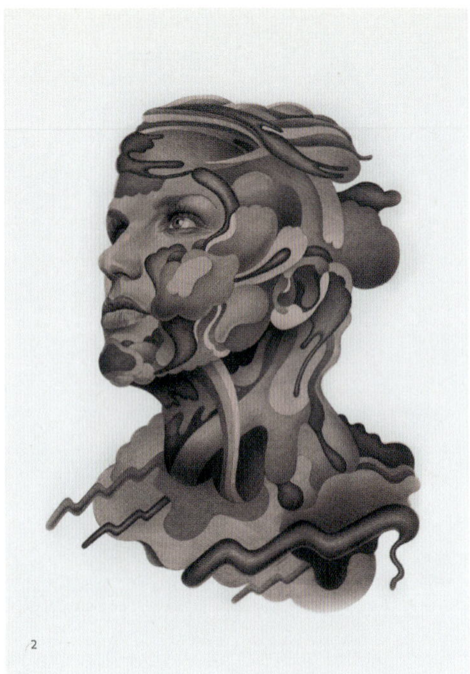

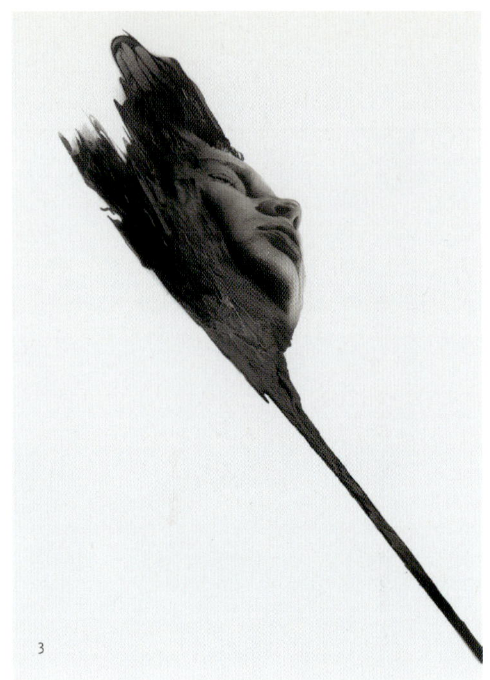

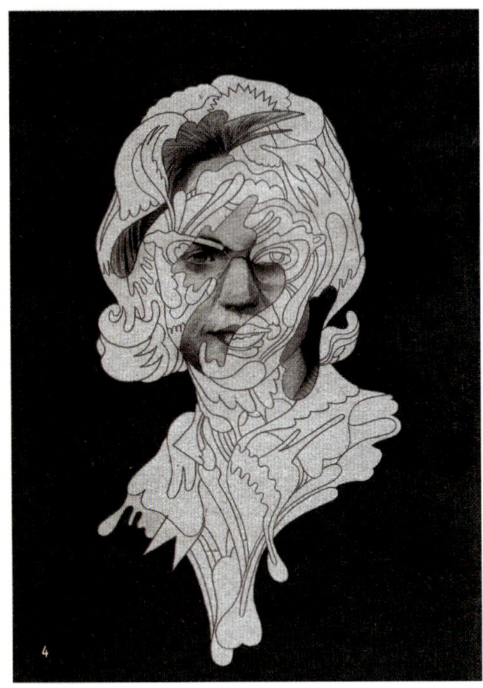

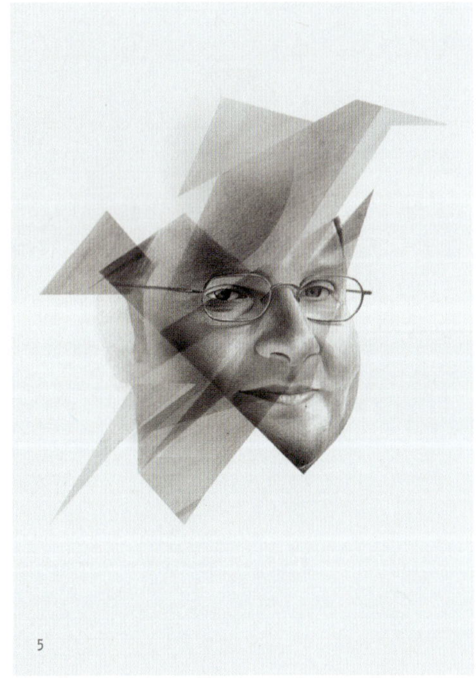

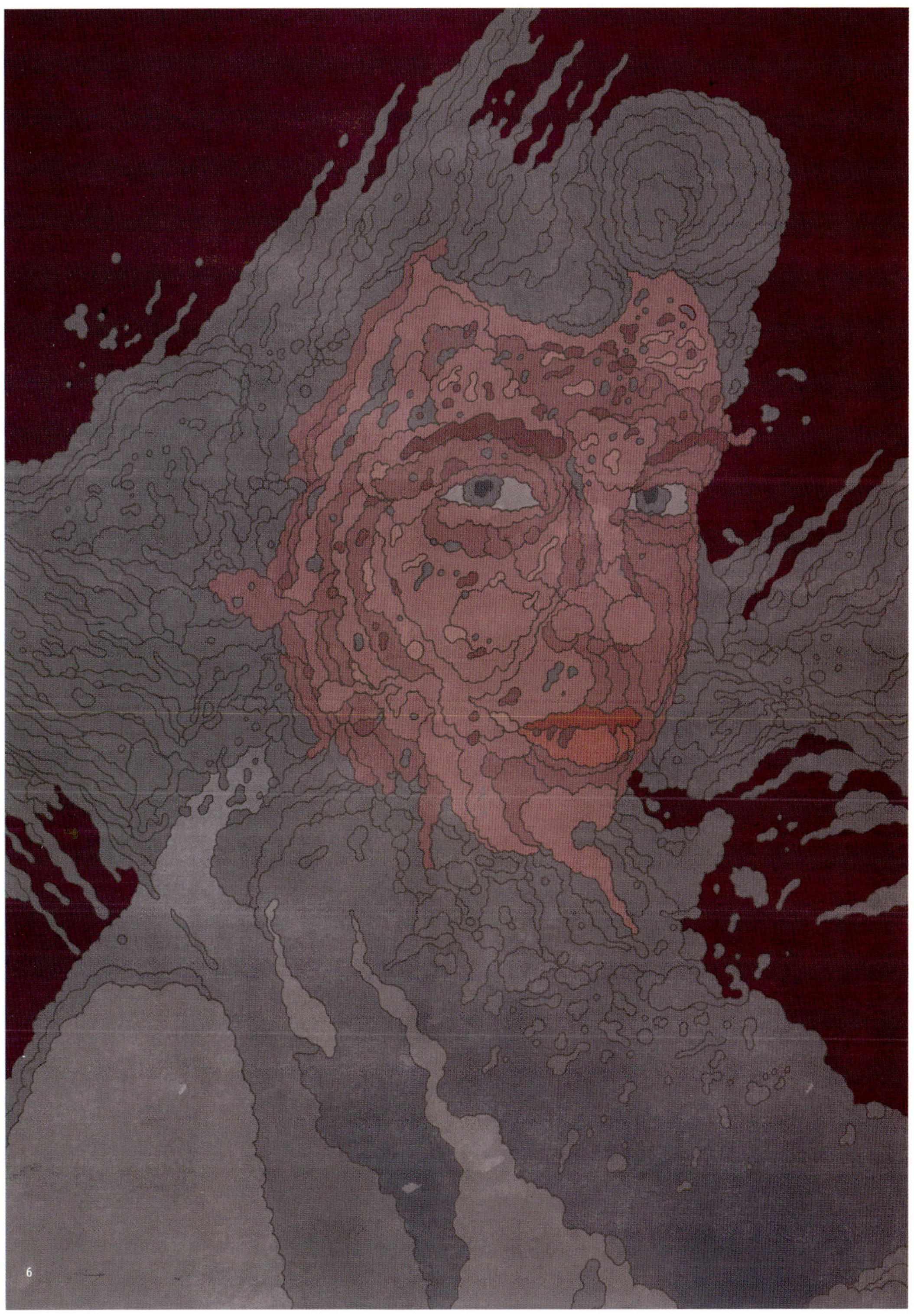

Sam Green
UK

www.sams-place.net

1. **Where does it hurt?** (2012). Howard Hughes Medical institute Bulletin. Pencil, acrylic on paper, Photoshop

2. **Female portrait** (2010). Personal work. Pencil on paper

3. **Surfacing 3** (2010). Personal work. Pencil on paper

4. **Female portrait** (2009). Personal work. Pencil on paper

5. **Old & New** (2010). Onlab & Birkhäuser Verlag. Pencil on paper

6. **Female portrait** (2010). Hugo and Marie. Pen on paper, Photoshop

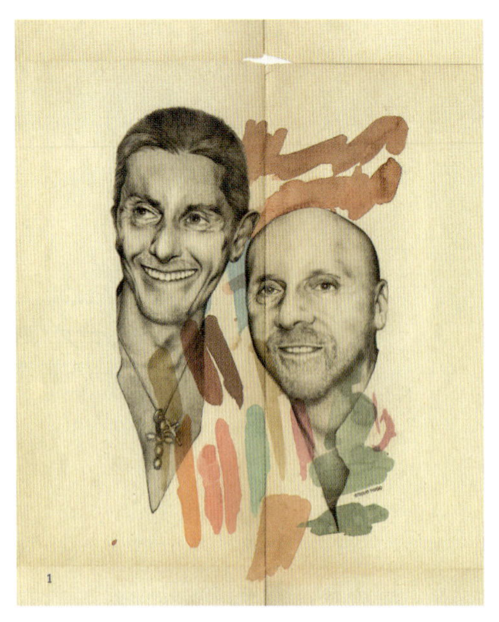

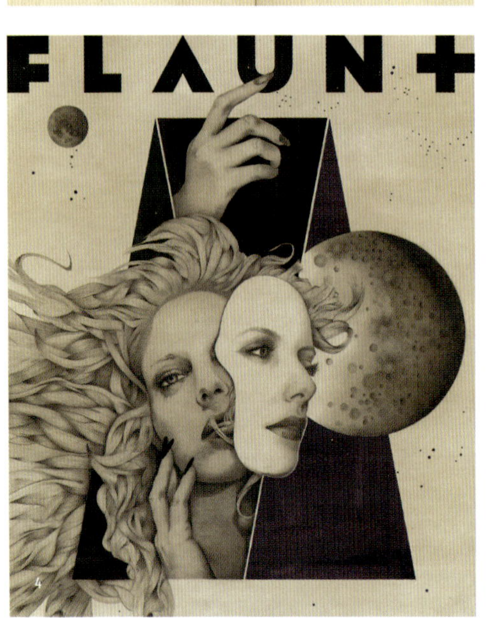

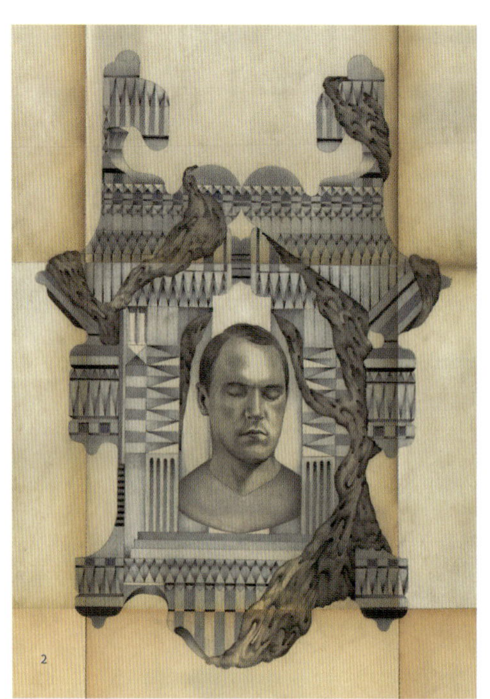

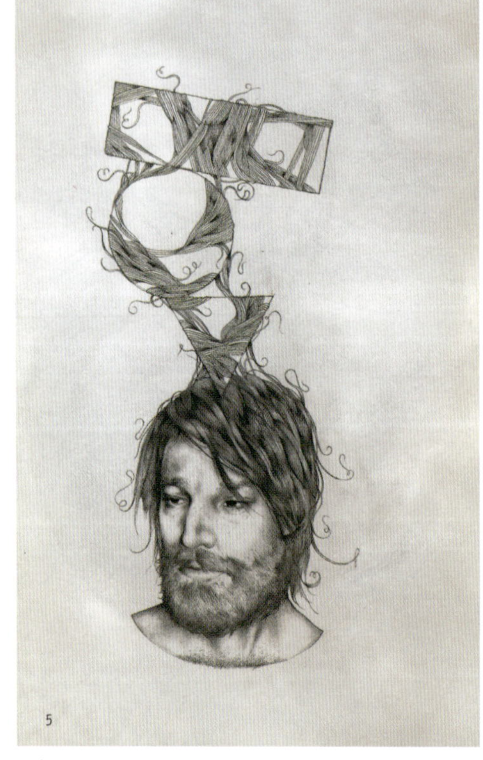
FLAUN+

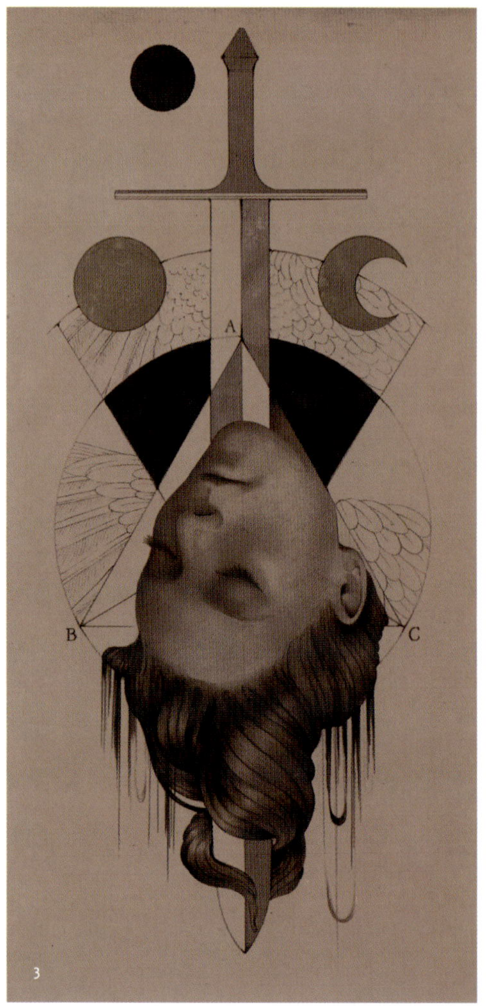

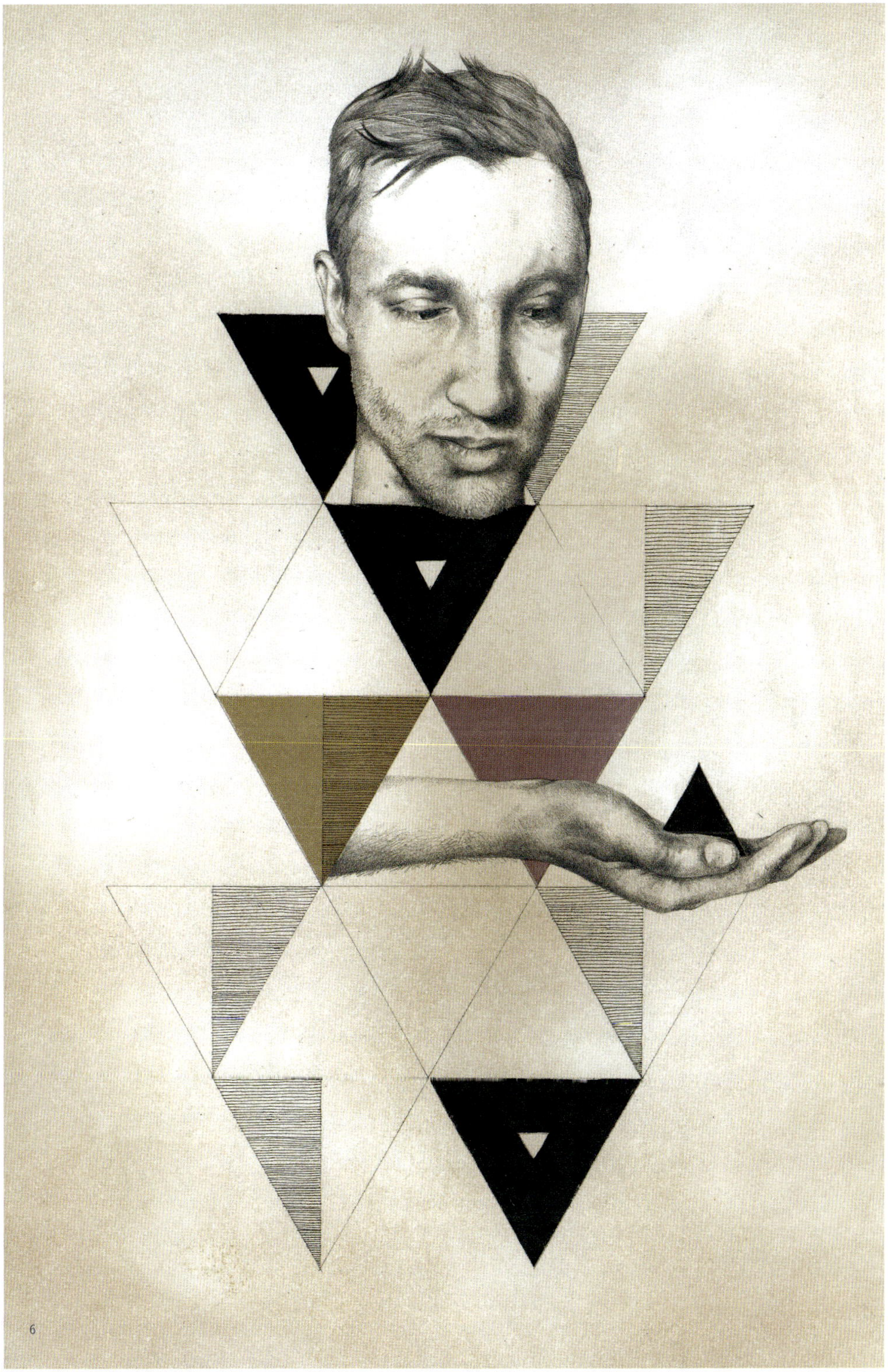

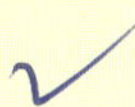

Mario Hugo
USA

Agency: Hugo & Marie
www.hugoandmarie.com

1. **Dolce & Gabbana** (2006). Giovanni Bianco GB65. Pencil, watercolor on found paper

2. **Image of a Cathedral** (2010). *Please! Magazine*. Pencil on found paper

3. **Dymphna in Effigy** (2008). *The Fader Magazine.*Pencil, wash on found paper

4. **Flaunt Magazine Issue 83** (2007). *Flaunt Magazine*. Pencil, china ink on found paper

5. **Hair Knots** (2006). Personal work. Pencil on found paper

6. **The Meaning of Life** (2006). Personal work. Pencil, china ink on found paper

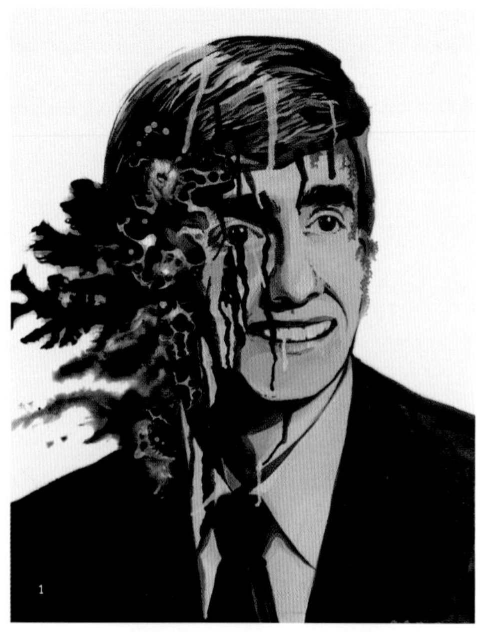
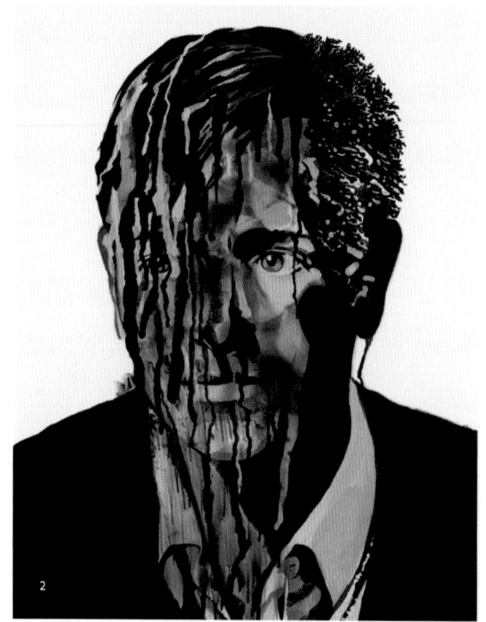
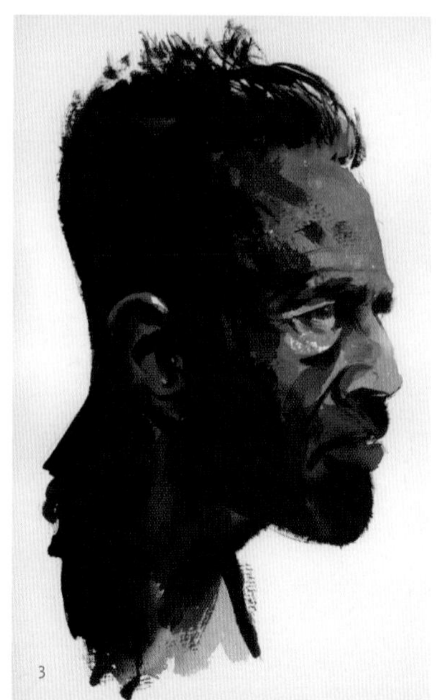
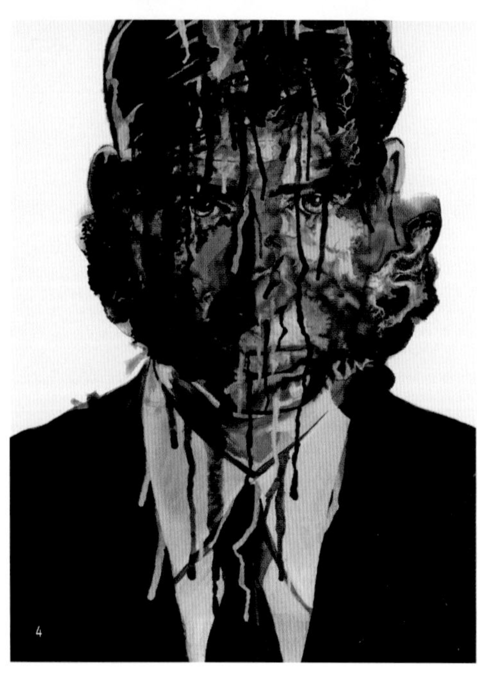
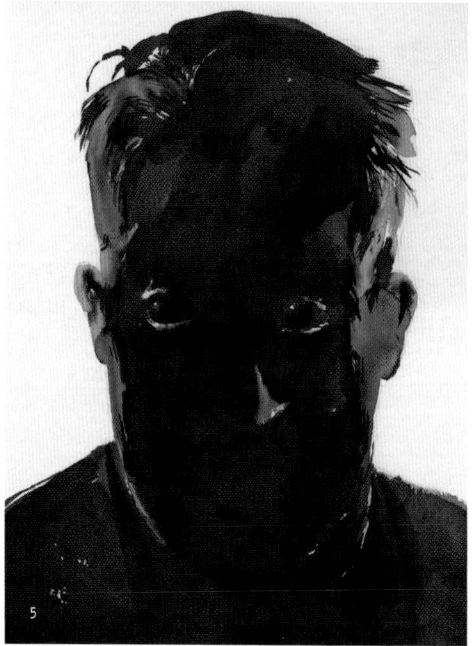

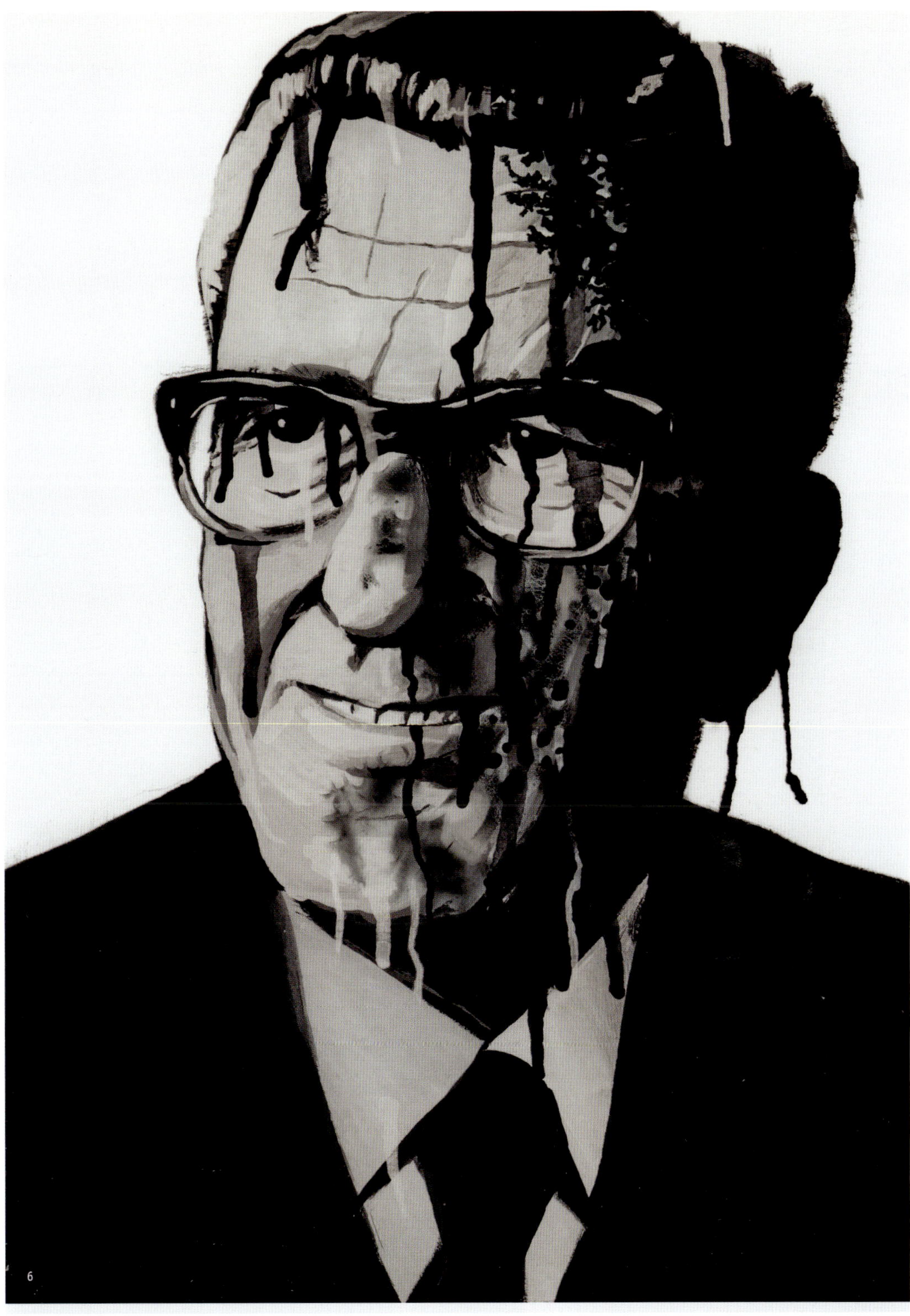

Fredrik Tjernström
Sweden

Agency: www.agentbauer.com
www.fredriktjernstrom.com

1. **From the series *The Faces** (2010).
   Personal work. Acrylic, ink and digital

2. **From the series *The Faces** (2010).
   Personal work. Acrylic, ink and digital

3. **From the series *The Brawlers** (2009).
   Personal work. Ink on paper

4. **From the series *The Faces** (2010).
   Personal work. Acrylic, ink and digital

5. **From the series *The Brawlers** (2008).
   Personal work. Ink on paper

6. **From the series *The Faces** (2010).
   Personal work. Acrylic, ink and digital

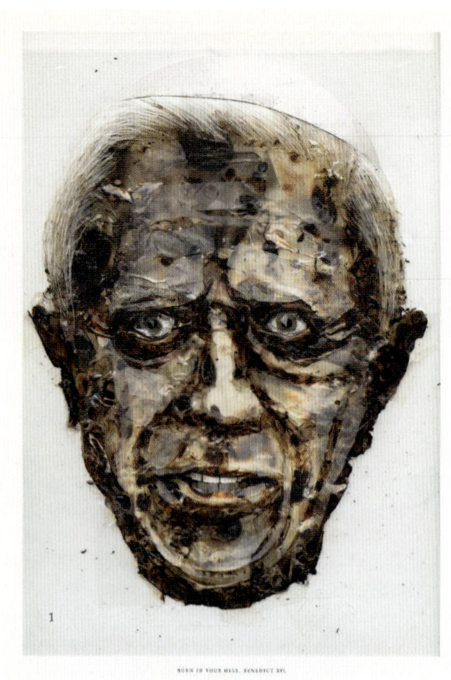

BURN IN YOUR HELL, BENEDICT XVI.

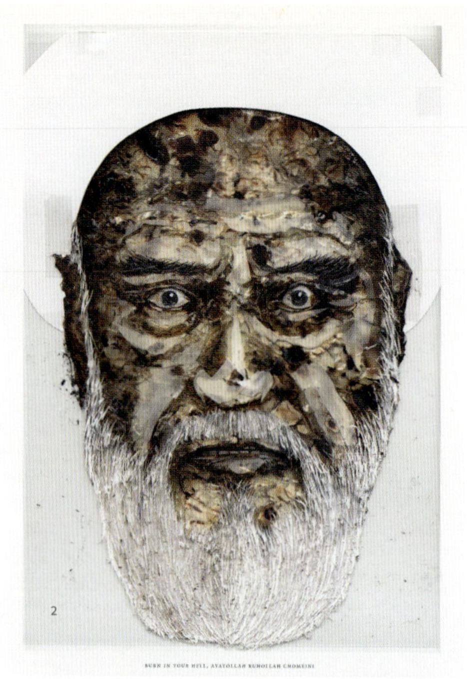

BURN IN YOUR HELL, AYATOLLAH RUHOLLAH CHOMEINI

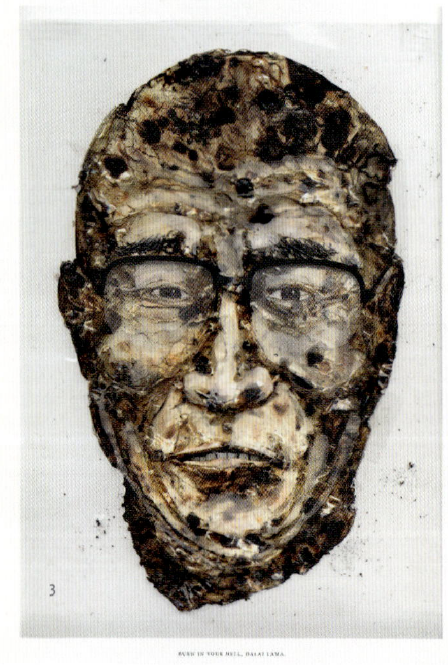

BURN IN YOUR HELL, DALAI LAMA.

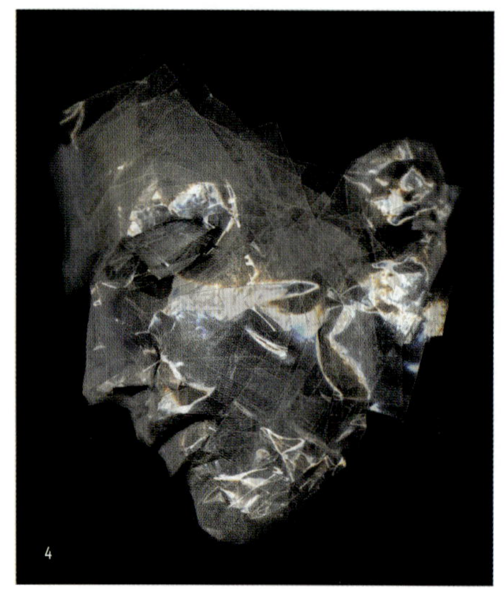

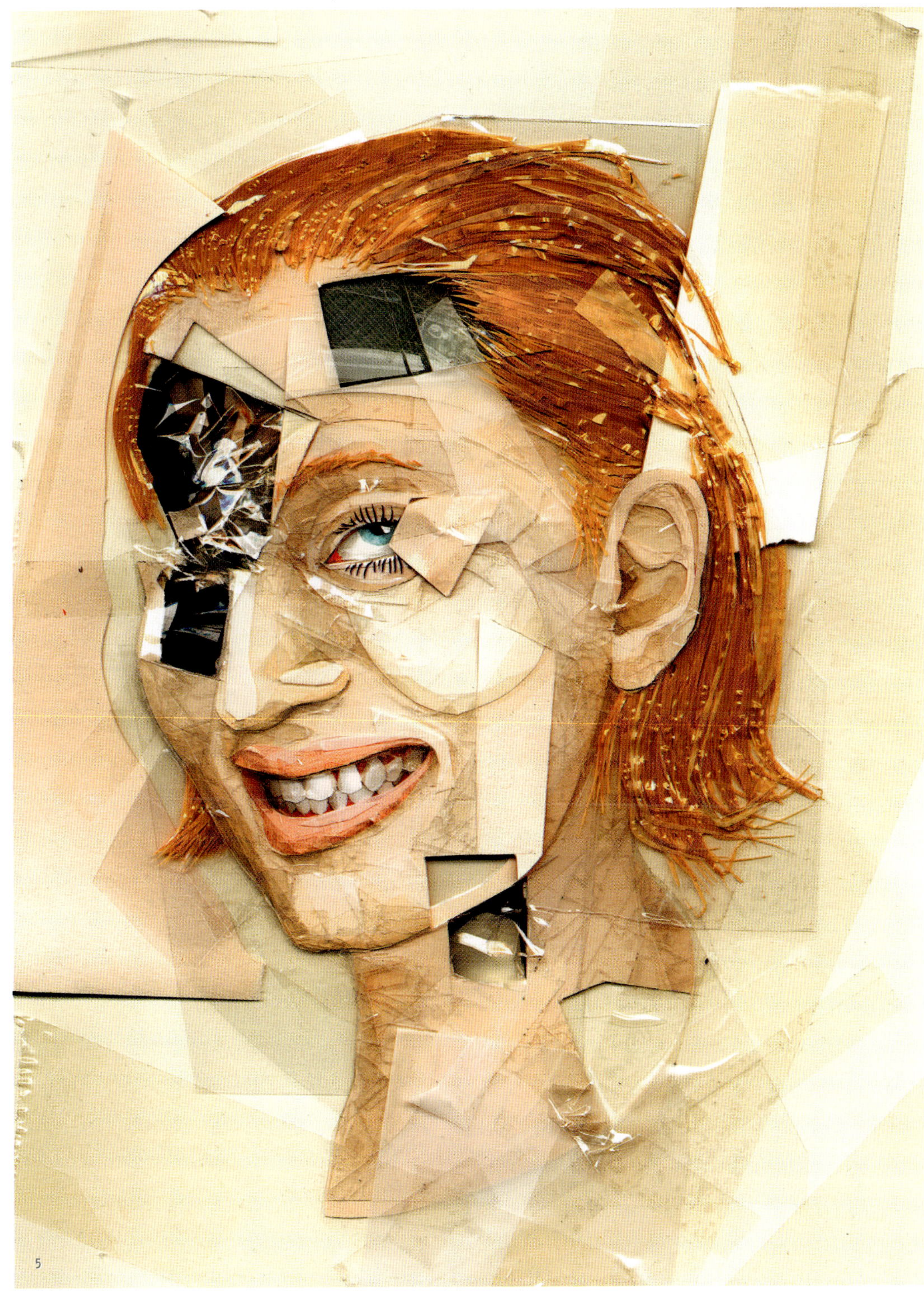

Herr Müller

Germany

www.ilikeyourbadbreathdaddy.de

1. **BURN IN YOUR HELL, BENEDICT XVI.** (2011). www.burninyourhell.com. Scotch tape, adhesive tape, paper, foil, fire

2. **BURN IN YOUR HELL, AYATOLAH RUHOLA CHOMEINI** (2011). www.burninyourhell.com. Scotch tape, adhesive tape, paper, foil, fire

3. **BURN IN YOUR HELL, DALAI LAMA** (2011). www.burninyourhell.com. Scotch tape, adhesive tape, paper, foil, fire

4. **Iron Curtis** (2011). Iron Curtis. Scotch tape, light

5. **Collateral 2** (2011). Exhibition. Scotch tape, adhesive tape, paper, foil

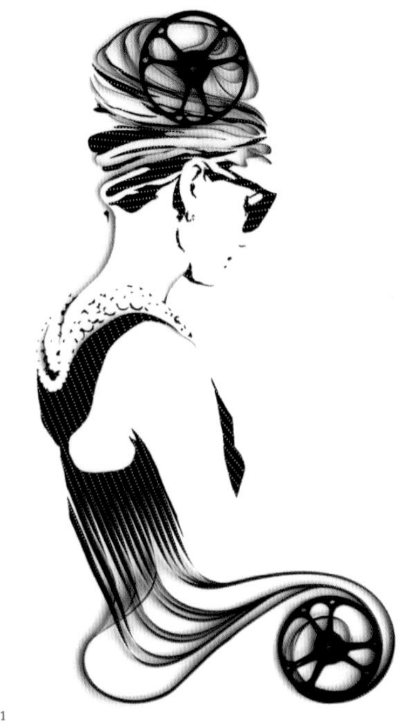

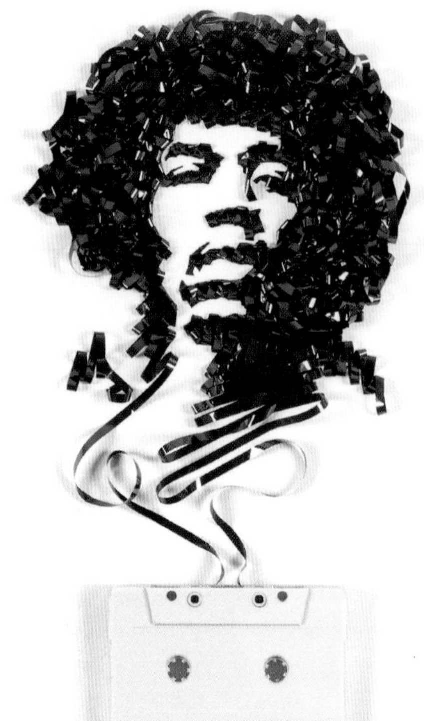

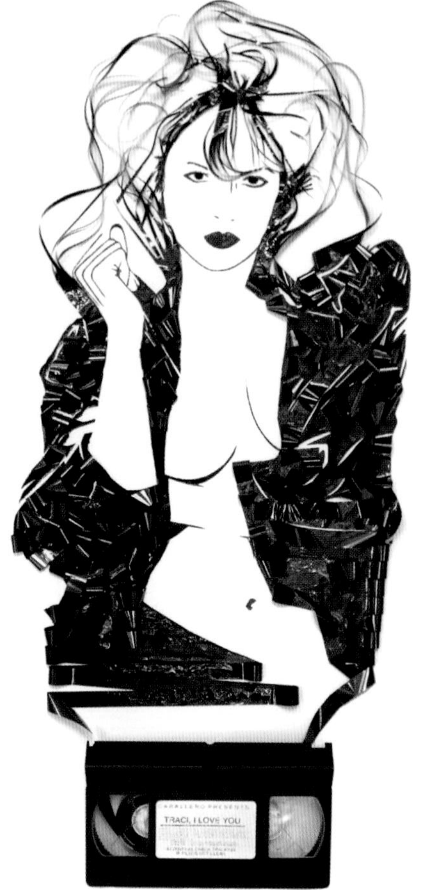

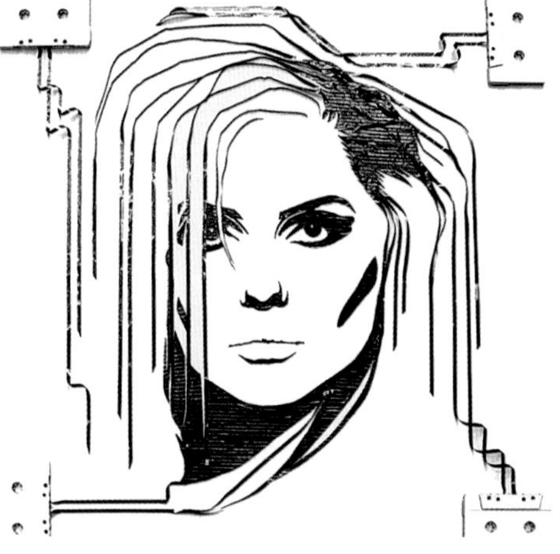

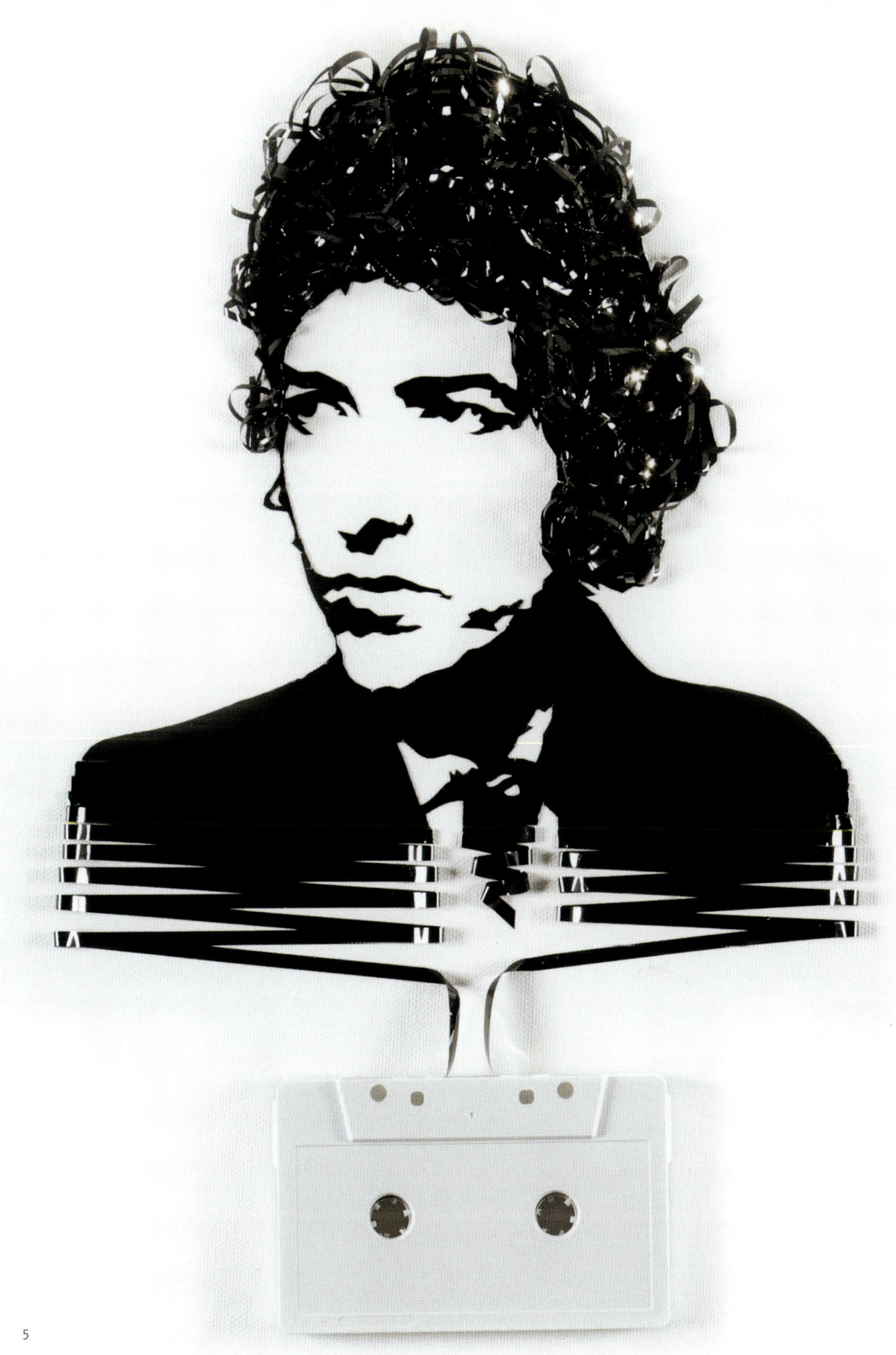

Erika Iris Simmons

USA

www.iri5.com

1. **Audrey Hepburn** (2011). 8mm film on canvas

2. **Jimi Hendrix** (2009). Cassette on canvas

3. **Traci Lords** (2010). VHS tape

4. **Debbie Harry of Blondie** (2010). Bumbershoot. Cassette

5. **Bob Dylan** (2009). Cassette on canvas

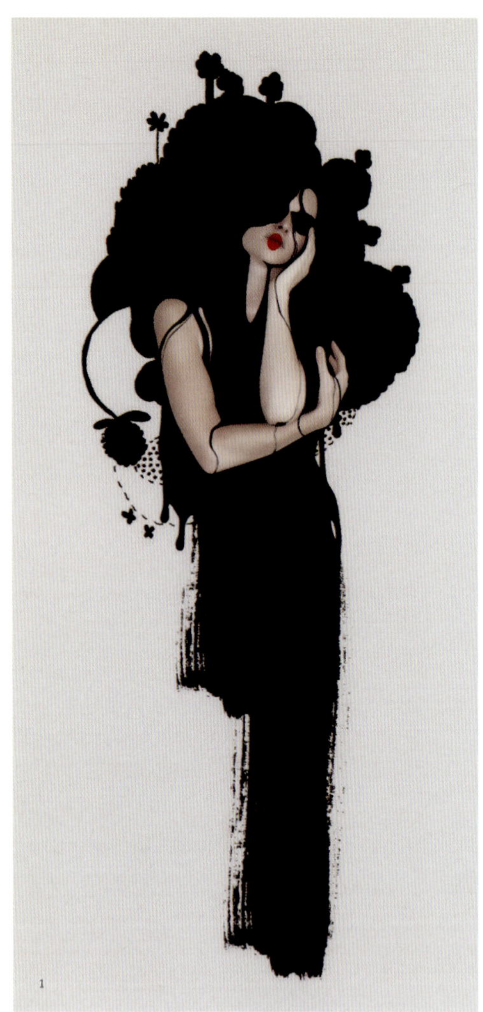

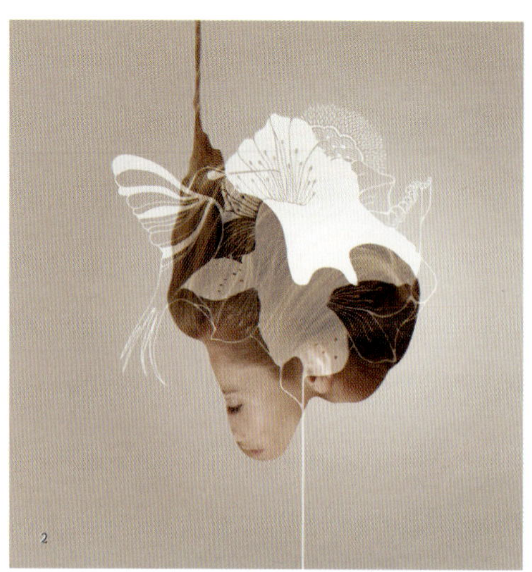

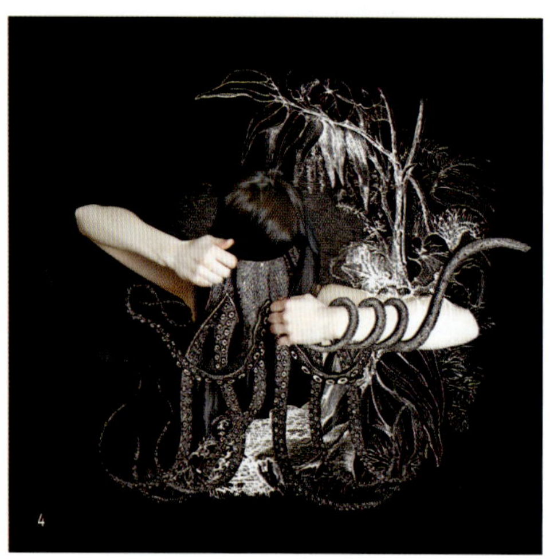

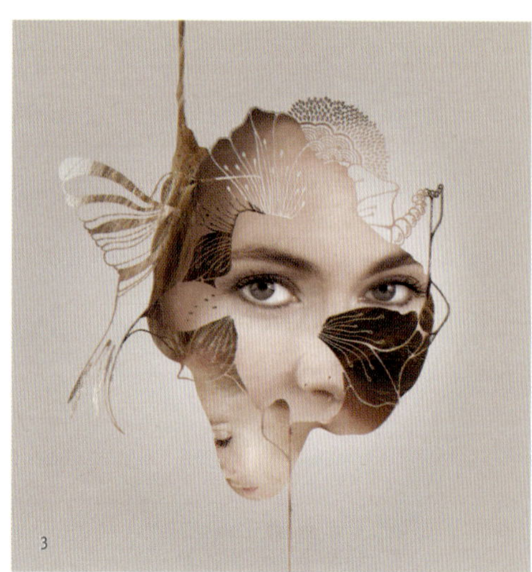

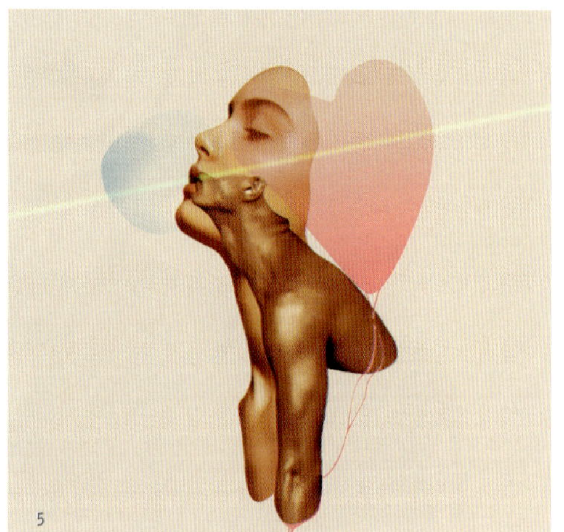

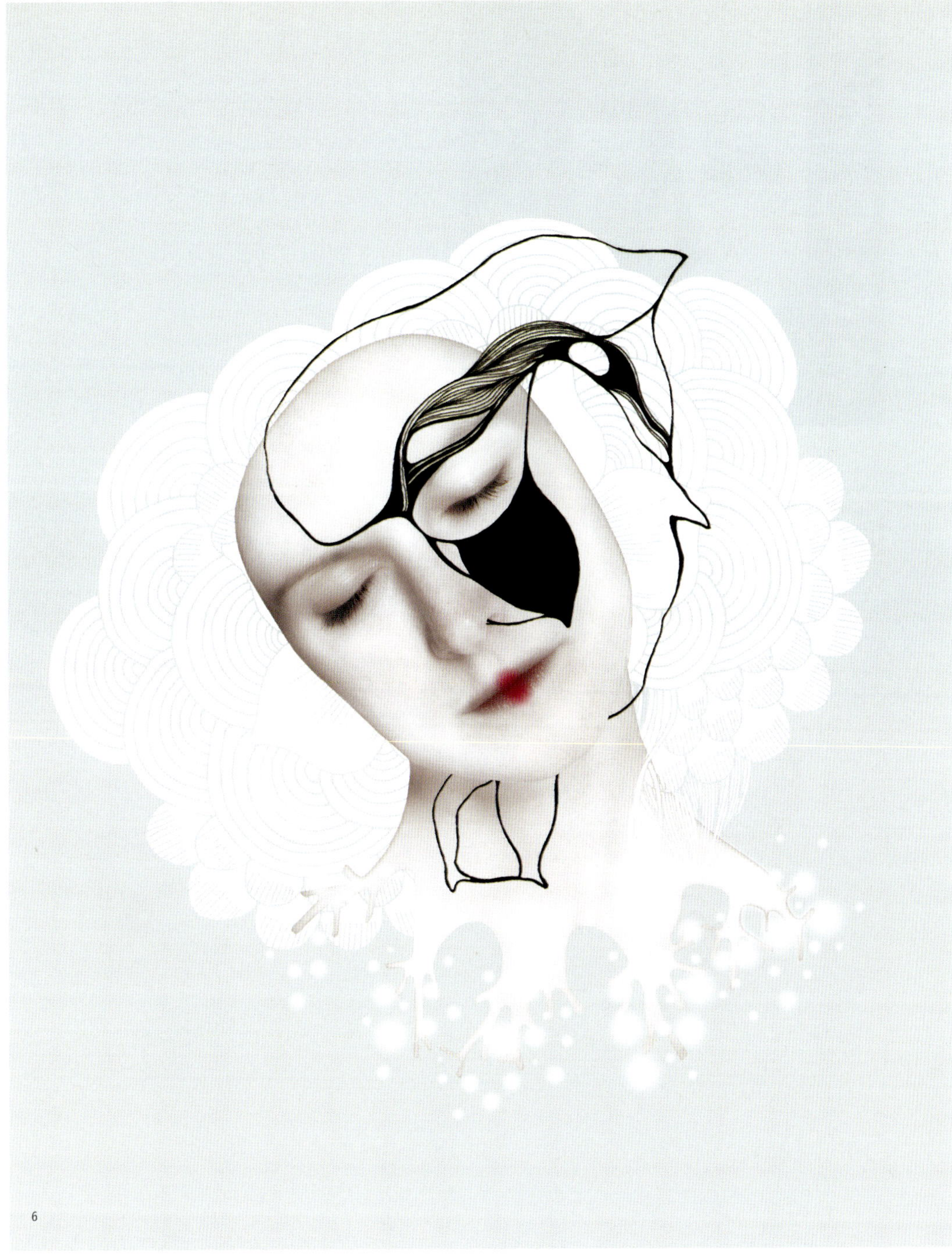

Géraldine Georges

Belgium

Agency: Colagene, Illustration Clinic
www.colagene.com/fr/illustration/
geraldine-georges

1. **Black Woman** (2008). Personal work

2. **No Title** (2009). Karin Clercq

3. **No Title** (2009). Karin Clercq

4. **Jungle** (2010). Personal work

5. **The Kiss** (2007). Personal work

6. **Snowwhite** (2009). Personal work

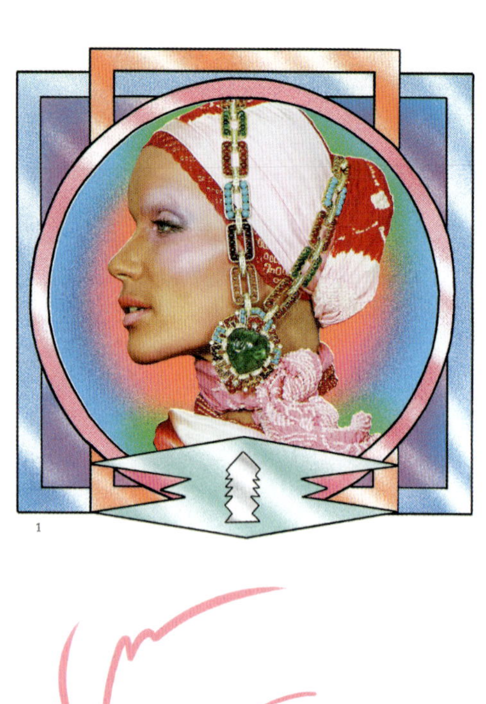

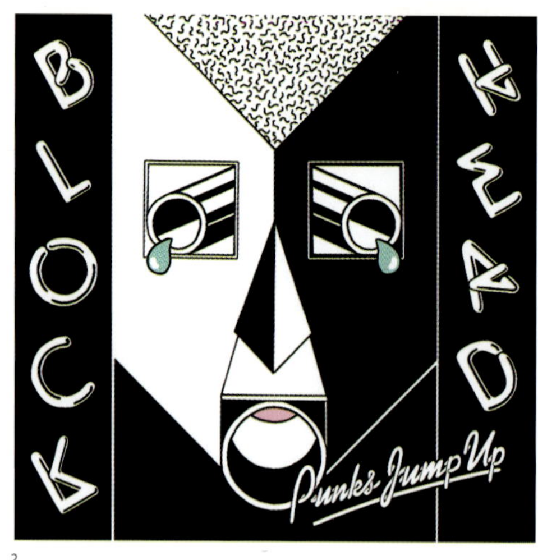
BLOCK
HEAD
Punks Jump Up

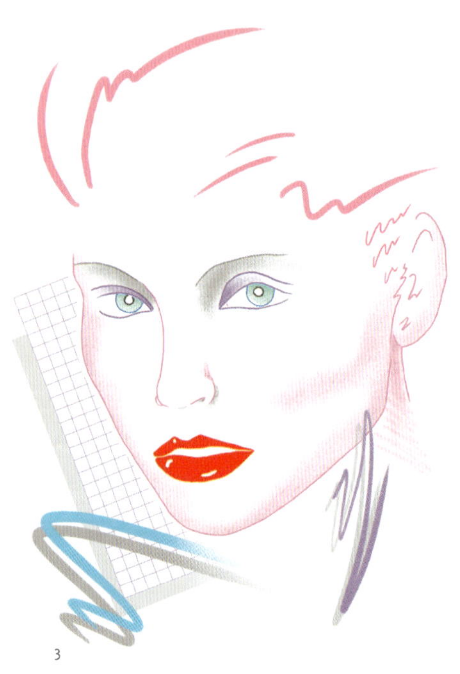

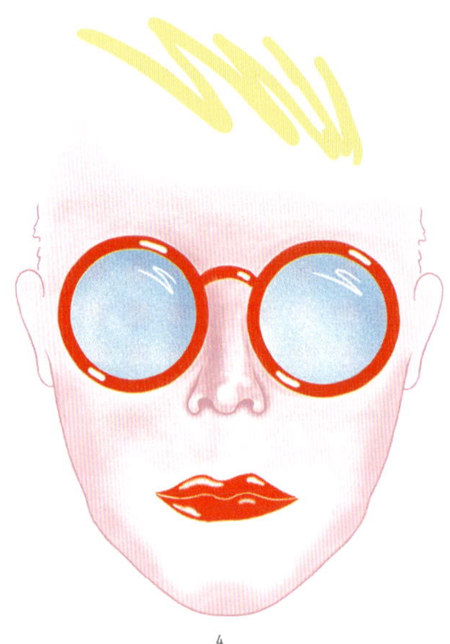

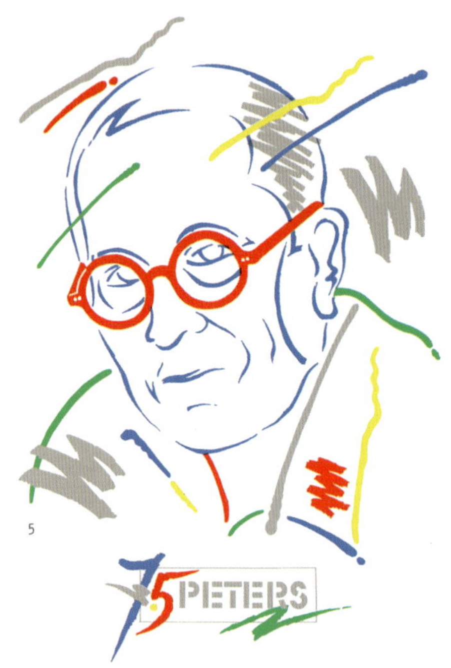
75 PETERS

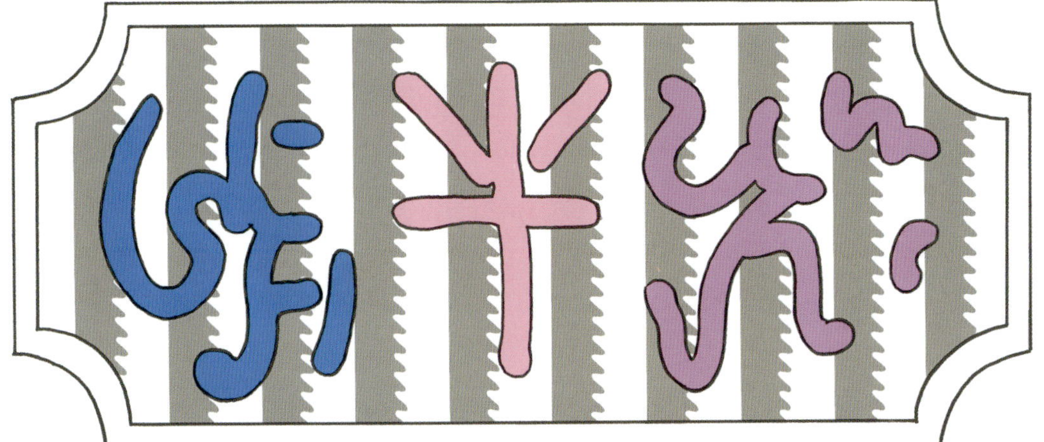

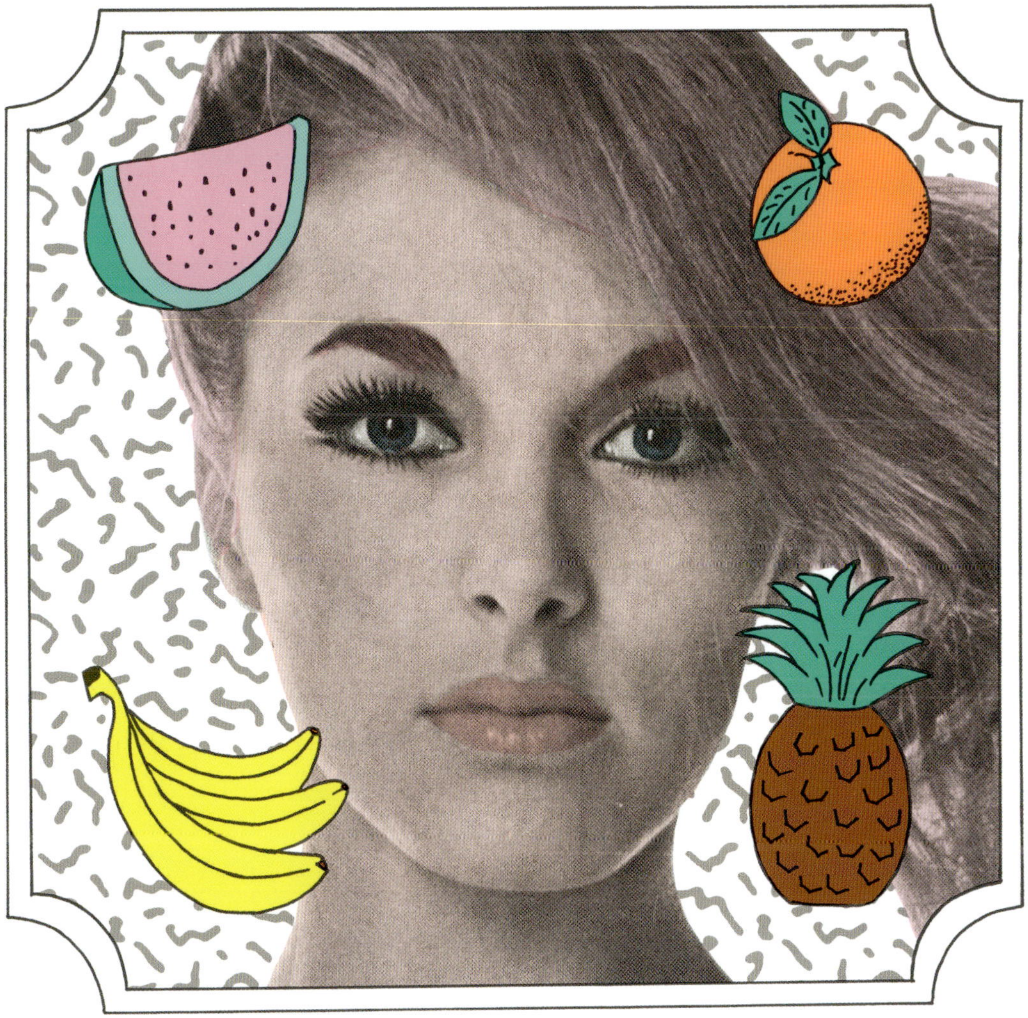

Michael Willis

UK

www.otherscenes.com

1. **Dream Portrait** (2010). Personal work. Mixed media

2. **Blockhead** (2011). Punks Jump Up / Kitsuné. Mixed media

3. **Untitled Portrait** (2011). Personal work. Mixed media

4. **Untitled Portrait** (2011). Personal work. Mixed media

5. **Sir Peter Cook** (2011). The Adam & Eve Project. Mixed media

6. **Mirror Portrait** (2011). Personal work. Mixed media

6

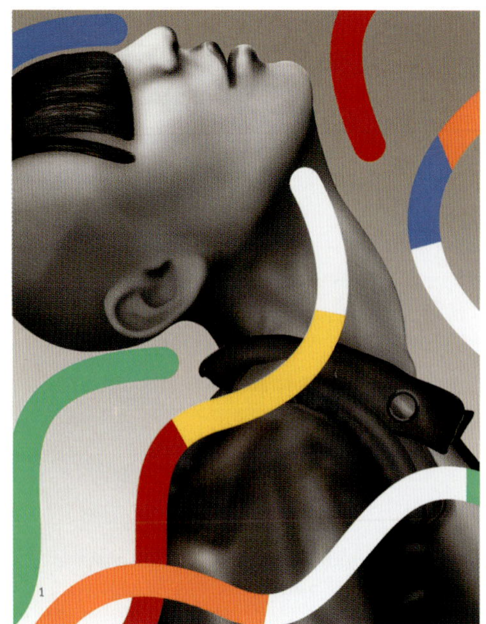

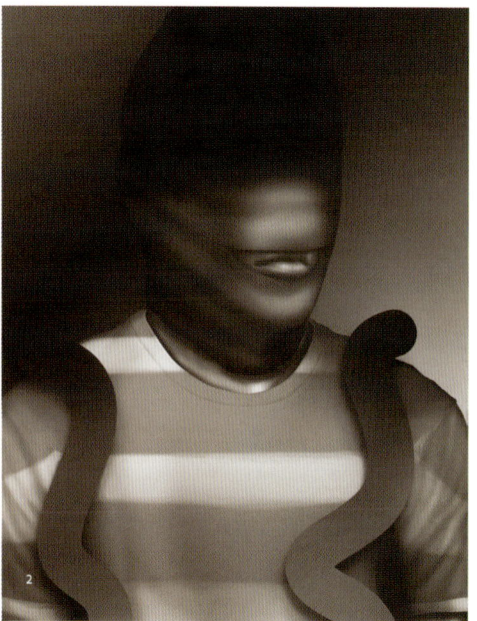

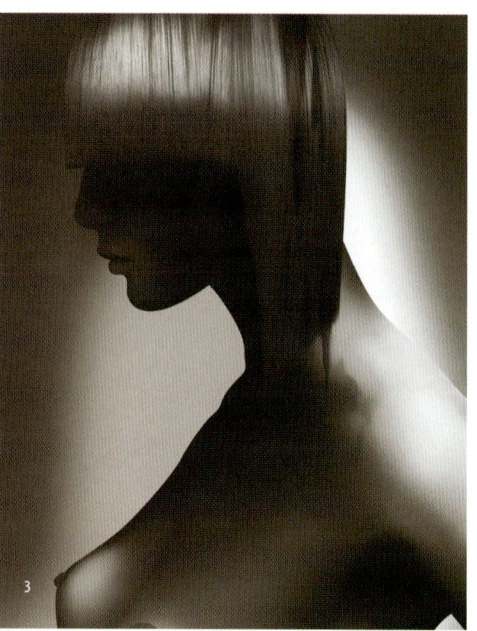

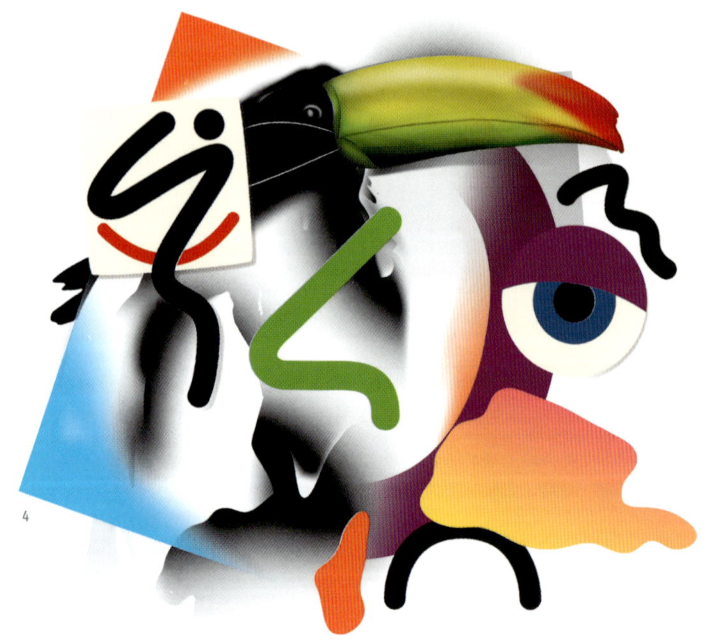

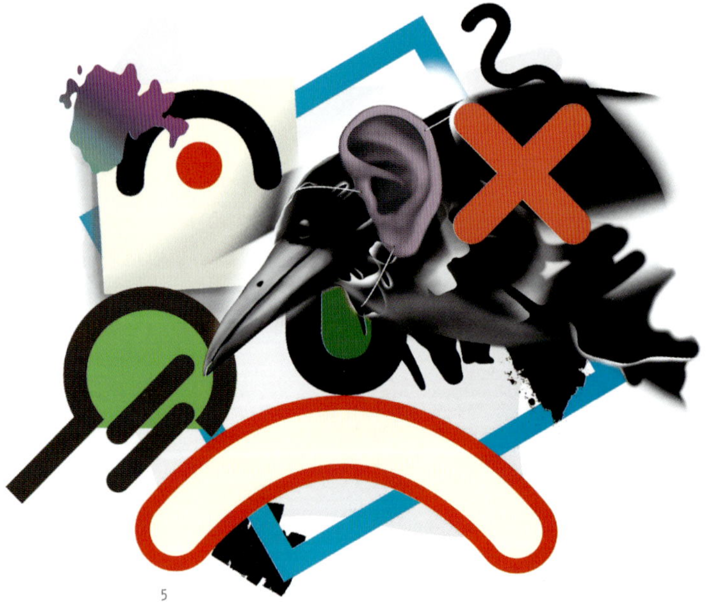

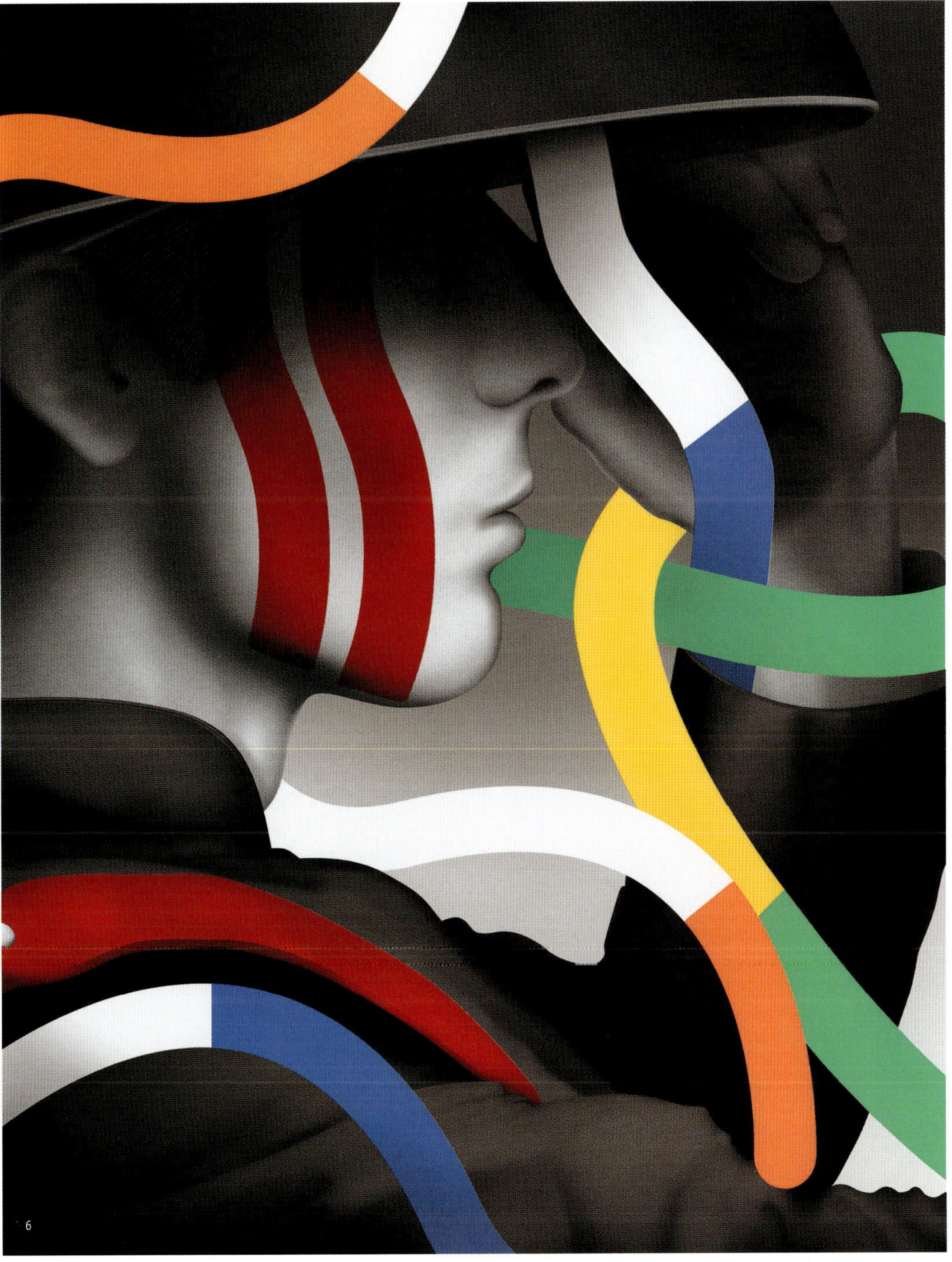

Dan Stafford
UK

www.dan-stafford.com

1. **Sophomore WAR! / All The Saints 1**
(2012)

2. **Kokon To Zai** (2012)

3. **Charlie Le Mindu** (2012)

4. **Murder 3** (2012)

5. **Murder 2** (2012)

6. **Sophomore WAR! / All The Saints 2**
(2012)

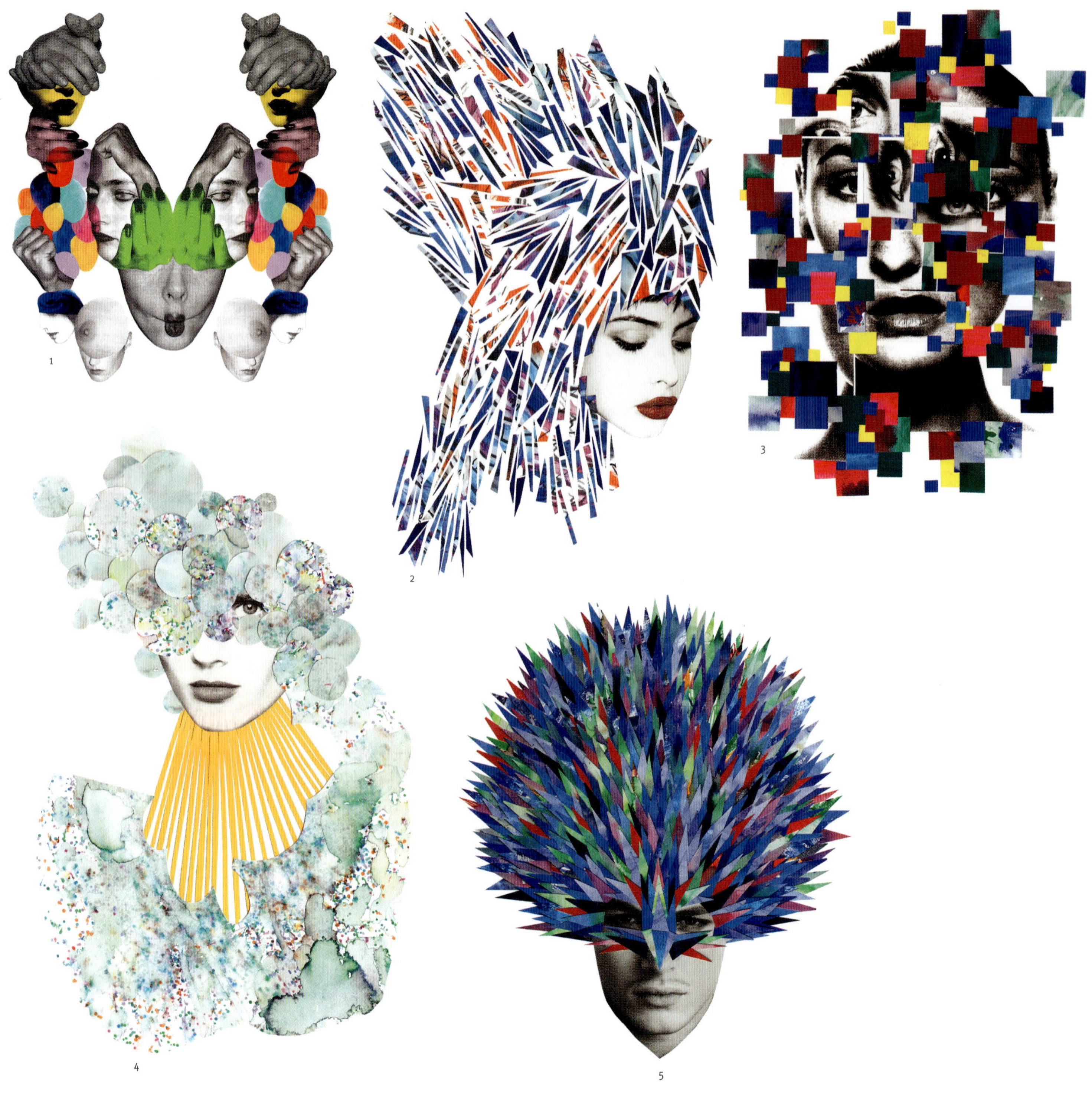

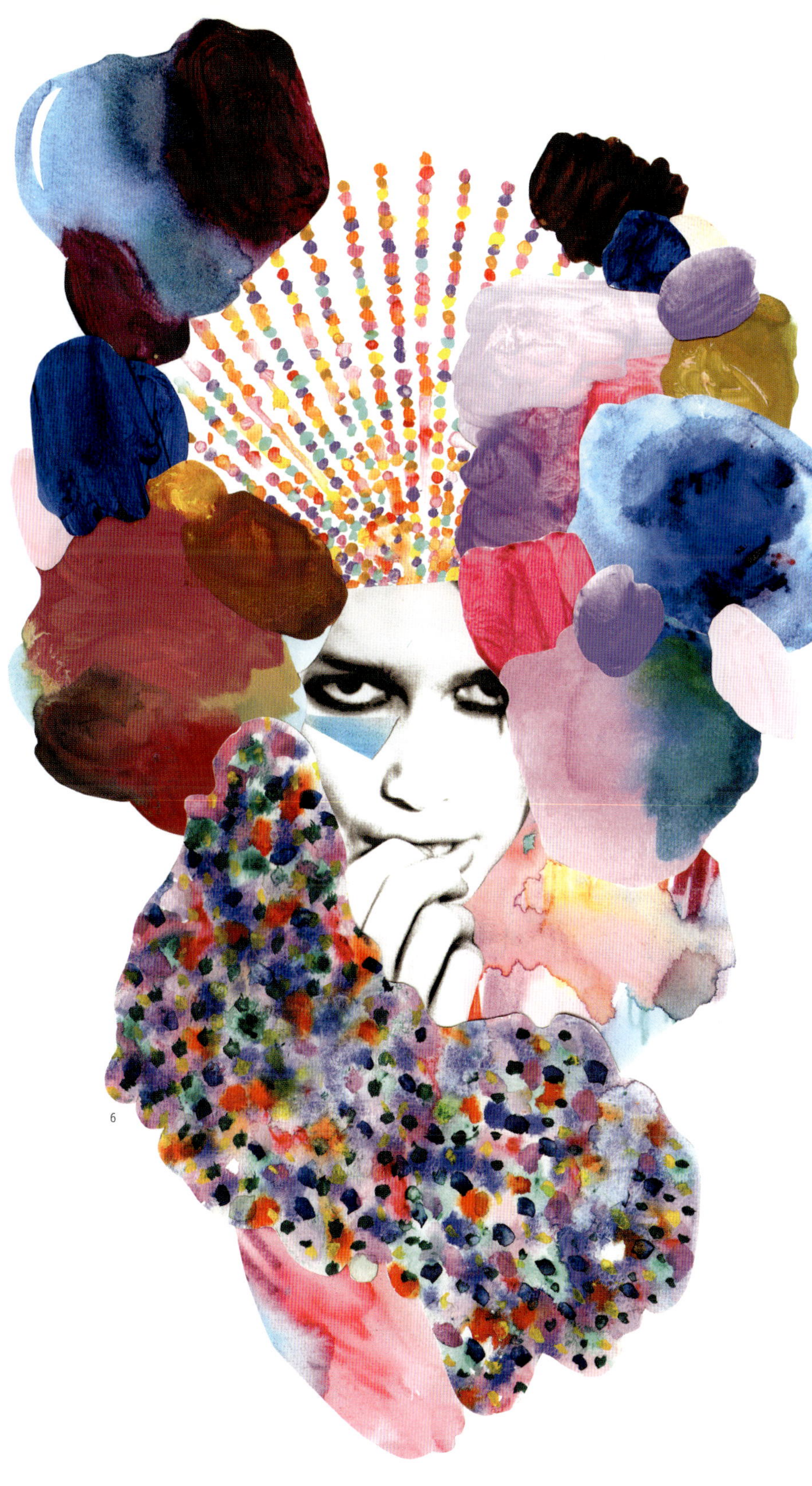

Niky Roehreke
USA

www.nikyniky.com

1. **Sweet Zeitgeist** (2011). *kinki magazine* Switzerland. Mixed media

2. **Winter Headpiece** (2011). Tokyo Vansankai exhibition. Mixed media

3. **Untitled** (2010). JOHN LAWRENCE SULLIVAN. Mixed media

4. **Spring Headpiece** (2011). Tokyo Vansankai exhibition. Mixed media

5. **Igel** (2011). Tokyo Vansankai exhibition. Mixed media

6. **Fighting Chance** (2011). Tokyo Vansankai exhibition. Mixed media

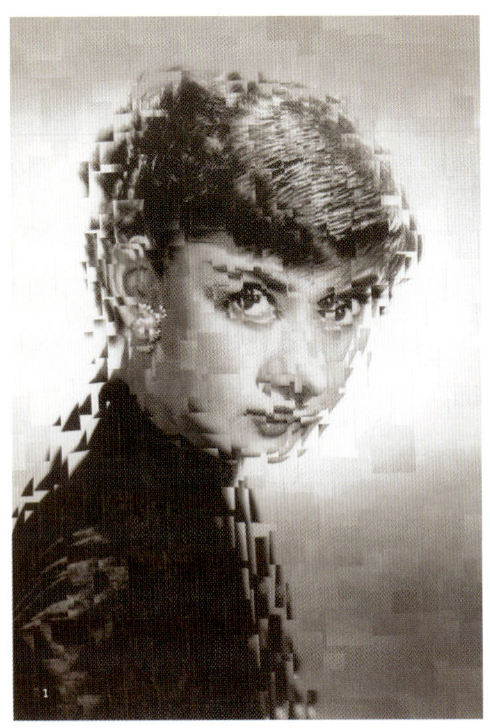

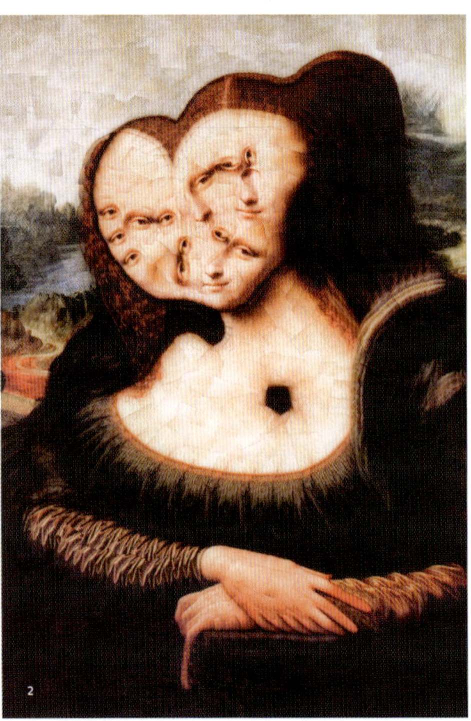

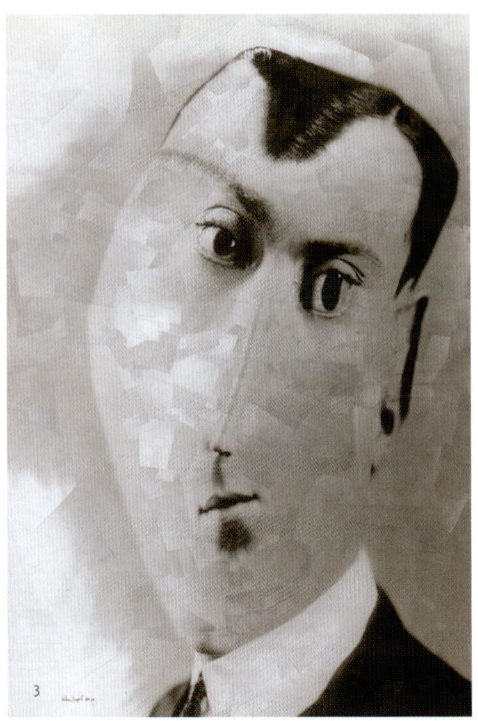

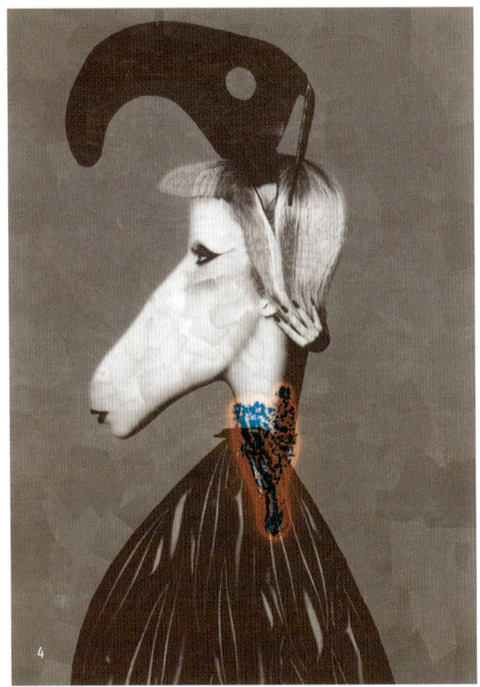

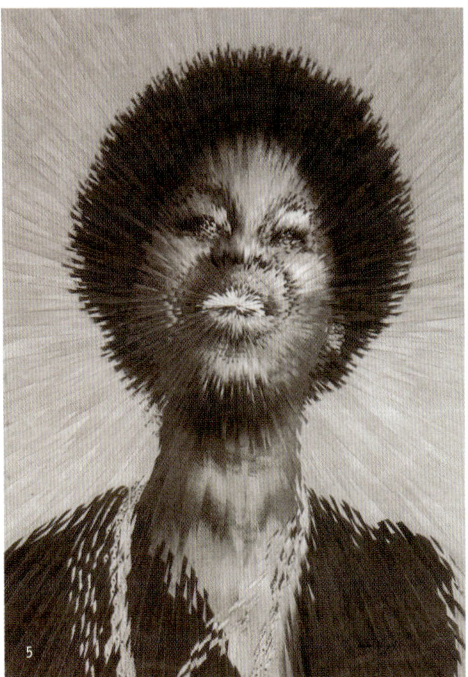

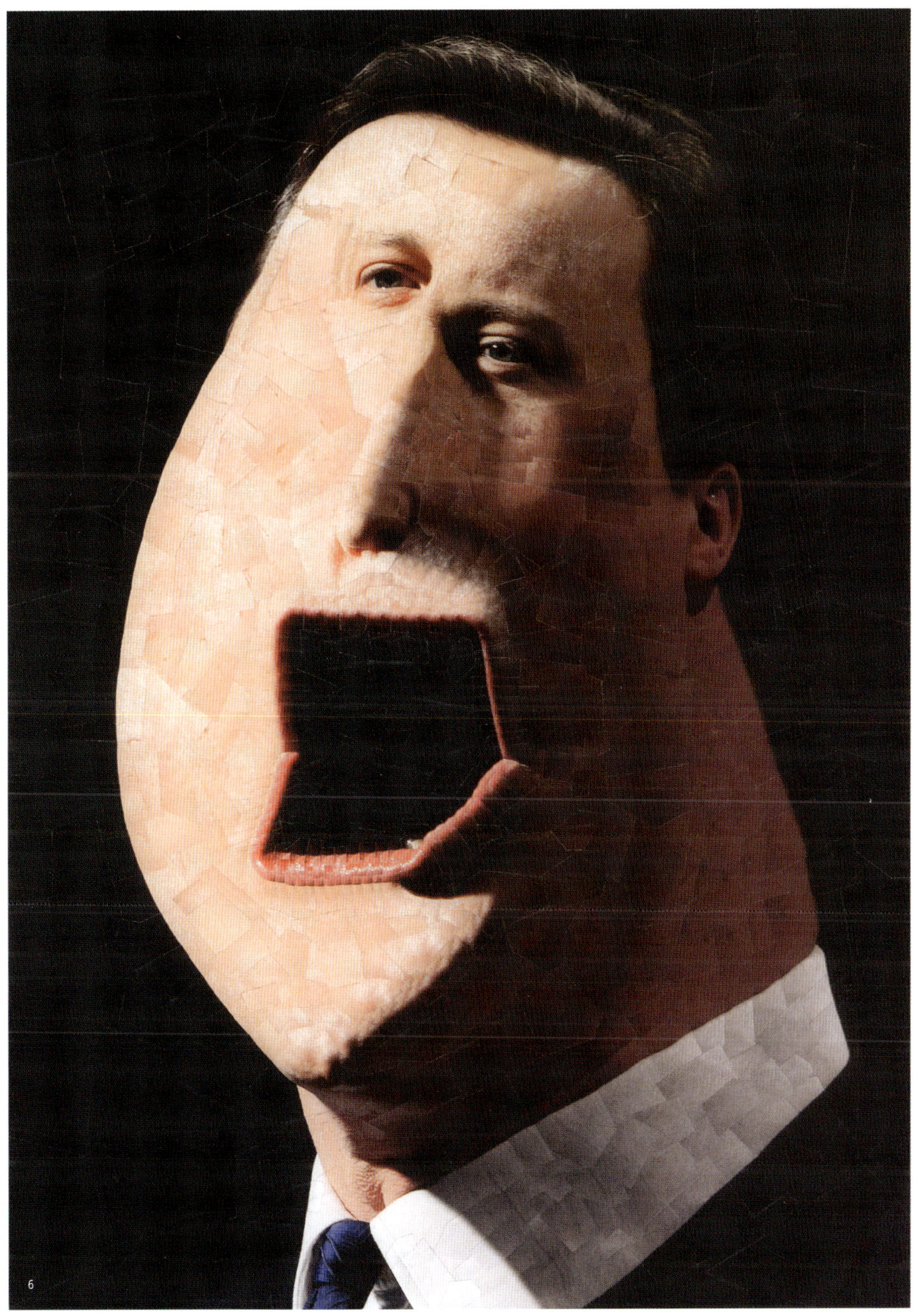

Lola Dupre

France

www.loladupre.com

1. **Exploding Audrey Hepburn #2** (2011). Private collector. Collage

2. **Mona Lisa** (2010). Private collector. Collage

3. **Buster Keaton #1** (2012). Personal work. Collage

4. **Gaga Hari** (2011). Private collector. Collage

5. **Nina Simone** (2011). Phone Booth Gallery. Collage

6. **David Cameron #4** (2011). Personal work. Collage

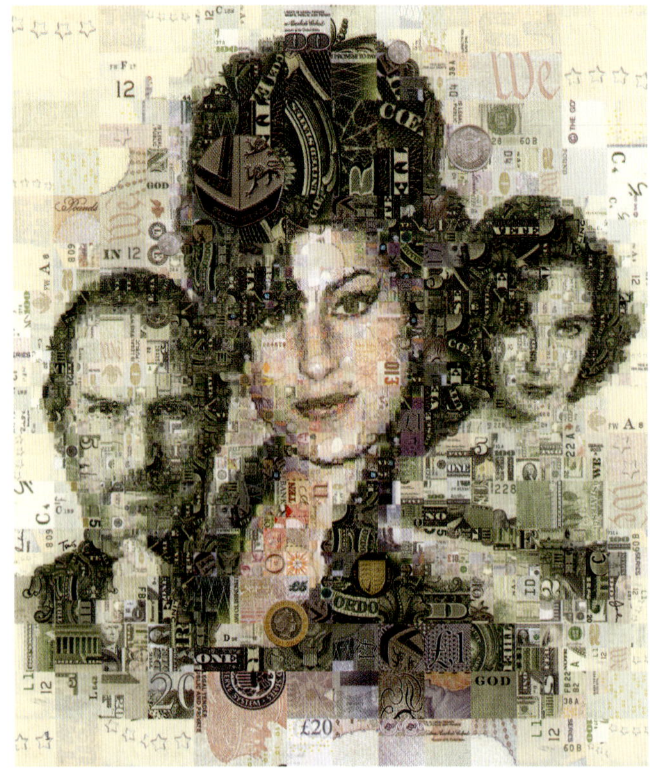

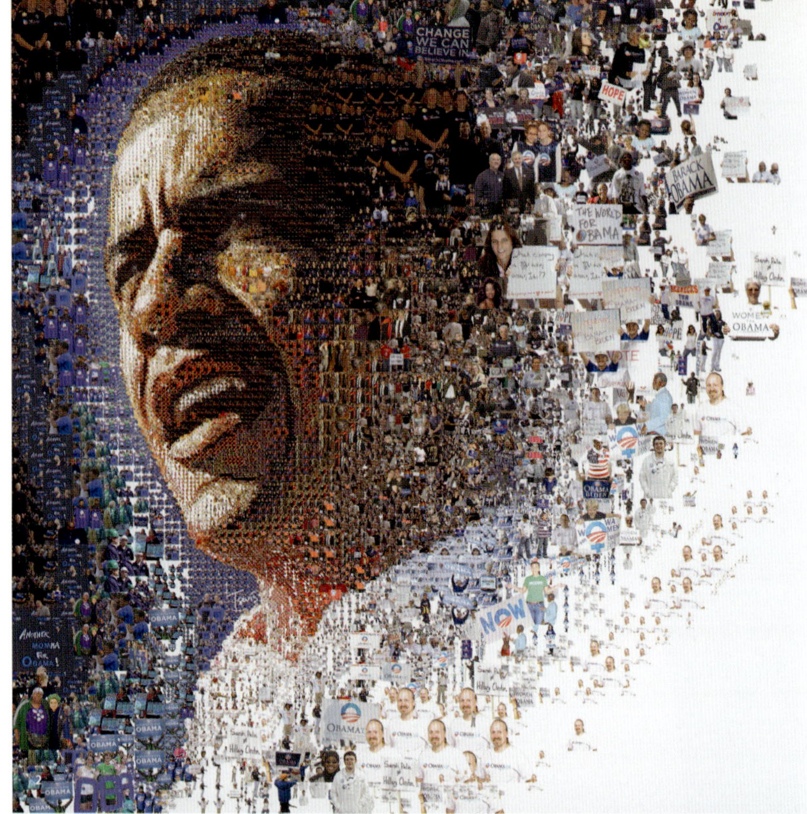

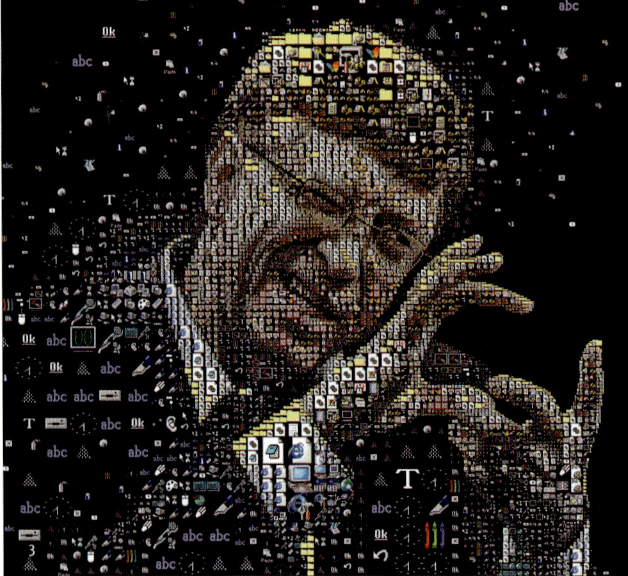

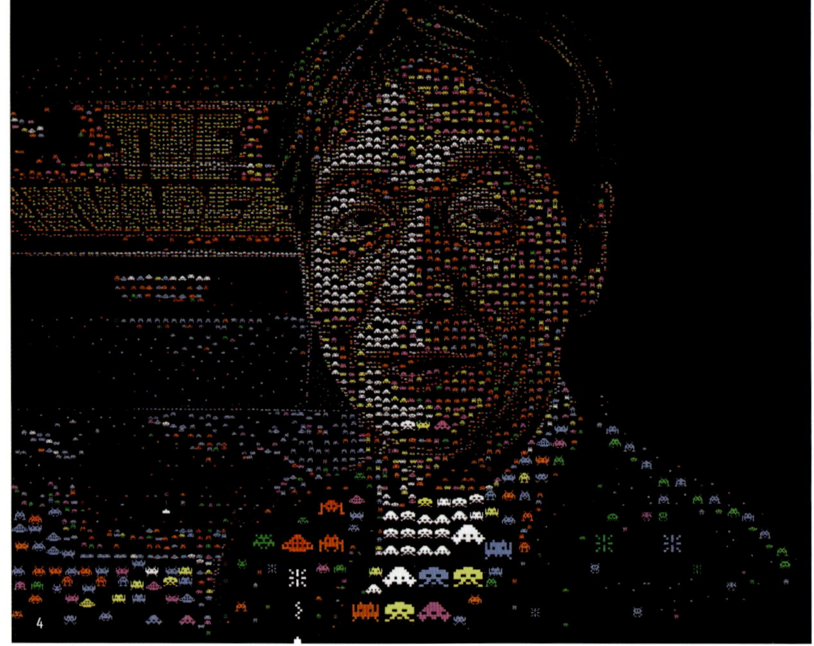

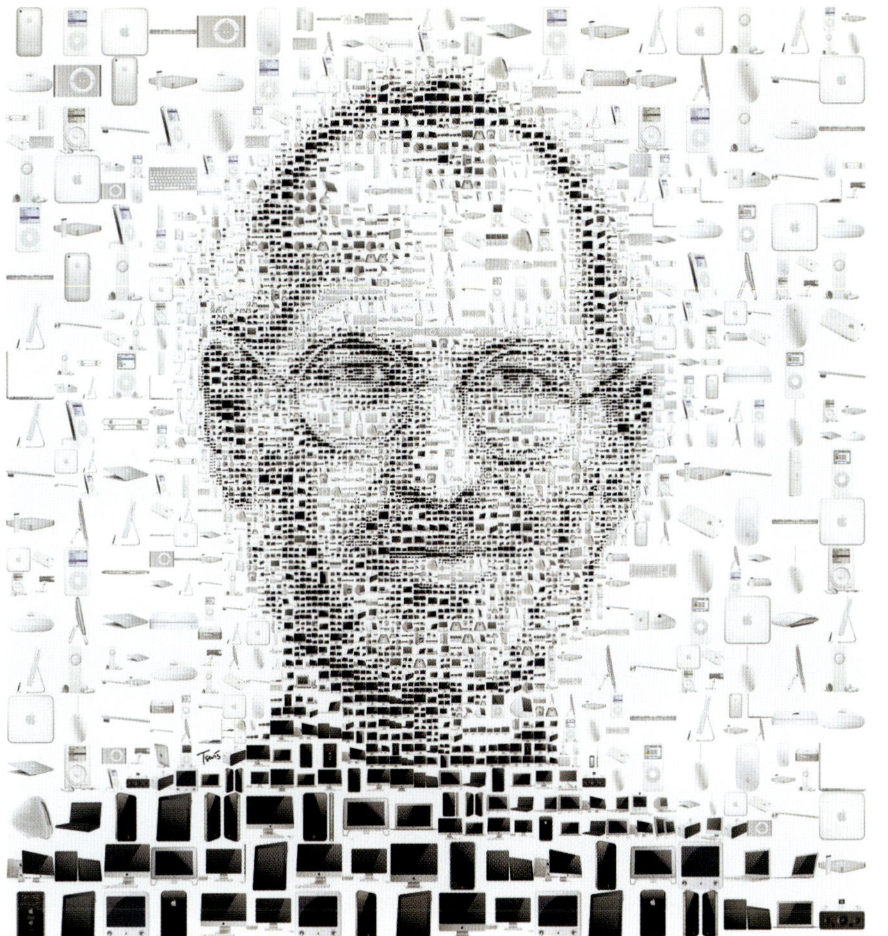

5

Charis Tsevis

Greece

www.tsevis.com

1. **Steve Jobs, Amy Winehouse and Liz Taylor, the 3 biggest losses of 2011** (2011). *Evening Standard*

2. **Barack Obama, American president** (2011). Personal work

3. **Bill Gates, American entrepreneur** (2011). DK, Penguin Books

4. **Tomohiro Nishikado, Japanese game developer** (2011). DK, Penguin Books

5. **Steve Jobs, American entrepreneur** (2011). *Panorama magazine*

Imaginary

Maybe all imaginary portraits are inherent self-portraits. The images
in this chapter have no pretense of portraying an actual person.
Instead, they reveal to us the perception of the artist, oscillating
between introspective self-reflection and radical abstraction. Some
of the portraits reflect our ideal of beauty, while others adhere to
a faux naive style. Yet all of them speak to us about the society in
which we live, and how the artist perceives the individual within it.

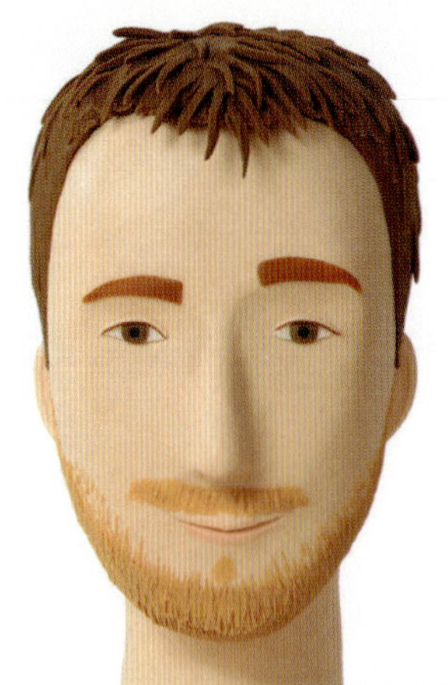
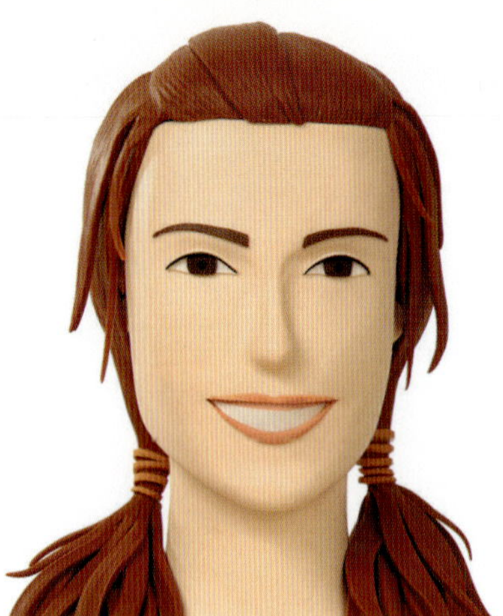
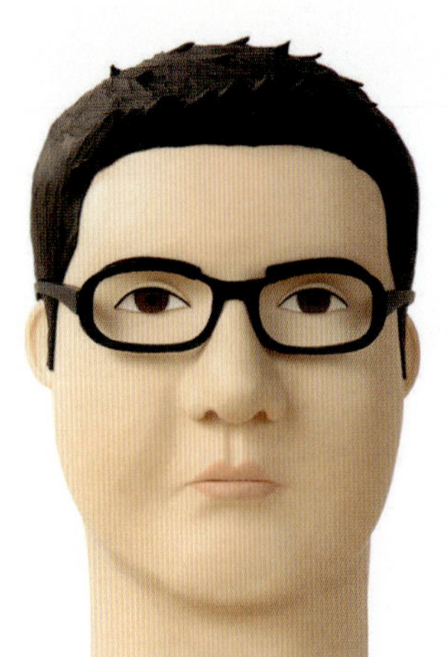
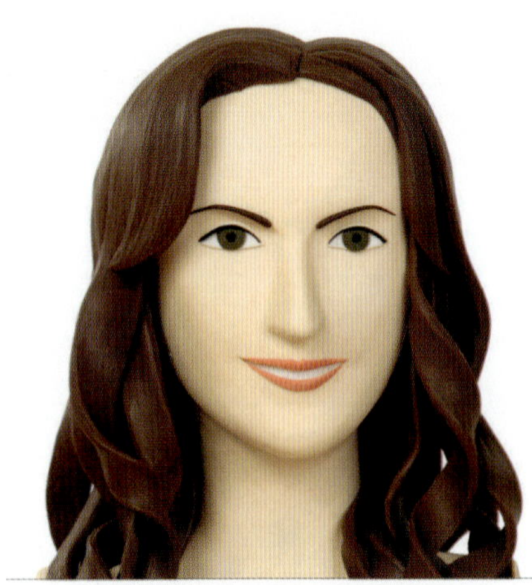
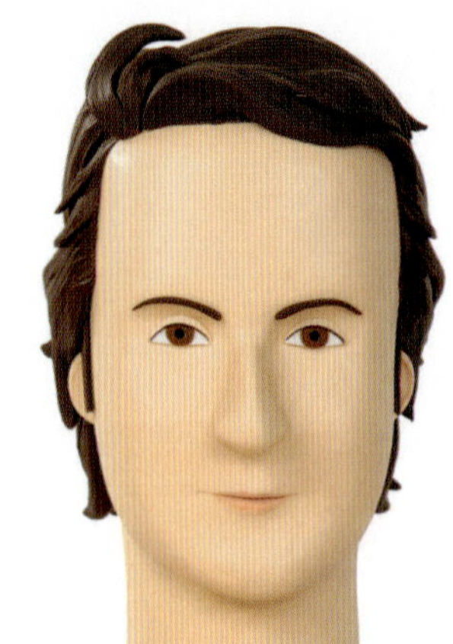
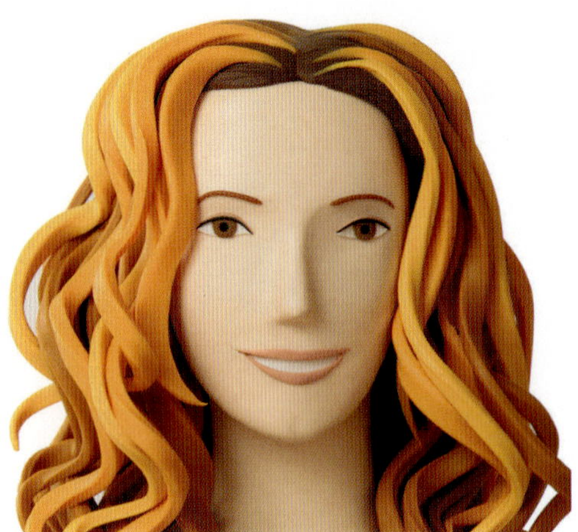
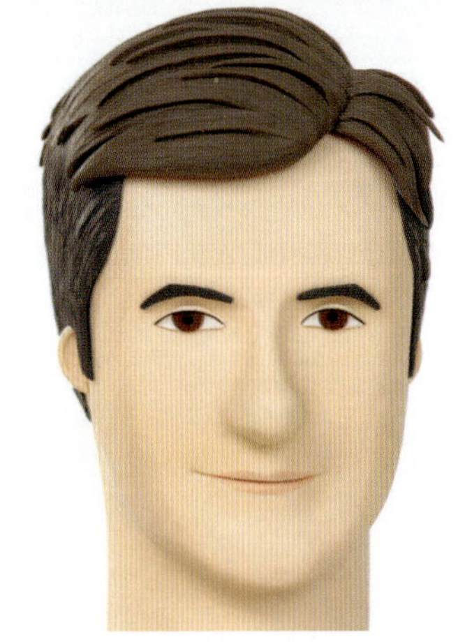
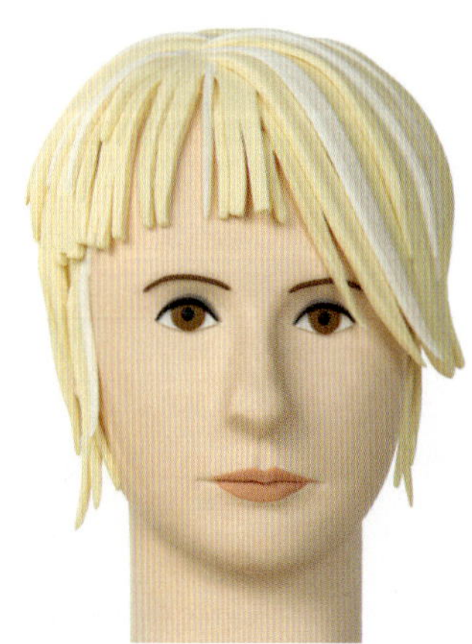
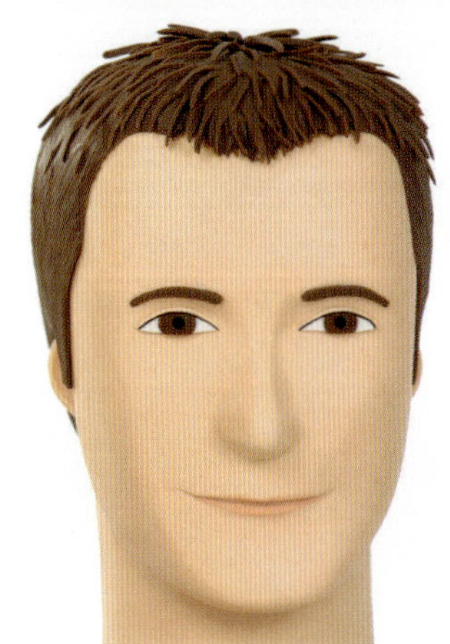

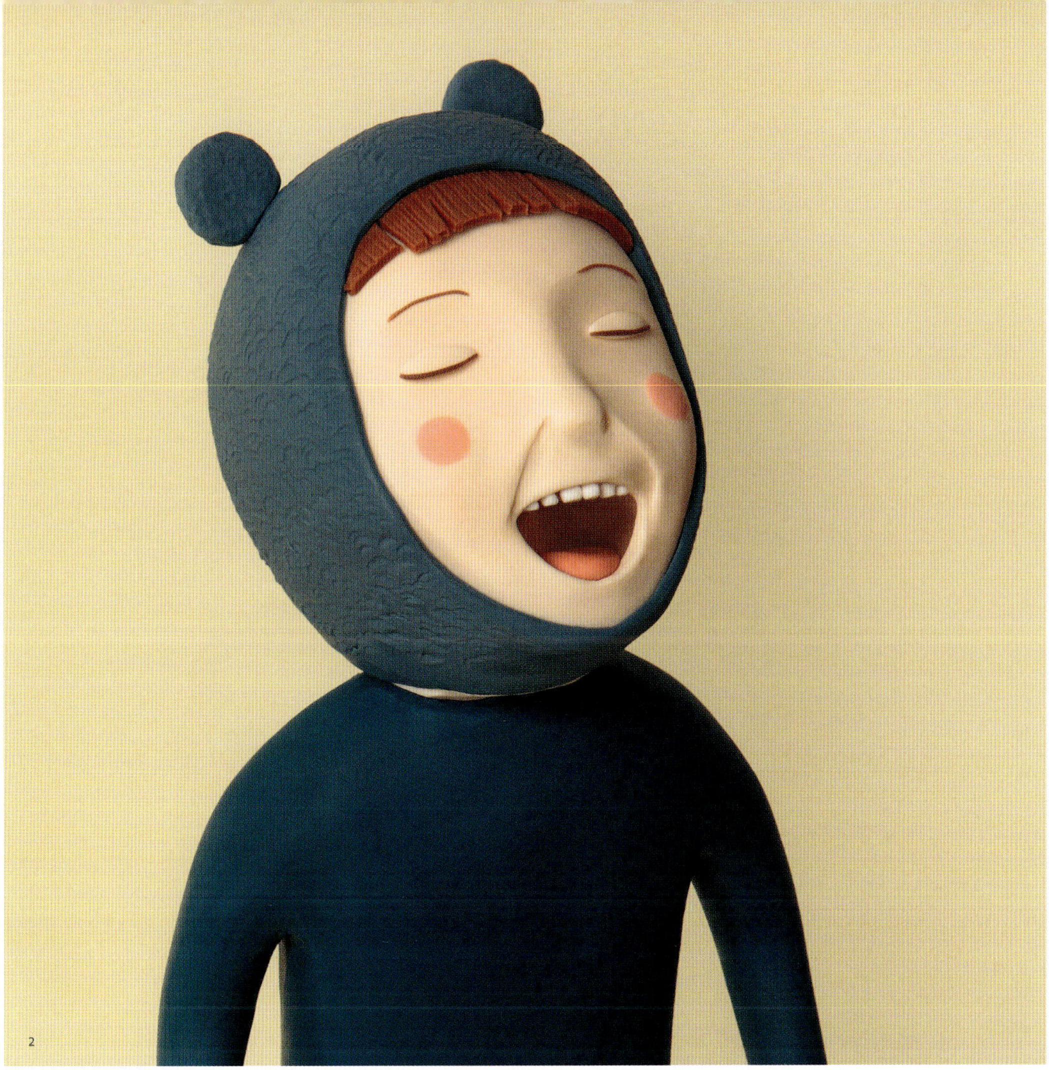

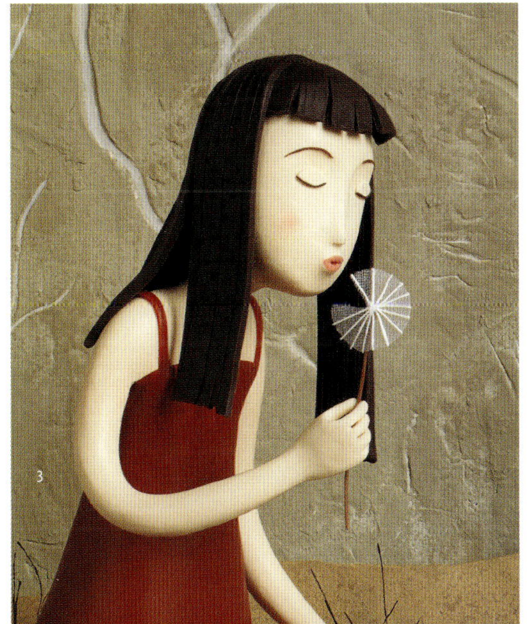

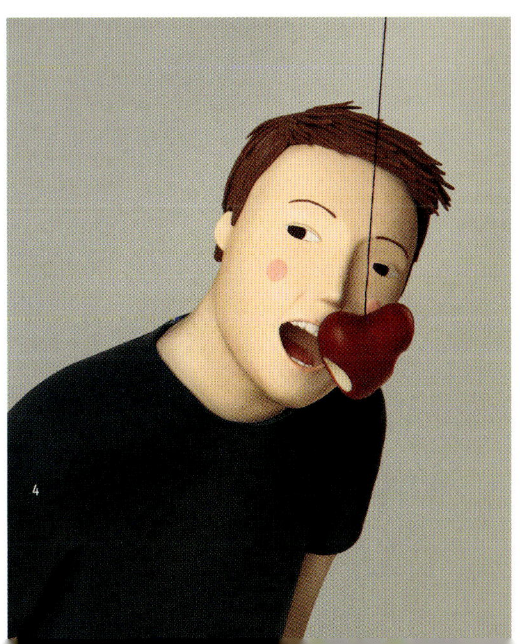

Irma Gruenholz

Spain

www.deplastilina.com

1. **Tv Hosts** (2010). Cuatro tv Channel. Assemblage

2. **Ito** (2009). Personal work. Assemblage

3. **Wishes** (2008). Personal work. Assemblage

4. **Play** (2009). Personal work. Assemblage

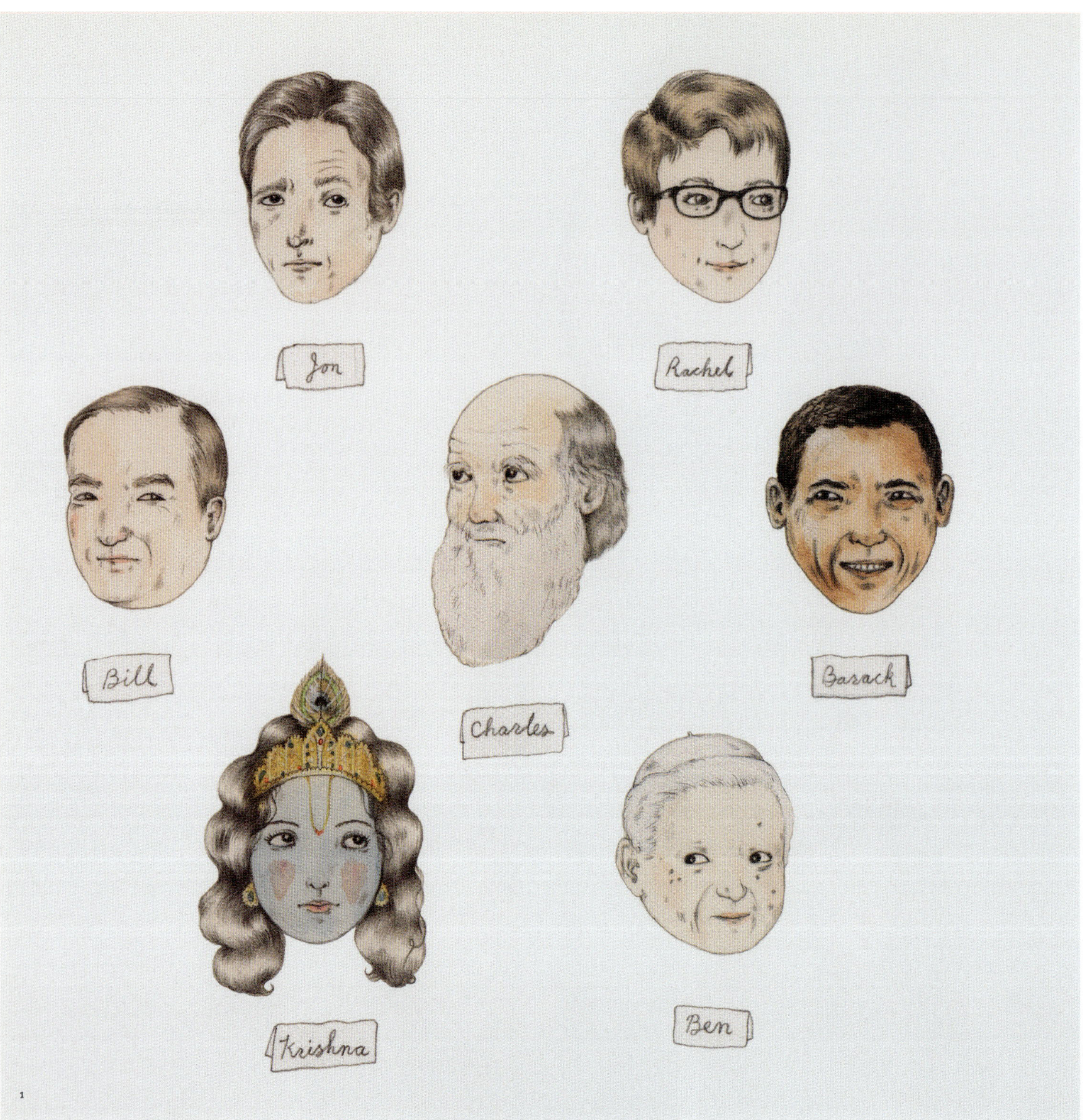
Jon
Rachel
Bill
Charles
Barack
Krishna
Ben

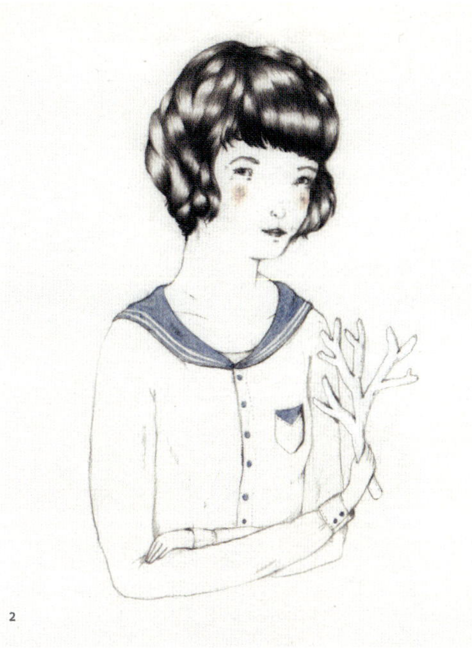

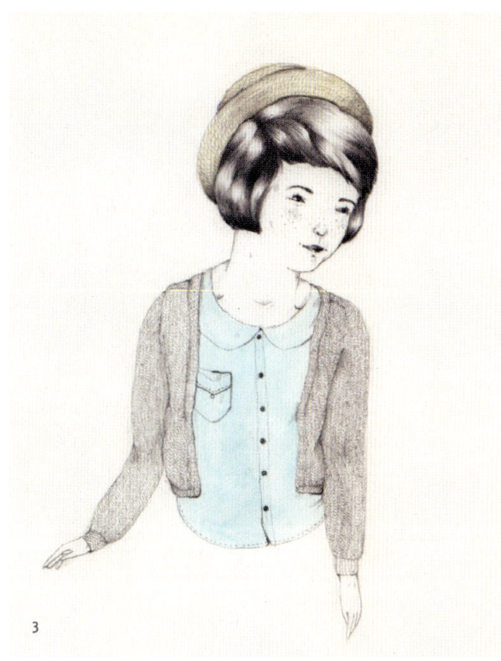

Sarah McNeil
New Zealand

www.400pencils.com

1. **Awkward Conversation** (2011). *Real Eats Magazine*. Pencil, gouache on paper

2. **Branch from the White Forest** (2009). Pencil, gouache on paper

3. **Straw Hat** (2008). Personal work. Pencil, ink on paper

4. **Tattoo Sweater and the Colours of Everything Inside** (2008). Personal work. Pencil, gouache on paper

5. **The Piper** (2009). *Once Upon* exhibition. Pencil, gouache on paper

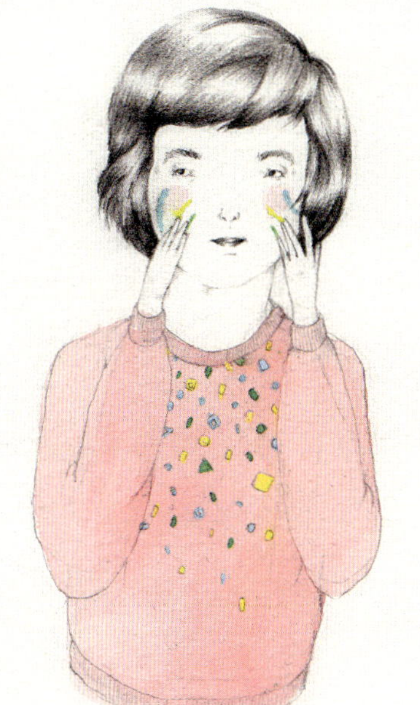

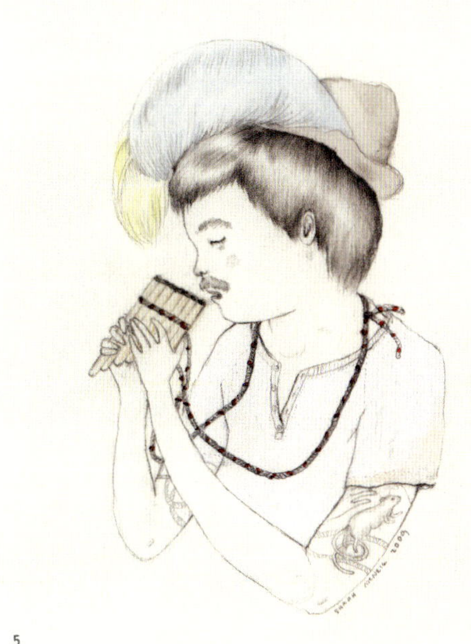

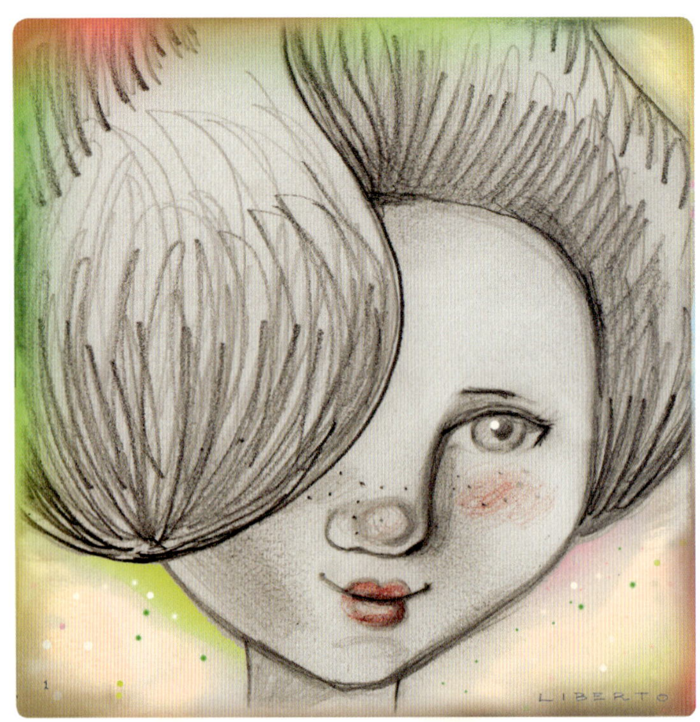

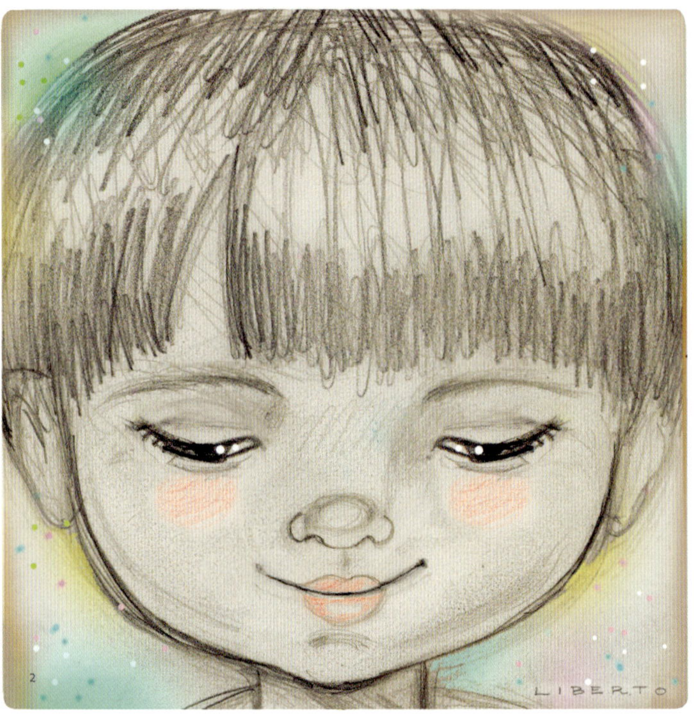

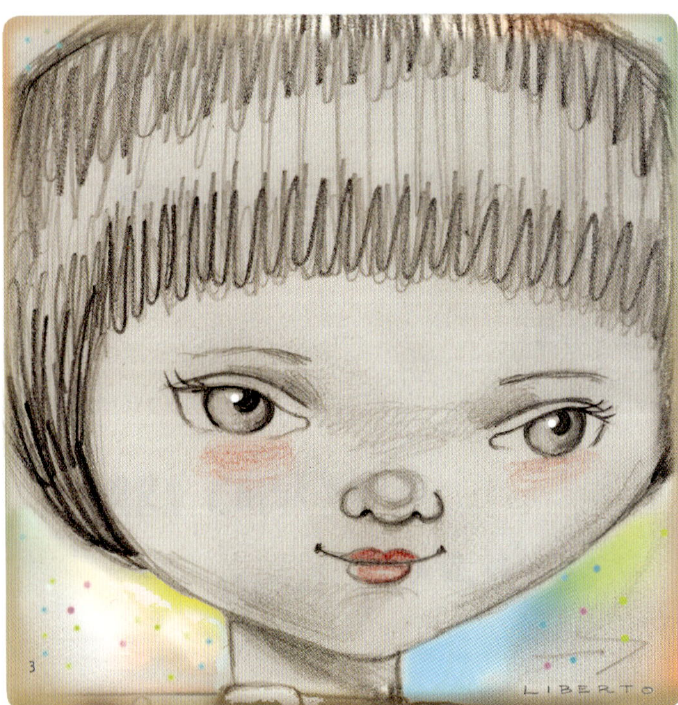

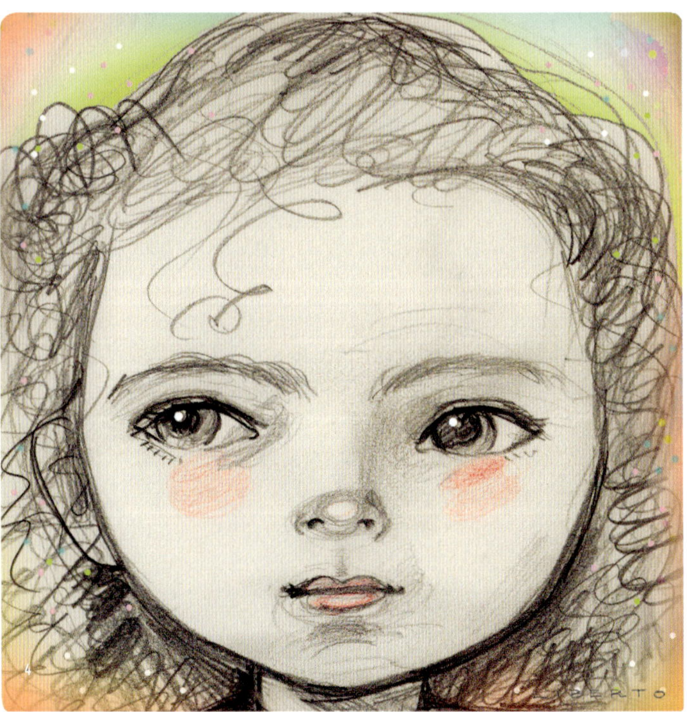

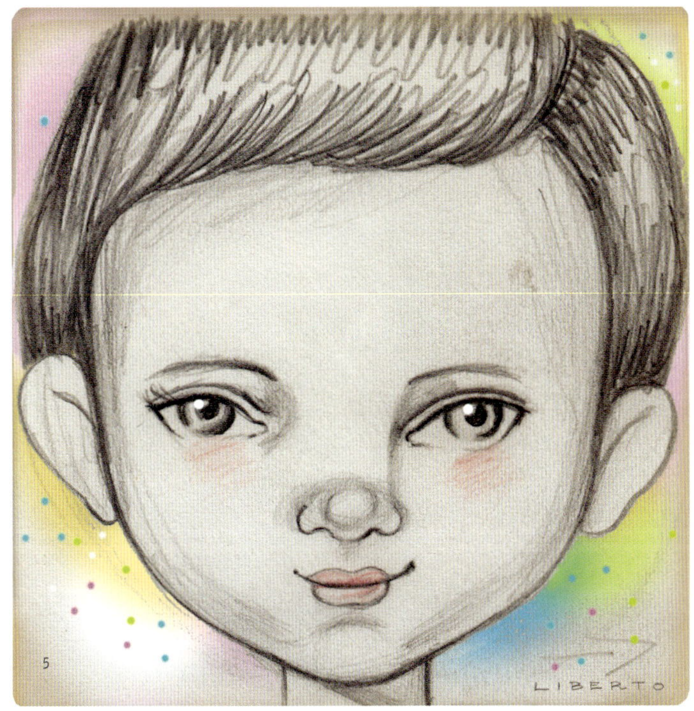

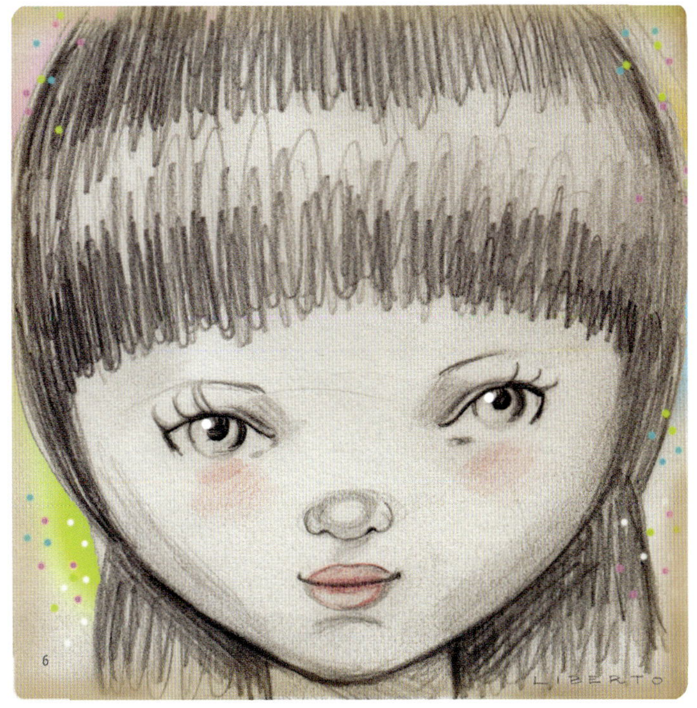

Gastón Liberto

Argentina

www.gastonliberto.com

1. **Retratos DIVINOS** (2009 - 2011). Personal work. Graphite, pastel, colored pencil

2. **Retratos DIVINOS** (2009 - 2011). Personal work. Graphite, pastel, colored pencil

3. **Retratos DIVINOS** (2009 - 2011). Personal work. Graphite, pastel, colored pencil

4. **Retratos DIVINOS** (2009 - 2011). Personal work. Graphite, pastel, colored pencil

5. **Retratos DIVINOS** (2009 - 2011). Personal work. Graphite, pastel, colored pencil

6. **Retratos DIVINOS** (2009 - 2011). Personal work. Graphite, pastel, colored pencil

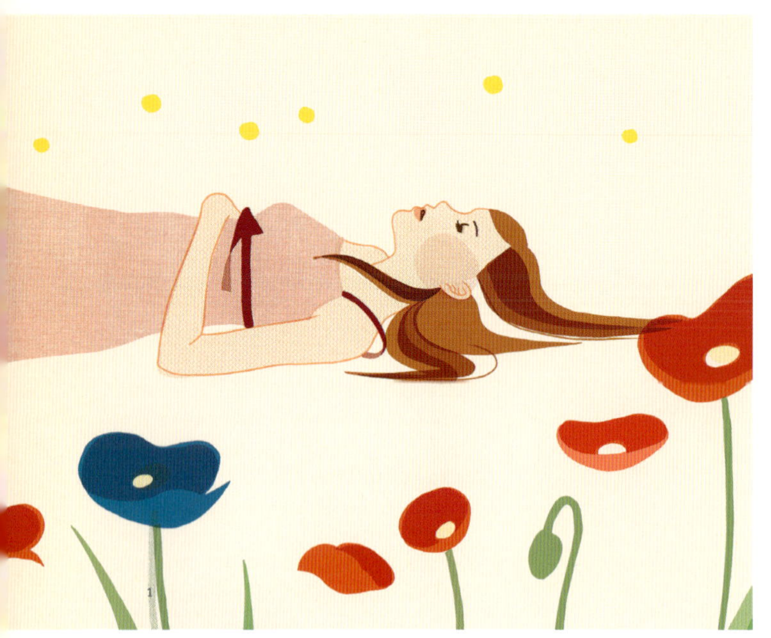

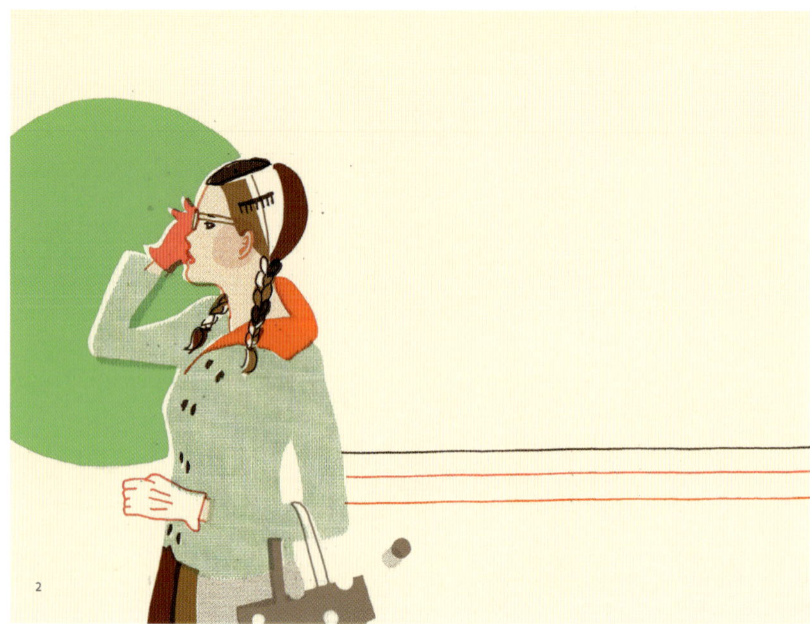

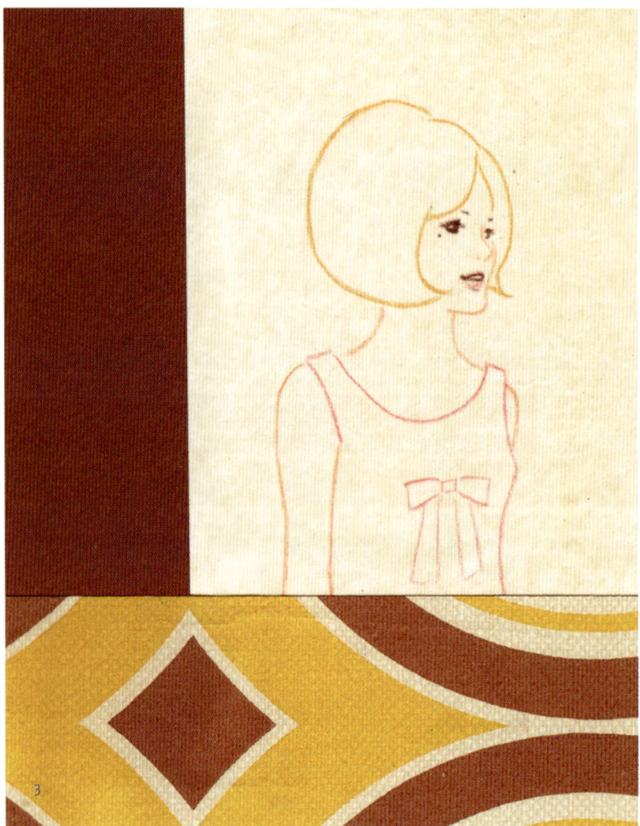

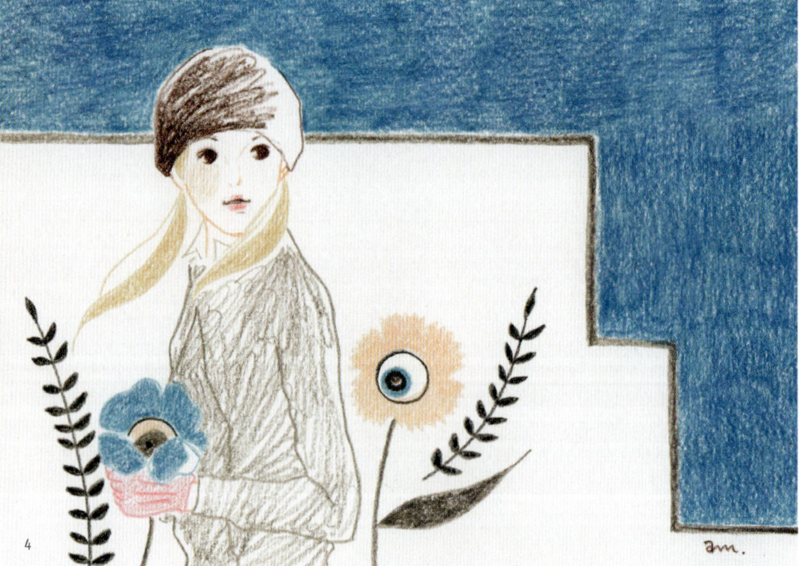

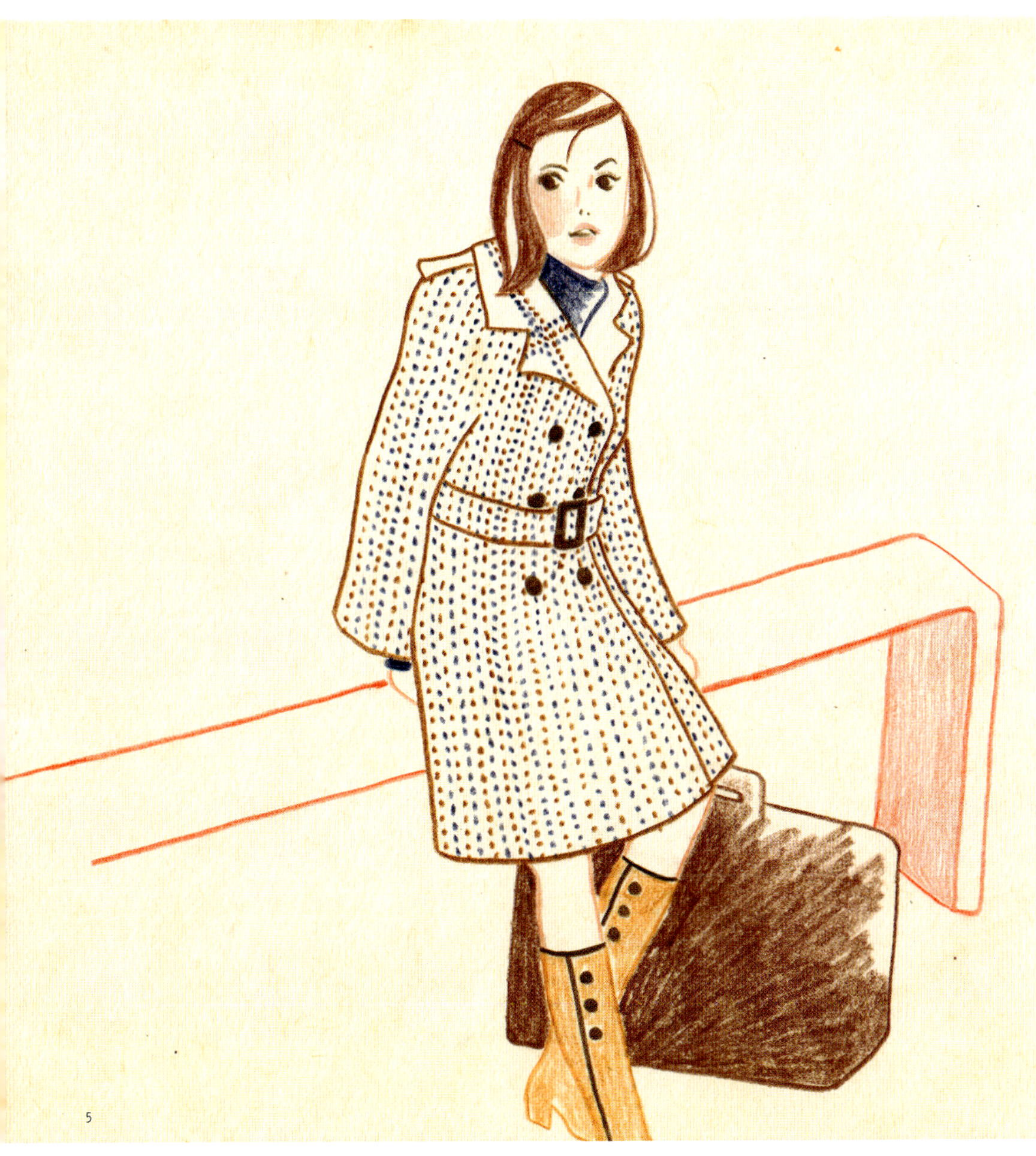

Asako Masunouchi

Japan

www.asako-masunouchi.com

1. **Avril** (2007). Mr.Brown & Vue sur la Ville. Felt pen, Photoshop

2. **It Will Be Found Later** (2007). Personal work. Felt pen, Photoshop

3. **Poupée de Son** (2007). Personal work. Color pencil, collage

4. **Belle Époque** (2008). Personal work. Color pencil

5. **I'll Write to You Soon** (2007). Velvet Morning. Color pencil

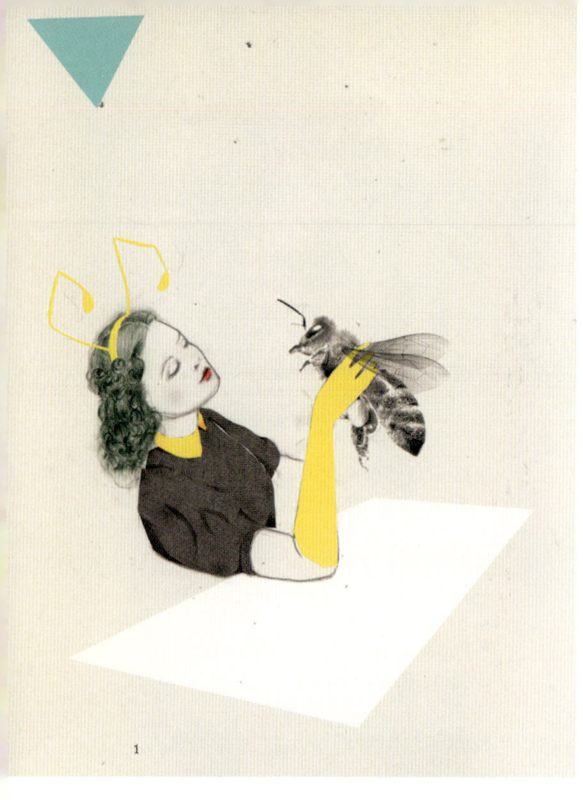

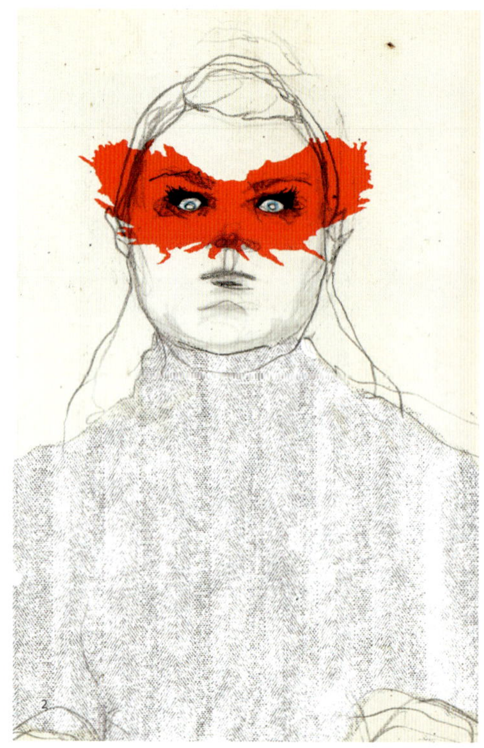

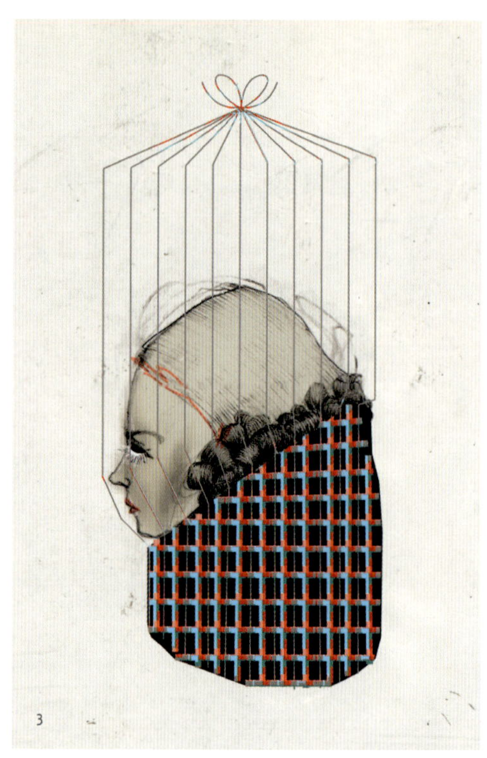

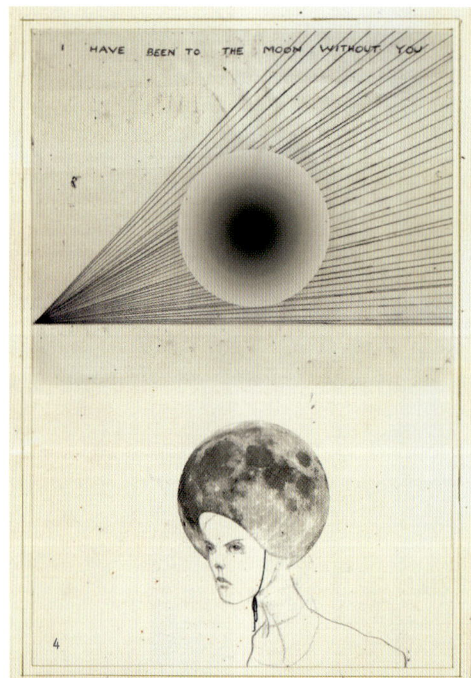
I HAVE BEEN TO THE MOON / WITHOUT YOU

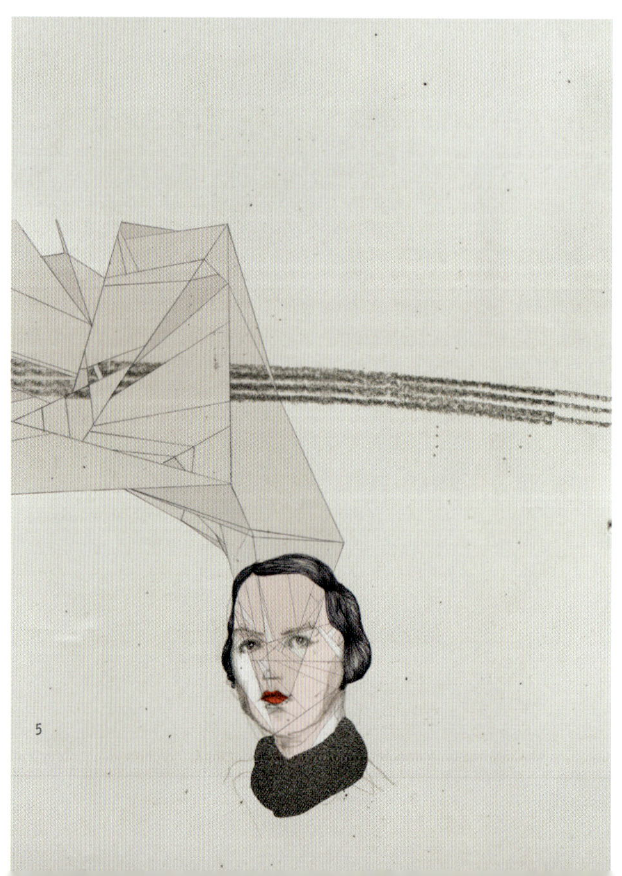

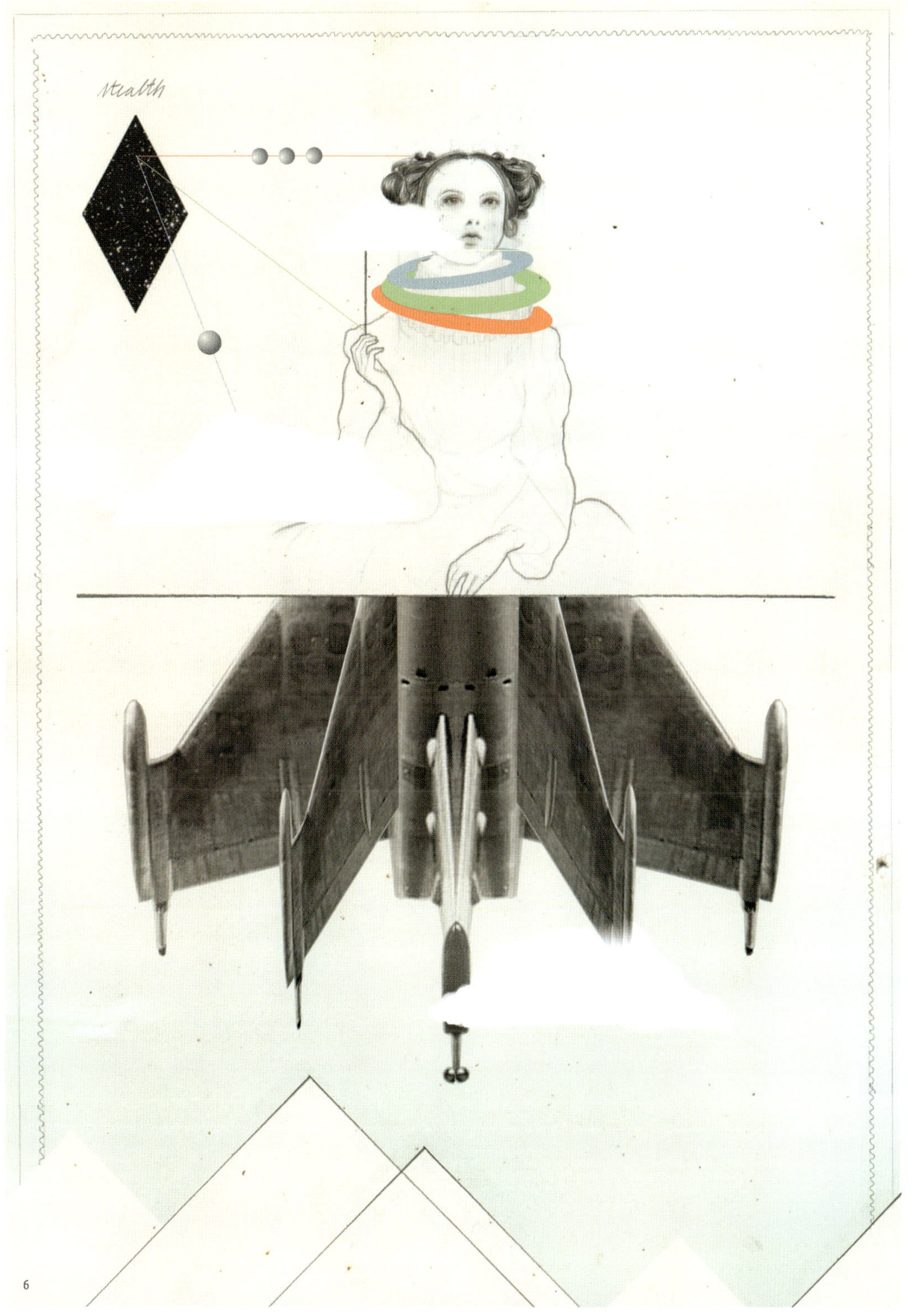

Tilman Faelker

Germany

www.tilmanfaelker.com

1. **Bee** (2010). Personal work. Hand drawing, digital collage

2. **Mask Girl** (2009). Personal work. Hand drawing, digital collage

3. **Pattern Girl** (2010). Bayrischer Rundfunk. Hand drawing, digital collage

4. **I've Been to the Moon Without You** (2011). Personal work. Hand drawing, digital collage

5. **Me and my Polygon** (2010). Personal work. Hand drawing, digital collage

6. **Stealth Girl** (2011). Personal work. Hand drawing, digital collage

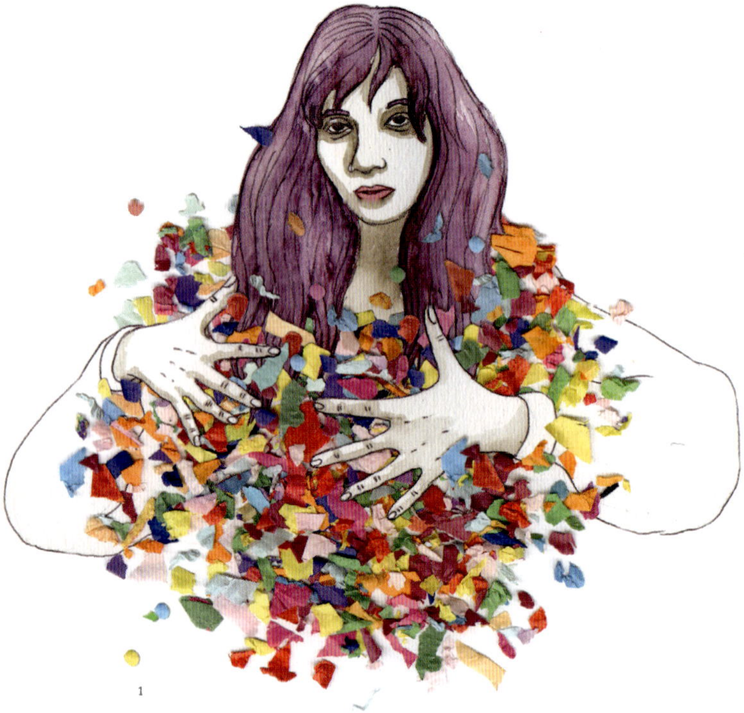

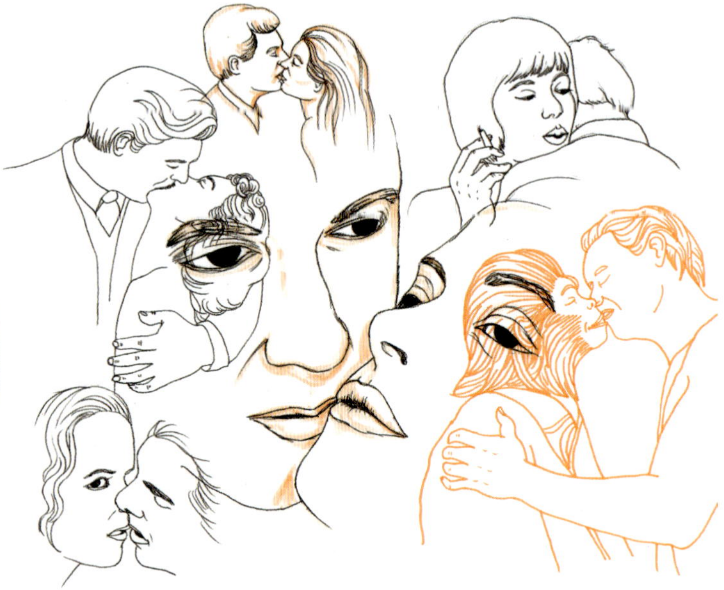

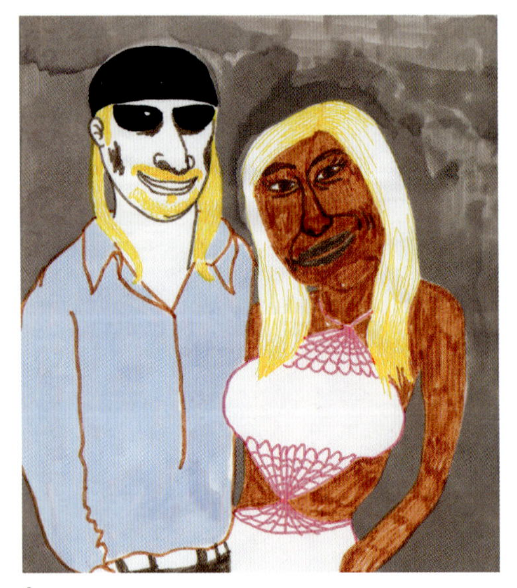

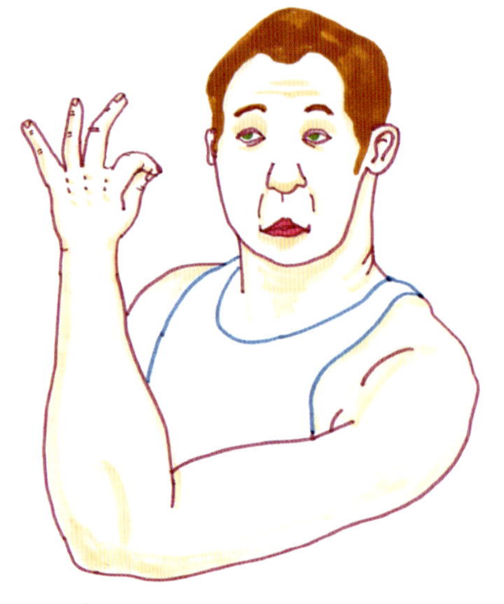

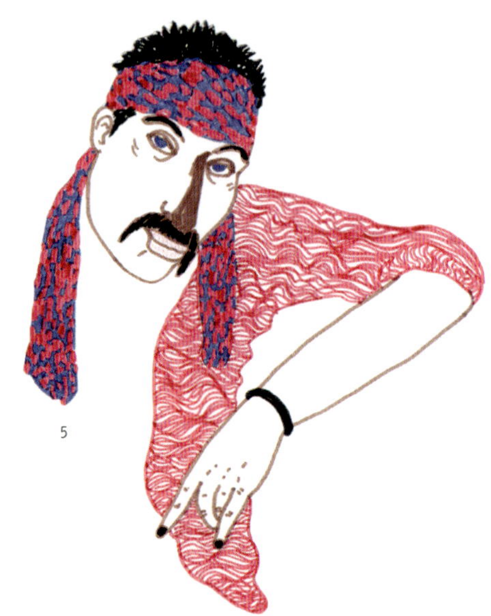

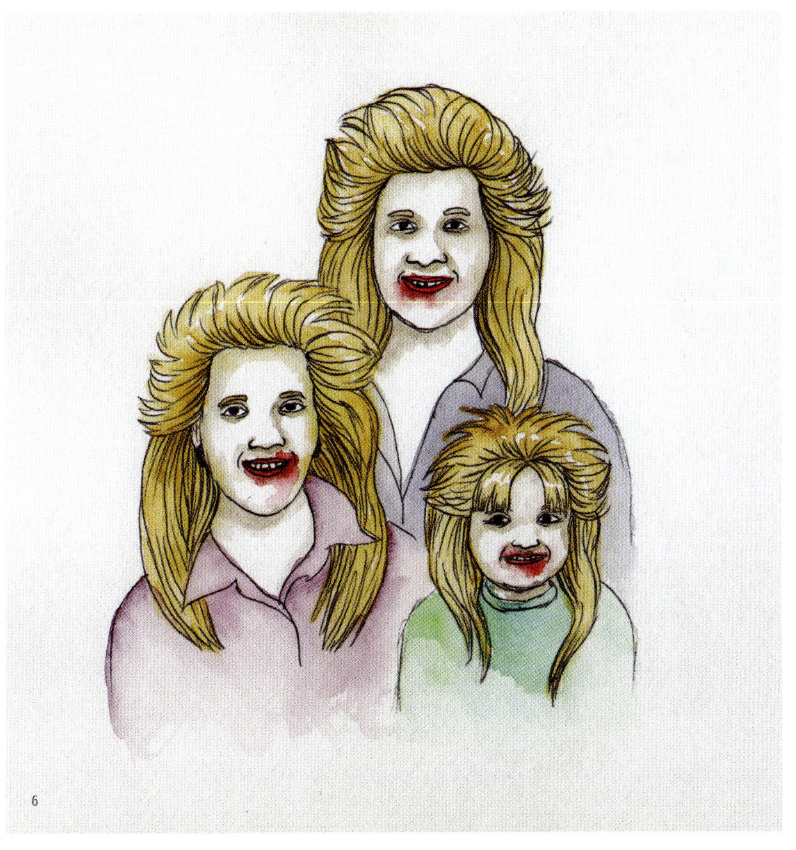

6

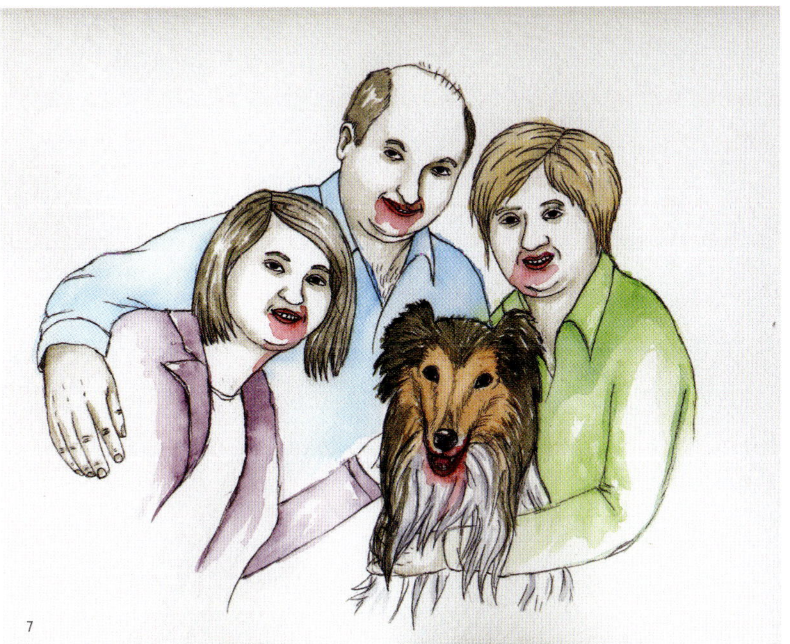

7

Sandra Haselsteiner

Germany

www.sandra-haselsteiner.de

1. **Confetti Drawing** (2010). Personal Work. Watercolor, confetti, digital

2. **Kisses** (2010). Schnitt. Marker, felt pen, ink pen, digital

3. **Pam + Kid** (2006). Personal Work. Marker, felt pen

4. **Shut Your Mouth** (2010). the drawbridge. Marker, felt pen

5. **Darkness** (2006). Personal Work. Felt pen

6. *You Are So Beautiful – We Are Family* (2009). Personal Work. Watercolor

7. *You Are So Beautiful – Hair* (2009). Personal Work. Watercolor

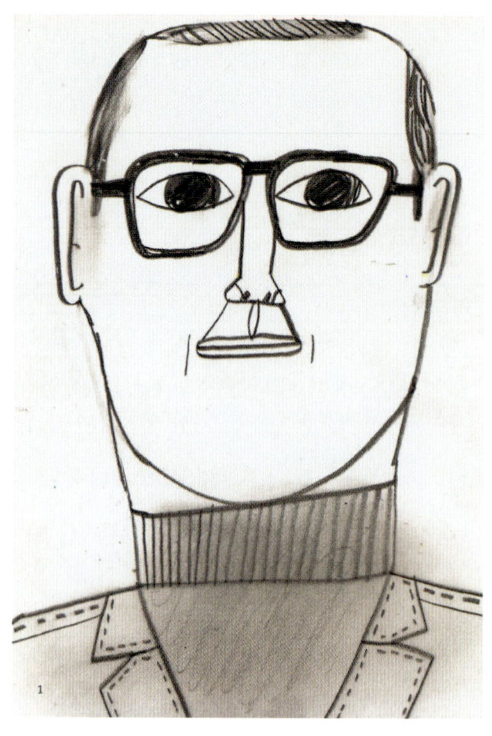

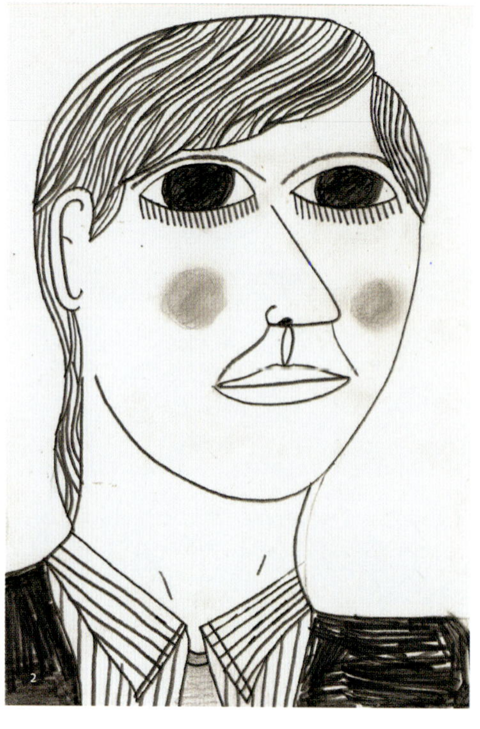

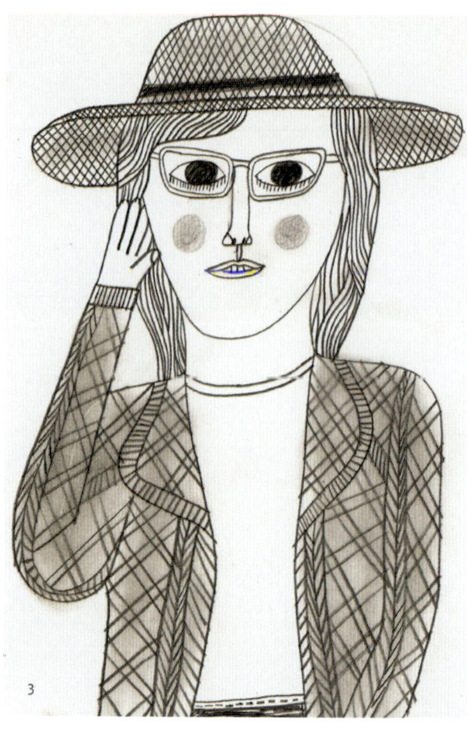

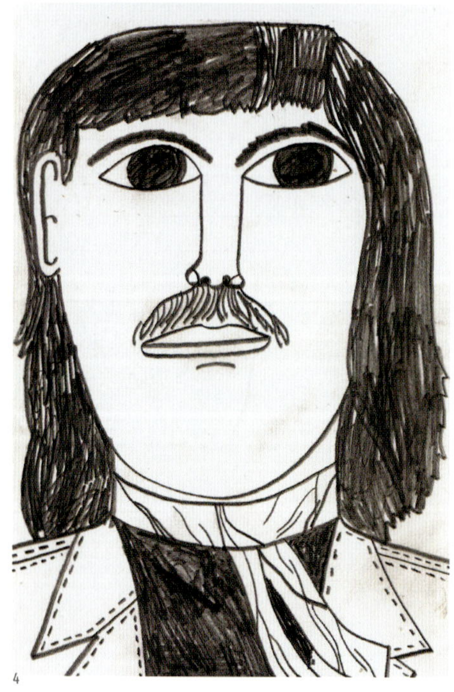

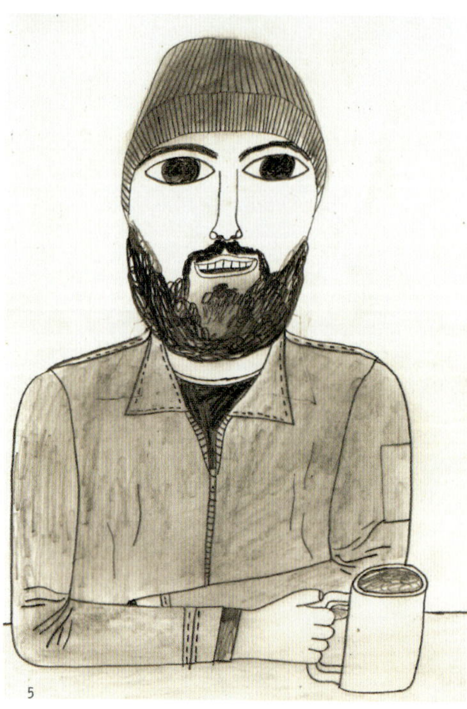

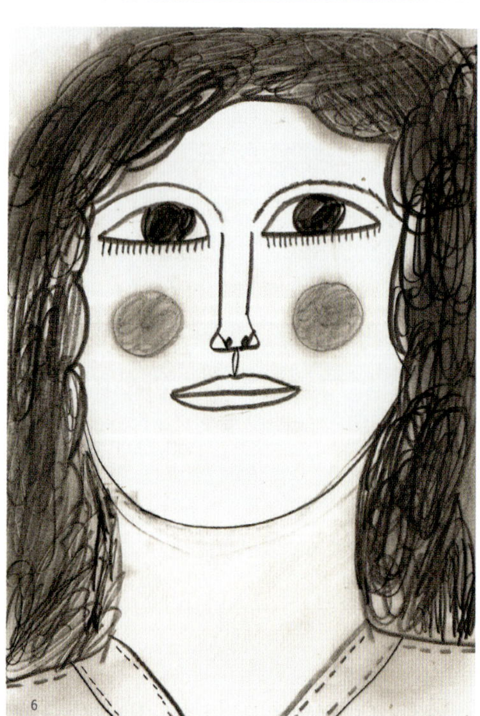

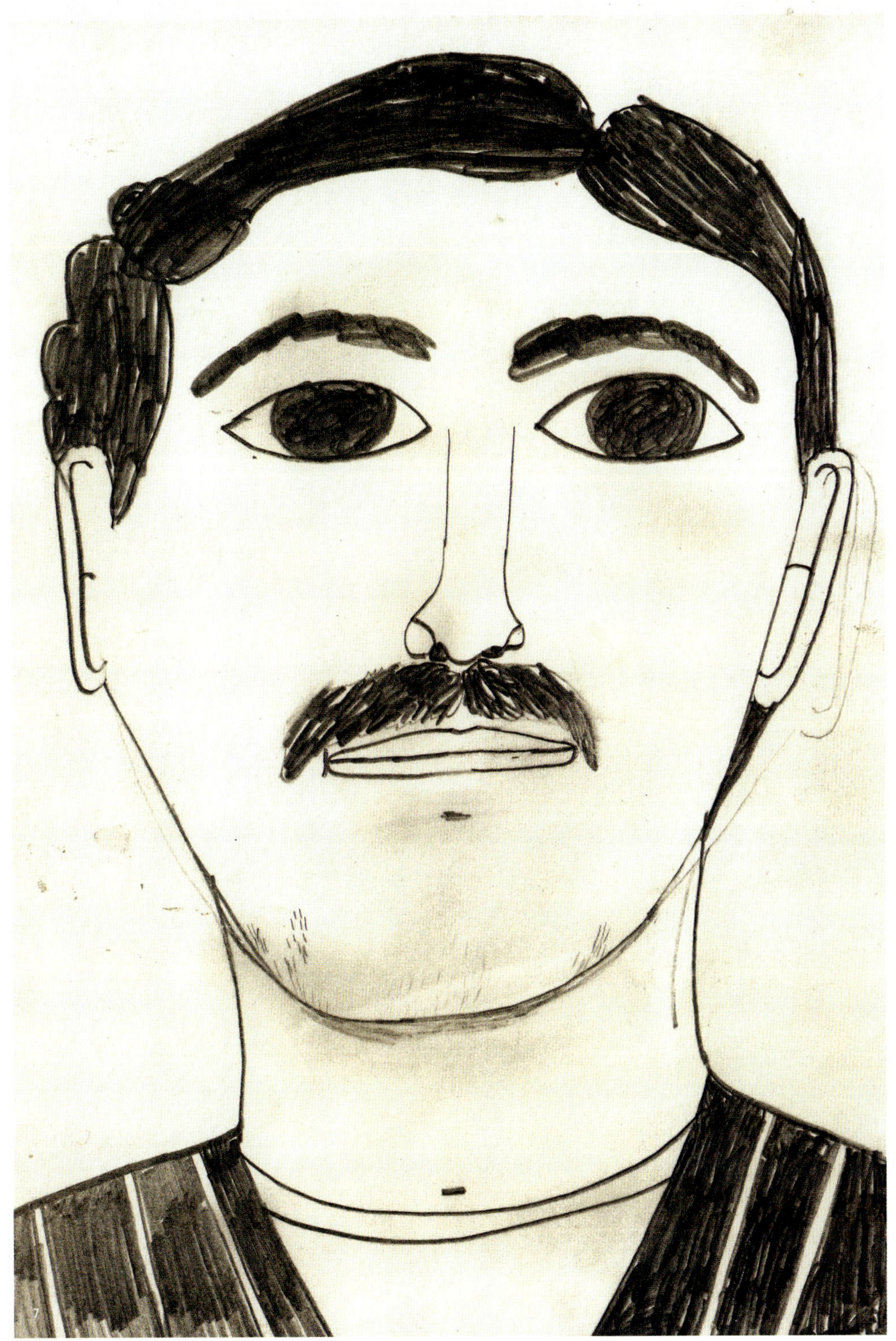

Marcus Oakley

UK

www.marcusoakley.com

1. **Andy** (2008-2010). Nieves. Pencil

2. **Clare** (2008-2010). Nieves. Pencil

3. **Hayley** (2008-2010). Nieves. Pencil

4. **Adam** (2008-2010). Nieves. Pencil

5. **French** (2008-2010). Nieves. Pencil

6. **Xuan** (2008-2010). Nieves. Pencil

7. **Joseph** (2008-2010). Nieves. Pencil

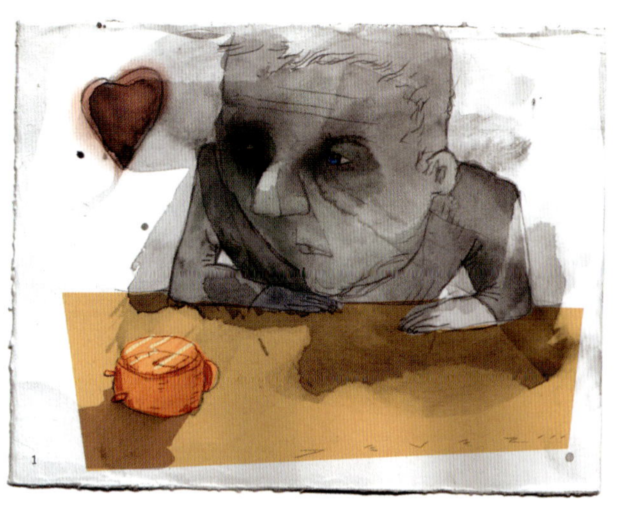

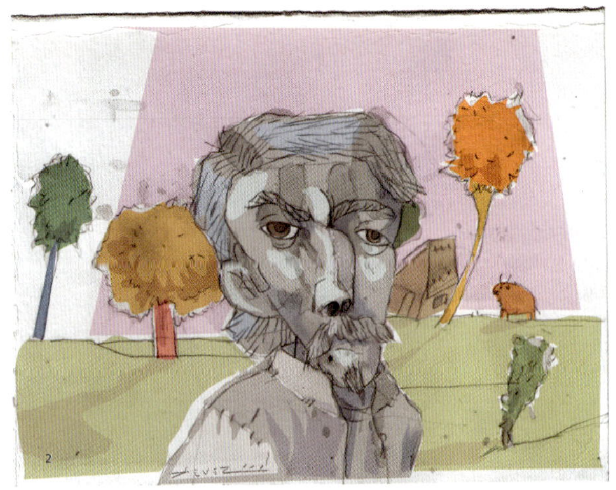

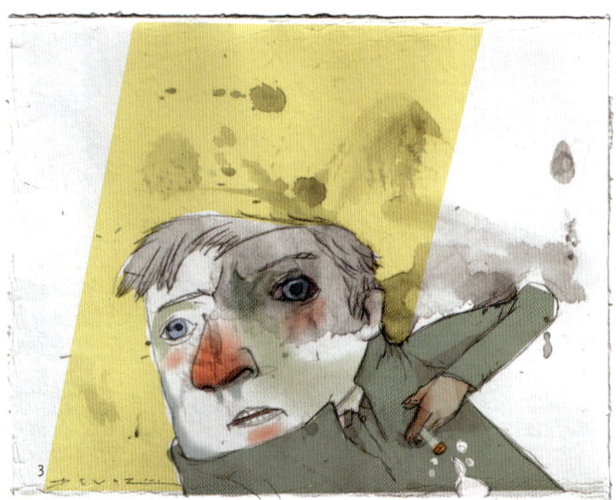

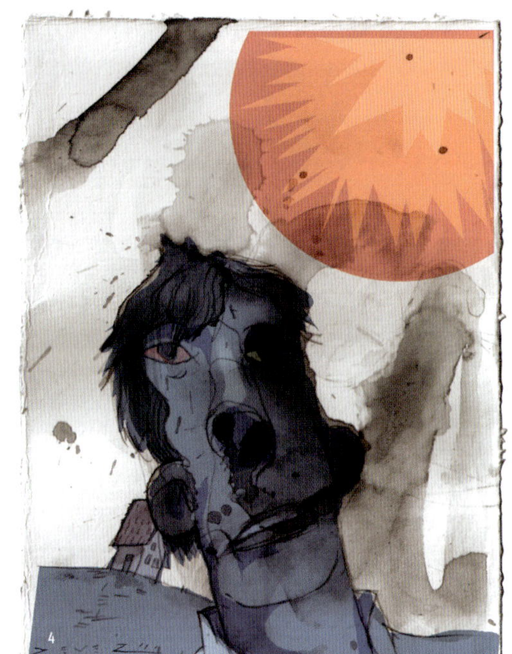

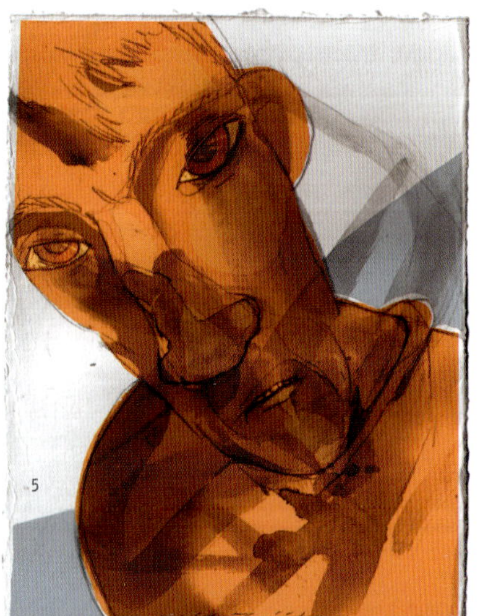

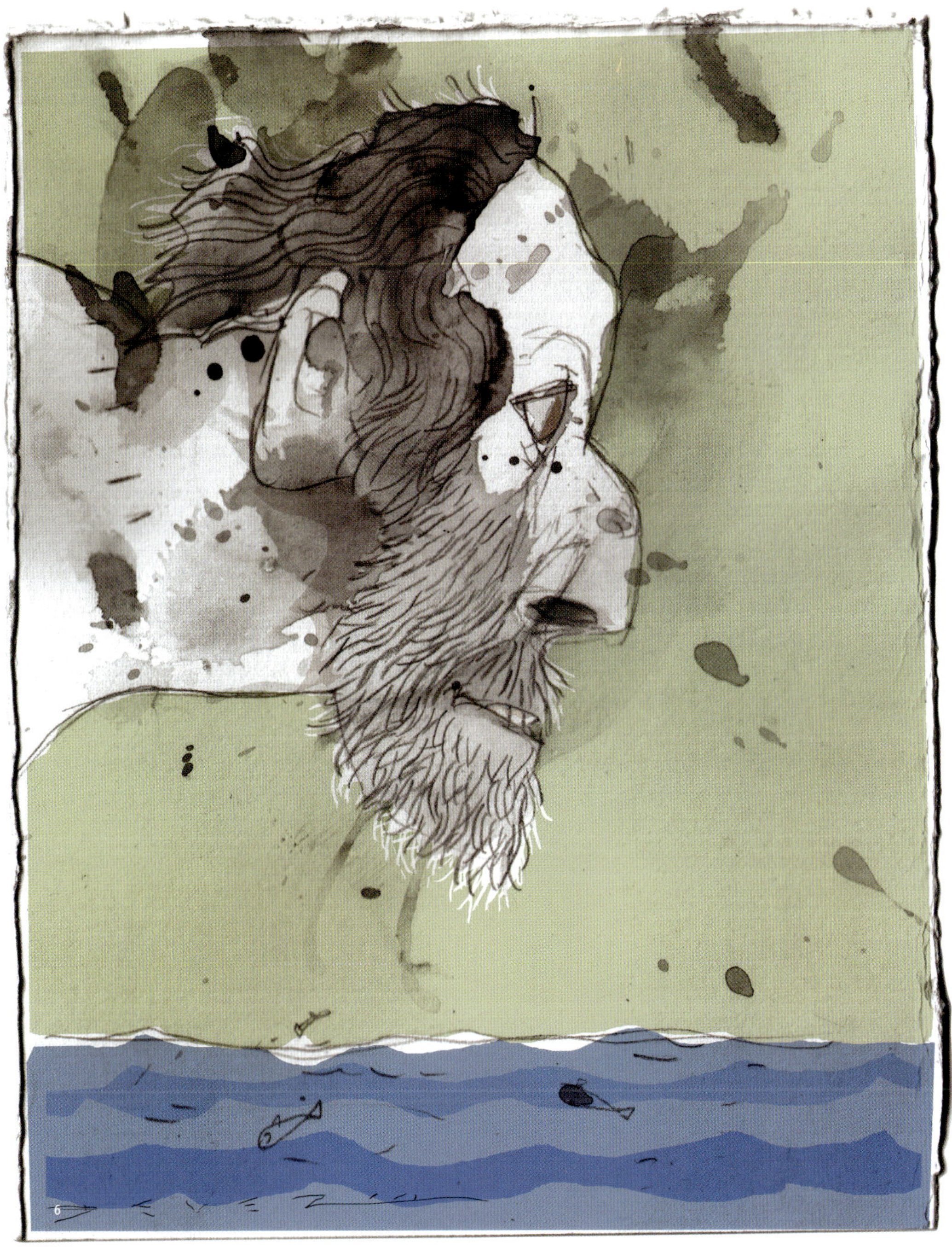

Gustavo Deveze
aka Jeneverito

Argentina

www.deveze.com.ar

1. **Heart Time** (2011). Personal work. Ink, pencil on paper, digital coloring

2. **Untitled** (2011). Personal work. Ink, pencil on paper, digital coloring

3. **Untitled** (2011). Personal work. Ink, pencil on paper, digital coloring

4. **Something Like Me** (2011). Personal work. Ink, pencil on paper, digital coloring

5. **Too Close** (2011). Personal work. Ink, pencil on paper, digital coloring

6. **Untitled** (2011). Personal work. Ink, pencil on paper, digital coloring

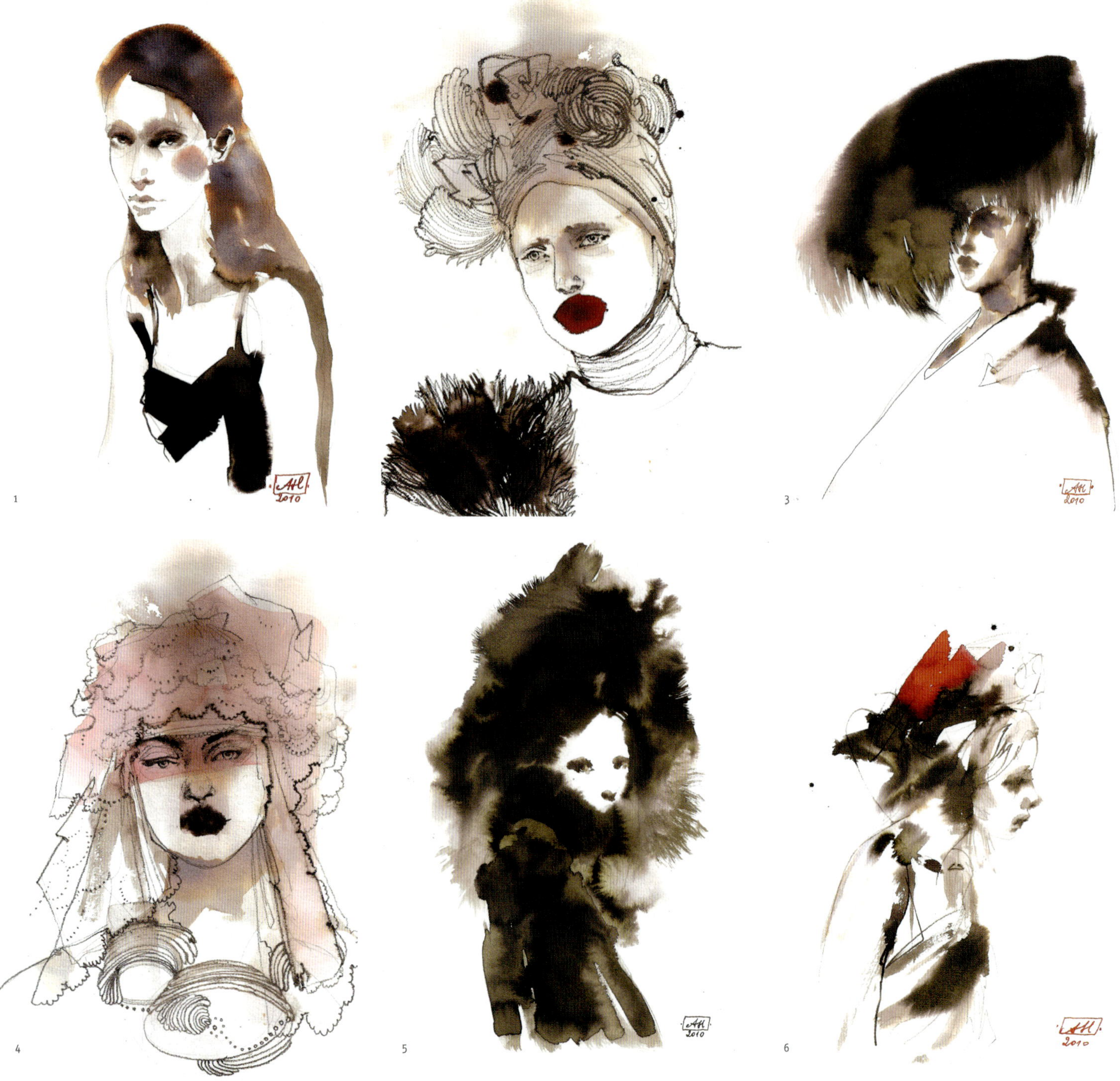

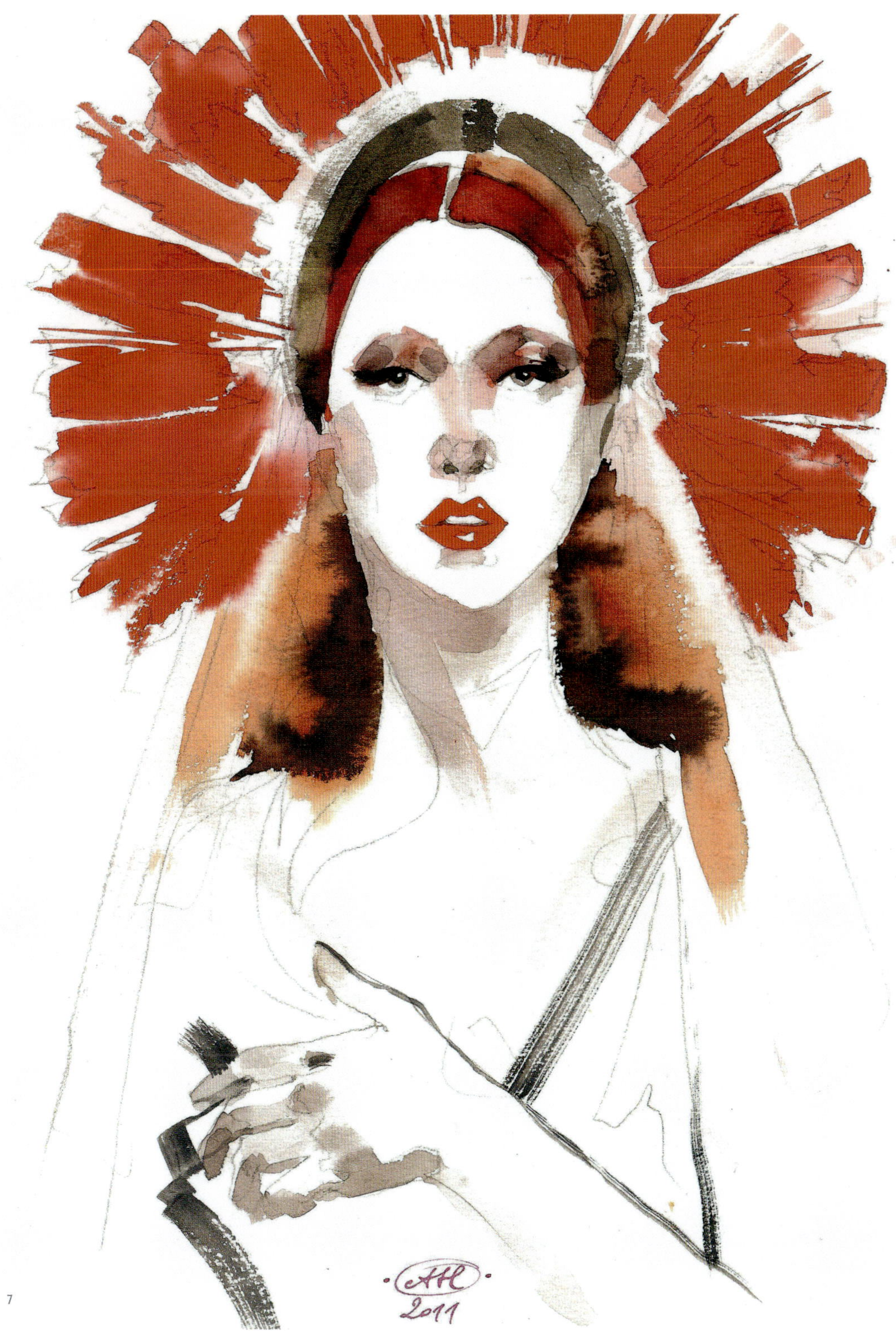

7

Anna Halarewicz

Poland

www.annahalarewicz.eu

1. **Pure Red & Black** (2011). Personal work. Watercolor, crayon, ink

2. **A Tribute to Alexander McQueen** (2011). Personal work. Watercolor, crayon, ink

3. **Pure Red & Black** (2011). Personal work. Watercolor, crayon, ink

4. **A Tribute to Alexander McQueen** (2011). Personal work. Watercolor, crayon, ink

5. **Pure Red & Black** (2011). Personal work. Watercolor, crayon, ink

6. **Pure Red & Black** (2011). Personal work. Watercolor, crayon, ink

7. **Pure Red & Black** (2011). Personal work. Watercolor, crayon, ink

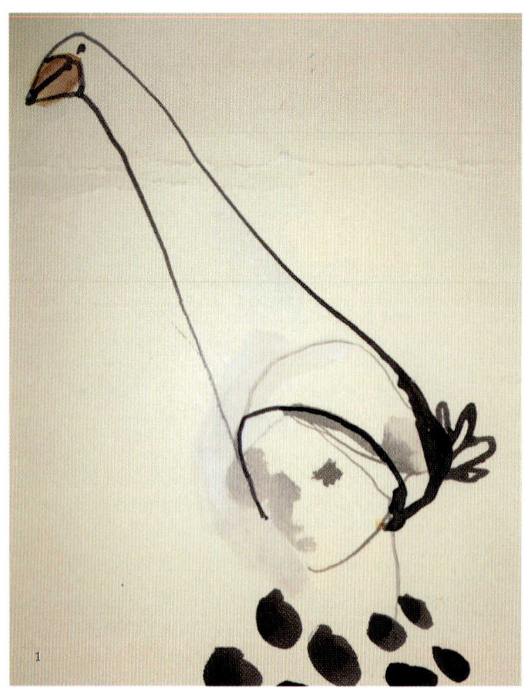

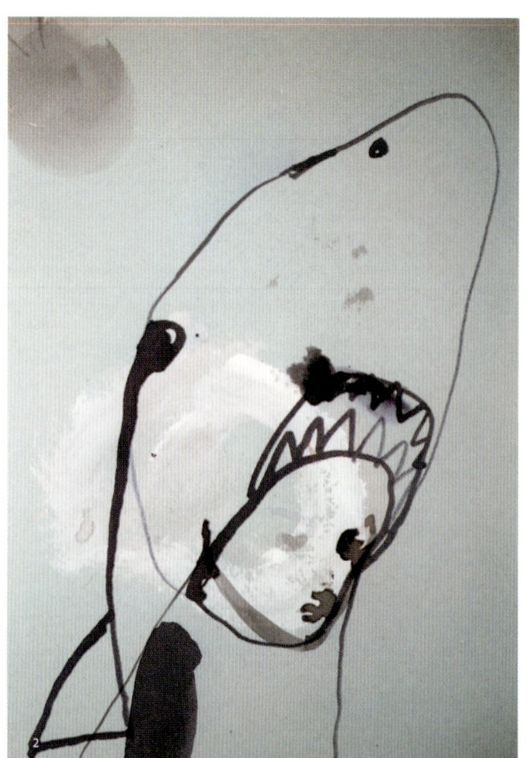

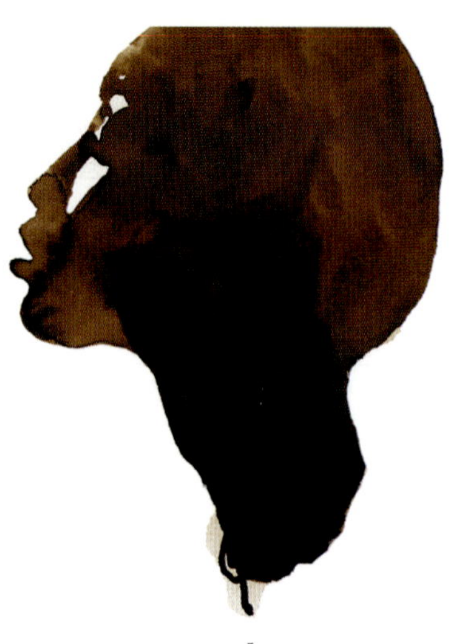

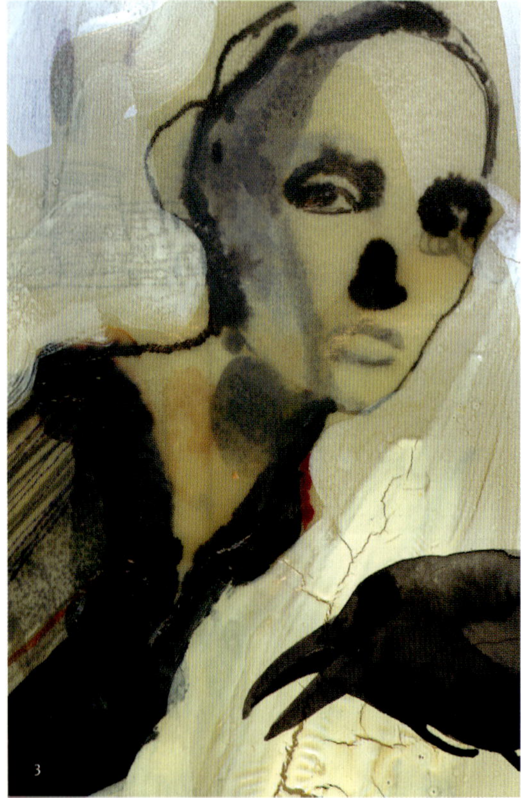

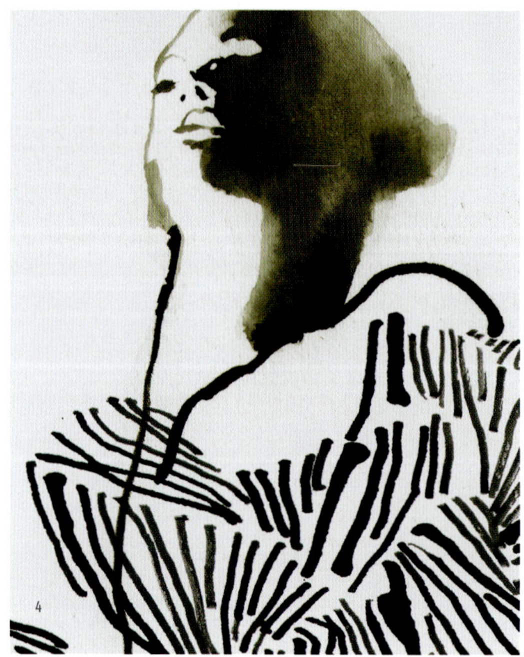

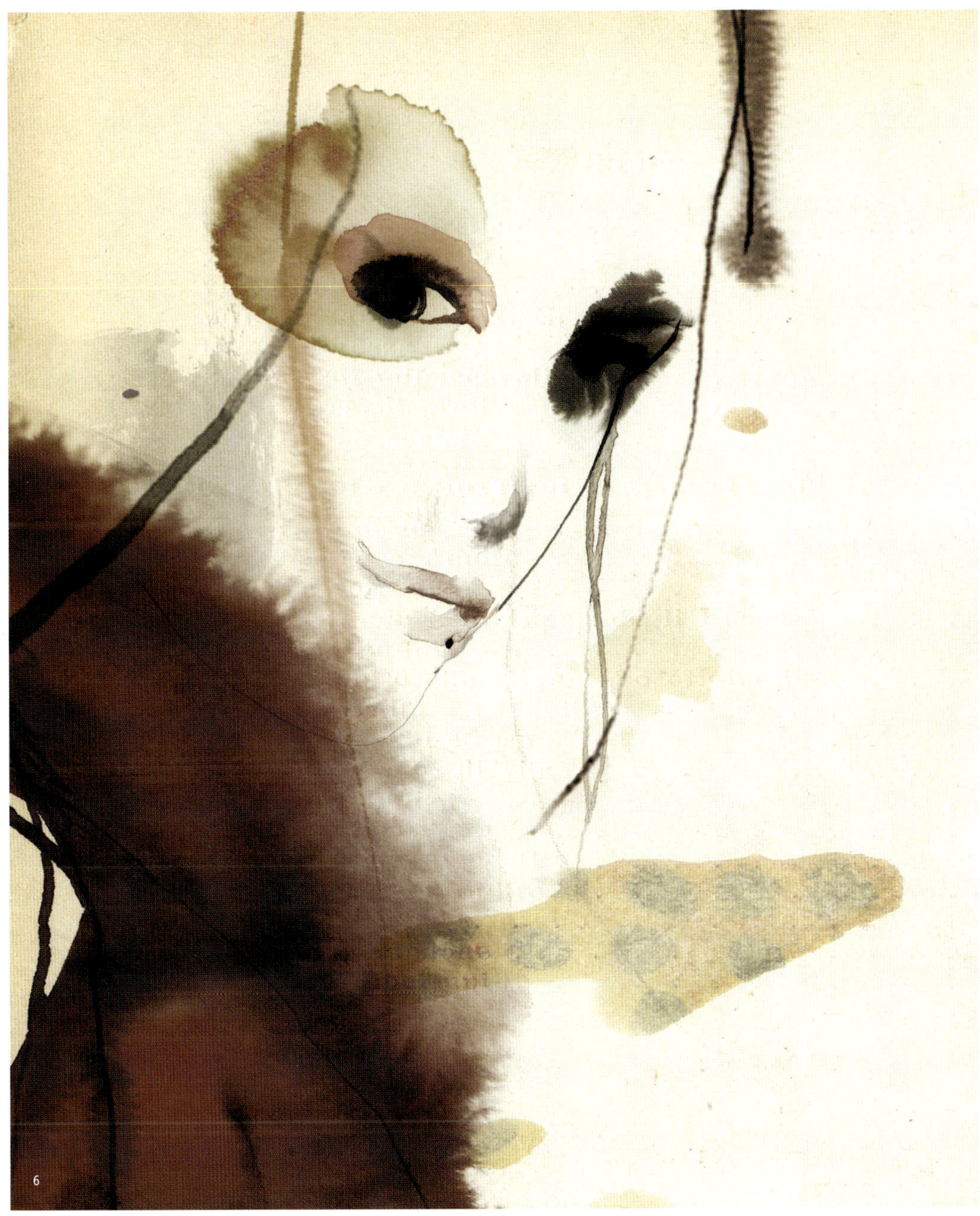

Daniel Egnéus
Sweden

www.danielegneus.com

1. **Hengirl** (2010). Personal work. Ink, watercolor, pencil

2. **Sharkgirl** (2010). Personal work. Ink, pencil

3. **Untitled (2011).** Il sole 2. Watercolor

4. **Woman_Raven** (2011). Personal work. Watercolor, varnish, pencil, ink

5. **Woman** (2011). Personal work. Watercolor

6. **Untitled** (2011). Personal work. Ink, watercolor, pencil

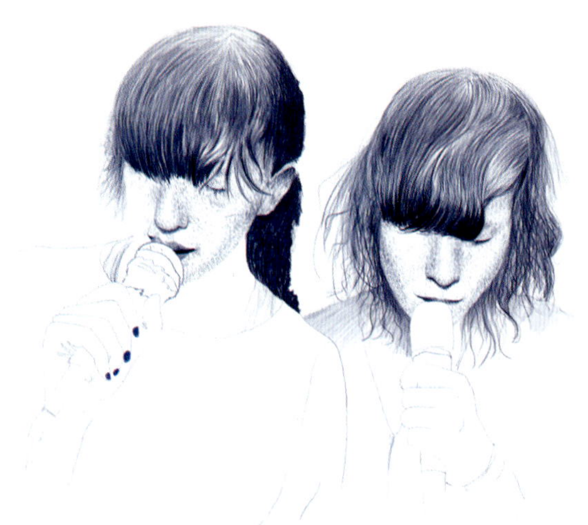

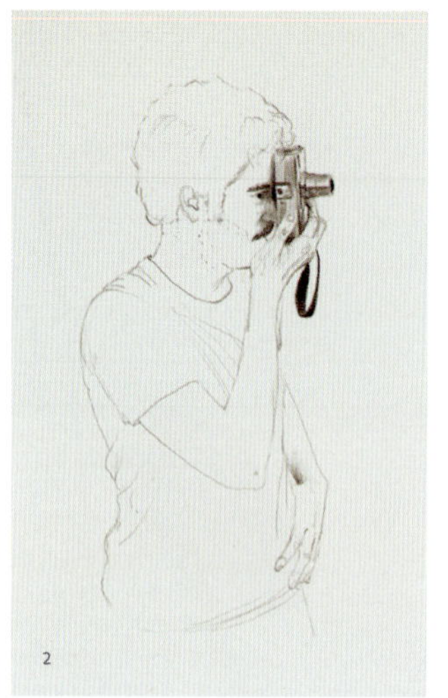

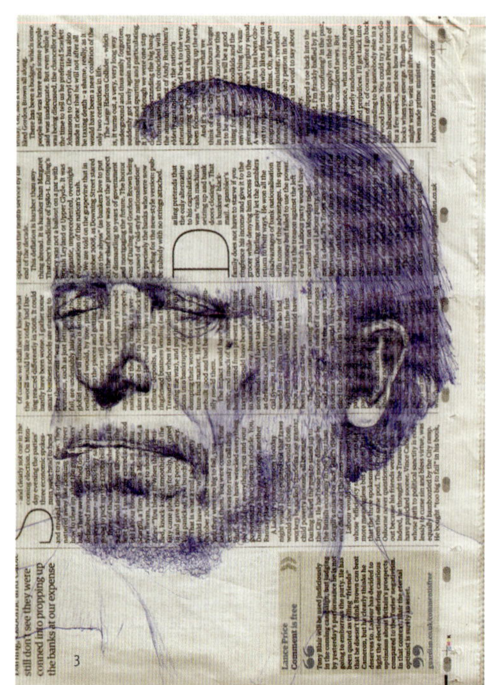

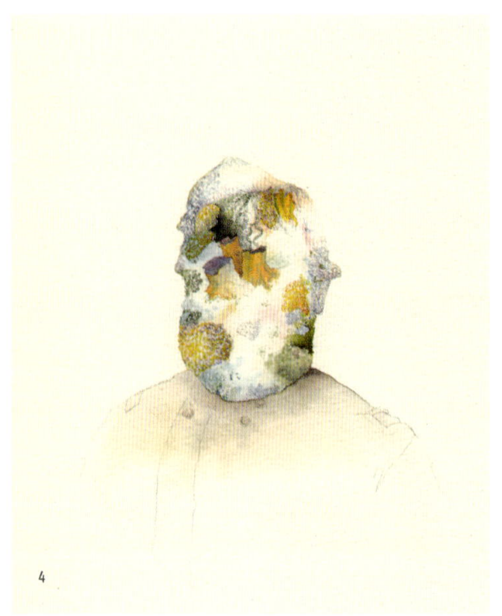

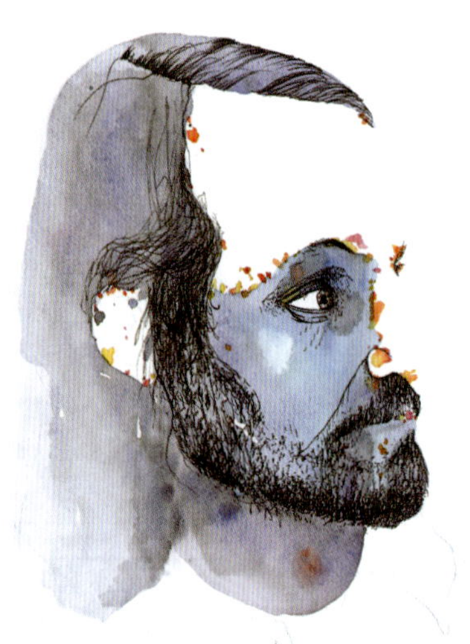

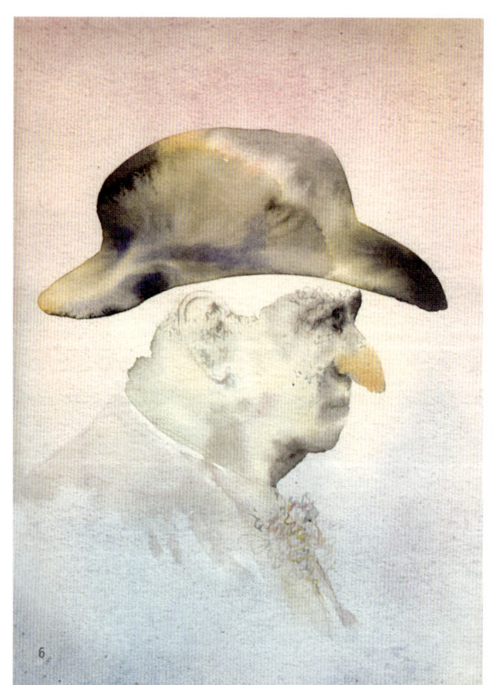

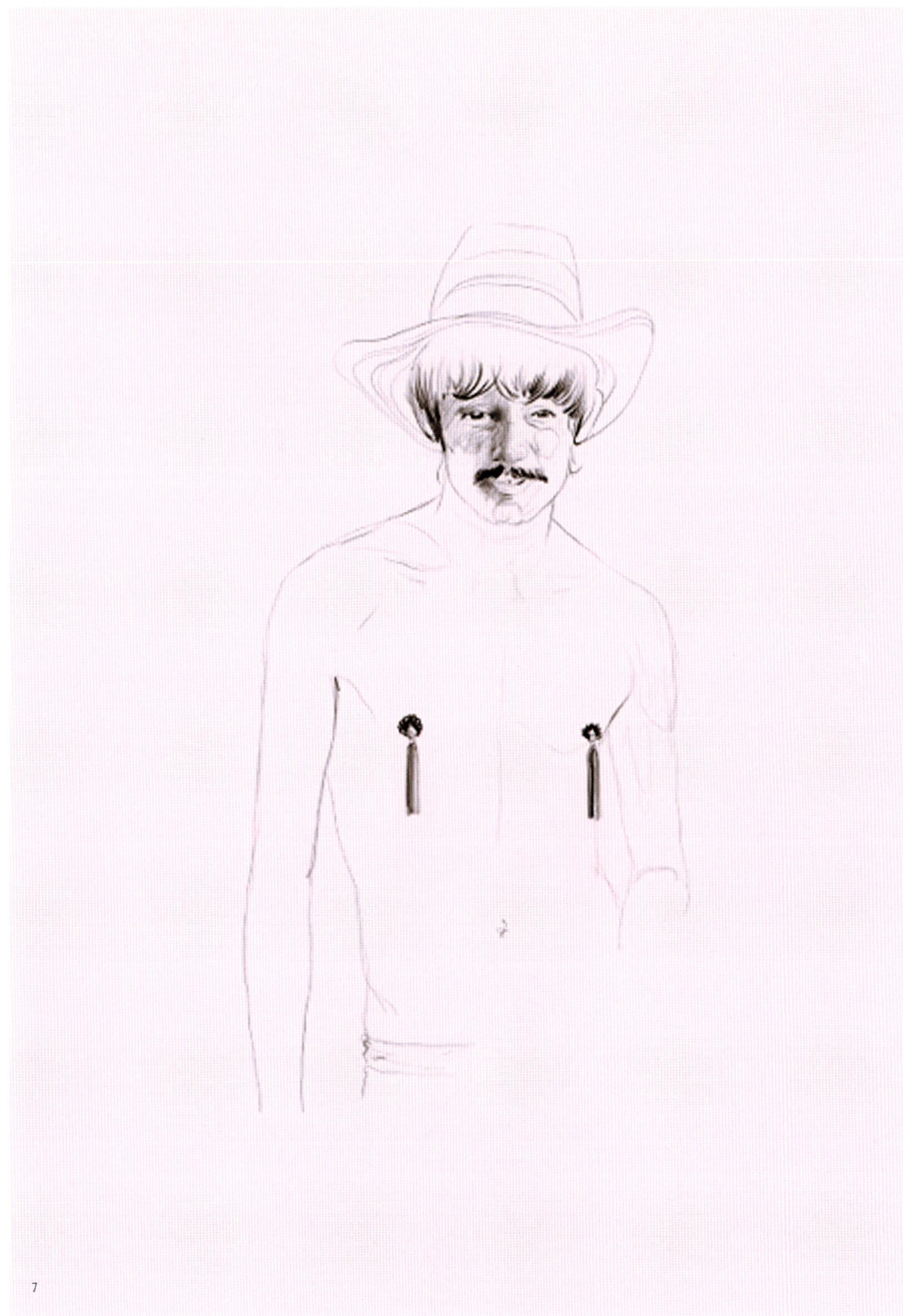

Elliot Beaumont

Australia

www.elliotbeaumont.tumblr.com

1. **Telepathe** (2010) *INTRO* magazine. Pen, digital

2. **Adrià Cañameras** (2010). Personal work. Pen, digital

3. **Mr Charles Bukowski** (2010). Personal work. Pen

4. **Mutualism** (2011). Personal work. Watercolor

5. **Vincent** (2009). Personal work. Watercolor

6. **Captain Walker** (2011). Personal work. Watercolor, pencil

7. **Coke Bartrina** (2010). Personal work. Pen, digital

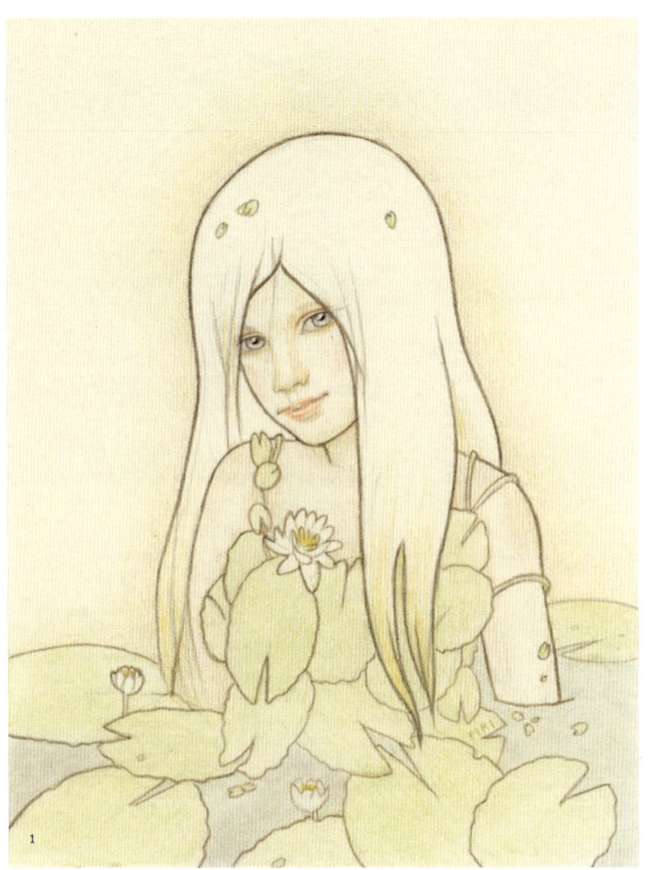

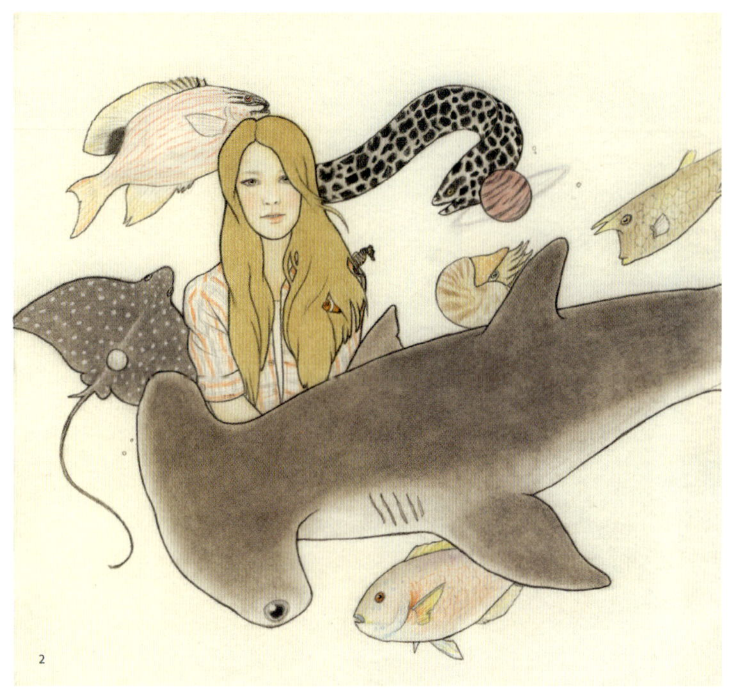

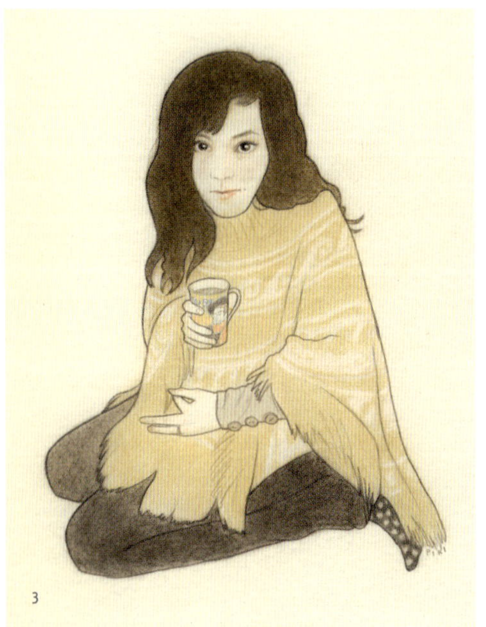

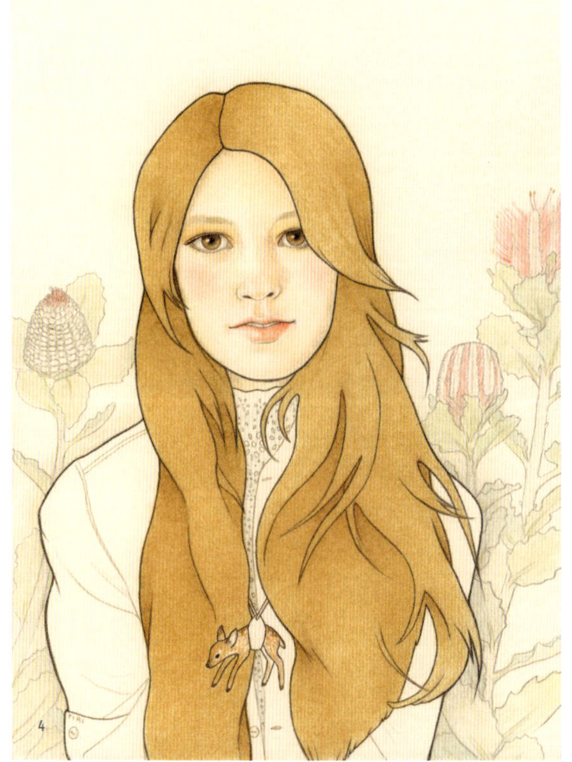

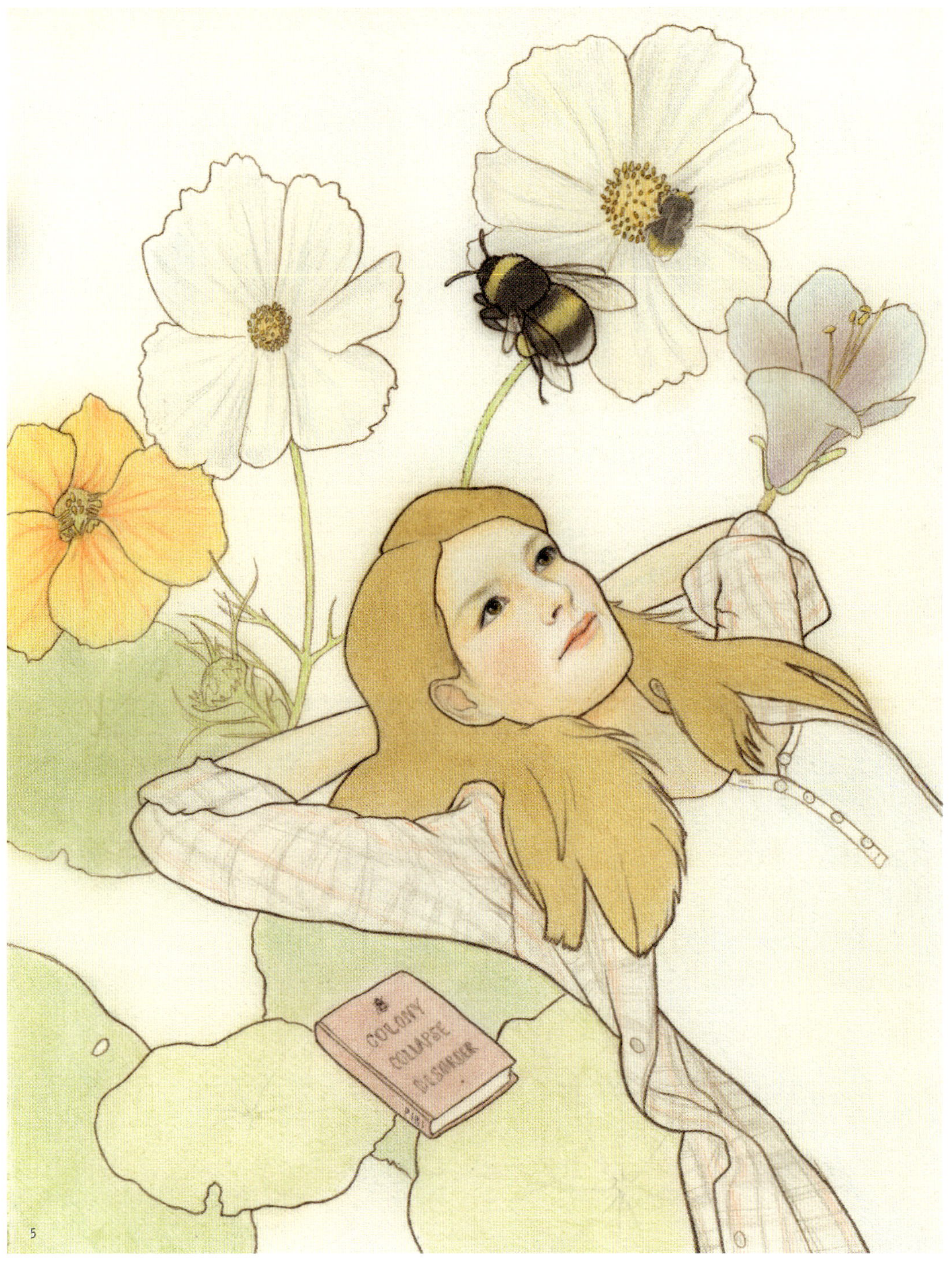

5

Lilly Piri
Australia

www.lillypiri.com
www.littlegalaxie.com

1. **Naiad** (2011). Personal work, sold to raise funds for the Queensland Flood relief. Colored pencil

2. **If I Had a Hammerhead** (2011). Personal work. Colored pencil

3. **What I wore Today** (Self Portrait) (2011). Personal work. Colored pencil

4. **Hier and There** (2011). Personal work. Colored pencil

5. **Flight of the Last Bumblebees** (2010). Personal work. Colored pencil

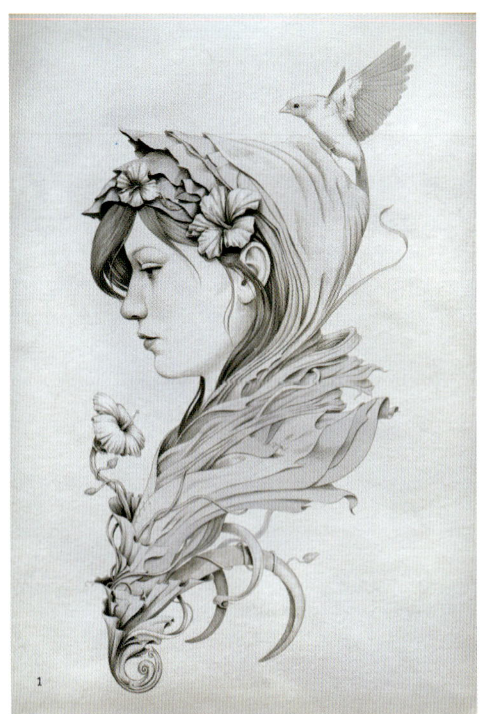

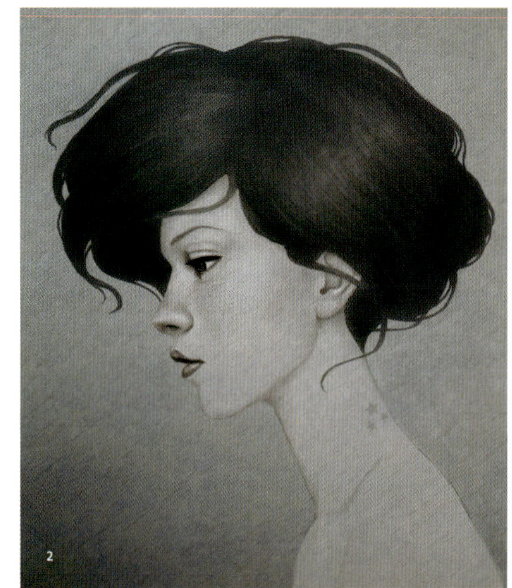

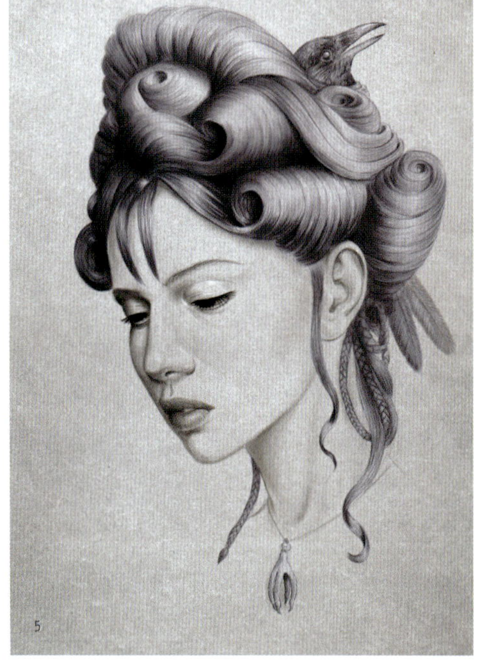

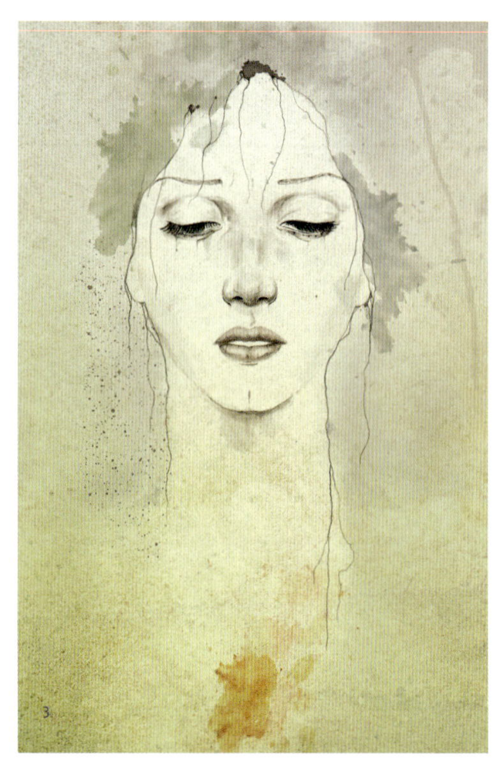

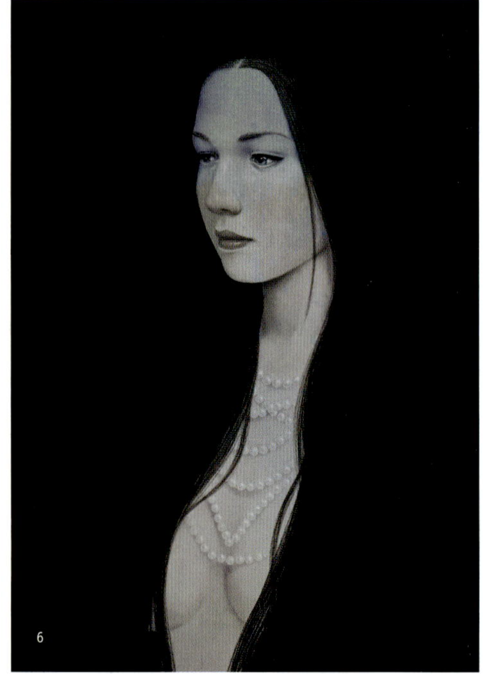

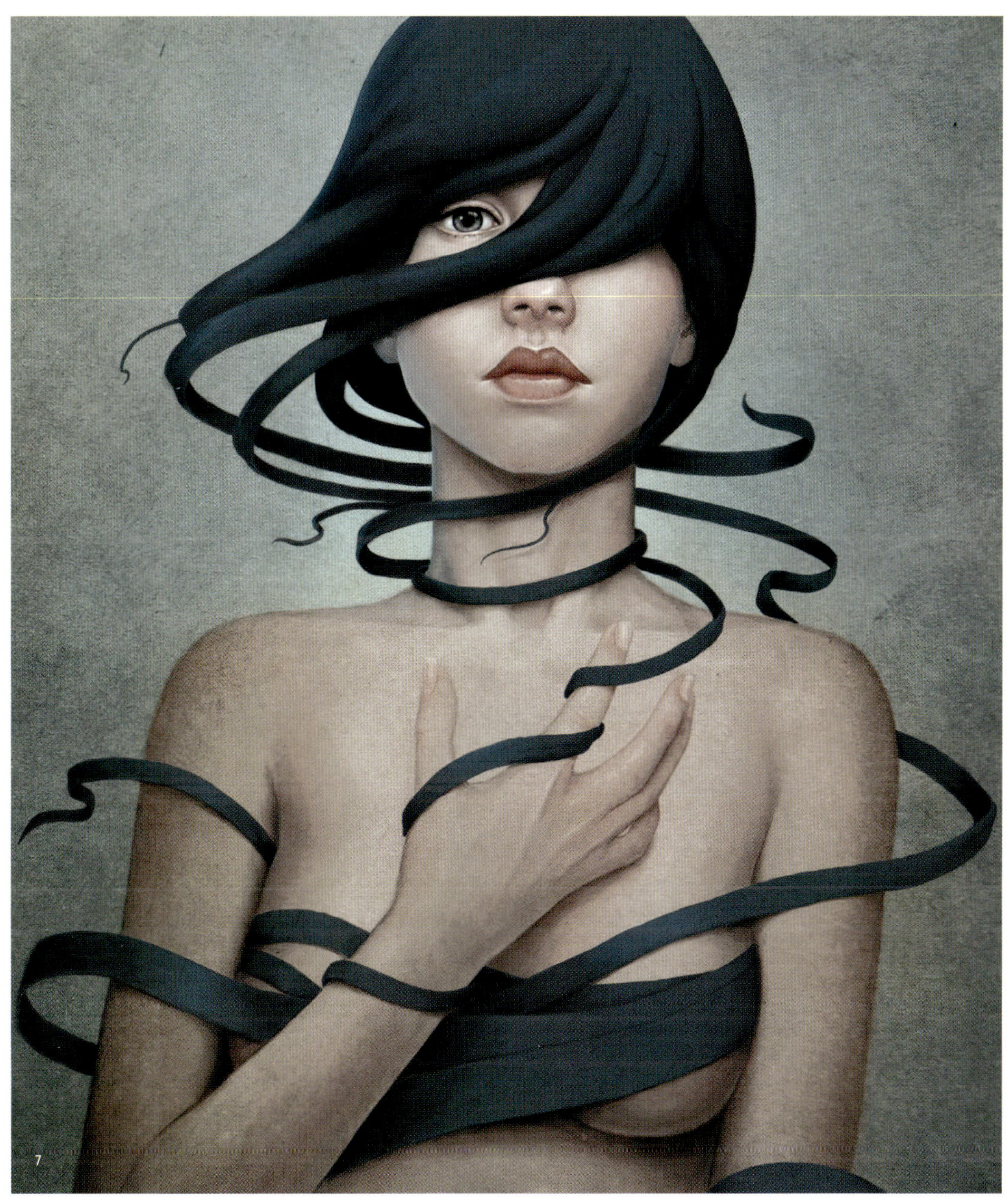

Diego Fernandez

Argentina

www.diegofernandez.daportfolio.com

1. **Hooded** (2011). Personal work. Photoshop

2. **Submarine** (2010). Personal work. Photoshop

3. **Raining** (2009). Personal work. Photoshop

4. **Daydreams** (2011). Personal work. Photoshop

5. **In Fashion** (2010). Personal work. Photoshop

6. **Pearls** (2010). Personal work. Photoshop

7. **Twisted** (2010). Personal work. Photoshop

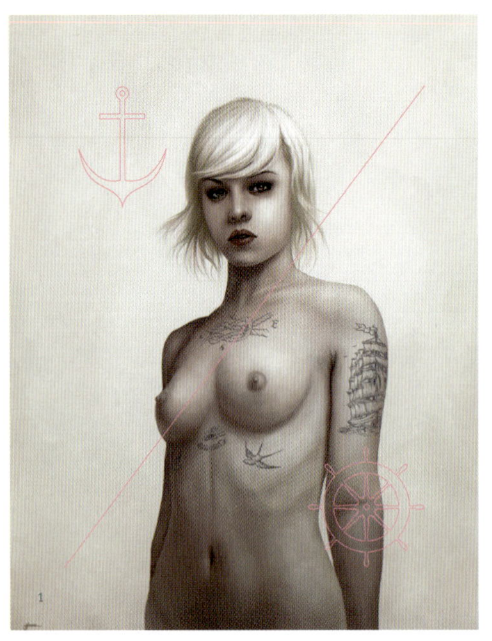

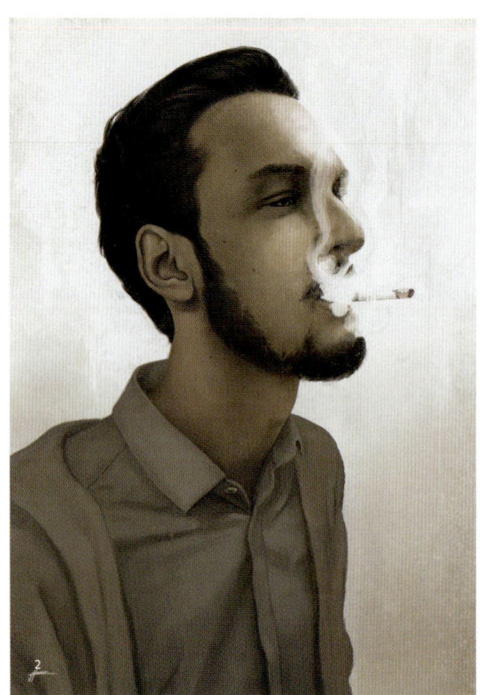

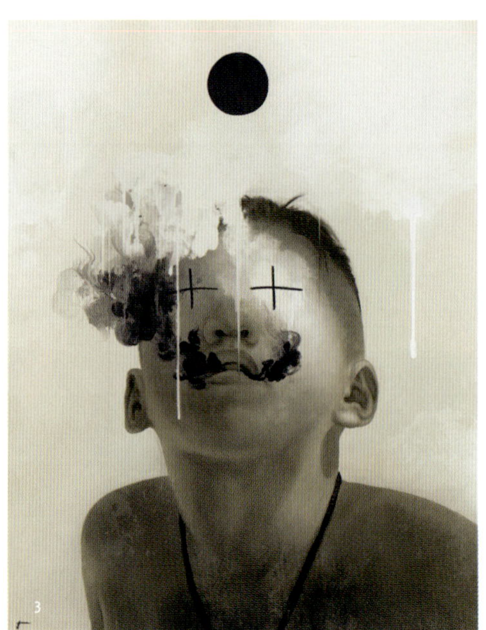

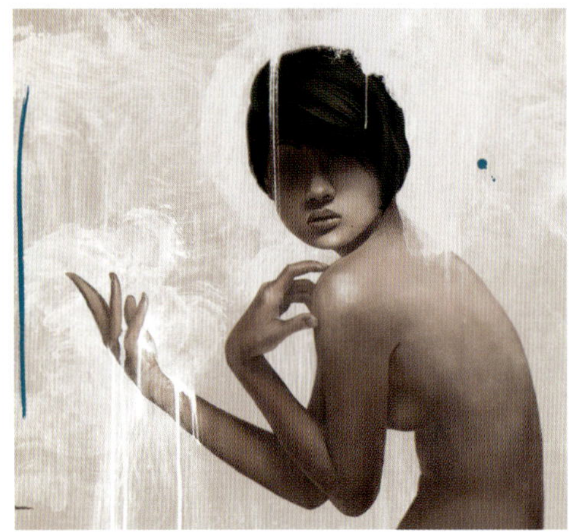

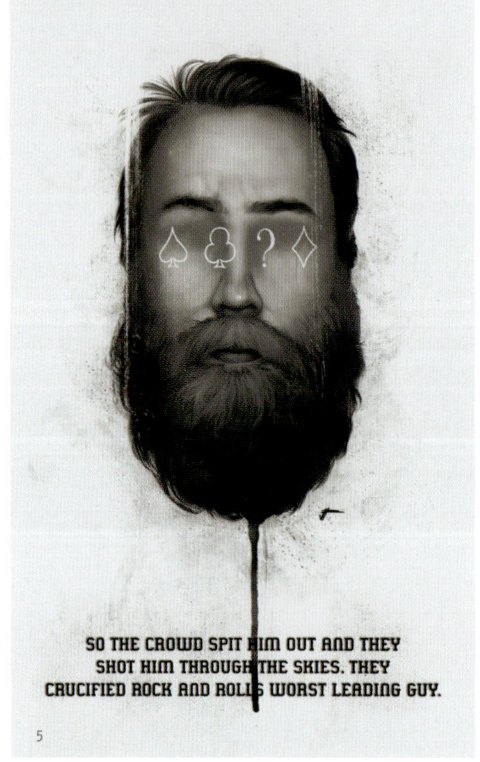

SO THE CROWD SPIT HIM OUT AND THEY
SHOT HIM THROUGH THE SKIES. THEY
CRUCIFIED ROCK AND ROLL'S WORST LEADING GUY.

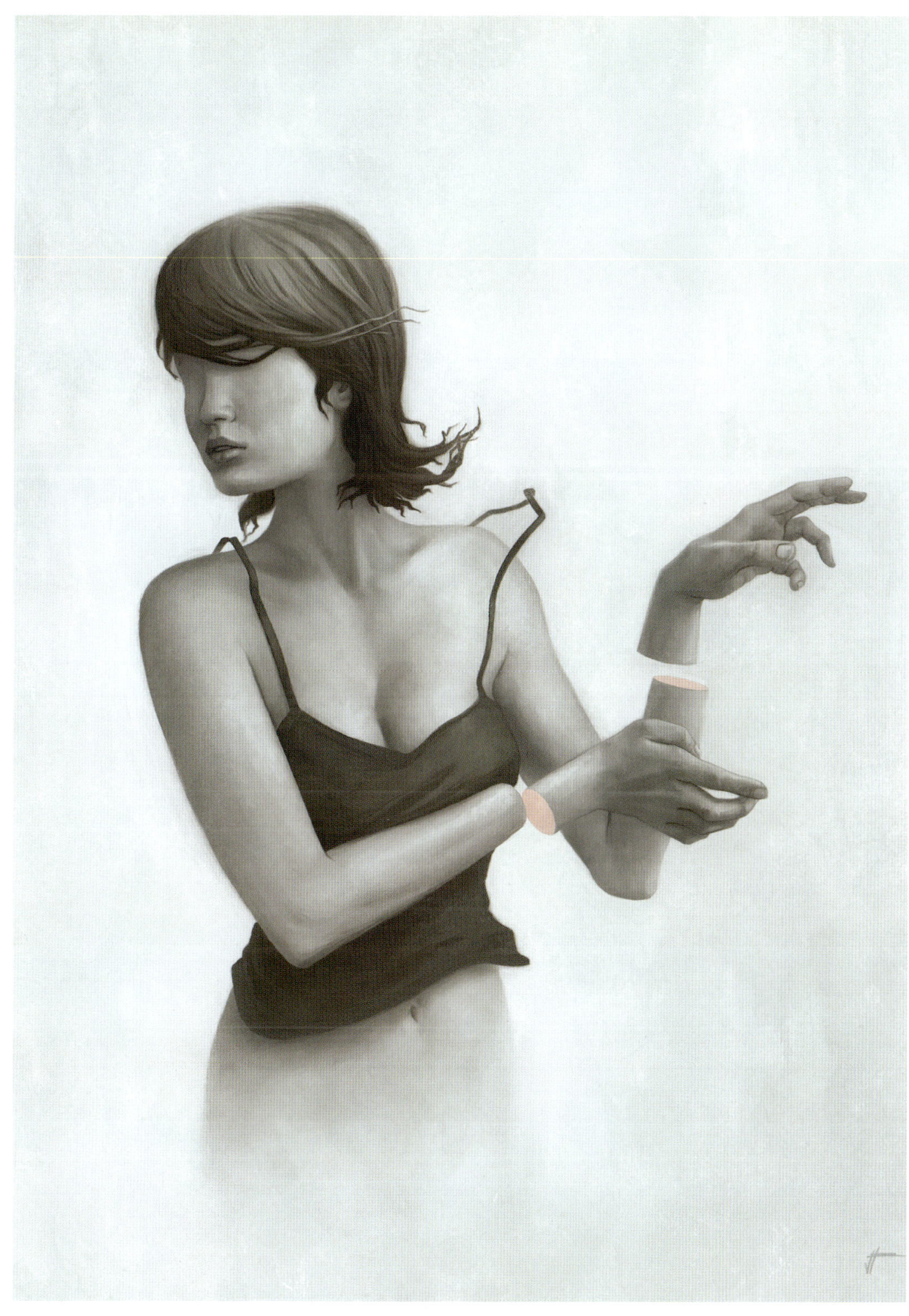

Valentin Fischer

Germany

www.valentinfischer.com

1. **Schwere See Mein Herz** (2010). Personal work. Photoshop, mixed media

2. **Feli** (2011). Henriques Coelho, Theodorou GBR. Photoshop, mixed media

3. **His Dying Elegance** (2010). Personal work. Photoshop, mixed media

4. **The Leading Guy** (2010). Personal work. Photoshop, mixed media

5. **The Leading Guy** (2010). MAGMA Brand Design. Photoshop, mixed media

6. **Carried Silence** (2011). Personal work. Photoshop, mixed media

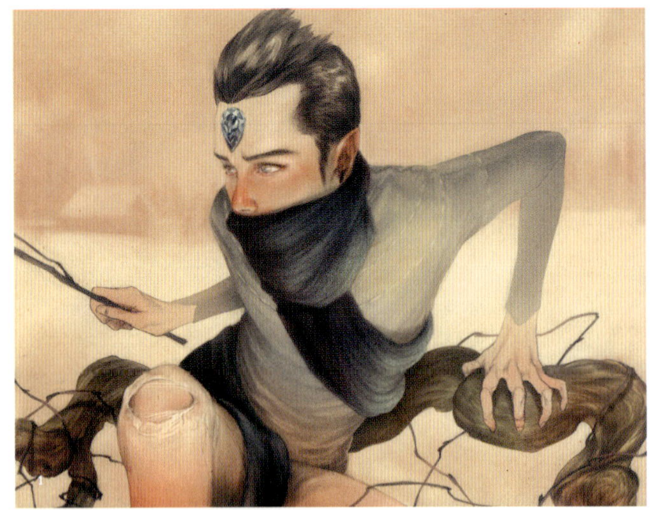

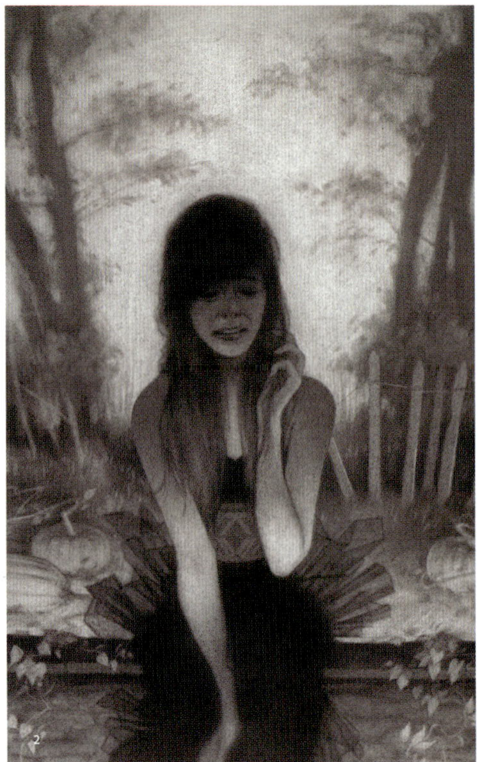

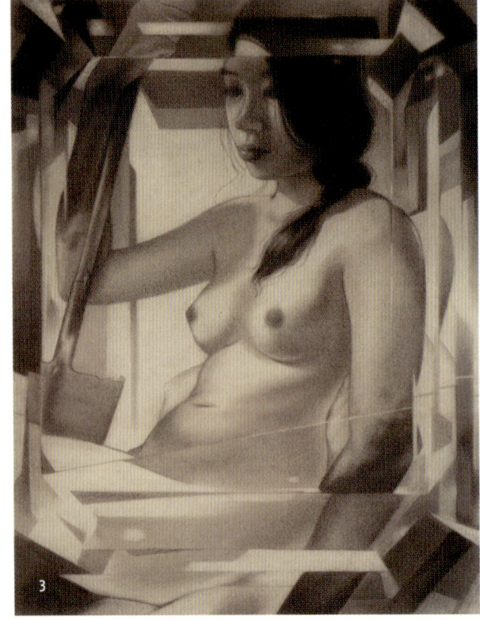

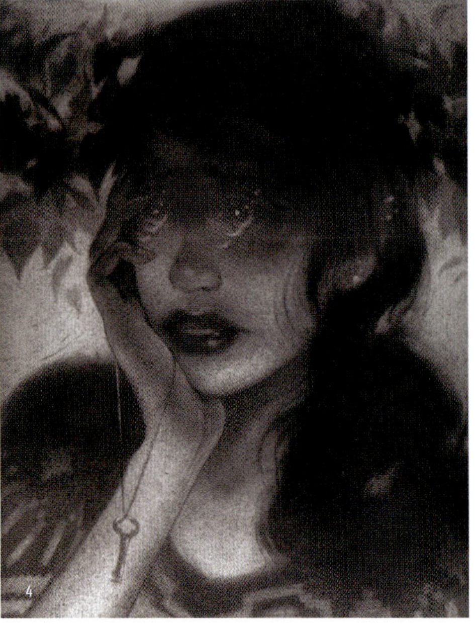

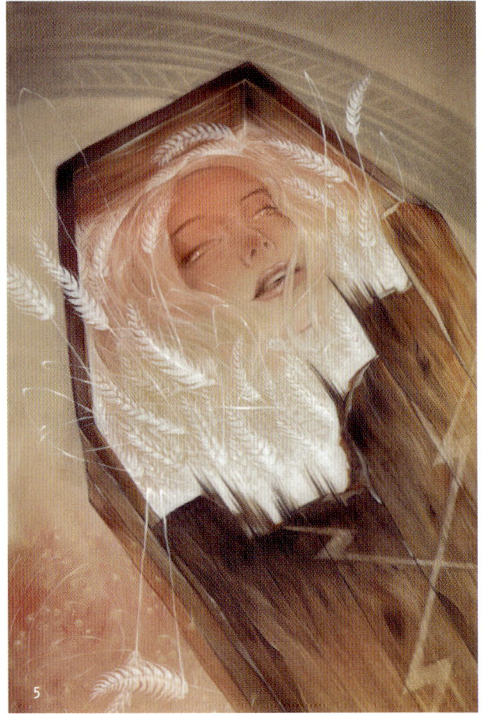

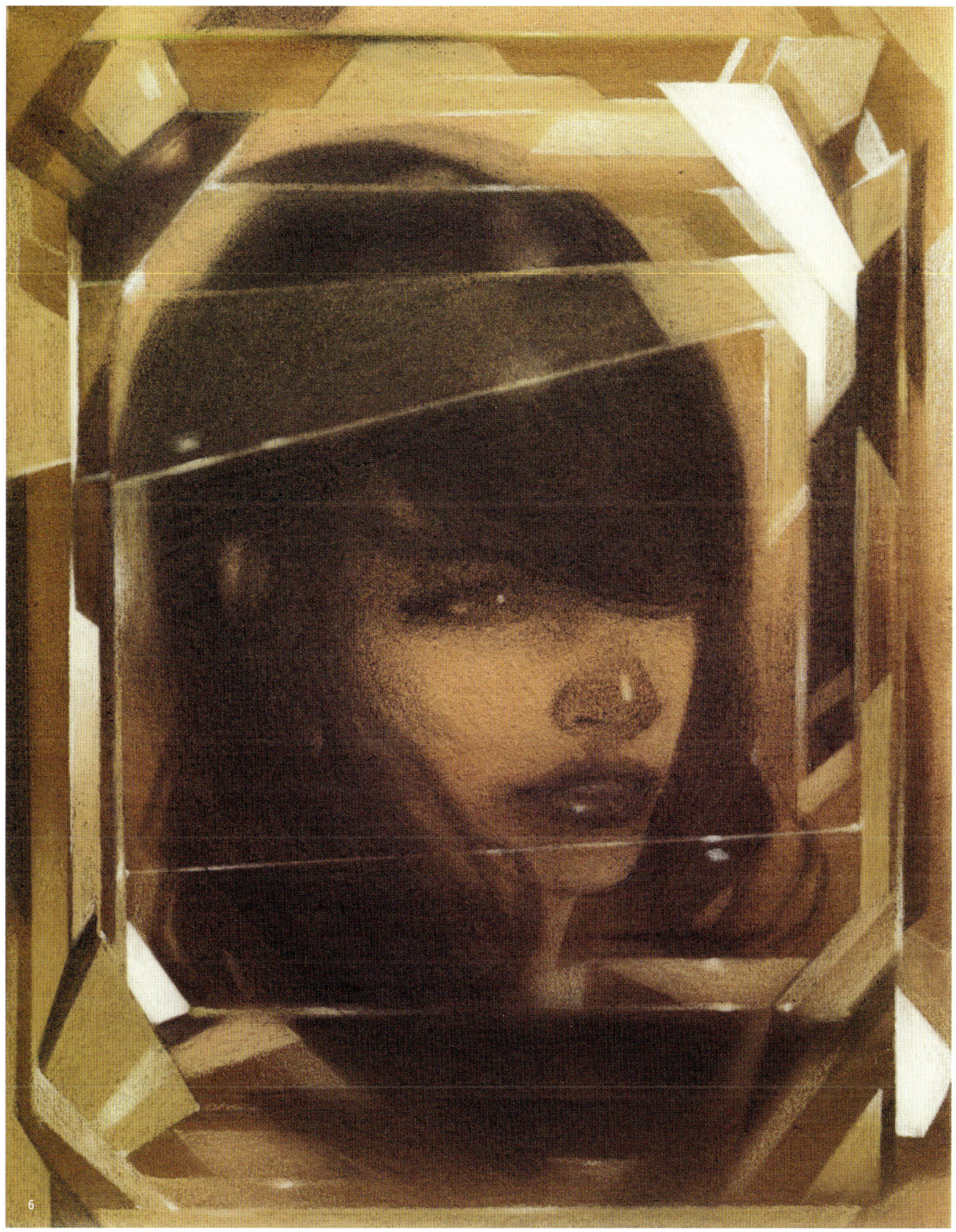

Sam Wolfe Connelly
USA

www.samwolfeconnelly.com

1. **Jack Frost** (2010). Personal work. Graphite, digital

2. **Alex** (2011). Personal work. Graphite

3. **Luster** (2011). Personal work. Graphite

4. **Bleary Night** (2011). Personal work. Graphite

5. **Pine Box** (2011). Personal work. Acrylic, colored pencil

6. **Vanadium** (2011). Personal work. Acrylic, colored pencil

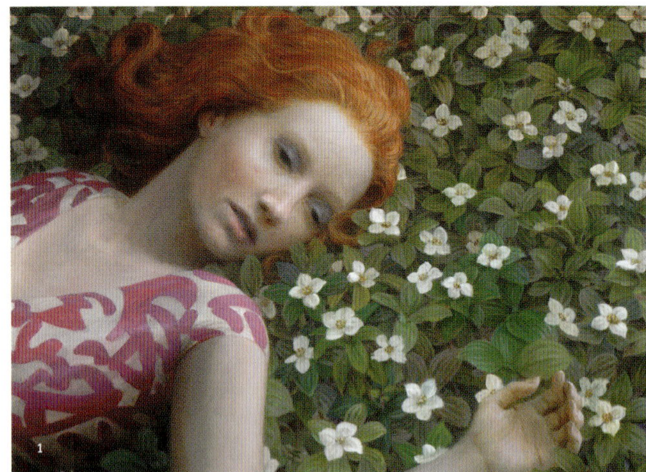

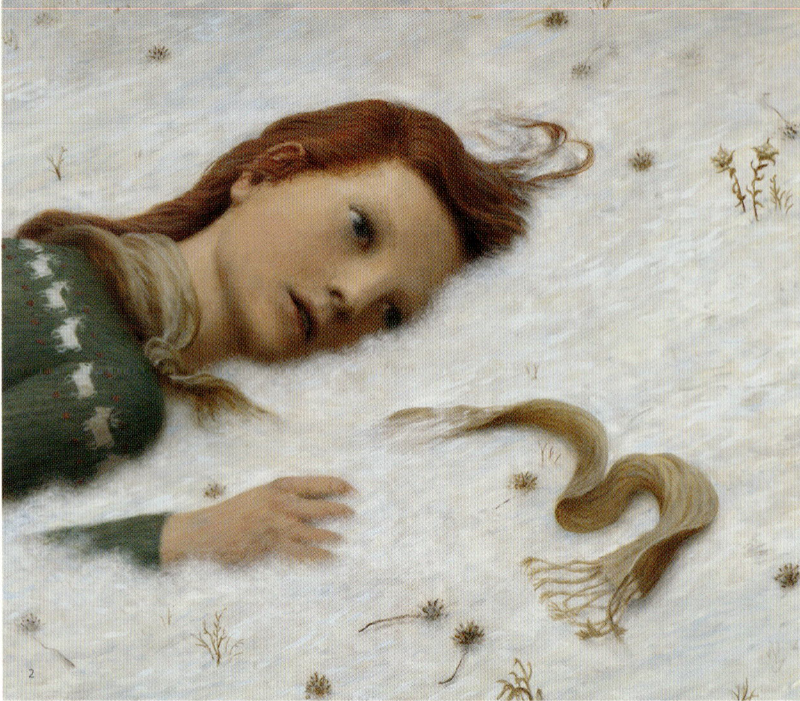

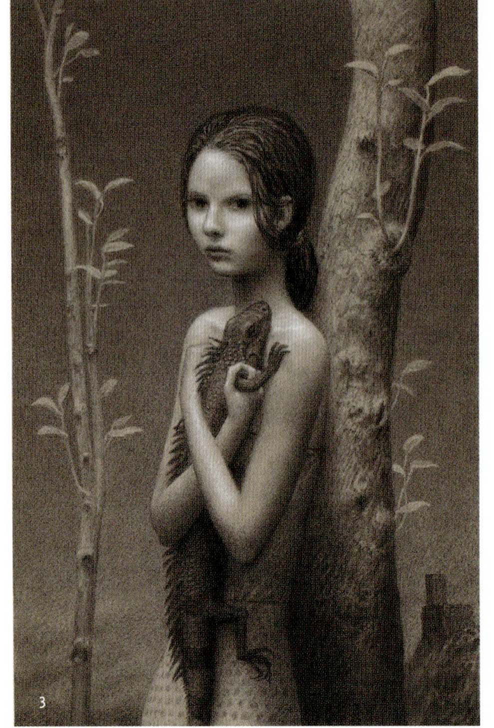

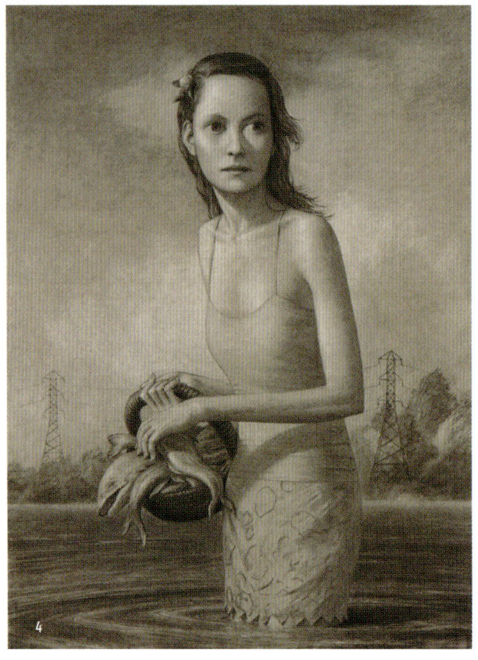

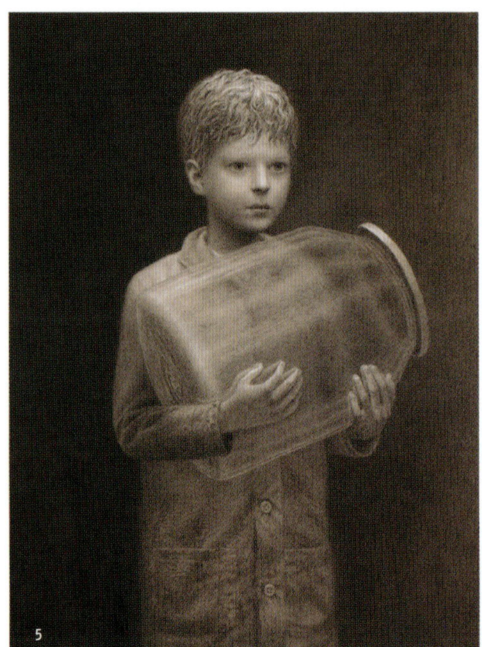

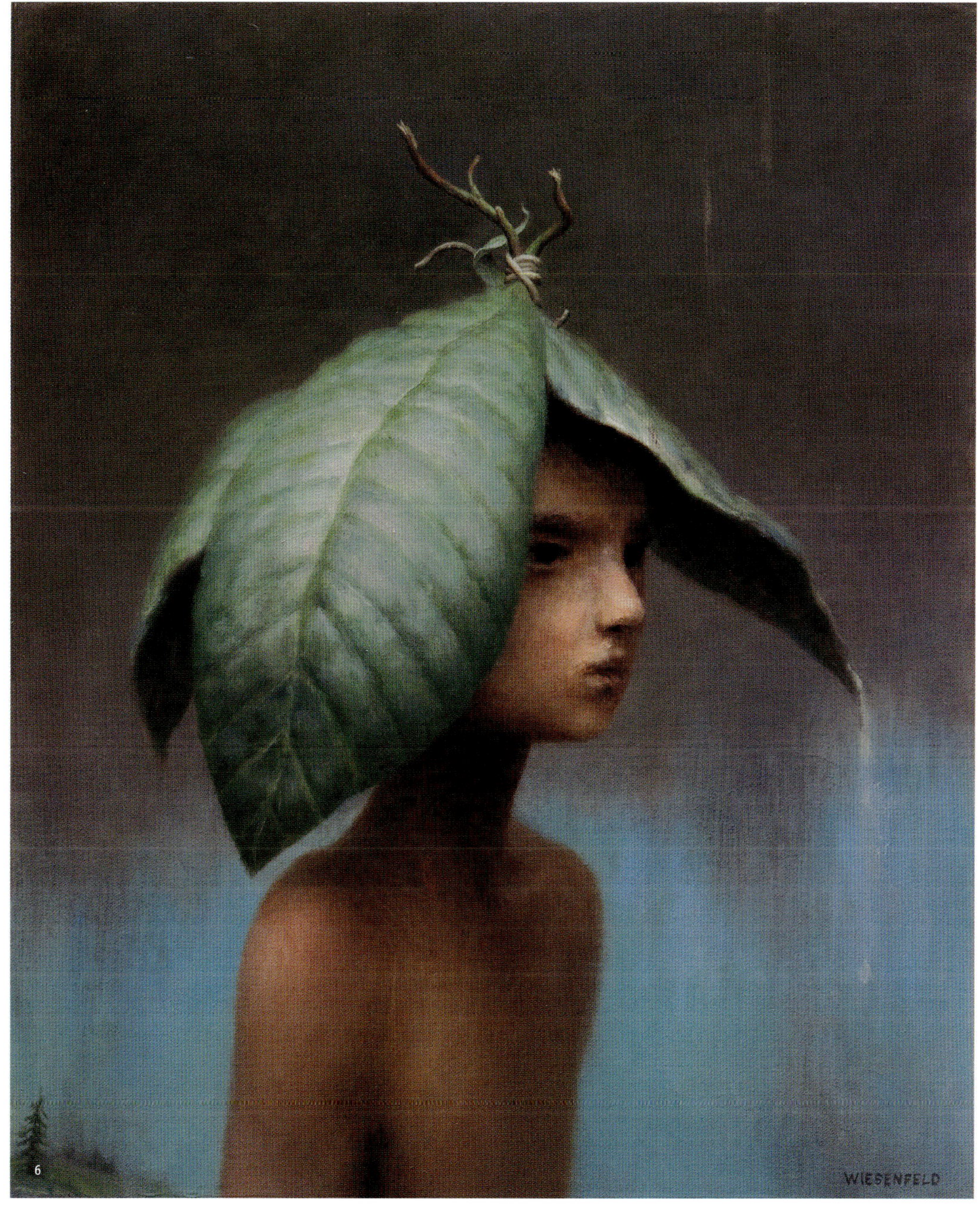

Aron Wiesenfeld
USA

www.aronwiesenfeld.com

1. **Flowerbed** (2007). Personal work. Oil on canvas

2. **Snowbed** (2011). Personal work. Oil on canvas

3. **Thicket** (2009). Personal work. Charcoal on paper

4. **The Fish Gatherer** (2006). Personal work. Charcoal on paper

5. **Thomas** (2011). Personal work. Charcoal on paper

6. **March** (2011). Personal work. Oil on canvas

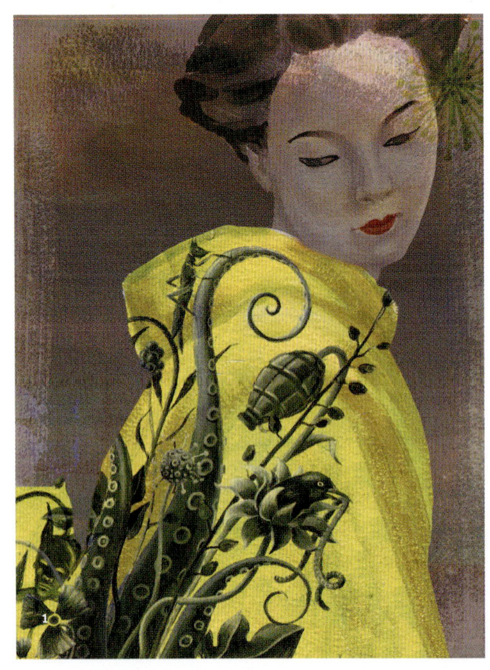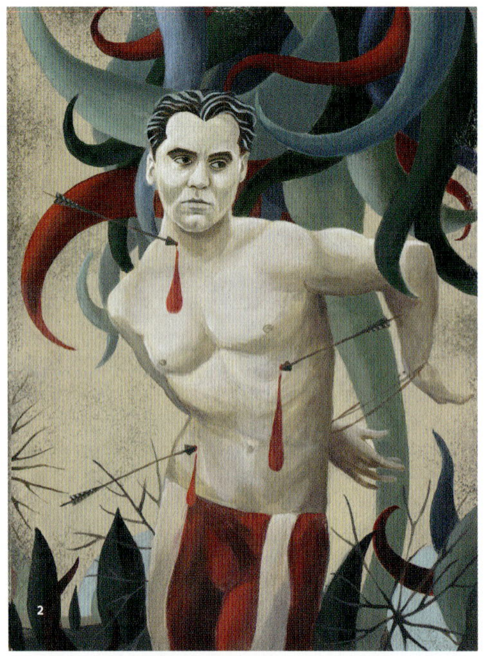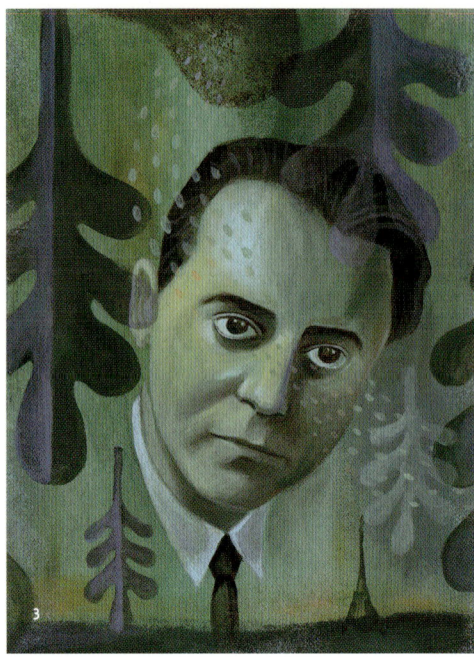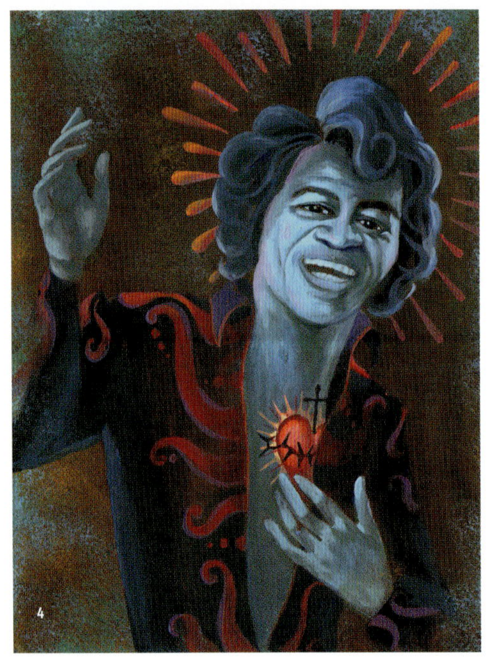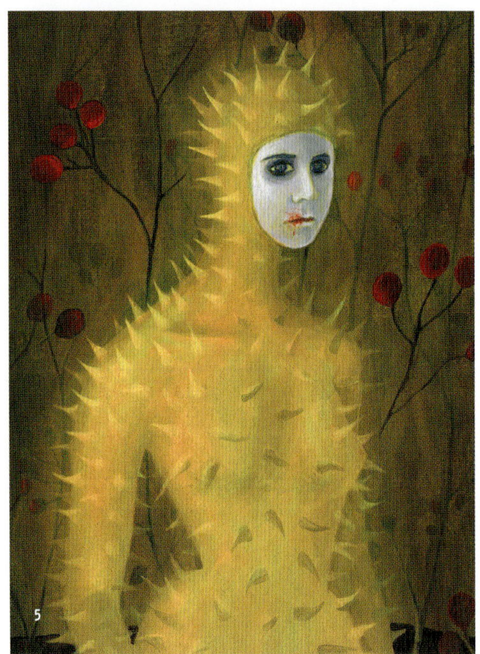

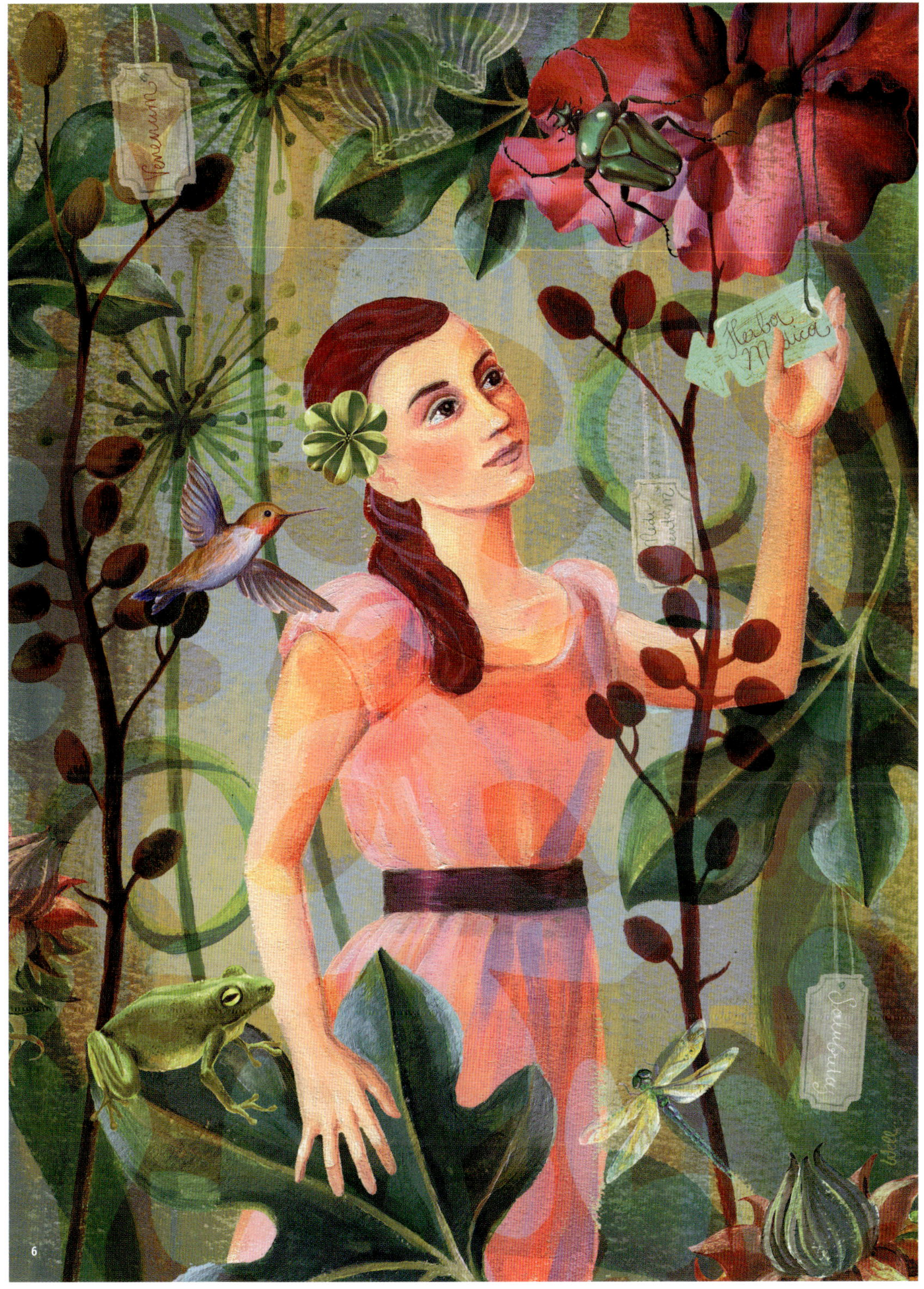

Alice Wellinger
Austria

www.alice-wellinger.com

1. **Don't Look Back** (2010). Personal work. Acrylic, digital

2. **Federico Carcia Lorca** (2011). Personal work. Acrylic on cardboard

3. **Ödön von Horvath** (2011). Personal work. Acrylic on cardboard

4. **James Brown** (2011). Personal work. Acrylic on cardboard

5. **Locked In** (2010). Personal work. Acrylic on cardboard

6. **Medizin aus dem Regenwald** (2010). *Vital Magazin*. Acrylic, digital

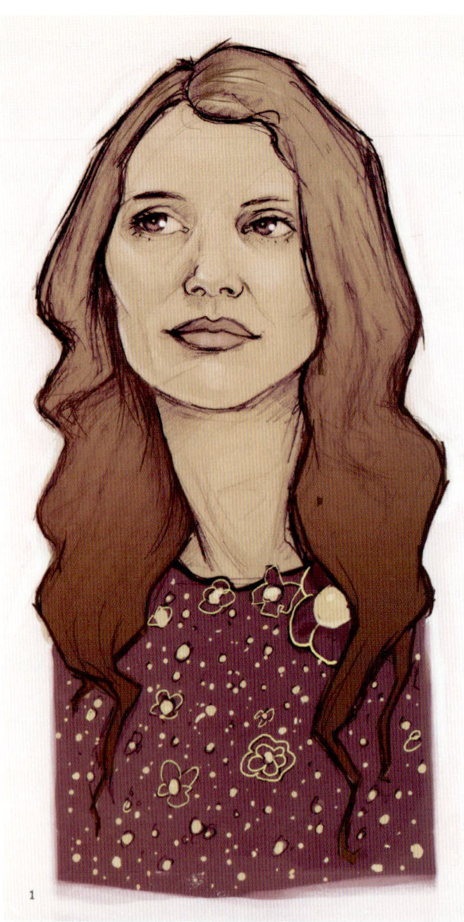

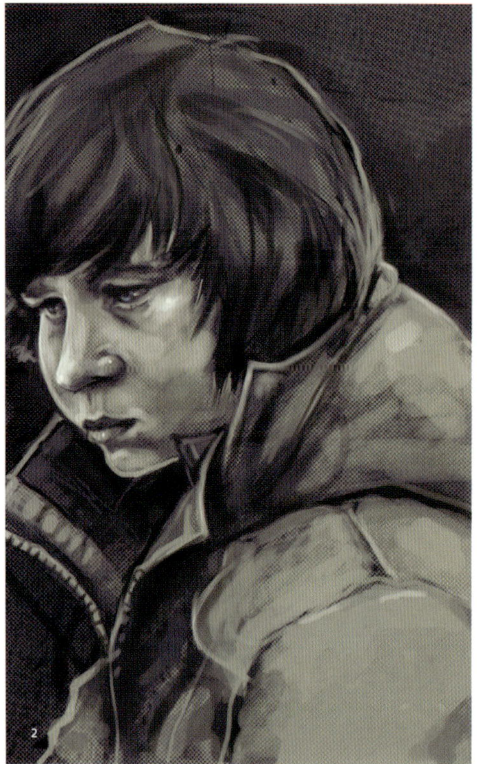

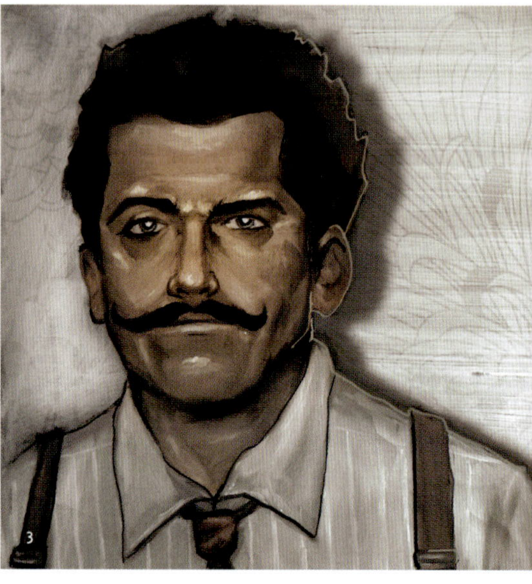

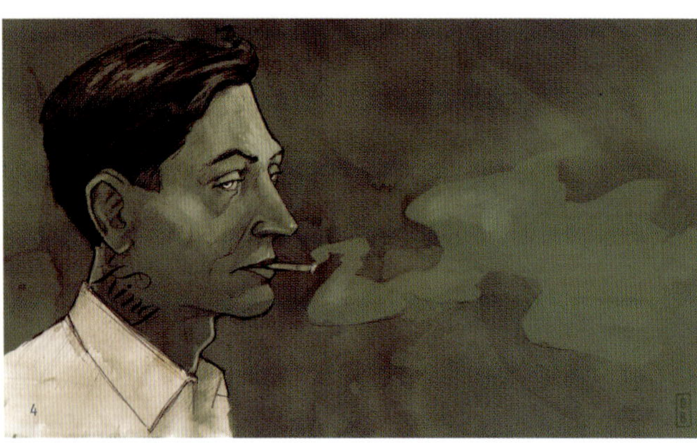

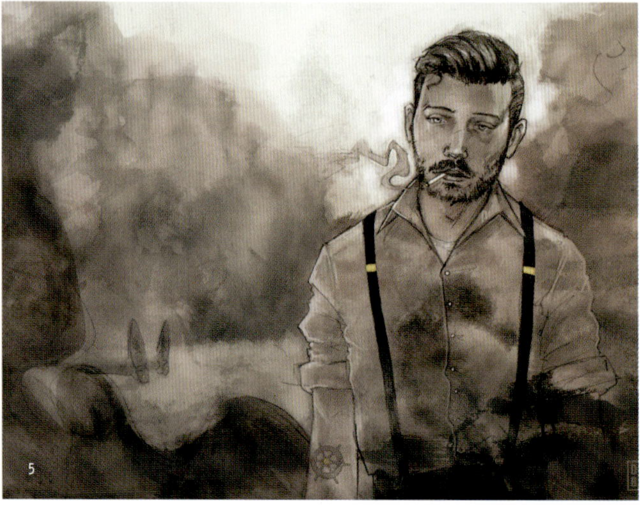

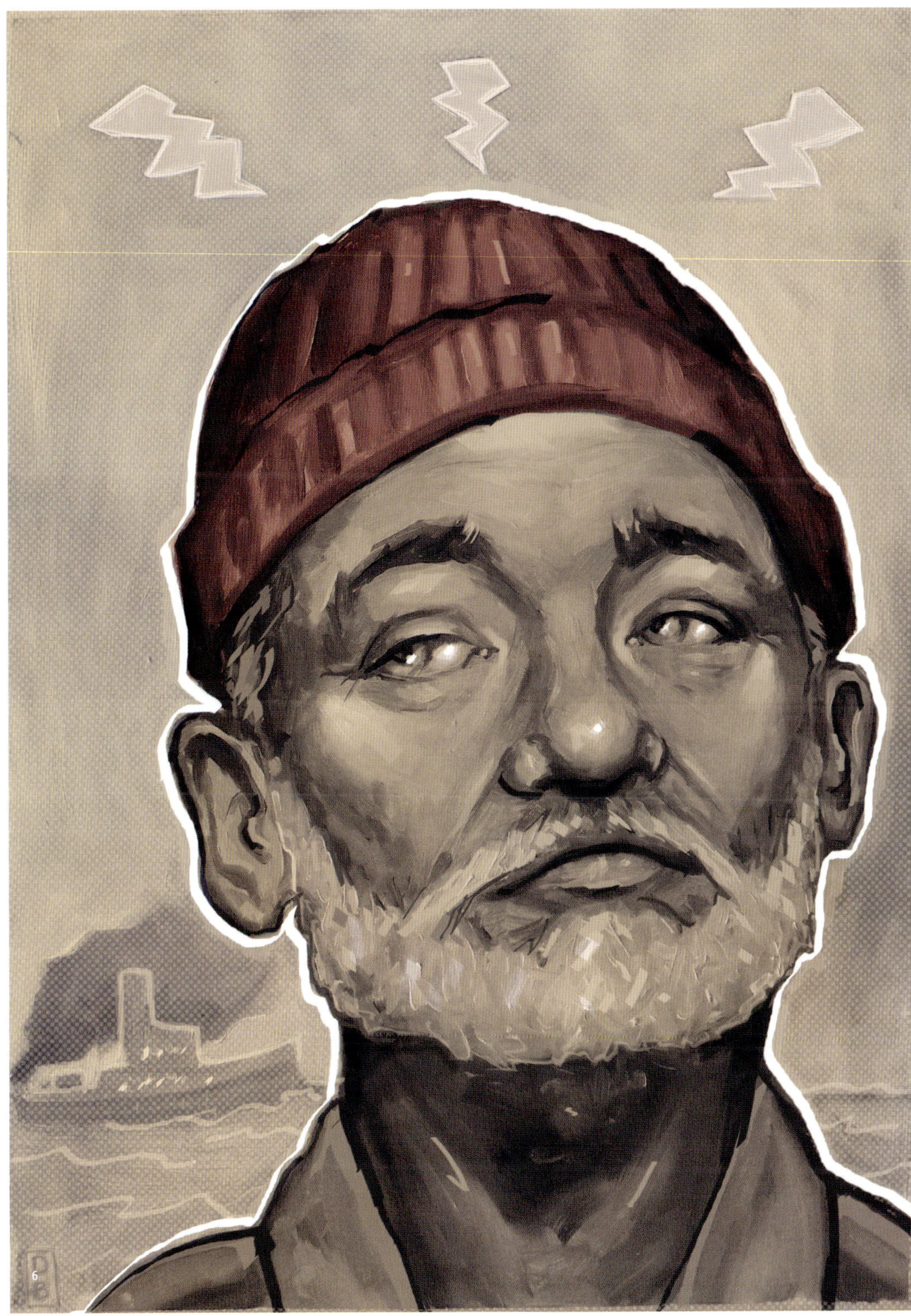

Dale C Bowers
UK

www.dalebowers.co.uk

1. **Anna** (2011). *FI Magazine*. Pencil, digital

2. **Red Letter** (2011). Poster for short film *Red Letter*. Digital

3. **The Red Phone Rings** (2011). Personal work. Oil, digital

4. **King** (2011). Personal work. Pencil, digital

5. **Smoke** (2011). Personal work. Pencil, digital

6. **Zissou** (2011). Personal work. Oil, digital

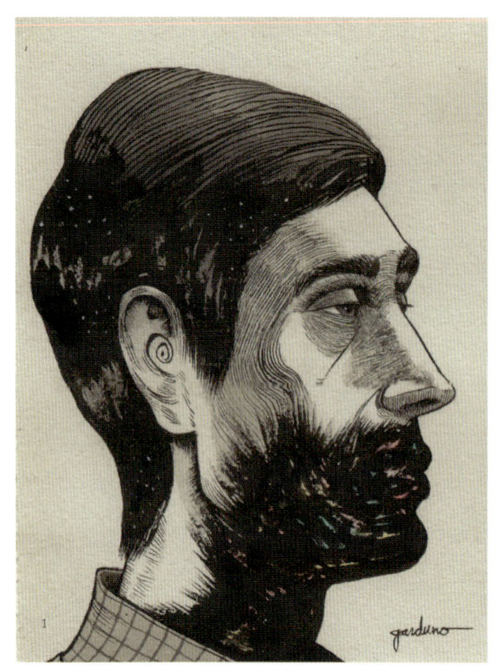

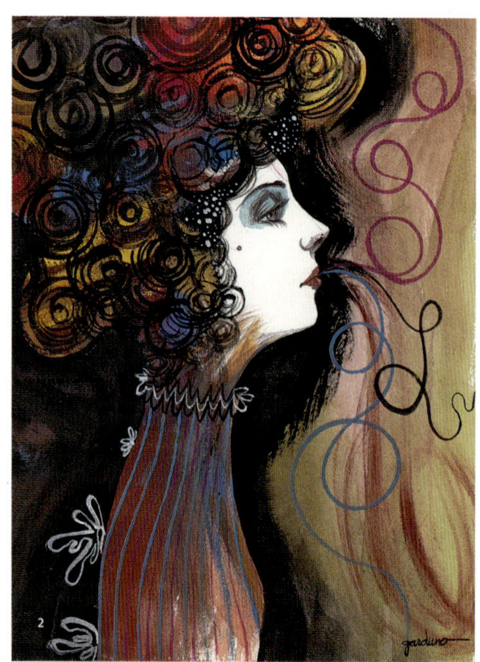

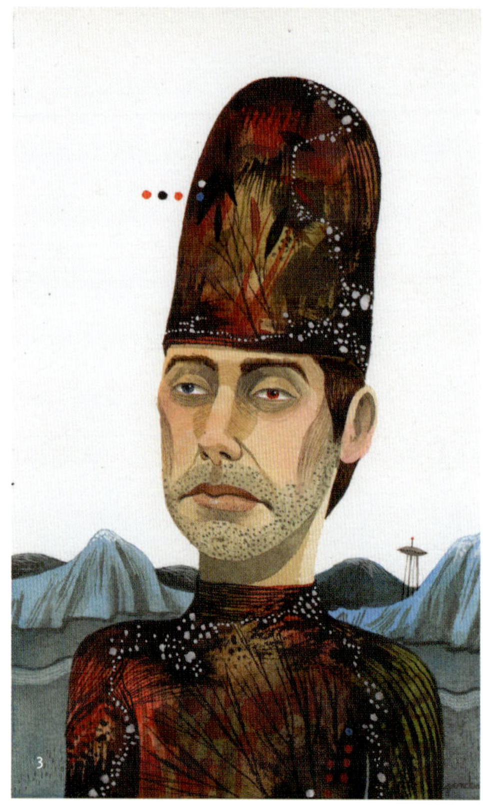

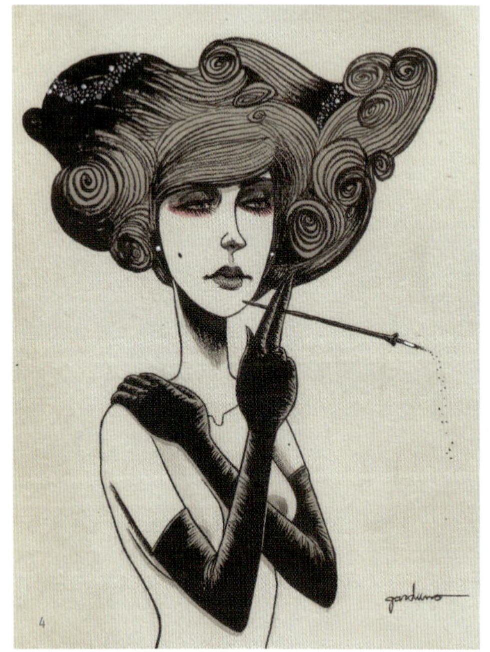

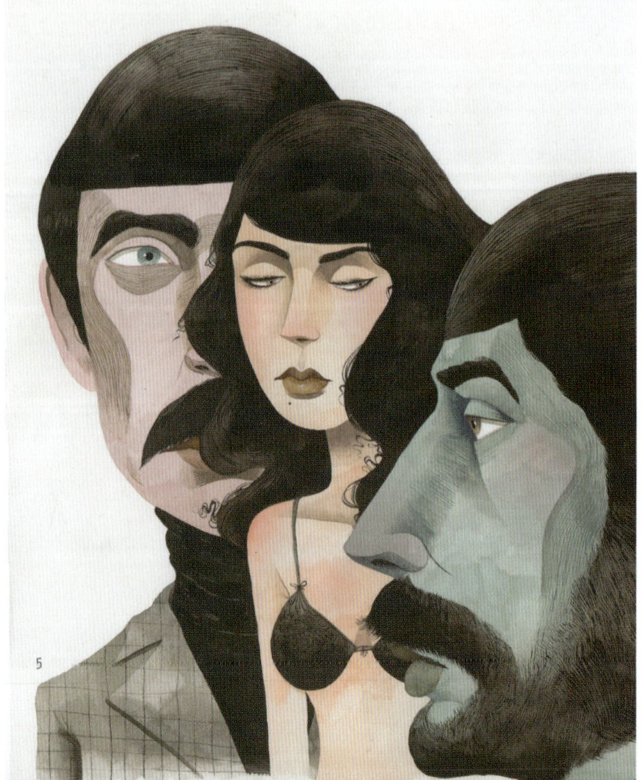

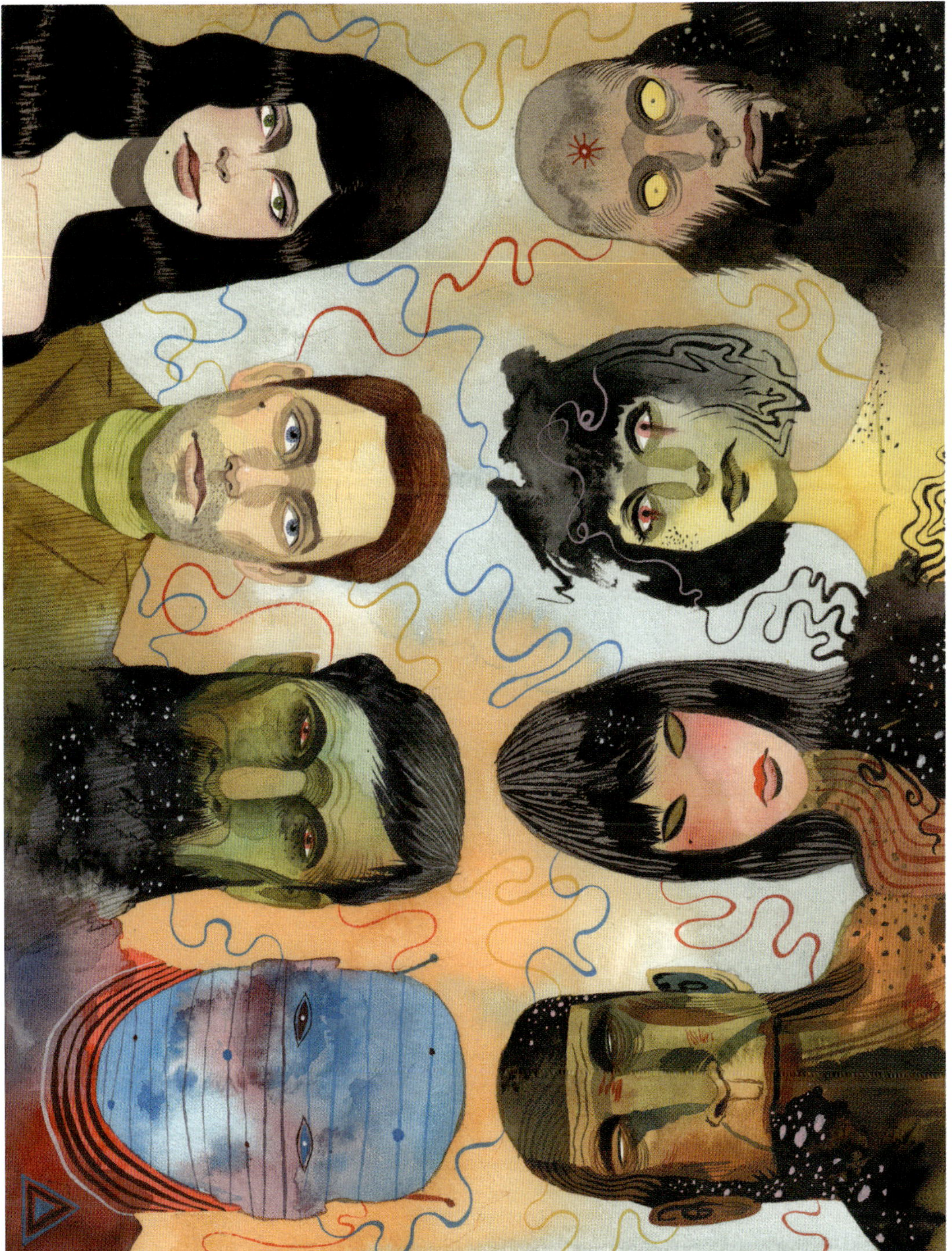

Ken Garduno
USA

www.kengarduno.com

1. **Birthday Party** (2011). Personal work. Acrylic ink, wash

2. **Bernadette** (2011). Personal work. Gouache

3. **Unmasked** (2011). Personal work. Acrylic ink, wash

4. **Narcissism** (2011). Personal work. Acrylic ink, wash

5. **Love Triangle** (2011). Personal work. Acrylic ink, wash

6. **We the People** (2011). Personal work. Acrylic ink, wash

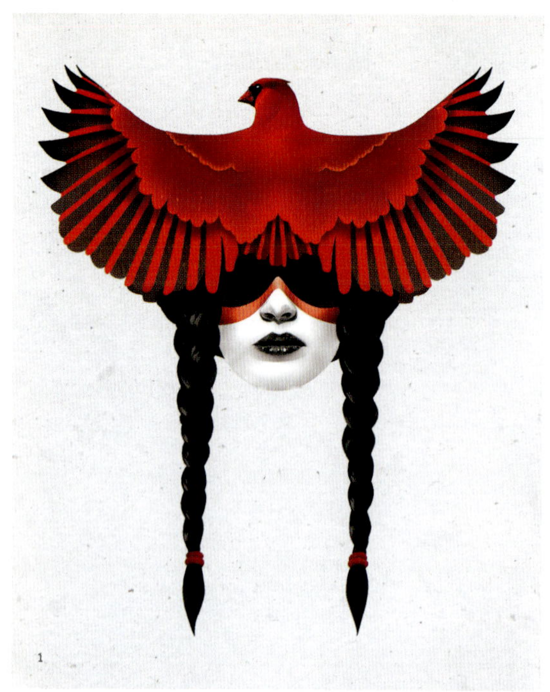

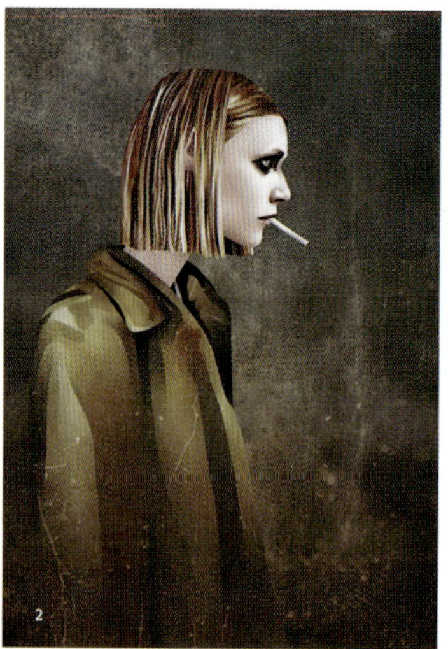

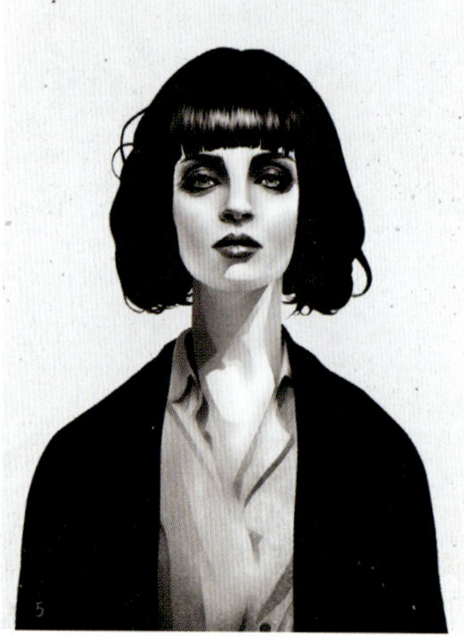

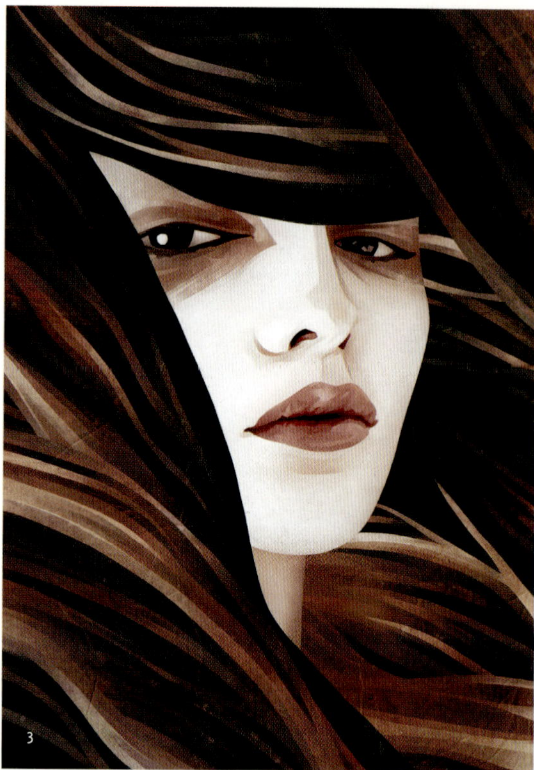

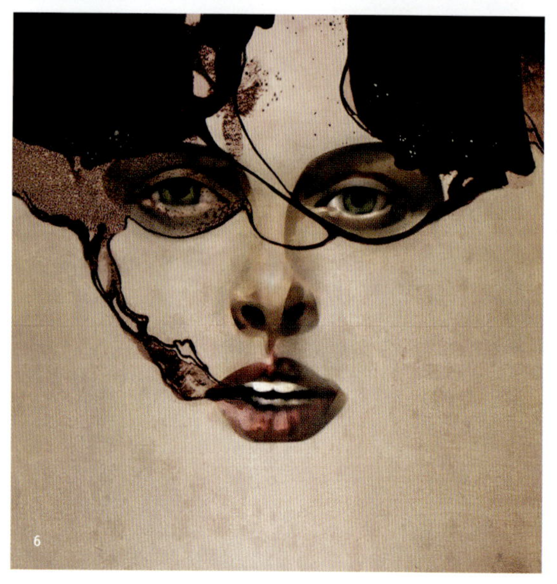

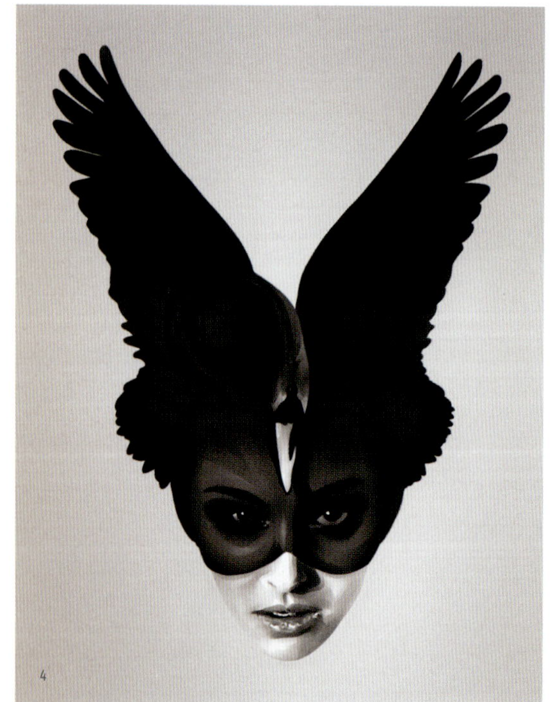

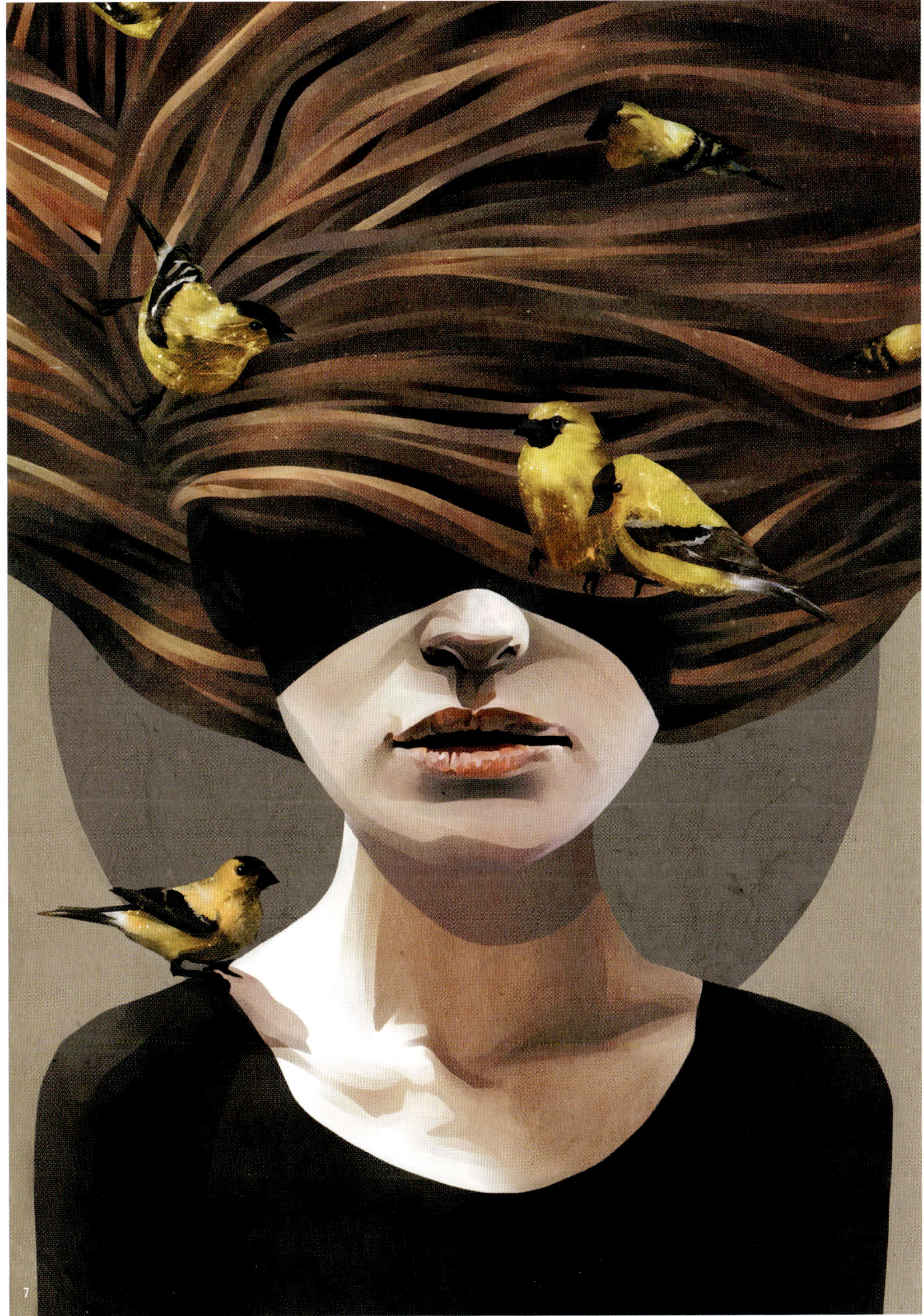

Ruben Ireland
UK

www.rubenireland.co.uk

1. **Cardinal Warrior** (2011). Sharpshirter. Digital

2. **Margot** (2011). Spoke Art Gallery *Bad Dad's 2* exhibition. Mixed media, digital

3. **Eye of the Storm** (2011). KneeDeepInSleep. Mixed media, digital

4. **It's My Time** (2010). Personal work. Mixed media, digital

5. **MrsMiaWallace** (2011). Personal work. Mixed media, digital

6. **Mind's Eye** (2010). A Future Without. Mixed media, digital

7. **Girl with Finches** (2011). ClickForArt. Mixed media, digital

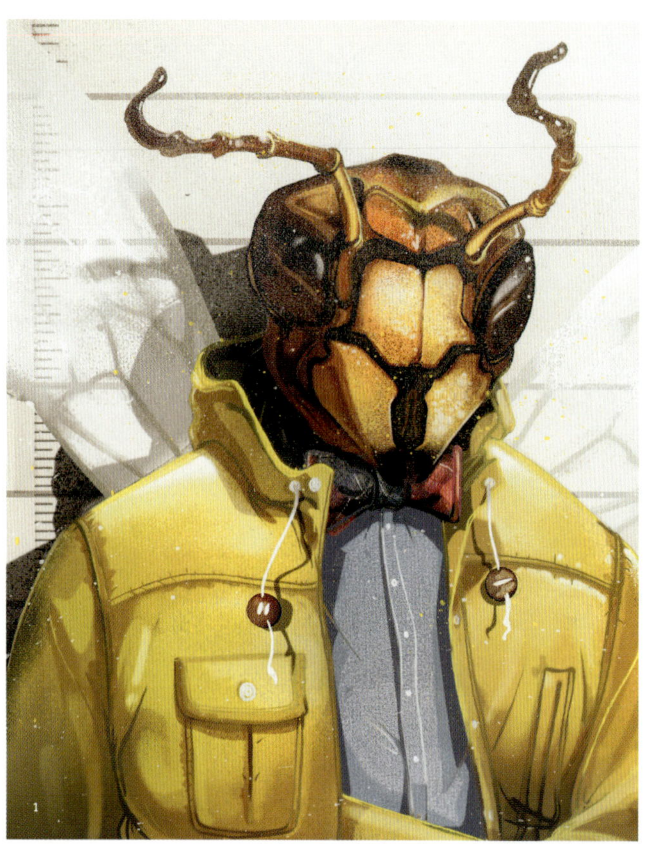

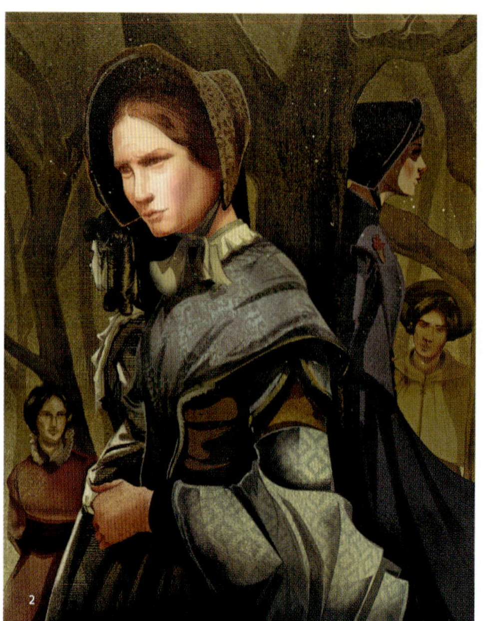

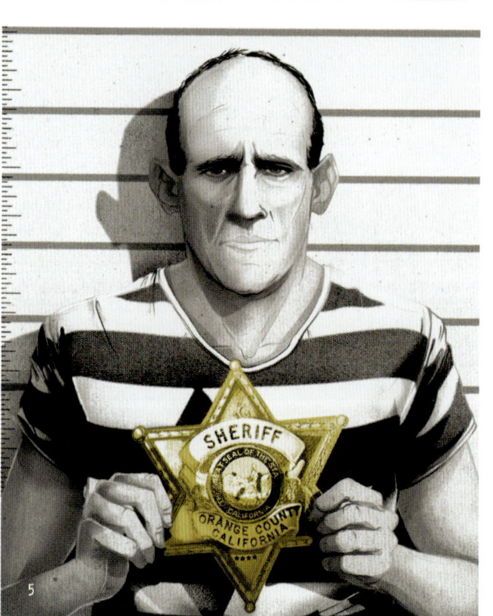

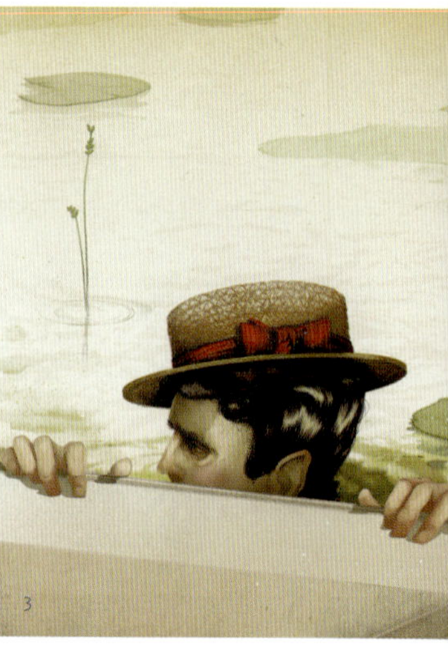

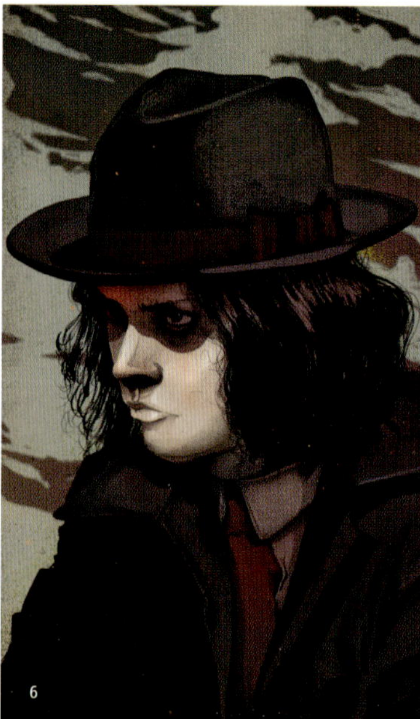
SHERIFF
ORANGE COUNTY
CALIFORNIA

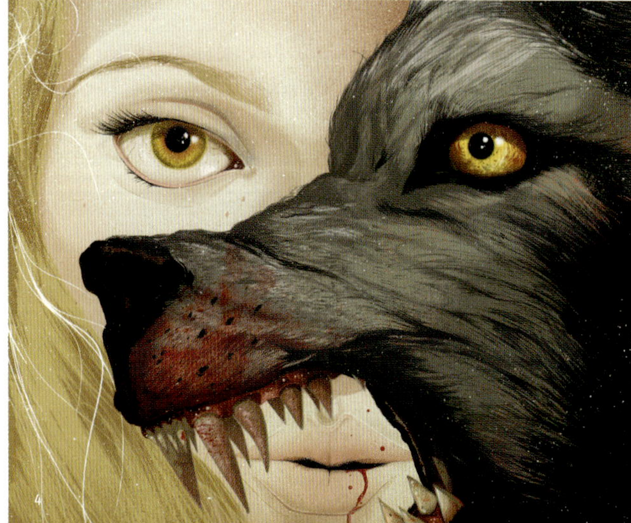

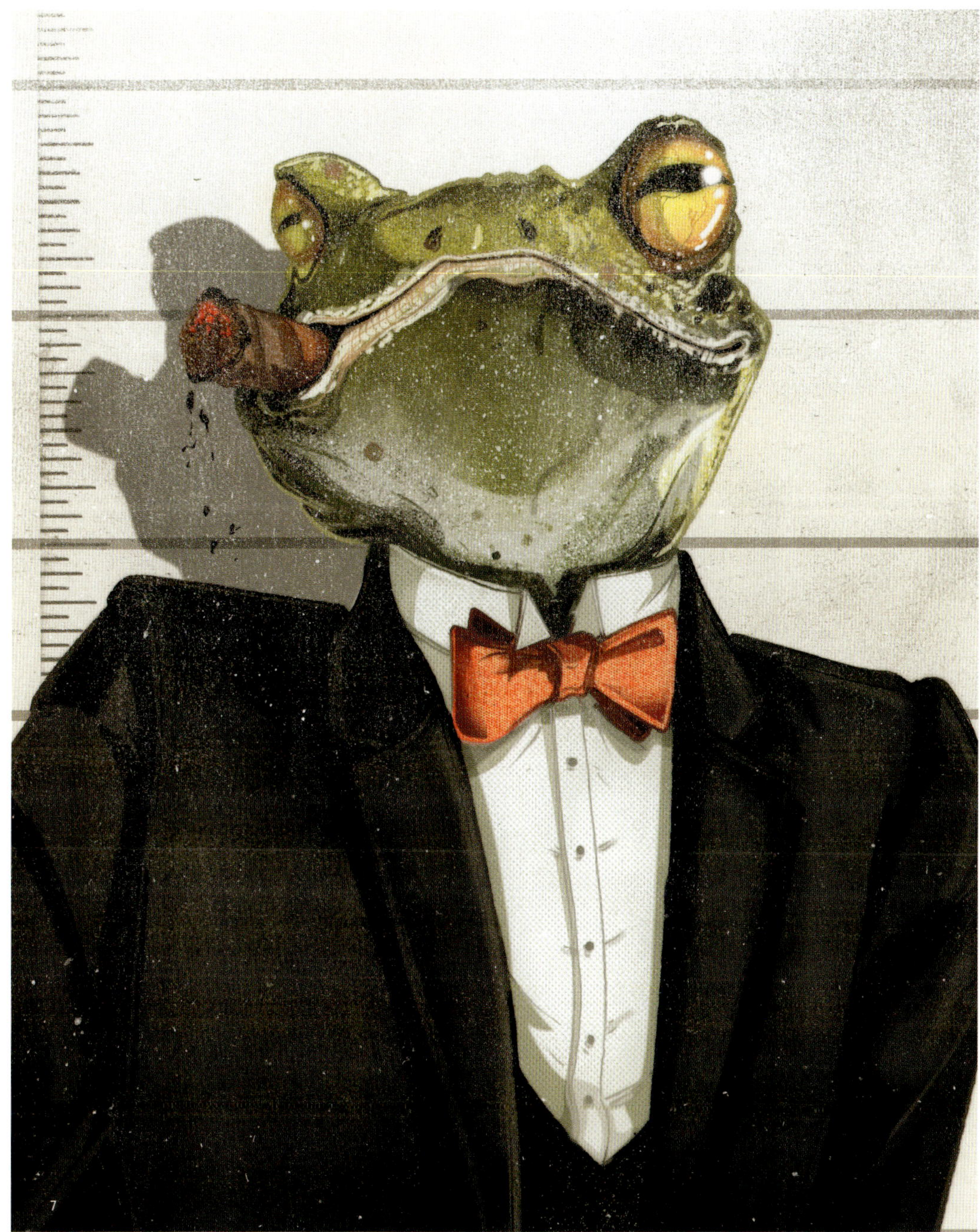

Jonathan Bartlett
USA

www.seejbdraw.com

1. **Sweet Honey** (2011). Pierrepont Hicks Tie Makers. Mixed media

2. **Jane Erye** (2011). *The Boston Globe*. Mixed media

3. **Wicker Skimmer** (2010). Personal work. Mixed media

4. **Wolfsbane** (2010). *The Los Angeles Times*. Mixed media

5. **Sheriff Mike Goes to Jail** (2010). *The OC Weekly*. Mixed media

6. **Jack White** (2010). Personal work. Mixed media

7. **Swamp King** (2011). Pierrepont Hicks Tie Makers. Mixed media

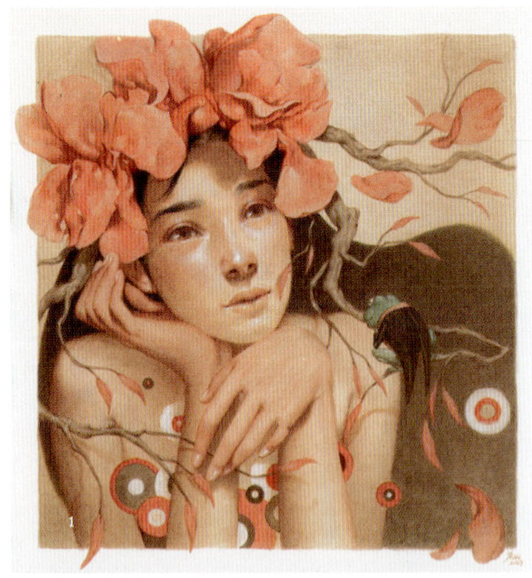

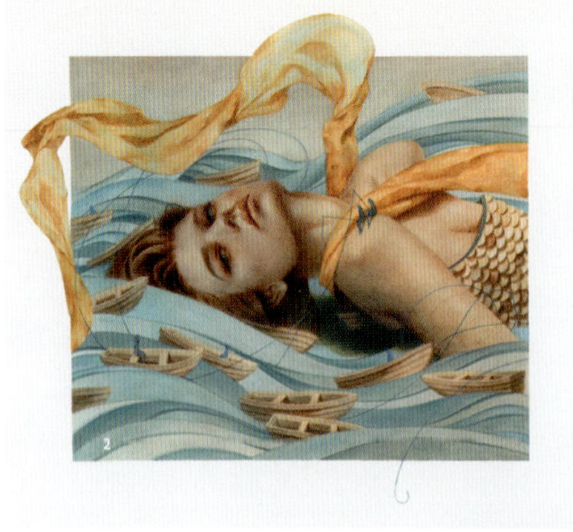

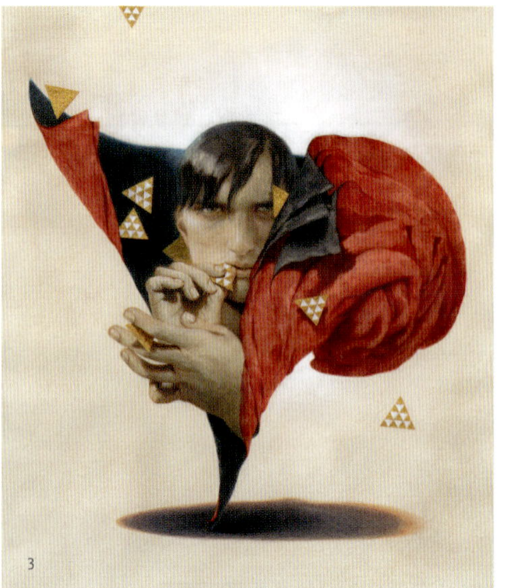

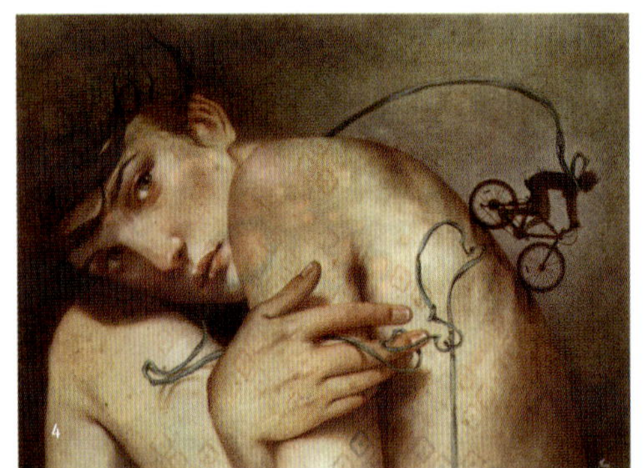

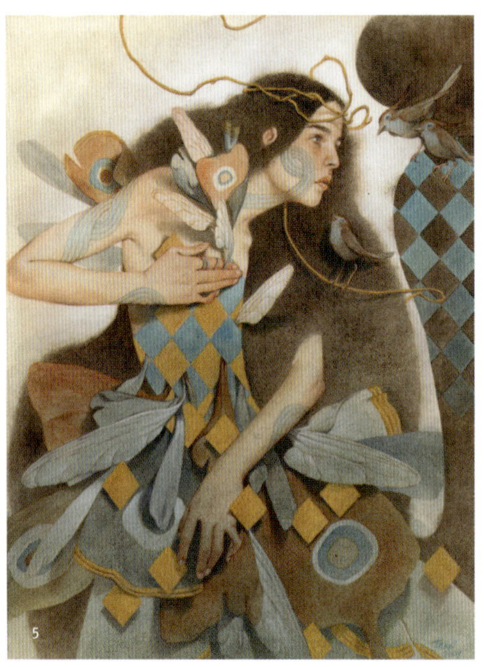

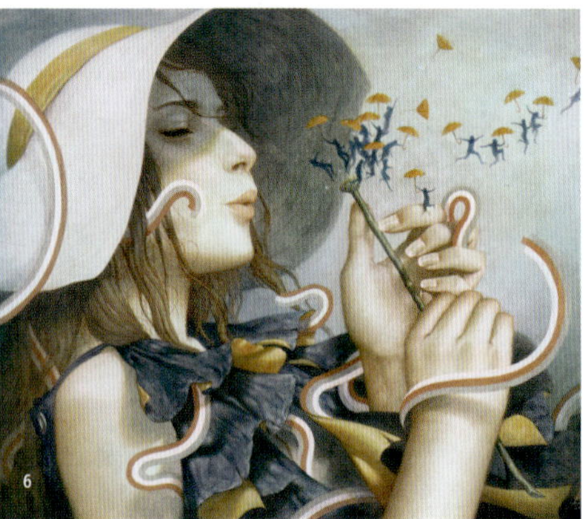

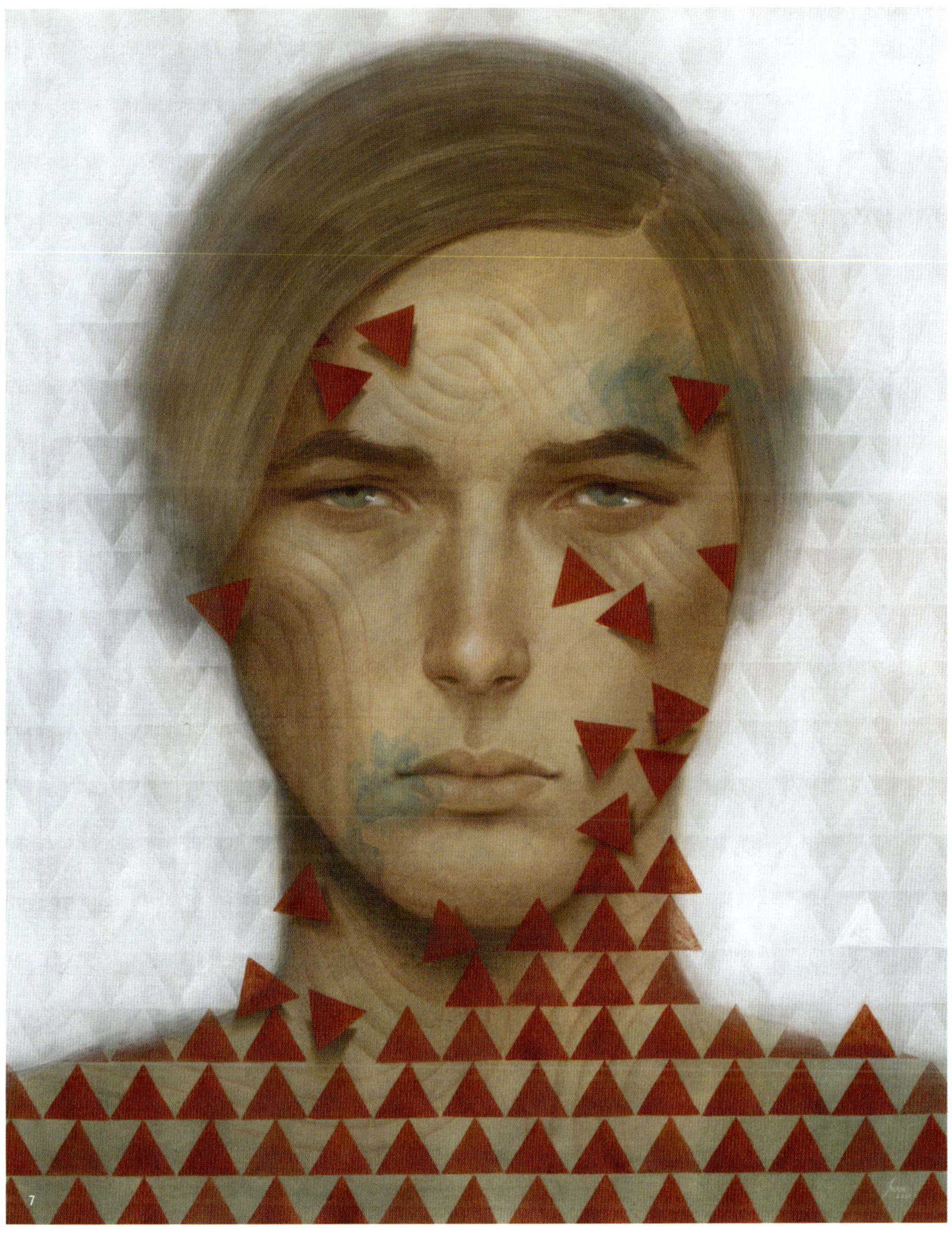

Tran Nguyen

USA

www.pockypuu.blogspot.com

1. **Bonjour Said the Prince** (2009). Personal work. Acrylic, colored pencil

2. **Cast into a Rippled Mentality** (2011). Personal work. Acrylic, colored pencil

3. **If the World Keeps Churning, Turning** (2010). Personal work. Acrylic, colored pencil

4. **The Man With the Occupied Hands** (2011). Personal work. Acrylic, colored pencil

5. **What the World Doesn't Know** (2010). Personal work. Acrylic, colored pencil

6. **Our Flutter - some Ordeal** (2009). Personal work. Acrylic, colored pencil

7. **Rearranging Your Cluttered Mind** (2010). Personal work. Acrylic, colored pencil

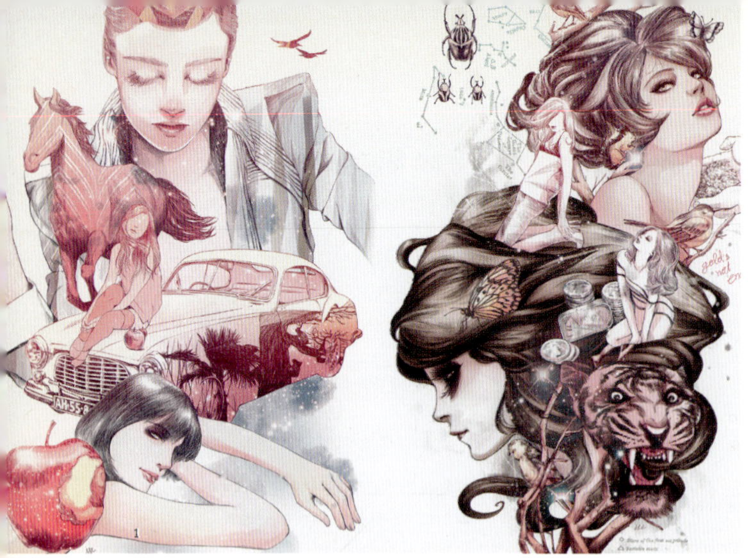

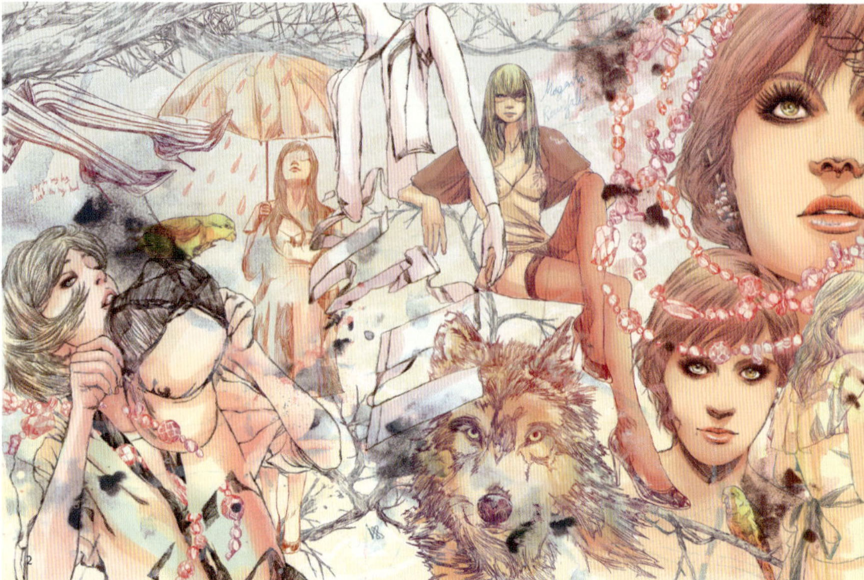

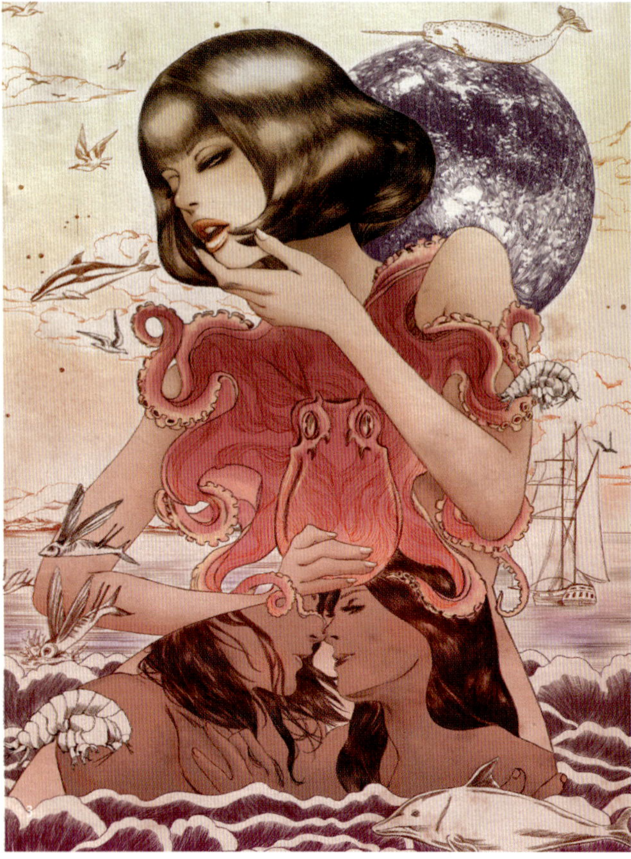

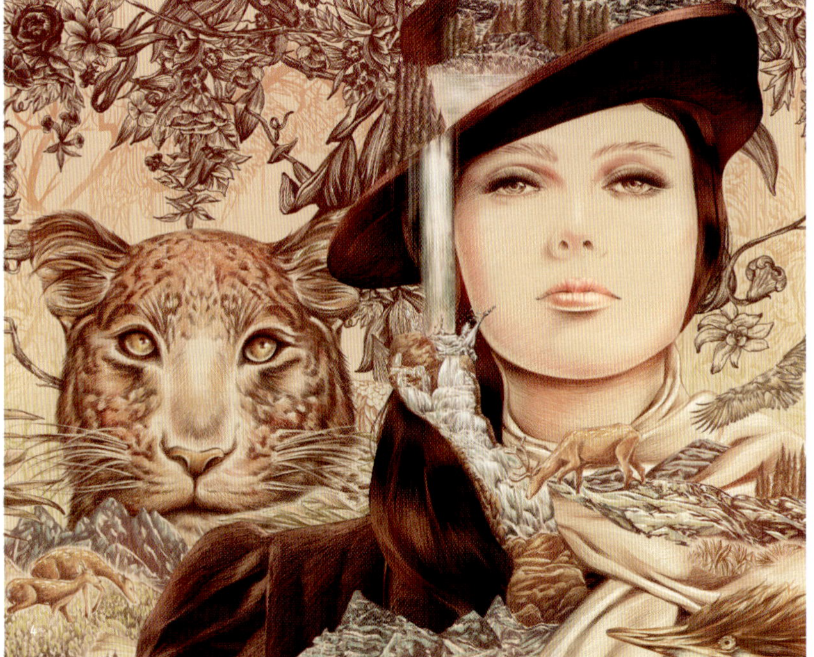

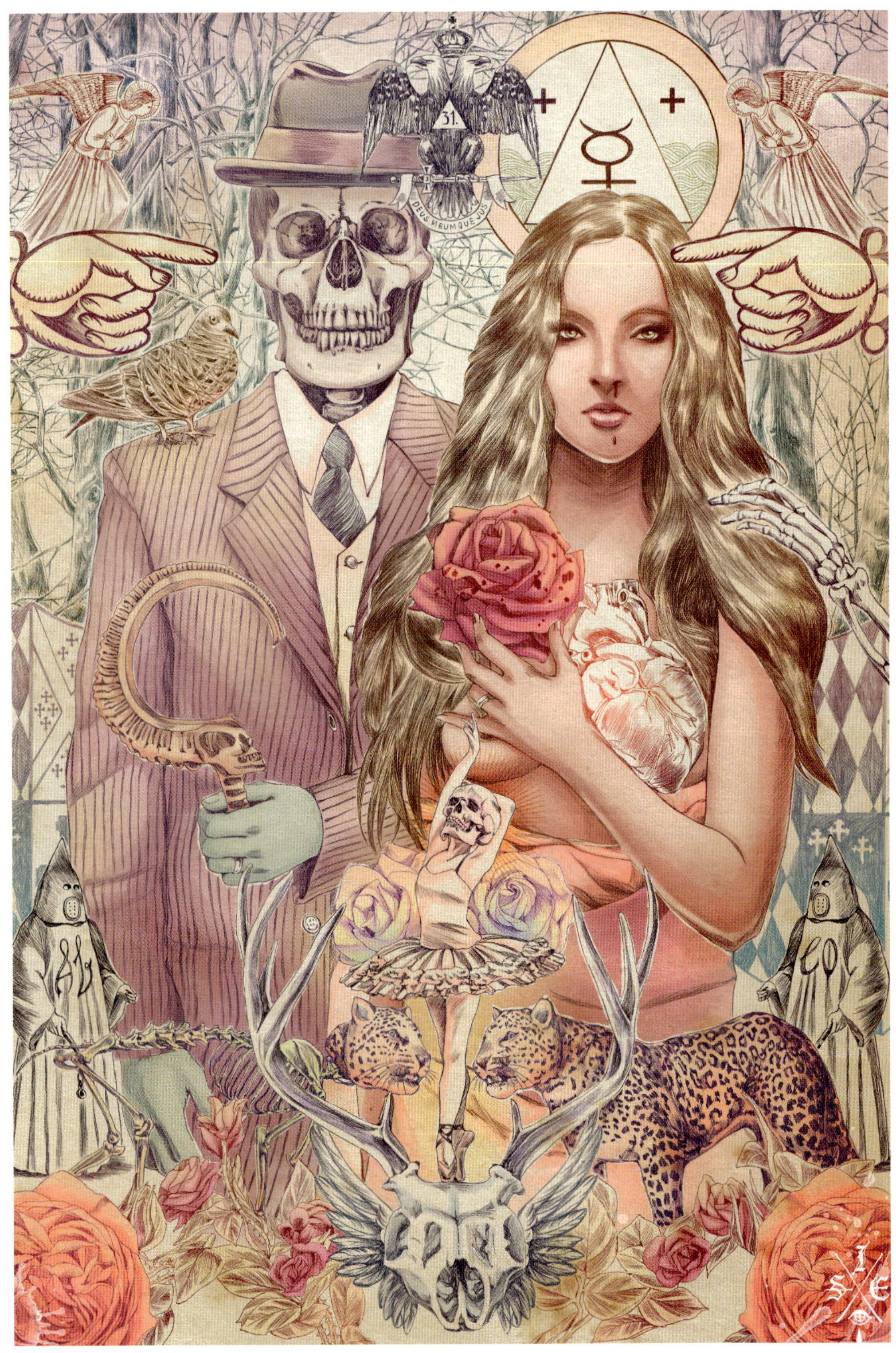

1. **Gold and Silver** (2009). *LIPS Magazine*

2. **Rainy** (2007). *Chick Happens Magazine*

3. **Octopus Lovers** (2009). Personal work

4. **True Nature** (2011). Personal work

5. **The Death** (2008). *LIPS Magazine*

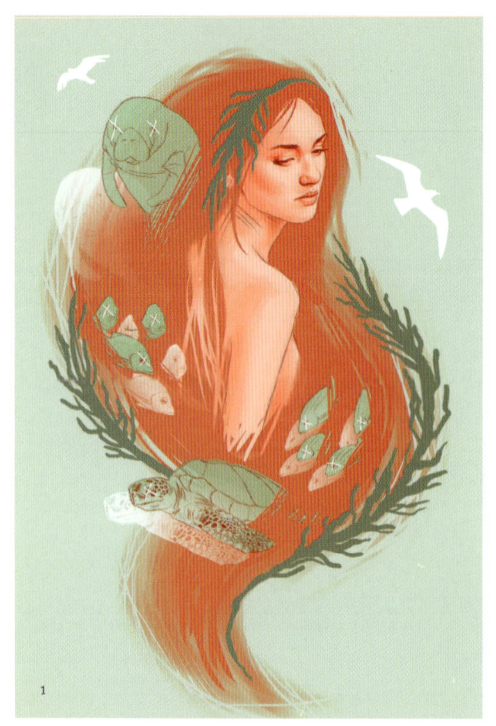

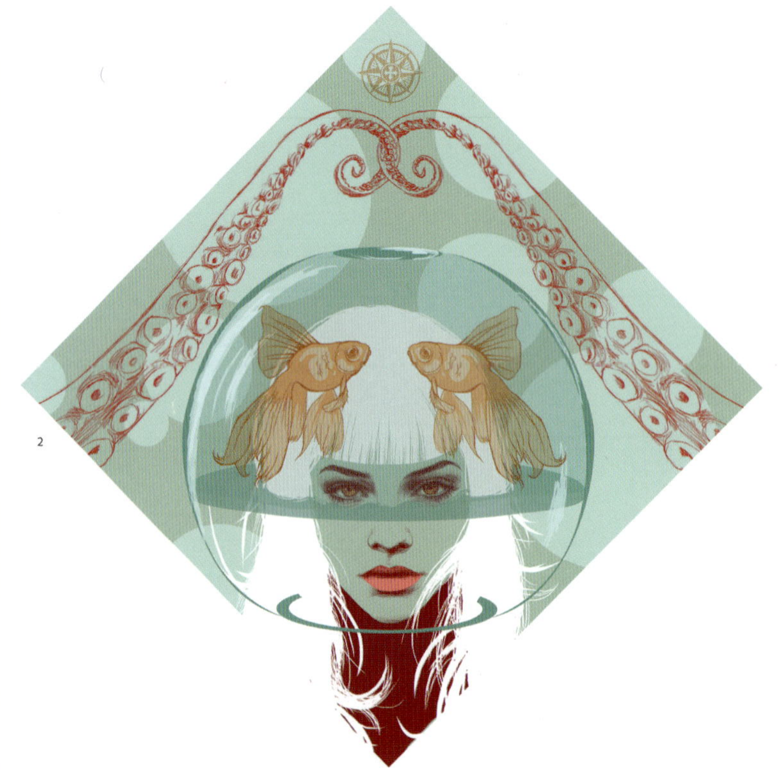

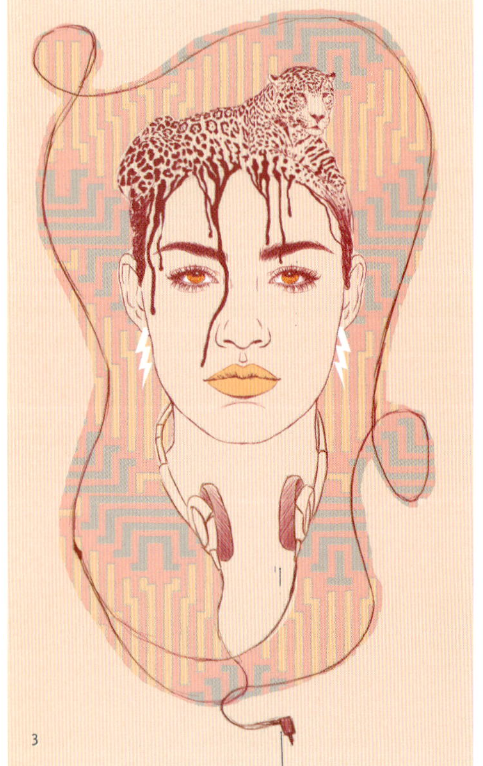

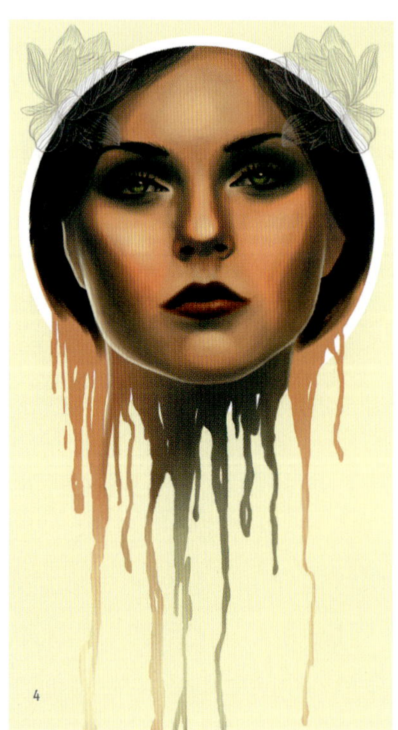

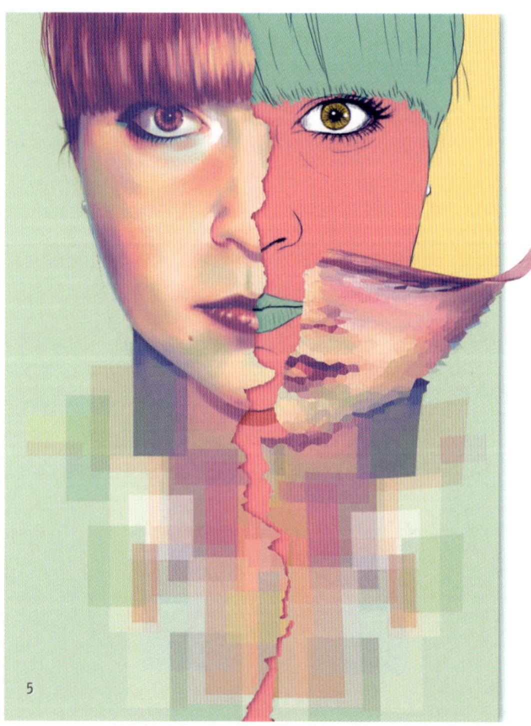

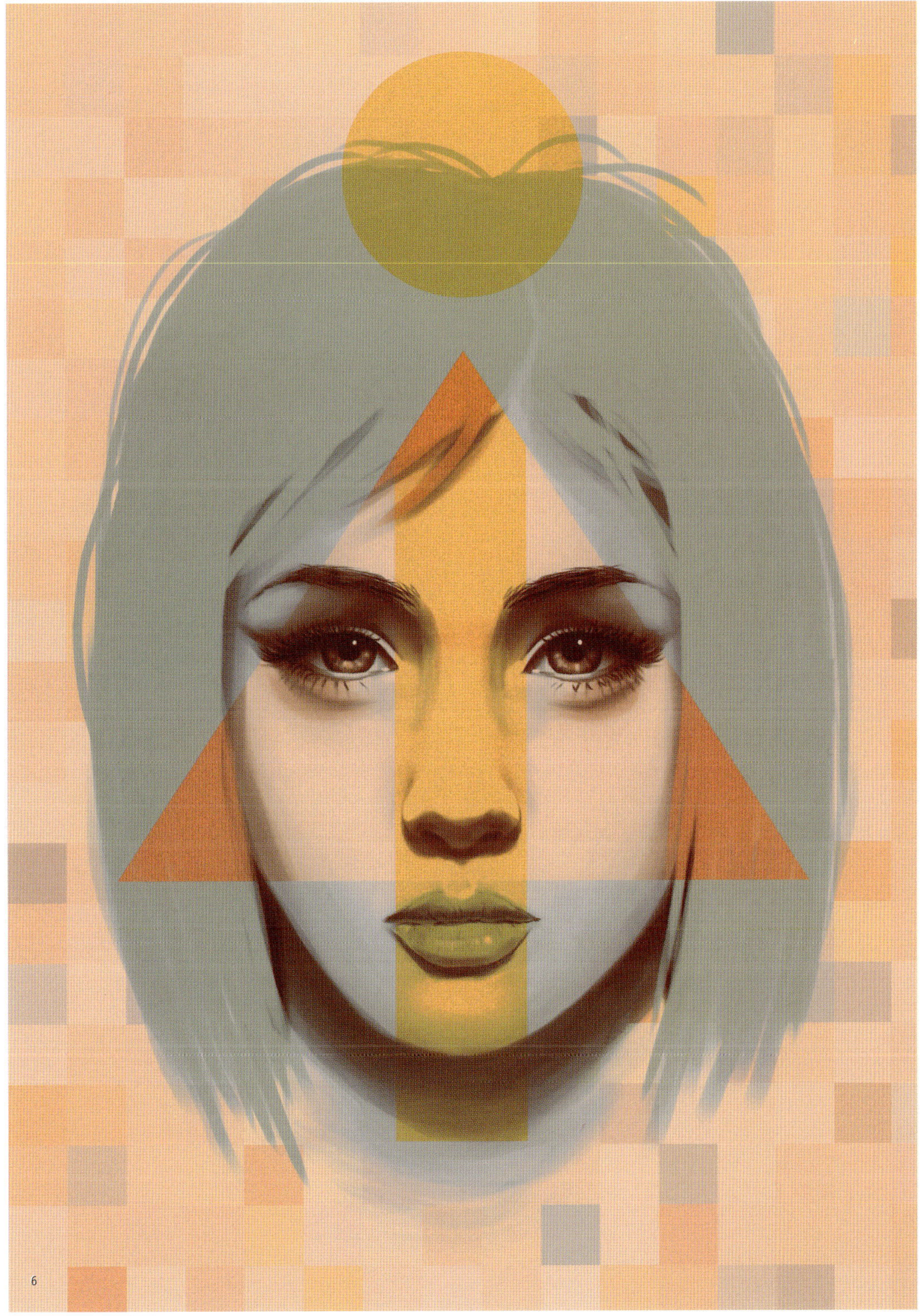

Isabel Arenas
USA

www.iarenasdesign.com

1. **Red Tide** (2011). Mote Marine Laboratory. Digital

2. **Nautical Surrealism** (2010). Personal work. Digital

3. **Flashback** (2011). Personal work. Digital

4. **Goddess** (2011). Personal work. Digital

5. **Self Portrait No.2** (2011). Personal work. Digital

6. **Reinvention** (2011). Personal work. Digital

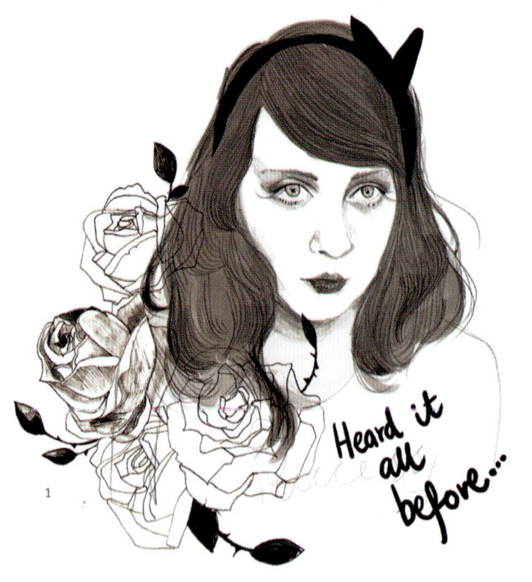
Heard it all before...

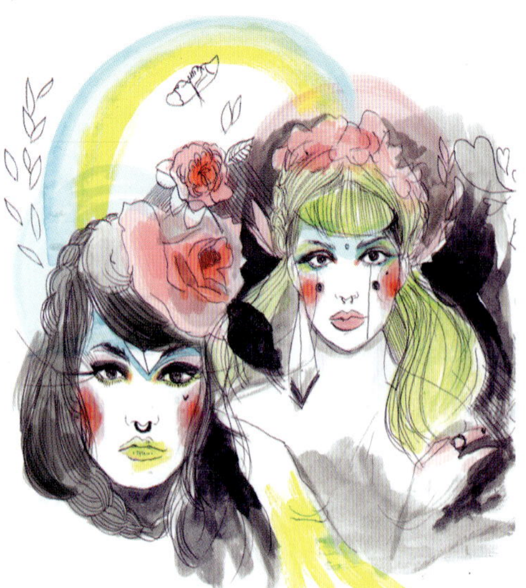

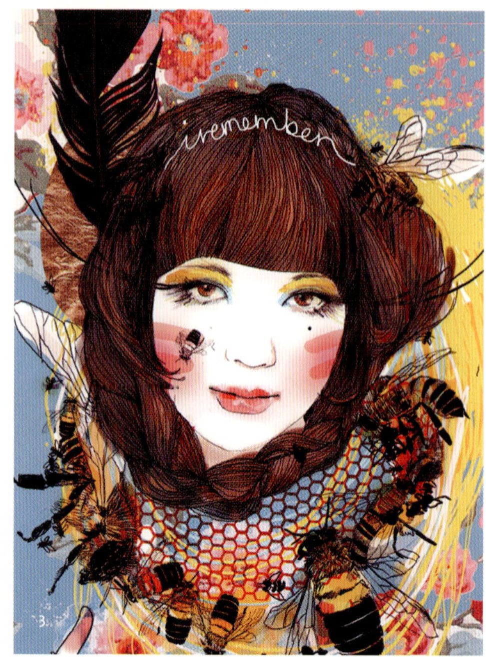
remember

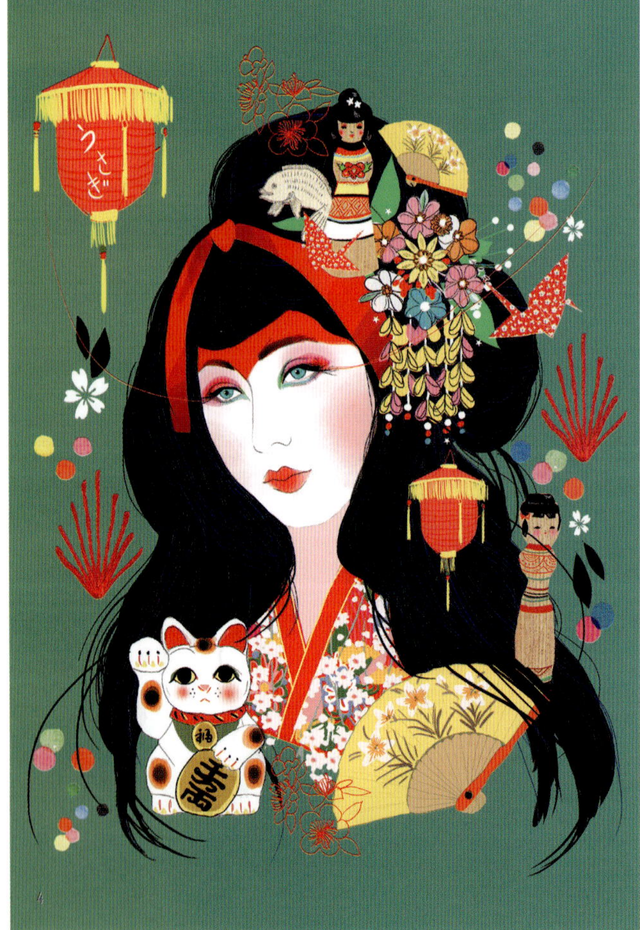

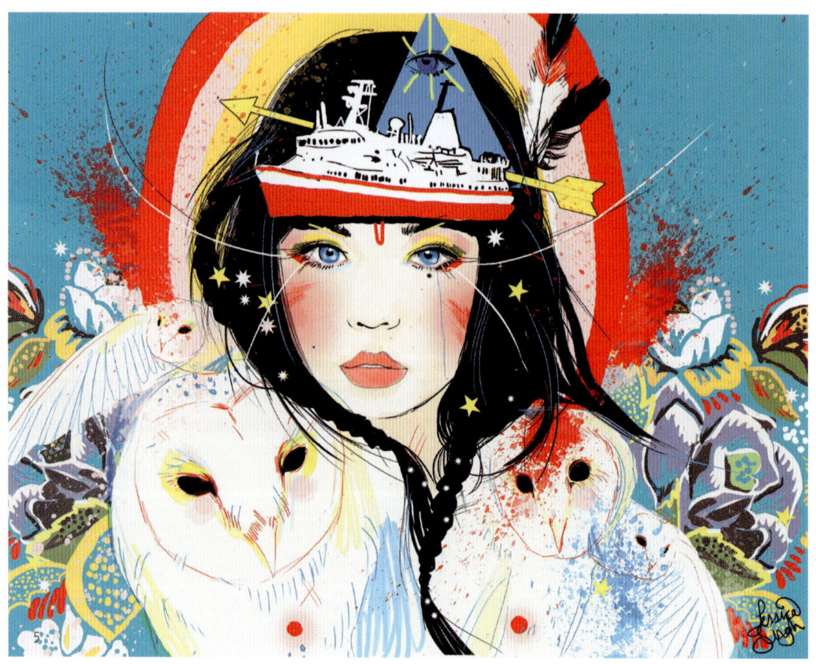

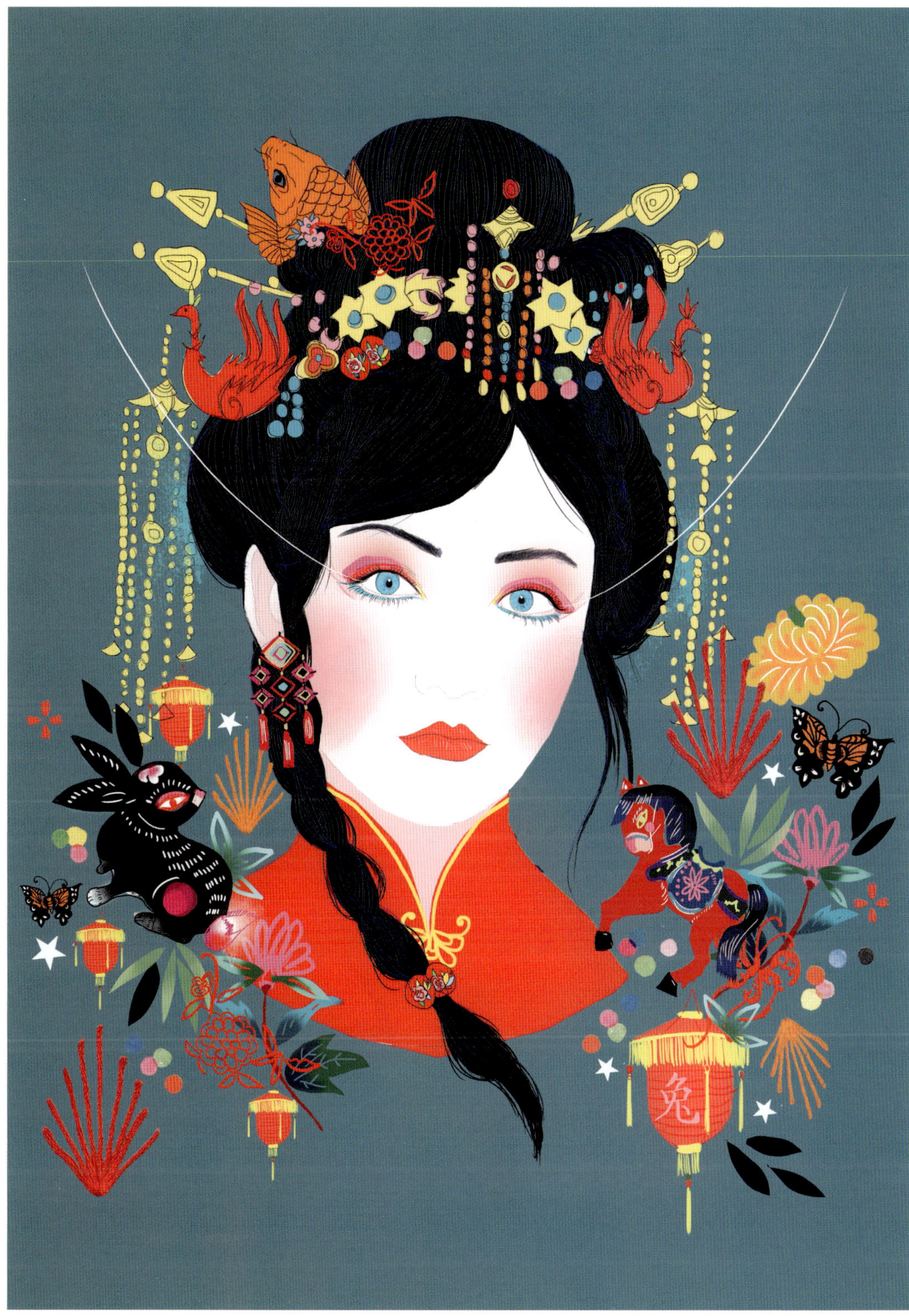

Jessica Singh

Australia

www.jessicasingh.com

1. **Long Gone Down** (2011). Personal work. Pencil, digital

2. **Rapunzel** (2011). Personal work. Ink, watercolor

3. **You Stung Me** (2009). Personal Work. Digital

4. **Usagi** (2011). Personal Work. Digital

5. **Sierra** (2010). Personal Work. Digital

6. **Xiao Baitu** (2011). Personal Work. Digital

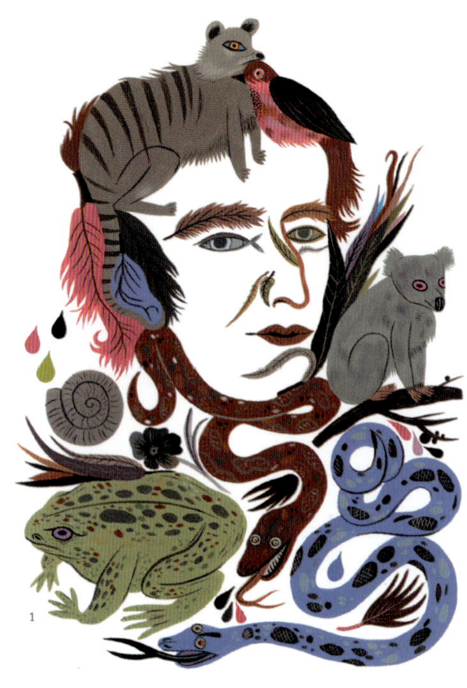

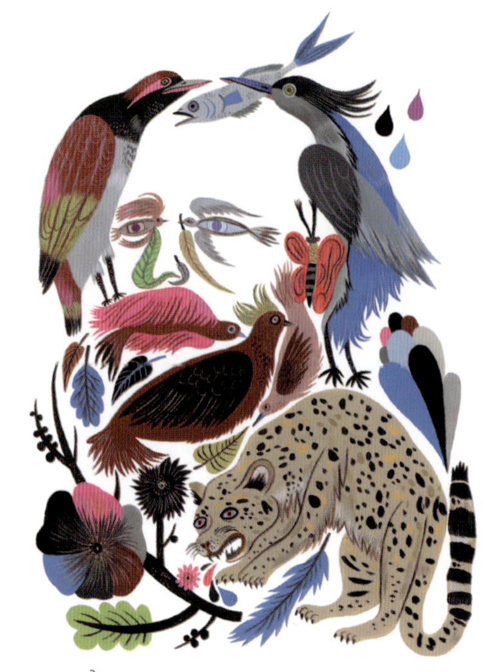

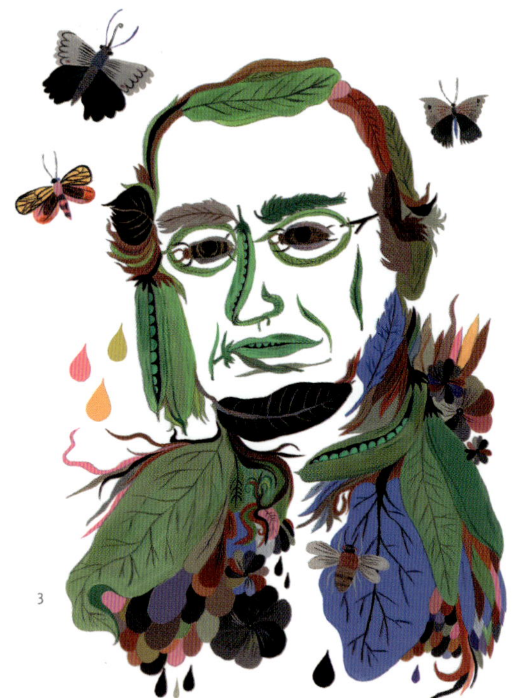

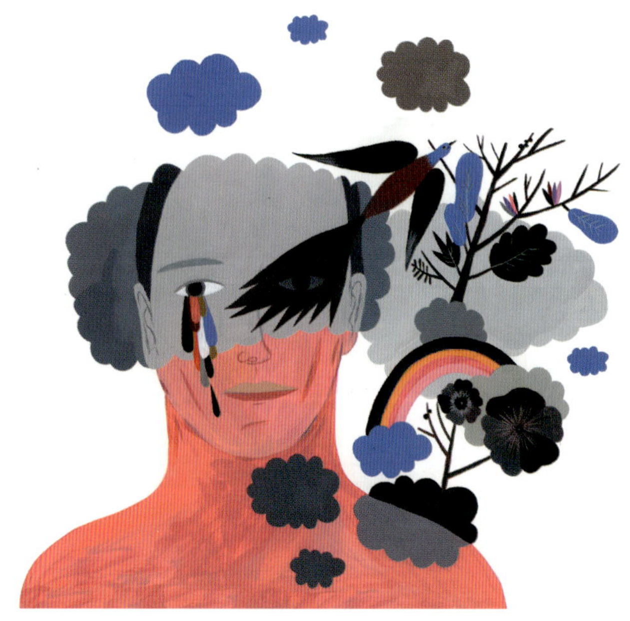

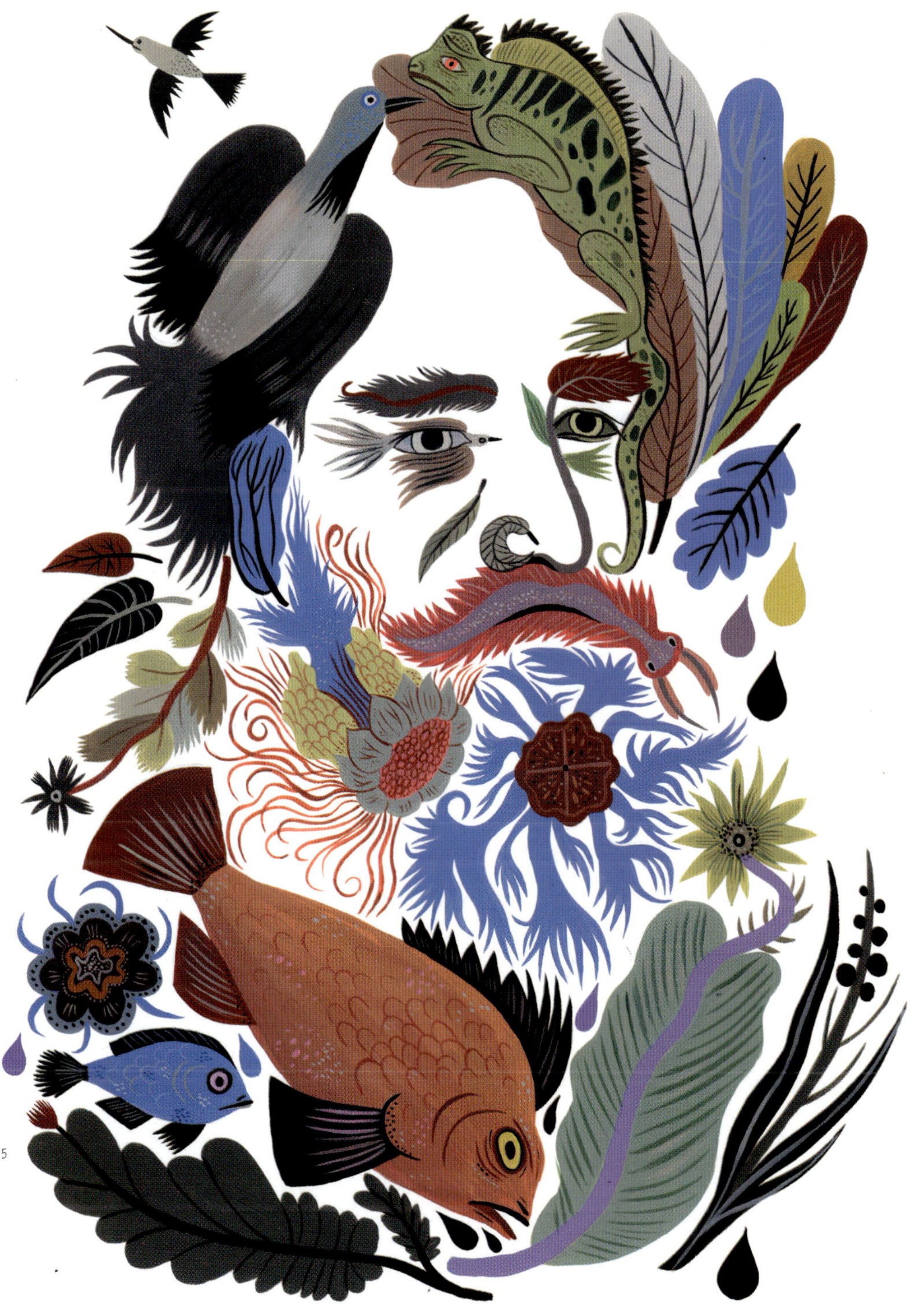

Carolin Löbbert
Germany

www.carolinloebbert.de

1. **Georges Cuvier** (2010). *Das Magazin*. Acrylic on bristol cardboard

2. **Alfred Brehm** (2010). *Das Magazin*. Acrylic on bristol cardboard

3. **Gregor Mendel** (2010). *Das Magazin*. Acrylic on bristol cardboard

4. **Träume vom Fliegen** (2008). Personal work. Acrylic on bristol cardboard

5. **Ernst Haeckel** (2010). *Das Magazin*. Acrylic on bristol cardboard

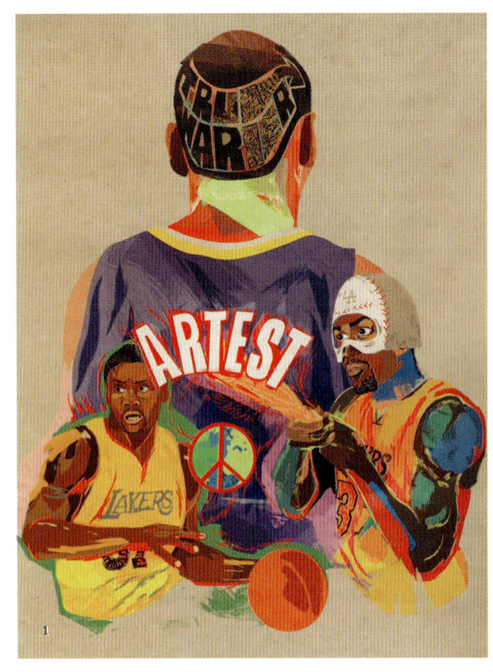

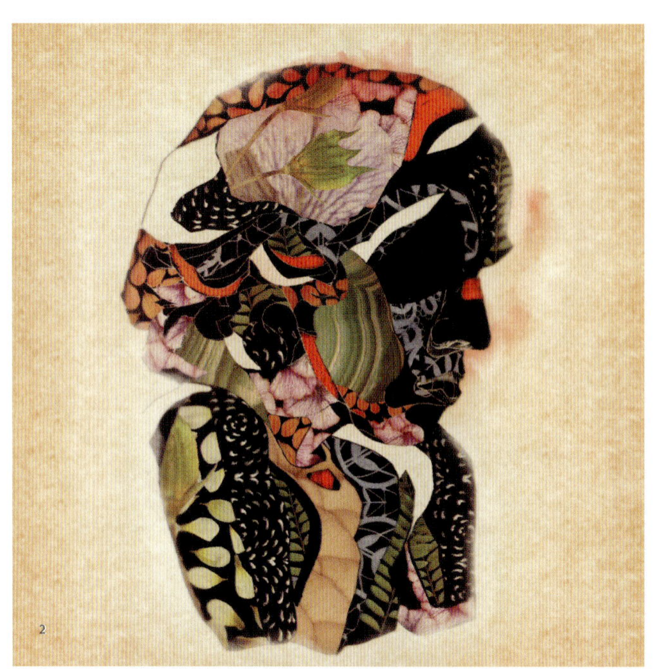

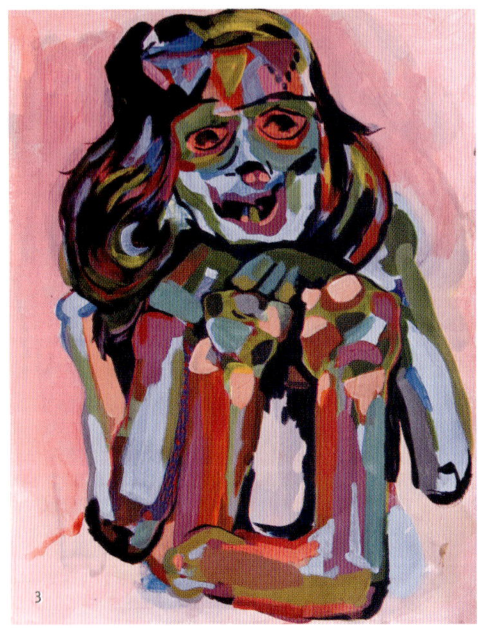

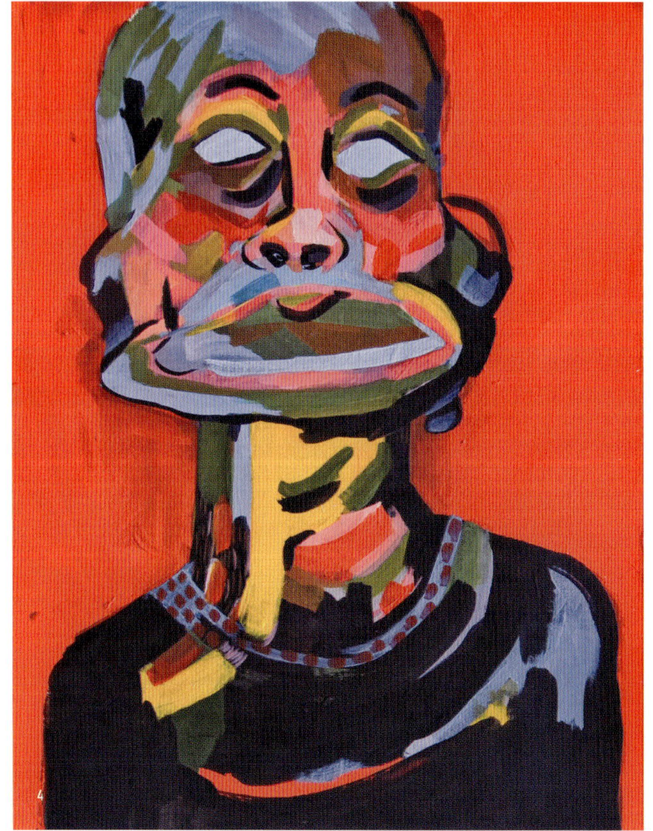

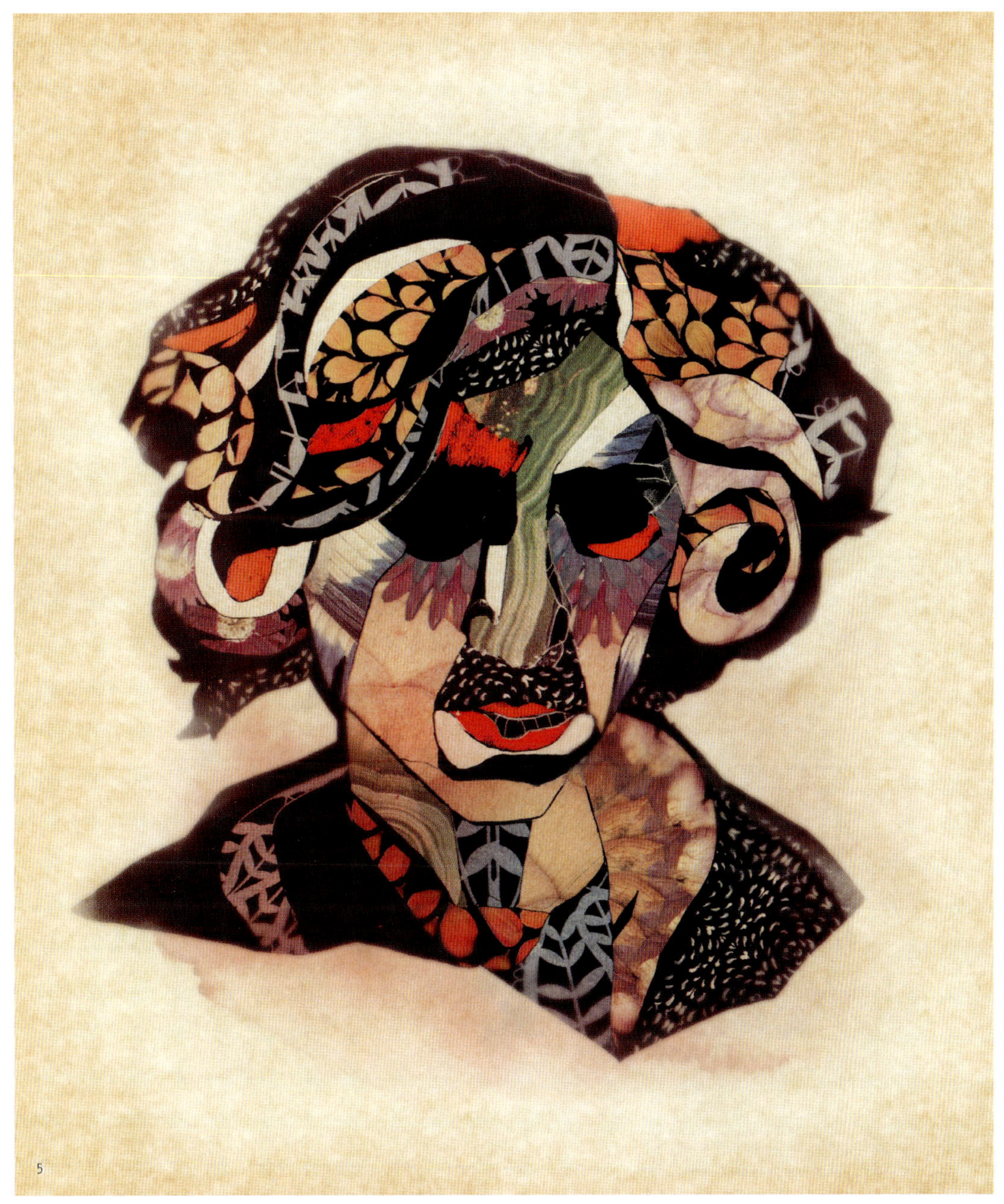

5

Sam Hoh
Australia

www.deepfriedsam.com

1. **Ron Artest** (2011). *Ball Street Journal.*
   Digital

2. **Wallflowers 1** (2009). Personal work.
   Collage, digital

3. **Nazca Mummy** (2011). Personal work.
   Acrylic on paper

4. **Africa** (2011). Personal work. Acrylic on
   paper

5. **Wallflowers 2** (2009). Personal work.
   Collage, digital

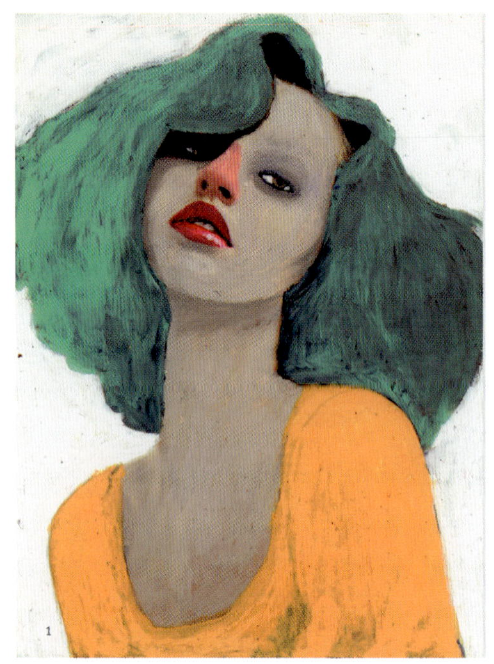

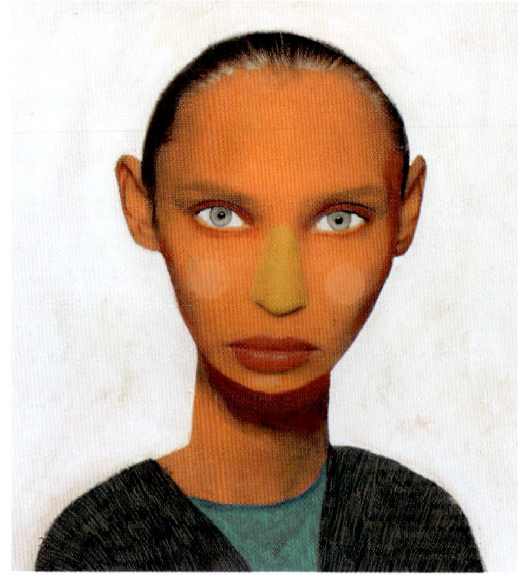

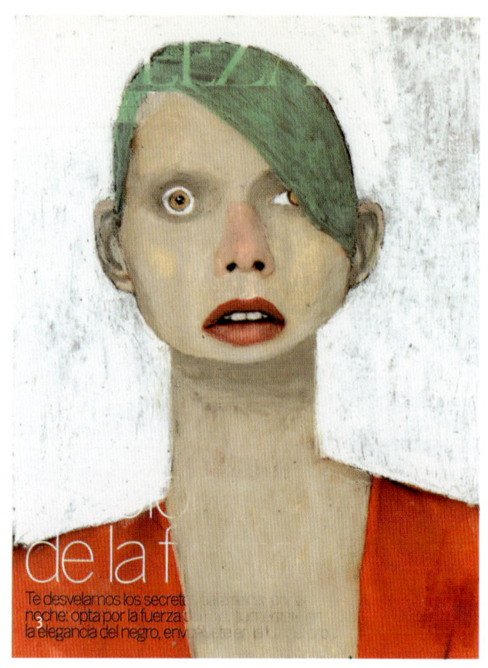

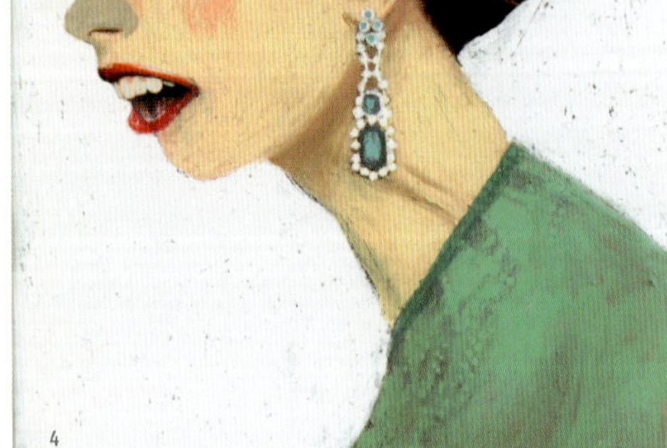

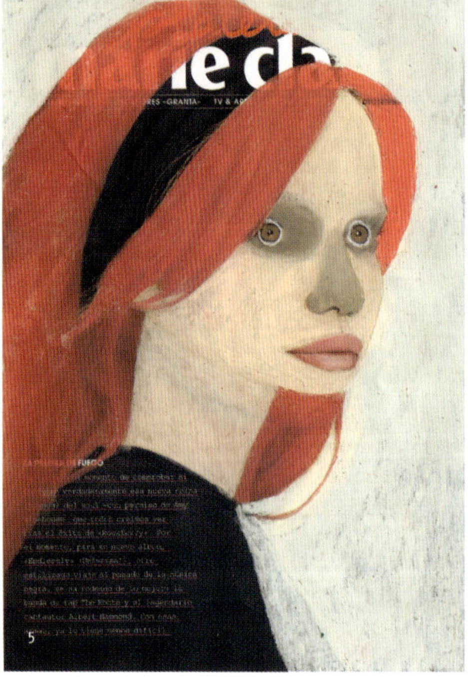

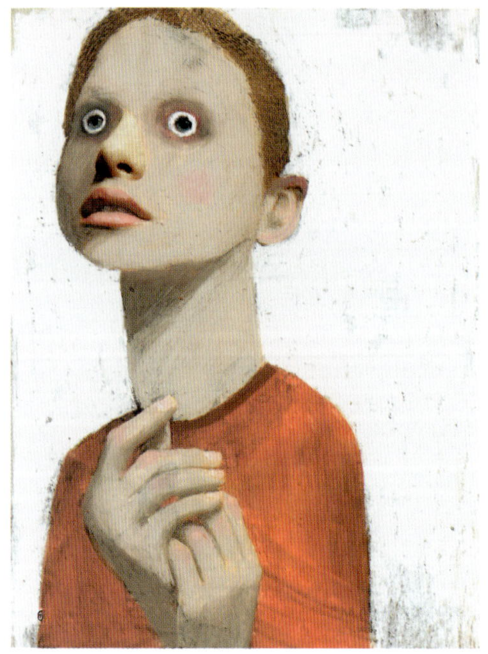

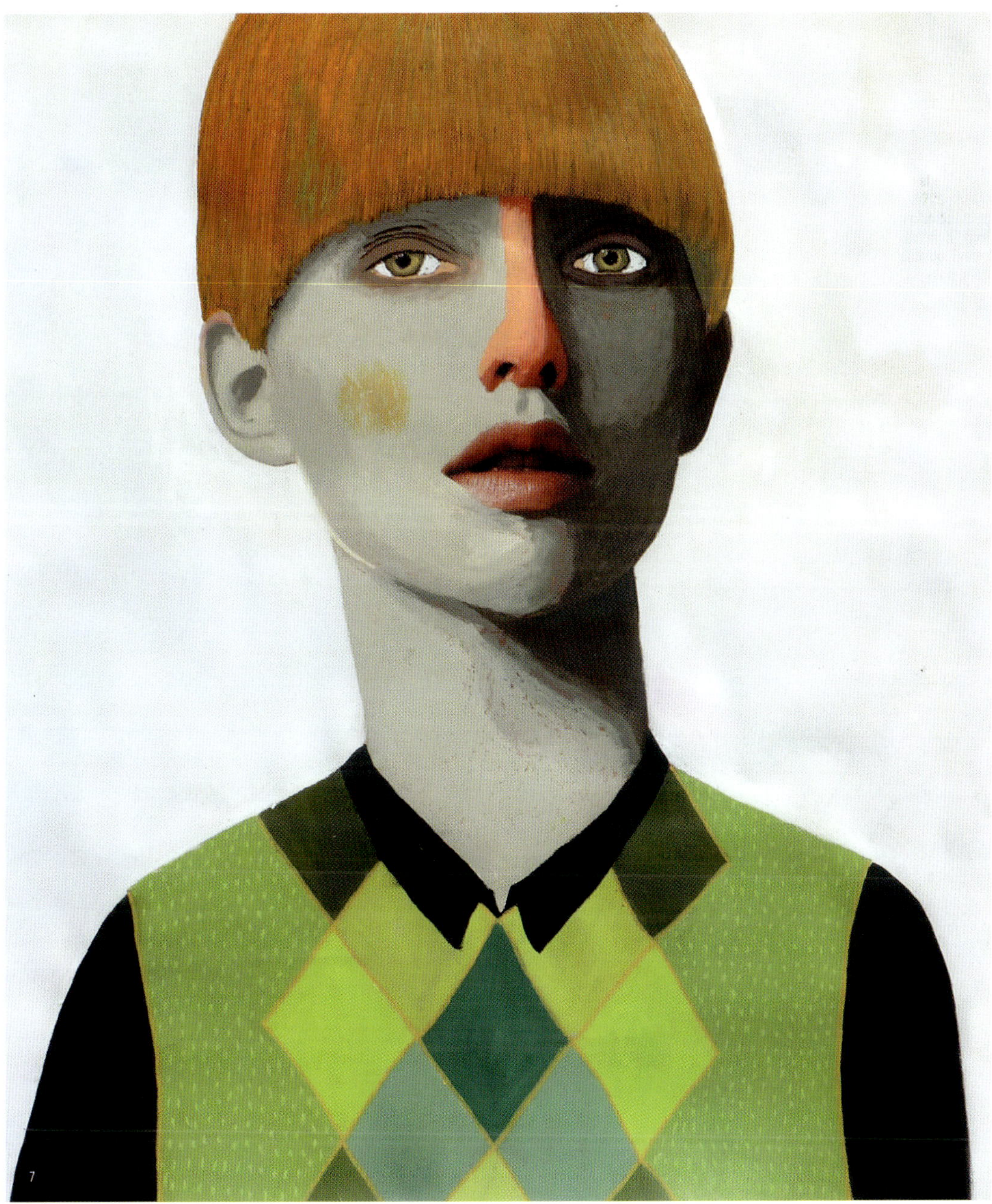

Guim Tió Zarraluki

Spain

www.guimtio.blogspot.com

1. **Maria** (2011). Personal work. Wax on magazine

2. **Orson** (2011). Tipos Infames books & wines. Mixed on digital print

3. **Olins** (2010). Personal work. Wax on magazine

4. **Dido** (2011). Corretger5 Gallery. Wax on magazine

5. **Claire** (2010). Artevistas Gallery. Wax on magazine

6. **Clark** (2011). *Body Snatchers* exhibition. Wax on magazine

7. **Silas** (2010). Personal work. Mixed on digital print

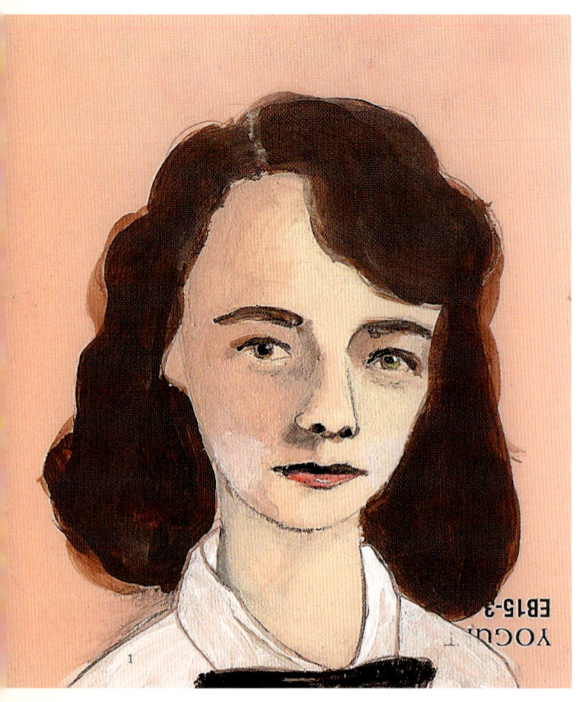
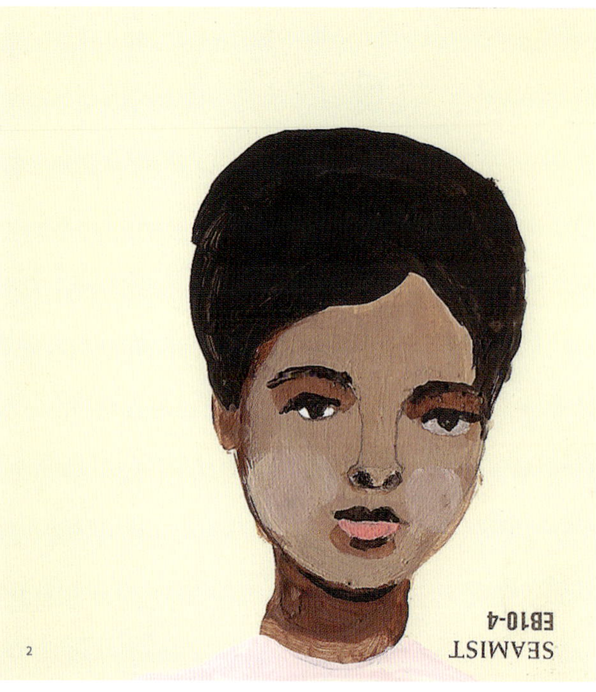
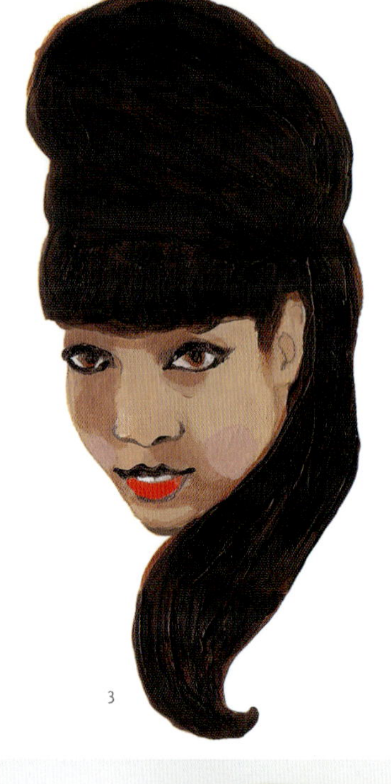
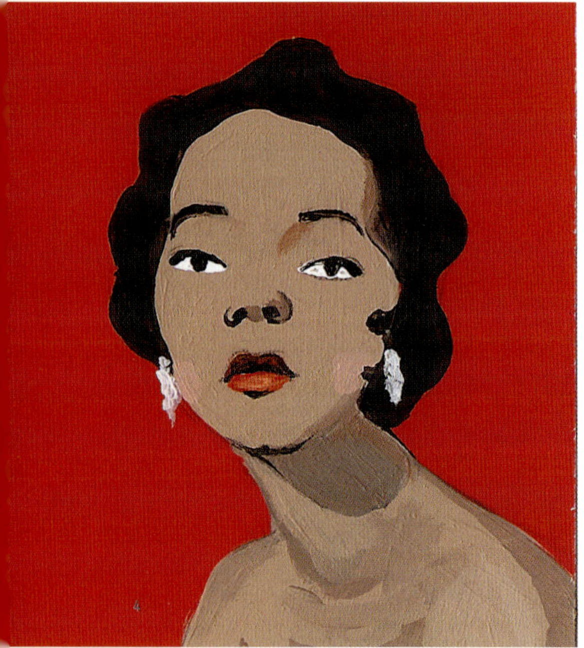
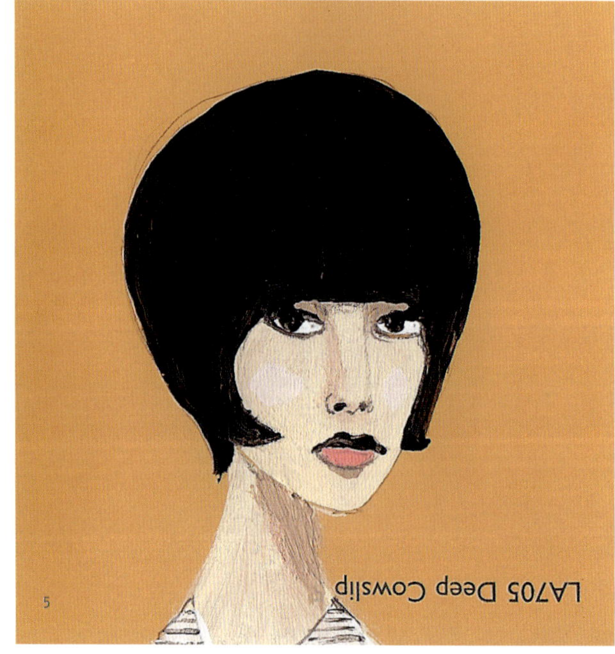
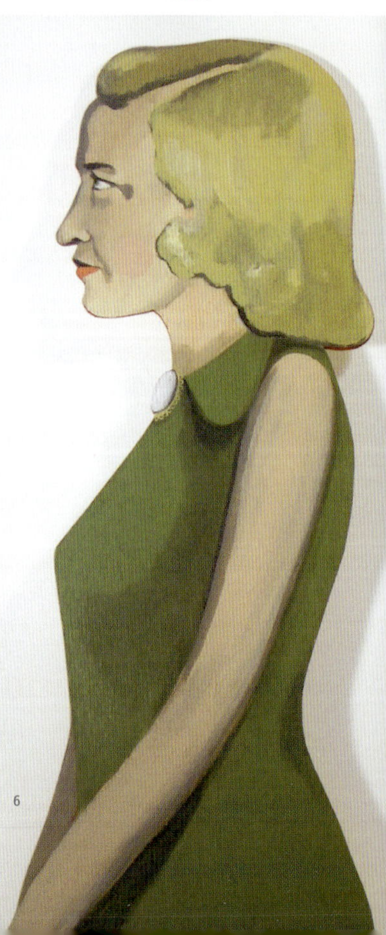

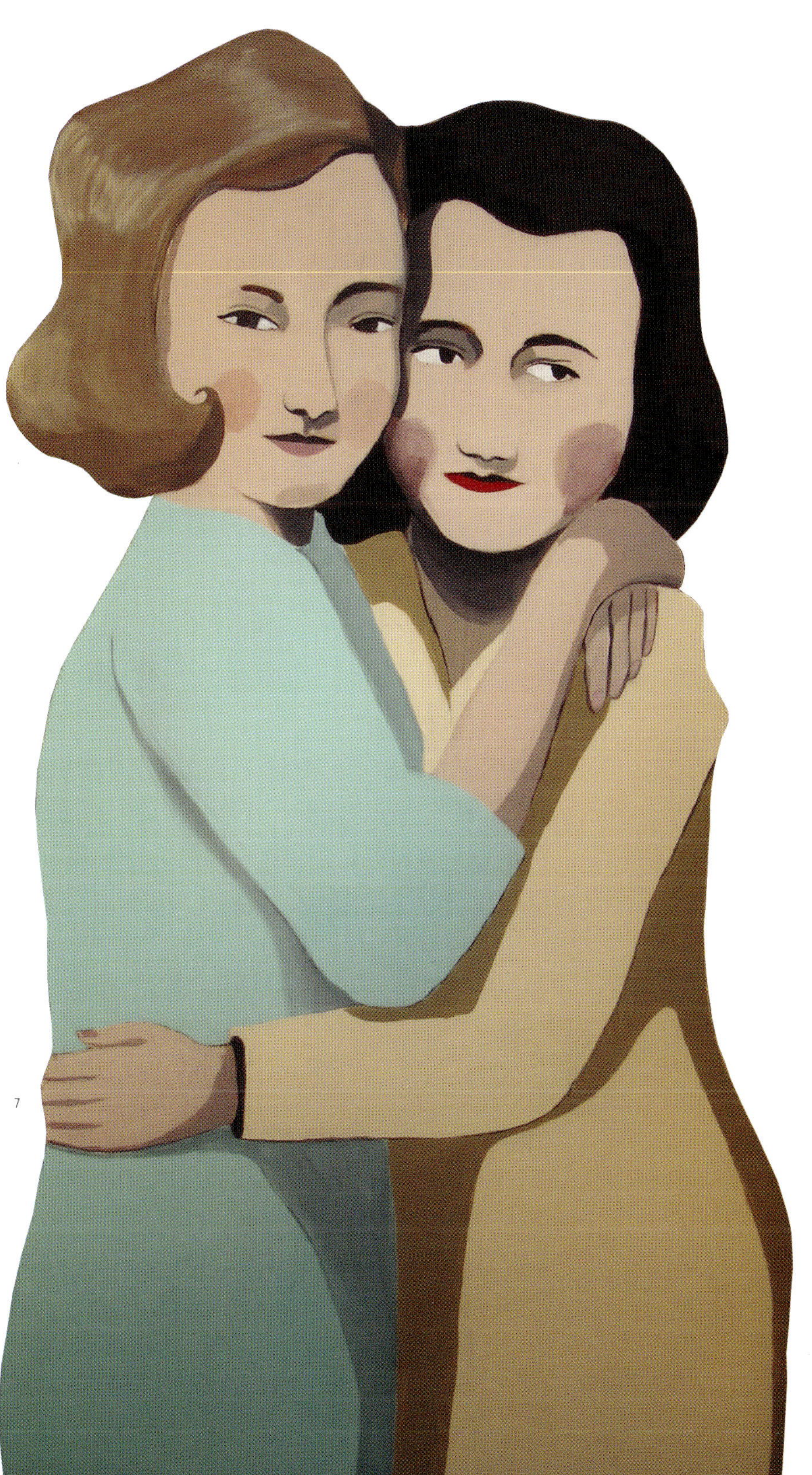

Jordan Grace Owens
USA

www.jordangrace.com

1. **Lucy** (2009). Personal work. Acrylic on paint sample

2. **Seamist** (2009). Personal work. Acrylic on paint sample

3. **Ronnie** (2010). Illustration for band poster. Acrylic on paper

4. **Lady on Red** (2009). Personal work. Acrylic on paint sample

5. **Deep Cowslip** (2009). Personal work. Acrylic on paint sample

6. **Green Dress** (in profile) (2010). Personal work. Acrylic on cut plywood

7. **Two Girls** (2011). Personal work. Acrylic on cut plywood

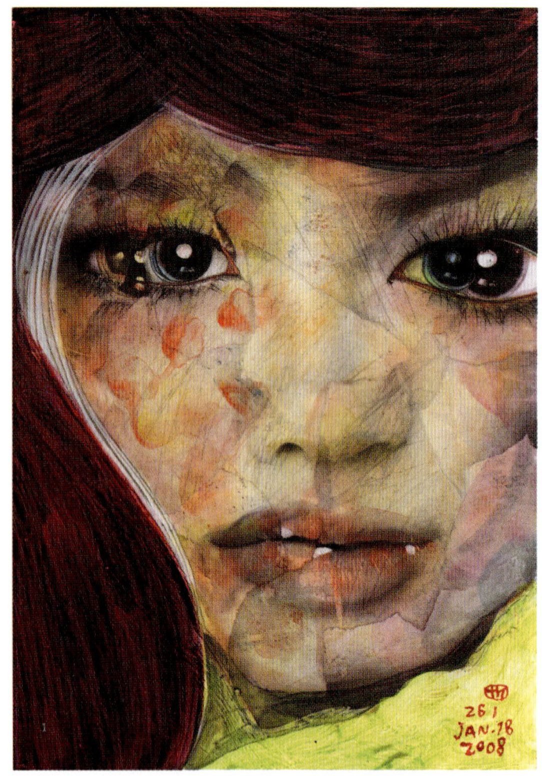

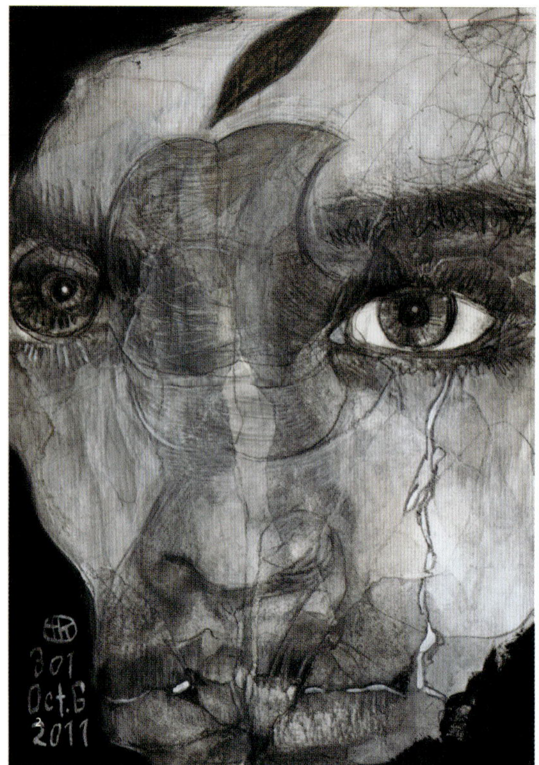

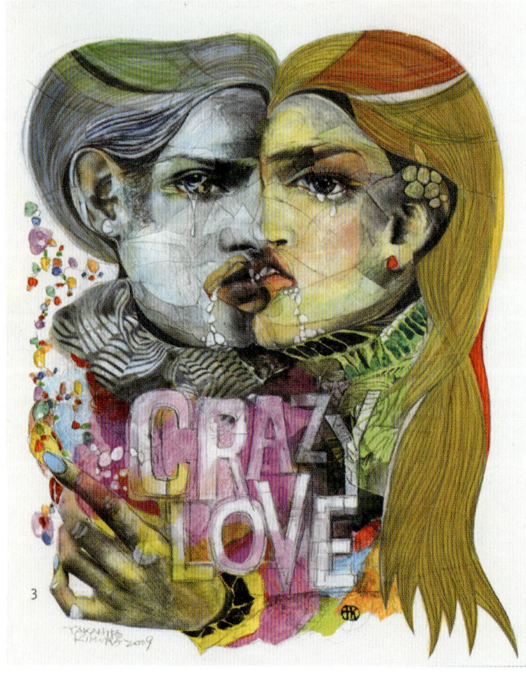
CRAZY
LOVE

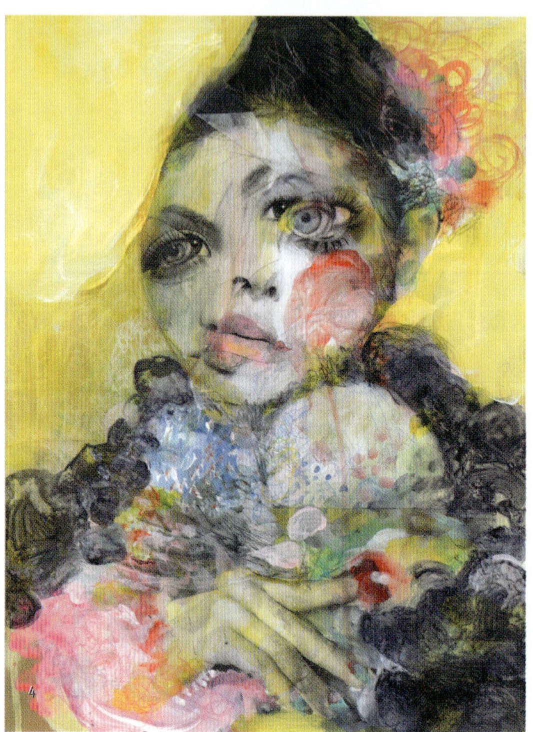

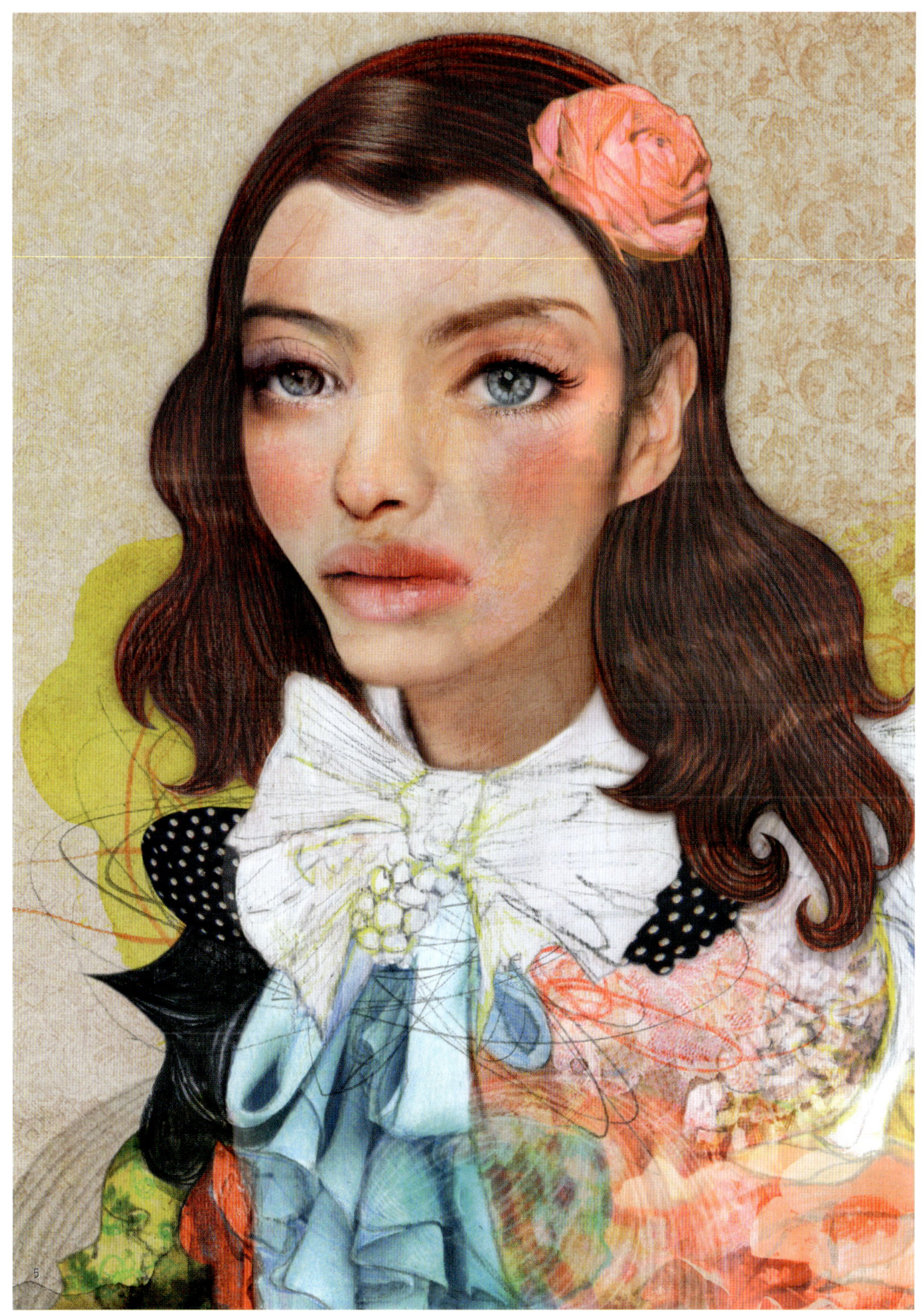

Takahiro Kimura

Japan

www.faceful.jp

1. **Broken Face 261** (2008). Collage on paper

2. **Broken Face 301** (2011). Collage on paper

3. **CRAZY LOVE** (2009). Collage on paper

4. **not ID 005** (2011). Collage on paper

5. **ATTRACTION001** (2011). Collage on paper

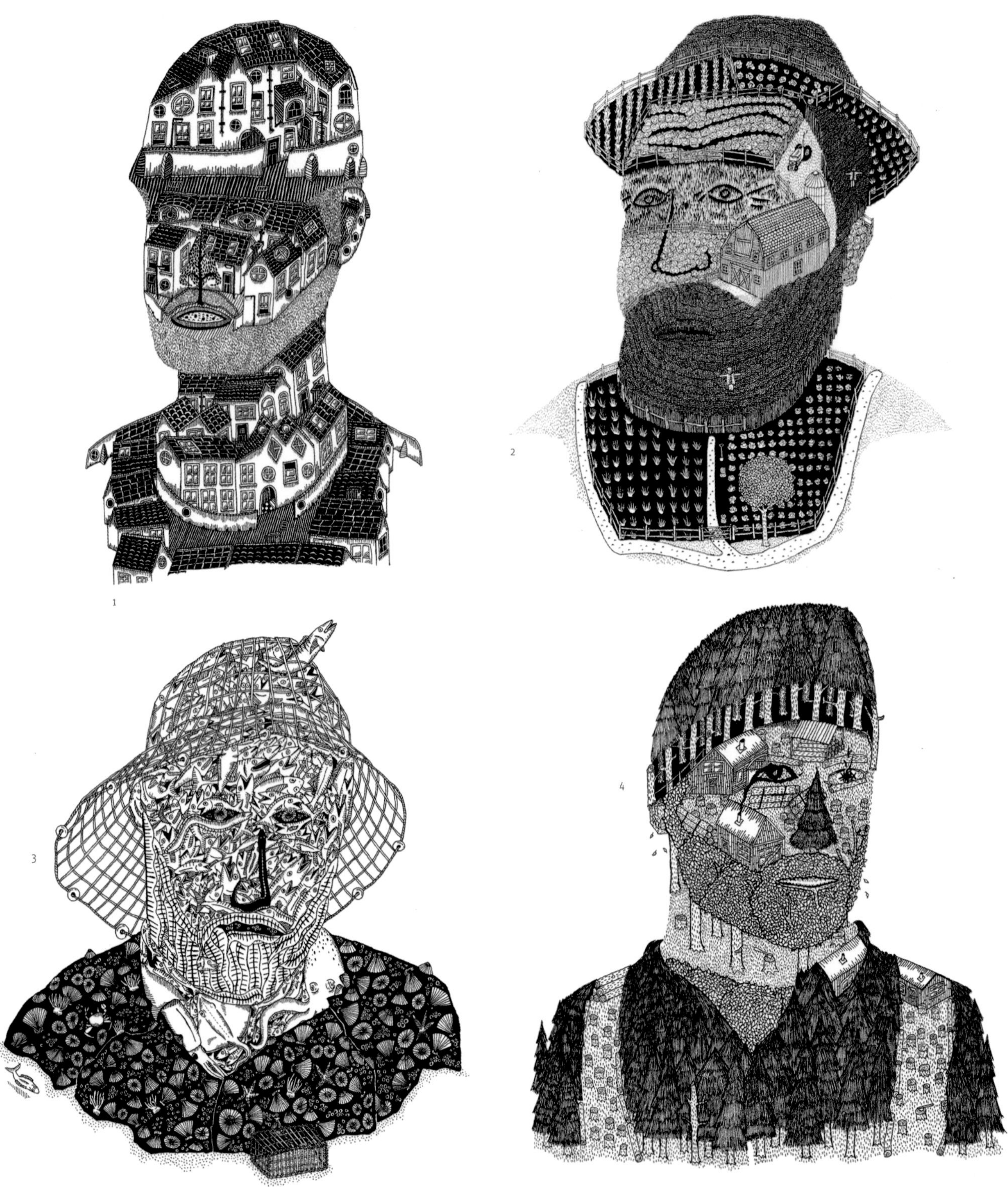

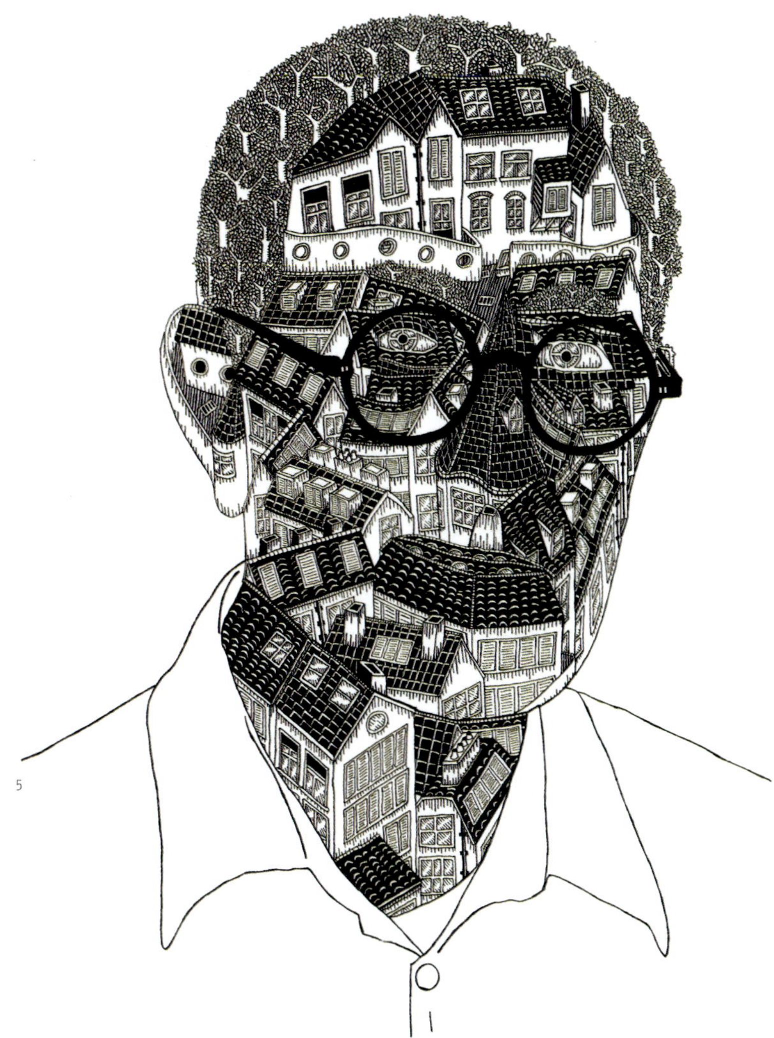

Aidan Meighan
UK

www.meighanillustrations.blogspot.com

1. **Builder** (2011). Personal work. Pen

2. **Farmer** (2011). Personal work. Pen

3. **Fisherman** (2011). Personal work. Pen

4. **Lumberjack** (2011). Personal work. Pen

5. **Sir Peter Cook** (2011). *75 Peters* show. Pen

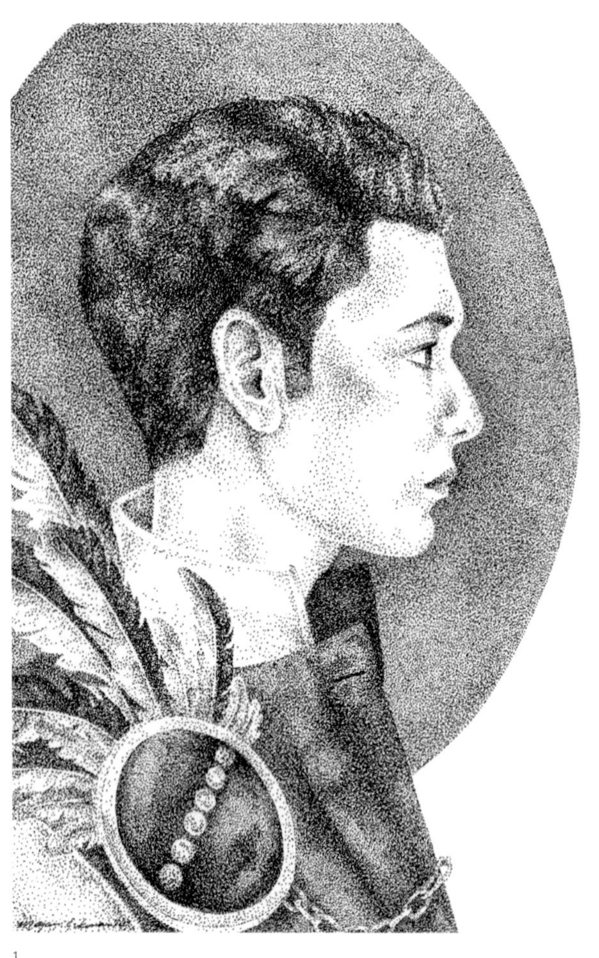

1

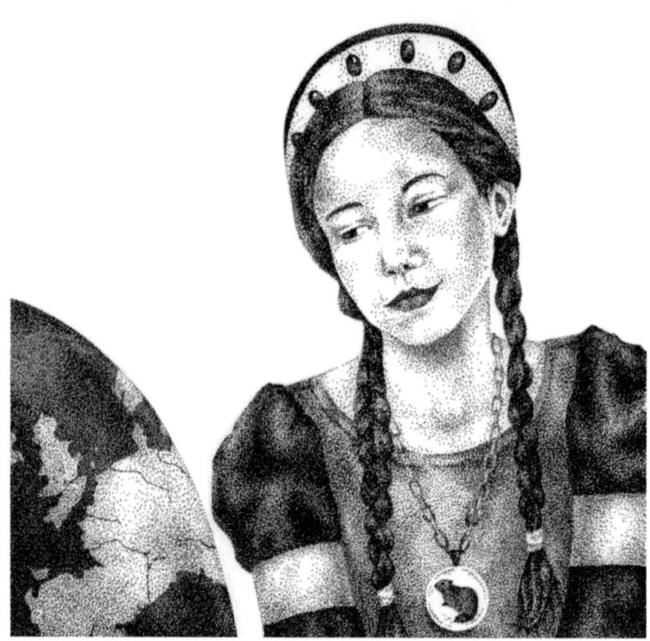

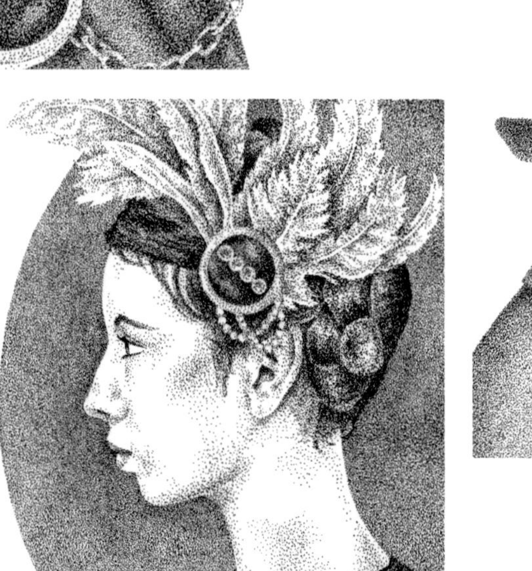

3

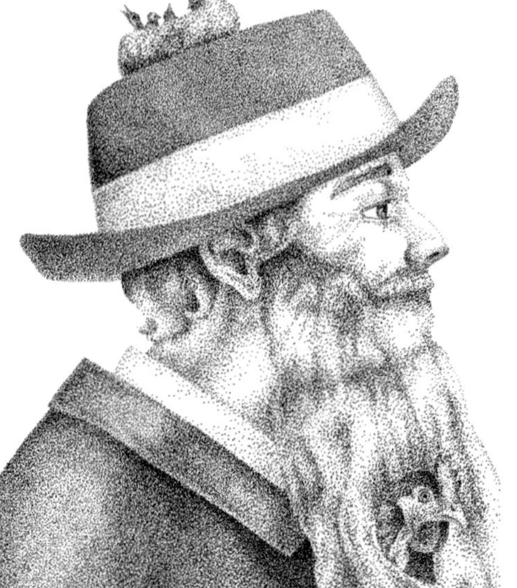

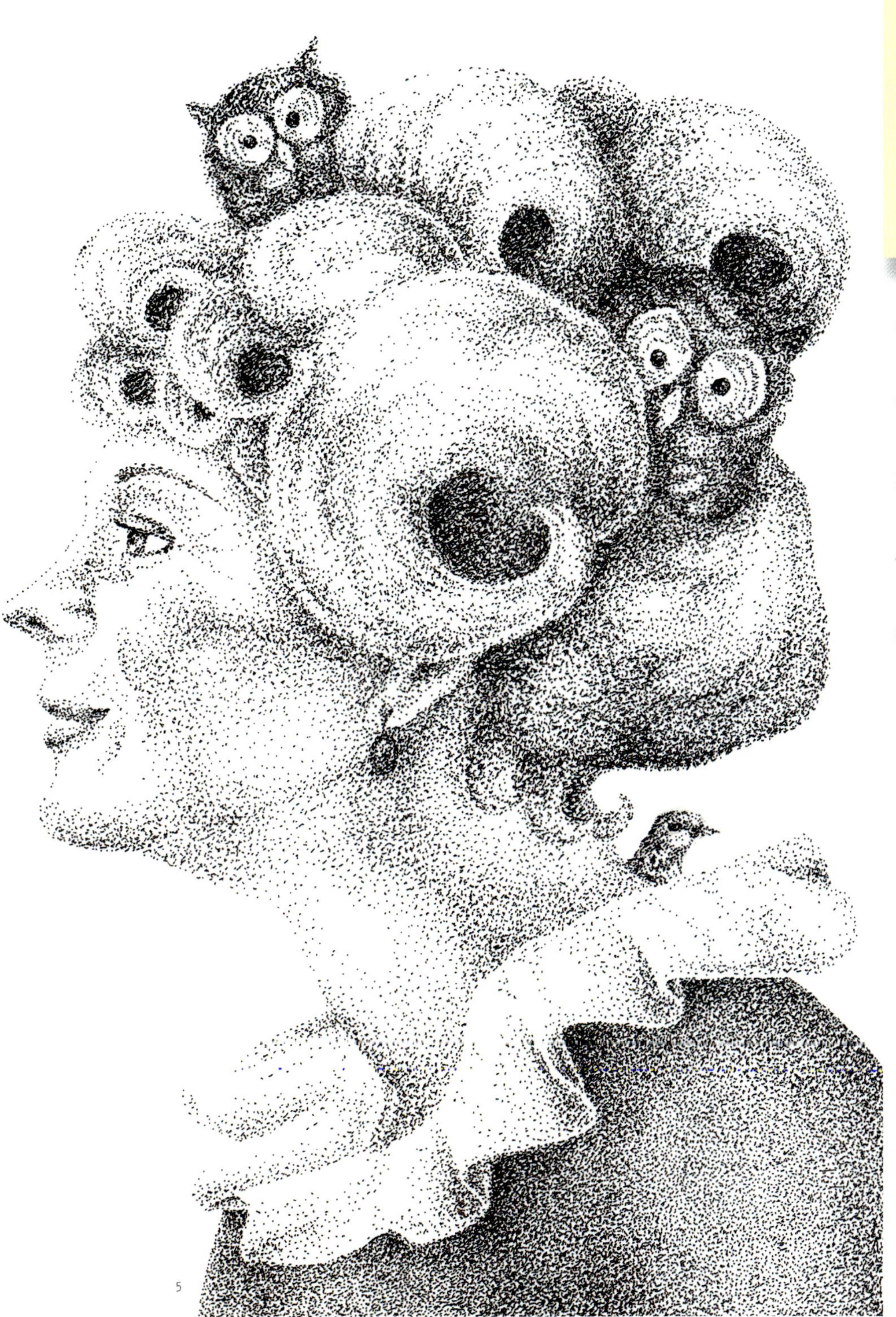

Megan Eckman
USA

www.studiomme.com

1. **Mister Mal Laird** (2011). Personal work. Pen, ink

2. **The Future Lady Marmot** (2012). Personal work. Pen, ink

3. **Miss Oste Rich** (2011). Personal work. Pen, ink

4. **Birds of a Feather** (2010). Personal work. Pen, ink

5. **Flock Together** (2010). Personal work. Pen, ink

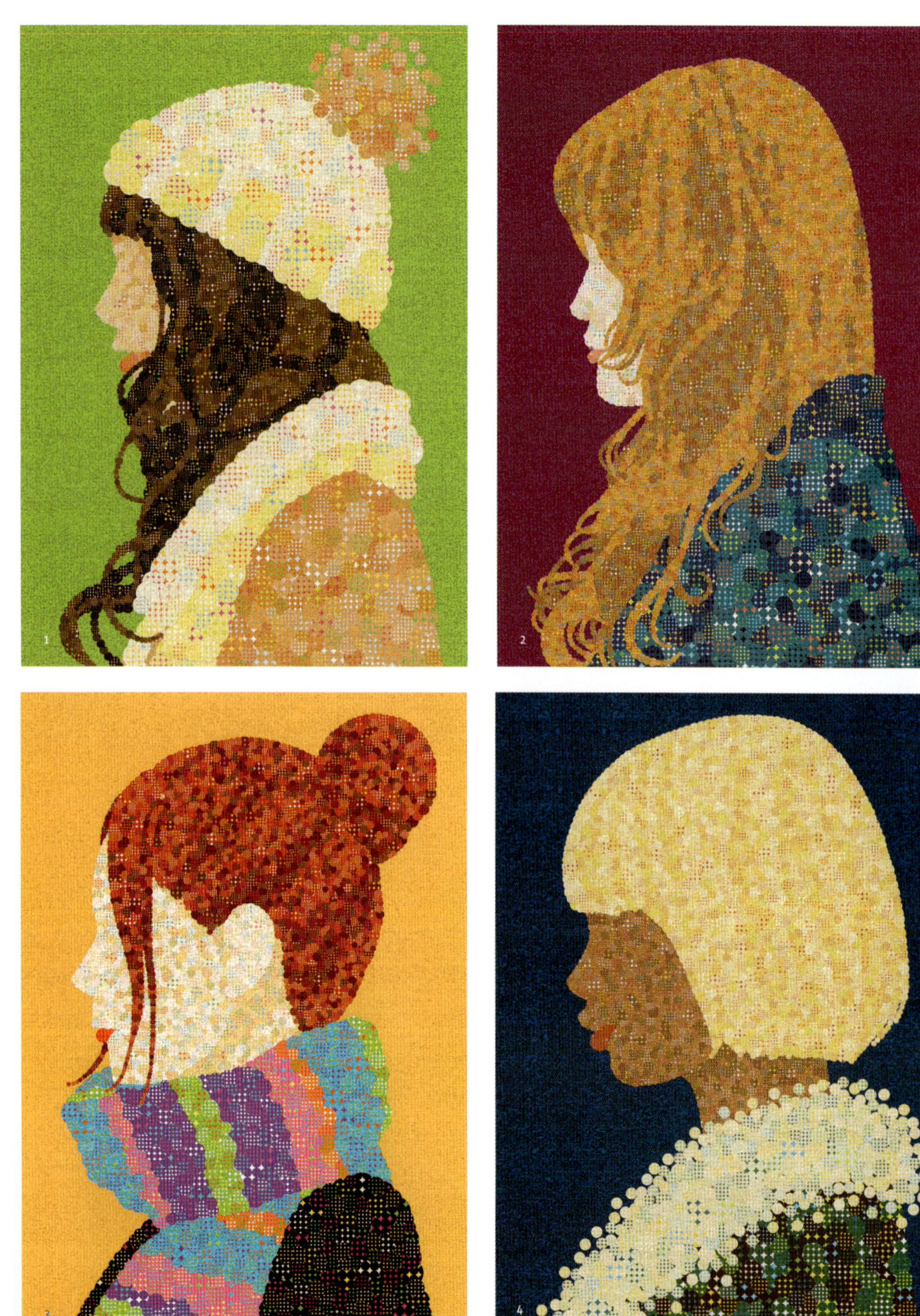

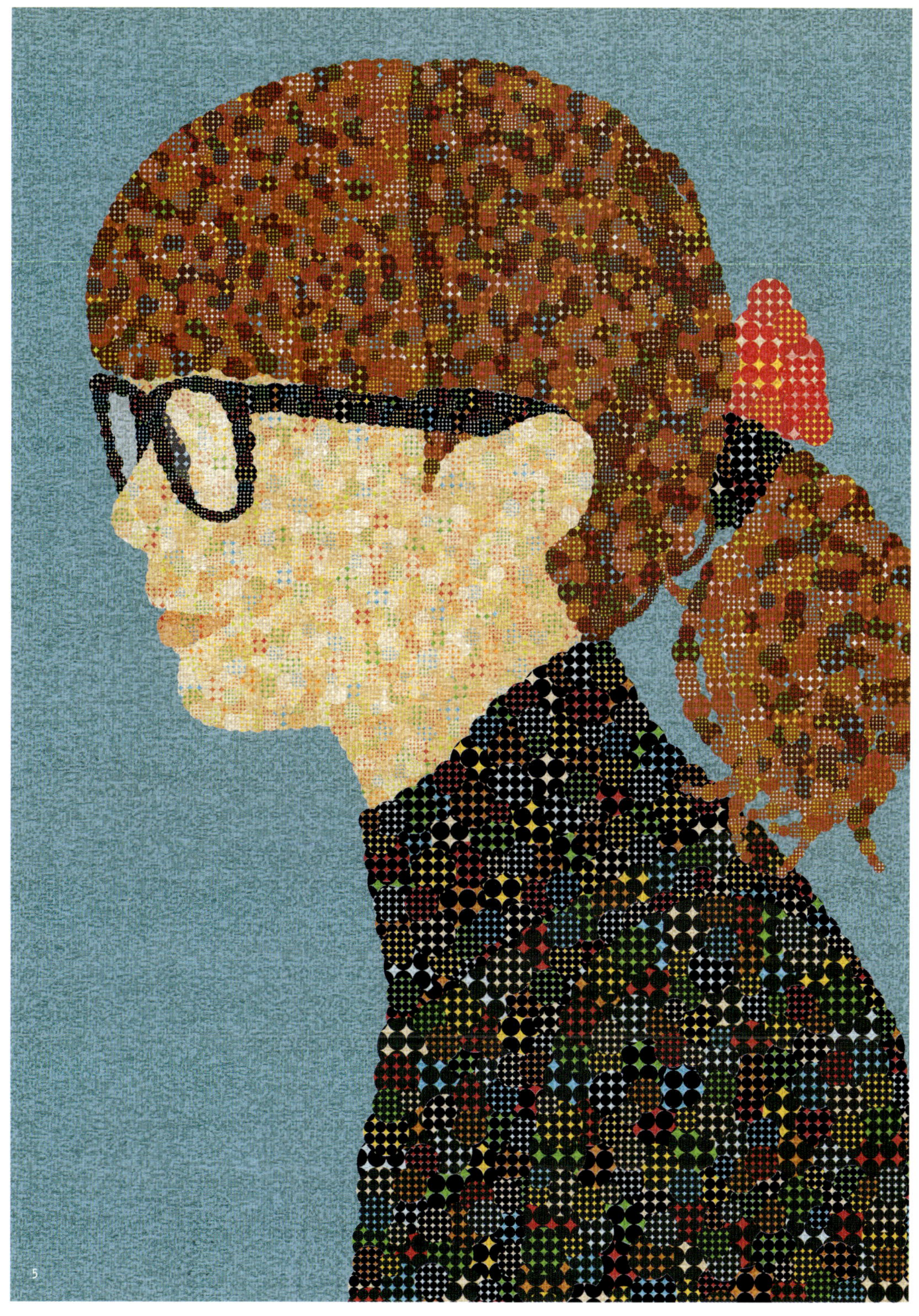

Begoberlin

Japan

begoberlin.web.fc2.com

1. **Friend's friends 1** (2011). Personal work for Shibuya1000 Urban Expo. CG

2. **Friend's friends 3** (2011). Personal work. CG

3. **Friend's friends 4** (2011). Personal work. CG

4. **Friend's friends 5** (2011). Personal work. CG

5. **Friend's friends 6** (2011). Personal work. CG

6. **Friend's friends 2** (2011). Personal work. CG

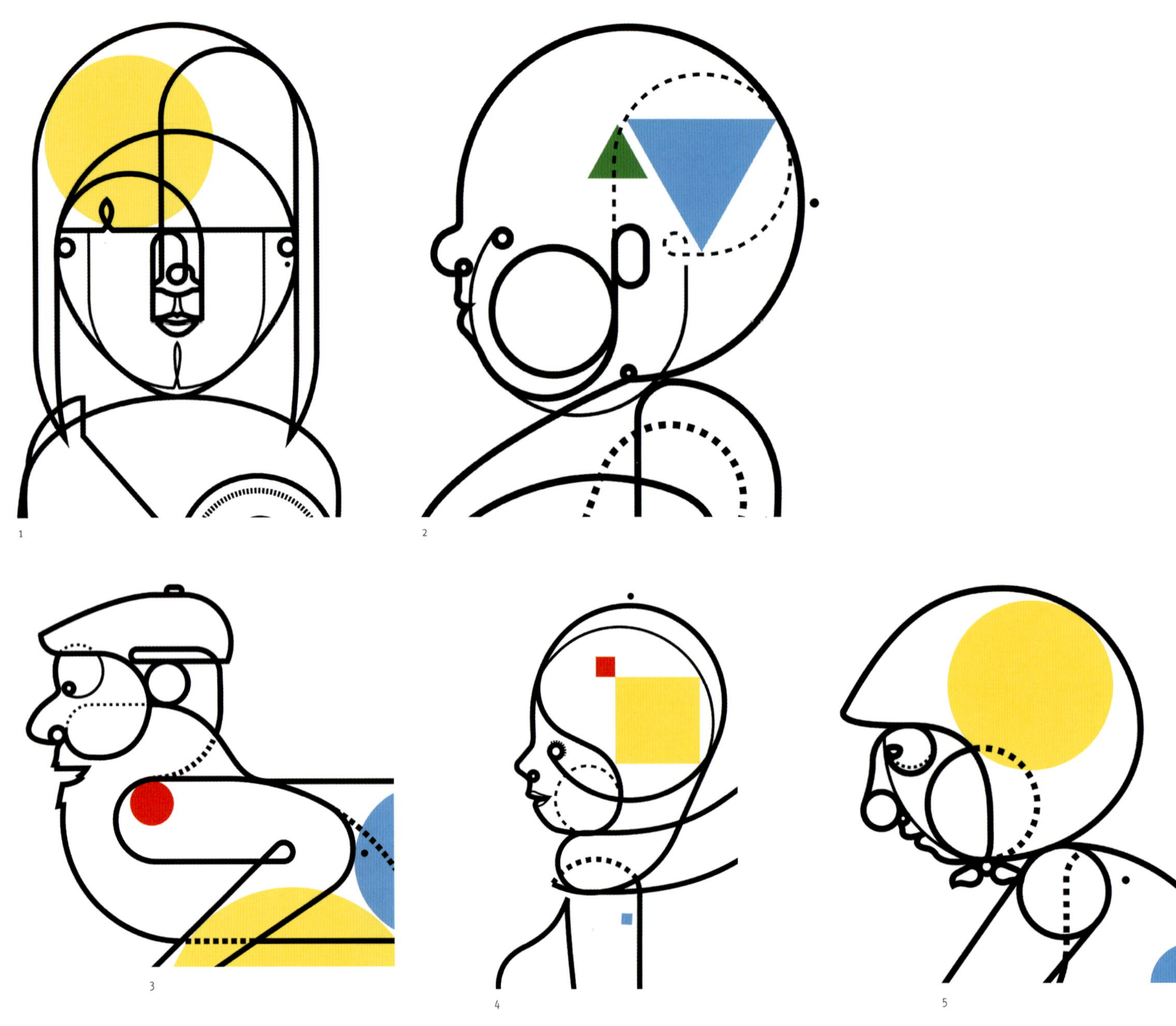

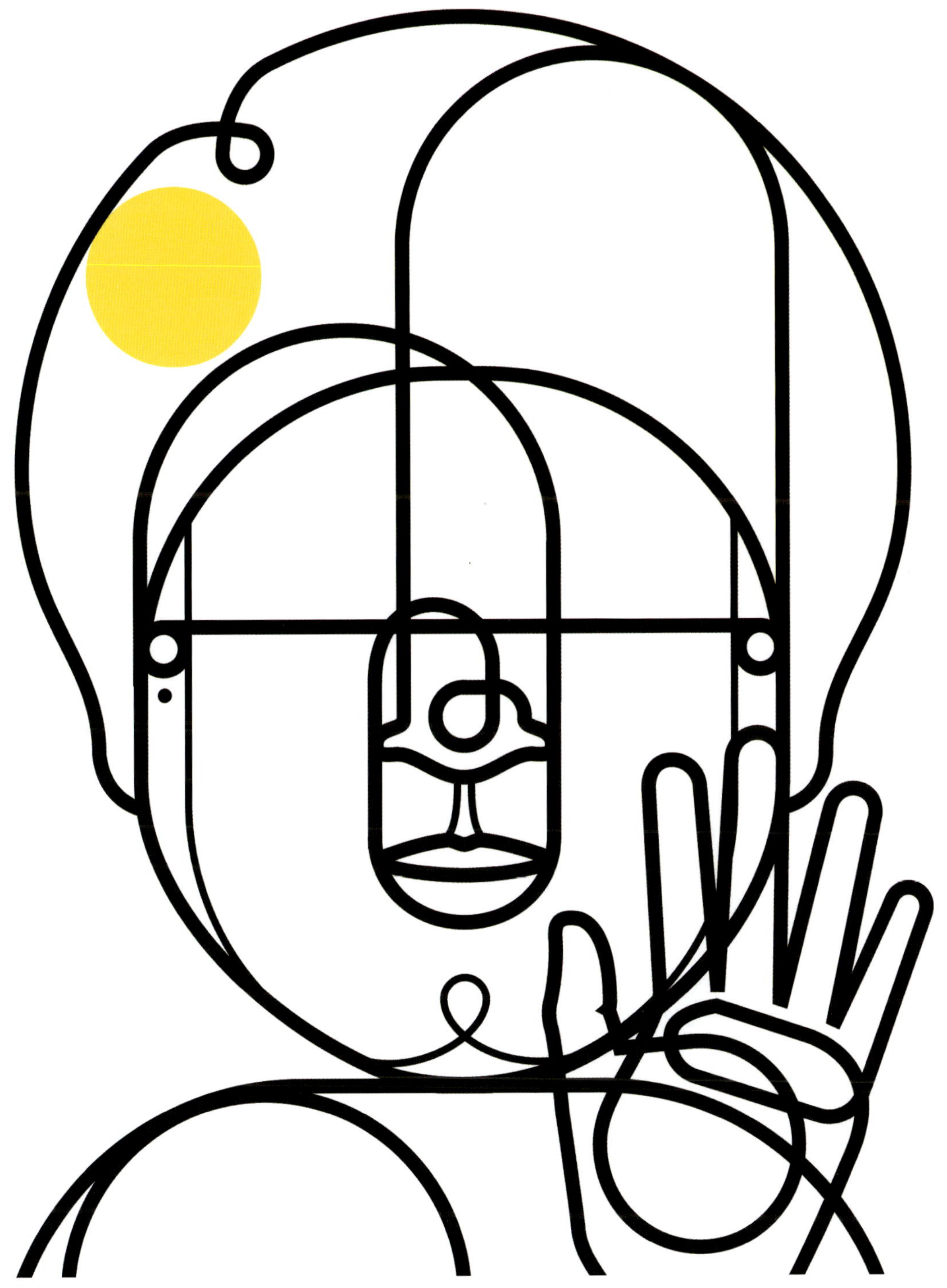

Will Scobie

UK

www.willscobie.co.uk

1. **Mar** (2009). Personal work. Digital

2. **Mr** (2010). Personal work. Digital

3. **Gramp** (2010). Personal work. Digital

4. **Lady** (2010). Personal work. Digital

5. **Mam** (2010). Personal work. Digital

6. **Pap** (2009). Personal work. Digital

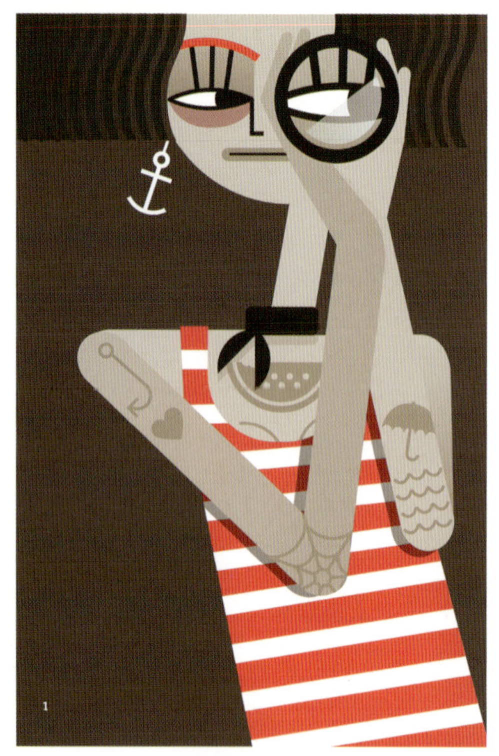

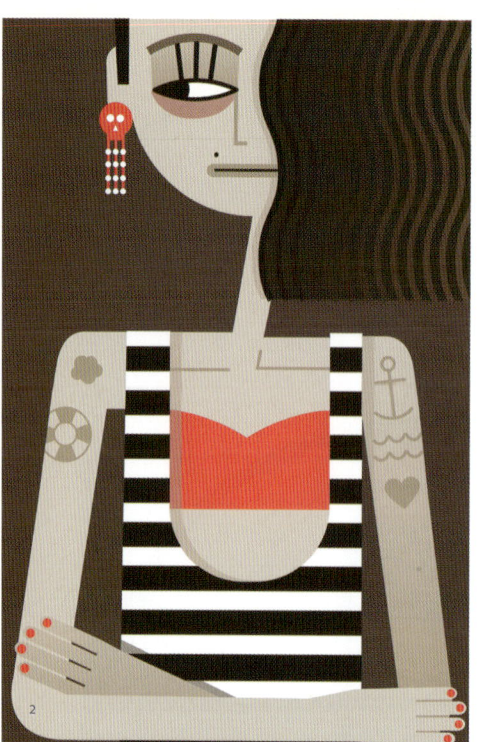

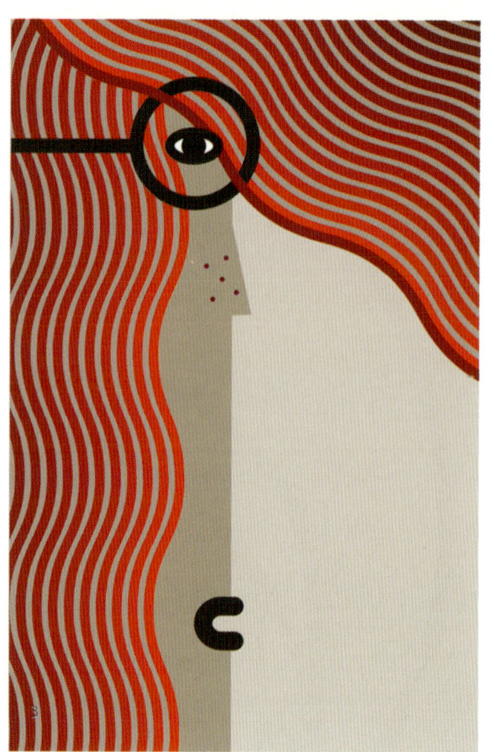

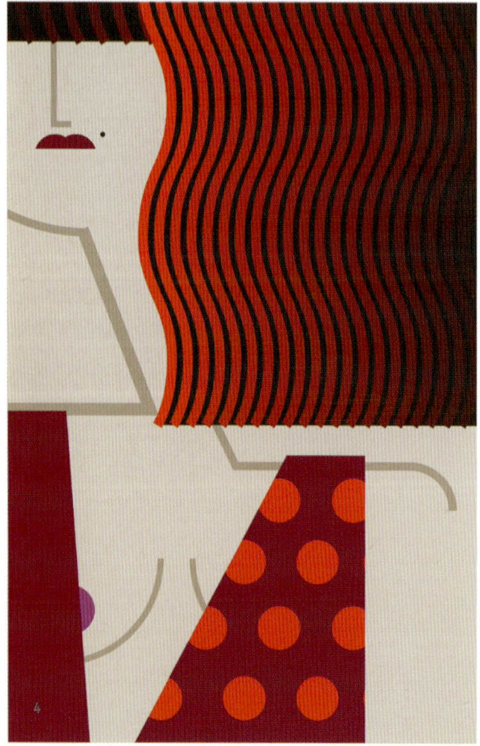

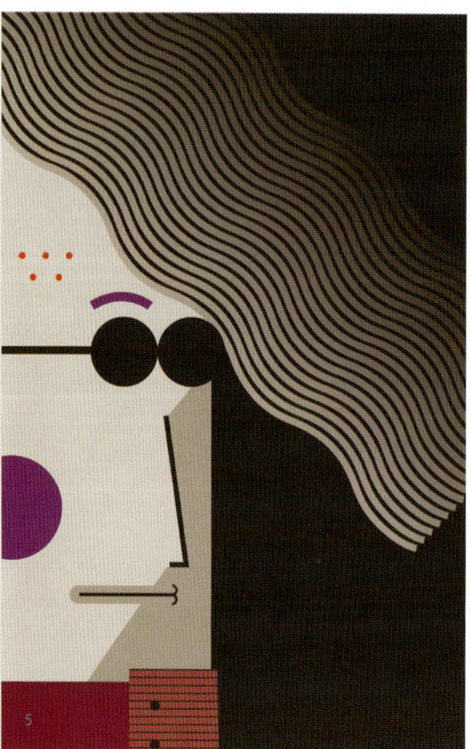

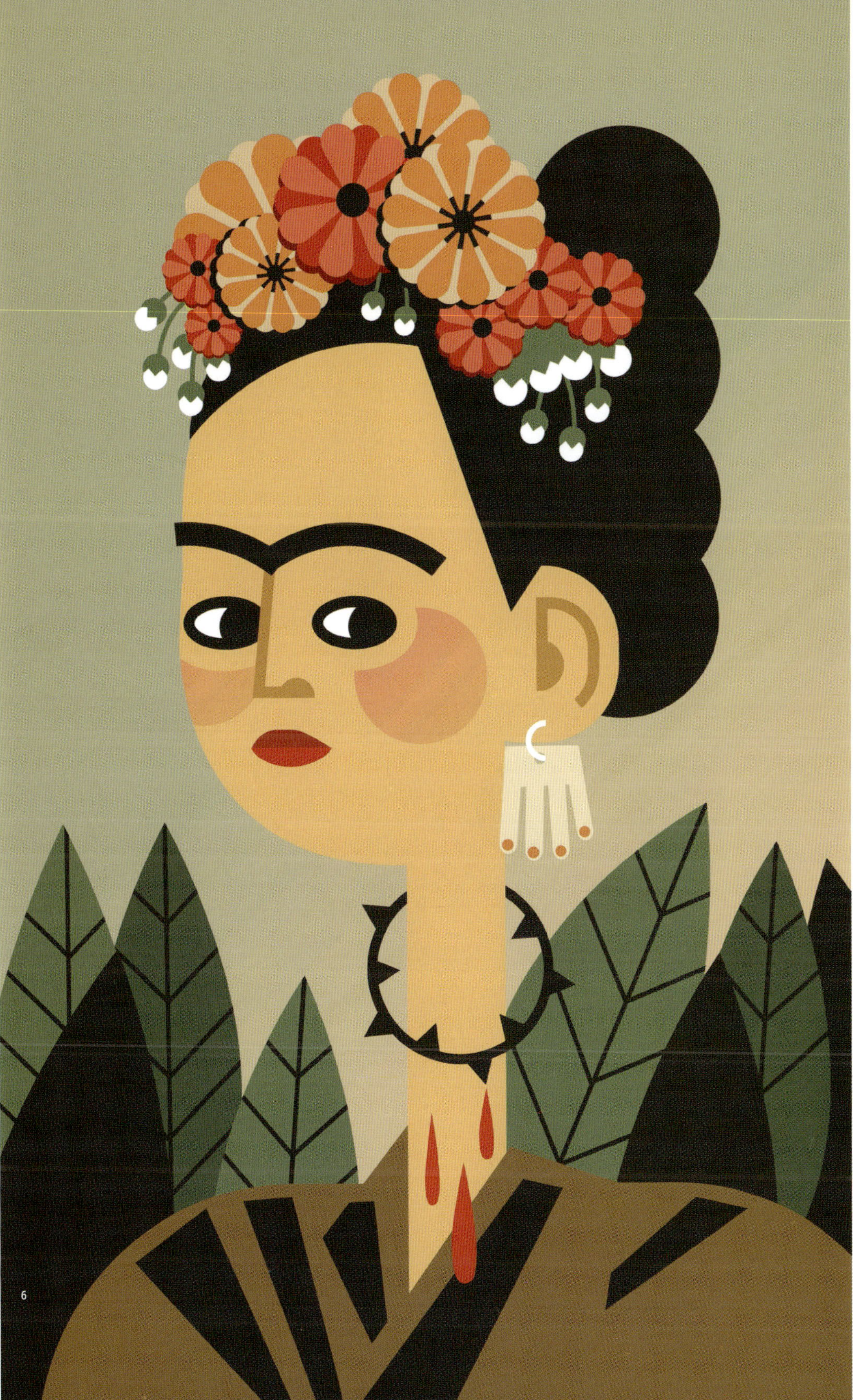

Claudia Carieri

Italy

www.claudiacarieri.com

1. **Sailor Girl** (2011). Poolga. Digital

2. **Sailor Girl** (2011). Poolga. Digital

3. **Portraits** (2011). Personal work. Digital

4. **Portraits** (2011). Personal work. Digital

5. **Portraits** (2011). Personal work. Digital

6. **Frida Kahlo Self Portrait** (2011). Personal work. Digital

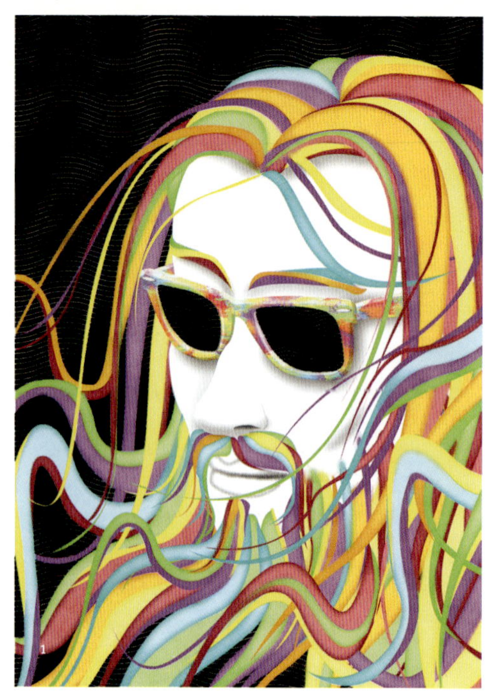

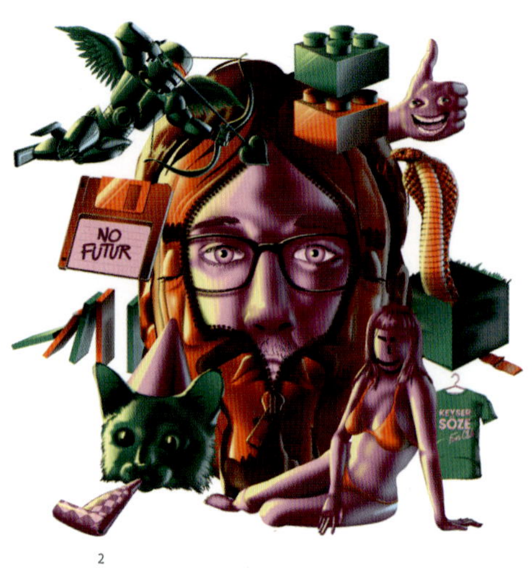

NO FUTUR
KEYSER
SOZE
2

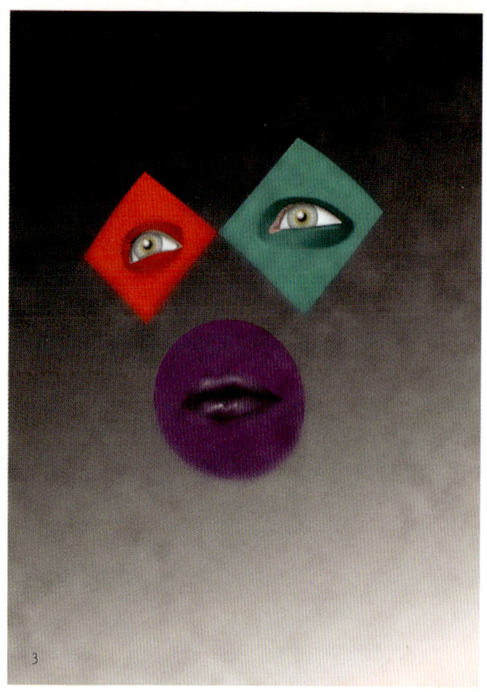

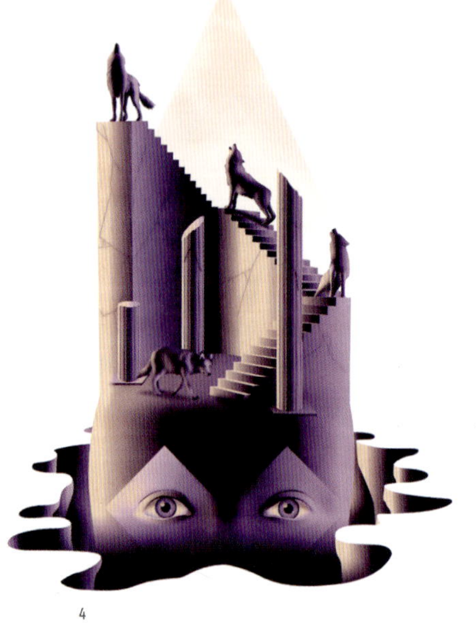

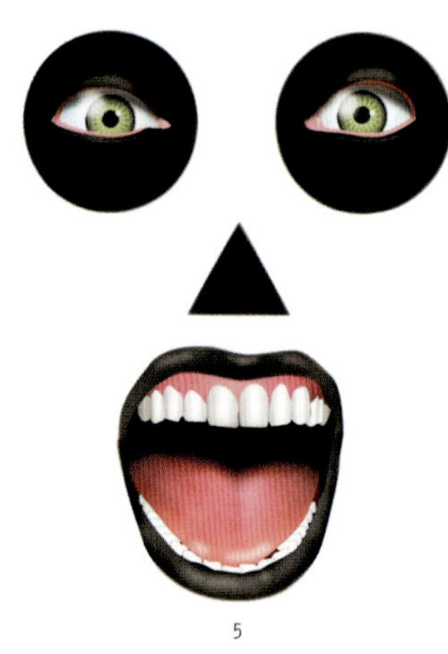

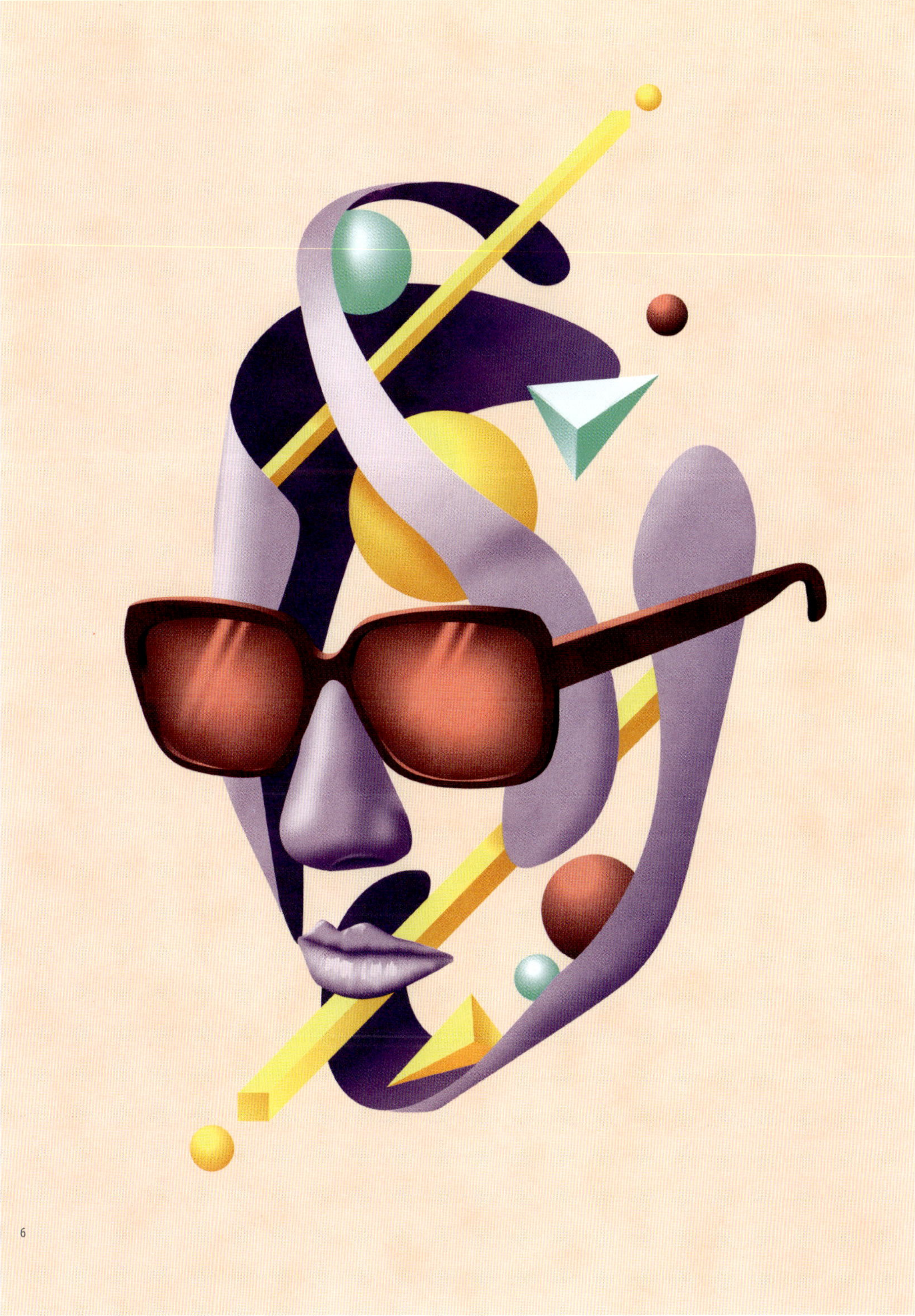

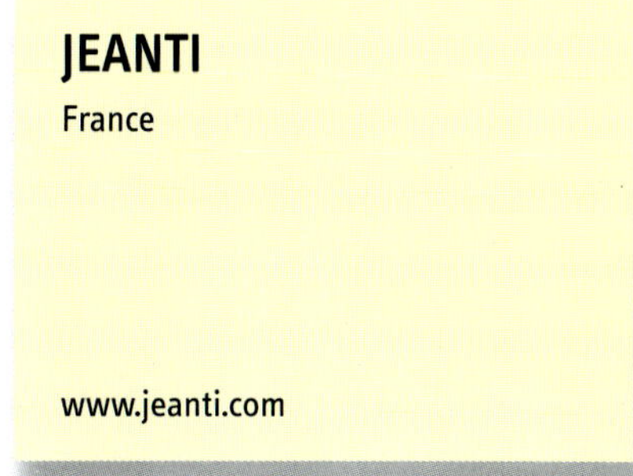

JEANTI
France

www.jeanti.com

1. **Colorfullman** (2010). Rayon proposal. Mixed media

2. **Geek** (2011). *Mc Donald's Air le Mag.* Mixed media

3. **Geo Eye 1** (2009). Personal work. Mixed media

4. **Heathen Shout** (2011). Personal work. Mixed media

5. **Skullhead** (2010). Personal work. Mixed media

6. **Metaréalism** (2011). Personal work. Mixed media

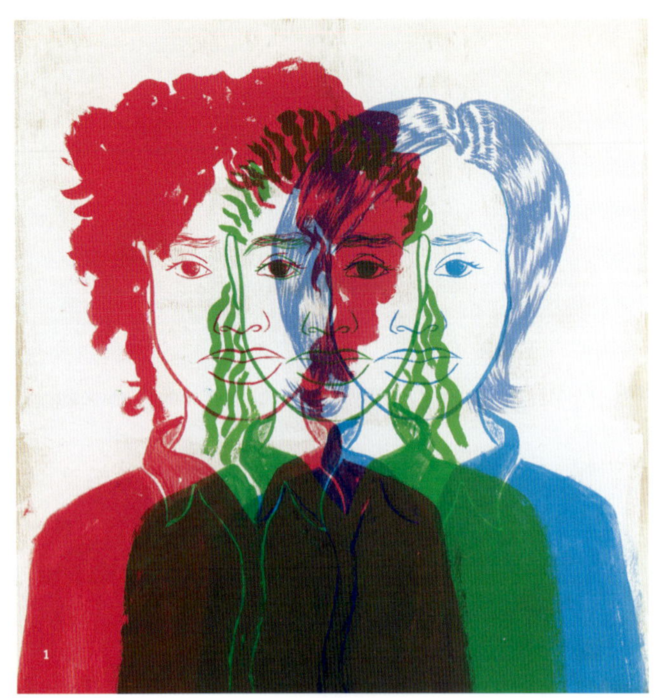

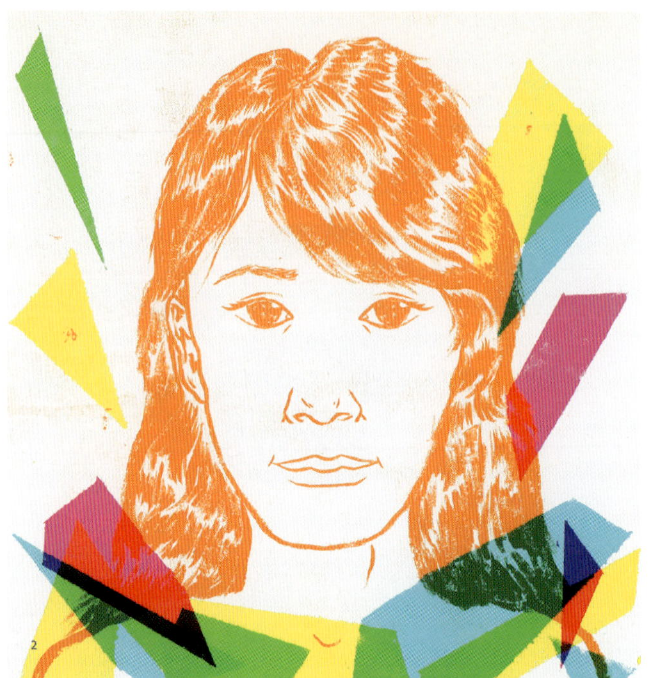

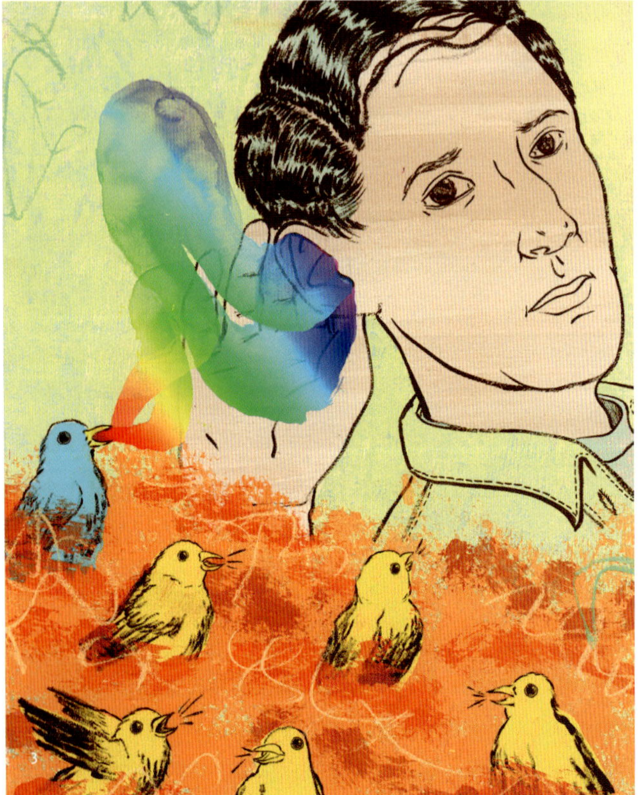

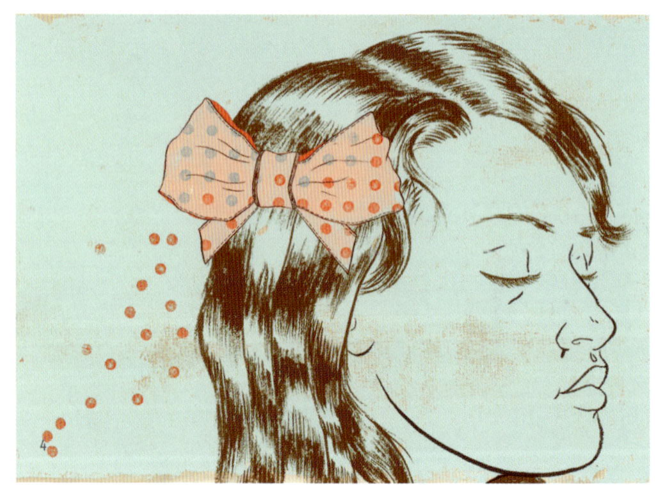

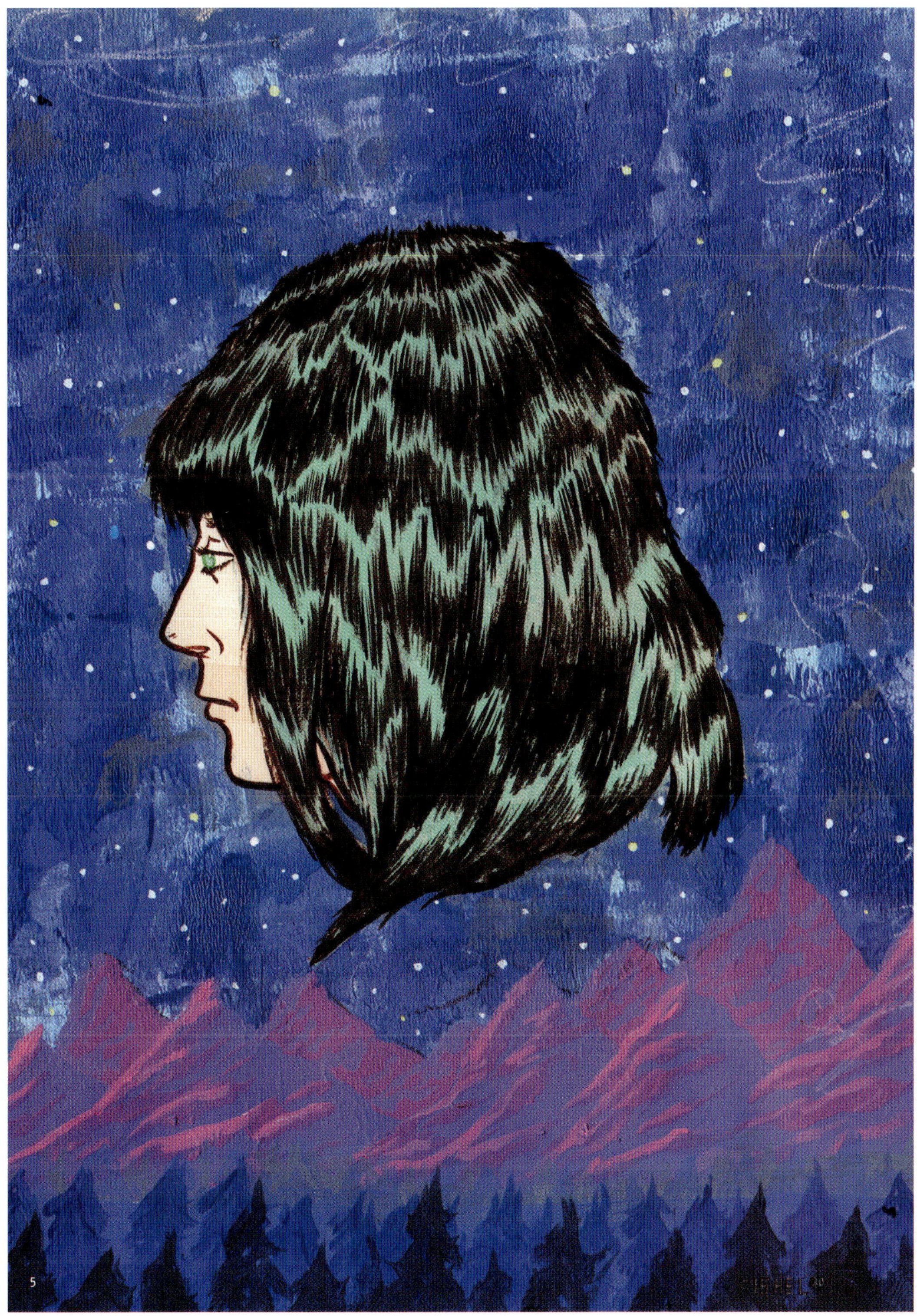

Daniel Fishel

UK

www.o-fishel.com

1. **Mistake Identity** (2009-2012). *Boston Globe.* Mixed media

2. **Happiness** (2009-2012). *Seattle Met.* Mixed media

3. **Deciphering between whistle blowers with poor information and good information** (2009-2012). *Nexus Magazine* (University of Toronto Law). Mixed media

4. **Lack of Motivation** (2009-2012). Personal work. Mixed media

5. **About the Other Night** (2009-2012). Personal work. Acrylic, ink on paper mounted to board

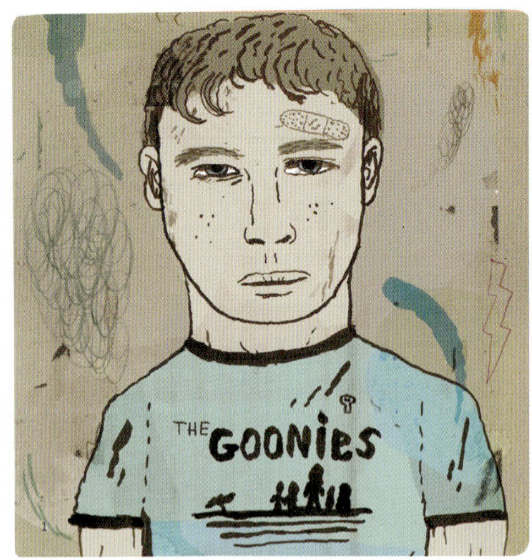

THE GOONIES

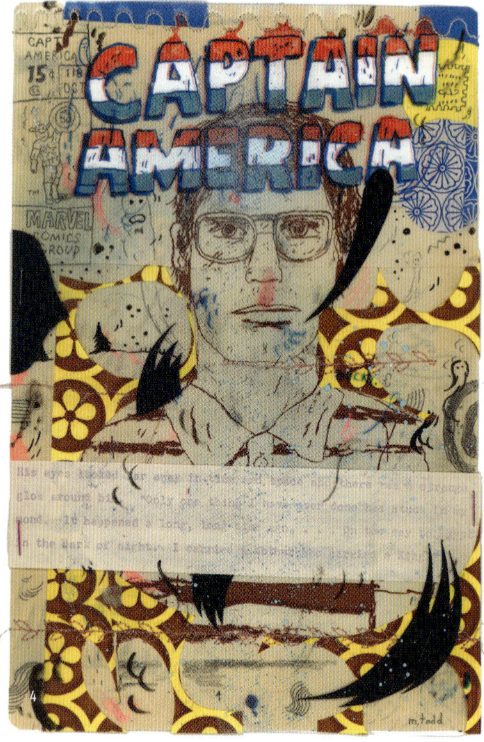

CAPTAIN
AMERICA
15¢
MARVEL
COMICS
GROUP
m.todd

MEGA BURGER!
MEGA BURGER
GLEN
TRAINEE
ASK ME ABOUT MY BIG BUNS
3

MARVEL COMICS
30¢ 15
APR
BATTLE.

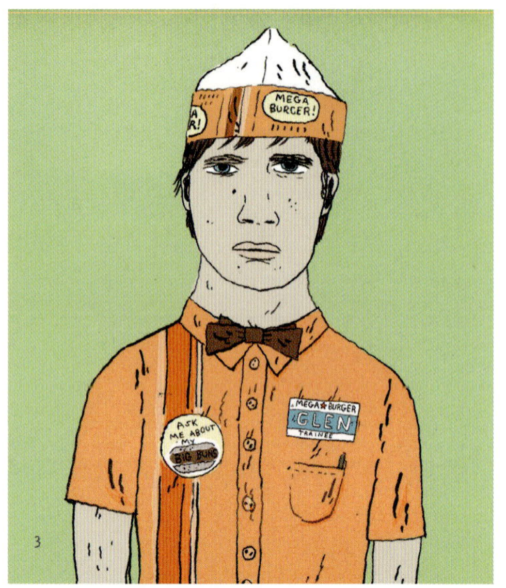

MARVEL COMICS GR
FANTASTIC FOUR
25¢ 168
LET
CA
YOUR
US
YOU
KNOW
IT
TORCH!
5

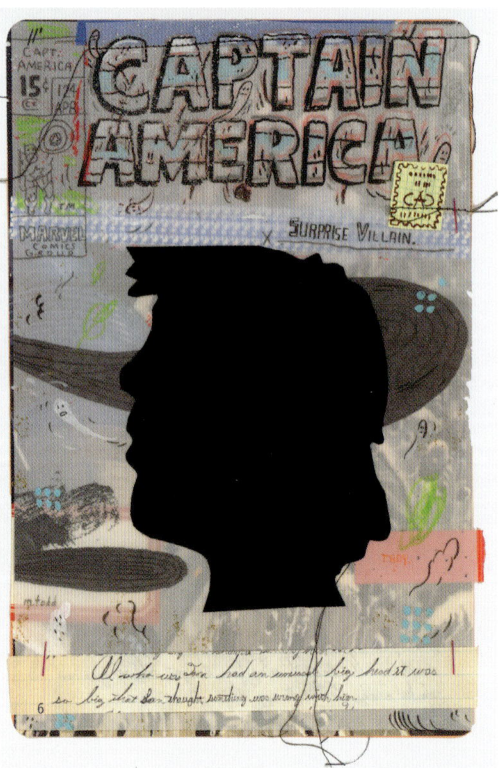

CAPTAIN
AMERICA
15¢
CAPT.
AMERICA
SURPRISE VILLAIN.
MARVEL
COMICS
m.todd
6

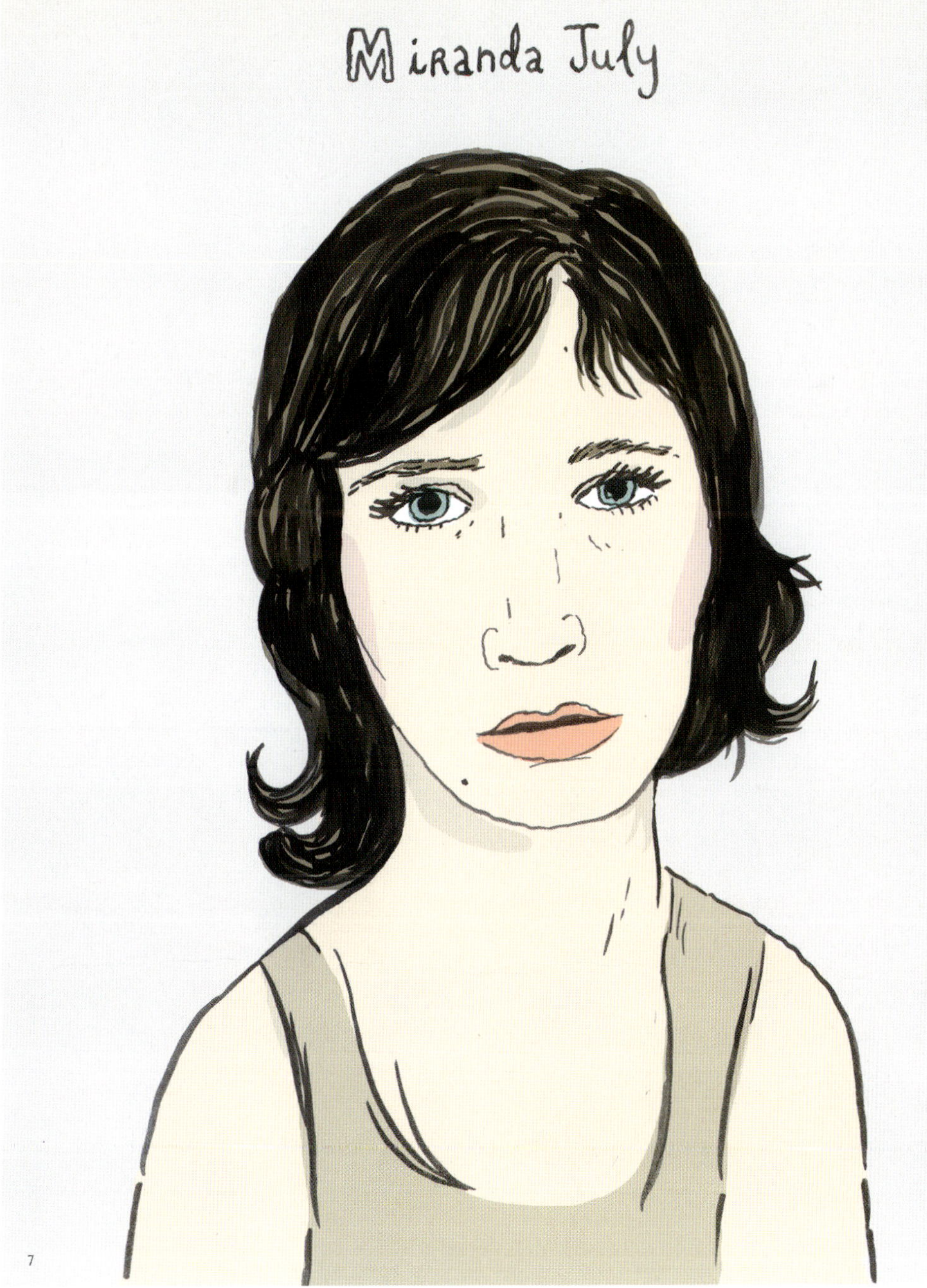

Mark Todd

USA

www.marktoddillustration.com

1. **Miranda July** (2009). *Los Angeles Times.* Mixed media

2. **Battle** (2011). Personal work. Cel-vinyl on panel

3. **Fast Food** (2009). Clearasil. Ink, digital

4. **Carried a King** (2010). Personal work

5. **Portrait** (2011). Personal work. Cel-vinyl on panel

6. **Surprise Villain** (2010). Personal work. Mixed media on paper

7. **Miranda July** (2010). *McSweeney's.* Ink, digital

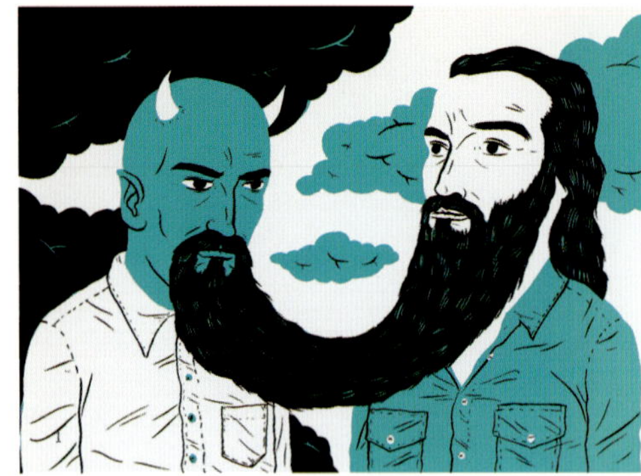

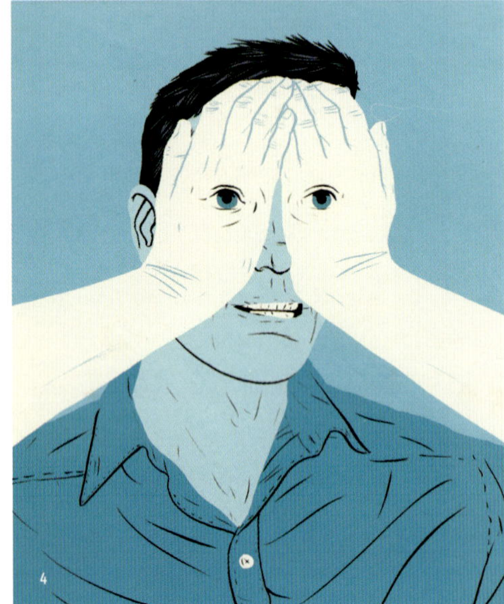

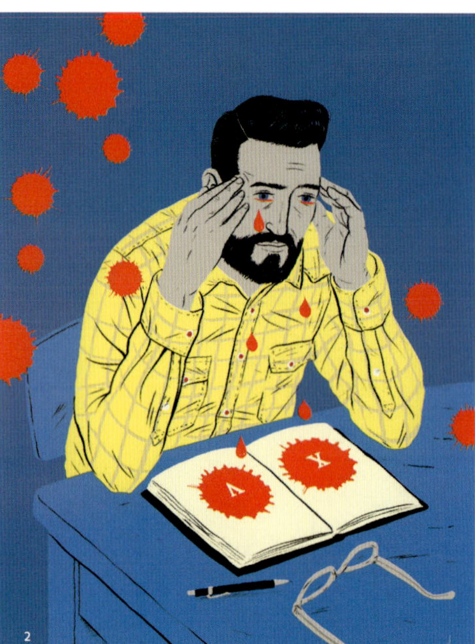

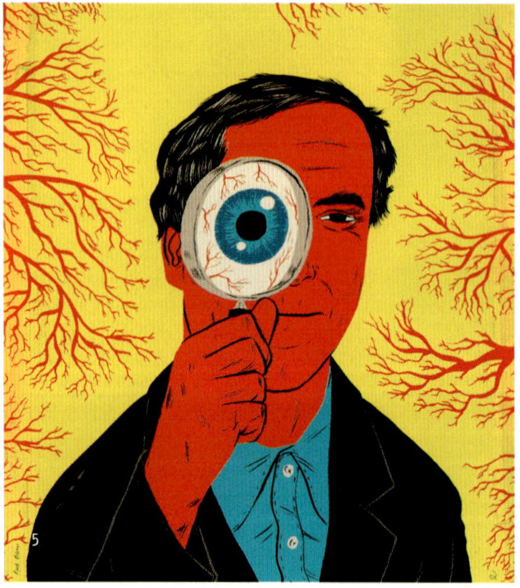

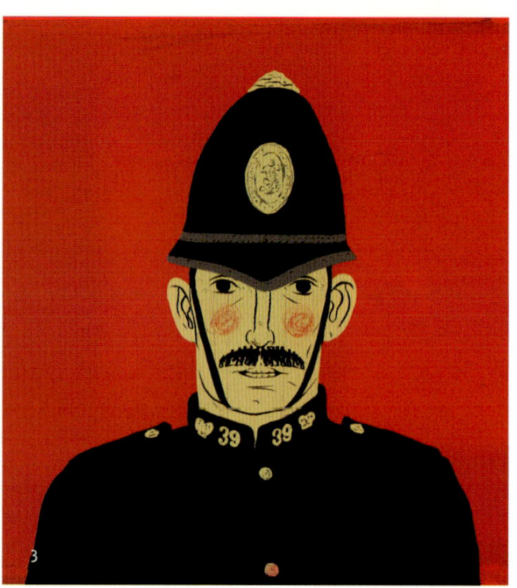

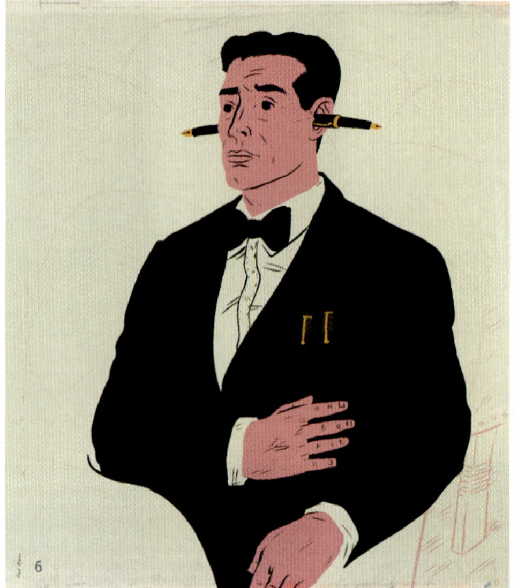

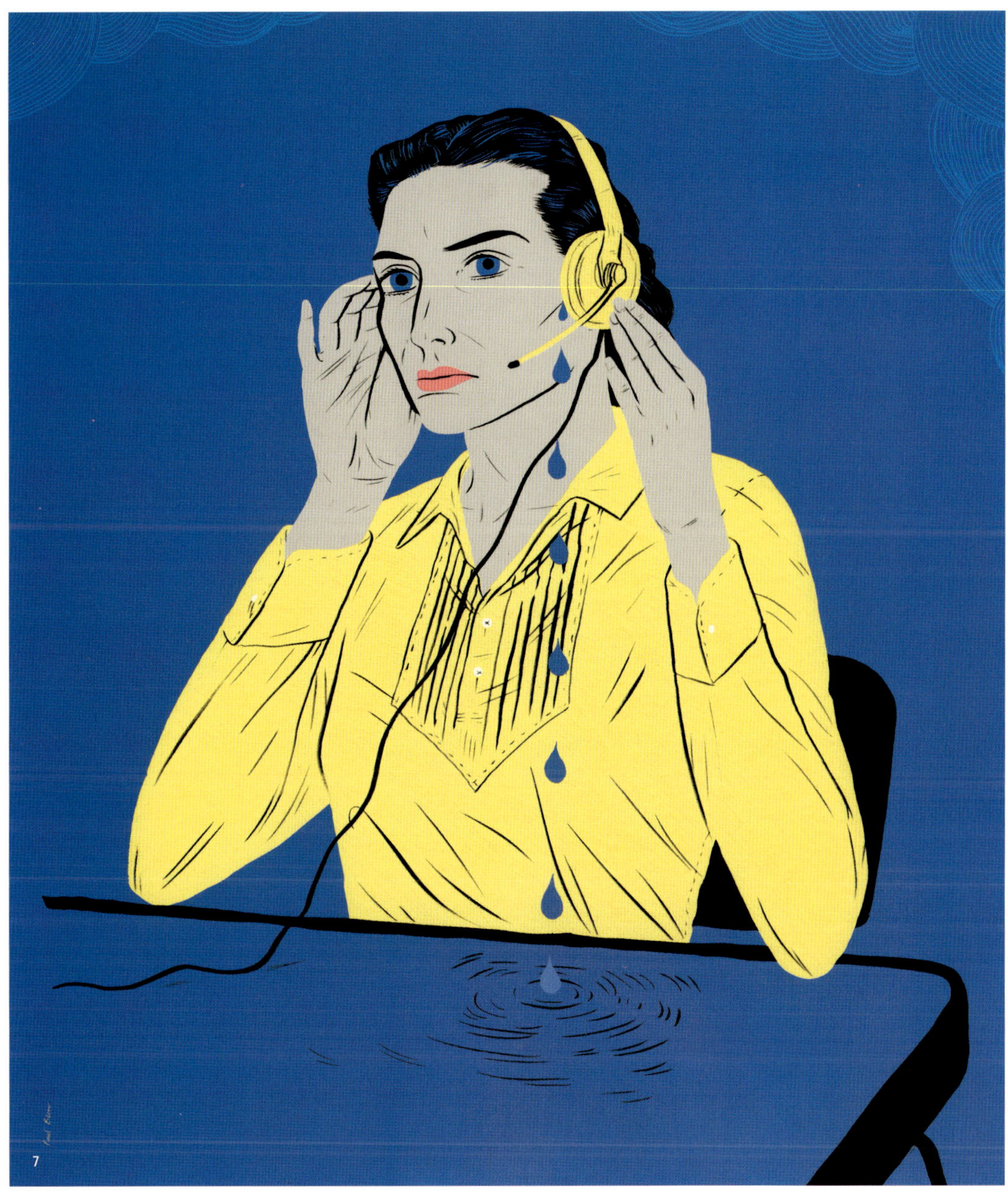

Paul Blow
UK

www.paulblow.com

1. **Gods and Monsters** (2009). *Nobrow Press.* Mixed media

2. **3x3** (2009). *3x3 Magazine.* Mixed media

3. **Riot** (2011). *Anorak Magazine.* Mixed media

4. **Open** (2008). Open Studios. Mixed media

5. **Jack Cashill** (2011). The Pitch. Mixed media

6. **Music Critic** (2011). *BBC Music Magazine.* Mixed media

7. **The Samaritan** (2009). *Independent Magazine.* Mixed media

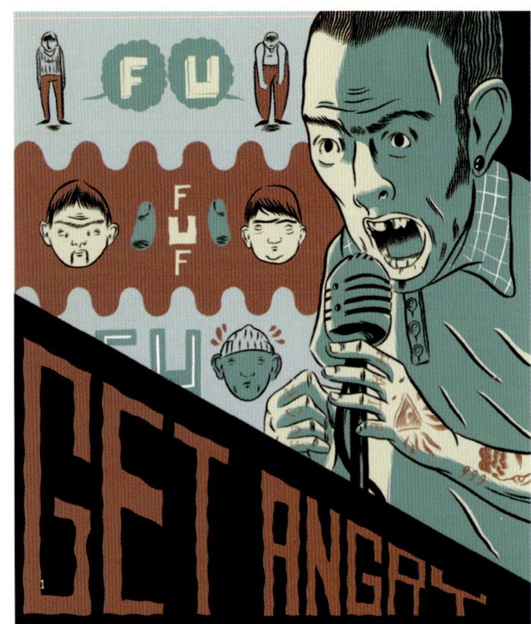

F U
F
U
F
GET ANGRY

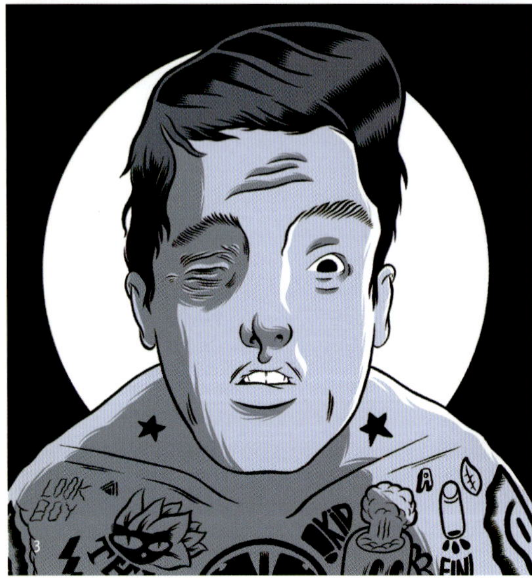

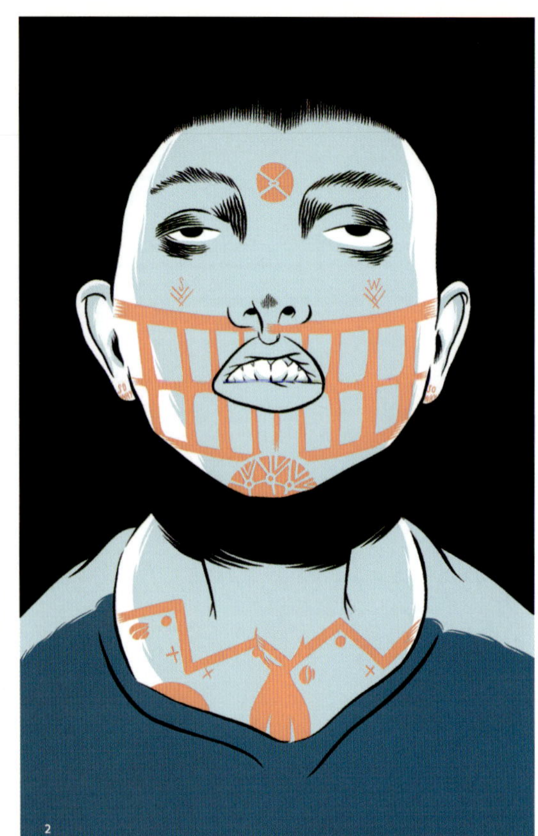

LOOK
BOY

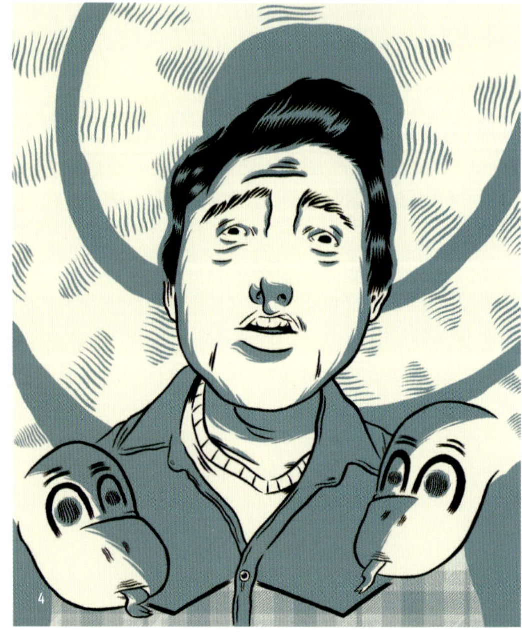

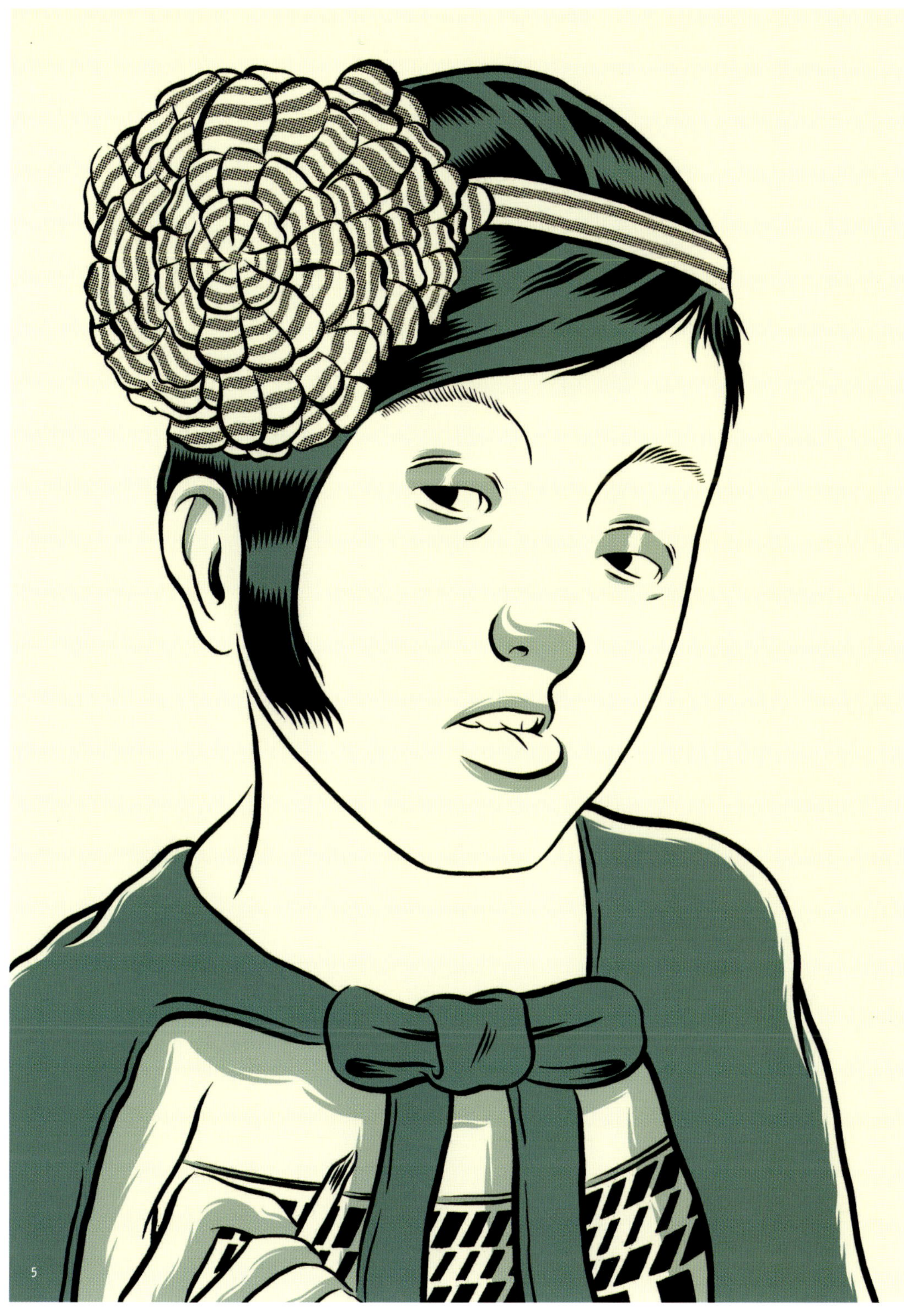

Pablo Vigo

Argentina

www.pablovigo.com

1. **Get Angry** (2011). Personal work. Mixed media

2. **Untitled** (2011). Personal work. Mixed media

3. **Boxer** (2011). Personal work. Mixed media

4. **Socket Snakes** (2011). Personal work. Mixed media

5. **Girl with Bow** (2011). Personal work. Mixed media

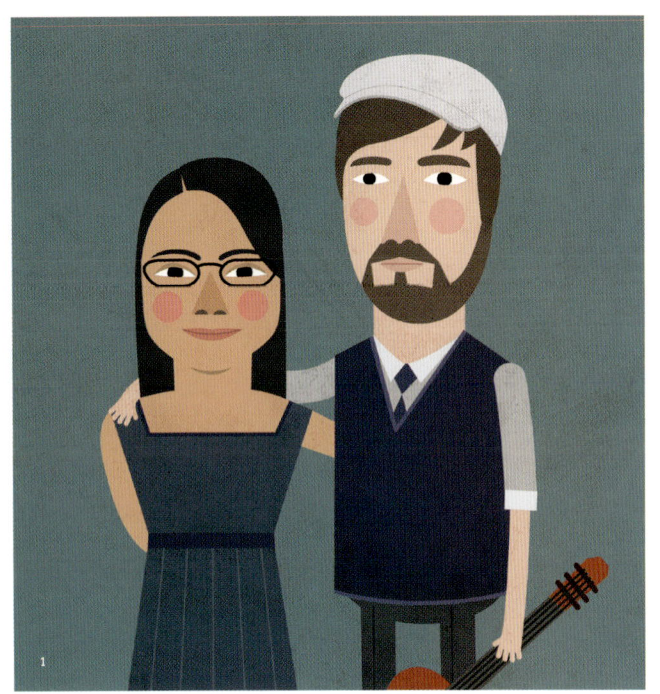

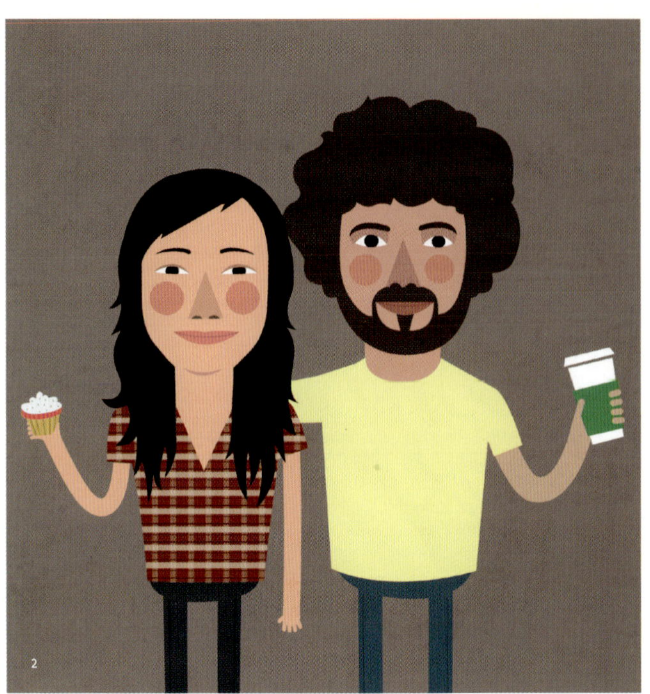

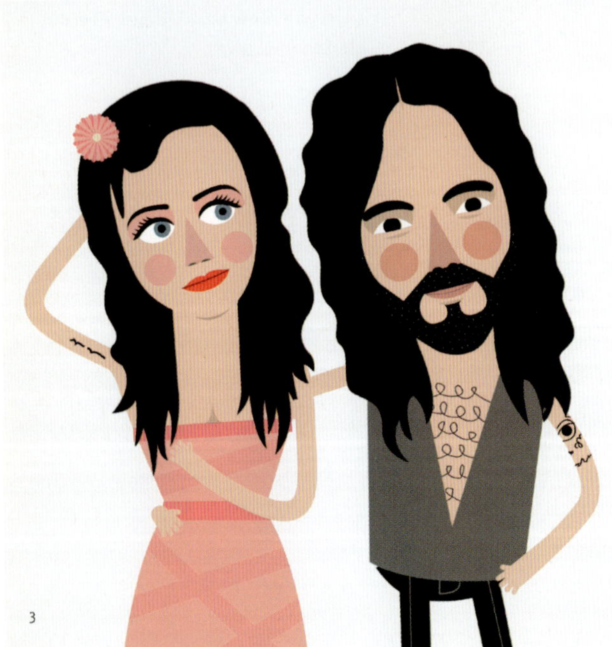

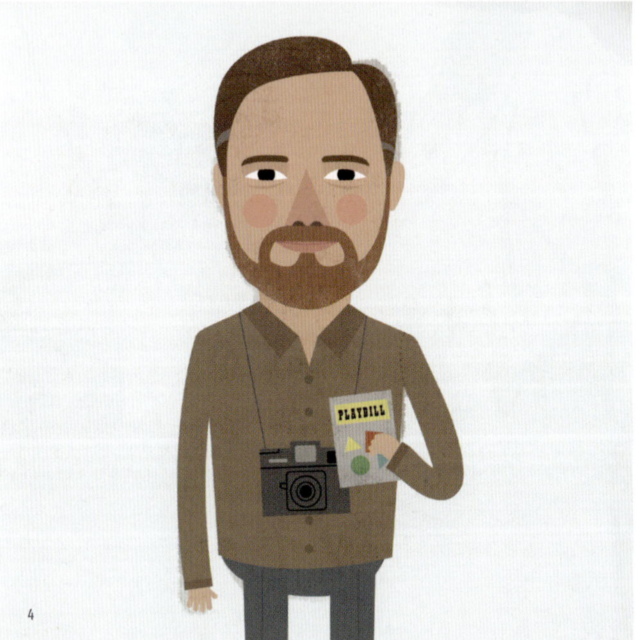

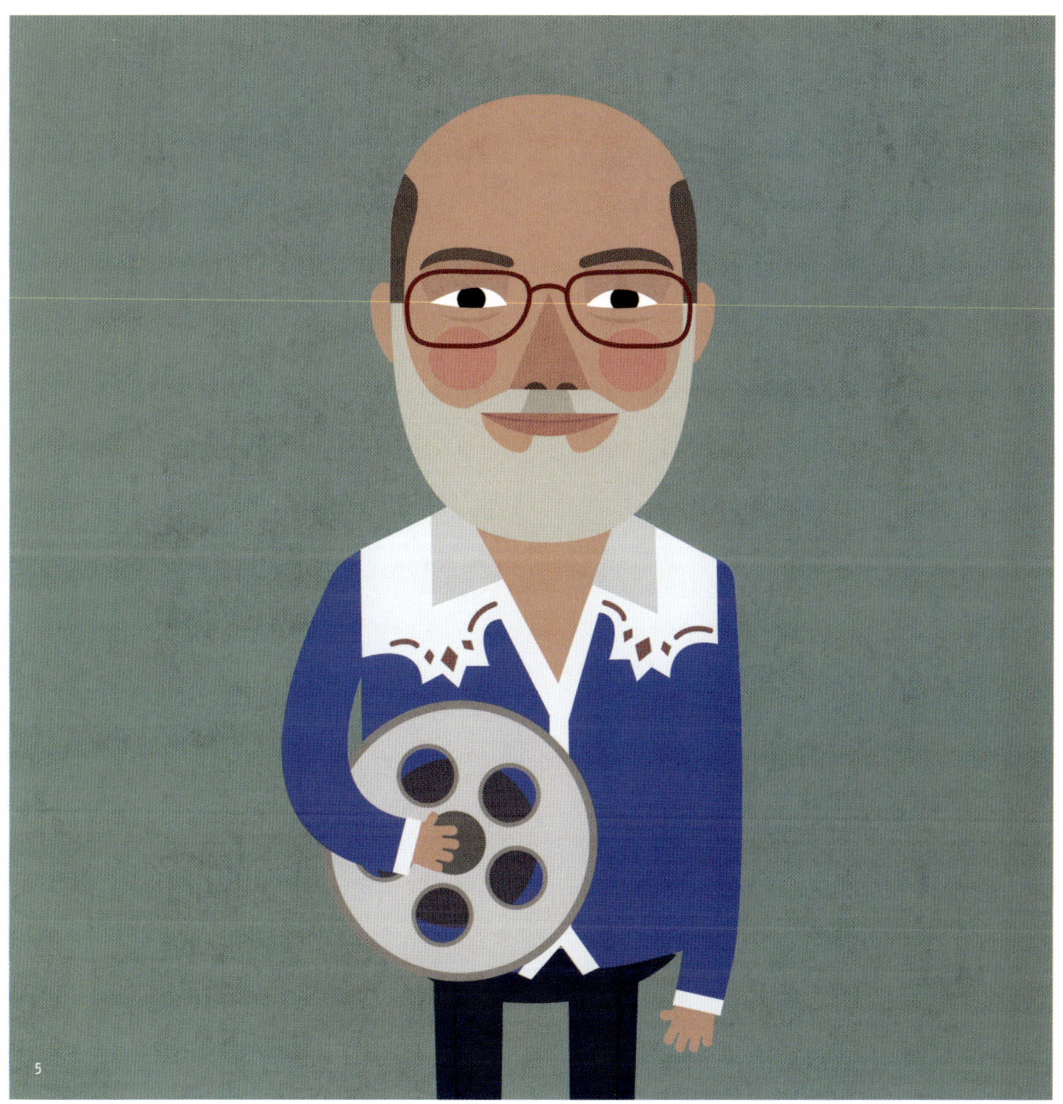

Ryan Feerer
USA

www.ryanfeerer.com

1. **Customer Portrait #4** (2010). Elsewares Customer. Digital

2. **Customer Portrait #7** (2010). Elsewares Customer. Digital

3. **Katie & Russell** (2011). *Sunday London Times*. Digital

4. **Customer Portrait #2** (2010). Elsewares Customer. Digital

5. **Customer Portrait #6** (2010). Elsewares Customer. Digital

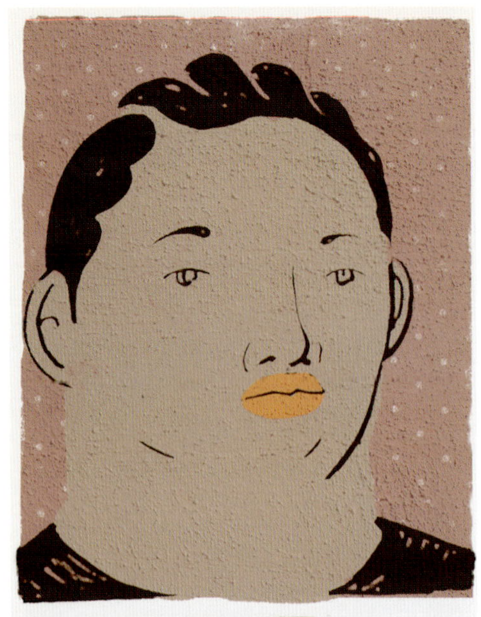

A is for Apathy

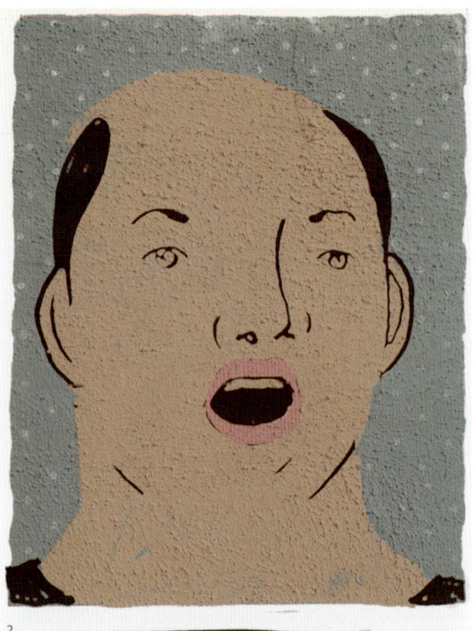

O is for Outrage

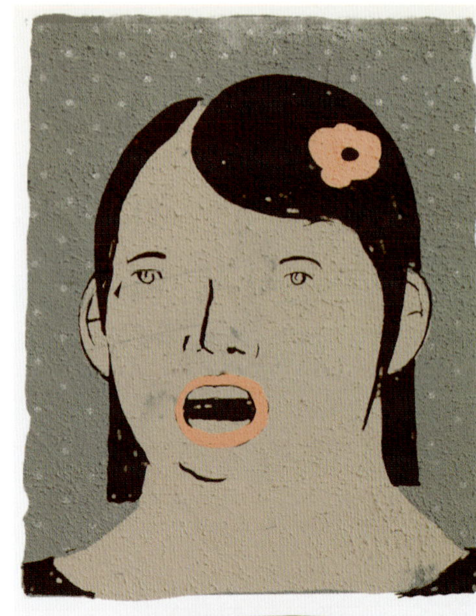

E is for Envy

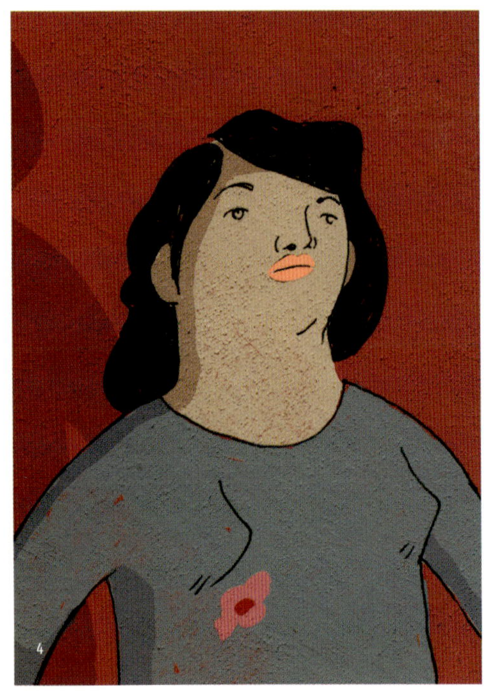

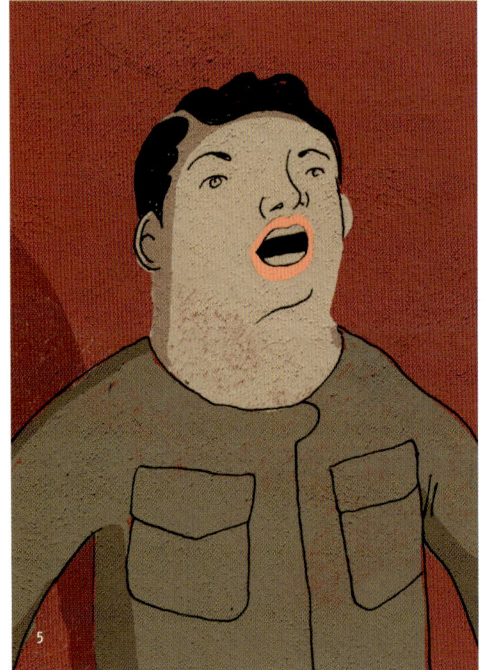

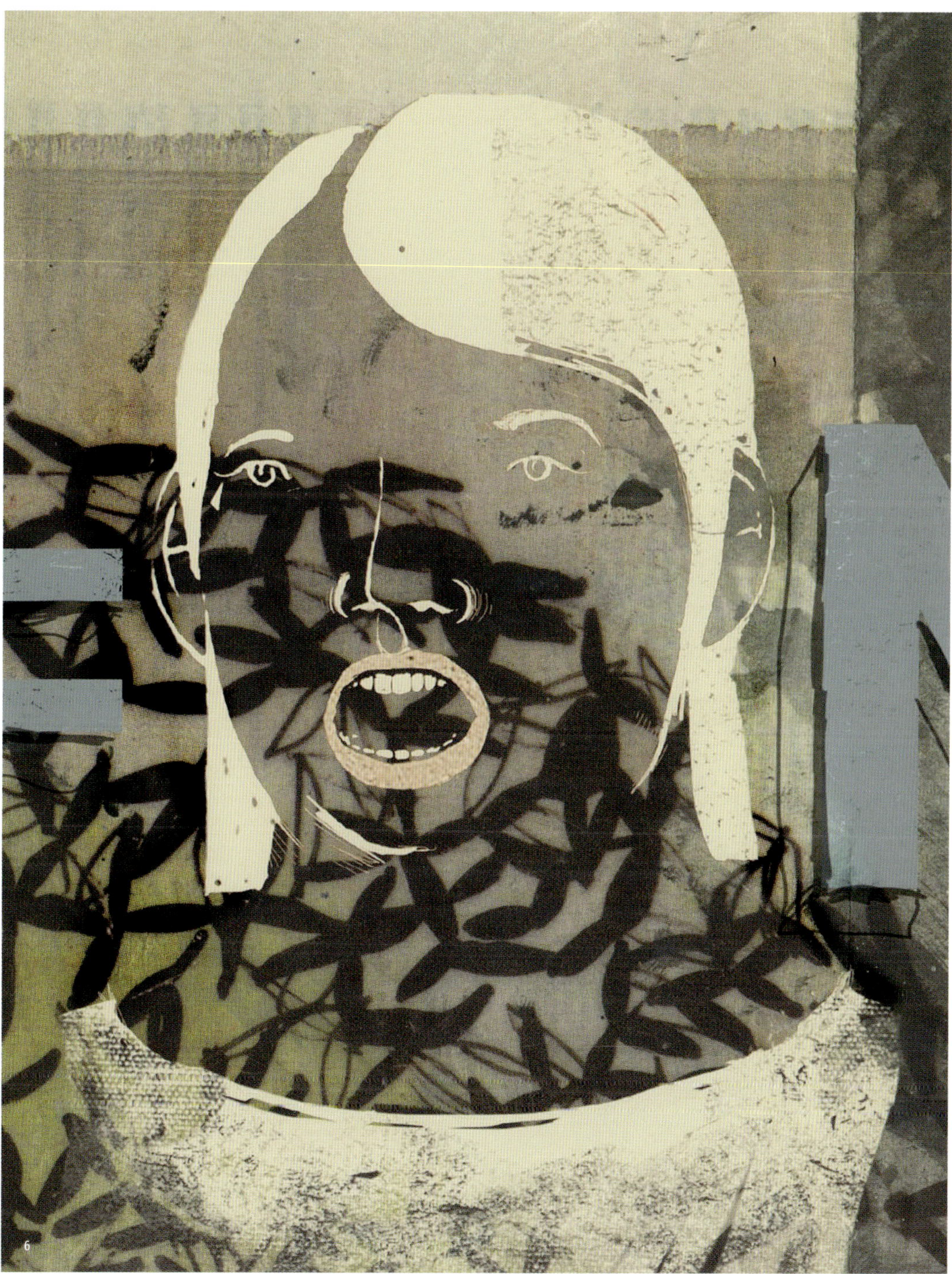

Bryce Wymer
USA

www.brycewymer.com

1. **A is for Apathy** (2011). Personal work. Textured gouache, India ink, digital

2. **O is for Outrage** (2011). Personal work. Textured gouache, India ink, digital

3. **E is for Envy** (2011). Personal work. Textured gouache, India ink, digital

4. **The Moby's 01** (2011). Personal work. Textured gouache, India ink, digital

5. **The Moby's 02** (2011). Personal work. Textured gouache, India ink, digital

6. **Hellen** (2011). Personal work. Gouache, India ink, collage on found object

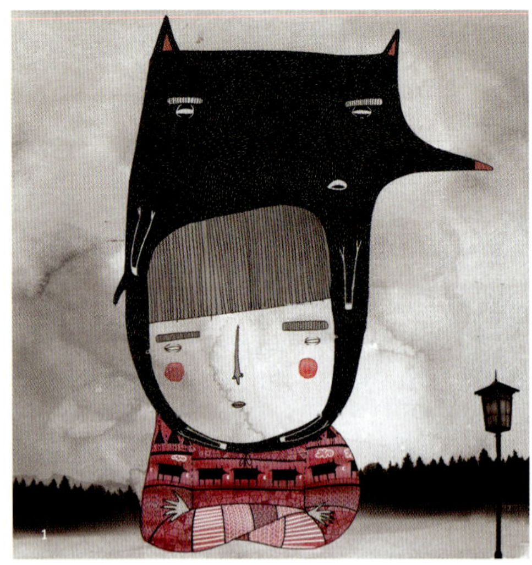

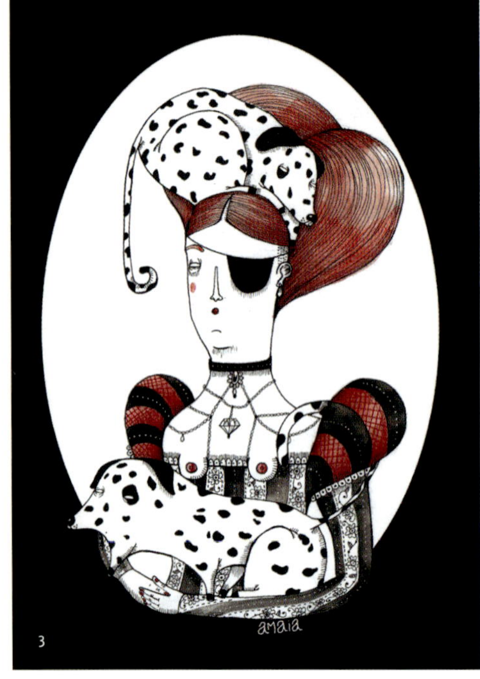

PARECÍAN DOS,
PERO ERAN
UNO SÓLO
PUM PUM !!
PUM PUM !!
amaia

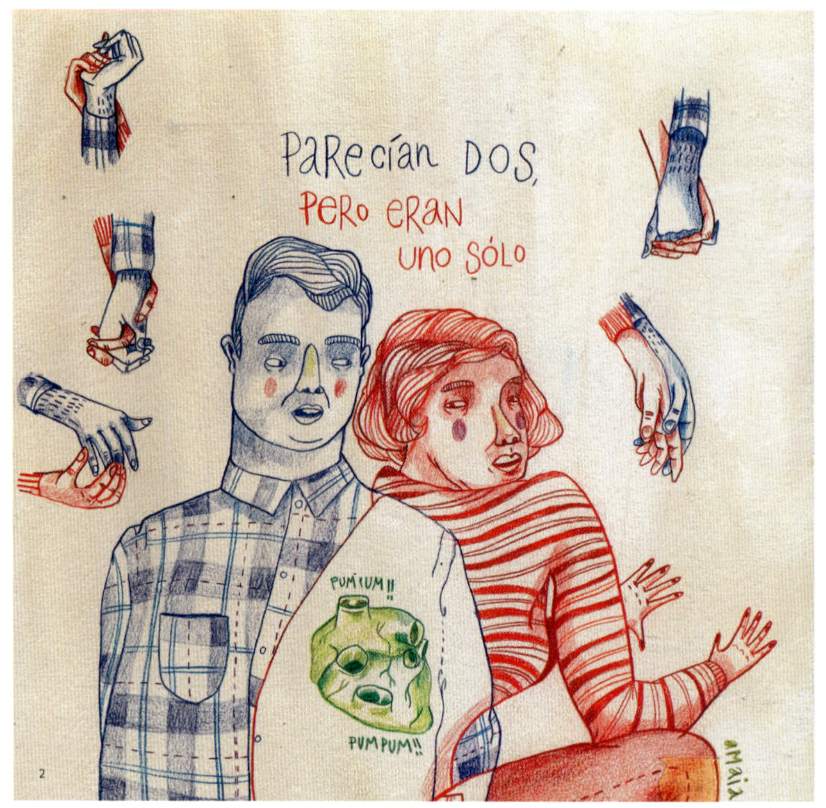

amaia

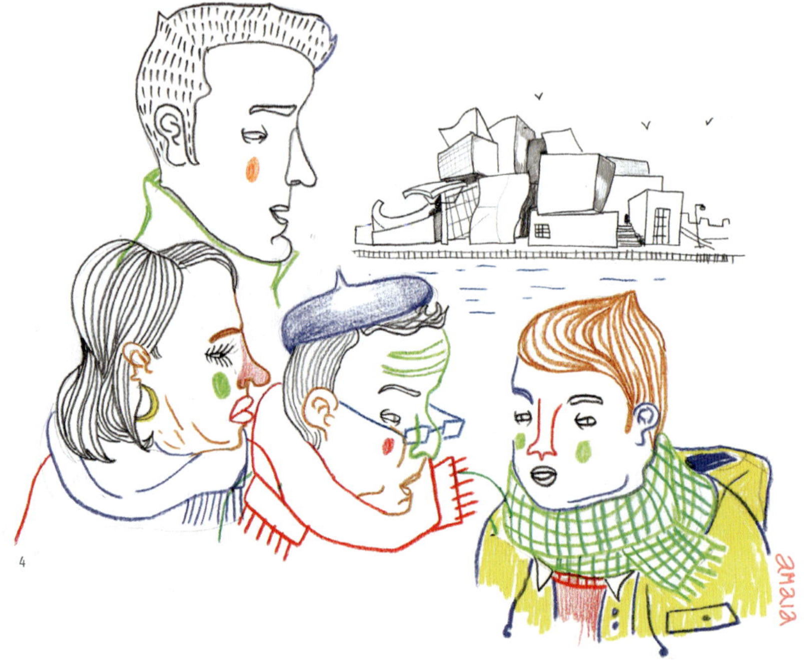

amaia

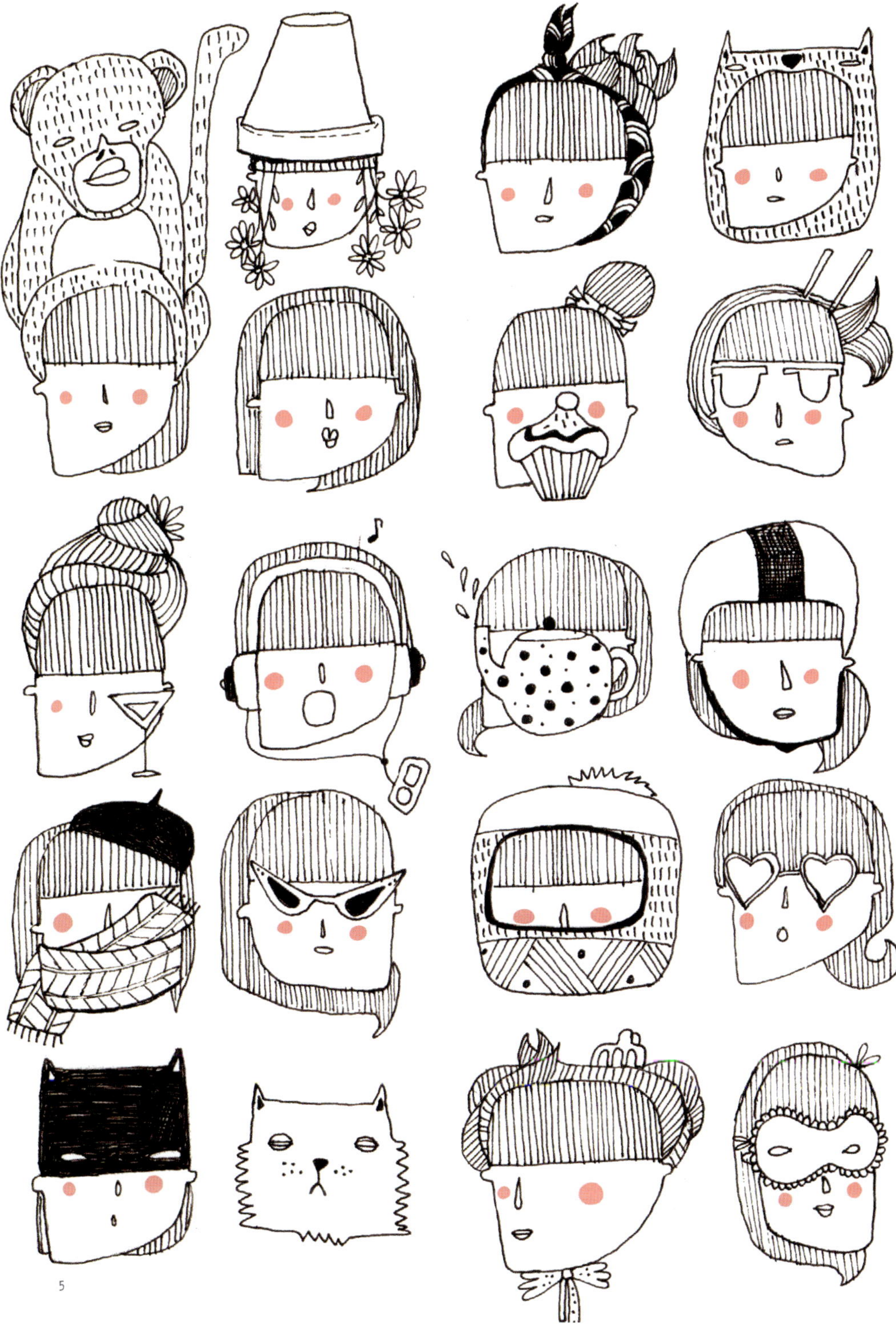

Amaia Arrazola
Spain

www.cargocollective.com/
amaiaarrazola

1. **Wolfhat** (2011). Exhibition work. Pencil, ink, Photoshop

2. **Translation** (2011). Charity Calendar. Pencil, color pencil, acrylic

3. **Miss New Century Gothic** (2011). Personal work. Pencil, ink, watercolor

4. **Bilbao** (2011). *Ling Magazine*. Pencil, watercolor

5. **Her** (2010). Personal work. Pencil, ink

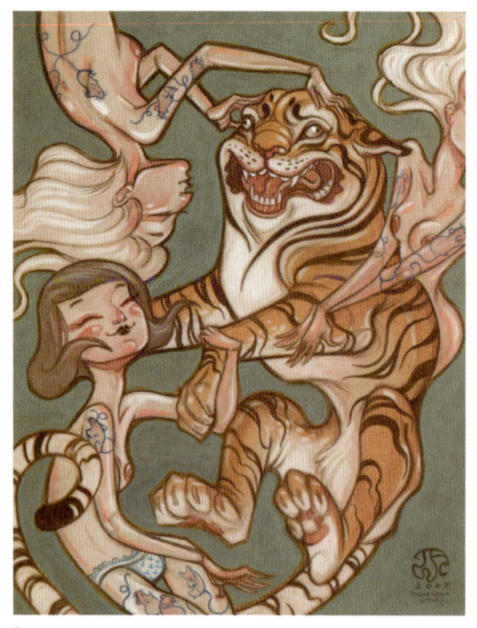

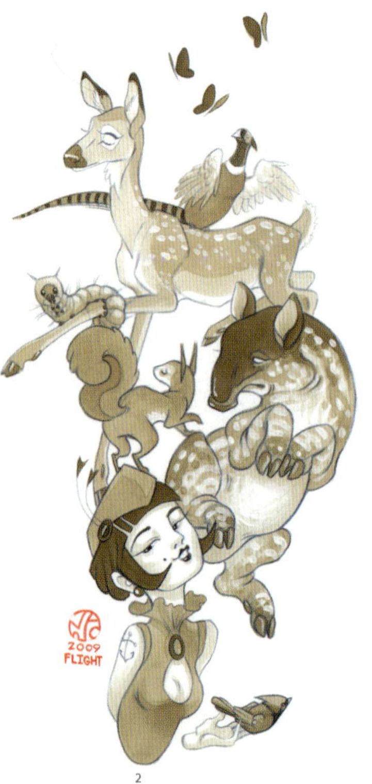
2009
FLIGHT

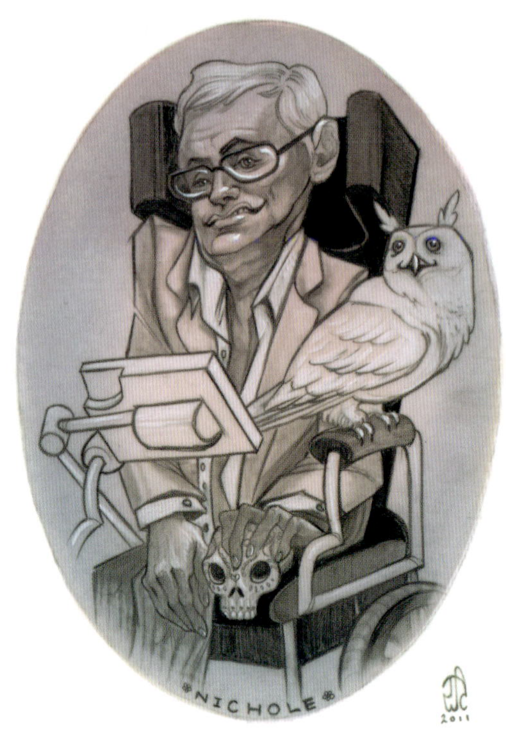
NICHOLE
2011

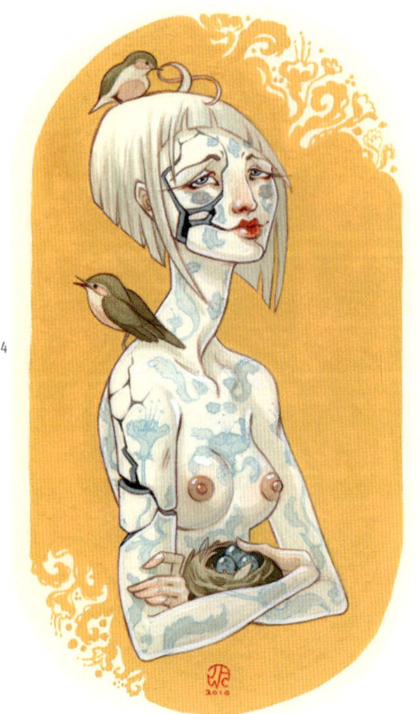

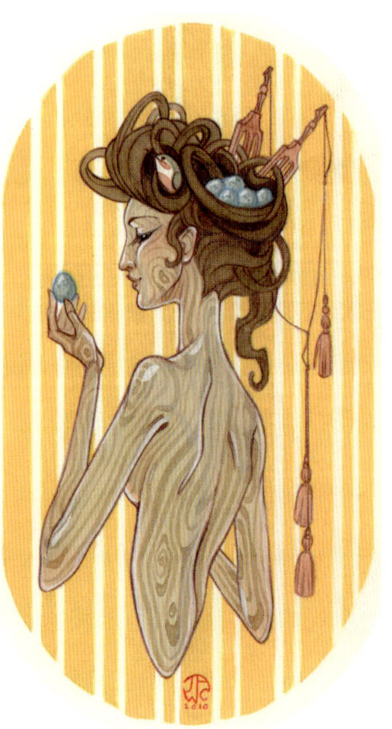

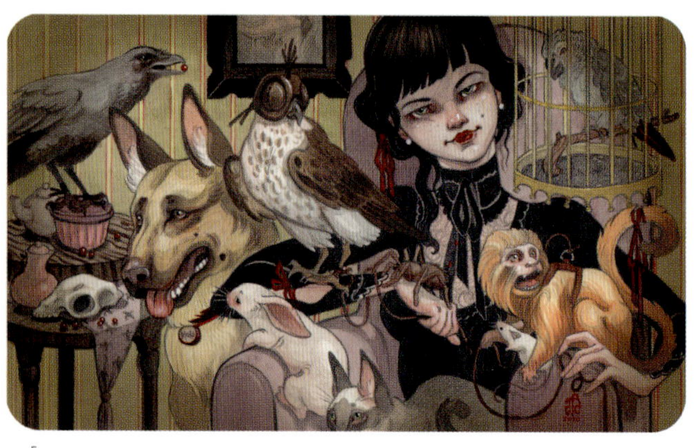

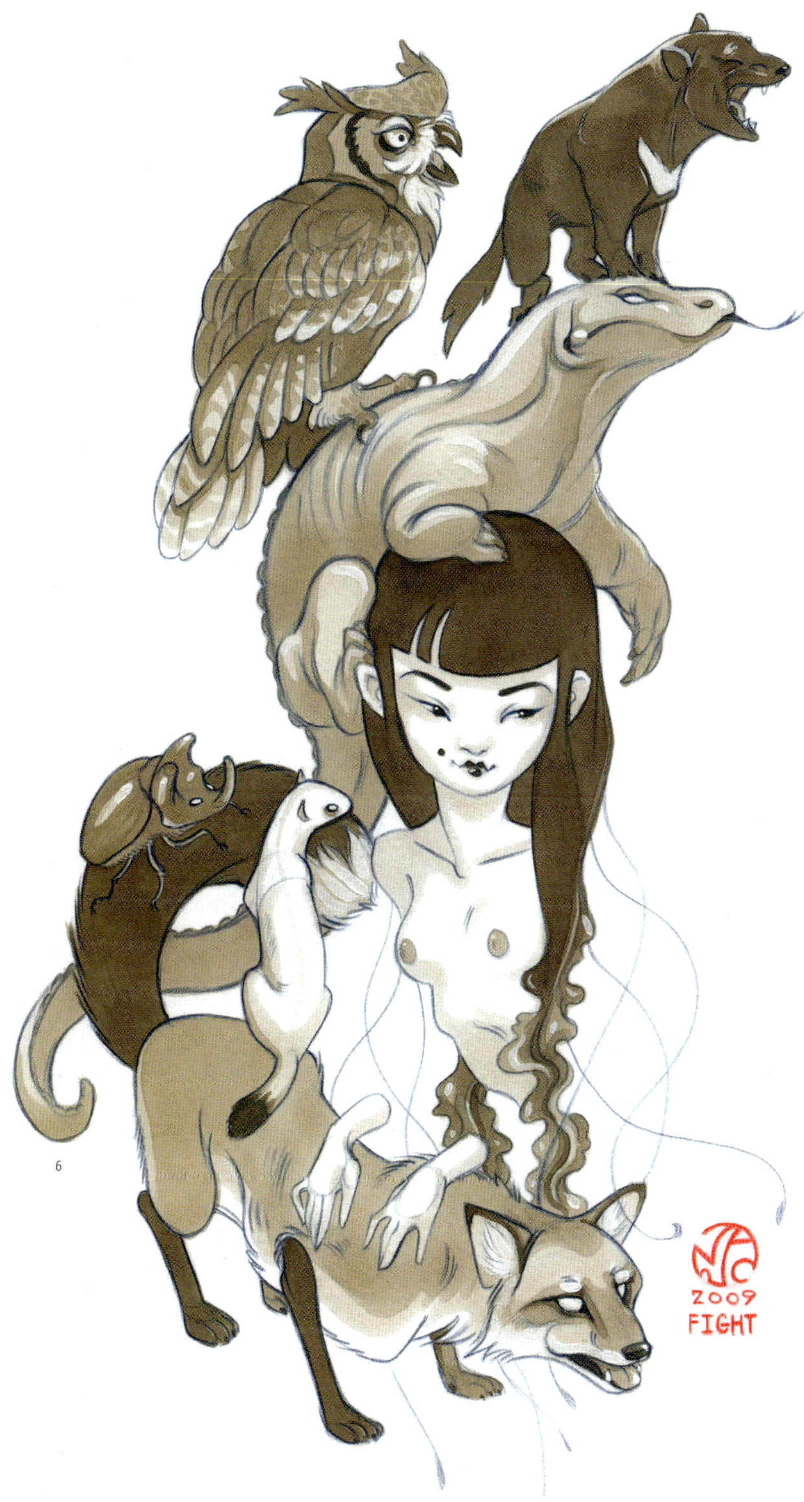

6

1. **Pied Piper** (2009). La Luz de Jesus Gallery. Acrylic

2. **Fight Flight** (2009). La Luz de Jesus Gallery. Ink, graphite

3. **Stephen Hawking** (2010). Private commission. Ink, graphite on frosted acetate

4. **Cracked / Tangled** (2010). La Luz de Jesus Gallery. Ink, gouache, col-erase

5. **Minions** (2010). *LA Weekly*. Ink, gouache, graphite

6. **Fight Flight** (2009). La Luz de Jesus Gallery. Ink, graphite

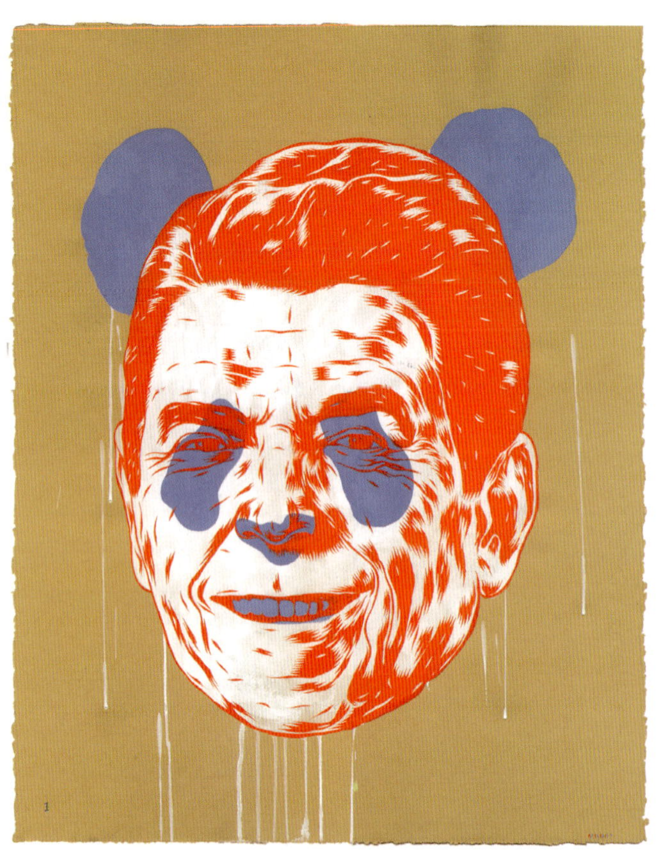

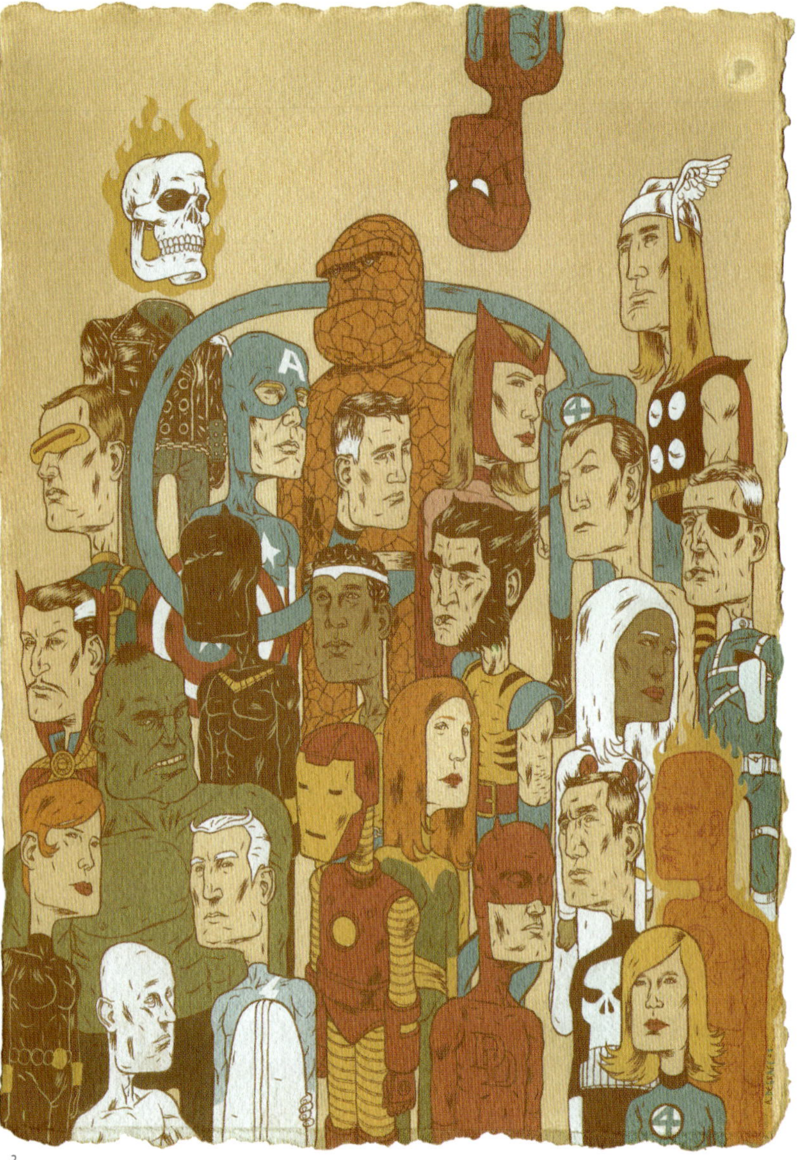

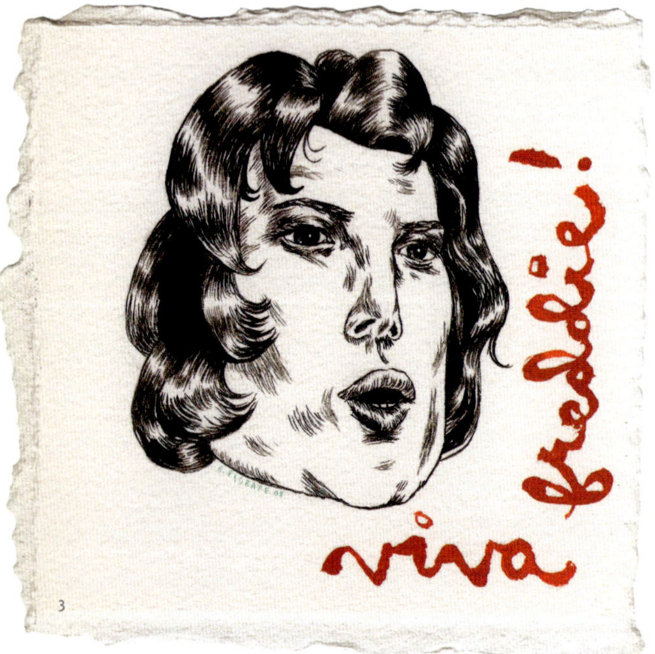

viva freddie!

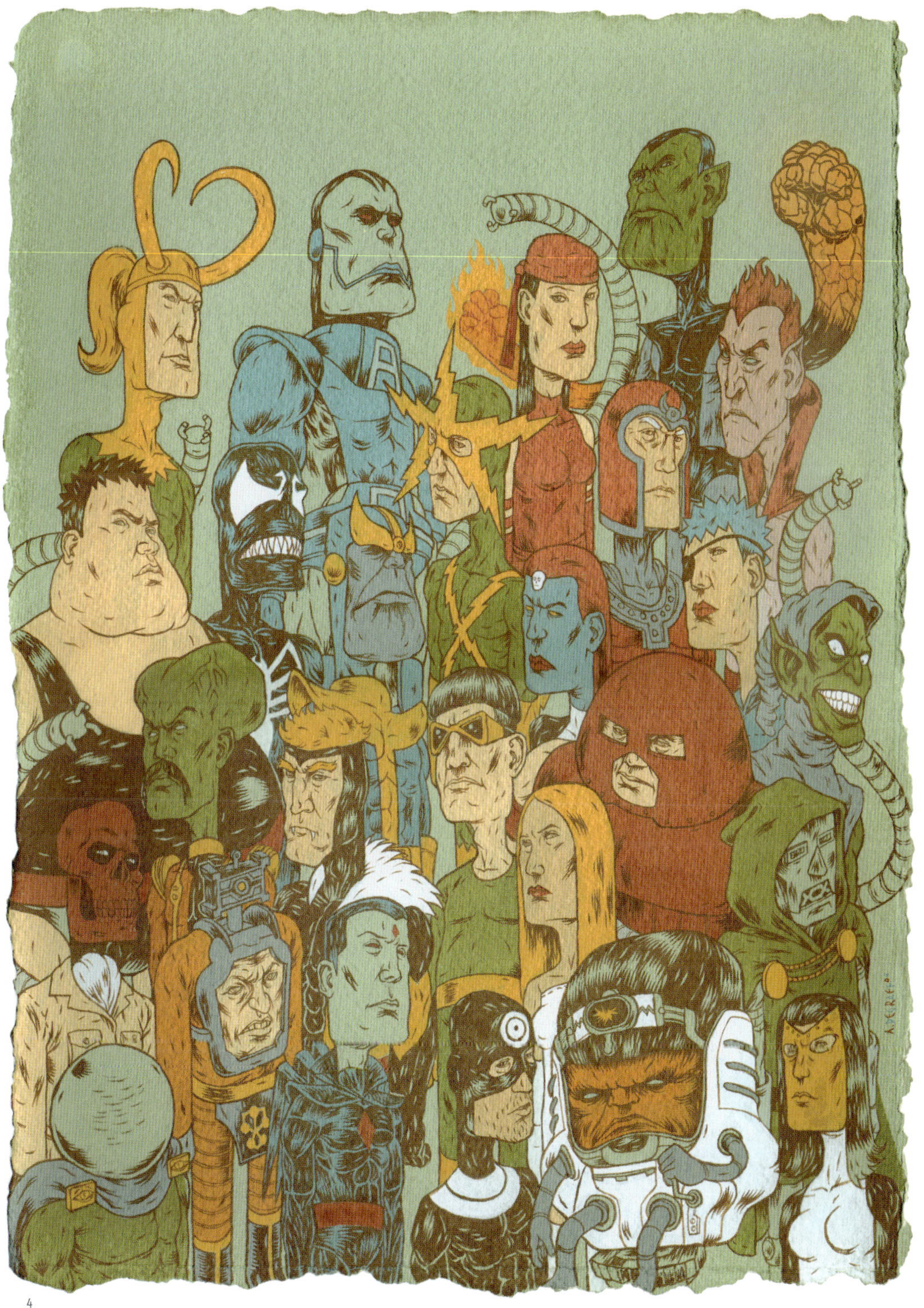

Andrew DeGraff
USA

www.andrewdegraff.com

1. **Endangerous** (2011). Gouache on paper

2. **Marvel Superheroes** (2009). Gouache on watercolor paper

3. **Viva Freddie** (2008). Ink, gouache on watercolor paper

4. **Marvel Supervillians** (2009). Gouache on watercolor paper

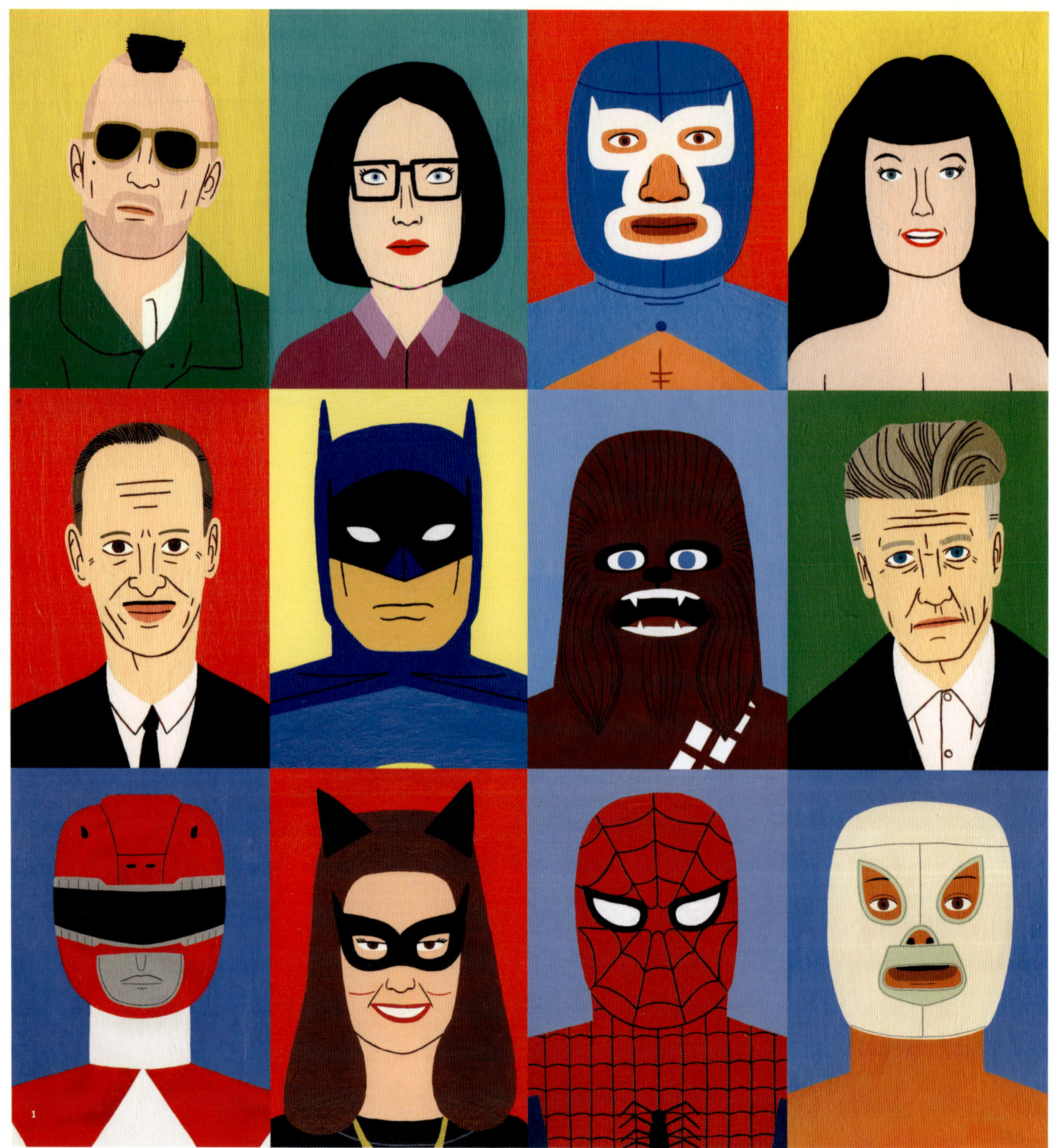

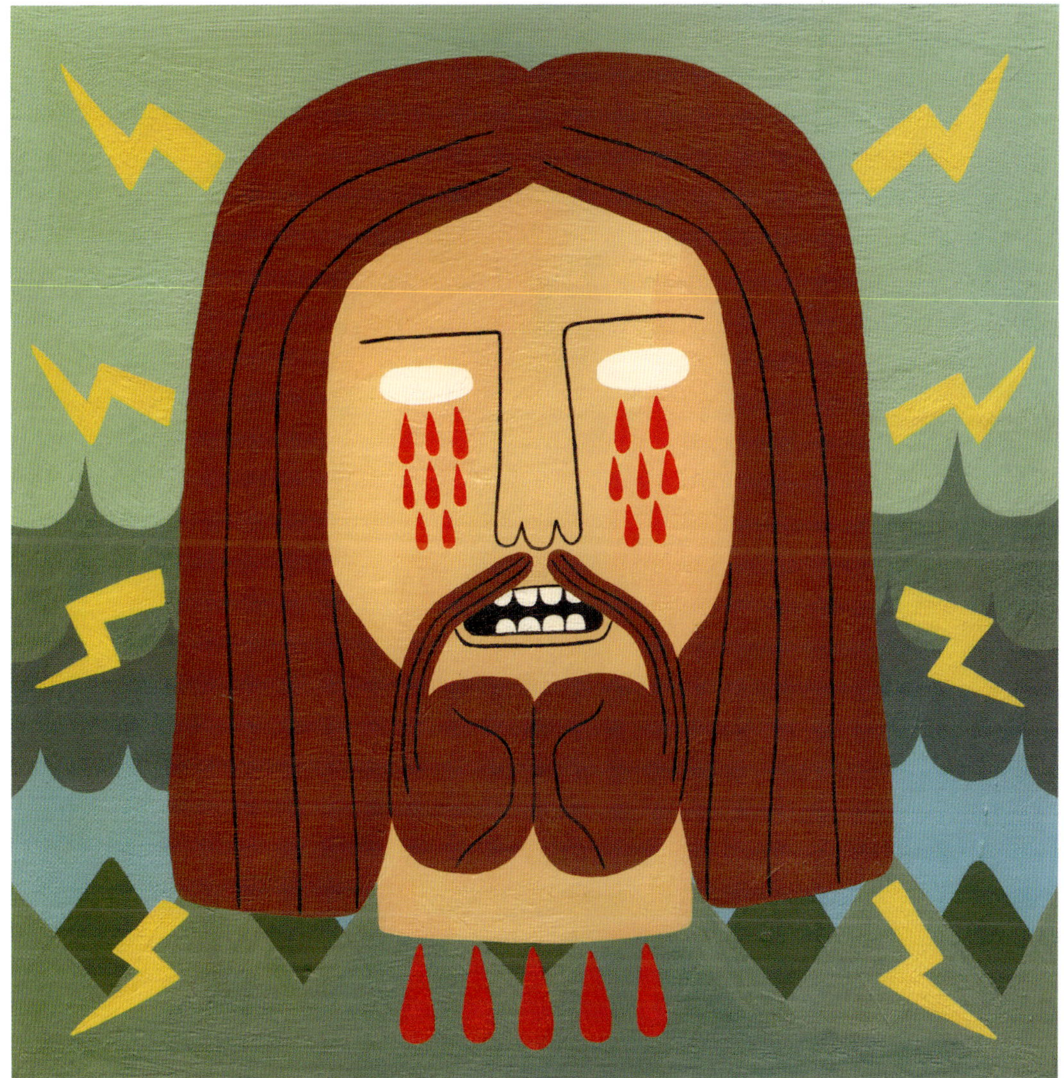

Jack Teagle
UK

www.jackteagle.co.uk

1. **Inspirational People** (2010). Nonamarmi. Acrylics

2. **Zeus** (2010). Personal work. Acrylics